CRUCIFIXION BY POWER

Essays on Guatemalan National Social Structure, 1944–1966

CRUCIFIXION BY POWER

based on field research by

RICHARD NEWBOLD ADAMS
MAVIS ANN BRYANT
FREDDA BULLARD
JERROLD BUTTREY
BRUCE CALDER
JOHN DURSTON
LARRY GRIMES
JULIO JIMÉNEZ
WILFORD LAWRENCE
BRIAN MURPHY
BRYAN ROBERTS
JOHN SLOAN
DEANNE LANOIX TERMINI
JERRY WEAVER
ALVAN ZÁRATE

Essays on Guatemalan National
Social Structure, 1944–1966

by RICHARD NEWBOLD ADAMS

with chapters by
Brian Murphy and Bryan Roberts

UNIVERSITY OF TEXAS PRESS, AUSTIN & LONDON

International Standard Book Number 0–292–70035–0
Library of Congress Catalog Card Number 79–121125
© 1970 by Richard Newbold Adams
All Rights Reserved
Printed by The University of Texas Printing Division, Austin
Bound by Universal Bookbindery, Inc., San Antonio

This book is written with the thought that

All the king's horses
And all the king's men
Couldn't put Humpty together again.

ACKNOWLEDGMENTS

Five institutions have contributed crucially to the gradual evolution of the formal research project that lasted from 1963 through 1967, the labors of which were the direct source of data on which the present book is based. The Institute of Latin American Studies (ILAS) of The University of Texas at Austin, under the direction of Dr. John P. Harrison, served as the home base of the research and provided funds and facilities during the entire period. The Seminario de Integración Social Guatemalteca, under the executive secretaryship of Lic. Flavio Rojas Lima, served as the informal home in Guatemala City and provided a multitude of services through the entire period and is publishing, jointly with the ILAS, Spanish editions of the monographic products of the research. The Consejo de Planificación Económica, under the direction of Lic. Antonio Palacios, cosponsored the period of most intensive research during the summer of 1965 and provided counsel and support that was essential to the project's operation. The United States Agency for International Development Mission to Guatemala, under the direction of Mr. Marvin Weismann, was the other cosponsor during the same summer and provided constant support, facilities, and sources of data that were crucial to the success of the work. Finally, the Ford Foundation, under a grant to the ILAS, provided the basic funding that made it possible to carry on the seminars and the student field research, as well as the many incidental expenses necessary for the continuity of a project of this scope over the period 1963–1966. It also subsequently supported much of the preparation of this manuscript. The responsible executives and innumerable staff members of all these institutions were invariably cooperative and helpful. As institutional entities, however, they in no way can be held responsible for the findings of the study, nor for the opinions expressed herein. They allowed free access to information and facilitated research, but in no way tried to influence the findings. In this day of national sensitivity to the activities of one's government and nationals, I believe these institutions participated in an entirely correct and disinterested manner, and my colleagues and I found it a pleasure to be associated with them. I hope that the nature of the product, while perhaps not always happy, will not embarrass them.

Specific acknowledgment should be made to individuals who have kindly commented on individual portions of the manuscript. They, too, are obviously not responsible for the final form, but their help is deeply appreciated: Fernando Aldana, Calvin P. Blair, Mavis Ann Bryant, Ira Buchler, Jerrold Buttrey, Bruce Calder, Marta Cehelsky, Ricardo Falla, S.J., Julio Jiménez, John Johnson, Anthony Leeds, Brian Murphy, Ing. Alfredo Obiols G., Frederick Pike, Ivan Vallier, and members of the Brookings Institution Conference on Politicization in Latin America. Roger Abrahams reviewed almost the entire manuscript.

Although the material in this volume is based on the field work specifically of those individuals listed on the title page, there have been many others who have worked with the project at one time or another. Because they did, in fact, form part of the general group, I want here to acknowledge the roles they played in the progress of the work. They are John Avant, Calvin P. Blair, Jack Brown, Donald Cole, Riet Delsing Durston, William Hazard, Bruce Hupp, Theodore Johnston, Michael Micklin, Stuart Pullin, Friedrich Sixel, Kay Sutherland Toness, Odin Toness, and Richard Wright.

Over the years that this project has been under way, I have had the regular counsel and personal support from a number of individuals whom I would like especially to mention. Dr. and Mrs. Donald Fiester and their children have given unsparingly of their hospitality and support; Lic. Jorge Skinner-Klee has provided help in uncountable ways, as well as intellectual criticism and insights; visits with Dr. and Mrs. Fernando Aldana have always been important parts of our trips to Guatemala; Walter and Marley Hannstein and Millie Schleisier know how very deep a debt I owe them in all my work in Guatemala; Dr. John Harrison, former director of the Institute of Latin American Studies, provided unfailing encouragement and understanding of the work upon which I was embarked and that rare combination of scholarly and personal concern that can make the academic community a good place in which to live.

Sr. Joaquin Noval, director of the Instituto Indigenista Nacional under the Arbenz government, and long an object of political persecution within his own country, has been an important contributor to the writer's search for a better understanding of Guatemala.

My family, of whom I am the only non-Guatemalan, must decide in due course whether the time this book has taken from them has been warranted; at least it facilitated periodic trips to our home in Guatemala from our home in Texas. To Betty, Walter, Tani, and Gina I always owe more than my frequently morose disposition allows me to express; perhaps some of it can be recognized in our concern and love for Guatemala.

The data for the maps were prepared by Mr. Ronald Venezia and, later, Mr. Steven Smith, and the maps themselves by Miss Gloria Goff. The manuscript preparation has been handled by Miss Pamela McBride and Mrs. Bonnie Swan, to whom I am very indebted for unfailing good humor and competence.

Austin, Texas   R.N.A.

CONTENTS

CRUCIFIXION BY POWER

Essays on Guatemalan National Social Structure, 1944–1966

Introduction

1. *The Purpose of the Study*

FROM 1950 UNTIL LATE 1956, I lived in Guatemala and had occasion to make a variety of studies of rural societies both there and in neighboring Central American countries. My interests at the time were of a traditional and applied anthropological nature, influenced by the fact that during most of the period I was an active advisor to the World Health Organization and the Institute of Nutrition of Central America and Panama. The 1954 revolution in Guatemala, supported directly by the United States and followed by the rejection of many of the advances made by the two revolutionary governments, reinforced a fact that was already evident to some of my colleagues: it was impossible to understand the life trajectories of peasant and poor peoples in contemporary society without understanding the larger society within which they lived; and it was equally necessary to see how the larger society related to the world.

Traditional anthropology, however, had neither the techniques nor the concepts to permit me to turn readily to a study that would elucidate these larger spheres. For the most part, anthropologists had chosen to study microareas, primarily the tribe or the community, but at that time were expanding into urban barrios, plantations, haciendas, and other fairly discrete, clearly bounded groupings. Julian Steward's major project in Puerto Rico was just pub-

lished[1] but, as will be noted in Chapter 1, seemed to fall short of
providing the links necessary to see how the larger whole worked
in a systematic way with the microspheres.

The question of underdevelopment had pushed itself into anthropology by this time and posed a further issue. Clearly, most societies
that anthropologists had been studying were underdeveloped; but
there was little within the anthropological literature that threw any
very direct light on the nature, causes, and processes of that condition. Just as the processes of change in peasant villages could not be
understood apart from a larger picture, so the process of development was impossible to understand from a study of fragments. An
automated factory and an Indian village will illustrate characteristics of, but not the structure of, the processes that have produced
these events.

Following my return to the United States in 1956, these problems gradually tended to formulate around three central issues:
(1) If a study is to be made that will clarify the relation between
the individual peasant and his community, and the world at large,
what scope should be used from the study? Obviously, we cannot
study a sample of peasants and a sample of nations. (2) If a study
is to identify these relations, what initial set of concepts will permit
us to relate the United Nations with a small village in some manner
that is not merely trivial? (3) If development is in some sense
growth and expansion, what is the connection between it and evolution, that theoretical area of anthropology that has usually been
concerned with growth and expansion?

The answer to the question of scope was that the basic unit of
investigation should be the *nation*. Of all the social units in the
modern world, this is the only one that claims, and is generally
recognized, to have sovereignty. Sovereignty is central to the question of appropriateness for study. The social group that claims it
will also claim the right to defend itself by any means against
threats to its integrity, and its action will usually receive approval
from at least some other nations. The nation can claim, then, some
kind of survival-unit quality. Since survival is necessary for continuity of culture and social organization, any study of societies
over great periods of time must focus on some kind of unit that will

---

[1] Citations will be given later to sources relevant to the discussion.

have sufficient continuity to sustain the study. No historic agrarian community has claimed and maintained sovereignty, and it probably could not have done so for long under neolithic conditions. The study of the tribe today is of continuing interest in part because it tells us something of what tribes may have been like when they were, in fact, sovereign. Cities have never been sovereign, apart from their state and hinterland. The nation, then, provided the appropriate focus for the study, both in regard to internal relations and operation in the larger world.

The answer to the question of concepts allowing one to relate the individual with larger organizations proved to lie in the realm of power.[2] The central defining feature about a nation is that it is a state that claims the ultimate authority of wielding power within its own domains. No matter what other aspects may be brought in for descriptive purposes, a profound discussion of the nation eventually finds its way to the central core that holds a nation together: the power structure. Some sort of intellectual framework could then be fashioned around the skeleton of power structure to give initial direction as to what we might study with some effectiveness and to yield basic descriptive material for the further development of concepts more appropriate to the macrosphere we wanted to analyze.

To the third question, concerned with growth and expansion, the answer that emerged was that development was itself, in a sense, evolution. It comprised that aspect of evolution having to do with the build-up of goods and human time usage, the expansion or growth of the material and economic side of life. More than this, however, with the concept of power in hand, it was not merely that technology and economics related development to a larger evolutionary framework, but that their concerns were part of a more inclusive subject matter. This, it turned out, was again power. For power had to do with the control of both individuals and goods, voters and laborers.

The three questions, then, were related closely by the answers found to them. By using a framework of power structure, we could initiate a study to seek the relationships that fixed the peasant in some position with respect to the nation; and these relationships, in

[2] See Appendix to Chapter 1 for statement on power.

turn, were directly involved in the question of development as it pertained to evolution.

The principal reason for choosing Guatemala for the study was that I was already reasonably familiar with it in some of its dimensions. Quite a number of field studies had been made of communities,[3] both Indian and Ladino, and there was available in the anthropological literature a reasonably broad, if irregular, set of reports on some phases of provincial and rural life. But other characteristics also recommended Guatemala. Principal among these was that it is a small country. It would be possible to have some comprehension of the whole through studies of only some of its parts. In this sense, its choice was dictated by a concern that has influenced the choice of many anthropological field sites. Second, as a practical matter, it was sufficiently close to the writer's home institution so that it would be possible to have students travel and work there without an extraordinary cost. But probably most important, in my own mind, is that the problems of understanding human society had been most challenging to me in Guatemala, and it was there that I felt it would be most rewarding to seek some of the answers.

A final reason for studying Guatemala was that the recent history of the country fell into three distinctly different phases: pre-1944, or the prerevolutionary period; 1944–1954, a revolutionary decade; and since 1954, the postrevolutionary period. These three distinctive periods made it possible to contrast relations under three national-international rubrics. Specifically, this division makes possible a comparison of the country during three phases of its own history. Before turning to the description of how the field study was carried out, it will be worthwhile to explore a little more fully the questions that have led to the study and the additional issue of how one is to work on such a wide and diverse set of phases of society and maintain his conceptual balance between matters of culture and social relations.

The method chosen utilizes social structure rather than cultural

---

[3] These studies have been summarized in Robert H. Ewald, *Bibliografía comentada sobre antropología social Guatemalteca, 1900–1955*. Since that time, additional anthropological material has been published by Benson Saler, Ruben Reina, Michael Mendelson, Alfredo Méndez, Joaquín Noval, Oscar Horst, and León Valladares; to these should be added the sociological monographs by Nathan Whetten and Mario Monteforte Toledo.

structure as the guide into the subject matter. This is dictated by conceptual and theoretical biases. As a social anthropologist, I believe that each variation in culture becomes significant when it marks a variation in social relationships. Whether a Guatemalan Indian woman wears one or another design on a *huipil* or makes one motion rather than another is of social significance when the subsequent chain of behavior goes in one direction rather than another. Conversely, if there are alternative paths that a series of behaviors may take, these alternatives must in some manner be signaled by perceptual differences in some cultural forms. Given these assumptions, one may approach the study of a culture and society either through exploring variations in the social behaviors, or through exploring variations in the cultural forms, or both. The study ideally should make the connection between the two, since the behavior is signaled by the formal differences, and the signal is only relevant if related to such behavioral differences.

Given the bias toward using social relations as a base, it then follows easily in what way the lines of power within a society provide an appropriate initial guide into the social structure of that society. Presumably, the major criterion in selecting any particular organizational or relational feature for this purpose is that it should lead into all corners of the society. Power structure appeals as a network of relations that is extensive, penetrating, salient, and definitive for the kind of society under study, the nation-state.

There are other systemic features that relate everyone in a society in one manner or another. Language is the most obvious, but the network it spreads is both too broad and too coarse. Also, while often an effective index of social differentials, languages tell us little of the substance of these differentials. Kinship also relates everyone in a society, but the prospect of formulating a genealogy for a population of over four million people is a little staggering as a field problem. Economic relationships, through both market and labor relationships, provide connecting links that tie people from all corners of a society into a single network. Here, however, there are two problems. One is that the connections, while important, are often fleeting, and make it extremely difficult to trace a network of interlocking relations for the entire society. While the patterns of such relations do permit the identification of subgroups, the very nature of a market economy is such as to bring shifts in marketing patterns with every change in abundance and scarcity of goods and services. The market is an extremely delicate system, and its very responsiveness to the changes in the natural and cultural environment makes it difficult to handle as a basic map. The second problem is that to make such a map would take almost as much time as the rest of the study. Using the community as a focus, as Steward did in his Puerto Rico study, fails to map out the relations that hold within the larger society. It is therefore necessary, as in Steward's work, to make a special sortie into history. The use of the government network would theoretically be satisfactory if the governments were all-powerful and omnipresent. They clearly are not, however, and there are wide and important areas where their absence is notable.

Power, then, as a basis for a preliminary understanding of the subject of study, seems to have much to recommend it. It is a feature of every social relationship; it spreads its effect differentially through the entire society; and every individual is related to every other in some manner that can be initially estimated on the basis of a general understanding of the larger system. Compared with the other linking systems, power provides more differentials of current significance than does language. It is not as delicate as is the market economy, it is not fragmented, as are communities, and, unlike kinships, it has at least one clear-cut boundary significance in a nation-state.

In the case of Guatemala, it is evident that the power system, while defining the nation-state, is not in any sense restricted to that unit. Quite the contrary. The power relations indicate where the boundaries are, but, like kinship and economic systems, have ramifications and linkages around the world. However, neither the power structure nor any other single approach to a society will serve to bring to the surface all matters of interest in an area as general and broad as national social structure. The very fact of using one device will restrict the number of aspects of any given event that may be touched; and it will not necessarily open up that event to a fuller analysis.

There are two reasons for this limitation. One has to do with the fact that any event is complex, and seeing it through one of its aspects is seeing only the part that, like an iceberg, is exposed to our view. In addition to this, we know something of those portions that are not readily perceptible. In any society, many events generate counterevents; the choice of one mode of study automatically eliminates the possibility of another. The male investigator will automatically find it difficult to study female culture, and the student of Guatemalan labor unions will find it difficult to spend most of his time studying the upper class. An investigator is, himself, a complex of characteristics and potentials, and these must find responsive aspects in the society he is studying for him to have real success in that study.

There are always elements of a society reluctant to admit the exercise of the power of a nation-state, and therefore events that might be subject to punishment, were they recognized at the national level, are hidden or masked. Phases of Indian organization, especially having to do with community land titles and details of religious *cofradía* organization, will seldom be opened to persons who, in a sense, "come down" from the national level. Similarly, farmers who may be systematically breaking the laws having to do with treatment of labor, or who suspect that their manner of life would be subject to ridicule or negative sanctions, will naturally not want it exposed to view. In a study of the present kind, it was not practical to attempt to study the *guerrilleros* in a detailed way, not merely because they might not have allowed it, but also because had we been successful in doing so, other members of the society and the government itself might not have been willing that we continue the study.

So it is that in any social situation where one is dealing with but one pole of a power relationship, the other members of that relationship may thereby prove to be unavailable for effective study. In the present case, I assumed that we had sufficient information for the moment on the nature of community organization, that it was specifically the national phase that was not being effectively studied. Since this was our goal, it seemed necessary to choose a method that would ignore or even obscure some areas about which we already had some knowledge.

The problem of development, which has been mentioned in connection with its relation to evolution, has another aspect that warrants being clarified in this preliminary chapter. The first obvious question that one must ask about development in Guatemala is whether it is, in fact, taking place? The answer to this is yes and no, depending on what is meant by development. The common North American view holds that development is taking place if there is some measure of wealth, income, or welfare per capita increase at some predetermined rate. Many Latin American economists and sociologists, however, would suggest that development is not occurring unless there is a significant broadening in distribution of such an increase.[4]

It may be worth noting in passing that this difference in viewpoint is probably not random, but is correlated with the kind of development being experienced within the two areas. Sheer gross increase per capita has been a popular criteria for determining development in those areas where primary development is occurring, where technological invention has primacy over social innovation and change.[5] In the areas of secondary or hinterland development, however, we find a significant proportion of planners and economists holding that it is not mere increase or growth, but the achievement of distribution of both what already exists and what may be gained through such increases. Distribution is as important as increase. Not all economists in areas of secondary development would agree to this, simply because they find their welfare in the benefits accruing to them by operating within the hinterland of primary development.

A substantive concern of this book is to indicate that, while development in terms of *increase* has occurred in Guatemala, it has not been accompanied by any readily demonstrable new differential in distribution. While there has been an important growth in power of the upper sector of the society, there has been no comparable increase in distribution. This means that Guatemala has developed only from the point of view of what is advantageous to nations of primary development.

The purpose of this book, then, is to examine various phases of Guatemalan society to learn something of the structure of that society and how it relates on the one hand to the peasant, provincial, and general lower-sector population that still comprise the great mass of the nation, and how it relates to the world at large on the other. By clarifying the relations as they extend from the extreme

[4] See, for example, the papers in Claudio Véliz, ed., *Obstacles to Change in Latin America.*

[5] See Richard N. Adams, *The Second Sowing.*

of the entire world as a macrocosm to the local level as the locus of individual activities, it is hoped that the question of development in Guatemala may be seen in a broad perspective that will clarify the major forces determining both why and how the development occurs.

The purpose of this volume necessarily involves both empirical reporting and theoretical constructions. In actual fact, the materials in Chapters 2 through 10 were written independently of Chapter 1. In them, we have tried to present something of the history and present condition of the national social structure of Guatemala. In the course of this, however, the other aspect of the central problem, that is, how to handle complex societies, continued to be of concern. Finally, I prepared Chapter 1, an extended exploration into the use of certain concepts that I believe go some way toward permitting us to better understand the nature of complex society and how it may be studied. I determined to put this chapter first in order that the reader who is conceptually curious and concerned with the theoretical problems could familiarize himself with these concepts before going into the more substantive portion of the volume. I have intentionally not rewritten these later chapters in terms of the concepts developed in Chapter 1, because it would, I believe, detract from the more general reader's interest. It is, of course, impossible to handle substance completely independently of theory. The last section of Chapter 1 deals with some of the substantive matter; Chapters 2 and 3, while specifically concerned with relating issues on development and the evolution of the power organization, constantly revert to theoretical issues. The remaining seven chapters in the volume, however, are more clearly devoted to substance; they too have their theoretical bias. Chapters 4 through 7 are concerned with cases of the development of the upper sector of Guatemalan society and its relation with the society as a whole. Chapters 8 through 10 look at the situation from the lower sector, specifically seeking to identify how access to power is limited by the more general structure. The book thus consists of four major parts, moving from the theoretical to the substantive.

Thus, while this volume is an attempt to relate what is happening on the regional and local levels of Guatemala with the events of the external world, to do this we have focused almost entirely at the middle range—the national level. We have carried out no basic field studies within local communities. The study must, then, be seen in the context of the research that has preceded it in Guatemala. It does not replace the local studies, but hopes to supplement them and bring certain aspects of the conditions they describe into a clearer focus. And, in doing this, it hopes to provide anthropology with some additional notions about how to study societies in a larger context.

2. *How the Study Was Made*

This section will go into some detail on the planning and course of events that have led to this volume and the other products of this study. The general reader may find this of little interest, and it is recommended that he move on to Chapter 1 or 2, depending on the nature of his interest. For the continuity of social science, however, it is important to keep on the record how these investigations are carried on, not because they should serve as an ideal model, but because they offer some experience that perhaps may make the next such investigation better.

This research project began as a device to provide general research and training for graduate students in Latin American studies at The University of Texas at Austin. As such, it went through three phases. Preliminary work was carried on in 1963–1964 while funding was uncertain and the writer was ascertaining the level of student and faculty interest in such a program. With the clear availability of Ford Foundation funding, intensive work began with seminar work in 1964 and a plan for summer field work in 1965. Following this, there were a few additional field studies and followup seminar work. The present volume will be the major product of the research as far as I am concerned. However, it is by no means the only product nor necessarily the most important. Many of the collaborators are publishing studies separately.

The written products of this project are being published, for the most part, under an arrangement with the Seminario de Integración Social Guatemalteca. Project funds have been set aside for the translation of all such manuscripts into Spanish in Guatemala. Those essays and monographs that the editorial council of the Seminario judges to be of value for publication in Guatemala are thereby translated and published by the Seminario jointly with the

Institute of Latin American Studies of The University of Texas at Austin in a series called *Estudios Centroamericanos*. Most of the publications of the project will, therefore, be in Spanish. It is up to each author to see to the publication of his work in English, should he wish to pursue the matter. This plan is based on my policy that materials concerning Guatemala should be made available to Guatemalans for whatever purpose they may wish to put them to. Scholars presumably may have access to the work in either English or Spanish.

The preliminary period saw two sets of field studies. During the summer of 1963, nine students accompanied me to Guatemala. Most had had no previous graduate training or field experience, and the summer's work was an introductory field training period. Each student worked for approximately a week in each of about eight communities. The rough manuscript notes on this work, covering approximately sixty communities, are now on deposit for consultation by scholars in the Latin American Collection, The University of Texas at Austin. In 1964 a reconnaissance was made of migration to El Petén with the aid of four students, and a field study of Poptún was started. Two studies were initiated in a barrio of a Central American capital city.

The summer of 1965 was the period of major field activity on the central problem of the project. For this, a general conceptual mapping plan was devised, and each student then prepared a research proposal around one substantive phase of Guatemalan society. Three faculty members joined the research effort and planned interrelated work on special topics. During this summer, the Consejo de Plantificación Económica and the U.S. Agency for International Development in Guatemala sponsored the faculty members, and the Ford Foundation supported the academic work of the students.

The remainder of this section will be devoted to a description of the conceptual mapping that served as the basis for most of the field studies during 1965 and a description of the various phases of the research at that time.

THE CONSTRUCTION OF A CONCEPTUAL MAP OF SOCIAL STRUCTURE

This study of a national social structure is an exercise in the context of discovery. Most of what goes under the name of "ethnography" is the same kind of activity. When the anthropologist sets out to describe for the first time a social organization or some other cultural picture, he is trying to make a series of statements about a particular aspect of reality. The statements he makes are not properly hypotheses, since they are statements about specific empirical events in the external world; they are not deduced from theory-like statements. Nevertheless, like hypotheses, they are propositions that need to be tested. They are empirically-based statements that state, in effect, that out there, in the external world, there is an event, A, and it is endowed with certain features, a_1, a_2, a_3. When the anthropologist makes a whole series of interconnected statements concerning certain relations that he believes hold true in that particular part of the external world at that point in time, he is making a *conceptual map*.

Just as empirical propositions are distinct from hypotheses, so are maps distinct from models, since the latter usually refer to a specific interpretation made on a theory. Nevertheless, maps, like ethnographic statements, should be testable. If we say that the military in Guatemala has a set of rural agents called *commisionados militares*, it should be possible to confirm or deny this. If we can be more specific and say that the role of these individuals differs in various parts of the country during the period of study in the summer of 1964, then it should be possible to determine through historical and/or ethnographic research whether this was true or not.

One problem in the construction of maps is that one must have some place to start. One cannot make a discovery with no preliminary knowledge. As in theory construction, there must be some "primitives," some accepted assumptions about the nature of the events. Many of these in ethnography are obvious, such as the fact that we are dealing with rational and affective human beings endowed with a wide range of behavioral potentials. It might even be worth mentioning that when the anthropologist or historian approaches his topic, he is making a basic assumption that there is something there at all. In the present study, the preliminary knowns were based on the anthropological and kindred research that had been carried on before and on the background knowledge and impressions that I had built up over a period of some years (1950–1963). The utility of this preliminary information is to establish at the outset a set of relationships that serve the investigator as a preliminary map, permitting him to plan his study more productively.

The formulation of preliminary maps is not an innovation in anthropology, but it has been slow to become regularized and formalized in the ethnographic literature. Linguists have for years had theories of phonemic systems and grammars that guided them in their investigation of any particular language. Similarly, students of kinship have assumptions about kin types, genealogical relationships, and recognized common patterns of relationships. One reason that the community study became so popular in anthropology was that it permitted the student to make various prior assumptions about the society he was to study.

Maps also present certain problems. The very fact that they can tell you where to go means that they also fail to tell you to go elsewhere. This is not a subtle influence; maps positively keep you on the road that has been drawn. The ethnographers' problem here is similar to that examined by Omar K. Moore in his paper on the use of divination to improve hunting.[6] By following the traditional paths, the wild game was hunted out; by using divination, the hunters inserted an element of randomness, leading them to seek directions that were not indicated by their conceptual, topographic maps.

The design of a preliminary conceptual map in the present study followed the lines suggested in the previous section. The power structure was selected as the basis for the map for reasons mentioned there. The form of this map is taken up in Chapter 3. Such a formulation, however, is merely the guide to lead us into the territory. From this it is possible to identify more clearly areas that might be studied in more detail. The major portion of our research was to explore such areas; each of these studies then led to the formulation of more detailed maps.

To explore the literature effectively before going into the field, and to conceptualize the kind of knowledge that was being accumulated, I designed a scheme for exploring a social area. Since this was used in some part as a guide by most of the student investigators involved in the study, and because it might contribute to formalizing

[6] Omar Khayyam Moore, "Divination: A New Perspective," *American Anthropologist* 59, no. 1 (1957): 69–74.

the process of ethnography, a modified version is presented herewith. It should, perhaps, be mentioned that the use of the terms, "relation," "networks," "social system," and "social structure," *are specific, in this instance, to this construction procedure,* while their usage in this context does not generally conflict with more general usages, except in the case of "social structure." The meaning of "structure" in the work of Levi-Strauss is so prevalent these days that it is probably worth noting that the complex picture we are here calling "structure" does not look much like his.

The problem in construction was to formulate a series of statements that might range in their applicability from gross and broad-scope relational systems, such as between "the military" and "the *guerrilleros*," to very microscopic sets of events, such as those constituting the relationship between a particular departmental governor and the local military commandant. It is not easy at the outset to know what relative level of knowledge two such statements might represent. One goal in the construction process was to be able to identify explicitly the quality or level of knowledge that any statement might have.

The manner developed for this permits the investigator to decide what level of knowledge is most suitable to his particular task. The method involves identifying different features concerning the events in question, and new features of knowledge can be added in the course of the investigation process, thus increasing the level of control that one exercises over the materials. The initial concept in the scheme is the *event* or *occurrence*, a primitive notion for the entire range of unique happenings that are observed by or reported to the investigator. Each of these by themselves occurs only once. The events of interest here are those that involve interaction, communication, or affective behavior between two or more *parties*. A party is any social actor or agency: an individual playing a specific role, such a collectivity as the entire population comprising a nation, or merely an effective agency of such a nation.

The basic concept for the construction is the *relation*. A relation is a set of events in which the investigator finds some consistency by focusing on certain features. These features are (1) that two or more parties are involved (not an exhaustive listing, but merely an identification of the consistent presence of some); (2) the approximate time-space dimension, similarities involved in the various events, and what commonalities may hold between them; and (3) the identification of some set of formal features that are common to the various events in the set. The relation, then, is a low-level concept formed to refer to a set of events when one has only very limited knowledge of the extensions and ramifications, not to speak of detailed features, of those events. Because there are literally thousands of relations that can be posited, the question is which ones give evidence of being of particular relevance to the observer's problem.

It should be noted that we are not starting with a concept of a group, nor will we resort to such a concept during the process of construction. In the practice of field work, however, the most obvious place to find well-established relations is to look into apparent groups. For this reason, groups are often an object of field study, but are not necessarily of conceptual importance. It should also be noted that each relation posited is, in fact, a construct, and as such might be available for testing. Since, however, nothing has yet been stated concerning the possible duration of the repetition of other events to fit into the set, it may be that a test would prove to be negative, since no further such events were happening. It is specifically the investigator's concern, however, to learn more about the proposed relations. For this, it is useful to find out more: (4) a history of the relationship; that is, how long has it been going on in its present form, and what was its predecessor? For example, a married couple might formerly have been student and professor. (5) Is it limited, or is it paralleled by other similar relationships in the society? It is wise to attempt a preliminary formulation of the variations in occurrence and form found among the members of the set.

The next step in the construction is to relate a number of relations into more inclusive sets of interdependent members, *networks*. The features necessary to identify a network are (6) the linked relational sets, (7) the time-space dimensions of these sets, and (8) the identification of formal features peculiar to the network as opposed to any specific relation that composes it. A network refers to a series of relationships that link various parties. To describe a network does not, however, necessarily tell us how the relations work except insofar as they provide raw data for a theory of communication. It is further necessary, therefore, to determine

the relative value of the various relations within a network before
we may deal with a social system. One can conceptually elevate the
network into a social system when he can additionally specify the
following: (9) the relative values attached to the member relations
and sets of relations by the parties in the network and (10) the
nature of the interdependence that holds between the different
components of the system, such that change in one component will
bring predictable changes in others.

The delineation of the values assigned to the various relations and
sets of relations and the knowledge of the interdependence that
holds between the parts, taken together with the formal data provided in the earlier steps, give the investigator all he should need
to describe the operation of the system under study. There still are
missing, however, two related items of information that are necessary to evaluate the importance of the various relations and components. The necessary data on a social structure are described
when the investigator can specify information concerning (11) the
time during which the varying relations and sets have held and
(12) the features, environmental or internal, sufficient and necessary for the continuing operation of the system. By delineating the
conditions that must exist for a system to operate, we have identified
the interrelation between the structure of the system and other
relevant structures. By identifying the time duration, which in turn
can be compared with the known relevant conditions, we have the
necessary information to make predictions concerning the structure.

How far the investigator wishes to carry his descriptions will
depend in part on his research interests. It may be that some relational set has come into being only recently, but that from the
point of view of the interests of the study, it is sufficiently important
to be pursued and described in terms of its structural conditions.
A case in the present study would be the expansion and elaboration
of upper-sector voluntary associations (Chapter 6).

Presumably the goal here is to have a description of a social
structure. To arrive at this, it is necessary to have at least the
various component parts here delineated. In many instances, our
knowledge is far from satisfactory on many aspects of a total structure, and we may in fact see little beyond the systemic or even network characteristics. We may only be aware of the fact that there

is a network and find it impossible to identify the systemic features. Finally, there will always be some relations that for some reason have not come under further study and, therefore, do not form a part of any known network. It is important to recognize that our knowledge, both before and after a study of the kind involved here, is imperfect and to try to be clear as to where our understanding is weak.

One of the most crucial steps in the process just described is the step from knowledge of a network to knowledge of a system. It is here that it is necessary to understand the operation of the relations as seen by the participants rather than simply as a set of observed regularities. This is of particular ethnographic interest. From the point of view of the science of culture and society, the step from the systemic to the structural is perhaps the most significant, for it is when we discuss structures that we are in a position to understand the conditions that control the perpetuation or variation of the events and, therefore, to formulate hypotheses or theories concerning them. It will be easier to reach theoretical statements when we have knowledge of the conditions affecting a given empirical case than when such knowledge is lacking.

THE PLAN OF THE STUDY

The plan of the study rested on two major bases: the mapping delineated above and the previous research that had been done. The majority of the earlier work had been anthropological community studies. From these we had a reasonably good basis for understanding some of the major features of the internal organization and current changes of the Indian communities. We knew considerably less about Ladino provincial populations. To understand the national structure as it affected the provincial areas, our model directed us to look to the center as well as to the peripheries. We therefore set up two phases of the ethnographic field study: regional and topical investigations.

In order to study the operation of various power structures that centered in Guatemala City but operated in the provinces, five departments were selected as regional study sites. They were chosen on the basis of wide sociological variation and to expose some of the major variations in the way that power related the center to these provincial areas. One investigator was to reside in each of the provincial capitals of these departments, and, using this as his center, try to determine the kind of relations and networks and, if possible, systems for which that town served as a center. The object was not to study the department as a whole, but to identify the extent of the various systems of relations that stemmed out from the provincial capital and, especially, to identify those relations and networks that tied the farther rural areas, via the provincial capital, to the national capital or other power centers.

The five departments chosen were Jutiapa, Escuintla, Chimaltenango, Quezaltenango, and Izabal. The first two were predominantly Ladino, Jutiapa representing a fairly old population that was stable, except for outmigration, and Escuintla being an area of heavy inmigration and recent agricultural development; the second two were heavily, although not completely, Indian in population. Chimaltenango, however, was only a few miles from the national capital, whereas Quezaltenango was some hours distant and contained the second largest city of the republic. Izabal was divided ethnically, with the northern section being predominantly Ladino of recent migration. When the study reached the field, it developed that the *guerrillero* activity in Izabal had made much of the population so nervous that it was unlikely that much information could be obtained by the techniques to be used in the time allowed. Alta Verapaz was substituted. This department contained the same basic Indian population as did northern Izabal, but very few Ladinos. It was, and continues to be, a somewhat isolated and independent area and is heavily Indian. Four of these studies (all but Quezaltenango) yielded sufficient data for comparative analysis.

Each investigator was to explore the commercial and local government networks, military networks (should they exist), local organizations of townspeople or rural people, political parties, and indeed, any sign of relations that might provide some understanding of the nature of the interrelations between the provincial people and the center. The topical studies consisted of the a priori identification of institutions and relational systems that we had reason, on the basis of the preliminary power map and rather long contact with Guatemala, to suppose would be relevant to the center-provincial power structure. Those that were ultimately decided upon were political parties; *campesino* organizations—leagues, unions, cooperatives (Chapter 9); associations of upper-sector peoples—large-scale farmers, businessmen (Chapter 6); the electoral process (Chapter 11); lawyers, and especially labor-law practices (Chapter 8); the military (Chapter 4); students; the Church (Chapter 5); bureaucracy; and upper-class genealogical structure. Subsequently, studies of two urban barrios of Guatemala City (Chapter 10) and of the development of cotton (Chapter 7) were carried out. As will be related in the body of the report, we were not equally successful in all of these areas, but in most instances enough basic data were collected to make at least a first approximation of the relative importance of the activities within the whole.

One investigator chose to study, and was assigned to, each of these topics as his (or her) special concern. The investigator then started through informal channels to bring together documentary and interview materials to permit him to construct a picture of the general nature of the relational systems to be studied. The relationship between the regional and topical investigators was of particular importance. The topical studies were started for the most part in Guatemala City, where attention was paid to the national focus of the activities. The investigators then followed out the relationships that held between the national center and the individuals in the five departments that were under special study. The regional investigators were taking as one of their special tasks the delineation of the local networks for each of the topical studies. This enabled the topical investigator to move from the national center to the provinces under a variety of local conditions and, in some instances, to move to the municipal level. In this way, for example, the student of *campesino* oganizations could use the regional investigator as his point of contact and source of background material in his study of *campesino* organizations at the local level.

A 2,500-person sample survey was also designed. This was carried out by a professional sociologist (Hazard) in cooperation with the various investigators on the project. The survey consisted of two kinds of materials. One was a set of questions that specifically related to one of the topical subjects and the answers, which were of particular interest to those investigators. The other consisted of a set of questions designed to locate the perceived power structure. The survey was carried out in five selected *municipios* in the five

departments already selected for special study. Within each of the
locales, a random sample of town and rural households was taken.
The *municipios* were systematically selected for variation in features available from the 1964 census: degree of ethnicity, Indian
language usage, literacy, use of shoes, percentage of population born
locally, and percentage of population resident in the municipal
capital. Unfortunately, as of the time of writing, the professional
sociologist has not found time to analyze or prepare a report on any
of this material.

Another semi-independent phase of the study concerned data for
the entire country that was available from the 1950 and 1964 censuses. This, too, was carried out by a faculty member, but has resulted, to date, in only one brief census study (by Zárate) and one
student project (by Termini). In view of the results currently
available from the sample survey and the census study, I can only
record that the student production from this project has been
much superior to the faculty performance.

Carried on somewhat independently, but specifically to be related
when the results are available, was the survey by C. P. Blair, an
economist, of one hundred industries, from one-man workshops to
large factories. The specific objective of this study was to examine
the nature of entrepreneurialism. For this, sites were selected from
the twenty-five *municipios* and the provincial capitals of the survey
and regional studies. A stratified random sample was taken of all
the industries and workshops in all these *municipios*. The results
of this study are still actively in analysis and will be published
separately.

The names of individual students and research assistants responsible for each of these studies or portions thereof are given in
the notes. As most were master's degree candidates, they went to
the field only with the specific preparation possible for this project,
but with a minimum of technical research training in any specific
social science. One result was that there was a considerable mortality of specific projects. This necessarily led to the loss of some
areas of particular interest (such as political parties), the weak
collection on some (the military), and to repetition of other studies
(the *campesino* movement and the Church). Some studies were still
under way at present writing (primary education and Quezaltenango urban Indians). To paraphrase Dr. Johnson's comment on

lady preachers, "It is not surprising that all these phases of the study were not done well, but that they were done at all."

One of the features of studying national social structure is that it places the investigator in a fairly visible position with respect to the subjects of his study. Modern anthropology has become acutely aware of, if not entirely comfortable with, the fact that the subject societies are increasingly literate and concerned with the reports made by investigators. Undesirable repercussions from community studies have been the most publicized of these cases. In a national-level study, however, the investigator is in a position with respect to the power structure that differs significantly from that which he may hold in a community.

In community-level studies, the investigator must adapt himself to the situation of the community and gain either overt or silent approval for his work. However, communities are in many instances under the direct control of larger systems, and it has often been the case that the investigator carried on his study in the face of quite considerable local opposition. This has been done in part with help from sympathetic locals, but also with backing from the outside. I say that a study can be carried on under these circumstances; this does not affirm that it will be a very profound or penetrating study. In the national situation, however, we are dealing with a sovereign entity, one for which there may be no superior power to turn to for support. While the large size of a nation may provide some ano-nymity, the fact that the investigator (in the present case) is a foreigner means that he must obtain entry privileges and conduct himself so that he is not prohibited from carrying out his study. Furthermore, it is important for him to develop fairly good working relationships at many different levels of society and, as is inevitably the case, with individuals of vastly different political complexions. To be both ethical and safe, some approval and sponsorship must be obtained from the government. The investigator's known attri-butes or references must be such that he can expect some coopera-tion from a few of the sectors of the society crucial to the study.

In the present case, the principal investigator had worked in Guatemala over a period of fifteen years and could depend upon the cooperation of some of his local friends. His contacts with the national government were few, however. They were sufficient for such local studies as he had carried on in the past, but were not well established enough for a broad national study. One possibility might have been to carry on the investigation as a series of small, partly disconnected studies and hope to piece them together in some final phase.

At the time, the Institute of Latin American Studies of The University of Texas at Austin was working under a grant from the Ford Foundation to study nationalization and development in Central America. Under this grant, two summers (1963 and 1964) of preliminary and rather specialized studies were carried out by a number of students and me. In the fall of 1964, the Guatemalan office of the Agency for International Development (AID) contacted me and inquired whether I would be willing to lead a team to study the situation in rural development in Guatemala, in order to provide them with assistance in deciding where they should place their rather meager resources. As I was involved in continuing research, and as the proposal sounded somewhat as if it would be a study of the "welfare" agencies of the country, I declined. I suggested a counterproposal, however, to the effect that we were embarked on a study of the national social structure and that, should the AID be willing to provide additional support for that study, it would enable us to carry it along at a much more rapid pace than would otherwise have been possible. AID was willing to do this only if an appropriate Guatemalan government agency would sponsor the work. The national Council for Economic Planning (CNPE) agreed to sponsor the work, and on this basis an agreement was reached. From the point of view of the question of carrying out studies in complex societies, there are some special features of the contractual arrangements that warrant attention.

This arrangement between the regular project from The University of Texas at Austin, AID in Guatemala, and CNPE worked out very well in practice. From the outset, planning of the project was carried out in open discussions with CNPE and AID in Guatemala. The actual plan was entirely created and directed by university staff members, although suggestions of CNPE and AID were taken and acted upon wherever possible. The object of the procedure was to retain the status of the research as academically designed and directed research, for which United States government financing and Guatemalan government sponsorship were necessary. The strict arrangements proved to be well worth the effort, since no real problems were encountered in the course of the research due to the nature of sponsorship or support. Basically, we were trying to provide for the scientific autonomy that a university permits, with the necessary financing and governmental approval that must be attendant on projects having the scope and size that national studies must have.

AID in Guatemala was willing to accept a situation that was somewhat anomalous in that the "reports" that would be available to them as a result of the study would be the standard academic products of regular research. No special written reports were to be prepared, but AID was to receive all final written material as soon as it was available. No "secret" or classified reports were to be made, and all products of the study were to be handled under standard scientific procedures. It was agreed that an impressionistic verbal report would be provided at the end of the actual field phase of the study, but that this material would also be available to anyone else who could legitimately request it. In the two months immediately following the 1965 field phase of the study, such a report was given nine times: five times to various United States Embassy and AID officials; three times to various groups of Guatemalan officials, including one session for the chief of state and the cabinet; and once for a private group of Quaker field-service personnel working in Guatemala. It was given to all groups that requested it. In addition to this, during the same period and the following year, portions of these preliminary materials were used in seminars and academic papers given at The University of Texas at Austin, Yale University, the Institut des Hautes Études de L'Amérique Latine for the Centre National de la Recherche Scientifique, Paris, the University of Minnesota, Indiana University, and the Brookings Institute, Washington, D.C.

PROJECT ORGANIZATION

The basic timetable set for the project was as follows:

November, 1964–May, 1965: Preliminary work at The University of Texas at Austin; training of students and preparation of the specific subprojects.

May, 1965–September, 1965: Field research in Guatemala; preparation of interim, impressionistic report.

September, 1965–August, 1966: Preparation of reports; preparation of final study.

The first two phases were completed as scheduled. The preparation of written materials occupied three and one half years after the end of the 1965 summer field work. The manuscript of the present book was finished in draft form in June, 1968. It was arranged that copies of all formally prepared written materials would be distributed as follows: one copy each to the Consejo Nacional de Planificación Económica, the Agency for International Development, the Seminario de Integración Social Guatemalteca (with the additional arrangement for publication in Spanish described in the Introduction), and The University of Texas at Austin Latin American Collection.

In preparation for the 1965 work, AID started in November of 1964 to air-mail three daily newspapers from Guatemala to the university staff. Students began a continuing analysis of these papers in connection with the special topics they had chosen. Fredda Bullard worked specifically on indexing all articles having to do with provincial activities and the work of agencies and organizations; similarly, all individuals who were associated in one way or another with such organizations or activities were noted. A general file was built up on the individuals and organizations, providing the reference to the news article in which they were mentioned. In addition to this, a daily abbreviated summary of relevant news items was prepared. The students conducting the research were thus enabled to have an index that could lead them rapidly to the newspaper materials relevant to their study planning.

In February, 1965, the planning seminar began. This seminar was overtly a planning seminar for the project, but students that might not have been able to participate in the field phase of the project were not thereby eliminated. As it was established, the term project for each student was to prepare a plan in as great detail as possible of the field project that he or she would carry out in Guatemala. The seminar sessions were devoted to current knowledge of the social structure of Guatemala, setting up the theoretical framework, examining the model that provided the basis of the work, and going into details about field procedures. Students who were unable to prepare a satisfactory project proposal did not participate in the field phase of the work.

Special emphasis was placed in the seminar (although more would have been desirable) on the delicate quality that any research such as this must necessarily have. Emphasis was placed on such matters as the need for security and safety of informants, and of being good investigators without developing a reputation for being nosy pests. As it turned out, Guatemala during the summer of 1965 was a madhouse filled with United States students carrying on a great deal of interviewing. Here again, the preparation that went into this project paid off since none of the project members became involved in any major bungles or offenses, and feedback from informants indicates that they were regarded as having been well prepared.

The position of the students in these matters was of particular concern. Although the faculty members of the project were being supported during the summer of 1965 from AID funds, the team of student investigators was not. Their support came from the Ford Foundation funds mentioned earlier. This arrangement was maintained for two reasons. In the first place, the project was still a training project as well as a research effort, and the Ford funds were specifically for the training of students. Since, in most cases, the students had no earlier experience in systematic research in Latin America, it was felt that they were primarily a university responsibility and should not become involved in funds established by contract with AID. In addition to this, the project director felt strongly that as students, and as people thus inexperienced, it was neither prudent nor wise to place them in a position where they would be expected to produce work of a professional level and take the responsibility that should in fact be borne by the faculty members responsible for the project. It was hoped, of course, that their products would be worthy of preparation for publication; but it could not be assumed at the outset that this would be the result.

Consequently, the arrangement was that the students would be responsible solely to the project director and would have absolutely no responsibility to AID. Their only responsibility to CNPE would be the same as that of any scholar or student doing research, namely, to provide their sponsor with the products of their research, and this was to be done automatically anyway through the project sponsor-

ship. The relationship between the students and AID did have
another side, however. Since they were not to be responsible to AID
and since they were responsible to the project director, it was
decided that they should have no connection or relations with AID
beyond that which would be necessary in the course of their research. In other words, had they been doing the same research
without the indirect AID connection that the project provided, they
might in some instances have sought out AID officials as informants.
We calculated that this was a perfectly appropriate relationship and
should not be interfered with. However, the students were given
strict instructions to provide no reports to AID or any other agency,
unless first prepared as an academic report for the project. AID,
for its part, cooperated well and made no demands upon the students above and beyond those it might have of any visiting scholar
who was using its data. It may sound as if this kind of arrangement
would be difficult to carry out in fact, but such did not prove to be
the case. The students were able to carry on their work as university
students and were not involved in AID or United States government
activities in any way, except as would be expected as U.S. citizens
abroad.

In the actual field operations, each of the four staff members
carried on essentially his own work, and the work of the survey
research, demographic research, and entrepreneurial study will be
reported in the appropriate places by the individuals responsible for
these areas. AID provided a headquarters in Guatemala City for
the field study and thus made it possible for the students and the
staff to have a center in which they might meet and discuss their
problems. In addition to this, AID assigned a secretary, a watchman,
a driver and car, and a young man recently out of the Peace Corps
as general assistant, as well as supplies and office equipment necessary for the work. Each student carried on his own research, sub-
mitting a copy of his notes periodically, and consulting with the
project director on matters related to his research or adjustment.

In the fall of 1965, all the students but one returned to The
University of Texas at Austin, and a write-up seminar was carried
on during the fall term. This involved periodic meetings with the
entire group in which each student prepared the plan of his report,
presented it to the group as a whole, and then had it discussed. This
allowed further interchange of materials as well as a critical panel

for the study plans. During the academic year 1965–66, the project continued to receive newspapers from Guatemala, now paid for by the project's Ford funds. During the summers of 1966 and 1967, additional students went to Guatemala. In 1966, Dr. Bryan Roberts of the University of Manchester and Dr. Friedrich Sixel of the University of Bonn carried on field research under the project. During his research, Dr. Roberts acted as faculty advisor for the students in the field. His own work, of which Chapter 10 of this volume is only a portion, has been most productive.

1 | The Study of Complex Societies

1. *The Anthropology of Complex Societies*

"THE CLASSICAL ANTHROPOLOGICAL STUDY takes a unit—a 'tribe' or 'society' or 'community'—and presents the behavior of its members in terms of a series of interlocking institutions, structures, norms, and values. It is not only anthropologists working in urban areas who have found this sort of assumption difficult to maintain, but also those who have been conducting 'tribal' studies in modern Africa (and presumably also elsewhere). They have found that the effect of groups and institutions not physically present in the tribal area influences the behavior of people in it. The unit of interacting relationships, in other words, is larger than the tribe."[1] It is not the intent of the present work to provide a history of anthropology's gradual migration into this new area, but it is worthwhile to detail some of the immediate intellectual antecedents of this widened perspective, since the successes and failures of earlier studies engendered the present work.

At the outset, it is worthwhile distinguishing what is characteristic about the anthropological approach from others that have been generally referred to as studies of "total societies." The difference lies both in the units of study and in the methods of study. Total

[1] J. Clyde Mitchell, "Theoretical Orientations in African Urban Studies," in Michael Banton, ed. *The Social Anthropology of Complex Societies*, p. 56.

society studies usually choose a limited set of variables, commonly ones that can be measured in specifically quantifiable terms. The variables, more often than not, concern individuals, either all individuals in the society, or all individuals of some particular kind (for example, all voters, all businessmen, all unwed mothers). The study then consists of determining certain characteristics of a sample of these individuals with respect to the subject matter under investigation. The studies are "total" in that the sample is assumed to have generalizable relevance for the entire population under study.[2] Total society studies are argued with apparently considerable confidence in the importance of the variables being studied. It is characteristic, then, that they are less likely to cast about for new variables than they are to try to clarify values of variables already thought to be important.

There remains in much anthropological field investigation a strong natural history element. The approach tends to be more like net fishing than spear fishing. By attempting a national study in our current state of knowledge, it is inevitable that the net will be crudely made and more will escape than are caught. Nevertheless, the virtue in this kind of approach is that it is likely to bring to the surface kinds of interrelations, patterns, and variables that were perhaps underrated or little recognized before.

It should not be thought, however, that anthropologists are of a single mind on the advisability of such studies. Julian Steward, whose pioneering work in this area in Puerto Rico has been so important to subsequent students, was most explicit: "The ethnographic method is applicable to sociocultural segments but not to national institutions."[3] Steward felt that the study of national-level institutions had to be understood "apart from the behavior of the individuals connected with them," and that the tried and true anthropological study focusing on small social segments would be useless under these circumstances. Devons and Gluckman express

---

[2] For a variety of papers on "total society" studies, see Samuel Z. Klausner, ed., *The Study of Total Societies*. Klausner says, "In practice . . . a student concerned with a total study selects the minimum of relevant variables from a minimum number of disciplines which enable him to predict phenomena with no more than some tolerable error" (p. 4).

[3] Julian Steward, "Levels of Sociocultural Integration: An Operational Concept," in *Theory of Culture Change*, p. 48.

reservations on another aspect of the approach. They argue that a more solid account will be produced if the anthropologist sticks to his discipline. "Properly applied, the duty of abstention involves a *rule of disciplined refusal to trespass* on the fields of others."[4] While not really defining "discipline," they seem to be referring to the subject matter of study, and, for social anthropology, this subject matter is "custom." The problem with this is that subject matter is only one or, at best, part of the defining features of a discipline. Method and technique are also central. This differentiation becomes important in the social sciences, where the object of the study is human behavior. Kenneth Boulding pointed out that the various so-called social science disciplines are not really different disciplines at all in the sense that physics and biology are different.[5]

To speak of an anthropological approach to national social structure does not include all the work of anthropologists who have written about nation-states or about complex societies. There have been studies based on a personality approach, such as those by Benedict, Mead, and Gorer; and there have been synthetic summaries, such as those of Lowie and Raymond Smith and Charles Wagley, based on considerable intimate knowledge but involving no specific study design and field research.

The notion that the focus of study of a contemporary society must, at some point, take into account a macrocosm rather than focusing on a microcosm became increasingly clear toward the end of the 1940's and found its first large-scale research effort in the work of Julian Steward and his colleagues in Puerto Rico.[6] Steward's goal was imaginative and pioneering, although it did little more than combine the historical and methodological approaches common to the time. It assumed that communities were not microcosms, but varying samples of a larger whole; the problem was to find how these pieces were articulated with each other.

---

[4] Ely Devons and Max Gluckman, "Conclusions: Modes and Consequences of Limiting a Field of Study," in M. Gluckman, ed., *Closed Systems and Open Minds*, p. 168. Italics in original.

[5] Kenneth E. Boulding, "Dare We Take the Social Sciences Seriously?" *American Behavioral Scientist* 10, no. 10 (June 1967): 12–16.

[6] Julian Steward, et al., *The People of Puerto Rico.* 1956. See also his *Theory of Culture Change.*

Attempts to deal with entire countries or some meaningful segment thereof on the basis of fresh field work, however, have been few. The early work of Robert Redfield concerned a part of two states of Mexico; John Bennett's recent study covered a portion of the Canadian great plains.[7] One of the principal modes of approach of increasing importance has been to focus on the city, but, to date, most anthropological efforts in this area have been on microsegments of the urban population. One of the very few studies explicitly attempting to span an entire nation is the combined work of E. H. Winter and T. O. Beidelman, who have produced a complementary set of studies on preindependence Tanganyika. This work fits the Steward mold perfectly in that it treats of two levels of society: the national level (studied by Winter), in which little field work is done, and one case of a local-level group based on field work (by Beidelman).[8] Following Steward in Colombia, Charles Wagley also initiated a set of related studies on communities in Brazil. Some years later, based on a broad literature and experience, he prepared a general volume on that country.[9]

Insofar as they have taken the nation as their general focus, these studies have generally conformed to an observation made by Eisenstadt:

Social anthropological studies dealing with this problem [of change] do not usually explain how new frameworks of social organization— new "social fields"—have emerged out of the older ones, or how the new institutional order and norms that develop have become crystallized. Nor do they systematically explain the forces which influence a

[7] Robert Redfield, *The Folk Cultures of Yucatan*; Steward, et al., *The People of Puerto Rico*; John Bennett, "Microcosm-Macrocosm Relationships in North American Agrarian Society," *American Anthropologist* 69, no. 5 (1967): 441–454.

[8] E. H. Winter and T. O. Beidelman, "Tanganyika: A Study of an African Society at National and Local Levels," in Julian Steward, ed., *Contemporary Change in Traditional Societies*, vol. 1, pp. 61–204.

[9] The studies included Marvin Harris, *Town and Country in Brazil*; Harry W. Hutchinson, *Village and Plantation Life in Northeastern Brazil*; and unpublished studies by Benjamin Zimmerman and Anthony Leeds. Charles Wagley himself contributed *Amazon Town: A Study of Man in the Tropics*, and the general volume, *An Introduction to Brazil*. From these studies also appeared *Race and Class in Rural Brazil*, under the editorship of Wagley.

different individual to choose between alternatives in the new situation. Rather, most of these studies take the existence of some of these new frameworks for granted. Starting off from this premise, they tend to investigate the different groupings that exist within them.[10]

While these efforts have each contributed to expanding the scope of our understanding of complex societies, they have also tended to bifurcate the local from the national-level phenomenon. The former tends to be seen as composed of individuals and groups, and the latter of institutions. There is a conceptual differentiation that, when bridged in the process of investigation and description, usually refers to specific instances of how the top affected the bottom, or occasionally the reverse. The relational complexities and structure are left as something of a no man's land.[11] Where theoretical and conceptual commentaries are necessary, it is generally thought to be beyond the province of the anthropologist to have serious ideas about the higher levels, but rather that he should focus on the lower levels and how they may articulate with the higher.

This has been illustrated in the course of the development of studies by Steward and his co-workers. They recognized that the national level must be described, but they felt that dependence upon the other social sciences was not only necessary, but also sufficient for this task, and that anthropologists should regard it as beyond the scope of their studies. Thus, they fully recognized and gave due credit to the general historical course of events at the higher levels and detailed some structural features where their own casual experience permitted. They did not treat the national level as a dynamic system, undergoing changes itself, interacting with the local level, and therefore necessarily shifting the nature of the relations between the two. Nor did they apply concepts that stood within the same conceptual system to both levels. "Modernization," for example, was a set of more or less fixed relational elements that

10 S. N. Eisenstadt, "Anthropological Studies of Complex Societies," *Current Anthropology* 2, no. 3 (1961): 209.

11 To be a no man's land does not mean that it is being totally ignored. Anthony Leeds' dissertation deals with it in a general way. The work of Alain Touraine and his colleagues specifically proposes the effect of lower-sector activity on the general direction of events. And, of course, Eric Wolf has pursued the role of individuals and small groups in this context.

stemmed from industrialized societies and that selectively affected traditional societies.[12]

The first important departure from Steward's approach was taken by Eric Wolf, a participant in the Puerto Rican study, in his paper "Aspects of Group Relations in a Complex Society."[13] Basing his observations in Mexico, Wolf focused attention on complex societies as networks of relations linking together various segments. The idea was related to an evolutionary view concerning the emergence of the nation, which he detailed elsewhere.[14] Three ideas introduced in the article were of particular importance. The first, and that which received most attention, was that the collection of the various grouplike parts of a nation could never provide a picture of the functioning of that nation. Rather, it was the interrelations that operated between the various sectors and groups that could provide the major guide for study. The second idea was less developed in the article, but was equally important: the linkage between these groups was accomplished by the appearance of "brokers," and these operated essentially within a power structure. "The study of these 'brokers' will prove increasingly rewarding, as anthropologists shift their attention from the internal organization of communities to the manner of their integration into larger systems."[15]

A final idea, mentioned but not pursued, was that "in dealing with the group relationships of a complex society, we cannot neglect to underline the fact that the exercise of power by some people over others enters into all of them, on all levels of integration. . . . These dictates of power are but aspects of group relationships, mediated in this case through the forms of an economic or political apparatus."[16] Wolf's statement served to crystallize a tendency that had been increasingly felt among those who were working at the community and regional levels of integration, but the very formulation of the

[12] See Steward's "Perspectives on Modernization: Introduction to the Studies," in Steward, ed., *Contemporary Change*, pp. 1–56.

[13] Eric Wolf, "Aspects of Group Relations in a Complex Society," *American Anthropologist* 58: 1065–1078.

[14] Eric Wolf, "La formación de la nación: Un ensayo de formulación," *Ciencias Sociales* 4 (1953): 50–62, 98–111, 146–171.

[15] Wolf, "Aspects of Group Relations," p. 1077.

[16] Ibid., p. 1067.

problem left the anthropologists with few new tools to attack the new subject matter. While Wolf emphasized that he was dealing with "groups of people," it was clear from the problems at hand that the real problem was how to deal with networks of relationships. In the late 1950's, "network theory" began to evolve, especially in England, in the hands of those who were working in the urban areas of Africa. "Brokers," as Wolf suggested, became an object of study. In the anthropologist's kit of tools, however, little seemed to develop in the area of power. Sophistication increased in the study of political systems, but power as a common factor saw little development in terms of theory.

An additional weakness of the Steward Puerto Rico study, as would have been the case with the Redfield and Bennett studies had they been specifically concerned with national-level definition, was the fact that the area chosen was not a nation. It became evident in working in Guatemala during the 1950's that things were happening there that could only be understood if one were to see the country in the context of being a nation in a community of nations. Nationalism, defensive styles, the development and operation of a military, *guerrilleros*, and many other features were not likely to play a strong role in modern Puerto Rico, specifically because it was not a nation-state. A more subtle difference is the distinctive role of the prime urban center: Guatemala City serves the nation of Guatemala; in Puerto Rico, it is hard to know whether the comparable center is San Juan or New York City. The inadequacy of the Puerto Rican rural context to handle the expanding population is solved by Harlem and other urban United States centers. Guatemala City may be less flamboyant and complex a center, but it is one in which the migrant remains Guatemalan; the Puerto Rican who goes to New York may be faced with an ultimate choice as to whether he can remain indefinitely Puerto Rican. So, while Steward tries to treat Puerto Rico as if it were a unit of study at the national level and finds in many respects that it is, we must also find that in many other respects it is not. To study a nation, one must choose a nation to study.

Yet another aspect of the anthropological approach to complex societies is less evident in the North American approaches. There is a commonality in the English-American social anthropological tradition that emphasizes functional interconnections and integration and distinguishes it from those sociological efforts that have been more heavily influenced by Marxian thought, where the emphasis on social conflict is a central principle. A good brief review of this historical dichotomy may be found in the early chapters of Lenski's recent effort to prepare a comprehensive theory on power in society.[17] Lenski sets the basic difference as that between the "haves" and "have-nots," a differentiation that dates back to the emergence of civilization. "Most modern theories of inequality fall into one or the other of two major categories. Those which stem from the conservative tradition are usually referred to as 'functionalist' theories. Those which have their roots in the radical tradition are commonly labeled 'conflict' theories."[18] Although Lenski's own concern has to do more with the significance of this in sociological theory, the same dichotomy exists in the anthropological traditions. Peter Worsley has expressed the tendency in terms that are particularly relevant to the present study: "He [the social anthropologist] is nurtured on a theoretical model which subordinated the analysis of power to the study of reciprocity; which muted the facts of interest, force, and conflict; and which highlighted complementariness and integrative value-systems. So in social situations, where the key decisions are taken *outside* the milieu; where commanding heights exist; where the decisions may be imposed and one-sided; in all these situations, the primary group orientation is no longer adequate."[19]

Another commentator added that "one area of research which is a fruitful one for those interested in an understanding of the mechanisms regulating 'the interrelations of social behavior to group and institutional structure' in complex societies is the study of power groups or 'government' in the broadest sense. . . . This centralization of power has resulted in the emergence of power-wielding institutions and groups which encroach upon and may dominate all other institutions of the society."[20] In the Latin American area, the same issue has been discussed in a slightly different vein in the

---

[17] Gerhard Lenski, *Power and Privilege.*

[18] Ibid., p. 15.

[19] P. Worsley, "Commentary on Eisenstadt," *Current Anthropology* 2, no. 3 (1961): 219.

[20] Laila Shukry El Hamamsy, "Commentary on Eisenstadt," *Current Anthropology* 2, no. 3 (1961): 216.

criticism by Bonfil Batalle concerning the failure of U.S. anthropologists to come to grips with the class system as it operates in Mexican society.[21]

While this criticism is certainly relevant, the situation under which field anthropology developed has also played a role in its biases. The long-standing interest in culture history and in primitive societies has led many anthropologists to study societies in which conflict was indeed played down in favor of consensus. The failure to deal at length with the conflict side of the issue in anthropology became clearer when the colonial empires began to break up after the Second World War. Primitive and peasant areas, long under the control of European nations, began to exercise their own desires for autonomy. It became evident that the European-American view of society differentiated administrative control—the exercise of domain power—from the confrontation of social units. As long as a non-Western society was under colonial control, aggressive efforts against the colonial ruler were regarded as an abnormality to be squashed. Real conflict was a matter for "mature nations,"— European powers. The collapse of political colonialism with the end of the Second World War suddenly enabled societies that had formerly been completely under domain control to make confrontations, to act like "mature powers." Social scientists who had assumed that the world was composed of a series of exclusive domains, bent upon a stable and gentlemanly cannibalism, found, instead, that the heretofore docile native wanted in on the goodies. The curtain that had been drawn around Marx by Western social scientists fell, and peoples once called "primitive" began to be seen as "underdeveloped"; nations earlier thought to be stable and advanced began to appear predatory and conflict ridden.

These two viewpoints are products of the sociology of knowledge in two ways: One is the fact of the political difference between the essentially conservative capitalist societies that produced most anthropologists in the first half of the twentieth century and the clear differentiation of the world into capitalist and socialist camps that

---

[21] See G. Bonfil Batalle, "Conservative Thought in Applied Anthropology: A Critique," *Human Organization* 25, no. 2 (1966): 92. See also, R. Stavenhagen, "Clase, colonialismo y aculturación: Ensayo sobre un sistema de relaciones interétnicas en Mesoamérica," *América Latina* 6, No. 4 (1963).

followed World War II. The other is that societies do, in fact, differ with respect to the relative role of conflict and consensus and that the anthropologist's focus, until World War II, was the primitive society where consensus had to dominate over conflict, and the latter, when expressed, did not occur on a class basis. Following the shift in the interest that perhaps began with Redfield's Yucatán work, the inadequacy of the conservative approach became an increasing obstacle. Both views of society have truth in them, but they sometimes speak to different situations and often to different aspects of the same situation. Since they have roots in the political differences of our times, however, it is unlikely that they will move rapidly toward a credible synthesis,[22] simply because the political dispositions of the participants, social scientists included, will constantly revive them. In the present context, however, as will be seen later in this chapter, they serve to clarify the processes of complex society when seen as different aspects of a single process.

2. *Operating Units*

One problem of general interest is how the concepts implicit in cultural evolution can be of help in understanding the complex societies of the modern world. While anthropology has become so tolerant of cultural evolution in recent years that one need not expect to be necessarily regarded as a political subversive for thinking about it, most such thinking has been on a scale concerned with a full course of evolution,[23] or has been focused on the dynamics of

[22] Lenski (*Power and Privilege*) thinks that a synthesis is possible. I. L. Horowitz, in a recent article, "The Norm of Illegitimacy: Toward a General Theory of Latin American Political Development," *Soundings* 51, no. 1 (1968): 8–32, seems to suggest there is a differentiation among modern states along this line.

"It is evident then that for Marx the essence of the state was power; while for Weber the core of the state is authority. Without wishing to resolve such a pervasive dualism in the sociological literature by fiat, for the purpose of this study I consider it quite feasible that certain societies do operate in Weberian terms, while others operate in terms of the Marxian conception."

I think it will be clear that this is not the differentiation being made here. We are concerned with structural processes common to all societies and not organizational preferences that may serve to differentiate them.

[23] Cf. Robert Carneiro and Stephen F. Tobias, "The Application of Scale Analysis to the Study of Cultural Evolution," *New York Academy of Sciences, Transactions*, 2nd ser. 26, no. 2, pp. 196–207.

sociopsychological relationships.[24] In an earlier volume,[25] an attempt was made to characterize the evolutionary development of Latin America in terms of a specialized evolution,[26] one which occurred in direct relationship to the fact that the more industrialized part of the world was technologically more advanced and would continue to be so indefinitely. The argument in that volume was that Latin American countries were unlikely to take the lead in general cultural evolution in the foreseeable future. The reason was that only a catastrophic situation would provide the circumstances that would enable them to take the lead. Latin American countries generally were deeply adapted to playing hinterland to the primary industrialized areas, and the problems of advancing both technologically and socioeconomically in order to take the lead in these developments would be very difficult.

The Guatemalan study was not carried on with the intent of using evolutionary concepts. However, in line with this interest, it seemed impossible to understand the evolving society of Guatemala apart from its subordinate adaptive relationship to the United States. It was not immediately apparent, however, just what was doing the adapting. There were some elements in Guatemala in perfect accord with the interests of the larger power; there were also those categorically opposed. And there were some quite uninterested. In one sense, Guatemala, as a nation, was adapting to the world; but in another, various of its parts were doing their own adaptation, sometimes in accord with the nation, sometimes in conflict with it. It became clear that to understand Guatemalan complexity and development it would be necessary to formulate a manner of seeing the relationship between these various parts within a wider framework.

"Development" has become the magic wand of contemporary civilization, but it becomes meaningful evolutionarily if seen as a sequence of changes a society may undergo that are advantageous to that society; it refers to events that will not only be specifically different for different societies, but which must, at some point, also

---

[24] Margaret Mead, *Continuities in Cultural Evolution.*

[25] Richard N. Adams, *The Second Sowing.*

[26] Marshall Sahlins, "Evolution: Specific and General," in Marshall D. Sahlins, and Elman R. Service, eds., *Evolution and Culture.*

become conflicting and competitive. If evolution is the universal process whereby life becomes more complex, development is the specific means whereby a given viable entity successfully improves its position with respect to its environment. If evolution involves cooperation and competition, natural selection and random variation, adaptation and destruction, then development also involves these very same processes. Both evolution and development involve experimentation on the part of a society with new ways of controlling the environment, new ways of organizing itself to adapt to the changing world, and new ways of exploiting both the social and natural resources within its reach. Development inherently requires social invention, both to improve the working of existing operating units and to spawn new units.

It is important in discussing development to make clear what unit is developing. In the contemporary world, the nation-state is often assumed to be the only appropriate one. However, the difference in definitions of development cited in the Introduction, the contrast of mere per capita increase as compared with an increased distribution, clearly suggests that to choose the nation is, in some circumstances, merely to answer one set of interests, that is, those interests standing to gain through the per capita increase. If, instead of the nation, we say that development may be an issue of any organized set of human beings, a poor family, a local community, a clique, a business firm, a military junta—that any such unit is concerned with maintaining and assuring, if not improving, its adequate control over the environment—then quite obviously there will be conflict between one of these and another. Particularly, there will be conflict between units interested in the same resources, and there will be efforts by those in control to see that others do not take that control from them.

Development is, then, inherently uneven. Since the various societies or their elements must, at any point in time, be competing within and among themselves to some degree, development for one portion of the whole must inherently mean loss for another. It would seem theoretically possible for various human groups in a completely open environment to survive without destructive competition. While this has been reported periodically, it is usually in circumstances where the technology is stagnant. When development is underway, however, it means that the society is, in some sense, expanding; and, insofar as other human groups are present, it usually means that they give way or survive competitively. Development, therefore, implies destruction as well as expansion; not only the destruction of converting natural resources into waste, but also the destruction of one portion of a society by another. This unevenness is amply visible and occurs in all dimensions. Geographically, it is evident in the exploitative relationship that necessarily holds between the highly developed nations and regions and the underdeveloped areas. In social organization, it is evident in the increasing differential between returns that accrue to the power holders and those available for subsequent distribution to the rest of the society. The unevenness occurs both within and among societies, so that it is in many instances not very helpful to attempt to insist upon whether there are national boundaries involved or not. Nations act as units, but so do sets of supranational power holders, as well as subnational entities.

A part of this picture of apparently rampant Darwinism is the growth of those social entities that are more successful at adaptation. The emergence of culture in the human species produced a form of adaptation that differentiates man from all other species. Without here going into the nature of culture that makes this possible, it is relevant to spell out the consequences in human social organization. Unlike most other species, there is as yet no known maximal unit of social organization aside from the world's total biomass nor any known minimal unit aside from the individual. Among social scientists, the family is often said to be a minimal unit, and the nation has been seen as a maximal unit. But the fact of the matter is that neither one nor the other of these satisfies the notions of maximum or minimum. In a biological sense, there must be men and women and some kind of organization to effect the continuation of the species. But very few people are motivated toward either matrimony or intercourse by visions of perpetuating the species. In fact, the minimum unit of survival, at any one time, is the individual. When societies are thrown upon their most difficult and reduced resources, many individuals search for themselves. The family, that variety of ways that men and women have institutionally arranged to keep each other available, is certainly an important unit, but by no means a constantly necessary or universal one. For many purposes and in many situations, it has proved to be effective. But in some it has not, and in those places the sexual, educational, and commissariat activities are taken care of in other ways.

The proposition that the nation is the maximum unit of survival is subject to even stronger doubts. Few nations could survive today in their present form were it not for derivative power in the form of economic help or military backing from certain other nations. Nations, like people and families, can only survive if there is a community of nations. But some nations are little more than paper-based fictions, whereas others are in fact multinational blocs masquerading under the guise of being separate sovereign entities.

To understand human social evolution, it helps if we can divest ourselves of preconceived notions as to the absolute necessity of certain kinds of social units. Rather, what has enabled the species to survive and what has particularly marked its organization has been the opportunistic and pragmatic quality that marks the shape and operation of every human social unit. In this regard, the individual, the nation, the nuclear family, the family band of a hunting and gathering group, and the clique of politicians who work together for their own individual self-promotion are all equally units of survival and collectively distinct from the limited types of units characteristic of most other species. The great variety of social organization in human social life has, of course, been made possible by culture, by the ability to redefine the form, content, meaning, and "function" of any given group. The question of the "universality" of particular kinds of human social units is more a matter of academic sociology than a human survival concern.

The cultural ability to change the organizational form and psychological meaning of social relationships marks one of the signal adaptive advantages that man has over other species. Within the human species, those groupings that are more adept at adjusting themselves have the advantage over those that are less able to change. Not only is it unlikely that any particular social type should be regarded as a "minimum" survival unit, but the basic nature of the human organization should also be seen as the basically amorphous relational set, that best fitted to a particular set of circumstances. Any effort to fix upon some unit as being the crucial, central, or most important social unit, whether it is the individual, the world, or somewhere in between, must be regarded by the jaundiced eye in the light of whether the chosen unit promises, under the current levels of knowledge, belief, and prejudice, to bring advantages of survival and/or development to the particular holder of the belief. While students of society pursue their study of particular forms, specific forms are usually not endowed with social values unless they are widely believed to have some advantage for the survival or development of some portion of the world's society.

Tangentially, at this point, it is probably worth noting why I use both "survival" and "development" here. The reason is that which formed the basis for my earlier distinction between the two sectors of Latin American society and which G. Lenski delineates clearly in his more general treatise.[27] When one's survival is threatened, survival is the principal general goal; when one lives in the midst of greater abundance, survival is no longer a basic necessity, and other developmental interests take over. If this general picture is reasonable, then we are not really interested in finding some particular social form or group that can be assumed to be a fundamental unit of human survival, but rather in asking about every observed network a series of questions that clearly identifies both the network and its parts in terms of the local operation. If these questions were answered, the procedure would go a long way in providing understanding of such units, in regard both to operations and to patterns of constituent features.

Some of the questions are as follows: (1) What is the composition of the network or unit in terms of subsets of individuals and in terms of the roles of the specific individuals; that is, what is its internal organization? (2) To what domains does the unit or network pertain in a subordinate capacity or in a superordinate capacity? (What is its position with respect to receiving and allocating derivative power?) (3) With what units is it a coordinate? What is the nature of the confrontation between these units? Is there a community of such units? (4) What aspects of the environment does it control? (What source of independent power, if any, does it have as a base?) (5) Considering both members and nonmembers, who is affected, positively or negatively, from the operation of this unit? (6) What restraints exist on the operation of the unit? What circumstances especially facilitate it?

These are basic questions about any unit of human organization

27 Lenski, *Power and Privilege.*

that must be answered if we want to know how it operates within the local context. Without at least having answers to these questions, we are in a very weak position to set forth propositions concerning whether a given unit is similar in operation to some formally similar unit elsewhere. In other words, scientific comparison should follow this basic inquiry, not precede it.

The social anthropologist has an investigative role that not only permits but also requires looking into these human social operations wherever they occur, no matter the level. This, of course, is where our view diverges from those of Steward, and Devons and Gluckman, cited earlier. The issue, however, is not whether we should mimic the study topics and methods of other social sciences, or that the so-called macroscopic cannot be understood within the same set of concepts and the same framework that we use for the "microscopic" events. In order to make meaningful propositions that relate the two areas, field investigation is important at higher as well as at lower levels.

This approach, however, presents problems in conceptualization. There seem to be few concepts that permit us to readily handle organized aggregates operating at the national level along with those operating in the more familiar local level. Some anthropologists who have worked in this area, particularly Steward and later Despres,[28] (influenced by M. G. Smith and Malinowski) have turned to the concept of *institution* to refer to those aggregates that work at the supralocal level. The purpose here, however, is not to multiply concepts, but rather to extend a few of them and see whether we cannot deal with these "national-level institutions" in the same terms that we deal with families, communities, voluntary associations, and other units. What is there in common among such formally distinct social entities as, for example, the household, the community, a chamber of commerce, a *panelinha*, a *bufete* of lawyers, a cooperative, a *campesino* league, or a political party? There are probably no formal features that will provide the necessary clue to their common qualities, because the major characteristics that

---

[28] Cf. Steward, "Perspectives on Modernization"; also Leo A. Despres, *Cultural Pluralism and Nationalist Politics in British Guiana*. Despres borrows the concept of "broker" from Wolf and applies it to those institutions that work at the regional and national levels.

are held in common are "functional"; they are all organizations of human beings that operate with more or less explicit agreed-upon cultural forms and common understanding and that attempt to obtain certain controls over their environment of advantage to their collective membership. It is in this last notion that we find the central commonality immediately relevant to them—these units and networks share the characteristic that *they are all devices that adapt to and exploit their environment.*

That some of these devices have the elusive quality of networks extending far beyond our ability to observe, while others conveniently perform within our view, does not alter this common characteristic. Similarly, that some are as large as nations or confederations, such as "United Nations," while others are cliques of two or three individuals or even single individuals again does not alter this fact. That some are explicitly composed of other smaller units, or that some intersect so that members common to the two find that the means and goals of each are somewhat contradictory, does not alter this feature. In short, human beings organize in order to grapple with some phase of the total environment, and the possibilities of such organizations are limited only by the qualities of the human beings themselves, the nature of the environment within which they operate, and the potential and limitations inherent in their organization.

Although this human ability to vary organization is limited, within these limitations the members of the species, by and large, change and readapt their organization in the face of new environmental threats to their continued existence. It is important to recognize that the factors determining whether one or another organization is more resilient, or more adaptable, depend upon many variables and can only be predicted with any certainty if many of these are known and taken into account. What we are dealing with, however, are adaptive units composed of human beings and their artifacts, often conceived of and organized in terms of components already known in other contexts; parts of many can reassemble into new configurations. The direction of social evolution depends upon how the units involved are differentiated, combined, and recombined. Each recombination offers a new object for possible cultural identification, definition, and evaluation, and ceases merely to be the aggregate sum of its original parts. Sometimes the original parts continue independently; sometimes they are assimilated and disappear from the scene as distinctive, culturally recognized entities.

The process is that which has become clear from linguistic study. The grammar of culture permits almost infinite recombinations into phrases; only some of these will become separately identified as clichés, repeated phrases, or separate concepts. The mechanics of group formation is slower than is that of language, and the parts are different. The general process, however, is comparable to that suggested by linguistics, and both may be referred to a common model.

The purpose of such analysis is to see things in terms of the nature of the objects being dealt with. The evidence for this nature rests entirely with the observed behavior. We may choose to believe what members of a group say of the goals, or we may not—there is always some credibility gap here—but we can describe its output. In other words, rather than deal with motivation where we have no reliable evidence for such an analysis, we choose a pose of studied ignorance, saying in effect that we do not know what the motivation may be (for example, the meaning aspect of the cultural potential), but we can seek consistencies through recurrent patterns of activity. It is not that motivation is unimportant; but events are only partially guided by explicit motives, and even when the motives dominate, they are usually complex and impossible to verify. Until the biochemistry and neurophysiology of motivation allow direct access, the human organism can for many purposes be more effectively considered as a "black box." Where we deal with social groups and networks, we are even more in such an illusory situation. Without detailed knowledge of the internal structure of the entity, we can better judge it by its actions.

We know there have been certain consistencies in the general evolution of human society. Organizations of greater scope have come into existence, and those of smaller scope have had their adaptive values readjusted to operate within the larger wholes. While today nations seem to dominate the earth as the major adaptive organization, there was a long period of human history when there were no states or nations; and there are present today some operative units that make one question just how viable an organization the nation may be.

In thinking about complex societies, we are concerned with some specific problems: (1) What kinds of units operate? (2) How do they operate to survive within the environment? (3) Given the course of general evolution, what elaboration of features will prove more adaptive to the evolving environment, and which are those that were possible for an earlier condition of human evolution but that today are either changing or disappearing?

We will here use the term "operating unit," or just "unit" to refer to any and all social relational sets that provide some focus of human activity; commonly they come into existence and have continuing existence for some period by virtue of producing some kind of consistent output peculiar to that unit. For an individual to be viewed as a component of an operating unit, it is sufficient that he have some consistent role that he plays with respect to some collectivity of individuals. Operating units are sociocultural entities and, as such, must meet two requirements: they must adapt, at least minimally, to relevant elements of the environment, both social and nonsocial; and they must receive sufficient recognition within the cognitive system of the other members in the environment that they receive license to act out their roles. These two aspects are important. One concerns the actual potential of the unit to operate in some specific way in a real environment given its composition, history, and physical circumstances. The other concerns what the people believe is the potential of the unit, the rules, the prescription, the proscriptions, and the special values they attach to it, in light of the environmental conditions as they are perceived. These two sets of circumstances will be referred to as the *reality potential* and the *cultural potential* of a unit.

The reality potential can probably only be accurately defined in categorical ways. Just as the physiological and biochemical structure of fish requires that they live in fluids of specific chemical composition, so internal composition of the Asociación General de Agricultores in 1948 made it impossible for its members to join together in concerted action against the changing national situation. The internal structure of the United Fruit Company limited it from acting as a military organization. The laborers on a 1940 Guatemalan farm were essentially co-opted politically within the farm-department-state power structure and were incapable of any separate concerted action. In the 1940's, the military was probably incapable of operating a government.

If we allow that the external behavior of a unit is contingent upon its internal organization and some specific environmental conditions, then it follows that the reality potential changes (1) as the internal organization changes, and/or (2) as the specific environmental conditions change. While it is difficult to treat reality potential apart from cultural potential of a unit, it is probably worthwhile to note some examples.

Under the revolutionary governments, Indian labor on many southwestern piedmont coffee farms was organized into local unions. This was done by changing *both* the internal organization *and* the external environment. Internally, a union organization was established with functionaries who would relate themselves in an aggressive way toward farm management, and others (sometimes not the same individuals) would relate themselves to outside services or obtain knowledge about such activities. Externally, it required the enactment of new labor laws that enabled the government to allow the laborers derived power and the activity of agents of the revolutionary movement to teach them how to organize, what to demand, and so forth.

The growth of administrative bureaus under the revolutionary governments was necessary if new governmental activities were to take place. Correspondingly, the government had to pressure the environment to change so that these new bureaus could carry on their appointed tasks. For example, not only did the Guatemalan Social Security Institute (IGSS) need its own organization, but the government also had to require employers to pay the money necessary to support that organization and had to organize labor to make use of the facilities offered.

It should be clear that reality potential is not a separable feature, but an analytic concept that becomes significant when compared with cultural potential. The cultural potential of a unit consists of the definition of the activities that its members expect of it (that is, the meanings they ascribe to it) and the definition of such activities that are ascribed to it by participants in the environment. It follows, then, that the cultural potential of a unit changes (1) as the definition of the unit as seen by its members changes, and/or (2) the definition as seen by relevant environmental members changes. Changes in meanings by either group will always be signaled by changes in form. That is, if changes are taking place in the way a survival unit is perceived, what its appropriate activities may be, what its value is to both members and nonmembers, then it is likely that this will be signaled by changes in ritual, in external, perceptible, formal features.

Of particular importance in the cultural potential is the fact that the form and meanings of units can change in response to elements that do not *directly* affect the reality potential. Cultural potential can change through cultural influences from the outside. New goals can be given to already existing organizations; new organizations can be conceived of and brought into being as imitations of models available elsewhere; units, in short, can constantly change their forms and meanings with no corresponding change in reality potential of adaptation. Indian labor had to be taught to organize; the laborers had to be taught that they had "new rights" under the new laws, and employers had to be taught to pay the social security fees. So it has been with all the more visible units during the changes that date (for present purposes) from the Ubico period to the present.

Action with respect to either of these potentials has an influence on the other. The effect of the reality on the cultural potential of a unit is fundamentally a test of reality. Individuals believe certain things are possible or not possible and act on those beliefs. If the concepts have reasonable (and crucial) congruence with experience, they are rewarded. If their beliefs do not work, then, over a period of time, variations are conceived of and tried. It is well documented that all belief systems carry a great amount of nontestable, nonverifiable content, and so most meanings do not change drastically merely due to failure in the external world. There are points, however, where some individuals lose their faith and try new meanings. Where they seem to be more satisfactory, they may be taken over by others, and the complex of meanings begins gradually to change and differentiate itself. The clear applicability of a set of definitions will usually at least guarantee their survival; their failure to work will not guarantee their demise, but it opens the way for innovation, trial and error, and efforts to find better ways.

The cultural potential affects the reality potential in two ways. First, a machine will not work unless people believe that it will and therefore start to operate it. Thus, the cultural potential determines (at any point in time) the possibility of the properties of an operating unit really being exploited—that is, the degree to which the reality potential will come into operation. Second, belief and knowledge may define some particular reality performance as being necessary, and the actual composition of the event will be experimented with and changed until its performance does approximate that dictated by the cultural potential. This is a kind of "reverse reality testing" and can produce self-fulfilling prophecies.

In choosing to use the generalized operating unit as the basic concept in our understanding of the evolution of Guatemalan society, we are not saying that some already existing concept may not be useful in the Guatemalan situation. Rather, we are simply withholding a decision, trying not to ascribe qualities that are not there. Nor are we suggesting that operating units have no structure. Using the construction method suggested in the Introduction, it is possible to keep track of many of the particular characteristics that a unit does have and to be able to be explicit not only about some of those characteristics, but also about our level of knowledge concerning them.

While it is not particularly useful to catalog the various forms that are known from other studies,[29] it is of use to specify here one dimension of variation among the units. This has to do with the degree, intensity, or tightness of their organization. Units may vary from a state of fragmentation to one of rigid internal organization. The degree of organization is directly correlated with internal responsibilities. For purposes of discussion, let us distinguish four steps of organization:

Fragmented Units: These consist of aggregates of individuals who recognize no internal unit organization beyond the fact that they have equivalent or parallel interests. Such units are, for example, migrant laborers converging on a farm at harvest time, two street vendors playing the same street, poverty-stricken families moving from different areas of the city into a new slum barrio, agrarian

---

[29] See, for example, Eric R. Wolf, "Kinship, Friendship, and Patron-Client Relations in Complex Societies," in Banton, ed., *The Social Anthropology of Complex Societies*, p. 16; Anthony Leeds, "Brazilian Careers and Social Structure," in D. Heath and Richard N. Adams, eds., *Contemporary Cultures and Societies of Latin America*; Ruben Reina, "Two Patterns of Friendship in a Guatemalan Community," *American Anthropologist* 61 (1959): 44–50.

colonists converging on newly opened colonization land, and travelers in a bus. All these have in common the facts that they are facing the same environment and sharing certain resource limitations, but there is no recognized or institutionalized internal organization beyond their physical arrangement.

Informal Units: These consist of sets of individuals who have formed a minimum of internal organization, marked principally by some recognition of reciprocity. The only power available to this kind of organization is the collective power of the individual members. The informal organization sets in, so to speak, when there is a mutual recognition that each will make his power available to the others on some basis. This level is reached, for example, in urban barrios, among migrant labor groups that travel together under a leader, friendships, the *promoción* relation among military officers, cliques, and temporary business "deals." The major recognized basis of interdependence is reciprocity.

Formal Units: The shift to what we are calling a formal organization is an important one. It involves, first, the availability to the group of some source of power beyond the mere collective power of the members. In part, this consists of the organization of the group to such a degree that it will act in concert for the common good. More than this, however, it also means the real manifestation of this concert through the control agent or office (an executive group or set of officers) together with some set of funds or resources placed at the disposal of the group for its benefit. In terms of substantive economic relations, the appearance of the formal unit is clear when the members do not receive merely on the basis of reciprocity, but on the basis of a redistributive system. Organizations that have reached this level fall under what M. G. Smith, following Henry Maine, has called a "corporate" group. Examples are plentiful: groups such as those described in Chapter 6, the government, political parties, the Church, labor syndicates after the revolutionary period, Indian communities, lay religious societies, or *bufetes* of lawyers. As Smith has expressed it, there is a "presumption of indefinite continuity."[30]

---

[30] M. G. Smith, "Political Anthropology," *International Encyclopedia of the Social Sciences* 12: 194.

Corporate Units: At the risk of terminological confusion,[31] this term has been chosen to designate the most extreme kind of formal unit, one that, besides the characteristics already noted, has the exclusive control over some power base beyond the aggregate membership, that has the control over its members to mobilize them for specific purposes, and that counts upon their loyalty as being total, with the possible exception of loyalty to the state as an allowable competitor. Such organizations include Indian communities in possession of community lands, the Catholic Church, certain Catholic groups, such as the Opus Dei and religious orders, business enterprises that demand such loyalty, labor unions during the revolutionary period, the Communist party, the Banco de Guatemala, the military officers' corps, and *guerrillero* bands. It is worth while distinguishing such groups from those that are formalized but not capable of such internal control, because the ability of a group to mobilize provides it with a degree of power that is not automatically available merely with paper formalization and election of officers.

In summary, any organized subset of the human species that tries itself out against elements in the environment is an operating unit. The effectiveness of these persons depends upon their internal degree of organization and their external environment. They differ from such groups in other species, however, because in addition to being merely allocated within the habitat and specialized with respect to particular niches, they may be readily able to change their form in order to adapt. In addition to these characteristics, they have one other: they are also located within a social universe of levels. The environment gives operating units a limited selection of other units with which to interact. This selection is made in great part by the structuring of society into *levels of articulation.*

3. *Levels of Articulation and Power Domains*

The operating units of a complex society carry out certain activities. In the course of this, it is inevitable that part of their en-

---

[31] This uses the term "corporate" following the more restricted meaning of Eric Wolf, "Closed Corporate Communities in Mesoamerica and Central Java," *Southwestern Journal of Anthropology* 13 (1957): 1–18, and "Types of Latin American Peasantry: A Preliminary Discussion," *American Anthropologist* 57, no. 3 (1955): 452–471.

vironment, either in a helpful or in an obstructive way, is made up
of other units of human society. When the units meet in confrontations, they find themselves either standing in superordinate-subordinate positions with respect to each other, or recognizing each
other as coordinates. When the latter is the case, the two units operate at the same *level of articulation.* When one exercises controls
over the other, the two operate in a *power domain.*

The concept of level of articulation is derived from Steward's
"level of integration." Although he mentioned a "family" level of
integration, Steward chose to deal with complex societies primarily
in terms of two levels: the community, or local, and the national
levels; ". . . a total national culture is divisible into two general
kinds of features: first, those that function and must be studied on
a national level; second, those that pertain to sociocultural segments
or subgroups of the population."[32] It was a very distinct finding in
the present study that if "levels" are to be used effectively, it is
necessary to regard the number as flexible, for a different number
might well operate from one situation to another. In fact, it was
specifically the variation in the number of levels that could provide
crucial indications about the nature of the society. More recently,
Steward came to a parallel conclusion, although he still holds that
the basic level is the family, a position to which I cannot subscribe.
In any case, he speaks not only of the nation-state level, but "many
higher level institutions" and says that "a state may have several internal levels of integration." He does not elaborate, but says that we
may hope for a fuller discussion in a forthcoming book.[33] Wolf has
carried Steward's concept further:

> The concept of levels of communal relations or levels of sociocultural
> integration is especially useful in the analysis of this type of change
> [such as the breakdown of Indian communities and haciendas], since
> it illuminates the manifold processes of conflict and accommodation
> which take place when the components of a socio-cultural system are
> rearranged to answer new needs, or taken up into more embracive
> systems. The concept itself, as old as St. Thomas Aquinas who spoke of
> five such levels—family, village, province, kingdom, and the empire

[32] Steward, "Levels of Sociocultural Integration," p. 48.
[33] Steward, "Perspectives on Modernization," pp. 24–25.

of Christendom—has had its most fruitful application and development in anthropology at the hands of Julian Steward.[34]

Wolf then states that there is integration both vertically and horizontally, but he does not differentiate clearly between the two. Finally, he points out that "the material indicating the nature of ties between levels of integration is still rudimentary. Our data are especially deficient in tracing the ties between region and superordinate state."[35]

The materials of the present study have made it clear not only that the number of levels varies with different cases, but also that the notion of "level" is really a set of intellectual categories into which articulations between units are placed in order to arrange them, relative to one another, in some sort of ordinal scale. For this purpose, we can speak grossly of such levels as the "individual," "family," "local" or "community," "regional," "national," and "supranational" or 'international." What occurs is a range of confrontations, oppositions, integrations; what we deal with conceptually is an arrangement of these for our convenience, one which we think has some theoretical utility.[36] It is important to see these levels as the loci where articulations occur and to understand that such articulations may occur between a great variety of operating units. It is also important to clearly distinguish the level and the various units that operate within it from any particular kind of unit. Thus, at what may be called generally a "local" level, there will be articulations among nuclear families, kinsmen, *compadres,* potential marital partners, potential in-laws, and so forth. There is no level that operates with only one kind of unit, and specific individuals may operate at a number of different levels.

The term "level of articulation" has been used rather than "level of integration" because the set of related concepts being proposed

[34] Eric Wolf, "Levels of Communal Relations," in *Handbook of Middle American Indians*, vol. 6, pp. 299–300.

[35] Ibid., p. 301.

[36] For Middle America, Wolf proposed the following series: "nuclear family, kindred, barrio or ward, community, constellation of town center with dependent communities, constellation of regional capital with satellite towns (given institutional form in Mexico as states, in Guatemala as departments), and, finally, state" (ibid., p. 300).

here goes somewhat beyond those proposed by Steward. In the present usage, all such levels involve *both* integration and opposition, cooperation and competition, coalitions and conflict. Steward, in a functionalist and Americanist tradition, tended to place his emphasis on the nonconflicting aspects of what happens at both the local and national level. Both the levels he chose to discuss, however, were levels of opposition as much as of integration. Two government ministries may cooperate in trying to gain something of common interest but are also likely to compete for parts of the national budget. What is common to all these events is that articulation takes place; the specific nature of that articulation depends, as we will see, on other factors, some of which are theoretically linked. If opposition is involved, it may vary along a range from simple competition through open conflict to the point where one or the other is eliminated or subordinated. If integration is the mode, the variation may extend from simple cooperation to coalition, to formal confederation, and, finally, to assimilation or incorporation as a single entity. The process, however, can rapidly shift from one to the other, just as political candidates shift their alliances in accordance with perceived benefits.

Just as levels of articulation provide us with an ordinal arrangement of units that stand in superordinate-subordinate position, so there is a conceptual system that may be applied to distinguish lateral relations among coordinates. The concept of power domain refers to any arrangement of units wherein two or more units have unequal control over each other's environment.[37] Wherever there is a distinctive difference in the relative power exercised by two units with respect to each other, there is a domain, and the two units pertain to different levels of articulation. Units in confrontation at one level will usually pertain to distinct domains. There is a direct relationship between levels of articulation and power domains: any set of operating units that meet in confrontation will thereby form a level of articulation and, at the same time, be differentiated into power domains. The converse of this is that any units pertaining to distinctive domains will tend to find their confrontation in accordance with confrontations already existing between members of those domains. The act of confrontation of units provides a common

[37] See appendix to this chapter for explanation of *power*.

organizational feature to both power domains and levels of articulation.

The relative level of a set of units is determined by the relative power of the units within their respective domains and how those domains are already articulated. An example is available in the case of the Alta Verapaz coffee growers. For the two decades following the Second World War, as will be described in more detail later, the large farmers of the area controlled their own farms, their own domains. They were organized at the regional level to control informally local coffee prices and to keep out individual outside competitive buyers. When they discovered, however, that under the international coffee arrangements they were at a disadvantage with respect to the other coffee regions of the country, they established a formal organization that pooled their power and allowed them to compete directly with other regional groups at the national level. Insofar as the local farmer depended only upon his own power, he could compete at the regional level; when he wanted to compete at the national level, he had to get more power. To do this, the new organization was formed. The amount of coordinated power available determined both the size and the scope of the domains involved on the one hand and the level of articulation on the other. The pooling of power both enlarged the domain and raised the level of articulation of the operators.

The level at which a unit operates does not necessarily change the amount of basic power over which it has control. However, individuals who have greater individual access to power (whether independent or derived) will tend to operate at as high a level as their power permits. The converse of this is also true: individuals wishing to perform at higher levels will have to seek out power sources that permit them to increase the level of their operation. In general, then, integration or opposition at higher levels implies that the units involved have access to a sufficiently broad base of power so that they can remain superordinate in their own domains and articulate effectively with their counterparts at the same level.

It will be seen from the use of the concepts of levels and domains that all operating units have some power base. These units may either hold direct control over some source of power (land, weapons, mass of people), or they can call upon some other power holder to use his power on their behalf. The first kind of power is independent, the second, derivative. In power domains, subordinate members are usually dependent upon superordinates for some derivative power; they will also usually hold some independent power. But, in a confrontation, they may use both sources. However, power can also be increased by formalization or incorporation of units more loosely organized. Since power is always used tactically, however, what may be enough for one confrontation may not be enough for another.

The particular level at which a unit operates sets certain restrictive conditions on the organization of the units involved. At the highest level, that of international activity, there can be no corporate or formal organization of the units involved. The units at this level will be either in opposition or in cooperation. Since there is no other set of units aside from the few at this level, they will not incorporate for a confrontation. There can never really be a world government, but only a moving set of alliances. This is important in attempting to forecast the development of Guatemala. It is out of the question that the basic oppositions visible in Guatemala will be solved through some sort of coordinate action at the international level. If anything, the oppositions inherent at the international level, together with the increase of power that is steadily taking place among the major powers, suggest that the opposing units at lower levels within Guatemala will have increasing derivative power to continue their strife. As will be argued in Chapter 4, the military in Guatemala could probably not have attempted successfully to run the government until very recently; by the same token, when Arbenz tried to neutralize the army, the Communist bloc and sympathetic Latin American powers were not capable of coming to his aid. In both instances, the units did not have sufficient available derivative power. Today, the amount of derivative power has increased so that the military is stronger, but there has also formed a countermilitary, the *guerrilleros*.

It is important for the internal organization of a unit whether its activities are directed at a higher or a lower level of articulation. When the Alta Verapaz *finqueros* were concerned with controlling the market for the Indian coffee in their own localities, the organization they had among themselves was essentially informal. They agreed on a reciprocal basis to cooperate to maintain a ceiling on coffee prices to be paid to the Indians. When these same *finqueros*, however, decided that cooperation was necessary to compete with other regional coffee-growing associations at the national level, they organized themselves formally, with a name, rules, and officers. This shift from an informal to a formal organization was necessary for a number of reasons. First, to defend themselves, they needed some allocation of powers by each member to some individual who could speak for all. This established the principle of a corporate authority for the whole. Since the various members were not all equals, they had to recognize that they were going to contribute their power to this organization and that the returns would not be equal for all of them; they had to recognize that, to have strength, they had to give up simple reciprocity as a basis of organization.

It is not the fact of "working at the same level" that requires this formalization, but rather, that working at a given level forces the opposing units to decide whether they should formalize or risk losing their power. Thus, degree of organization is an adaptive matter; failure to intensify the degree of organization may mean further loss of power. The actual confrontations that lead a unit to increase its degree of organization may be due to a variety of circumstances; all, however, stem basically from the question of seeking superior adaptive circumstances. The corporate Indian communities, the Banco de Guatemala, the military, and the Church are all cases of formalization and extension of controls by the collectivity (not to be challenged by an individual member) over some basis of power and their own action.

Just as new levels can come into being, as they do when societies gain more power, so they may, theoretically, disappear. Since we live in an age of expansion and growth, this is less immediately evident in the events about us. However, it did occur when the power of the Spanish Empire had been so reduced that it could no longer provide derivative power to the member colonies to control them, so that they broke up into separate states. Indeed, it seems to be the case that each level has its own diachronic pattern. The cyclical configurations differ from one level to another. For the individual, the life cycle dominates; for the family the domestic cycle; for the community there are annual, as well as other, cycles. For nations, there may be political cycles or some longer patterns of domination or subjugation. This is a subject that cannot be explored in terms of the materials gathered during the course of this study, but the data suggest that there may be a periodicity of human events that is determined by the levels of articulation at which the particular social units are operating.

Another way of seeing the variation in modes of articulation is to look at decision makers in terms of being elites within their respective levels. Elites, in this sense, may appear at any level of articulation. Since a level is a set of points where coordinate power holders interact, it should be clear that they cannot for long be monolithic blocs. Members of an elite hold power severally because each holds power independently of others. Just as their best interests will, from time to time, be served by cooperating with each other, so on occasion they will come into conflict. Thus, both conflict and cooperation are implicit within any elite set. This is illustrated in various instances in the discussion of upper-sector interest groups (Chapter 6), where the intergroup relations provide an irregular counterpoint of cooperative joint interest (usually as against the government and/or the consumer) and of competitive self-interest against each other.

Articulation between elements at different levels of articulation is more complicated than that at any given level. It occurs in a number of different ways. First, there are the vertical relationships that occur within single domains. Second, there are those that occur between domains (that is, where superordinate and subordinate lie within two or more separate domains). Third, there are cases where units come into being between levels. In each of these three kinds of situations, two different questions arise: what is the nature of the power relations that exist between the units or parties involved; and what are the specific kinds of units involved, the processes of action available to them, and the individuals that compose them?

Within single domains, the power situation is classically that of subordinates being dependent for derivative power on superordinates, the latter controlling certain phases of the former for the continuing maintenance of their power. The most obvious of these in Guatemala are the relations holding within agrarian and business enterprises, and within government ministries and agencies; the role of the priest within the Church hierarchy; the obvious hierarchy of the military (such as the relation holding between the *comisionado militar* and his superior officers); between the schoolteacher and the education ministry officials; and the interaction between the farm owner, administrator, foreman, and the laborer. The relationship between superordinates and subordinates, it must be remembered, is one that exists between operating units. There may well be similar operating units at different levels that are not within a domain. The voters who readily swing their votes are only temporarily within the domain of their political agent; and the local labor union may not actually be controlled at all by the federation.

Vertical relations between distinctive domains may be highly unstable, tentative, and tenuous, though with a potential for initiating more stable links for the future. Or they may be fairly stable ties that are relics of periods when the units involved were correlates. Examples of the first include political party agents trying to win members and bargaining with migrant labor, the attempt of a government extension agent to get the tobacco farmers to organize, the attempts of *guerrilleros* to win loyalty from peasant communities or the Protestant preacher attempting to gain converts. In crossing domain lines at different levels, participants cannot be entirely sure of the outcome. In some cases, of course, there are institutionalized ways of crossing these lines, as is the case at public markets. But even under these circumstances, regular participants will eventually work out a coordinate understanding, or one will become superordinate. The uncertainty of the role of the labor inspectors illustrates the problems of crossing domains. Some of them subordinate themselves to the domains of the local and regional *finqueros*; others try to retain their role as government agent and representative of the people and act coordinately to the *finqueros*.

Possibly of greater interest are those vertical, interdomain relations that continue to bind individuals or units that are not coordinate, but whose relationship is maintained because of reciprocal or mutual interests. Some of the relations have been dealt with by Wolf.[38] Much of the discussion of "cultural brokers" has emphasized dealing between different levels, but it also concerns individuals who actually operate in distinctive domains. Kinship, affinity, friendship, clique membership, market relations, seller-buyer re-

[38] Eric Wolf, "Kinship, Friendship, and Patron-Client Relations in Complex Societies," in Banton, ed., *The Social Anthropology of Complex Societies*, pp. 1–22.

lations, lawyer-client relations, and the various processes of social
mobility whereby the individual moves from one position to another
—all are devices that operate to connect what otherwise may be
independent domains. Some such connections involve an exercise
of power; others depend on more general questions of influence.
Few of these relations have come under study in the present investigation. They have been the focus of increasing interest on the
part of anthropologists, however, presumably because, following
Steward's line of reasoning concerning the anthropological study
of higher-level institutions and units, they are more clearly subject
to traditional methods of anthropological microfield inquiry.

The third kind of interlevel articulation is most commonly seen
in cases where operating units tactically insert new units between
two levels or in another level with the specific purpose of introducing change into the system. Although this has been explored in an
earlier paper,[39] it should be mentioned here that a single unit never
becomes established by itself at some level. It will eventually seek
out confrontation and find its appropriate locale within the general
pattern of levels and domains. It is easier to see some of the theoretical relations that hold between domains with the assistance of
diagrams:

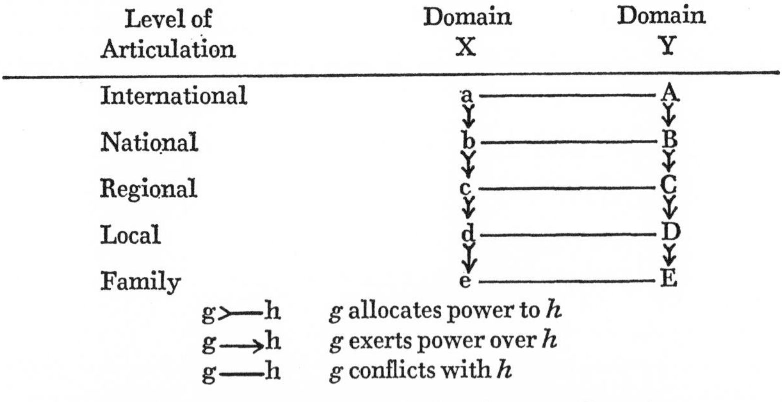

Level of Articulation	Domain X	Domain Y
International	a	A
National	b	B
Regional	c	C
Local	d	D
Family	e	E

g>—h   g allocates power to h
g —→h   g exerts power over h
g ——h   g conflicts with h

FIGURE 1–1. Theoretical Relations between Domains

[39] Richard N. Adams, "Power and Power Domains," *América Latina* 9, no.
2 (1966).

Figure 1–1 shows the basic pattern of relations where there is no independent power at lower levels. Higher levels allow derivative power to lower units within their domain. Units at every level may have confrontations with units of other domains; the relative amount of power available to it determines where any particular unit may operate.

Figure 1–1 also illustrates a theoretical relationship. Since the superordinates concentrate more power than any subordinate (where there is no lower-level independent power), the pattern of confrontation of the higher level will be reproduced at the lower levels *if* the higher-level units so wish. If A and a are in conflict, then T and e will conflict. Figure 1–1, however, shows an ideal system that only occasionally is realized. One such case was the support of the Castillo Armas insurgency against the revolutionary government. Figure 1–2 shows the same figure with a highly simplified version of the operating units involved.

Level of Articulation	Revolutionary Government	Insurgency
International	Iron Curtain (arms) ———	U.S. (cash and arms)
National	Arbenz ———	Castillo
Regional	Agrarian Comités ———	farmers
Local	campesinos ———	campesinos
Family		

FIGURE 1–2. Operating Units

Figures 1–1 and 1–2 show a situation in which there was little or no significant independent power. Where independent power does exist, the process is reversed, but the pattern remains the same. In Figure 1–3, *B1* and *B2* incorporate their power, as do *B3* and *B4*. In each case, they thereby form a new operating unit that allocates power to their agent at a higher level in order to contest their competitor at the higher level.

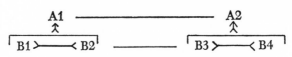

FIGURE 1–3. Allocation of Power

The *B*'s here may be coffee planters who organize regionally to compete with planters of another region; or they may be voters who put up a candidate to compete for them with other candidates. Most situations, of course, involve both derivative and independent power, and therefore the real situations are the product of the power values in a combined allocation and application of power, as in Figure 1–4:

$$\begin{array}{ccc} \text{A1} & \text{---------} & \text{A2} \\ \text{B1/B2} & \text{---------} & \text{B3/B4} \end{array}$$

FIGURE 1–4. Combined Allocation and Application of Power

This situation can be further simplified. Since *A1* and *B1/B2* are each allocating power to the other, and this is paralleled in the other set, then each set may be taken as a distinctive operating unit, as indicated in Figure 1–5, where *X1* stands for the first set and *X2* for the second:

X1 ————————— X2

FIGURE 1–5. Distinctive Operating Units

This transformation illustrates that the issue of being precise about location of levels is only heuristically useful because, in fact, levels are determined by the relative amount of power available and the way in which the units combine or fail to combine. Since an *X* is likely to be stronger than most particular *B*'s, it pays other *B*'s either to join some *X* or to organize themselves into a new one. This is what the coffee planters of the Alta Verapaz (cited earlier) did when they found that the eastern and western growers were getting a bigger share of the national market through having organized to operate at higher levels.

The Thirteenth of November military revolt was a case where there had been an *X*, that is, the combination of the government (*A*) with the military (*B*), and one member of the *B*'s separated out to challenge the rest of the unit (Figure 1–6):

FIGURE 1–6. Separation of an Operating Unit

B2 failed in the revolt. But the *A/B1* combination was not strong enough without *B2* and therefore invited them back. *B2* then further split within itself, some refusing to return and starting the *guerrillero* units (*B2.2*); others returned (*B2.1*). The *guerrillero* units then sought derived power from the outside, from Cuba and elements in Mexico (*A3*):

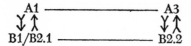

FIGURE 1–7. Separation and Combination of Operating Units

Obviously, Figure 1–7 is essentially the same in organization to that in Figure 1–4 and can be handled the same way: both may be converted to *X*'s (Figure 1–5).

One further example will be appropriate because it illustrates the beginning of what happened in Guatemala in recent years.

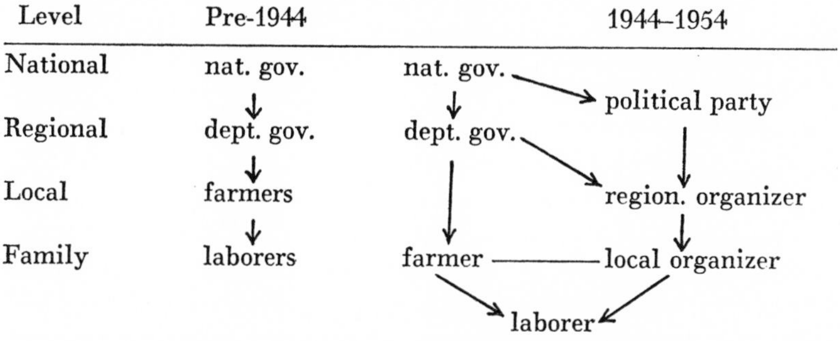

Level	Pre-1944	1944–1954
National	nat. gov.	nat. gov. → political party
Regional	dept. gov.	dept. gov.
Local	farmers	region. organizer
Family	laborers	farmer — local organizer
		laborer

FIGURE 1–8. Unitary and Multiple Domains

In this case, the pre-1944 situation was what is called a unitary domain, where the power was controlled through a single line of access. With the revolution, the political parties (along with other elements to be described in Chapter 8) received derivative power from the governments, and this they then allocated to the lower levels. This set up a multiple domain, giving the laborers multiple access to power and bypassing the unique controls formerly held by the farmer. It should be noted here that the new channels were set up as organizational devices by the government in order to destroy the unique domain system. The only way to get at the lowest level as a power source was to bypass the intermediate units. This placed the farmer in conflict with the local labor leader because both had sufficient power for confrontation.

These few examples illustrate some more general propositions. First, operating units are not fixed in composition; they are made up of parts that may separate or merge, and it is not always possible without knowledge of the internal composition to learn just how these fissions may occur. Second, the opposition between units on different levels of different domains will usually reformulate through the reorganization of the domain, so that the units will seek out opposition they believe they can confront successfully. Third, derivative power is very important to units in lower levels. Since their position in lower levels is due to the fact that they have relatively little access to power, the availability of power from higher levels can be of particular importance.

Depending upon the instance under investigation, it may be the case that the focusing on level relationships will be more fruitful than domains, or the reverse. But since the operation of a unit fundamentally establishes both the organization of domains and levels, it is preferable to keep both sets of interrelationships in mind.

The operation of levels of articulation can be visualized in various ways. One is to place the different units of each domain as they relate to a given individual. Figures 1–9 and 1–10 provide two schematized views of the operation of a number of domains that have particular relevance to a *campesino*-laborer on the one hand and a coffee *finquero* on the other. Neither diagram pretends to be complete; they merely illustrate ways that different domains relate the individual with units at different levels of integration. The concentric circles only suggest the various levels, just as the identification of operating units are hypothetical and cannot be precise in an illustration of a generalized case.

Taken together, levels of articulation and power domains set forth the basic relationships among operating units. The levels ac-

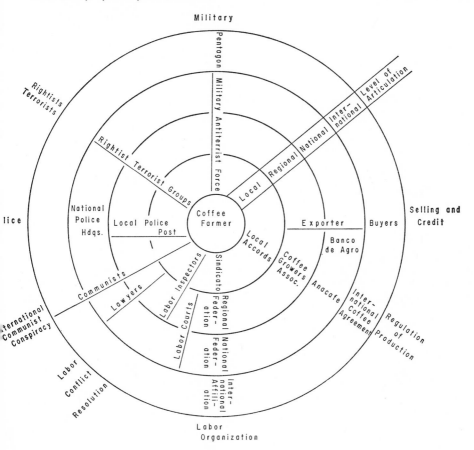

FIGURE 1–9. Idealized *Finquero*-Centered View of Relations between Selected Domains

count for the dimension of coordination, competition, and integration; and the domains account for the dimension of superordination/subordination. It should be clear, now, that the nature of the levels in any particular instance is a matter of ethnographic reality. General zones of levels, such as the "international," "national," "local," and probably "regional" and "family" are good approximations for beginning the study of a particular society. However, it is necessary to become specific in any particular case, because these

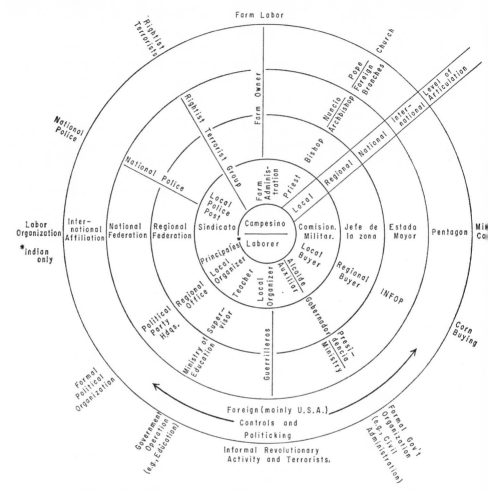

Figure 1–10. Idealized *Campesino*/Laborer-Centered View of Relations
of Selected Domains at Different Levels

concepts are really cross-cultural in nature and not ethnographic.

Relating the ethnographic with the cross-cultural is important, because it is through levels of articulation that the linkages that hold between different units in different parts of the world can be ascertained. From this, one would suppose that the higher the level, the greater the possibility of cross-cultural coincidence. This poses an interesting question for cultural relativism. Anthropologists have usually accepted the situation in which an ethnographic description could not use the same concepts as an ethnological, comparative study. The use of levels of articulation, however, specifically relate operating units within totally distinct cultural systems. It proposes, in effect, that any sociocultural system may organize itself internally as it may wish, but no matter what its internal features its organization has to cope with the environment, and part of that environment is the rest of mankind as presented through confrontations with units at different levels of articulation.

It becomes evident that every level of articulation will require of its participating units some common communicative forms and thereby manifest a culture peculiar to itself. The Useems have written of the "third culture" in the area of intercultural relations at the middle levels of articulation.[40] The concept of levels suggests that these "third cultures" will be specific to particular levels, and that we may, therefore, expect to find a variety of "third cultures": not only Western-trained intellectuals, but also hippie yoga buffs, the jet set, and internationally oriented academics. The forms and language of diplomacy and spying, for example, which derived mainly from the Western traditions as colonialism spread that level of articulation across the world, are common to all national agents working at the international level.

As one moves into lower levels, however, the concomitant effect of domains is felt. Domains become the restricting devices that select which units at lower levels will come into confrontation or association with which others. "National culture" refers to some coherent set of form-meanings associated with a national domain. Since power domains change rather rapidly with the change in power availability, and culture changes in accord also with psychological limits, there can never be expected to be a sharp one-to-one relationship between a "culture" and a "domain." The longer a domain exists, the more opportunity will there be for a consistent culture to evolve.

[40] See John Useem, Ruth Useem, and John Donoghue, "Men in the Middle of the Third Culture," *Human Organization* 22, no. 3 (fall 1963): 169–179; also, John Useem, "The Community of Man: A Study of the Third Culture," *Centennial Review* 7, no. 4 (fall 1963): 481–498.

At all levels, however, units and the domains within which they operate are subject to the realities of the environment and must adapt. The issue of adaptation and the differentiation between a diachronic adaptive sequence that approximates general evolution and one that is essentially similar to specific evolution is the subject of the remaining sections of this chapter.

4. *Elemental Processes of Adaptation*

Most discussion of adaptation in cultural evolution relates human action with the natural environment. The focus here is more on the adaptation of any unit to the *total* environment and especially to other units within the sociocultural sphere. There is talk in the anthropological literature of seeking out "basic diachronic processes" that will provide formulations as useful as some of the structural studies have for synchronism. Although only the surface of this problem may be touched in the present study, I feel sure that the formulation of diachronic processes will most effectively emerge from a concern with adaptation.

John Bennett discusses adaptation in the sense it is used here: ". . . an adaptive process does not imply complete control—only partial control and also a change of some kind in order to accommodate to that portion of the system that remains out of control." However, he then goes on to argue: "The analogy of adaptation to the natural environment comes to mind, but this analogy is defective for two reasons. In the first place, the environment, especially weather and especially moisture, is often completely unpredictable. . . . In the second place, the environmental analogy is defective insofar as the habitat does not respond actively to the cues thrown out by the enterprisers."[41] Bennett underplays the value of seeing the continuity of environment as a totality of habitat *and* society and fails to point out the similarities. There are, for example, phases of the natural habitat that are much more predictable than any government bureau: that day will come and be followed by night; that summer will be followed by autumn and winter; and that prevailing winds will prevail, and so forth. Every habitat has its more and less predictable features. The same holds for society.

[41] John W. Bennett, "Microcosm-Macrocosm Relationships in North America Agrarian Society," *American Anthropologist* 69, no. 5 (1967): 451–452.

One can predict that government bureaus will follow certain patterns. But, in the spring of 1968, there is no one that sounds convincing with predictions about elections or assassinations or the outcome of a war. The sociocultural environment also has its unpredictable phases.

Bennett's second point, that habitats do not respond, is also a narrow view. The entire process of plant and animal domestication is premised on the assumption that a habitat will respond to certain stimuli. If the right kind of seed is placed in the right kind of ground at the right time and the right conditions ensue, then there will be a crop. This is not a one-sided action. It is a mutual effort. A concatination of men do certain things, and a concatination of non-human events do certain things. Each requires the other. To reverse Bennett's comment, in domesticating the habitat, man "is not simply at the mercy of external forces, but can actively mold these forces, in ever-varying ways and degrees, to benefit the individual and the community."[42] In view of this, the habitat will, in the present essay, be regarded within the same frame of reference as society. There are obviously important behavioral differences, because the higher the society evolves its levels of articulation, the more differentiated becomes the articulation with the habitat.

Steward has commented, "As technology develops and sub-societies become more dependent upon the larger society, direct adaptation to the local environment decreases."[43] This notion that more complex societies and higher levels of integration (using Steward's term) within them are less dependent upon the natural environment is, in a sense, true. However, it should be kept in mind that very few aspects of the so-called natural environment are not mediated by cultural practices and that even in the most advanced society the habitat (now increasingly affected by man) still has a regular and direct effect on man. Guatemala City, even with its fairly dependable winds, is subject to a cloud of diesel smoke from the urban buses, and pollution of the water from the springs and rivers is becoming a greater problem of environmental sanitation as the population increases. The differentiation suggested by Steward

[42] Ibid., p. 542.
[43] Julian Steward, "Cultural Ecology," *International Encyclopedia of the Social Sciences* 4 (1968): 342.

(and common in much of the general thinking on the subject) is misleading in that man at higher levels of organization is not really less articulated with his environment, but more articulated with parts of the environment that he or his predecessors have already modified and left in a deteriorating condition or as waste. There is, however, clearly a greater survival of some operating units at the higher levels in Guatemala; that is, individuals who have worked effectively at the higher levels have obviously greater access to medical services and are likely to live longer. The survival advantages at the upper levels are not merely a greater control over the environment, but also a variety of roles for each individual; in addition, a larger unit may fragment into a smaller set of units, and the parts usually can survive in that manner. The peasant family cannot readily fragment into its component parts and expect all to survive equally well.

An important aspect of the environment of any unit is where it stands with respect to other levels of articulation. This is evident in Figure 1–10. For the *campesino*, the next immediate level of articulation of direct contact provides a personal environment. The local police, the farm administration, the priest, the *comisionado militar*, the local grain buyer, the teacher, the local party organizer, the local labor organizer or organization, all of these are units with which he may have direct confrontation and to which he may look for facilitation or from which he expects inhibition. Moving up a level, however, the environment of the individuals at the next level is immediately dual, with problems of articulation reaching both up and down.

Whereas the *campesino*'s contacts with the bishop may be non-existent, for the priest both the *campesino* and the bishop are of importance; similarly, the *comisionado militar*, the alcalde, the teacher, and so on, are all facing two directions. Clearly, the issue of which one receives more attention revolves around which one provides the greater basis of power, is more facilitating, and is more dangerous. Since most power is concentrated at the higher levels of articulation, the intermediate levels tend to respond more readily to the higher levels than to the lower. The power from the larger system that is felt at the lower levels is mediated in Guatemala through these intermediate levels. The set of units that comprise a local lower sector, in many instances, never articulates directly with the fluctuating outside world. The mediating levels tend to provide a rather more constant environment for the lower sector units than would be the case were they answering directly to outside changes.

This aspect of peasant and labor adaptation is often overlooked. When it is said that Indians live in a world of their own, it may be forgotten that this would be impossible except for the fact that unless there is some positive set of competitive lower-level units to challenge the Indian's "world," and unless the mediating levels above them are drastically altered in their organization and responses, there is little stimulus from the outside to force a new adaptive stance on the part of the Indian communities. It was precisely because such a set of events occurred that the revolutionary period was so significant in spite of its failure as a political movement.

Some of the ways in which the higher levels maintain a constant environment for the lower sectors are worth mentioning. Wages for work in large farms are not adjusted to the world price, nor to the income of the farmer or country as a whole. Rather, the relation between the upper-sector coffee growers and the Indian laborers is such as to allow the grower to survive in the face of the worst foreseeable coffee-price situation. The grower argues that he cannot afford to raise wages during good years because the prices and income are likely to go down, and then he would go bankrupt. For the growing units (the farms) to survive, they must keep their payments to labor at the lowest common denominator. This lowest common denominator means that the laborer receives a more or less constant wage, whether the prices in a given year are good or bad. The grower and the intermediate operator then take advantage of the surplus during a good year and are protected from losses during the poor years.

The owners of the *fincas de mozos* (see Chapter 8) have a similar situation. By providing land at no cost for subsistence cultivation to Indians, the grower has guaranteed labor as he needs it, not as the laborer may need it. The growers' attitudes toward labor organizations have an element of this in them too. Since it is a risk that a union may fall into the hands of an aggressive and hostile organizer, it is safer to be categorically against all labor organizations.

This role of the intermediate levels of articulation is extremely important since it reflects not only on the channeling of wealth, but also on the entire view of how one thinks about complex societies. Bennett, in his Great Plains study, found that the interplay between what he regards as the "macrocosm" and the "microcosm" is a central feature: "The 'complex society,' then, in the North American context, is [one] in which there is interplay between local and external, microcosm and macrocosm—not one in which a single center of power dominates the entire society. North American agrarian society retains this characteristic interplay, a combination of autonomy and cultural distinctiveness, with varying degrees of acceptance of externally derived frames."[44]

In Guatemalan society, however, it is clear that the effect of the intermediate levels of articulation, combined with the concentration of power at the top, produces a situation in which this interplay is still limited and much less reciprocal. It would be misleading to suppose that the situation described by Bennett is somehow characteristic of "more advanced" or "more modern" societies if, by those terms, there is the implication that Guatemalan society is destined to become more like them. Societies like those of Guatemala, where there is no primary leadership in technological advance, are likely to continue (whether under socialist or capitalist governments) with more and more highly concentrated control over power; the intermediate levels will probably continue to provide an important phase of the total environment for the lower sectors.

In view of the severe variations on the adaptive process at the various levels of articulation, adaptation can be thought of as occurring also at these levels; the problems faced by operating units can be discussed in terms of "levels of adaptation." Among the principal problems are (1) the availability of the power base, (2) ability for physical mobility, (3) multiplicity of possible roles, (4) intensity of degree of organization, (5) potential for expansion, and (6) the possibility of disappearance.

The formation of a unit immediately implies articulation with elements in the environment. These articulations in turn imply that certain features are particularly relevant to the unit. Some features facilitate and provide a framework within which the unit may progress and perhaps consolidate; other features inhibit and require

[44] Bennett, "Microcosm–Macrocosm Relationships," p. 452.

either that the unit adjust, that it change itself slightly, or that it force a change in the environment. The facilitating features may involve other units that go so far as to cooperate and assist it; the inhibiting aspects may go so far as to compete with it and even challenge and openly conflict with it. A niche, then, comprises at least three sets of factors: the power bases of the unit (those phases of the environment that are controlled and that provide the where-withal for operation), the facilitating phases, and the inhibiting phases.

The power base is of particular importance because in some degree it sets the framework for other phases of the environment to facilitate, inhibit, or be nonactive. In general, the greater the power base of a unit, the higher will be the level of articulation or confrontation of the unit with other units. In crude terms, a unit with one gun will be unlikely to confront a unit with a hundred guns for an extended period. For exactly the same reason, the peasant with only five *cuerdas* of land will be hard put to confront the *finquero* with five *caballerías*; the laborer who controls the work of one man per day (himself) will find it difficult to confront the employer who controls the wages and working situation of five hundred laborers; the artisan who needs credit to produce fifty hats a week is in a poor position to confront reciprocally the creditor who controls enough funds to choose between fifty such credit risks. But the local political organizer who controls five hundred votes can confront the presidential candidate who must get those votes to be elected. If the individual with one gun can get more, then a successful confrontation may be made, but, if so, the confrontation has been raised to a higher level, to that of the unit controlling the one hundred. Similarly, units of peasants or of laborers or of credit clients may, through their organized control over the power that each has, confront the higher level operator.

Power, then, may consist of many kinds of controls, specifically including the organization of human beings. No matter what the source, if it has some degree of dependability, greater power will inherently raise the level of articulation of its user. When a government agent pressed small tobacco growers to organize against the major tobacco company, and the growers told him that the monopoly of buying gave the company such control that the growers perceived no advantage in such an organization, they might also have perceived that the government agent himself did not command enough derivative power with the domain of the government to confront the company directly. Crass as it may sound, the kind of question Stalin asked concerning how many divisions the pope could command is a basic question for any social operating unit. For the amount of power that any unit can in fact command determines, in great part, the ultimate success of its adaptation.

Physical mobility is used by the peasant or laboring family that needs a niche similar to that which it has had but which is no longer available locally. The priest whose cooperatives were successful in Quiché was moved to another post for a while, the politician who is possibly troublesome to the government becomes a diplomat, the entrepreneurial grower knows he can move to new agrarian areas, and so on. All societies have constructed themselves so that certain kinds of environment are peculiarly useful to them, and there are multiple instances of these environments. The individual unit that can readjust its behavior to take advantage of another niche similar to that to which it is accustomed will probably survive.

Internal organization for survival, however, characterizes units at all levels of articulation. The *bufete* of lawyers, in which each member plays a specific role with respect to the range of possible clients, is a unit with broad adaptive powers (see Chapter 8). It survives changes in government, changes in income of its members, and innovations in the agrarian, industrial, and commercial climate of the nation. The government bureaucrat, long practiced in how to run an office, can move readily from the ministry of education to that of agriculture when a government changes, so that while his specific salary, location of office, immediate co-workers, and substantive activities change, his basic knowledge allows him to continue within a common type of governmental niche.

Most units at higher levels have multiple roles available to them. Not all are as consciously planned or as broadly based as the *bufete* of lawyers or the multiple-crop grower. The newspaperman can become a bank executive or an importer of veterinary supplies. The higher the level of articulation, the more experience is often necessary to allow the individual the sufficiently broad background to play out such a variety of roles. But whether he is president of the country, a university professor, a colonel in the army, or a practicing lawyer, his general background makes it possible to operate in a number of different niches at a high level, just as the practice with muscle permits the laborer to carry out a variety of unskilled roles. It is probably worth noting, then, that multiple role-playing is an important organizational characteristic of any unit that is required to adapt to new circumstances at higher levels.[45]

While physical mobility permits a unit to escape the threats of a particular environment and multiple role-playing permits it to seek out another facet, the change in degree of organization is usually brought into play under specifically threatening circumstances that do not allow mobility or role-playing as a resolution. The shift from a fragmented laboring mass to a disgruntled, informally organized set of laborers or from the latter to a formalized syndicate organization are changes that take place internally when the nature of the environment is threatening to the laboring force. The shift from a set of individual farmers to the corporately organized co-owners of a piece of communal property signals a shift from a group of people who may be individually shorn of their properties to a group that stands together to corporately defend the basis of their power. When there is no other basis of power, corporate defense is often the best defense. However, the reverse is also true. When a basis of power is lost, the units may find that individual survival is more likely with a reduction in degree of organization. Thus, when *guerrilleros* are too hard-pressed by the government military forces, they split up into smaller, less centralized groups. When the government, as during the Peralta period, made it difficult for some political parties to organize and operate openly at the national level, they tended to break up into smaller parts and attempted to continue in that form. However, fragmentation implies a loss of power and is therefore a dangerous game. It can mean ultimate dissolution of the unit. So it is that some political parties have been unable to re-form since the Peralta administration, and a great many labor unions that are still legally on the books from the days of the revolution have been unable to reestablish themselves as active, formal organizations. They have not had a sufficient basis of power, even though they retain legal authorization.

Such fragmentation occurs annually in segments of the lower

[45] Anthony Leeds has illustrated this well in "Brazilian Careers and Social Structure," pp. 379–404.

sector. Indian families that must migrate to coffee or cotton harvest leave their communities and go to the coast; individuals, usually the men, may leave their families for the same purpose. It has become the habitual way of dealing with the limited power available in the home territory. In this case, the fragmentation is accompanied by a minor, temporary change in roles.

It must be taken as a matter of definition that all units do have some kind of organization. It would probably be difficult to argue that the people walking down Sixth Avenue in Guatemala City comprise a unit, even though they have things in common that brought them there, a mode of walking, devices for avoiding collisions with vehicles and other people, a high level of concern with marketing and prices, and so on. The Sixth Avenue crowd, organized though it is, might be difficult to recognize as a unit. If, however, we accept as identifying criteria the features of organization and not the precise membership at any point in time, then it is easy to recognize it as such. For example, this organization can take on different features: instead of a more or less even north-south movement, everyone seems to be moving north toward the National Palace; and instead of a random mixture of men and women, it seems to become heavy with men; and instead of a random mixture of ages, there seem to be few infants and very small children and a heavy proportion of active adults; and instead of merchants opening their stores, they are frantically bringing down their metal shutters— then we recognize that we are not dealing with a random collection bent on commerce and bureaucratic business, but a unit heading for some sort of public demonstration.

From many standpoints, one of the most interesting aspects of a unit is its potential for expansion. Expansion is the way that some units survive while others do not, and, if reasonably based on reality, is probably an important index of successful adaptation. It is also central to our understanding, for it is through expansion that many confrontations occur. Real expansion must rest fundamentally on an expanded power base, not merely an elaboration of the images of cultural potential. A paper organization may increase, or the enthusiasm may grow, but without concomitant increased control over the environment, the reality potential does not change. Every operating unit may be said to be composed of certain critical elements, basically those elements providing its base and those permitting it to act. It should be possible to distinguish between those units that, once in being, seem to have little or no growth potential (potential to gain and increase their power base), and those having such a potential. Obviously, within the latter, there is also the question as to what distinguishes those units acting on this potential from those that do not.

Basically, an expanding unit is one that increases critical inputs over outputs. If it is the members' time in some specific activity that is crucial, then it is more effective man-hours of such activity, with some accumulated product; if it is cash investment, then it is increased funds for that purpose; if it is farming, then it is more land, more coffee trees, more crop, more income. Expansion is part of the entire question of development, but it is only part. Since the expansion of one unit may mean the simultaneous decline (through competition) of another, expansion in itself does not constitute development unless it may be said that it is occurring absolutely across some level of articulation. Land redistribution that removes control from one individual and allows it to a multiplicity of others obviously does not comprise development, since it does not lead to an increase per capita and may even amount to a decrease. Expansion within levels, however, often tends to be limited and cyclical, with some units being on the ascendency for some period, while others take over later. Thus, a peasant family may so subdivide the inheritance that in the next generation some other individual is more successful, and the remnants of the wealthy family find themselves without their former base.

A significant change in the expansion of a unit at any level takes place when the unit finds that it is beginning to adapt to a higher level. The entrepreneurial peasant who has been successful in buying up land locally and using his neighbors as hired help not only begins to confront the village storekeeper as a credit agent, but also moves to the departmental capital or center and confronts others who operate at the regional level. From there, success places him increasingly in contact with those who operate at the higher levels. As this occurs, his enterprises expand, becoming more valuable, and he becomes more powerful. Of course, there is in all this the contrast between the cultural and reality potential. If his real power does not match the cultural potential, then he may find suddenly that he has gone bankrupt or that someone with greater power has discovered his weaknesses and has taken advantage of them.

Socioeconomic mobility of the kind just described is not extremely common in Guatemala, but it does occur and is a recognized process. It does not mean instant social acceptance by the traditional society that occupies the higher levels, but it does mean that articulation, confrontation, competition, and sometimes cooperation will be available. The upwardly mobile person who wishes to sustain himself at higher levels of articulation must consolidate his controls in fact. This can be more easily done the higher up one is. Since more power is concentrated by units that articulate higher up, so more power becomes accessible (through fair or foul means) to those who can operate at those higher levels. But along with the movement upward, the individual or unit must also learn the devices that are appropriate to and peculiar to the higher levels. He has to learn the ways of banks before he can effectively exploit them; in order to marry into a wealthy family, the individual must show some ability to manage the manners and customs of that level of society. All of this is part of adaptation.

Further expansion at the highest levels of a national society force one into the international sphere. Indeed, in a country like Guatemala, where so much of the real basis of power rests in the control over some portion of an export market and some facets of foreign political action, the aggressively expanding unit will presumably move into the international area almost as soon as it is working at the national level.

Expansion is a process that can be undertaken only by some units. At every level of articulation, most units will be more involved in survival than in expansion. Very few peasants or laborers are successful in expanding their operations to a regional level of operation; few who operate at the regional level successfully break into a broad national operation; and few of those, in turn, succeed in operating at the international level. It is here that one can see most clearly the analogy to the process of natural selection. In a sense, there is at each level a set of comparable species; those operating at higher levels have achieved a greater control over the environment and thereby, in a sense, comprise a different genus. Those "higher level" units also will be relatively more specialized and complex and therefore involved in a much more intricate adaptation.

If expansion is one index of successful adaptation, it is because we accept survival as a criterion of success. However, as Alfred Emerson has pointed out, death is also adaptive in that it allows other members to further readapt to the changing environment. It is certainly the case that contemporary human social organizations tend to be cluttered with operating units of little reality potential but a tenacious cultural potential. Like mutations, however, it is probably the case that most operating units never really come alive because their own construction does not meet minimum survival needs. Disappearance of units is probably much more common than may be allowed.

In dealing with disappearance, the fading away of a unit that cannot exist unless operating with respect to specific environmental stimuli must be distinguished from the failure of a unit in a confrontation, where it is literally unsuccessful in mastering the environment that it has set as its goal to conquer. Among the most outstanding examples of the second type are Guatemalan political parties. The first is illustrated by a failing commercial venture that misjudged its market. Disappearance among operating units is, in one sense, even more adaptive than among living species. It has been pointed out that environment is a relative concept: ". . . its bounds are not set, but vary according to the social units isolated for purposes of analysis. Thus, factors that for one purpose may be regarded as external may for another purpose or in a different context be regarded as internal."[46] Because of this quality, operating units often are so transformed that some, seeming to have disappeared, have merely taken on a new form not immediately recognizable.

Since the existence of a social unit is seldom coterminous with any specific set of organisms, the units can and do continue well beyond any particular membership. A social unit may see continuity in one of three distinctive ways: (1) through continuity of forms, that is, the nature of the power base, the behaviors of the members, and so forth (2) through continuity of meaning, for example, the

[46] Eisenstadt, "Anthropological Studies of Complex Societies," pp. 292–293, referring to the view of A. L. Epstein in "The Network and Urban Social Organization," *Rhodes-Livingston Journal* 29 (1961): 29–62.

way it is thought of, the role it is believed to be playing in the larger society, the purposes and goals ascribed to it, and (3) through continuity in membership, that is, the continuing presence of particular individuals of specific other units within it. Since the cultural aspect of a unit can change with variations in form and meaning, it is frequently the case that a continuity of form will hide the fact that meanings have changed; but it is equally the case that a continuity of meaning keeps reappearing under a variety of formal guises. One unclear result of the present study is the degree to which the Catholic Church in Guatemala is representative of a continuity of form but a change in meaning, and also the degree to which the meanings have been changing (Chapter 5). Quite obviously, one would not rashly speak of the "disappearance" of the Catholic Church merely because it was becoming liberalized. However, if it became actually revolutionary, such characterization might be appropriate.

Since changes in any phase of a unit may be adaptive as well as "disappearing," the disappearance of an operating unit is really part of a larger adaptative picture. For a unit to succeed, some phase of it must disappear. Real and total disappearance of all phases can usually come about only through a sudden destruction of membership, such as Castro's elimination of the Bautista officer corps in Cuba. This suggests why a "revolution" is so difficult. The Guatemalan revolution of 1944–1954 initiated many new operating units but did not destroy most of the old ones. The failure to do this, by whatever means, contributed to its own destruction.

5. *Structure and Organization*

In describing the sets of relationships that simultaneously comprise the central adaptive (the central diachronic) processes of this complex society and the macroscopic design of the system as a whole, it will be necessary to use two terms that have been given a multitude of meanings in the social science literature and that therefore may be expected to bring some confusion to relating this argument with those that have preceded it. The two terms are *organization* and *structure*. The referents of these terms may be illustrated by contrasting two kinds of changes that are repeatedly cited in this volume: the fluctuation in the locus of power within the society, and a concomitant unidirectional concentration of power in the government and upper sector.

Later chapters detail specific cases concerning the military, labor-court action, and the expansion of cotton cultivation, wherein there has been a unidirectional concentration of power in the hands of the government and the upper sector. This is evident in the laws passed in the Ubico period with respect to the control of laborers and *campesinos*, and it can clearly be dated back at least to the liberal revolution of García Granados and Justo Rufino Barrios. At the same time, a great deal of material in this volume describes the variations in organizational emphasis, the shifting of allocation of derivative power, the rise and fall of whole sets of such units as *campesino* organizations, political parties, and specific interest groups. Arbenz promoted the cultivation of cotton, a device destined to bring increasing power to individuals of the upper sector, and, at the same time, was promoting the formation and action of rural labor unions to contest the power of the landlords. The postrevolutionary governments effectively stopped all but minimal labor organization but, at the same time, allowed the labor courts to continue to operate in a way somewhat favorable to the laborer. There were, in other words, two apparently distinct processes going on at the same time. One continually drew the strings of control into the center; the other set one part of the society against another.

It is the set of patterns illustrated by these two major processes that are referred to here as *structure* and *organization*. Since the term "structure" has been so important in social science, and especially in recent anthropology, it is important to be explicit as to its usage here. It does not refer to the Levi-Strauss usage wherein "structure" refers to a statement proposing related points that, through transformation rules, permit one to predict a later state of the system.[47] Nor does it follow the differentiation made by Firth, who saw structure more as the rules laid down by a society, while the contrasting social organization referred to the actual behavior of the members of the society.[48]

Structure here refers to a set of conditions within which the social organization of a series of events takes place. Organization includes the policies, specific operating behaviors, rules, and relational sets that comprise the conduct (specifically adaptive) of operating units

[47] Cf. Claude Levi-Strauss, *The Savage Mind.*
[48] Cf. Raymond W. Firth, *Elements of Social Organization.*

at any point in time. Thus, structure must be seen as the framework of some set of parts with reference to some set of events. Structure must be identified in terms of the events that it conditions and for which it provides a framework and backdrop. It may also be seen as the conjunction of the relevant social, cultural, and natural environmental elements within which some series of events takes place and which provides the conditions initiating those events. With this general notion, it is possible to abstract phases of a total structure, such as the power structure in the present case, and to speak specifically of the power structure of those parts, referring to a set of conditions that determines the limits of the operation of those parts.

Chapter 8 describes various structural features that inhibit access by the *campesino* to wealth and justice, singling out the policy of the government as a separate event, which either operates congruently with the structure (thereby probably introducing more rigidity into it) or operates contrary to it (thereby introducing new elements that will weaken the structure). When the military added political reporting to the duties of the *comisionados militares*, they introduced a new relationship into a structure that was already well defined. The new relationship did serve to strengthen the military establishment as an organization. However, in the countryside, the new activities of the *comisionado* led him to come into conflict with elements of the environment that he did not affect previously. The rural environment, with its traditional factions and hatreds, served the personal interest of various parties and led to the assassination of some *comisionados*.

It should be clear that, while neither structure nor organization is fixed, these elements change in accordance with different sets of factors. They are also characterized by different patterns of change. Organizational events seem to follow one another with some pattern of fluctuation, sometimes similar to an action-reaction formula, other times to the conjunction of independent events leading to specific historical outcomes. Structure, within the time scope of the present study, shows itself as what appears to be a unidirectional set of changes or a set of constants, a set of variables that answers to conditions that, in this instance, are not changing. In looking at any specific event, the issue is to single out those conditions that are beyond the control of the operating units in the event and that therefore act as the conditions under which the event will find its outcome. These elements are the structure of that event. The factors and conditions that fall within the control of the participating units, the relations that are the result of those manipulations and efforts, are organizational.

An important illustration is the case of government. Students of government have often shown preference for describing government in one of two ways. By some, it is projected as a controlling and regulating institution, comprising various administrative organs and political activities; in this view, it deals with the society but stands slightly apart from it. The other view sees it as the conjunction of the major power controllers of the society, as the operating unit reflecting the interests of those powers. Of course, both these views are true in the sense that government does act in these ways. It helps to clarify the picture, however, if these two views of government are differentiated in terms of organization and structure. The government is composed of related operating units acting in various capacities; it is a set of parts, organized in various activities of regulation and promotion within the society at large. This organization comes into being and continues and adapts at any point in time to the realities that surround it. It fluctuates in terms of new people taking control of governmental institutions, of emphasis being placed on first one, then another, kind of policy, regulation, or service. It is, in short, a highly complex organization, answering the conflicting demands of its own component units and the other units of the society.

It is also, however, a structural system within the total society. No matter who runs it, there is always a government; no matter which party or set of local interests may have dominant influence, it still continues to mediate these interests into regulatory, political, and administrative activities. And most important, it exists by virtue of the fact that it controls a great deal of power. This power is not just that which is in the immediate domain of the government as an organization, such as the regulatory controls exercised through the police, military, and other agents. Of greater importance is that it serves in some harmony with the major domain interests of the society, since it depends upon those domains for its basic power support.

One of the notions proposed in this study is that the Guatemalan military has advanced in its control of the country to the point where it exercises an extraordinary amount of power within and beyond the governmental framework. Political observers from Edmund Burke to the present day have observed that no people can continually be ruled by force: "The use of force alone is but temporary. It may subdue for a moment; but it does not remove the necessity of subduing again; and a nation is not governed which is perpetually to be conquered."[49] Morton Fried puts it in sociologese: ". . . the state . . . cannot constantly mobilize its force at each point in its structure."[50] The direction of events in Guatemala during the three years of the Peralta regime was not a rule by force, but a temporary rule in which all the major cabinet posts were occupied by military men. The nature of the increased control by the military in Guatemala, and indeed in most Latin American countries, is not in the form of the classical police-state, but rather through the fact of common interests being held by the military and a controlling segment of the conservative upper sector of the society. The increased strength of the military has taken place as an *organizational* phase of the structural centralization of power. We know that centralization has occurred in other ways too. A serious question is whether structural centralization of power in the government could take place in the absence of organizational growth of military power. The answer is probably affirmative, but it could only be demonstrated by comparative study.

The military is (along with the various police) the organizational element of the government providing the greatest tactical concentration of force. A government, as a structure, may increase its concentration of power in various ways. It can reflect the specific concentration of powers of the society at large merely with a police force. However, organizationally, a government is the focal point of the major powers, a focus of contention, the locus of major confrontations within the society. As such, the contending powers themselves value an increase in their own controls, and there will always be some that value the available derivative power of a military force. Since the military is itself an organization, an operating

---

[49] Quoted by Lenski in *Power and Privilege*, p. 51.

[50] M. Fried, "State: The Institution," *International Encyclopedia of the Social Sciences* 15 (1968): 148.

unit in terms of this analysis, it has all the same predispositions concerning its own security and progress that other units do. The major difference is that it has the basic control of force as an independent power base.

The distinction between structure and organization is useful in an understanding of any society, but crucial in tracing relationships in complex societies. However, treating the two as dichotomous concepts is misleading. Both are themselves complex products of a set of independent variables. The variables that affect structure are most easily identified in the habitat and in levels above that of the confrontation; those that determine organization are more readily seen within the confrontation level and below. The confrontations at the higher levels involve the greater concentrations of power in the society, the greater bases of power. As such, they are both more unwieldy and more responsible for setting the gross frameworks within which lower levels operate. Those at the lower levels involve smaller concentrations of power, more individual cases of them, and therefore greater possible variation in the outcomes. This last accounts for why organizations tend to dominate our perceptions; we are constantly aware of the changes in social organization that surround us, but much less aware (if aware at all) of those occurring at higher levels; they are discovered as structural conditions when lower units try to act.

The differences may be seen in contrasting three cases of control: that of the *campesino* seasonal migrant, the wealthy owner of a number of coffee farms, and the U.S. State Department official concerned with Latin America. The first is organized within a family group, a community, some of whose members go to pick coffee every year on the coast. The degree of organization of the migrant's family is affected by the structural economic limitations, including the necessity to obtain cash. The structure within which the *campesino* works is that of the large farm system with seasonal labor as an intrinsic part. The wealthy farmer operates within a structure of much broader scope. The world coffee market and its attendant price fluctuations and export possibilities, together with the possibility of socialist-bloc buyers, are things over which he has no control. Nor, in company with the *campesino*, does he have control over the vagaries of the natural environment, whether it will be a good coffee year or not. He can, however, affect the organization of his farms, determine the number of migrant pickers he needs, make sure that fertilizers get in and new seedbeds are planted, and so forth. He can also have some effect, through confrontation, with operators of his government, including the military.

The U.S. State Department has few direct controls over what goes on in Guatemala but has considerable controls that it can affect, for example, with respect to the international coffee agreements, the role of the United States as a market for Guatemalan coffee, the threat of armed intervention, and the availability of loans. But these controls have to be coordinated with the U.S. coffee buyers, importers, constituents of congressmen, and others. Similarly, in the broader coffee market, the State Department acts in confrontation with other national agents and is deeply influenced by the broader structure of world power domination as between the Communist and non-Communist countries. The members of the Third World tend to take a back seat in its concerns. Its decisions concerning Guatemala are made not in terms merely of a rational appraisal of Guatemala, but what is best for the U.S. in the world confrontations for control. For the State Department, the structure also includes certain natural environmental features, such as the totally uncontrollable fact of Chinese national growth, the development of Arab strength, the competition for outer space, and the fact that even its erstwhile friends such as France, can be rapidly converted into serious international competitors. All of these are structural facts.

The Guatemalan *campesino*, landowner, and the U.S. State Department are all operating units. They all work within limits set by a larger structure, and all try to manipulate their controls so that the outcome will be to their advantage. But what may be organizational concerns at a higher level become structural concerns at the lower. It was suggested earlier that the pattern of change of the structural phase is somewhat different from the social organizational. The former tends to be unidirectional, the latter fluctuating. A major characteristic of the structure within which most Guatemalan units operate is an escalation of power concentration at the higher levels. For the *campesino*, this means greater concentration of power within the upper sector and government. For the government, it means greater concentration of power in the United States and Mexico.

6. *Structural Escalation*

Structural escalation refers to the process whereby the contenders for power find that in order to retain and secure their positions they must constantly further strengthen their controls. The process is composed of a simple set of steps: (1) a confrontation occurs between a set of units at any level; (2) some (or one) of the units are successful in obtaining new power sources to superordinate themselves over others, (3) in the process of doing this, they have, of course, strengthened themselves and, by superordination, find themselves now in confrontations with units at higher levels of articulation. The process then repeats itself. When a unit is at the highest level of articulation, the first two steps simply keep repeating themselves, constantly attempting to bring new power bases under their control. The fact that some units are particularly concerned with this process does not mean that all units are equally concerned. The rationale at any point in time, however, is likely to be survival; in order to survive, the unit must superordinate, gain more power.

Events contributing to structural escalation can be found throughout the periods here under consideration. Ubico legally brought labor control directly under the domain of the central government. The vagrancy law, which dated at first from the liberal beginnings under Barrios, continued on the books following the revolution of 1944, although the government control over labor through the personal work records was abolished. The major change was that there were no specified punishments for vagrancy. In this way, however, the government kept its legal control over lower-sector individuals through a law that had been associated with earlier more oppressive regimes. The exercise of this governmental right seems to have dropped into disuse in most parts of the country, but it will be seen that a local interpretation was apparently (at the time of the study in 1965) still in use as a device in the Alta Verapaz.

The revolutionary period was a time during which major changes were introduced into the nation as a whole and which brought the chains of control directly into the hands of the government. Under

Ubico, Guatemala could almost have been characterized as a country with a lower sector controlled by the upper sector and the latter controlled by Ubico. This, in spite of Ubico's personal controls, still left the upper sector in the crucial position of being the mediator between the government and the lower sector and thereby allocated to it much of the derived power that the government had to give out. The revolutionary government selectively removed power from the upper sector and granted it to the lower. By this means, it gained more direct control over the population of both sectors. The mass organization of the lower sector was among the primary devices. The aim of the revolutionary government was not to destroy the upper sector, but to break its power and thereby strengthen the lower sector but, more than anything else, it sought to strengthen the government. The Banco de Guatemala, for example, was started as a way of removing the control over government finances from the older Banco Agrícola Mercantil, a private bank in the hands of the leading members of the older upper strata of the country. The land expropriated during Arbenz' agrarian reform was distributed not as property, but in nontransferable rental. This provided the government greater control. The extension of the franchise and the organization of the local political party agents served the same purposes. In the Ladino communities, party people sympathetic to the government were often hostile to the more traditional upper class. In a parallel way, the older traditional Indian political organizations were undermined. The cumulative effect was to weaken the traditional control devices in the provinces.

In Chapter 8, it is pointed out that although the revolutionary period began with a rise in individual legal cases brought against the government, this increase was severely slowed down before the end of the period, and it never became a significant element of the legal picture again. Without being able to do further research on this, it appears at the outset as if the first enthusiasm of the revolution led its leaders to encourage a degree of challenge to the government that they later had to reject and prohibit.

Perhaps the most important feature of the attempts of the revolutionary governments was the introduction of devices to bring power to the government itself without being dependent on the derivative power of any extranational group. It was part of the nationalistic mode to reject dependence on foreign derivative power and to incorporate the controls within the country. The contrast may be seen clearly in comparing it with the way the postrevolutionary governments continued the process of centralization. Instead of emphasizing the nationalistic control, the counterrevolution itself was a product of the direct aid of the United States government. Immediately upon the confirmation of the new government, the United Fruit Company gave a large land area to the government for distribution to lower sector people, and the United States technical, economic, and military aid efforts were rapidly stepped up. Until the end of Ydígoras' regime, efforts by the government to gain control were regularly neutralized by the fact that there was a continued dependence on the United States and a concomitant inability to gain the confidence of the broad range of provincial peoples. No political party was regarded as having sufficient power or potential to warrant great confidence, and most such parties were temporary efforts. "Parties constantly emerge, split, and die; few parties last for any significant length of time. Parties, being temporary coalitions of men, cannot be relied upon by political leaders as solid bases of support."[51]

During this period, there were various attempts to formulate a coherent opposition by revolutionary-inclined parties, but, of these, only the Partido Revolucionario survived, and this was not an easy task. The Communist party (PGT) reformed in Mexico but could not play a very active role in Guatemala, since it was specifically outlawed. With the failure of the Thirteenth of November military revolt and the beginning of *guerrillero* activity, another phase of postrevolutionary activity got under way. The military had become markedly stronger, and the government, now under the military control of Peralta, overtly promoted the formation of stronger upper-sector interest groups.

Structural escalation has some directly perceptible manifestations, the most obvious being nationalism and nationalization.[52]

---

[51] John W. Sloan, "The Electoral Game in Guatemala," Ph.D. dissertation, University of Texas at Austin, 1968, p. 222.

[52] "Nationalization" here does not refer to the process whereby a government takes over ownership of private property, but rather the process whereby a population that has been dealt with through semiautonomous intermediary institutions and operating units comes under direct contact and control from the na-

Nationalism is the expression, used at all levels of integration, of what is believed to be the best way to achieve greater control for the sovereign domain. Nationalization is the idiom for the process whereby the nation can attempt to achieve greater internal and external controls. It is a salable doctrine because the activities at the national level are somewhat visible from the lower levels of the society; as the lower levels increasingly recognize their derivative power needs, they can identify with higher-level confrontations.

Internally, it pursues a policy of increased controls through more direct links with various levels of the society, bypassing the intermediate levels in order to gain direct controls over the lower levels. The expression "national integration" refers not to an integrative process at distinctive levels, but the process of multiple articulations between levels. Externally, nationalization is an attempt to incorporate the nation-state as an operating unit that can count on the directed participation of most, if not all, sectors of a society in the decisions made by the government at the national level. This is externally oriented because the issue is the confrontation with other nation-states in the competition for the various resources available throughout the world.

Since it is the nation-state government that is the principal beneficiary in this process, the government, no matter what its political color, finds nationalism to be generally an advantageous public ideology and doctrine. The promotion of centralization of power in the area of government therefore becomes an organizational goal for every government. The consistency of this organizational process provides the mechanism for world-wide structural escalation. By exactly the same token, it is a part of the structural situation within which lower-level operating units within any nation-state find themselves. It often requires that the poor remain poor for the benefit of nationalism, and that the rich become richer in order to strengthen the nation.

In this sense, then, nationalism is an idiom that is of specific benefit to some national-level operators, but is also one that must be

---

tional government. It involves the "internal acculturation" of the people and their political identification with the nation-state as the ultimate regulatory authority.

reinterpreted to be useful at the lower levels. The benefits of nationalism are clearly different for a Guatemalan Indian and the owners of the major beer industries. It is one thing to argue that Indians should be loyal; it is quite another to have a device to improve market possibilities and to keep out foreign competitors. The obvious nationalistic concern of various of the interest groups described in Chapter 6 finds its only rationale in the benefits that will accrue to the local industrialists. If nationalism at this level of articulation were much more than this, then presumably it would be equally visible among the coffee and other export crop producers and businessmen. The split of the Cámara de Industrias from the Cámara de Comercio, discussed in Chapter 6, reflected this differentiating interest.

In this sense, then, nationalization must be seen as a doctrine and trend that is thoroughly adaptive in the sense that it is the response of a series of competitive high-level operating units to the fact of survival in a world dominated by a few technological superpowers. Internationalism, so called, is merely the converse doctrine, the accommodative side of the confrontation of nations at the international level. It is a process, however, that requires the constant effort on the part of the interested parties to reorganize the national societies. Hence the series of social organizational events sponsored by the government and others, in the effort to centralize power. In Guatemala, the export-dependent portion of the upper sector maintains the international accommodation, and the internally dependent portion emphasizes protective nationalism. As has been pointed out by many writers, the Indians seem to be outside this process, a feeling generally shared by the Indians themselves. They are little interested in either the export or the local industrial and market development and see no advantage for themselves in either.

Although structural escalation appears to be unidirectional when viewed within the scope of the present study of Guatemala and of the current world, it is not inevitable that it will continue indefinitely. While it is not within the scope of this study to explore the future, it seems clear that the factors leading to escalation can also lead to destructive strife, and it is not out of the question that what are today known as nations may become subordinated to some other level of integration. Given the nature of complex societies as outlined herein, however, it is difficult to see how this could occur without changing the role of technology in human social structure or involving the participation of residents of other planets in some larger solar, astral, or cosmic level of articulation.

While structural escalation is somewhat analogous to the process of general evolution, organizational fluctuation is similar to specific evolution. The latter is the process whereby units at various levels confront each other, reorganize, become strong, weaken, emerge, disappear, and in general produce the fluctuating course that we know as human history. It is possible to find within specific periods fairly cyclical regularities, such as changes in government, the rise and decline of commercial houses, the ascendency and fall of a politician and his entourage, or the expansion of a particular crop with growth in the world market and its decline with the collapse of that market. Each organizational effort has its own individual history, and this history is, in a sense, terminal. The history of the internal politics of a provincial town fluctuates with the rise and fall of factions, of innovators, of efforts to better oneself at the expense of others. At the lower levels of articulation, these may have little importance for what happens in the broader scope or at higher levels of articulation. However, at any point in time, there is a set of interdependencies that clearly relates to events at other levels. There is always some variety of contests and competitions under way, just as there will be coalitions and cooperative efforts. This happens constantly between the "ins" and "outs" in the governmental process and between the various entrepreneurs attempting to operate over the same power base or in the same environmental niche. Basically, the features that lead to organizational variation are the same that ultimately contribute to structural change. They operate more immediately, however, and at the lower levels of integration.

A major difference between the organization and the structure is that the latter acts as a set of factors in the former. The structural situation at any point in time sets the basic conditions within which organizational processes occur. As the latter evolve, they bring into being new circumstances that may contribute to the nature of the structure. The mechanics of structural escalation require a series of organizational events, the preponderance of which have a cumulative effect.

7. *The Nation and the Individual*

There has been no rigid definition in anthropological studies as to what constitutes a "complex society," and it is probably just as well. Whatever else may be involved, it seems wise to consider complexity a matter of degree; a society is more or less complex. This is not hiding behind relativism, because it is possible to set some criteria for judgment on the matter.

In the evolution of human society, in different places at different times, the nature of the controls within the society has made an important shift. From a situation in which the governing of the society was based on the collective power of the various parts, organized in an informal way, the controls were formalized and gave the parties in charge the advantage of controls independent of the collective allocations for the express purpose of governing the society. Subsequent addition of power and its incorporation merely made the society more controllable. It has proved convenient to think of the degree of complexity as being determined by the degree of concentration of power, the crucial change probably occurring with the appearance of the state. It was the state that found it necessary to bring special controls to bear on the population to keep it within the society and out of the power of another state.

Since this is a power-based definition of complexity, it inevitably entails a further characterization in terms of levels of articulation. As more power is brought to bear, the level of articulation wherein this power is exercised increases. Complex societies are, in this view, those societies that have formulated a level of articulation beyond that of the locality, and in which there are confrontations between such higher-level units. Complexity is a quality that emerges with the appearance of a community of states and higher-level units. By the same token, the units that operate at these higher levels are formal controllers of domains that relate a number of levels.

The region is a consequence of complexity. To be a region, a geographical area must be part of a larger whole. The totality of the situation in which complexity emerges, then, is the existence of a set of statelike entities, each of which is composed of a set of communities and regions and which confront one another at an interstate level of articulation.

The present study is not concerned with the earlier evolutionary situation of a multiplicity of states, but its more complex and advanced counterpart, the multiplicity of nations. Nations, being a product of industrial technology, are based on incredibly more power than preindustrial states ever had access to; they allow for a much more complex set of levels of articulation and interpenetration of domains. Part of this complexity is the fact that nations are inevitably involved in multiple domains, either through having and exploiting them, or through recognizing that they are implicit and are systematically attempting to destroy or restrict them. This range between the poles of pluralism and totalitarianism is typical of nations, and a given nation, at a point in its history, may appear almost anywhere along the continuum. The fact of multiplicity of domains, however, gives the nation a basic structure, another characteristic that is of particular importance. Quite the contrary of old generals, nations do not fade away; they have to be killed. Because they are inherently composed of multiple domains, various of which have differential but common interests and controls, nations may change regimes, but they do not simply collapse and break up into smaller parts. Such decomposition can happen to states and to nationally centered colonial empires (of the nineteenth-century variety); but the industrially based nation, be it in the vanguard of technological primacy, or in the hinterland of agrarian mercantilism, lives in a community of such nations. The only way that one of these nations can cease to be a nation is literally to be conquered and assimilated or incorporated by a stronger neighbor. The internal multiple-domain system means that there is a cultural identification of being a nation, expressed in a wide variety of ways, that deprives the individual citizens of the alternative of merely collectively shifting their allegiance to some other nation.

While complexity may then be said to have started long before nations came into existence, nation complexity is a very special kind and has to be recognized as such. The quality of being incapable of self-disintegration, it should be noted, is probably not true of any other kind of operating units. The human individual, the family, the community, and even the state, can disintegrate simply by removing the power base upon which it is founded. The nation, however, both internally and externally, has set forth its cultural potential in terms of a Weberian legitimate authority that must be recognized by all other nations in order that they can retain their own controls. This means that to destroy a nation, the task must be overtly done by other nations.

As an aside, this quality of the nation today makes it an ambiguous entity in the world community. At one and the same time, it is recognized increasingly as an anachronistic social unit, but no other viable social units have been invented to replace it in such a way that both local and regional order is maintained, on the one hand, and world order is at least a promise, on the other. So the world juggles along on the constant brink of international catastrophe.

The individual operator in this context is faced with a structure that severely limits what he may accomplish. Interestingly enough, this structure has the same effect on both the student of complex society and the operator who wishes to change the society. While it is hardly novel to suggest that the student of contemporary societies cannot study them without participating in them, it may not be adequately recognized that the kind of participation required of him has the same structural limitations as affect the individuals who are trying to introduce change into the society.

Looking first to the investigator, the complex of levels and domains in which he works defines for him an area of organization and an area of structure. There are many things that he can confront and observe and about which he can obtain direct information. But there is also an area concerning which he must infer, because he cannot confront it directly—there is the possible as well as the probable. That is, depending on where the investigator is standing within the system, there will be sets of events wholly obscured to him, as well as some that he may find merely difficult to study. Direct observation requires essentially what is equivalent to confrontation. This means that he must be operating at the same level of articulation at which the events are taking place. Concomitantly, direct observation also requires certain controls, such as knowing when events are to occur and being capable of getting data concerning them. For these, the student must have access to the domains involved. The investigator who does not operate in confrontation at the levels where events are being generated cannot effectively study them. To achieve this, he may try to be accepted as a unit operating within that level and thereby having access to interviews; or he may get access to the documentation produced in the course of the events and, as does the historian, vicariously construct a myth of the events.

But the serious student is more than a recorder and an antiquarian; he wants to understand the events and see them within a larger perspective. To do this, he must make inferences about things which, given his particular position, are impossible to witness or confront directly. So it is that the student, like any other member of the society, finds that he must construct a picture of the structure, those variables and factors that he cannot know directly in any sense but which he knows must, in some form or another, be in operation. The situation is one of structure and organization. Essentially, the student can confront events at the level where he is operating. As such, he is experiencing the organizational, not the structural. Among the kinds of information he may gather will be various views concerning how the structure is composed. But these data will merely be folk knowledge; he must evaluate them along with behavioral and documentary information and other data. To say that an investigator has good control over his data means that he has operated effectively in confrontation with the events involved and, if contemporaneous, is a part of the organizational facts of those events.

The importance of being at the level of confrontation is patent concerning events being generated at higher levels. The political scientist who wishes to capture the nature of a presidential campaign must be able to have direct confrontations with the leading participants; inability to do this, either personally or through adequate documentation, makes his study impossible. Is the same equally true of working at lower levels? Experience in anthropology suggests that it is. It is essential for the ethnographer to work in continuing intimate contact with the society he wishes to study because he must participate in continuing confrontations at the level where that society is working. If he arrives from the outside, seen as an operator working from a higher level, the kind of relationships that he establishes and the kind of information that he is obtaining will be conditioned by the fact that he is seen as a power wielder, possibly a superordinate of the domain, or merely an outsider, not even pertinent to the domain system at all.

The sociology of knowledge of complex societies requires, then, that the investigator find the means of inserting himself into the level of the society that he wishes to investigate. It may, of course, be possible for him to play multiple roles and work at various levels. To do this well, it helps to be an accomplished dissimilator. Anyone who has tried working at various levels of a society knows there is often a variety of ways of accomplishing it. However, it is also necessary to work in the other dimension, within the necessary domains. Just as events take place at levels, so they also take place within a domain structure. As long as the units involved are informal or merely formal, there may be no major problems in finding a way to work within these domains. However, when a domain has become corporate, severe problems may be placed in the way of the investigator. Since incorporation involves exclusion as well as inclusion, it means that the investigator has to find a way of convincing the domain operators that it is to their advantage to allow him to make the necessary confrontations within the domain. The problems of studying the military in Guatemala, or getting data on corporate businesses, illustrate this.

The investigator's problem is a consequence of the difference between organization and structure. He can study organization because that falls within his area of potential confrontation. He cannot, however, directly study what is beyond this. The difference is common to all sciences. The geologist, looking at the earth and being unable to control it, must infer its structure. Those phases of it, however, which he may bring to his laboratory or which he may experiment with allow him direct confrontation with the events and, thereby, direct observation. Physicists inferred much about the structure of the atom, but it was not until they had built an atomic pile and were able to confront the events with control that they could bring these events out of the realm of structure into the realm of organization.

The dilemma of the investigator is enlarged to full proportion by the changer of cultures. Fundamentally, he faces the same constructions as the investigator, but in a much more frustrating way. He wishes not merely to derive a pretty picture of the events, but he wants his control to be manifested in changing the future course of the event, in changing its organization. As will be clear, we are speaking here of all kinds of change agents: the extension agent, the politician, the reformer, the revolutionary, the socially mobile entrepreneur, and others. By the same reasoning as followed above, the individual can only bring change directly into events generated at the level of articulation at which he is operating, or in those events over which he has control by virtue of being superordinate within a domain. By tactical calculation, he may indirectly influence events elsewhere through the manipulation of those that he directly controls, but this is a different matter.

It would follow, then, that the individual does not change the structure of the events among which he works, but he may change the structure of those that operate within the same domain or that he may confront at his own level. How, then, does the operator succeed in coming to grips with the structural variables that confine him? One way is through possible tactical manipulation of the kind just mentioned, but this is tenuous, depends upon lucky circumstances, and usually has a low probability of success. The only way that he has a real chance of success is for the individual to operate at the level where the events are generated. In its simplest form, this involves obtaining enough power to begin one's operations at the higher level necessary to confront or control those variables that determine those events in which one is interested. This, obviously, presents problems. Not only is there the issue of gaining the power necessary to operate at higher levels, but also there is the problem of knowledge as to what real factors are actually operating in the structure. The lower-level politician whose ambition is to move up in the political structure does so by obtaining power. But once he has moved up, he finds that his view of how the political system operated was wrong. His notions about how the system worked were born of having operated on a lower level and having inferred how the structure was composed. When he moves up and begins to confront the elements of the structure at their own levels, he finds his knowledge had been inferential and wrong. He now forms new knowledge and faces a whole new structural area where he lacks control.

There is bound to be a difference between the real variables that are affecting a given event and how the structure that includes those variables is seen by an individual within their control. This characterizes the problem faced by the change agent. He can really introduce change only into those areas where he has some possibility of control. He cannot introduce change (at least directly) into areas where he has no such possibility. As with the investigator, this is equally true for levels above and below his operations. The extension agent (described later) who tried to get tobacco farmers to organize found that the structure surrounding the farmers stemmed from a higher level of control. The market was controlled by the tobacco company. If the agent wanted to effectively change the organization of the tobacco farmers, he would have to bring power to bear on those variables that were being controlled by the company, which form a specifically monopolistic buying situation. To do this, he would have to confront the company by bringing a competitive company into the operation, or he would have to find a power holder greater than the company, such as the government, which could pass legislation concerning how the company or the farmers were supposed to act. But the agent, working at the local level, could not effect any change. Nor could he, in his situation, effect any change at the higher levels.

It is equally true, however, that if such an agent had wished to change the organization of the family of the farmers with whom he was working, he would have encountered the same problem of working at the wrong level. Coming from the government, as he would have, he would have had controls over some elements of the local situation. But unless the government had real power over the organization of the family, the agent could probably do little about it. It is here that a multiplicity of domains offers a structural situation quite parallel to that just described. Since there is a whole series of distinct families involved, each a domain in itself, the individual who wishes to change the family organization must do one of two things. He must get control of the structural features in the society that account for the organization of the family and manipulate these. For example, where low income and lack of significant occupational differential set the scene for lack of status differentiation among men, thereby leading to woman-headed households and an interchangeability of males, it would be necessary to raise the income levels in the community, so that men could begin to differentiate themselves in social ranking and a man would begin to take on some special value. With this, the woman would find it more worthwhile to try to stay with him.

Failing in this (and it seems likely that he probably would fail), our agent would try another tack and move to the direct confrontation with the families. Were he to do this, such a confrontation might result in his marrying one of the women and insisting in daily confrontation that he was not going to have the household broken up. He might win (or lose) in the confrontation, but at least he would be dealing directly with the problem. Of course, he would probably have no effect on any other family in the community, since the control that he might exercise would be only over his own family domain.

The example of family organization indicates that it is not beyond the realm of possibilities to change such an organization, but that it is fatuous to waste one's time in trying to do it unless one is willing to deal with the structure. One cannot change the structure of local events any more than of national-level events if one does not have controls. Merely being at the national level and being able to control matters concerning which side of the street cars drive on or how much budget an extension agent may have to draw on does not mean that there is any direct control over the structure features that determine the organization of rural families.

The same is true in matters of voting. The person who best controls a vote is one who has direct domain over, or stands in superordination to, a population wherein the control of the vote is an explicit issue; or one who can confront the voters and attempt to bring his persuasion to bear on them. As will be illustrated later, voting usually answers a complex set of factors, and these will differ from one place to another. Real control over the vote means real control over or confrontation with the particular factors that are structural in each case. Such control is obviously all but impossible in any sort of pluralistic situation but quite possible under a unitary domain such as currently holds in Haiti and formerly held in Guatemala under Estrada Cabrera and Ubico.

To summarize, then, in order to promote cultural or social change, the promoter must stand in a situation where he can either confront the units involved at the level where the events are generated, or he must have the power to act as a superordinate in a domain where the events to be changed are part of the things controlled by the domain. This suggests why the Ladino governments of Guatemala have been so uniformly unsuccessful in their efforts to introduce change into the way of life of the Indians. They have worked through agents who almost never worked at the same levels of articulation with the Indians, and they more often than not were trying to change things that fell outside the domains of government control entirely. Even though coming from higher levels of articulation, the change agents among the Indians have not been themselves structural to the way of life of the Indians. To change events, one must change the structural variables that produce them, and to change those variables, one must work at the level where those variables are organizational.

While cases from Guatemala will be reviewed in the next section, there is one general illustration, also specific to Guatemala, that may be mentioned here. That is the case of structural escalation. It was proposed earlier that structural escalation is effectively irreversible given the current nature of world social organization and its relation to technology. The same question can be asked of escalation, however, that can be asked of any set of human social organizational events. Within whose control does it lie? And the answer would seem to be that it is quite beyond the control of anyone. It is composed of confrontations at all the higher levels of articulation, of consistent confrontations over the access to power. In a sociological sense, then, it is hard to find any argument that indicates how this process might be slowed down.

Beyond this, however, it is probably a matter in which the sociological is merely an aspect of a deeper structure. The whole course of recent evolution has been toward the greater and greater extraction of energy from the environment, with all the concomitant power that this entails. Structural escalation is, in one sense, merely the sociological aspect of this accelerating general evolution. Human culture has been eminently successful in discovering new ways to secure energy and to harness it, and there is nothing in the general manner of scientific methodology and technique that indicates this will decrease in the future. The process whereby society exploits these technological advances follows closely behind the technical products of the new knowledge. And there is no single controller of this process because its real locus lies within the process of the confrontation of the major controllers of power and within the individuals long since trained within those systems to see the nation as a sacred value. This is the basis of the rationalizations that follow on each new expanding step. To speak of the value, however, is merely a shorthand term to characterize the way in which nations are viewed. The principal argument in behalf of the nation as a sovereign and indestructible entity stems from the level of articulation within which the domain rulers of the nation have their interests. Since a nation is not merely a government but is, at the same time, a collection of contenders for the control of that government, there is a set of individuals all of whom find their own power position to be based not merely on trying to get the advantages of the controls that government has to offer, but also on defending the system that makes these advantages continually available. And so it is at each successively lower level.

Structural escalation is structural to all levels of articulation, and, as such, to stem its movement the operators would have to work at all levels. It exists as the major issue at stake common to all confrontations; to inhibit it, confrontations would have to be stopped. Given these circumstances, it is hard to see why it cannot be considered, from the point of view of human society, a human, social, or culturally produced process that is inherent in the structure of complex society.

In summary, then, a complex society is one in which power has increased to the point that there are sovereign entities that have control sufficient to maintain continuing internal order and to participate in continuing external competition. This complexity is so arranged that for everyone and every unit within a society there is an area of structure defined in terms of the power available to the unit in question and described in terms of levels of articulation and domains of power. Agents of change can expect some success insofar as they can direct themselves toward events within their general level of confrontation or domain of control. To be sure that such confrontations can be made, the operator must stand in a position where he potentially controls the power necessary to the task.

8. *Two Kinds of Culture Change*

It was proposed in the previous section that to change events, one must change the structural variables that produce them. In terms of the present analysis, there are two situations within which this may be done. The first is where a superordinate within a domain exercises his specific controls toward the ends of changing certain events within his domain. This kind of change has two important characteristics. One is that the desired changes must relate to matters over which the superordinate has control. The greater this general control, however, the more the ramifications will be the specific manipulations within his power. The other is that culture change within domains is essentially accomplished through restriction of alternatives. The Indian in his village is constrained not to do things that are inappropriate to being an Indian. The permanent laborer on a farm is constrained not to misbehave. Orders invariably are restricting events; they either select one alternative out of many that should be followed or require that some specific set of alternatives should be eschewed. To achieve change through a domain, however, it is necessary that the superordinate really have effective power, that he can in fact control the environment of the subordinate so that failure to conform will result in some sort of more disagreeable restriction, such as being ostracized from the village or being fired from the farm.

The second situation in which events change is between coordinates in confrontation, two units operating at the same level of articulation. In this situation, it is possible for one of the units to make some set of alternatives so attractive that the other will voluntarily choose it; or it is possible for a unit to be so frustrated in the confrontation that it resorts to inventing something. The principle that differentiates confrontations at a single level from the domain situation is that there are no systemic, overt restrictions on the alternatives available. Of course, there are the limitations set by knowledge and ability or sheer lack of cleverness in adapting an idea to the problem being confronted. But there is no consistent restriction by one party on the alternative choices of another, except as may be set by the particular conditions of the specific situation. Two individuals or groups in confrontation have essentially an "open market" in which they may select for themselves an old behavior or an innovation in order to cope with the problem at hand.

Contrasting the domain with the confrontation, the former is essentially encapsulating and constrictive, restricting the operating unit to a niche that is not of its own making. It is adaptive but in terms of what is adaptively advantageous for the superordinate, not what is advantageous for the subordinate. The latter, on the other hand, allows choice from among the alternatives available, such that the unit adapts in terms of what it sees to be most advantageous for itself. In this situation, the operator can select from the entire

range available, borrowing from any source within which he has
had contact. In neither instance is the selection entirely random,
for there will always be other factors influencing or determining
the decisions arrived at. But in the domain, there is a systematic
selectivity in favor of those activities that will benefit an operator
at a higher level of articulation.

It will be obvious that it is unlikely that a superordinate will
allow conduct on the part of a subordinate that would threaten the
superordinate's own advantageous position; and he would probably
positively inhibit any innovation that would threaten his own controls. As a result, culture change as mediated in domains is usually
of a conservative nature; that is, it is designed to conserve the advantage of the decision maker. Decisions made in the course of
confrontations, however, would be random in this respect; that is,
the alternative chosen would be that deemed to be most advantageous whether a novelty or not. (It is assumed in this, however,
that the rational judgment as to whether something is advantageous
or not will include the question of handling the ramifications of the
fact of novelty. So the rejection of an innovation because of its new-
ness is also an adaptive decision.)

Among the major changes in the Indian acculturation pattern in
Guatemala were those that took place in response to the revolution
and, incidentally, also to the earlier introduction of the *intendente*
system by Ubico.[53] Ubico's innovation had some consequences because it introduced a new controller in the municipal domain. Of
much greater importance were the changes introduced by the revolution and described in Chapter 3. Political parties, labor unions, and
mass organizations provided the *campesino* and laborer with a device whereby they could, through a power-based organization, confront the employers directly. Of course, it would be misleading to
jump to the conclusion that these organizations did not in themselves, by virtue of acting in the capacity of superordinates within
their own domains, also submit the lower-level members to restrictions of choice. But, at the same time, they opened up an entirely
new range of choices, far beyond the restrictions existing under the
farm domains.

[53] See Richard N. Adams, ed., *Political Changes in Guatemalan Indian Communities*; and idem, "Nationalization," in *Handbook of Middle American Indians*, vol. 6, pp. 479–481.

One of Arévalo's efforts during his presidency was to invite Latin Americans and others who might be able to contribute to Guatemala's development to come and work in the country. It was precisely this kind of open search for new devices that could occur when working out of a given level of articulation and that would be restricted when working within a domain. Within the ten-year course of the revolution, the new domain powers of the parties, unions, and similar organizations, as well as those of the government, began to promise their own restrictions, but, again, at the time the range of alternatives had been immeasurably broader than they had been under Ubico or previous regimes.

Contemporary Guatemala is under the domain of the United States in many respects, primarily commercially and diplomatically (the latter includes the military). Because of this, and because of the public and private U.S. agencies operating within the country, there is pressure on the Guatemalans to accept what is being offered from that source and to reject what may be available from other sources. The Guatemalan army is expected to equip itself with U.S. military supplies; its workers and peasants are expected to be trained in leadership programs supported by the Agency for International Development; in earlier days, great emphasis was placed by U.S. agricultural experts on the U.S. agricultural extension system. And today the credit union system, the Mormon church, U.S. Catholic missionaries and material aid, the Peace Corps, and others are all doing their bit to impress on their Guatemalan friends the virtues and necessity of doing things the American way.

It should be kept in mind that the nature of the pressure on the Guatemalans to accept or conform to many of these suggestions is usually not overtly heavy. The alternatives are given, and the Guatemalans make the choice. The fact that the alternatives are strongly influenced by the dominant power, however, means that they are not really equally available alternatives. The United States is not enthusiastic when Latin American countries accept military hardware from European countries, and it is not entirely pleased when it loses commerce to other countries.

Within Guatemala, the domains also operate to restrict choice. As has been explained earlier, farm labor is free under the law to organize, but farmers find it very difficult to make a union organization in any sense an effective tool. The predisposition of the

Peralta government to throw organizers in jails as political agitators, combined with the restriction of unions to be nonpolitical, sets some stringent limitations on real alternatives open to these organizations.

The National Economic Planning Council drew up a table, presented here in a modified form as Table 1–1, which tried to suggest

TABLE 1–1

Territorial Extent of the Administrative Activities for Development of the Ministries and Decentralized Dependencies of the State

Ministry or Agency	Level of Effective Administration			Primary Function	
	Department	Municipio	Village	Service	Control
Ministry of Foreign Affairs	no	no	no	—	—
Ministry of Economy	yes*	no	no	—	—
Bank of Guatemala	yes*	no	no	—	—
Ministry of Agriculture	yes*	yes*	no	X	
Ministry of Communications	yes	yes*	no	X	
Ministry of Public Health	yes	yes*	no	X	
Ministry of Labor	yes*	yes*	no	X	X
National Police‡	yes	yes	no		X
Various Agencies (INFOP, IGSS, INFOM, FYDEP, INTA)	yes*	yes*	no	X	
Secretary of Welfare	yes*	yes*	yes*	X	
Ministry of Government	yes	yes	yes		X
Ministry of Education	yes	yes	yes	X	
Ministry of Hacienda	yes	yes	yes*		X
Ministry of Defense	yes	yes*	yes†		X

SOURCE: Modified from table following p. 226 in Secretaria General del Consejo Nacional Planificación Económica, *La Situación del Desarrollo Económico y Social de Guatemala*, Ju: 1965, Guatemala.

  * Listed as "partial"
  †Listed as "no"
  ‡ Not listed

the levels at which various of the major government ministries operated. While very general and not differentiating between the various subdivisions of the bureaus, it does serve to indicate the degree to which the government exercises direct controls. It does not indicate, of course, the effect of legal restrictions that may relate specifically to the work of some ministry, but the actual presence of ministerial agents at the level is indicated. Obviously, the estimations given in Table 1–1 are crude, and issue could be taken with a number of cases as to how really effective certain of the offices are at the departmental or municipal levels. The council's estimates included many as being only partially effective (as is noted on the table). In general, the differentiation made by the table suggests some interesting contrasts.

In the first place, some of the differences are to be expected. The Ministries of Foreign Affairs and of Economy and the Bank of Guatemala are concerned with matters that are not readily translatable to direct agents at the municipal or village level. Of the remaining, however, it is possible for all the organizations mentioned to operate at all three levels, and the fact that some do this weakly or not at all indicates qualities of the operation of the system. Scaling the differences of those reaching only the municipal level and those reaching the village level is interesting if one compares the major activities of the organizations. If we distinguish between control and service activities, it turns out that of the five organizations that reach the village level, three are concerned primarily with control; while of the six reaching only to the municipal level, four are concerned with service, one with control, and one with both. Apparently, the more likely an agency is to be concerned with service, the less likely it is to reach out to the village level. This is the opposite of what one might be led to expect or hope.

The basic reason is probably the obvious one: the central government has been concerned with the exercise of power over the country as a whole, and the issue of giving services was limited to those that were needed by the upper sector in their development of export agriculture. During the prerevolutionary period, the subsistence population commanded and received no special services, apart from those required by municipal government. The revolutionary period saw an attempt to develop the rural and provincial school system because education was felt to be necessary for meaningful political participation of the population. The Ministry of Defense has become more active in recent years (see Chapter 4), and a part of this has been the activation of their *comisionados militares*. Both the Secretariat of Public Welfare and the Ministry of Hacienda have agents in only limited areas. The first was a relatively new agency at the time of the study and reached little beyond the department of Chimaltenango, where its field headquarters was located. The Ministry of Hacienda's agents were concerned with contraband and clandestine production of liquor and placed their agents in areas relevant to those matters.

Those other ministries concerned with services, especially agriculture, communications, public health, and labor, together with the various agencies charged with working in the provinces, are unfortunately marked by their inability to extend themselves far into the provincial areas. A major exception to this is the Instituto de Transformación Agraria (INTA), which has worked, and continues to work, in very limited colonization areas. But these, too, work out of municipal headquarters.

A characteristic of government ministries and related agencies is, then, that they tend to operate no lower than the municipal headquarters unless they are concerned with some aspect of control. Where this is the case, then they may be expected to extend the placement of their agents more widely in order to accomplish that control. Given this generalization, one may ask why it is that the national police are not found in every village. The answer probably lies in the fact that the national police are concerned with civil order and the maintenance of national laws. The small and more isolated villages generally can handle their own public order through local means and need resort to the national police only in time of special trouble. Many larger *municipios* have their own municipal police for handling local matters. The extent and level of action of the national police, then, is perhaps more a gauge of the degree to which the provinces are of general concern to the central government beyond the special activities of the other government agencies. When special problems are newly recognized, such as control of contraband or infractions of the labor code, special agents from the relevant ministries handle them.

The effect of domain-sponsored culture change is felt principally by the permanent members of the domain. However, there are temporary restrictions on those who may move in only temporarily, as occurs with migrant labor. The highland Indians, who comprise the greater part of the seasonal migrants, become involved in seasonal labor in a quite insulated manner. They are ordinarily contracted in groups in their home community, with the wages established ahead of time. Sometimes, they will be accompanied by the individual who has done the contracting in their behalf. They live on the farm during the period and then return to their homes. They have no particularly telling experience insofar as urban influences are concerned, and they do not have enough money to go off on frequent weekend sprees (Chapter 8 notes that they accumulate an average of eighteen dollars to take home out of the entire seasonal labor). The farms, therefore, do not act as important culture-transmitting devices, and the Indians apparently are as little affected by the cultural alternatives offered them as are the Indian merchants described years ago by Redfield.[54]

Efforts at positive, directed culture change on the part of domain members suffer from the question of whether the superordinate in the domain really has the power to induce the subordinate to take the desired actions. Where legal pressure and, therefore, threat of arrest can be brought to bear, it is still a matter of limiting the alternatives. The requirement of voting, for example, may seem from the outside to be to the advantage of the citizen; but if it is required by law, the alternative left is to break the law and suffer the consequences. The change that accompanies confrontation is of a very different kind. Certainly the single most outstanding process that has produced culture change among low-income Guatemalans has been the permanent migration of people from the highlands, primarily the eastern area. The permanent migrant has to confront the fact of adaptation to a new environment and, as such, must make the choice between the alternatives available. Since the choice includes whether he wishes to submit himself to a domain, this is an important kind of decision.

Among the migrants interviewed in El Petén were some Ladinos from Jutiapa who had first opted to obtain land in the colonization in Nueva Concepción, Escuintla. Upon arrival there, they had found

[54] Robert Redfield, "Primitive Merchants of Guatemala," *Quarterly Journal of Inter-American Relations* 1, no. 4 (1938): 42–56.

that the land had long since been allocated, and their only local alternatives were to work for other *parcelarios* or on cotton or sugar- cane farms. They did not want to be laborers, however, and heard from a friend that land was available in El Petén. The small group of related families then moved to the north, into a region on the main road between Poptún and Flores. Since they had arrived too late for a crop that year, they collected leaves that were in demand by North American florists and intended to keep up this forest- gathering activity until they could get their cultivations going the next year.[55] This is a clear case of successive confrontations, suc- cessive selections between real alternatives (to avoid restrictions by subnational domains), and adaptation to the chosen circumstances. The cases described by Roberts in Chapter 10 provide another il- lustration of how, given free alternatives, different families will opt for different forms of adaptation, some seeking security and others being willing to gamble on more tenuous possibilities. His illustra- tion of how *colonia*-dwellers decide whether to move from one part of Guatemala City to another indicates the care that is taken in coming to such decisions.

Material from Zárate's review of migration, indicated in Table 1–2, shows that there is a great deal of movement out of Guatemala as well as into it, and this is confirmed in Roberts' account. Many of the migrants find they are really involved in a continuing re- adaptation. Some such patterns are illustrated in Roberts' descrip- tion of the social organization of the urban barrios. Others may be seen in the attempts to reestablish rural labor syndicates and *campesino* organizations (Chapter 9). Among the important aspects is the fact that for many of the migrants, there is no clear-cut differentiation between urban and rural adaptability. Many who migrated to the south coast have then gone to the metropolis. For some, the metropolis is more a staging center for subsequent rural sorties. The importance of the metropolis is suggested by material in Table 1–2. In nineteen of the nation's twenty-two active depart- ments, the department of Guatemala was among the first five de- partments of origin for incoming migrants. It was the leading de-

---

[55] Richard N. Adams, *Migraciones Internas en Guatemala: Expansión Agraria de los Indígenas Kekchíes hacia El Petén*, Estudios Centroamericanos No. 1, p. 22.

TABLE 1–2

Interdepartmental Migrants, Guatemala, 1964 (5% Sample)

Department	Number of Migrants	% of Migrants Born in Five Departments Contributing Largest Number of Migrants					Five Leading Departments as % of Total Migrants
Izabal	2,647	Zacapa	34.6	Alta Verapaz	7.9		87.0
		Chiquimula	29.5	Jutiapa	5.9		
		El Progreso	9.1				
Escuintla	5,665	Guatemala	18.1	Suchitepéquez	7.7		64.4
		Santa Rosa	16.2	Chimaltenango	6.7		
		Jutiapa	15.7				
Retalhuleu	1,671	Quezaltenango	24.4	Escuintla	8.4		65.6
		Suchitepéquez	17.5	Santa Rosa	6.7		
		San Marcos	8.6				
Guatemala	9,922	Santa Rosa	11.2	Escuintla	8.1		44.2
		Quezaltenango	8.9	Sacatepéquez	7.3		
		Chimaltenango	8.7				
El Petén	296	Alta Verapaz	53.7	Izabal	5.1		83.2
		Baja Verapaz	10.5	El Progreso	5.1		
		Guatemala	9.8				
Suchitepéquez	1,724	El Quiché	13.4	Sololá	9.5		53.1
		Retalhuleu	12.1	Guatemala	8.2		
		Escuintla	9.9				
El Progreso	461	Guatemala	31.9	Zacapa	10.2		85.5
		Jalapa	23.2	Izabal	8.9		
		Baja Verapaz	11.3				
Santa Rosa	947	Guatemala	31.4	Escuintla	10.2		87.3
		Jutiapa	31.4	Chimaltenango	1.6		
		Jalapa	12.6				
Zacapa	558	Chiquimula	28.3	Guatemala	12.5		81.2
		El Progreso	16.8	Jalapa	9.0		
		Izabal	14.7				
Quezaltenango	1,493	San Marcos	33.6	Retalhuleu	9.3		78.7
		Huehuetenango	16.0	Guatemala	9.2		
		Totonicapán	10.6				
Sacatepéquez	379	Guatemala	37.7	Santa Rosa	4.7		84.9
		Chimaltenango	24.0	Suchitepéquez	2.1		
		Escuintla	16.4				

(Table 1–2, continued)

Department	Number of Migrants	% of Migrants Born in Five Departments Contributing Largest Number of Migrants				Five Leading Departments as % of Total Migrants
Jalapa	331	Jutiapa	36.9	Santa Rosa	7.9	84.9
		Guatemala	19.3	El Progreso	3.9	
		Chiquimula	16.9			
Chimaltenango	516	El Quiché	31.2	Suchitepéquez	8.3	83.7
		Guatemala	22.3	Escuintla	6.6	
		Sacatepéquez	14.3			
Baja Verapaz	238	Alta Verapaz	31.9	El Progreso	9.7	78.6
		Guatemala	20.2	Suchitepéquez	5.0	
		El Quiché	11.8			
Chiquimula	309	Zacapa	22.3	Izabal	12.9	79.1
		Jutiapa	21.3	Jalapa	9.7	
		Guatemala	14.9			
Sololá	229	El Quiché	26.2	Chimaltenango	9.6	76.6
		Suchitepéquez	21.0	Quezaltenango	8.2	
		Guatemala	11.8			
Jutiapa	367	Santa Rosa	23.2	Escuintla	11.7	77.5
		Jalapa	19.1	Chiquimula	8.4	
		Guatemala	16.1			
San Marcos	567	Quezaltenango	29.8	Suchitepéquez	8.8	72.5
		Huehuetenango	17.3	Retalhuleu	5.1	
		Guatemala	11.5			
Alta Verapaz	300	Baja Verapaz	42.0	El Progreso	6.0	76.7
		Guatemala	14.3	El Petén	5.7	
		El Quiché	8.7			
El Quiché	288	Huehuetenango	28.1	Alta Verapaz	9.0	63.2
		Totonicapán	14.9	Chimaltenango	8.0	
		Guatemala	13.2			
Totonicapán	124	Quezaltenango	33.0	El Quiché	9.7	71.8
		Guatemala	10.5	Jutiapa	8.9	
		Huehuetenango	9.7			
Huehuetenango	240	San Marcos	45.0	Quezaltenango	9.2	84.2
		El Quiché	12.5	Totonicapán	5.8	
		Guatemala	11.7			

SOURCE: Alvan Zárate, "Migraciones internas de Guatemala," *Estudios Centroamericanos*, No. 1 Seminario de Integración Social Guatemalteca, Guatemala, 1967, Table 7.

partment of origin for Escuintla, El Progreso, Santa Rosa, and Sacatepéquez. Unfortunately, the figures available do not permit us to know what proportion of these emigrants from the department of Guatemala actually came from the metropolitan area; nor can we tell what proportion of them was adapting at the lower levels of articulation. It is probably safe to assume that in each case the proportion was large.

This suggests that the differentiation between the five zones outlined in the last section has further ramifications. The metropolitan zone not only is the center of urbanization, but it also is a center that is responsible for the urbanization (in terms of adaptive values) of the provinces, both rural and urban. Ruben Reina recently described an extreme case of this displaced urbanism, in the unlikely context of Flores, the capital of the department of El Petén.[56] The Flores case is exaggerated, but only because the department as a whole is so underpopulated and without a clear-cut immediate hinterland. Most particularly, however, it is the new lowland zones that are the recipients of the multileveled articulation that is structurally the central feature of urban development.

There are many ways of analyzing culture change. The distinction proposed here has to do with setting the context of choice within the general framework of the analysis of complex society. It can be argued, for example, that political development carried out entirely within the domain restrictions of a higher political power must necessarily so limit the choices that the possibility of achieving innovations that will materially add to the adaptability of the populations involved is very low.[57] Nor should it be thought that the argument applies to only one major domain, such as the United States. It is equally applicable with respect to the restrictions imposed by domains controlled by socialist or Communist countries, or by other nations trying to thread their way through the political maze of the modern world. It is as true at lower levels as it is when the domains are articulated in upper levels. Indian communities are as

[56] Ruben Reina, "The Urban World View of a Tropical Forest Community in the Absence of a City, Petén, Guatemala," *Human Organization* 23, no. 4 (1964): 265–277.

[57] This point is argued in my statement in, "Hearings before the Subcommittee on American Republics Affairs," of the Committee on Foreign Relations, United States Senate, 19th Congress, 2nd Session, 5 March, pp. 204–212.

restrictive concerning what is permissible as is the Guatemalan government or the United States.

The issue is that a context of confrontation will usually allow a wider set of choices and for many people will always be more readily acceptable, even if overtly harsher. The issue at this point is to recognize that the structure of complex societies sets different kinds of limits on change and, at the same time, channels change in courses favorable to the holders of power at the higher levels of articulation.

Adaptation, in the sociocultural evolution of complex societies, is a process that occurs within all domains and at all levels of articulation. The crux of the process, however, is how the variations at one level affect those at higher and lower levels and how the growth within one domain or set of domains affects that in others. The change is deterministic in the sense that there are limited alternatives as to what can happen from one point in time to the next and that there are cumulative processes that bring into being structural consequences not always seen by the manipulators of the operating units in the organizational processes.

The analysis of adaptation by units in levels of integration not only suggests one way the various parts of a complex society are tied together, but also theoretically proposes structural relations operating between them. It also suggests that the contemporary world is in the grip of a structural process that is beyond the control of any organizational entity in existence. If this is determinism, then it is so because the complexity of human social structure is beyond the control of human beings, not because it is beyond the effects of the natural environment and natural processes to eliminate human beings altogether. It suggests, however, that control is a function of knowledge and therefore that only by knowledge can human beings possibly bring themselves under control. There is evidence, however, that even knowledge is subject to the structural and organizational characteristics described here; and, if so, it is the task of each investigation to seek out the areas of relative control, as it will be there that the application of knowledge can most readily contribute to improved adaptation.

Appendix to Chapter I

The following is a statement on the definition of power as used in this book. It is reproduced from my "Power and Power Domains," *América Latina* 9, no. 2 (1966): 3–5, 8–11.

The Concept of Power

The concept of power introduced here has been developed to make explicit certain of the variables that are central to its understanding. *Power, in general, refers to the tactical control that is exercised by a party over the environment; power in a social relationship, therefore, refers to the control that one party holds over the environment of another party.* To understand power in the evolution of culture, it is important to see it as something that exists, in a sense, both in and apart from social relationships. The term "environment" is used broadly here to include the entire set of features relevant to the control of all parties involved in a social relationship. With respect to any given social relationship, other individuals or parties may be considered as parts of the environment. As between two parties, power refers to an aspect of a total relationship, that aspect which concerns the relative control that each party has over the environments of the others. A further feature must be noted in this general statement; the term "relative" is included because the actual control over aspects of an environment is a *tactical* matter. That is, I may have a gun, and you none; but my ownership of the gun gives me no power over you if I have made the tactical blunder of not having it in my possession.

The basic notion is that power ultimately refers to an actual physical control that one party may have with respect to another. The reason that most relationships are not reduced to physical struggles is that parties to them can make rational decisions based on their estimates of tactical power and other factors. Power is usually exercised, therefore, through the common recognition by two parties of the tactical control each has, and through the rational decision by one to do what the other wants. Each estimates his own tactical control, compares it to the other, and decides he may or may not be superior. We are reducing the use of power to the rational evaluation of a situation in which an individual decides to do what is best for him. This notion involves the concept of culture. If two individuals face each other, and one threatens the other with a gun, the power that the first has over the second is that he may take his life. For this to make sense to the other, however, they must share a minimal common culture; i.e., they must both know (or believe) that the gun is loaded and that it can, in fact, kill a person; and they must agree that a person will value his life sufficiently to do as he is bid rather than choose death as an alternative.

An analysis of power in any situation requires an understanding of the physical relationships that exist, i.e., what specific aspects are controlled, how great is that control, what are the tactical possibilities of mobilizing the control at some point in time when it needs to be exercised. This social power, then, is based on an essentially physical control, and presumably could be measured in those terms. It also requires an understanding of the participants' culture and cognitive systems; further, if the parties have very distinct cultures, it requires some understanding of the particular ways that the two different cognitive processes perceive the forms of the other culture. Elements of the environment and the relative tactical access to it will be differentially estimated and evaluated, and the indicators of power behavior will vary greatly from one society to another.

In defining the exercise of power as the tactical control of the environment of another party, we are not referring to a stock-piling of force, but to the particular condition and manipulation of force to which different parties may have access. Kenneth Boulding, apropos of a comment to the effect that there were enough thermonuclear bombs to kill the entire population, remarked that there were also enough hands on earth to strangle everyone in the world! Clearly, the issue is the tactical application of any such available force, not its mere existence. Power may be exercised when a person points a gun at another, withholds a salary check, places the other in jail, threatens to remove his political support, and so on. Anything that serves to change the environment of another party in a threatening way provides the basis for the exercise of power.

While this exercise rests on the tactical manipulation of things, the way it is perceived may vary widely. For the threat of power to be effectively exercised, the parties must have common understanding, i.e., must, to some degree, share the same culture. Their ideas must be so similar that the powerholder can predict the rational response of the other party because it is a rational response familiar to the culture. Further, both parties must understand the kinds of restrictions being laid through the control exercised over the environment by the powerholder. If a sorcerer says that he will change me into a frog if I fail to do what he wishes, we simply are not sharing culture enough for it to be effective: becoming a frog is not a serious alternative for me.

This aspect of power wielding is crucial; the fact that power claims may be forced into a direct check with reality affords the opportunity to learn. A person who continually threatens, but is unable to make good on the threat, can ultimately be ignored. Experience provides a test of the validity of the way power is perceived. If no test is given, cognitive patterns may diverge widely from an external description of the same event.

There are two features of the present concept of power that are crucial for its understanding and utilization. First, power is assumed to exist as an aspect of all social relationships. That is, wherever human beings set up a relationship, for whatever reason, there is inherently involved a relative control of the environment of each party by the other. Quite obviously, it is equally important to recognize that the power aspect of a relationship may not be manifest. It may be latent because of a lack of knowledge that it exists or that it could be mobilized; or it may be unused because of a rational decision to leave it unused. Power is not something that is always in use, therefore.

Second, power in a social relationship is always reciprocal. That is to say, wherever there is a social relationship, there is always power available to *both* parties. Even in the extreme case of the man in a dungeon, it must be recognized that he does hold some threat to the environment of his jailer. Should he escape or should he die at an inappropriate time or under inappropriate circumstances, his jailer would be in trouble. Obviously, the relative differential of power as between the jailer and prisoner is enormous; but this must not obscure the fact that it is a differential, and not a case of total control by one, and an absence of control by the other. Could it be demonstrated that the prisoner in fact had no power of threat over his jailer, that he was, as it were, forgotten, then it must also be argued that the social relationship has ceased to exist, and with it the power aspect.

The Structure of Power

Although cultures vary in the way power is perceived and handled, there are features common to power structure in general. A basic concept is that of the power domain. A power domain exists when one party has greater control over the environment of a second than does the second over the environment of the first. The inferior party of a power domain always has some power, too. The fact that the superior wants to control the inferior means, implicitly, that a failure to control him is a threat to the superior. So a power domain is a polar social relationship. All relationships, it must be noted, have a power aspect. It may be the case that the power aspect is ignored in a specific interaction, but it is nevertheless always potential and available for introduction into the dialogue. There can be said to be completely one-sided power in a relationship only when the inferior has ceased to be a social object; and if this occurs it is equally the case that the relationship has ceased to exist. It is the two-directional quality of a power domain that establishes it, even if the parties involved may not be happy with the situation. Both Russia and the United States exercise a superior domain position with respect to Cuba; in one case, Cuba likes it; in another, it does not. It is the quality of the power relations in a domain, however, that Cuba can use either against the other.

There are some basic kinds of relations that develop within and between domains. Domains may be of two kinds: those involving equals, and those involving unequals. The relation between a superordinate and subordinate in a domain involves the inferior's recognition that the superior has limited the inferior's range of alternative actions. The superior can make binding decisions concerning the inferior, whereas the latter may only suggest, request, or beg. The superior has the discretion as to when to change the inferior's possible alternatives.

Two kinds of power sources can be distinguished in these relationships. If the powerholder has the control in his own hands and does not need to turn to another party for aid, then he holds *independent power* and exercises an *independent domain*. If he depends upon another party, however, he is exercising *derivative power* and has a *derivative domain*; he stands, in short, within the domain of the third party, upon whom he depends for at least some of his power.

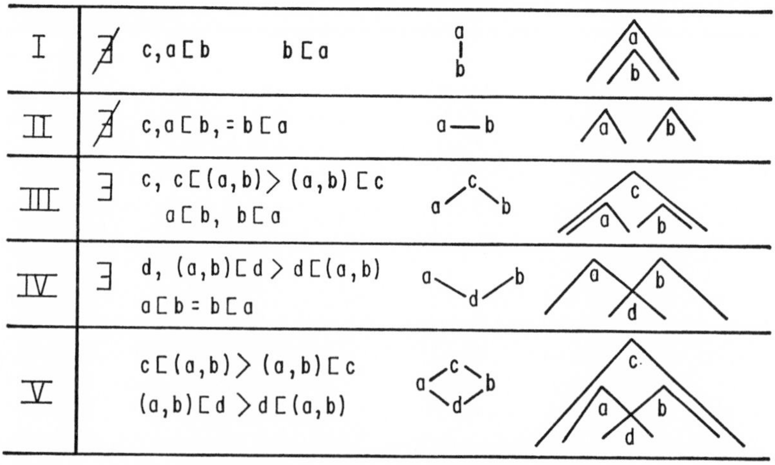

I	$\not\exists$ c, aСb bСa
II	$\not\exists$ c, aСb, = bСa
III	$\exists$ c, cС(a,b) > (a,b)Сc aСb, bСa
IV	$\exists$ d, (a,b)Сd > dС(a,b) aСb = bСa
V	cС(a,b) > (a,b)Сc (a,b)Сd > dС(a,b)

FIGURE 1–11. Basic Power Structures

The 19th century hacienda system, as it was practiced in Mexico, the Andes, and the *estancia* and *fundo* system of southern South America, provide cases of simple power domains. Each hacienda or *estancia* was essentially in control of the population that was dependent upon it. There was no other authority or source of power to which the *colono* or tenant could turn, because the landlords had complete rights of exclusion. It may be argued that they obtained these rights from the government, and legally that is so. But in fact, they exercised these rights without help from, or recourse to, the government.

There are three different circumstances in which relations between equals occur, and they have quite different effects on the behavior of the parties involved. They are: two inferiors within a larger domain (Fig. 1–11, III); two independent domains with no particular area of overlapping interest (Fig. 1–11, IV); and two independent domains with an area of overlapping interest.

The presence of two inferiors within a single domain is illustrated by the relation between two *colonos*, or two tenants, on a 19th century latifundium. Each could receive what he needed only from the patron, who, as such, could use one to threaten the other; i.e., each was available to the patron to use as he wished. When the issues were of no interest to the patron, the *colonos* were in a situation of two equals, neither of whom had any more power than the other. Within a single domain, each inferior under these circumstances has derivative power that he may exercise against the other, providing the superior grants it. This kind of situation is that of many Latin American governments when controlling the internal development of their countries. It has been used by the government of Mexico with considerable success in situations in which both business and industrial enterprise, on the one hand, and labor, on the other, were subordinate to governmental control, and the government could therefore push one or the other, depending upon the direction in which it wished affairs to move. In this relationship of inferiors within the domain of a superior, an important aspect is that one inferior may be induced by immediate gain to exercise derivative power against the other, thereby destroying any tendencies toward reciprocity between the two inferiors. When disputes and disagreements arise, they must be taken to the superior for resolution, thus enhancing his control.

The relation between two independent domains with no overlapping interests may almost be said, by definition, not to exist. They are important, however, because of what an inferior within one may do when the presence of another is known. Latin American borders are most convenient for individuals who have broken the law in one country.

Until extradition is recognized, the alleged bandit may skip from one sovereign state to another to avoid capture. Of even more importance is the fact that the right of exile is so recognized in the case of political refugees. The quality of the relationship between independent equals is essentially the kind described earlier for members of primitive bands within which no power is wielded, where each has approximately an equal possibility of making his neighbor uncomfortable, but equally needs him in time of stress. Each individual observes the rights of the other to insure respect of his own. These relationships are characterized by reciprocities, by attempting to use influence and persuasion. Power activities in these situations consist mainly of correcting or punishing someone who has offended the group as a whole, and this is done principally by "ganging up" on the offender, sometimes collectively, sometimes through an individual agent representing the group. This is the way it works in most preagricultural societies, and, indeed, in any group in which the power differential between any two members continues to be insignificant over extended periods.

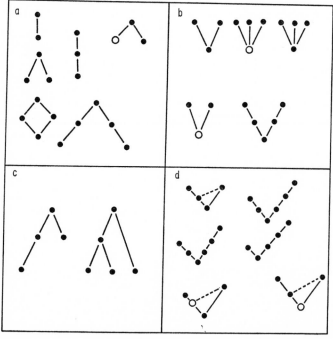

FIGURE 1–12. Some Simple Power Domain Structural Patterns

When two domains have an area of common interest, one in which each controls part of the environment of a third, there exists a basis for conflict. As opposed to the condition in which a single independent controls a single inferior, which we might call a *unitary domain*, the situation in which two or more sovereigns control a third is a *multiple domain* (Fig. 1–12). Whether or not conflict occurs under these circumstances depends upon whether the two superiors find any conflict of interest. Certainly, the church and state have, in Latin America, seen both kinds of situations. Under these circumstances, however, the inferior may find himself in a situation in which he can play one superior off against the other, thus extracting benefits from both. This is the situation that many underdeveloped countries find themselves in with respect to the world power blocs. It should be noted, as in the case of Cuba cited earlier, that it makes no difference, under these circumstances, whether the powers involved are friendly.

A further feature of interest here is that domains appear in groups. Although there is not time to explore this here, it appears that it is for practical purposes impossible to have a single independent domain for any length of time. If it occurred that one domain actually became independent and superior over all others, its fate would be to dissolve into a number of competing domains. A way of expressing this is that a domain can only be independent in a community of independents. Part of the explanation for this lies, surely, in the problem inherent in competitive exclusion; part also lies in the nature of the organization of the power controllers in the superior set.

2 | Structure and Development in Guatemala

STRUCTURAL ESCALATION is a world-wide phenomenon. While Guatemala illustrates the basic processes involved, there are, nonetheless, particular circumstances that condition the Guatemalan scene. These conditions, or structural features, are by no means unique to Guatemala, but they are fundamental to the framework within which the Guatemalan story is enacted. There are three such features that are clearly prime movers in Guatemalan social evolution. The population is growing at possibly the world's fastest rate; certain foreign nations, particularly the United States and Cuba, see in Guatemala an important area of control; and, related to the second, the internal bases of power in Guatemala have been expanding. Demographic growth is due to better public health controls over mortality; while it is true that the Guatemalans could reject these controls, world pressure is strong to accept them. Similarly, the interest of foreign powers in Guatemala can hardly be ignored, even if all Guatemalans wished it might be (and many do not). And the internal growth of power reflects a structural escalation of operating units to extend their controls, both through calling upon external derivative power and opening up new internal sources.

Development, as was indicated in the introduction, can be seen in various ways. In one sense, it might be defined as those increases in power related to the system of production (if the North American usage is followed), or production and consumption (if the underdeveloped-nations definition is followed). A significant portion of the inputs for Guatemalan development must come from the outside. This fact reflects the external world's collective commitment to that development. Because it is an inherent part of the multiple external-domain interests and a part of the increasing power bases within Guatemala, economic development in Guatemala is also a structural feature, a condition over which individual Guatemalans have really very little control.

The purpose of this chapter is to show that Guatemala is developing and growing, and that the development has been channeled in part by the resources of the natural environment, and in part by the geographical variations of the power structure. Economic change is occurring, but, if anything, it is reinforcing the existing power structure, not substantially modifying it.

1. *Demographic Composition*

As is the case with the populations of its Central American neighbors, Guatemala's population is rapidly expanding. The causes are generally attributed to the effects of public health on death rate in a situation where the birth rate has not significantly declined. The growth rate between 1950 and 1964 was 3.1 percent,[1] and the increase in urbanization has not affected it. While the growth has taken place across the entire country, its effects have varied. The pattern of population distribution in Guatemala finds the major nonurban density in the Indian central and western highlands. Until twenty-five years ago, the Pacific coastal area, the lowlands of the northeast, and El Petén were very underpopulated, the first two areas holding principally two major United Fruit Company centers and a scattering of local small-scale cattle ranches and subsistence farmers. While less densely populated than the west, eastern Guatemala has been under a mixture of latifundia and minifundia that has provided very little room for population expansion. The broad highland area, then, from the Indian west through the Ladino east, is the scene of the natural increase of the population and the home of the basic cultures of Guatemala.

This expansion of population has resulted in migration of peoples

[1] Departamento de Censos y Encuestas, *Censos 1964: Población; Resultados de Tabulación por Muestra,* p. 7.

out of both these old regions into three major zones: the northeast and northern lowlands, the south coast (really the south central and southwest coast, as the highlands come down close to the sea in the east), and metropolitan Guatemala. Movement to the northeast is the least of these. Metropolitan Guatemala includes principally the *municipio* of Guatemala but should also include the immediately suburban and extraurban areas of Mixco, Villa Nueva, San José Pinula, Chinautla, and possibly also the string of communities to the north of Amatitlán and Amatitlán itself. Most of the data are given by department, however, and therefore figures for the entire department of Guatemala are usually cited. The south coastal area of importance includes the lowland portions of the departments of Escuintla, Retalhuleu, Suchitepéquez, Quezaltenango, and San Marcos. Departmental statistics for the last two departments include such large highland sectors that they provide us with little refined information, and the figures we will refer to here will be those of the first departments named. The northeast includes specifically the department of Izabal, and the north is the department of El Petén. Table 2–1 shows how the departments vary in the percentage of native born recorded in the 1964 census. It will be seen that while Izabal has the lowest percentage of native born, metropolitan Guatemala and the three southwest coast departments account for a greater absolute migration.

Map 2–1 shows the percentage of population growth by *municipio* for the country as a whole; Map 2–2 shows the percentage of people in the 1964 census who were not resident in their *municipio* of birth. It is clear from these two maps that the general change in population distribution has been most profoundly influenced by these movements. Map 2–3 and Map 2–4 show specifically how the increase in population from the east and the central and western highlands have served to people the northeast and south coastal areas. Table 2–2 shows that of the total migration in the country, 80 percent is Ladino, and that 92.1 percent and 75.9 percent respectively of Izabal and El Petén migration, and 91 percent and 73 percent of the Escuintla and Retalhuleu migrants are Ladino. Map 2–4 shows that the Indian population, in total much less than Ladino, but still significant, is also moving to these two major in-migration areas. The provincial population growth of the past twenty-five years has pressed so heavily that the older populated

TABLE 2-1
Native Population, Guatemala, 1964

| Department | Native Population | Born in Same Department | | Born in Other Departments | | | | |
		Number	Percent	Total Number	Adjoining Number	Adjoining Percent	Nonadjoining Number	Nonadjoining Percent
Republic	208,213	178,941	86.0	29,272	15,908	7.6	13,364	6.4
Izabal	5,313	2,666	50.2	2,647	1,131	21.3	1,516	28.5
Escuintla	12,392	6,727	54.3	5,665	2,942	23.7	2,723	22.0
Retalhuleu	5,604	3,933	70.2	1,671	845	15.1	826	14.7
Guatemala	38,060	28,138	73.9	9,922	4,717	12.4	5,205	13.7
El Petén	1,322	1,026	77.6	296	173	13.1	123	9.3
Suchitepéquez	9,006	7,282	80.9	1,724	745	8.3	979	10.9
El Progreso	3,280	2,819	85.9	461	359	11.0	102	3.1
Santa Rosa	7,967	7,020	88.1	947	812	10.2	135	1.7
Zacapa	4,890	4,332	88.6	558	387	7.9	171	3.5
Quezaltenango	13,227	11,734	88.7	1,493	1,152	8.7	341	2.6
Sacatepéquez	3,986	3,607	90.5	379	296	7.4	83	2.1
Jalapa	4,933	4,602	93.3	331	286	5.8	45	0.9
Chimaltenango ...	8,077	7,561	93.6	516	452	5.6	64	0.8
Baja Verapaz	4,781	4,543	95.0	238	177	3.7	61	1.3
Chiquimula	7,164	6,855	95.7	309	165	2.3	144	2.0
Sololá	5,418	5,189	95.8	229	160	3.0	69	1.3
Jutiapa	9,144	8,777	96.0	367	186	2.0	181	2.0
San Marcos	16,378	15,811	96.5	567	296	1.8	271	1.7
El Quiché	12,758	12,470	97.7	288	195	1.5	93	0.7
Alta Verapaz	13,145	12,845	97.7	300	188	1.4	112	0.9
Huehuetenango ...	14,244	14,004	98.3	240	174	1.2	66	0.5
Totonicapán	7,124	7,000	98.3	124	70	1.0	54	0.8

SOURCE: Data from Guatemala, Dirección General de Estadística, 7° Censo de Población, 1964, 5% Sample. Table from Alvan O. Zárate, "Principales Patrones de Migración Interna en Guatemala," *Estudios Centroamericanos*, No. 3, Seminario de Integración Social Guatemalteca, Guatemala, 1967, Table 1.

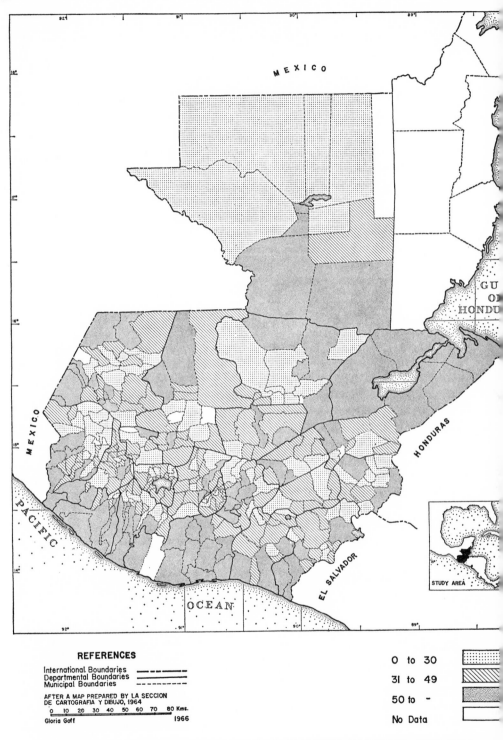

REFERENCES

International Boundaries
Departmental Boundaries
Municipal Boundaries

AFTER A MAP PREPARED BY LA SECCION
DE CARTOGRAFIA Y DIBUJO, 1964

0 10 20 30 40 50 60 70 80 Kms.

Gloria Goff   1966

0 to 30

31 to 49

50 to -

No Data

MAP 2–1. PERCENTAGE OF POPULATION GROWTH, 1950–1964

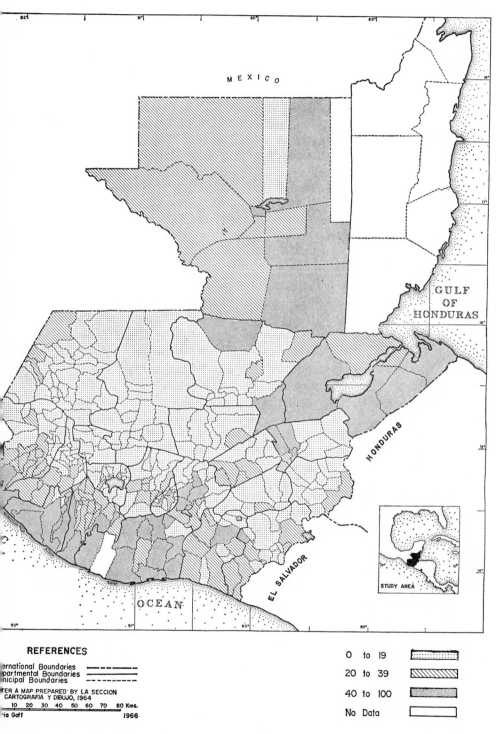

O C E A N·

GULF
OF
HONDURAS

HONDURAS

EL SALVADOR

STUDY AREA

REFERENCES

ternational Boundaries
partmental Boundaries
nicipal Boundaries

ER A MAP PREPARED BY LA SECCION
CARTOGRAFIA Y DIBUJO, 1964

10   20   30   40   50   60   70   80 Kms.

ia Goff   1966

O   to   19

20   to   39

40   to   100

No   Data

MAP 2–2. PERCENTAGE OF MIGRANTS, 1964

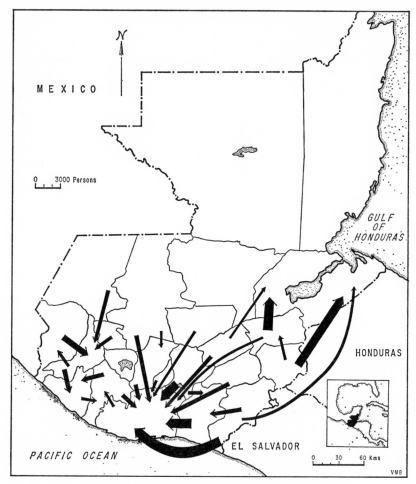

MAP 2–3. LADINO MIGRATION STREAMS

areas of the eastern and western highlands, caught in the grip of
their structural limitations, have experienced heavy migration of
their peoples into the new areas.

The migration has, of course, also contributed to the urbanization
of both metropolitan Guatemala and certain provincial regions.
Guatemala City increased from 284,276 to 572,937 between 1950

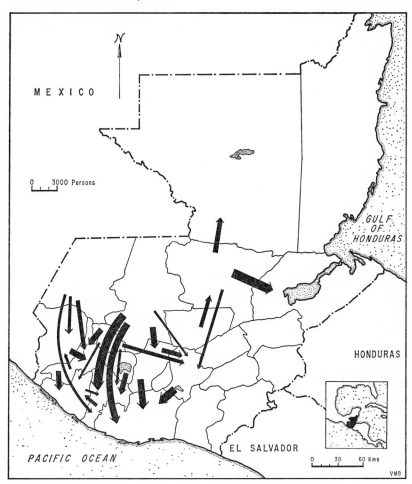

MAP 2–4. INDIAN MIGRATION STREAMS

and 1964.[2] This does not, as has already been indicated, reflect the
real extent of urbanization of this area, because it does not include
the outlying centers that have also grown as a part of the metropolitan centralization. Of equal importance is the fact that provincial urbanization has also been taking place and that it (like the

[2] Ibid.

TABLE 2–2

Five Percent Sample of Migrants, Guatemala, 1964

Department	% of total native population Indian	Total migrants		Intradepartmental migrants		Interdepartmental migrants	
		Number	Percent	Number	Percent	Number	Percent
Republic	43.3	46,488	100.0	17,219	100.0	29,269	100.0
Indian		9,238	19.9	5,137	29.8	4,101	14.0
Ladino		37,250	80.1	12,082	70.2	25,168	86.0
Totonicapán	95.4						
Indian		134	59.6	90	89.1	44	35.5
Ladino		91	40.4	11	10.9	80	64.5
Sololá	92.6						
Indian		171	51.0	67	63.2	104	45.4
Ladino		164	49.0	39	36.8	125	54.6
Alta Verapaz	91.9						
Indian		1,230	79.0	1,099	87.3	131	43.7
Ladino		326	21.0	160	12.7	169	56.3
El Quiché	84.7						
Indian		321	50.4	192	55.0	129	44.8
Ladino		316	49.6	157	45.0	159	55.2
Chimaltenango	76.1						
Indian		533	51.6	303	58.6	230	44.7
Ladino		499	48.4	214	41.4	285	55.3
Huehuetenango	67.5						
Indian		443	42.1	382	47.0	61	25.4
Ladino		610	57.9	431	53.0	179	74.6
San Marcos	60.6						
Indian		1,265	46.1	1,074	49.1	191	33.9
Ladino		1,477	53.9	1,110	50.9	367	66.1
Suchitepéquez	54.0						
Indian		1,152	38.9	564	45.6	588	34.1
Ladino		1,808	61.1	672	54.4	1,136	65.9
Quezaltenango	54.0						
Indian		916	35.1	426	38.1	490	32.8
Ladino		1,694	64.9	691	61.9	1,003	67.2
Baja Verapaz	52.3						
Indian		137	28.3	65	26.4	72	30.3
Ladino		347	71.7	181	73.6	166	69.7
Chiquimula	49.7						
Indian		129	20.0	99	29.5	30	9.7
Ladino		516	80.0	237	70.5	279	90.3

(*Table 2–2, Continued*)

epartment	% of total native population Indian	Total migrants Number	Percent	Intradepartmental migrants Number	Percent	Interdepartmental migrants Number	Percent
ɪcatepéquez	45.5						
Indian		138	21.2	68	24.4	70	18.7
Ladino		514	78.8	209	75.5	305	81.3
ɪlapa	42.7						
Indian		126	21.3	89	34.2	37	11.2
Ladino		465	78.7	171	65.8	294	88.8
etalhuleu	33.9						
Indian		616	27.0	201	32.7	415	24.8
Ladino		1,669	73.0	413	67.3	1,256	75.2
ɪ Petén	24.9						
Indian		125	24.2	13	5.9	112	37.8
Ladino		392	75.8	208	94.1	184	62.2
abal	11.5						
Indian		246	7.9	26	5.6	220	8.3
Ladino		2,862	92.1	435	94.4	2,427	91.7
acapa	11.4						
Indian		105	10.5	45	10.2	60	12.0
Ladino		896	89.5	398	89.8	498	88.0
uatemala	10.3						
Indian		781	5.9	301	8.9	480	4.8
Ladino		12,523	94.1	3,079	91.1	9,444	95.2
scuintla	7.1						
Indian		617	9.0	28	2.3	589	10.4
Ladino		6,267	91.0	1,191	97.7	5,076	89.6
anta Rosa	0.9						
Indian		42	2.2	1	0.1	41	4.3
Ladino		1,830	97.8	924	99.9	906	95.7
l Progreso	0.4						
Indian		6	1.0	1	0.5	5	1.1
Ladino		658	99.0	202	99.5	456	98.9
ɪtiapa	0.4						
Indian		5	0.4	3	0.3	2	0.5
Ladino		1,314	99.6	949	99.7	365	99.5

ᴏᴜʀᴄᴇ: Data from Guatemala, Dirección General de Estadística, 7°Censo de Población, 1964. ʼable from Alvan O. Zárate, "Principales Patrones de Migración Interna en Guatemala," *Estudios 'entroamericanos,* No. 3, Seminario de Integracion Social Guatemalteca, Guatemala, 1967, ʼable 5.

Crucifixion by Power

provincial rural population) is selectively distributed. Between 1950
and 1964, the number of cities of Guatemala with a population of
over 10,000 has increased from five to fourteen (see Table 2–3). Of
these, five (Escuintla, Mazatenango, Retalhuleu, Coatepeque, and
Tiquisate) are on the formerly minimally populated south coast,
with a total urban population of 82,709; three (Chiquimula, Zacapa,
and Jalapa) are in the east, with a total urban population of 35,968.
The northeast has not seen such urban growth. While Quezaltenango is still the second largest city of the republic, its rate of
growth has been far below that of many of the others. In comparing
the portion that metropolitan Guatemala composes of the entire

TABLE 2–3. Guatemalan Cities with a Population over Ten Thousand

	1950	
Guatemala City		284,276
Quezaltenango		27,672
Puerto Barrios		15,155
Mazatenango		11,067
Antigua		10,996
Total		349,218
	1964	
Guatemala City		572,937
Quezaltenango		45,195
Escuintla		24,832
Puerto Barrios		22,242
Mazatenango		19,506
Chiquimula		14,760
Retalhuleu		14,366
Coatepeque		13,657
Antigua		13,576
Amatitlan		12,225
Zacapa		11,173
Tiquisate		10,348
Huehuetenango		10,185
Jalapa		10,035
Total		795,037

SOURCE: Deanne Lanoix Termini, "Socioeconomic and Demographic Characteris-
tics of the Population of Guatemala City with Special Reference to Migrant–
Non-migrant Differences," M.A. Thesis, University of Texas at Austin, 1968,
Table 1.

urban population in centers over ten thousand for the two census years, we find that the metropolitan area has declined from forming 81.4 percent of the total in 1950, to 72.1 percent in 1964. Thus, while the greatest absolute urban growth has been in the metropolitan zone, the proportion that it accounts for of the total urban growth is declining, particularly in favor of the south coast. The structural details of this will be discussed in the final section of this chapter.

Map 2–5 shows that metropolitan Guatemala has received migrants from almost every department of the republic, although the major inputs have been from neighboring Escuintla and Chimaltenango and from Quezaltenango. This migration is almost entirely Ladino in composition, either because they were Ladinos when they arrived or because they have converted to being Ladinos since their arrival. In any case, only 3.5 percent of the metropolitan population was classified as being Indian, and 5.4 percent of the migrant population was so classified.[3]

It is clear from this very brief review that the growing population of Guatemala has already clearly established the new pattern for the country as a whole. The older agrarian-based highland areas are not growing with anything like the acceleration of the lowland areas and the metropolis. Indeed, as Table 2–4 shows, only the six departments singled out here as being the core areas of these new zones can show a positive net migration in the 1964 census. The area of greatest loss is the east, as one would suspect by the fact of Ladino dominance in the immigration streams. The actual composition of these new populations is distinctive. The migrants are generally in the able-bodied age groups. While the metropolitan area has a higher proportion of women than men,[4] the agrarian migration of Indians into El Petén is composed almost entirely of family units.[5] It should not be thought, however, that these migration pat-

[3] Deanne Lanoix Termini, "Socio-Economic and Demographic Characteristics of the Population of Guatemala City with Special Reference to Migrant–Non-Migrant Differences," M.A. thesis The University of Texas at Austin, 1968, Table 8, p. 35. The reader is referred to this source for further demographic analysis of the metropolitan population.

[4] Ibid., Chapter 2.

[5] Richard N. Adams, *Migraciones Internas en Guatemala: Expansión Agraria de los Indígenas Kekchíes hacia El Petén*, Estudios Centroamericanos No. 1, Table 4.

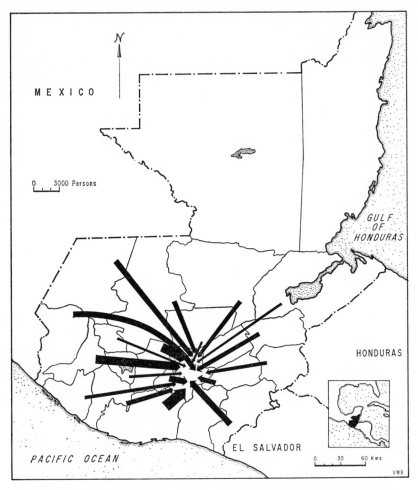

Map 2–5. TOTAL MIGRATION TO THE DEPARTMENT OF
GUATEMALA

terns are due simply to a movement from "full" areas to "empty"
areas. Indeed, the Indian highlands are much "fuller" than the
Ladino east, but are providing only one-fifth the number of migrants. And since cities get "full" by spreading out, metropolitan
Guatemala can hardly be characterized as "empty."

TABLE 2–4

Net Migration by Department, Guatemala, 1964

Department	Number born in department living elsewhere minus those living in department born elsewhere	Net migrants as percent of total native population
Escuintla	+ 4,098	+ 45.7
Izabal	+ 2,075	+ 39.1
Guatemala	+ 7,190	+ 18.9
Retalhuleu	+ 902	+ 16.0
El Petén	+ 195	+ 14.8
Suchitepéquez	+ 176	+ 2.0
Quezaltenango	− 296	− 2.2
Sololá	− 192	− 3.5
Alta Verapaz	− 588	− 4.5
San Marcos	− 870	− 5.3
Huehuetenango	− 861	− 6.0
Chimaltenango	− 1,061	− 6.4
Totonicapán	− 570	− 8.0
El Quiché	− 1,146	− 9.0
Sacatepéquez	− 672	− 9.5
Baja Verapaz	− 560	− 11.7
El Progreso	− 916	− 14.1
Chiquimula	− 1,189	− 16.6
Santa Rosa	− 1,496	− 18.8
Jalapa	− 1,011	− 20.5
Jutiapa	− 2,021	− 22.1
Zacapa	− 1,187	− 24.3

SOURCE: Data from Guatemala, Dirección General de Estadística, 7° Censo de Población, 1964, 5% sample. Table from Alvan O. Zárate, "Principales Patrones de Migración Interna en Guatemala," *Estudios Centroamericanos*, No. 3, Seminario de Integración Social Guatemalteca, Guatemala, 1967, Table 3.

2. *The Changing International Domains*

Modern Guatemala is bounded by certain geographical and historical conditions that are nonetheless important for being obvious. It is a small country, the population in 1964 being set at 4,284,473. A study on the basis of 1961 estimated populations ranked it eightieth in size among 133 of the world's nations.[6] It is the

[6] Bruce M. Russett, et al., *World Handbook of Political and Social Indicators*, p. 19.

largest of the Central American countries in population, however, and, having been the seat of the colonial *audiencia*, has retained something of the pride of that position. Since Mexico could hardly be threatened by Guatemala, there have been no military problems along their borders, although the disposition of British Honduras has been a matter of some contention. With the rest of the Central American countries, there has been a continuing fraternal bickering and, in the past, invasions and border disputes. The growth of the Central American Common Market, however, has probably provided a basis for cooperation in the future.

Guatemala has always been involved in international domains, but there have been important changes in their character and scope. Following independence in 1821, Guatemala left the domain of Spain and underwent fifty years of fluctuating alliances and schisms over the liberal-conservative division that dominated Central American politics in the nineteenth century. During this period, the major foreign competitor for influence was England, but as the United States expanded into Texas and Mexican California, the northern neighbor grew steadily in importance. The rapid rise of coffee growing under the liberal regimes of the latter part of the century brought in strong commercial interests from Europe, predominantly from Germany.

The importance of foreign ownership and controls is illustrated by figures cited by Jones. In 1914, of a total coffee production of 1,046,236 quintals, nearly half was produced by foreigners, and a third of the total was German owned. In the crop year of 1935–1936, of a total of approximately 1,162,000 quintals of coffee exported, 64 percent was exported by German firms, 18 percent by North American firms, 7 percent by Netherlands firms, 5 percent by Guatemalan firms, and 4 percent by British firms. By this time, almost half the production and 95 percent of the trade were in the hands of foreigners.[7] The German agricultural interests were concentrated in the coffee zones, the southwestern piedmont, and Alta Verapaz. Both areas were somewhat isolated from Guatemala City. The southwest found its center in Quezaltenango, with the port of Champerico as the outlet; Alta Verapaz had direct egress to Germany through Lake Izabal and the Atlantic coast. German imperial

---

[7] Chester Lloyd Jones, *Guatemala, Past and Present*, pp. 207–208.

whereas the private operator has shown a slight, but consistent, preference for combining with a Guatemalan. This doubtless reflects the fact that the dangers to the small owner are greater, and Guatemalan backing can help protect him, whereas the larger corporations feel they are strong enough to defend themselves.

The United States has many extensions of interest in Guatemala besides the purely commercial and industrial. One listing of U.S. voluntary agencies working in the rural areas alone identified fifty-two groups, with over five hundred personnel and a monetary commitment of over three million dollars from the United States for the year 1965 (Table 2–7). It is particularly interesting that the great emphasis of this voluntary work was, at that time, in the two highland areas, both the western Indian and the eastern Ladino. Very little work was done on either the south coast or in the northeast and north.

The interest of the United States government has been expressed in various ways, both through direct and indirect military assistance (see Chapter 4) and through extensive and continuing economic and technical aid. Explicitly, however, and continuingly, there has been a concern with trying to stem political radicalism, and a great many of the other efforts are subordinated to this issue of gaining "stability."

The failure of the revolution in 1954 may be attributed to a number of factors, but one was specifically that when Arbenz needed

TABLE 2–7

Voluntary Agency Activity in the Development of Rural Guatemala

| | Number of Personnel | | | | |
| | U.S. Supported | | | | |
Nature of Sponsorship	U.S.	Guate-malan	Third country	Number of Groups	Funding, Fiscal Year 1965
Catholic	200	299	33	22	$1,238,000
Protestant	273	243	1	14	1,463,460
Nonreligious	56	63	1	16	512,270
Total	529	605	35	52	$3,213,730

SOURCE: Agency for International Development, *List of American Voluntary Agencies Maintaining Programs in Rural Guatemala*, Unclassified, pp. 10, 19.

help from the outside, presumably from the socialist bloc, they were unable to come to his aid. An attempt to neutralize the army by arming the peasant agrarian committees with imported arms was stopped by the army and contributed to the military's decision to abandon him to the forces of the Liberation Army of Castillo Armas. Most specifically, the financial and material aid from the United States made the last possible.

The failures of the Arbenz regime were not repeated in Cuba. The Cuban revolution was able to get public support and defense from Russia, it eliminated the core of the old army, thus removing it as a self-interest group, and it was able to bring its case before the United Nations, an action Guatemala was prevented effectively from performing. In the years that followed the end of the revolution in Guatemala, the Partido Guatemalteco de Trabajo (PGT) regrouped in Mexico. With the failure of the Thirteenth of November movement against Ydígoras, *guerrillero* activities began in the northeast. Today, the country is effectively in a state of clandestine civil war. This has been possible because of the open support of many socialist nations for the *guerrillero* forces and because Cuba makes a public foreign policy of encouraging as much internal activity in its neighbors as possible. The *guerrilleros* have long since had methods of keeping themselves in arms and money, primarily by channeling material out of army supplies and through robbery and kidnapping.

Structurally, the appearance of open socialist support from Cuba and the Old World has placed Guatemala under multiple domains. Although the dominance of the United States is unquestionable, it no longer has exclusive superordination, and its domain is no longer unitary. The antigovernment interests can receive support at the international level from friendly socialist nations. This is an important change in the structure of Guatemala and one which cannot escape having extraordinary consequences in the long run. In addition, the newly awakened commercial and political interests of Mexico in Guatemala and the emergence of the Central American Common Market promise to have significant consequences.

Prior to the Second World War, then, Guatemala was primarily under the international domains of the United States and Germany. That war eliminated Germany as an effective actor and left the

United States supreme. The revolutionary governments attempted to gain derivative power from the socialist bloc, but were unsuccessful. Later, following the success of Castro in Cuba, insurgent elements within Guatemala were able to form, to seek and obtain support from the outside, and to confront the government directly. In this way, Guatemala once again came under a second international domain. In a minor way, other economic interests, primarily Japan and Mexico, as well as various European countries, were becoming more active too.

3. *Changing Bases of Internal Power*

All operating units must have some basis of power, either from independent sources or derived through the mediation of another unit. There are important differences between these two kinds of sources. Most notably, the unit in question has the primary decision-making capacity over independent sources, whereas it has access to derived power sources only through the discretion of the super-ordinate party that makes it available. As a result, the manipulation and dependability of derived power is contingent upon the cultural potentials of the unit to a much greater degree than is the case with independent power. For instance, the *finquero* may control his own land directly, but his annual credit is contingent upon a bank's decision, his police protection is contingent upon the local police agent's discretion, while his defense against his laborers' complaints depends on the preferences of the labor inspector and labor court.

Independent power bases are usually discernible and discrete. They consist of pieces of land, particular sets of weaponry, a specific set of individuals organized to a particular degree, and so forth. Derived power, however, comes from a complex of sources that are available to a third party, and the exact composition of the complex may be unknown to the unit that is depending on the source for derived power. The complex is usually itself a mixture of derived and independent sources and, in many cases, is entirely composed of derived sources. Superordinate power holders, then, may have very little independent power at any point in time and may, instead, depend on the effective tactical manipulation of derived power sources. It is for this reason that derived power depends to a great extent on the cultural potential assigned it. All complex societies depend on the utilization of derivative power. The sources of independent power do not increase rapidly in proportion to the numbers of people who manipulate and benefit from them.

Finally, and inevitably in view of the above, the manner of allocating or granting derived power may be entirely distinct from the real base. Thus, while a *finquero* may have a variety of power sources to depend on, the form and manner of granting derived power to his employees is through the opportunity to work for wages or to have land to cultivate.

Derived power is particularly important in complex societies because it allows the tactical manipulation of various sources so that power granted may be in a different form than that received. Power thus has something of the quality of cash: it is negotiable in a variety of circumstances. Derived power is also a scattered potential that can be mobilized at a given point in time to be allocated where it may be needed tactically and then shifted or even used simultaneously to aid another unit in an entirely different confrontation. As Fried pointed out, however, a government seldom has enough power to bring it to bear on all points in the system simultaneously.[9]

Guatemala has a limited set and range of internal independent power sources. They consist principally of land for agricultural purposes, limited mineral resources under exploitation, fairly mobile unskilled labor, some industrial capital, limited local savings, a certain amount of weaponry, and the mass action of the populace available to any country. Neither the materials nor the time available for this study are sufficient for an exhaustive review of the power sources available to the various units operating in Guatemalan society. The way in which these bases have been changing, however, can be illustrated through a review of some cases. The first will illustrate the power concentrated during the revolutionary period and then lost with the failure of the revolution (unions and mass organizations); the second will provide a parallel of concentration during the postrevolutionary period (the *finquero*); the last will illustrate a continuity of growth in concentration (the military and the government in general).

The major contribution of the revolutionary governments to the

---

[9] Morton H. Fried, "The State: The Institution," *International Encyclopedia of the Social Sciences* 15 (1968): 149.

general organizational adaptation of Guatemala was the introduction of mass lower-sector organizations and the provision of derivative power to these organizations. Under Ubico there had been no such organizations except those controlled by the military forces, and these were fragmented and scattered over much of the country. The revolutionary governments provided the basic impetus for the information by granting legality to the lower sector to organize and then bringing to bear governmental sources of support directly to the organizations and by inhibiting counteraction in the inevitable confrontations at the local and regional levels. The basic supportive action came through establishing a labor law and institutionalizing labor courts and procedures to educate and promote the activity of laborers and peasants in matters concerning their own rights and welfare. Of equal importance was the removal of such governmental protection from the landowners and employers. By "looking the other way," the often excessive and illegal activities of agitators and organizers were made easier, and the effective response of the *finqueros* was stifled at the local and regional levels. The general direction of governmental action in this respect became crystallized as the years progressed, and it became clear that the derivative power of the government was itself not enough to overcome the lack of experience and traditional fear in the lower sector about the punitive consequences of acting in concert against the landowners. The attempt during the Arbenz period to provide the agrarian committees with arms was to have provided the lower sector with a source of independent power that would then have been available to the government as derivative power in its contest with the opposition.

When the labor unions and *campesino* leagues began to reform slowly in the postrevolutionary period, the government did not grant them the legal right to political action, but limited them entirely to "economic" activity. The available paths for improvement of their condition through completely nonpolitical action were so totally restricted that it was equivalent to allowing them no effective power to confront the major protagonists, the *finqueros*. Under the postrevolutionary government, not only were the inhibitions formerly obstructing the *finqueros* removed, but important changes in their own bases of power rapidly evolved also. Prior to the revolution, credit was generally available to a few favored clients. Laborers were under effective control, since the government allowed effective local and regional power to be administered by farmers and local authorities. The postrevolutionary government stopped not only effective political organization among laborers, but also organization of almost any kind. They provided new credit facilities for the farmers and returned much of the land that had been expropriated under the revolutionary agrarian reform. At the same time, new technological knowledge was being made available to them through international sources. Coffee technology was being improved for the first time in its recent history, and with this came new credits, new machinery, and the possibility to develop skilled labor. Although the *finquero* was more subordinated to the sources of derived power than even during the time of Ubico, he was granted a visible absolute increase in the power available to him.

While the laborer experienced a simultaneous rise and decline of available power bases and the *finquero* had the benefit of a delayed increase, the government and the military saw a steady increase. Some changes that occurred in power bases are suggested here, although subsequent chapters take up various parts of the subjects in detail. The military has, by way of independent power, access to weaponry and funds for their acquisition and upkeep, the organized and fairly highly disciplined troops and officer corps, and an intelligence system for information extending throughout the entire country. In all respects, these bases have increased over the past twenty-five years. In addition to these independent sources, they have the governmental budgetary allocations necessary to keep the establishment going and the resources of the United States military establishment and the inter-American defense organization. An interesting question presents itself in examining this growth. According to apparently reliable sources, the budgetary allocations to the military have not grown any faster than have the general governmental expenditures since the beginning of the revolutionary period. Table 2–8 shows that, while there was a pronounced decrease with the fall of Ubico and a slight increase during the immediate postrevolutionary period, in general the proportion has remained fairly constant since 1946.

How, then, can it be said that the Guatemalan military establishment has significantly increased its bases of power? The answer apparently lies in a situation possibly unique to Guatemala. Unlike

TABLE 2–8

Defense Expenditures as a Percentage of Total Annual
Government Expenditures, 1938–1965

Year	%	Year	%	Year	%
1939	17.1	1948	8.5	1957	7.8
1940	16.4	1949	10.7	1958	8.5
1941	18.7	1950	10.5	1959	9.2
1942	17.4	1951	10.8	1960	10.0
1943	16.5	1952	10.0	1961	9.4
1944	13.7	1953	10.0	1962	8.3
1945	19.1	1954	9.4	1963	10.0
1946	11.6	1955	9.3	1964	10.3
1947	10.8	1956	8.6	1965	10.8

SOURCE: Joseph E. Loftus, *Latin American Defense Expenditures, 1938–1965,*
Memorandum RM-5310-PR/ISA, The Rand Corporation, Santa Monica, 1968,
Table 5.

many other Latin American countries that have expanded their
military forces in manpower and costs, the Guatemalan military
has apparently held down the size of the military in favor of increasing expenditure per man. A study by Loftus (Table 2–9) shows
that of all the Latin American nations for which there were data,
Guatemala had the greatest increase of defense expenditures per
member of the armed forces between 1955 and 1965. Furthermore,
as of 1965, this figure was the greatest of any Central American or
Caribbean nation (except Mexico) and larger than that of Bolivia,
Brazil, Ecuador, Paraguay, and Peru. While the cost of the military
in the national budget has not increased, the amount devoted to material, perquisites, and other expenditures must have increased
more than that recorded elsewhere in Latin America.

The growth of the government has also been great during this
entire period, but the increase has been in both personnel and costs.
Weaver (Table 2–10) estimates that the size of the public employee force increased over two and one-half times between 1950
and 1966. This is almost five times the rate of growth of the general
population, which was about 53.6 percent.

Unfortunately, while the field studies upon which the major
portion of this book is based were designed to study the social
structure of Guatemala at the national level, it was not possible to
mount a meaningful study of the span of the Guatemalan govern-

TABLE 2–9
Defense Expenditures per Member of the Armed Forces

Country	1955	1960	1965	Percentage Change 1955–1965
South America				
Argentina	$1,858	$2,178	$2,114	114%
Bolivia	—	267	—	—
Brazil	2,634	1,204	1,363[a]	52
Chile	2,974	2,524	2,144	72
Colombia	5,453	2.057	2,438	45
Ecuador	919	1,233	1,233	134
Paraguay	—	438	500[a]	—
Peru	2,051	1,002	811[a]	26
Uruguay	—	1,612	—	—
Venezuela	6,108	7,591	5,911	97
Central America				
Costa Rica	$1,833	$1,833/~2,000[b]	$1,917/~2,000[b]	—
Cuba	—	—	—	—
Dominican Republic	—	1,856	1,539	—
El Salvador	899	897	1,288	143%
Guatemala	857	1,143	1,763	206
Haiti	889	932	1,109	125
Honduras	703	1,281	1,225	174
Mexico	1,186	1,485	2,345	198
Nicaragua	—	1,490	1,380[a]	—
Panama	—	—	—	—

SOURCE: Joseph E. Loftus, *Latin American Defense Expenditures, 1938–1965*, Memorandum RM-5310-PR/ISA, The Rand Corporation, Santa Monica, 1968, Table 11, percentages added.

[a] Total defense expenditure figures for 1964 used in the absence of data for 1965.

[b] Beginning in 1959, the functional expenditure category "defense" used by Costa Rica in reporting to the United Nations *Statistical Yearbook* was changed to "justice, police, and other security forces." This change was made with no indication of what expenditures once classified as "defense" were to be included in this category. Accordingly, assuming the continuance of the 1948 legislative ceiling of 1,200 men for the security forces, the author has adopted a ~$2,000 figure for 1960 and 1965—approximately the 1958 level.

ment's growth in power. There is little question that the military, both as a part of and apart from the rest of the bureaucracy, has expanded in important ways. A future study will have to point out the various ways in which the government is using this vast increase

TABLE 2–10

Number of Government Employees during Selected Years

Year	Number of Employees
1950	15,500
1954	22,300
1957	27,900
1963	37,500
1966	40,000

SOURCE: Secretaria General del Consejo Nacional de Planificación Económica, *Situación del Desarrollo Económico y Social de Guatemala (Diagnostico General)*, Guatemala City, July 1965, Table 3. Figures for 1963 and 1966 were computed by Jerry Weaver from the national budgets.

in personnel in its other branches. There is no question, however, that the nation as a whole provided increasing internal basis for power, and the economic growth during the period confirms this.

4. Development and the Resource Base

Every society depends to a greater or lesser degree on elements extracted from the natural environment and conversion of those elements into needed goods. No special attempt has been made in this study to bring together all the available data, but it is important to establish that there has been development of the resources that form the major basis of independent power in Guatemala. The major Guatemalan resource is agriculture. Unfortunately, figures for the period prior to 1950 are not readily available; as a consequence, the present notes on development will stress the recent period.

Various studies leave no doubt that there has been economic development during the past two decades. Table 2–11 shows the annual rate of growth by major branches of economic activity between 1950 and 1964. Growth was much faster in the 1960–1964 period than during the preceding decade. The major expansion was in banking, utilities, industry, transport, and commerce, but agriculture also saw some growth. Table 2–12 shows that over the period 1960–1965 the basic structure of this production remained relatively unchanged. Agriculture's portion of the total economy declined slightly, and industry gained slightly. This gain of in-

Table 2–11
Annual Rate of Growth by Sectors, 1950–1964

	1950–64	1950–60	1960–6
1. Agriculture, forestry, hunting, & fishing	3.3%	2.9%	4.3%
2. Manufacturing industry	5.9	4.4	9.8
3. Other sectors	4.7	4.1	6.2
3.1 Operation of mines & quarries	0.7	2.7	— 4.1
3.2 Construction	0.9	— 0.1	3.4
3.3 Electricity, gas, water, & sanitary services	9.6	8.1	13.5
3.4 Transport, storage, & communications	6.9	6.7	7.3
3.5 Wholesale & retail commerce	5.0	4.2	7.2
3.6 Banking, insurance, & real estate property	7.9	5.3	14.7
3.7 Ownership of housing	4.1	3.1	6.6
3.8 Private services	4.8	4.9	4.3
3.9 Public & defense administration	2.8	4.3	—0.9
Gross domestic product	4.5	3.8	6.1

Source: CIAP/277, *El esfuerzo interno y las necesidades de financiamiento externo para*
desarrollo de Guatemala, fourth quarter; and estimates of the committee. Alliance for Progres
Evaluación del plan de desarrollo económico y social de Guatemala, 1965–69. Report presented
the government of Guatemala by the ad hoc committee, August 1966, p. 79.

dustry occurred after 1962, however, as it remained between 12 and 13 percent from 1950 through 1961.[10]

The gain in agriculture was principally in nonfood crops, crops destined for export. Table 2–13 shows the relative and absolute growth of agriculture and food crops based on the period of 1952/3–1954/5. In a crude and cruel way, the four columns of this table show what has happened in Guatemalan development. The gross agricultural product has increased from an index of 100 to 189 in a period of ten years. This is a respectable increase. Even when recalculated on a per capita basis, the increase is from 100 to 141, still respectable. However, the next two sets of figures make it clear that this entire gain is relevant to the export sector, for food crops have an absolute increase of only 1 to 135; and when this is calculated on a per capita basis, it turns out that there has been essentially no increase at all. The fact that the agricultural increase is principally in the export crops is indicated in another way in Table 2–14. This shows that the increase in land use from 1950 to 1962 was 20–25

[10] Calculated from Banco de Guatemala, *Informe de Guatemala, 1961–65,* Table 2.

TABLE 2-12
Gross Domestic Product of Guatemala by Sectors, 1960–1965

	Millions of Dollars at 1960 Prices						Percent Distribution		Annual Rate of Growth					
	1960	1961	1962	1963	1964	1965ᵃ	1960	1965	1960–1965	1960–1961	1961–1962	1962–1963	1963–1964	1964–1965
Gross domestic product	1,020.5	1,059.3	1,086.7	1,223.5	1,295.6	1,366.6	100.0	100.0	6.0	3.8	2.6	12.6	5.9	5.5
Farming	311.3	316.3	331.3	371.1	369.5	382.0	30.5	28.0	4.2	1.6	4.7	12.0	−0.4	3.4
Mines & quarries	2.0	1.3	0.4	1.6	1.7	1.7	0.2	0.1	−3.2	−35.0	−69.2	300.0	6.3	—
Industry	129.6	137.2	143.3	168.1	188.7	197.1	12.7	14.4	8.8	5.9	4.4	17.3	12.3	4.5
Construction	21.4	25.7	22.9	19.6	24.5	25.2	2.1	1.8	3.3	20.1	−10.9	−14.4	25.0	2.9
Eletricity, gas	7.1	7.9	8.6	10.8	11.8	14.6	0.7	1.1	15.5	11.3	8.9	25.6	9.3	23.7
Transportation	49.0	53.9	65.8	57.8	65.0	71.9	4.8	5.3	8.0	10.0	22.1	−12.2	12.5	10.6
Commerce	281.7	287.6	285.6	341.4	372.1	389.9	27.6	28.5	6.7	2.1	−0.7	19.5	9.0	4.8
Banking, insurance	15.3	16.8	20.6	23.9	26.5	29.6	1.5	2.2	14.1	9.8	22.6	16.0	10.9	11.7
Ownership of housing	79.6	80.9	82.2	100.2	103.0	106.6	7.8	7.8	6.0	1.6	1.6	21.9	2.8	3.5
Public administration	61.2	67.9	59.6	58.7	59.0	71.3	6.0	5.2	3.1	10.9	−12.2	−1.5	0.5	20.8
Services	62.3	63.8	66.4	70.3	73.8	76.7	6.1	5.6	4.2	2.4	4.1	5.9	5.0	3.9

SOURCE: United Nations, Economic Commission for Latin America, *Estudio Económico de América Latina*, 1965, (E/CN.12/752).
ᵃ Provisional figures.

TABLE 2–13

Indices of Guatemalan Agricultural and Food Production

	Total Agricultural Production Index		Food Production Index	
Period	Production	Per Capita Production	Production	Per Capita Production
1952/53–1954/55	100	100	100	100
1958–59	125	108	116	100
1959/60	131	110	119	100
1960/61	135	110	122	99
1961/62	151	119	127	100
1962/63	175*	135*	133*	102*
1963/64	189†	141†	135†	101†

SOURCE: Commission for Economic Development, *Economic Development of Central Americ*
New York, November, 1964, p. 49. Table 6.
* Preliminary figures
† Estimated figures

TABLE 2–14

Increase in Land Use by Selected Crops, 1950–1962

Crops of Primarily Domestic Consumption	Thousands of Hectares in 1950	Absolute Increase 1950–1962	Relative Increase
Corn and beans	5,365.0	117.1	21.8%
Wheat and rice	45.0	0.4	0.9
Garden crops and potatoes	4.5	1.1	25.0
Cultivated pasturage	232.5	50.9	21.9
Export Crops			
Bananas and plantains	20.5	—11.6	—56.8
Essential oils	4.2	4.8	115.0
Cotton	1.6	47.2	283.5
Coffee, rubber, cocoa, and fruit	153.8	281.5	77.3
Sugar	15.4	12.3	79.6
Total Land in Agricultural Use	2,056.8	50.3	2.4%

SOURCE: Guatemala, Secretaria General del Consejo Nacional de Planificación Económico, *I Situación del Desarrollo Económico y Social de Guatemala*, June 1965, pp. 113–114.
NOTE: Other classes of use not shown here include land in rest, natural pasturage, etc.

percent in basic food crop areas, but (with one exception) between 77 percent and 283 percent in export crop lands. The exception to this was the banana lands that, because of the United Fruit Company's withdrawal, were reduced by more than half.

The overall picture of development from 1950 to 1964 shows an increase of the gross geographic product per capita from 263 to 310 dollars a year (the quetzal equals the dollar). One report wistfully reports: "Lamentably, there are no statistical indices that permit us to establish how the distribution of income may have evolved . . . even though there have been some political steps tending towards a better distribution of income. The only assertion possible is that there exists a concentration of a very high percentage of the national income in a very small percent of the population."[11] From the above data, it may be inferred that the greater part of the increase was not in the subsistence sector, but in the export economy and industrial sector.

Growth in industry has been of some importance, and the sector as a whole shows a 70 percent increase in production over the twelve years from 1950 to 1962.[12] As was mentioned, the major upswing has been good, as indicated in Table 2–12. However, there is some question whether the recent rates may be sustained over a long period.

Some indication of the way in which development is affecting the population may be had by the change in economic activity manifest between 1950 and 1964. Table 2–15 shows that the agriculture sector has declined from 68.2 percent of the total to 64.7 percent. The sectors that have gained over this period have been business, transport, and services; industry is not among them. This would indicate a shift toward an urban-based population, but the relative figures are somewhat misleading. The absolute figures show that the total increment in agricultural employment (176,850) still exceeded all the other sectors combined (147,550).

In short, as is summarized in Table 2–16, Guatemala experienced economic development during the period under consideration. The

[11] Departamento de Censos y Encuestas, *Censos 1964*, p. 3.

[12] Secretaría General del Consejo Nacional de Planificación Económica, *Diagnóstico del Sector Industrial, Período 1950–1962*, p. 259.

TABLE 2–15
Economically Active Population, Ten Years and Older

Branch of Activity	1950 Population	%	1964 Population	%	Increase	% Increase in 14 years	Average Annual Increase	% per year
Agriculture, forestry, hunting and fishing	659,550	68.2	836,400[a]	64.7	176,850	26.8	12,632	1.9
Mining	1,441	0.2	2,160	0.2	719	49.9	51	3.6
Manufacturing	111,538	11.5	148,600	11.5	37,062	33.2	2,647	2.4
Construction	26,427	2.7	34,320	2.7	7,893	29.9	563	2.1
Electricity, gas, water, and sanitary services	244	0.1	1,680	0.1	458	35.0	31	2.5
Commerce	52,561	5.4	82,300	6.4	29,739	56.6	2,124	4.0
Transport, storage, and communication	15,352	1.6	28,020	2.2	12,668	82.5	904	5.9
Services	95,705	9.9	148,000	11.5	52,295	54.6	3,735	3.9
Activities not well classified	3,996	0.4	9,540	0.6	5,544	138.7	396	9.9
New workers	—	—	1,200	0.1	1,200	—	85	—
Total	967,814	100.0	1,292,220	100.0	324,406	33.5	23,171	2.4

SOURCE: Guatemala, Director General of Statistics
[a] 5% sample of preliminary figures.

TABLE 2–16

Change in the Gross National Product and Prices in Guatemala, 1950–1965

	Gross Internal Product (in millions of quetzales, 1958)	Index of Wholesale Prices (1958=100)	Gross National Product (in millions of quetzales for each year)	Annual Rates of Growth of the GIP to prices in 1958
1950	722.3	94.1	679.7	—
1951	732.5	99.2	726.7	1.4%
1952	747.7	98.2	734.3	2.1
1953	775.3	98.5	763.7	3.7
1954	789.6	103.4	816.5	1.8
1955	809.1	99.8	807.5	2.5
1956	882.7	99.6	879.2	9.1
1957	932.5	99.0	923.2	5.6
1958	970.9	100.0	970.9	4.1
1959	1,018.1	100.8	1,026.3	4.9
1960	1,047.9	99.4	1,041.6	2.9
1961	1,067.0	98.3	1,048.9	1.8
1962	1,098.2	99.8	1,096.0	2.9
1963	1,208.3	99.3	1,199.8	10.0
1964	1,318.6	102.8	1,355.5	9.1
1965	1,403.9	100.7	1,413.7	6.5

SOURCE: *El esfuerzo interno y las necesidades de financiamiento externo para el desarrollo de Guatemala*, CIES/277, Cuadro 3; *Informe de la República de Guatemala 1961–1965*, Conferencia el CIES, March 1966, p. 2; estimaciones del Consejo Nacional de Planificación del 14-IV-1966. eries prepared converting the 1950 base published by the Bank of Guatemala to the 1958 base.

growth has been concentrated in the agricultural export sector and in industry, transport, banking, and commerce after 1962. Of particular interest is the pattern of growth. Low during the revolutionary period, it rose sharply in 1956 to decline gradually until the advent of the Peralta government (1963) when it again rose sharply. As has been seen, the growth has been in the upper sector. From Table 2–16, it is evident that the political control by the upper sector has been important for such gross measures of growth.

5. *The Structure of Regional Development*

The pattern of migration outlined earlier suggests five major areas of Guatemalan growth: the old areas of the Indian western highlands, the Ladino eastern highlands, the northeast and north,

the new provincial areas of the south coast, and metropolitan Guatemala. In a very real sense, these regions have formed themselves
through the operation of progressive adaptation of the population.
There are still questions to be explored regarding how this regionalization has occurred, and, specifically, how it is related to national
structural escalation on the one hand and to local adaptive niche
hunting on the other.

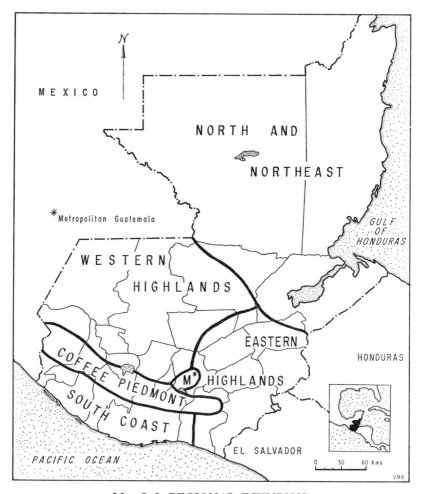

MAP 2–6. REGIONAL DIVISIONS

Regionalization, or the formation of distinctive regions, is one consequence of growth. For present purposes, however, I would propose that growth takes place when (1) there are confrontations for expansion or due to the necessity for survival, (2) there are available within the reality potential the elements or factors of production (resources, capital, labor, and also a market), and (3) the existing domains do not inhibit the success of a unit in moving to a higher level of articulation.

In comparing the five regions, the only major element that inhibits possible growth is the last: the presence of restrictive domains. In all the regions, there are confrontations for survival; capital is not categorically unavailable in any, although it is to a wide range of people of the two old regions. Labor is abundant in the old regions and is available by migration in the new regions. The market for all regions is essentially outside the regions themselves, but available. The negative features in the general picture are to be found basically in the domain structure.

THE INDIAN WESTERN HIGHLANDS

This area is comprised mainly of small landholdings, although there are some latifundia. Table 2–17 shows that all the departments in which Indians form over one-half of the population are in this area (see also Maps 2–6 and 2–7). The technology is agrarian and primitive, and any major step in development will require a shift away from its current dependence on manpower. That this kind of innovation is possible is illustrated by the success of the textile factory in Cantel.[13]

The closed-domain structure of the western highlands has long since been a factor in the pattern of survival of the population. A symbiotic relationship has developed over the past century with the coffee farms of the southern piedmont. As the pressure grew on the minifundia owners and the coffee cultivation expanded, the need for cash by the Indians was complemented by the need for seasonal labor by the farms. This pressure has been felt at different times in different communities, but it began as early as the end of the last century in some places and is now widespread over most of the area. It is complemented by a parallel pattern of seasonal migration pre-

---

[13] Manning Nash, *Machine Age Maya*.

TABLE 2–17
Indian Population of Guatemala

	1950			1964*		
Department	Total Population	Indian	% Indian	Total Population	Indian	% Indian
Totonicapán	99,434	96,054	96.6	142,873	134,596	94.2
Sololá	82,869	77,750	93.8	107,429	100,822	93.1
Alta Verapaz	188,758	176,231	93.4	263,160	241,820	92.0
El Quiché	174,882	146,398	83.7	255,280	216,340	84.9
Chimaltenango	122,310	94,774	77.5	161,760	123,060	76.1
Huehuetenango	198,872	146,127	73.5	285,180	192,620	67.5
San Marcos	230,039	165,964	72.1	328,420	198,840	60.5
Suchitepéquez	125,196	84,359	67.4	182,524	98.570	54.0
Quezaltenango	183,588	124,756	68.0	270,100	149,331	55.4
Baja Verapaz	66,432	38,927	58.6	95,680	50,040	52.3
Chíquimula	112,837	70,096	62.1	145,800	72,380	49.6
Sacatepéquez	59,975	30,722	51.2	79,120	36,040	45.5
Jalapa	75,091	37,897	50.5	99,300	42,340	42.4
Retalhuleu	66,066	34,040	51.5	115,977	37,236	32.1
El Petén	15,897	4,466	28.1	27,720	6,900	24.9
Izabal	55,191	8,109	14.7	114,380	13,100	11.9
Zacapa	69,533	13,140	18.9	98,560	11,260	11.3
Guatemala	441,085	80,807	18.3	792,594	80,804	10.2
Escuintla	123,809	19,628	15.9	266,488	32,637	13.9
Santa Rosa	109,812	10,450	9.5	158,505	2,963	1.9
El Progreso	47,678	4,321	9.1	64,866	263	<0.1
Jutiapa	138,768	26,709	19.2	189,460	840	<0.1
Total	2,788,122	1,491,725	53.5%	4,245,176	1,842,802	43.4%

SOURCE: Data from the Dirección General de Estadística y Censos.

ferred by some highlanders who go to the coastal areas to rent land and plant additional crops. These individuals supplement the limited yield of the highland plots with the lowland production and commute between the two.[14] This, it should be noted, is done by both Indians and Ladinos of the area.

The domain structure of the western highlands is comprised primarily of a series of separate communities under the complementary

[14] See Ruben Reina, *Chinautla: A Guatemalan Indian Community*, and Richard N. Adams, *Cultural Surveys of Panama-Nicaragua-Guatemala-El Salvador-Honduras*, p. 305.

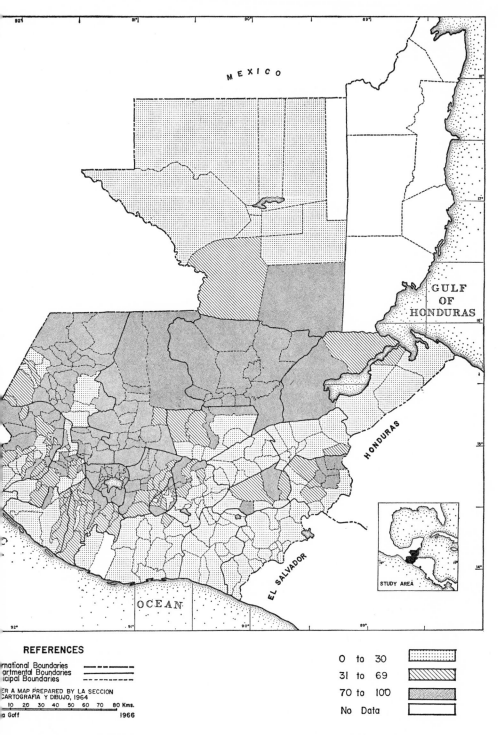

MAP 2–7. PERCENTAGE OF INDIANS IN POPULATION, 1964

controls of Indian civic and religious leaders and Ladino commercial interests. The variation in this pattern is to be found in the following: In a few instances, the Indians have taken over the commercial interests, as is strikingly the case in Quezaltenango. In some there are Ladino domains controlled from the outside, principally in the form of the *finca de mozo* system. Ladinos have control of almost all domains with external relationships; this holds for government posts of towns with significant Ladino minorities and provincial capitals. There are few higher-level domain structures that are in some sense fundamentally Indian. The communities have no serious confrontations (except for occasional squabbles over the allocation of woodland resources and similar problems) but maintain rather a high degree of sociocultural isolation from each other. The *gremial triguero*, described in Chapter 6, is one of the few cases of a predominantly Indian organization that extends beyond one community, and in this case its Indian leadership was in serious difficulty at the time of the study. In short, the Indian has developed no basis for unity beyond the local community.

THE EASTERN HIGHLAND REGION

Also long established is the eastern highland region. However, the population density there is much lower than in the west, and the domain patterns differ. Instead of a predominance of minifundia with a few latifundia, the eastern highlands have a much broader spectrum of small, middle-sized, and large producers. The general tenure system is comparable in its rigidity, however, although the variety of forms is much broader. Besides large coffee farms and other holdings, there are some Indian communities, with communal holdings (such as will be described for the people of the Montaña de Jalapa and has been reported for some remnant groups in Jutiapa) and some cases of the classical Ladino domination over the Indians, as seems to be the case in San Luis Jilotepeque.[15] There are instances of Ladino community lands, such as Quesada,[16] and there are all sorts of holdings of varying sizes but of generally low production.

[15] See John Gillin, *The Culture of Security in San Carlos;* and Melvin Tumin, *Caste in a Peasant Society.*
[16] Cf. Adams, *Cultural Surveys,* p. 398.

The range of domain structure of the eastern highlands is illustrated in Durston's study of Jutiapa.[17] The general consequence has been similar to that in the western highlands, but much more telling. Ladino migration, as already indicated, has been much heavier than Indian migration. Also, the Ladinos have not had immediately adjacent to them a developing region in need of seasonal labor, as the Indians have in the piedmont coffee zone. Since there is no study of the agrarian and migration situation in the east, it is not easy to know precisely why permanent migration rather than seasonal migration became the Ladino solution. It may be the case that there has always been greater mobility within the area and that the large movements of the past two decades have been merely an increase, not the start, of a new pattern. It is also probably the case, however, that there are more predatory farmers, willing to drive small farmers out of the region, and more small-scale renters than has been the case where the population has been entirely Indian. This was the area where the revolutionary law of forced rentals was particularly significant.

A factor that needs further study is the relation between the eastern highlands of Guatemala and the adjacent countries of El Salvador and Honduras. It was pointed out some years ago that the relative increase in density of population as one moves from west to east along the south coast tends to place Jutiapa in a position intermediate between Santa Rosa and neighboring Ahuachapan in El Salvador.[18] Since the opening of the Common Market and the attendant relaxation on border crossing by Central American nationals, there has been a heavy influx of Salvadoreans into Jutiapa and central Guatemala. Municipal authorities in some of the border *municipios* were locally renowned for selling citizenship identification to incoming Salvadorean laborers. This means, of course, that it is impossible to know with precision just how much of the immigration out of the southeast is of Guatemalan origin and how much due either directly or indirectly to Salvadorean immigration. The whole question of border relations of Latin American nations is one that needs study.

[17] John Durston, "Power Structure in a Rural Region of Guatemala: the Department of Jutiapa." M.A. thesis, The University of Texas at Austin, 1966. This material is reviewed in Chapter 3, section 5, of this volume.

[18] Richard Adams, *Encuesta sobre los ladinos de Guatemala.*

Taken together, the highland regions of the east and the west are similar in that they are relatively overpopulated and that their domain structures are the provincial relics of the past. Their adaptive stance still works, however, since the pressures of population growth are absorbed by emigration. The variation in the eastern region probably offers more immediate possibilities for growth than is the case in the west.

THE NORTHEAST AND NORTHERN LOWLANDS

The northeast and northern lowlands have been an area of little occupation until recently. In the census of 1950, El Petén had a population density of 0.4 persons per square kilometer, and the figure for Izabal was only 6.1. In 1964 these figures had risen to 0.8 and 13 respectively. The percentage of the total national population, collectively for the two departments, rose in the same period from 2.6 to 3.2. The department of Izabal, however, had the nation's highest annual rate of growth—5.3 percent for the intercensal period. El Petén followed only Escuintla and Guatemala with a rate of 4.0.[19]

Formerly, the major populations of importance in this region were those related to the United Fruit Company's plantation at Bananera and the town of Puerto Barrios. The El Petén population was small, scattered, and economically important mainly because of its chicle production, using seasonal labor dependent primarily upon migration from Alta Verapaz. It is hard to discuss the domain structure of these regions because of lack of information. It has been argued that movement into the region had been low because of the general lack of enthusiasm for the lowlands among all highlanders, especially Indians. This preference, however, did not stop movement when the pressure became strong enough. In short, there were not very many domains because there were not very many people. Bananera drew principally upon the eastern highlands and neighboring Honduras.

Movement into the area in the intervening period, while primarily Ladino, has also had a significant Indian component. Fifty-

19 Departamento de Censos y Encuestas, Dirección General de Estadística, Ministerio de Economía, *Censos 1964, Población, Resultados de tabulación por muestra,* pp. 15, 19.

three percent of the immigration into El Petén came from Alta Verapaz, and 7.9 percent of the Izabal migrants came from the same area. This migration was almost entirely Indian.[20] For Izabal immigration, the departments of Zacapa and Chiquimula alone accounted for 64.1 percent. Izabal is being somewhat split, with the half north of the lake becoming Indian in character and the part to the south forming an extension of the eastern Ladino population.

THE SOUTH COAST

The region lying mainly from Escuintla to the west is here referred to as the south coast. Santa Rosa is transitional with the eastern highlands. In the first part of this century, this area was regarded as an unhealthy lowland region and was occupied principally by scattered cattle farmers and their employees. Again, it was a United Fruit Company center, this time at Tiquisate, that formed the major single enterprise in the area. However, labor for Tiquisate came from both the east and the western highlands.

It is harder to differentiate the figures in order to demonstrate the growth of the coastal region because the two major departments concerned, Escuintla and Retalhuleu, also have significant highland zones. The densities for 1950 were, respectively, twenty-eight and thirty-six per square kilometer, and these figures rose in 1964 to fifty-seven and sixty-one. Presumably, the major growth was in the coastal areas. Equally important, however, is that the proportion of the total national population of the two departments rose from 6.8 to 8.7 percent.

The movement of peoples into the south coast was already evident in 1950, as it had been in the northeast.[21] In both areas, the opening up of land for colonization was an important impetus, not merely in settling people on the land, but because it brought many more who found that there was no more land available, but were willing to subordinate themselves as labor. Of equal, possibly of greater, importance was the introduction and growth of cotton (see Chapter 7). This, together with the increase in sugar and the smaller

[20] See Alvan Zárate, "Migraciones internas de Guatemala," *Estudios Centro-americanos* No. 1; and Adams, *Migraciones Internas.*

[21] Jorge Arias B., "Migración interna en Guatemala," *Estadística* 20, no. 76 (1962): 519–527.

growth of rubber, cacao, and other lowland products, has essentially opened the south coast as a major agrarian region of the republic. Since much of this growth was in export agriculture, however, and not subsistence agriculture, the pattern of settlement is currently mixed. Large-scale operations account for most of the new land opened up. It was also pointed out that important urbanization has taken place in this zone, with the city of Escuintla now the third largest city of the republic, and Mazatenango, Retalhuleu, Coatepeque, and Tiquisate (merely a company community in 1950) now all over ten thousand in size.

Movement into Escuintla has been principally from the neighboring departments as well as Jutiapa and Suchitepéquez. It is almost ten to one Ladino over Indian in composition. The proportion of migrant Indians in Retalhuleu is much higher, being 27 percent, and in Suchitepéquez it has reached 38.9 percent. Presumably there are similar proportions in coastal Quezaltenango and San Marcos, but the data at hand do not permit us to differentiate them.

The delineation of the new domain structure for the two new regions is not easy. Materials from the present study make it clear that, for Escuintla, the major new operations are sponsored from the national level of articulation (see last section of Chapter 3). The boom in cotton is entirely from that source, and we may assume that the same is true for the other major export crops. However, there is also present a respectable number of colonists, smaller operators who fall directly under the domain of the government, except in those cases where they have committed themselves to an export crop and thereby become involved with the larger producers in marketing arrangements. By roughly comparing the derivative power allowed by the Arbenz government to the agrarian reformist with that allowed by the postrevolutionary governments to the colonists, the development of the colonization areas is shown to be desultory, subject to much bureaucratic politicking, and receiving little consistent support from the government. Basically, the colonists are subordinated to a combination of government and commercial domains, whereas the larger producers find themselves working at higher levels. Regional commercial and marketing activities are clearly more important on the south coast than in the northeast. The relative growth of cities in the former area is a sufficient

index of this, and the course of cotton development illustrates the
various activities at the higher levels.

The area labeled metropolitan Guatemala is, of course, Guatemala City and its immediate developing environs. As might be expected, it has seen the greatest population growth of any area in the
country, with the municipal population more than doubling during
the intercensal period. Both the internal growth and the domain
structure of the metropolis are at present unstudied, and there is
little that can be said here about them. The metropolis is, of course,
the center of almost all upper-level activities; it provides the source
of almost all the sources of credit, of marketing arrangements for
export and import, and, therefore, for the major portion of the national income. It has the concentration of professionals: 84.6 percent
(see Chapter 8) of the lawyers are there, and the figures are probably similar for doctors and other specialists, as well as for most of
the government offices and employees. The department of Guatemala's proportion of the total population increased from 15.8 percent in 1950 to 18.5 percent in 1964. Bryan Roberts' contribution
(Chapter 10), shows something of what is happening within two
small segments of the large and complex city area. The geographic
dimensions of the metropolitan zone are a matter of arbitrary definition. It makes some sense to include the growing industrial belt
down to Amatitlán and possibly on to Escuintla. It certainly includes the neighboring communities of Mixco and Chinautla, two
Indian communities that are now being overwhelmed by Ladino
suburban movement. Even Chimaltenango is, in a sense, a suburban
adjunct of Guatemala City, and Antigua serves as the residence of
some who commute daily to the center.

The preceding discussion sketches out some of the major features of the five macroregions of Guatemalan national society. This
paints, obviously, with too broad a brush. It is necessary both to see
how these work and to have a more accurate picture. To do this,
some specific subsidiary areas and some exceptional enclaves can
be singled out.

In the Indian highlands there are two processes that contrast with the general picture. Just as there has been a movement to the lowlands of the northeast and south, so there has also been a movement to the lowlands of northern Quiché and western Huehuetenango. The Zona Reina of the Quiché-Huehuetenango border has long been one of the agrarian El Dorados of Guatemala, and movements into the zone by both large-scale operations and Indians from neighboring Huehuetenango have been encouraged for some time. Difficulty of access, however, has made it more a promise than a performance. Along the Mexican border there is another lowland area that was the scene years ago of a Ladino migration and settlement. In the past few years there has been a significant Indian movement, an agrarian migration parallel in kind to that of the Kekchi Indian movement into El Petén. In a very real way, the Indian population is spilling over steadily into all the available neighboring lowland zones. The extension of the Indian area of occupation is, in this sense, spreading. In the north and west, however, the Indians are probably not subject to the same acculturating influences that they are in the south; they do not come under the already existing commercial and agrarian domains that allocate them to subordinate niches within the local structure.

Another Indian development is the significant expansion of their domination of commerce in Quezaltenango.[22] On a microscale, the Indians of this western center have broken through the subsistence line and formed commercial and industrial domains of their own and, at the same time, forged a new kind of Indian middle- and upper-strata society. Children of the more successful families have continued their education into and through secondary school, and some have continued into the university. This is not a special case of the underprivileged, but simply the fact that the Indians who have achieved economic success have followed the basic pattern of affluence set by their Ladino predecessors. Economic affluence, then, like politicization, occurs independently of whether the individual may be Indian or Ladino. While generally on a smaller scale than some of the major Ladino enterprises, the Indian expansion has

[22] See Bruce Hupp, "The Indians of Quezaltenango City," M.A. thesis, The University of Texas at Austin, 1969.

been accounting for more and more of the commercial activities within the city of Quezaltenango. This economic success, however, does not mean that the Indians have achieved a comparable political importance. It has not given them access to new sources of power at the national level, or at least there is little evidence that they have successfully used it in this way. Even with control of much of the business activity, they seem not to have established a broad general domain of power.

It has been noted that there are important Indian enclaves in the eastern highlands (Map 2–6). These comprise the Pocoman of Jalapa and the Chorti of Chiquimula, as well as the community-land dwellers of the Montaña de Jalapa and Jutiapa remnants. There is no evidence as to the recent developments within the first two of these populations, but there are Ladino encroachments into the Jalapa area, and it seems not unlikely that some of the Jutiapa "Indians" may have joined the ranks of Ladino emigrants. The 1964 census takers evidently have not classified the Jutiapa remnants as Indian. Table 2–17 indicates that the reported number dropped from 26,709 in 1950 to 840 in 1964.

Besides the enclaves, there is a major set of regions in which the Indian populations and Ladinos are in direct contact at the same level of articulation, not merely in domain relations, such as in western towns. The lower piedmont *municipios* of the south coast from San Marcos to Escuintla are a mixture of Indians and Ladinos. The departments of Sacatepéquez, Guatemala, and Baja Verapaz are composed of a checkerboard of Ladino and Indian *municipios*, with the former dominating as one moves east, and the latter to the west. While there have been some studies of these communities, there is no clear pattern evident as yet beyond a general half-way acculturation that has been earlier characterized as "modified Indian."[23] A study by G. A. Moore of Alotenango, on the upper side of this belt, suggests that there may well be a flourishing of certain ritual aspects of Indian culture.[24] It seems to be the case, however, that in spite of a reasonably large number of studies over the past thirty years,

[23] Cf. Adams, *Cultural Surveys*, p. 271.
[24] G. A. Moore, "Social and Ritual Change in a Guatemalan Town," Ph.D. dissertation, Columbia University, 1966.

there is only a very spotty structural picture of the process of ac-culturation.[25] This broad zone of direct day-to-day contact, coupled with the inevitable confrontations that must occur under such cir-cumstances, should provide an especially likely ground for such in-vestigation.

In the country as a whole, there are two old regions with avail-able labor and two new regions with available resources and metropolitan Guatemala acting as the source of capital that is both following and preceding the labor into the two new areas in their growth. The two new regions may be said to be the product of the extension of upper-level activity from the metropolis to a zone that is simultaneously filling with available labor. These two factors supplement one another and prove to be a convenience. The upper levels, however, clearly dominate the domain structures. Labor in the cotton area is more or less at the mercy of the planters, as it is among coffee-farm harvesters. There are, presumably, now emerg-ing in the new areas a new set of domains and domain relationships that are not yet studied. Scattered information suggests that these are evolving on an intra-area, competitive basis that is still viable and unsettled.

This pattern has been supplemented by the emphasis of the post-revolutionary governments on encouraging foreign investment. The projected nickel mining on the north side of Izabal will introduce into that area an entirely new developmental element. But the gross picture is the extension of a domain system that is already well known to the country at large. The major difference in the new area is that there is less possibility of the emergence of a strong regional level of articulation. In Chapter 3, the case of Escuintla will illustrate how the major controls are held by individuals operating at the national level. With the rapid private transportation possible by both road and air, the two new regions of Guatemala are likely to become at once a part of the national level. In contrast, there will be a weak regional level, composed of commercial, administrative, and service activities, but with little local power.

[25] One manner of approaching this would be to bring more modern ethno-logical techniques to focus on related communities, such as might be done with Magdalena Milpas Altas and San Miguel Milpas Altas. The latter has now been studied by Joaquín Noval, (*Materiales Etnográficos de San Miguel*, Cuadernos de Antropología, 3), and the former by the present writer and others.

Whether these suggested macroregions continue to be distinctive will, obviously, depend upon many local adaptive factors. It is possible, however, to contrast the general regional structure of the nation in the Ubico period with its emergent form and to see how the new regionalization directly relates to the changing operations, the shifting locus of domains, and the level of articulation. In the prerevolutionary period, the country was made up of a series of mircoregional domains of varying size, from large latifundia to small Indian communities and Ladino peasant holdings. The cumulative effects of the revolutionary and postrevolutionary decades have been to raise much of the activity concerning Guatemala to the international level and to increase greatly the amount and kind of activity at the national level. This has meant directly removing the control over many of the microregions to the center. This involved not direct control from a single focus, but the formation of new networks of relations, first through the lower sector in the revolutionary period, and later through the upper sector in the postrevolutionary period. In this way, structural escalation has progressed through both periods.

These new networks, and the new controls over both the new and some of the older power bases, have not destroyed the fabric of the older highland society, but they have co-opted important parts of it. The Ladinos of the western highlands became less and less oriented to the particular locale and region in which they resided and upon which they depended for their income. Their orientation followed the lines of power that more and more clearly derived from operating units focusing in the metropolis. The Indian population and the peasants of the east did not make these new connections; they were variously tied to the regional and community domains within which their power was localized and controlled. However, the fact of demographic growth within these areas inexorably forced the budding off of the new generation. There were no more resources for the expanding population, and, failing to have access to the power that is necessary for higher-level articulations and that would permit them to confront and challenge at the regional or national level, they had to move to the area where they could either find haven within expanding domains or establish their own small operations with little competition. Both happened; the first principally in the metropolis and in later phases on the south coast, and the second in earlier south coast phases and continuing today in the north.

It should not be forgotten that this is the second phase in a major structural shift in recent Guatemalan history. The first occurred with the official impetus given to coffee and the encouraging of foreign entrepreneurs to undertake that exploitation. During the period of 1870 to 1930, this growth, which also was a major articulation at the national level, focused on the southwestern piedmont (see Map 2–7) as the new area for development. As today, the entrepreneurs came in from the outside, many from abroad, brought the basic capital resources and knowledge, and drew upon the labor from the Indian highlands. At that time, the increasing population pressures in the highlands forced the Indians into seasonal labor. This was arranged for by the labor controls set up under Barrios, and these continued in general effect until the revolution, even though (as is indicated in Chapter 3) there were important legal shifts by Ubico. The peopling of the piedmont, then, was an earlier parallel to what is happening in the lowlands today. Under the liberal governments that controlled the country until the revolution, Guatemala City became the recognized national center of the country. Quezaltenango and Cobán, as important as they had been as regional centers, nevertheless gradually became clearly subordinate. The Second World War conveniently provided the basis for breaking the regional power that had existed with the strength of the German-oriented society. The United States, in confrontation with Germany, removed the Germans from Guatemala. While this further paved the way for growth of the metropolis, it also paved the way for the United States to become the major operator at the international level of articulation.

The location of Guatemala City on the line of division between the western Indian highlands and the eastern Ladino region provided a convenient locus for contact with both the south and northeast. This contact was made early by the railroads and later strengthened by the revolutionary government's commitment to open a road to the Atlantic. The geographical connecting of the metropolis with these new areas was central to future development.

The regional structuring of the nation has therefore directly reflected the shifts in operations in domains and the levels of articulation as units reached out to find and exploit new bases of power.

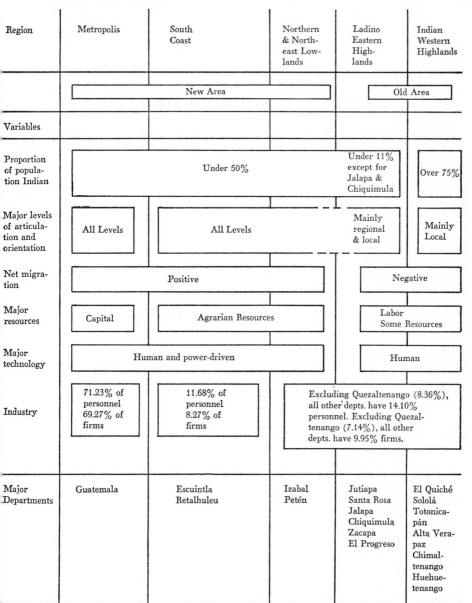

Region	Metropolis	South Coast	Northern & North-east Lowlands	Ladino Eastern Highlands	Indian Western Highlands
		New Area		Old Area	
Variables					
Proportion of population Indian		Under 50%		Under 11% except for Jalapa & Chiquimula	Over 75%
Major levels of articulation and orientation	All Levels	All Levels		Mainly regional & local	Mainly Local
Net migration		Positive		Negative	
Major resources	Capital	Agrarian Resources		Labor Some Resources	
Major technology		Human and power-driven		Human	
Industry	71.23% of personnel 69.27% of firms	11.68% of personnel 8.27% of firms	Excluding Quezaltenango (8.36%), all other depts. have 14.10% personnel. Excluding Quezaltenango (7.14%), all other depts. have 9.95% firms.		
Major Departments	Guatemala	Escuintla Retalhuleu	Izabal Petén	Jutiapa Santa Rosa Jalapa Chiquimula Zacapa El Progreso	El Quiché Sololá Totonicapán Alta Verapaz Chimaltenango Huehuetenango

TABLE 2–18
Variables in the Macroregions of Contemporary Guatemala

TABLE 2–19
Distribution of Manufacturing, 1966

Department Reported	Number of Establishments	Percentage of Total	Number of Employees	Percentage of Total
(Municipio of Guatemala)	(1,357)	(66.45)	(34,470)	(65.33)
Guatemala	1,400	69.27	37,586	71.23
El Progreso	10	0.50	108	.20
Sacatepéquez	34	1.68	605	1.15
Chimaltenango	11	0.54	666	1.26
Escuintla	104	5.15	4,744	8.99
Santa Rosa	16	0.79	205	0.39
Sololá	6	0.30	35	0.07
Totonicapan	3	0.15	89	0.17
Quezaltenango	169	8.36	3,772	7.14
Suchitepéquez	58	2.87	660	1.25
Retalhuleu	63	3.12	1,417	2.69
San Marcos	35	1.73	340	0.64
Huehuetenango	16	0.79	170	0.32
El Quiché	4	0.20	24	0.05
Baja Verapaz	5	0.25	36	0.07
Alta Verapaz	11	0.54	662	1.25
El Petén	4	0.20	282	.53
Izabal	25	1.24	759	1.44
Zacapa	23	1.14	307	0.58
Chiquimula	8	0.39	75	0.15
Jalapa	5	0.25	141	0.27
Jutiapa	11	0.54	82	0.16
Total	2,021	100.00%	52,765	100.00%

SOURCE: Bruce E. Bechtol, *Guatemalan Manufacturing 1966: A Preliminary Geographic Analysis*, Institute of International Studies, University of Oregon, manuscript, n.d., Table 1, p. 4.

Today the highland domains, with their symbiotic coffee belt, are gradually being eroded, while the lowlands are being formed under the escalation of a growing structure. The power foci and confrontations are increasingly at the national and international levels, and the country is differentiating into new macroregions.

It is possible, in a gross way, to arrange these five major regions in order of their relative degree of growth and development. Table 2–18 suggests the variation between a number of factors within these regions. The major variation in the two older regions has to do with the relative presence of an Indian population. In comparing the levels of articulation that are prominent, the higher levels gradually become increasingly important as one moves from the right side of the table to the left. The same is true of the general orientation of peoples who are permanent residents of the regions. Three variables clearly set off the pair of older regions from all the new regions: net migration, kinds of major resources, and the major technological base. Finally, the two older regions and the north lowlands stand approximately in the same level of industrial development. While almost 70 percent of the industry is concentrated in the department of Guatemala, the two departments of Escuintla and Retalhuleu account for another 10 percent. Among the remainder, Quezaltenango accounts for about 8 percent, and the rest is scattered throughout the rest of the country. Table 2–19 provides the specific information.

This comparison of variables does not try to take account of the enclaves and marginal areas discussed earlier, but it does show that even among themselves, there are important differences both within the old and the new and that, for most purposes, each area and its particular internal variations ought to be treated separately. Taken together, however, they provide a coherent whole, showing how the varying power structure of the nation has developed over the countryside.

3 | The Organization of Power, 1944–1966

IF WE ACCEPT THAT GUATEMALA has been developing, and that its growth has been directed in part by the power structure, then it is appropriate to look into the nature and development of the power structure itself. The first three parts of this chapter examine the broad changes that have occurred in the three periods of concern, and the fourth points up certain consequences in the recent political picture. The final section looks to the regional variations in the contemporary picture.

1. *The Situation Prior to 1944*

For more than a decade prior to the 1944 revolution, Guatemala was governed by Jorge Ubico, a Latin American personalistic caudillo. Unfortunately, knowledge of this era is already somewhat legendary, since few records of events of the time have been systematically brought to light. Moreover, the earlier dictator in the classic tradition, Estrada Cabrera, so influenced the Guatemalan scene that today it is difficult to be sure whether incidents casually attributed to Ubico actually may not have occurred during the Cabrera regime, or the reverse. The tendency to see Ubico simply as an extension of the Cabrera type needs to be qualified. There were important changes in the Ubico period that, if ignored, can only distort understanding of the evolving Guatemalan society.

Ubico was, legend has it, highly personalistic and individualistic in his operations. He was a dictator in the fullest meaning of that term. The flamboyance of his behavior, the peculiarities of his tastes, the strength of his control are all continuing subjects of discussion among his contemporaries. Less recognized is that some innovations made under his government have played a crucial role in structural escalation.[1]

When Ubico took over, the world was deep in a depression, and the price of Guatemalan coffee, the major cash income of the country, had dropped so low that it was increasingly difficult both to sell coffee abroad and to produce it at home. The wages of the 1930's were extraordinarily low, and even if Guatemalan producers of the time really cared about increasing the wages, they would have found it all but impossible. The few attempts to improve the generally depressed condition of the lower sector came almost solely from revolutionary efforts, such as exploded in El Salvador in the early 1930's.[2] Dictatorial repression had been the usual and accepted local means of control, and Ubico continued in this tradition.

An important feature of the Ubico period is that it instituted important changes over previous regimes in the direction of greater nationalization and increasing central government control. Prior to Ubico's government, there had been "elections" in Guatemala. Mayors were elected, but through the brashest kind of plebiscite. Ruth Bunzel describes the election procedures in Chichicastenango, when the Indians were herded in to put their mark in favor of the government's candidate for local offices.[3] Although a real study of the Ubico period is needed to fully explore these changes, he did two things that were specifically designed to shift the locus of power that had generally rested locally and regionally in the hands of the local upper class and bring it into more direct control from the center. One of these was to eliminate local elections and institute the *intendente* system. The other was to eliminate the practice of

---

[1] A good independent summary of labor legislation during the prerevolutionary period may be found in Frank Griffith Dawson, "Labor Legislation and Social Integration in Guatemala: 1871–1944," *American Journal of Comparative Law* 14 (1965): 124–142.

[2] J. Schlesinger, *Revolución Comunista.*

[3] Ruth Bunzel, *Chichicastenango: A Guatemalan Village.*

debt peonage and use solely a vagrancy law to provide a stable work force. These two acts have been overlooked by some students of politics because their search has been focused on "democratic advances" rather than changes in structure.

The *intendente* replaced the alcalde. Instead of having a local alcalde, chosen by the local upper class and therefore representative of their interests, Ubico appointed *intendentes* whom he sent (usually from other areas of the country) into the towns to act as mayors. The *intendentes* did not occupy a post indefinitely; Ubico did not want them to become too involved in the welfare of the local upper class. He was more interested in their loyalty to him than to the population. Above the *intendentes,* the *jefes políticos* were, in the same manner, responsible for departmental and regional affairs. Formerly, under alcaldes, the local upper class or caciques had broad controls over what happened within the immediate area. The control exercised by the central government was mediated through the locally selected officials. By imposing *intendentes,* Ubico removed this control from the local upper class and forced them to answer, through the *intendente,* to him. The local upper class found they had to answer more often to the demands of the *intendente* and that he was not their servant. His welfare was dependent upon how well he worked for Ubico, not how friendly he was locally.

The shift from debt peonage to vagrancy control had a parallel structural effect. The situation in which the laborer or *campesino* found himself was a complex of legal structures and local practice. Under Legislative Decree 243 of 1894, an employer was given the right to take measures against workers accused of failing in their work obligations. Local authorities were "strictly obliged to issue an order for arrest and to facilitate the means to effect the arrest. When the laborer was caught, the *patrones* or their agents had the right to request that the laborer be returned to the farm, or to be sent to the Company of Zapadores to work off the debt."[4] The debt, in the latter instance, was paid off at the rate of two reales a day. The Company of Zapadores, as stated in a regulation and accompanying act of September 1, 1930,[5] consisted of a special set of army battalions

---

[4] Jorge Skinner-Klée, *Legislación Indigenista de Guatemala*, pp. 76–83. Quote from Article 15, p. 78; my translation.

[5] Ibid., pp. 103, 107.

specifically composed of Indians from designated *municipios*. They were to serve the usual two years of military service, but in "time of peace," they were to be under the ministry responsible for road work, and they were to construct the country's highway system. Each *municipalidad* was responsible for providing ten Indians twice a year; there were also reserve battalions that provided additional labor as needed.

It was the practice during this period, and previously, for *finqueros* to assure themselves of sufficient manpower by paying wages in advance to bring labor to the farms and then keeping the new migrants constantly in debt, thus preventing them from disentangling themselves from their labor obligations. All these restrictive provisions were additionally backed up with a vagrancy law (Decree No. 222 of September 14, 1878, signed by J. Rufino Barrios), which provided for imprisoning individuals who were denounced as vagrants.

For the specific control of *mandamientos de mozos*, that is, groups of *campesinos* brought to the farms for work, a note was sent to all *jefes políticos* in 1893,[6] pointing out that the president was concerned that such labor should be equally distributed among the various owners of farms of the department. To be sure of this, the *jefe político* was ordered to force the laborers who were accused of failing in their obligations to either pay their debts, arrange something with their *patrón*, or be sent to the city to be placed in the Company of Zapadores. Clearly, the preferable situation for the laborer was to go back to work for the *patrón*.

Under Ubico, there were subtle but important changes in this system. The Company of Zapadores evidently was abandoned as a means of assuring road work, and in 1933, Decree No. 147 set up a road-work (*vialidad*) system.[7] Under this ruling, all individuals were subject to two weeks a year of road work. They could avoid this by paying a dollar each week, and those funds would be used instead. The *jefe político* was responsible for carrying out periodic censuses in order to identify who should be doing such work. This meant that road work was no longer directly related to military

[6] Alfonso Bauer Paíz, *Catalogación de Leyes y Disposiciones de Guatemala del Período 1872 a 1930*, p. 110.

[7] Skinner-Klée, *Legislación*, pp. 107–108.

service, nor could it be used as punishment for failure to appear for service on private farms.

In 1934, Ubico issued a decree prohibiting *patrones* from paying laborers in advance, for the purpose of bringing the laborer into debt and thereby controlling him.[8] This prohibition was extremely important because it removed from the hands of the owners and administrators their easiest weapon for directly controlling labor. The same year, however, Ubico promulgated a new law that made vagrancy a criminal offense,[9] and in the following year he issued a regulation,[10] to assure the supply of labor to the farms and utilized the vagrancy law as a sanction. The new regulation required every laborer to work at least one hundred days a year. Each had to have at least ten *cuerdas* of land himself, or had to have such work registered in a *libreto* by the farm owners or administrators. Those failing to fulfill the requirement were to be arrested for vagrancy. Since the only proof a laborer had that he had fulfilled the required work was an annotation by the *patrón* and the corresponding record that the *patrón* was required to keep in his own books, it was the common occurrence that the *patrón* would keep a laborer on simply by refusing to sign the books.

The structural change, while obscured by the fact that the laborer was little better off than before, consisted in the fact that the removal of debt peonage made it illegal for the *finquero* to impress individuals into farm work. Under the new regulation, the farmer who did so was breaking the law. It appears that the central government did not take specific steps to assure the laborer of just treatment; so the change sponsored by Ubico was a legal change, pointing in the direction of central governmental control rather than local control.

The Indian population of Guatemala continued to live generally in independent communities.[11] They traditionally worked under a set of elders and through a religious-political system, or through a

---

[8] Ibid., pp. 108–109. Legislative Decree 1995, May 7, 1934.

[9] Ibid., pp. 110–114. Decree 1996, May 10, 1934.

[10] Ibid., pp. 118–119. September 24, 1935.

[11] For this period see Bunzel, *Chichicastenango*; Oliver La Farge, *Santa Eulalia*; La Farge and D. Byers, *The Year Bearer's People*; Charles Wagley, *Santiago Chimaltenango*; Sol Tax, "The *Municipios* of the Midwestern Highlands of Guatemala," *American Anthropologist* 39 (1937): 423–433.

cacique, with or without some combination of the former. In practice, the *intendente* as often as not found it easier to work through these already existent organizations. This was especially true where the Indians were predominantly monolingual, and there were few Ladinos in the community. As a result, the structure of the Indian towns was not so immediately affected as was that of the Ladino communities, where the local upper class had formerly exercised more complete control.

The power structure in this period was unitary in the sense that the lines of power were direct from any member of the population to some immediate authority who was responsible to Ubico. Ubico was the only one who had the right to cross-cut this set of channels, and he did this through flying visits to towns throughout the country.[12] Similarly, individuals who felt they could make some progress by dealing directly with Ubico himself would take matters to him in Guatemala City. It was a matter that Ubico himself would determine. But few laborers dared bypass their employer to appeal to the *jefe político*, and no one found a court of appeal should he somehow offend the president.

This kind of organization was clearly more a relic of an Estrada Cabrera period than a precursor of the Arévalo-Arbenz period. But the structure that underlay the specific organization was clearly immediate. The revolution of 1944, calling as it did for common action throughout much of the country, could only have occurred where centralized government had already become a recognized fact. The Ubico period in Guatemala was the formative period during which the power of the regional caciques, the local upper class, and the local farmers lost its regional autonomy and became firmly dependent upon Guatemala City. The Second World War helped this process by leading to the dispossession of many of the German farmers.

Since organizational forms often outlast their usefulness, it is important to look at certain of those that flourished during the pre-1944 revolution period. Those that warrant attention are the local upper class, the military, the intellectuals, and the *campesinos*

---

[12] See F. Hernández de León, *Viajes presidenciales*, cited by Ruben Reina in *Chinautla: A Guatemalan Indian Community*, pp. 63–65. These trips are now legendary in many communities.

(Indians and Ladinos). The local upper class varied regionally and, in some instances, profoundly. Perhaps the most distinctive regional variation was Cobán, or rather, the section of Alta Verapaz and neighboring Baja Verapaz and Izabal that was strongly colored by the presence of German and some English coffee producers. Here, linked with commercial houses in Hamburg,[13] flourished an agricultural colony in which Germans, English, and Guatemalans alike learned Kekchí, thereby increasing their control over the Indian *campesinos*. During the period immediately prior to the Second World War, the Nazi Bund operated openly. The degree of isolation is exemplified by the stories of German *finqueros* who had never visited Guatemala City, sending their shirts down the Polochic River and to Hamburg for laundering.

But over most of the country, the local upper class did in fact have some kin as well as commercial relations with other sections of the country. As has classically been the case with small ruling elites, the available spouses in a local community were few, and wives had to be sought from the outside. This was especially true in the Indian area where the Ladinos formed a minute portion of the total population. Although these relationships existed, formal organization based on common kin, commercial, and economic interests were limited because there was little threat to those interests. Occasionally an individual or family would prove to be exceptionally successful in agriculture or business, and there would be a tendency for some members of the family to move to Guatemala City. In this manner the local upper class was directly linked to the urban system and moved up a level of articulation. Even this, however, stimulated little formal organizational development beyond participation in the Asociación General de Agricultores (AGA) or the Cámara de Comercio.

The military, during the Ubico period, was composed both of graduates of the national military academy, the Politécnica, and of men commissioned independently. One focus of training was engineering, and Ubico utilized the young officers to direct the extensive road building that marked his regime. The training received in

[13] Dr. Arden King has, for some years, been compiling material on the development and operation of this German colony. See also *Deutschtum in der Alta Verapaz*, a collection of articles written by members in the German community on the fiftieth anniversary of the German Club in Cobán.

the Politécnica was rigid, and apparently the dropout rate was fairly high. Indeed, military discipline was characteristic of other urban secondary schools during this period, and some of the young radicals who led the movement against Ubico remember well the harsh discipline to which they were subjected in these school years. The military itself, however, had already an established tradition by the time of Ubico, and through military connections with the United States, a few officers were sent there for further training.

The intellectuals under Ubico were subject to the choice of keeping quiet or leaving the country. As might be expected, this kept San Carlos University ineffective as an intellectual center, as well as assuring that Ubico would be ignorant of the currents of dissatisfaction and discontent that were growing about him. The accumulated exiles played a strong role in the revolution of 1944. This group took the leadership in many of the measures, both liberal and radical, that marked the course of the revolution.

In general, while Ubico succeeded in keeping the military well within control, in eliminating the contrary intellectuals from the country, and in subtly subverting the monopoly of control over the *campesinos* by the local upper class, he neither wanted nor attempted to destroy the general social control exercised locally by the upper class over the *campesinos*. The local upper class provided the leadership in the services and commerce that surrounded the production of coffee and bananas, the two major export crops and sources of income. The local officials who now were responsible for the road law, vagrancy law, and agricultural labor law worked specifically to assure that local farms did have sufficient labor. The *campesino*, especially the Indian, was no better off.

The development of coffee growing in the southwest piedmont and northern highlands (Alta Verapaz) and the simultaneous availability of Indian populations as labor may have been coincidental, but were surely complementary. Under the vagrancy law, the Indians, most of whom had already reached a state of minifundio, were readily forced to work on the large farms. This continued the practice already established during the latter part of the nineteenth century. This may be contrasted with the Ladino population of the *oriente* (the eastern highland) where the *campesino* was much less likely to be called under the vagrancy law and where coffee did not grow so well. In a sense, the complementary ecologies of the Indian and coffee made the road and vagrancy laws much more viable in the Indian than in non-Indian areas.

The effects of coffee labor on Indian communities have generally been assumed to have been culturally destructive. In one sense this was true. Each year some seasonal migrant coffee pickers would remain in the coffee area adding to the piedmont Indian population. These Indians naturally became detached from the organizations of their own communities and were reinstituted under the authority of the owners and administrators of the farms. Those who returned annually to their own Indian communities and cultivations, however, brought with them the small but important amounts of cash necessary to keep these towns going. As the Indian population grew and the highland minifundio problem increased, this seasonal work provided crucial input for the maintenance of the communities. As a result, rather than bringing about the destruction of the Indian community, the increase in coffee growing in the southwest piedmont served to consolidate it in a period when population growth might have had much more destructive consequences.

The Ubico period saw a gradual growth of the seasonal migration, as well as a continuation of the Indian communities. In the *oriente*, the population growth continued at a rate even greater than that of the Indians, but the entire area was much more underpopulated and the growth was not so keenly felt. The pressure in the *oriente* really began to become evident during the latter part of the 1940's. The result was that by the 1944 revolution, the Indians, who had long been accustomed to seasonal migration, were adjusted to moving about the country without their home communities suffering serious social disorganization. The Ladinos of the *oriente*, however, had not developed in this way. When the pressures came for them to move, they had no patterned mode of meeting the problems involved and, specifically, no pattern of using seasonal migration as an escape valve. Ubico, of course, allowed no effective rural organizations to be established to protect or further the interests of the *campesinos*. Whatever favors the *campesinos* may have expected were dispensed personally by Ubico or by the *jefes políticos* whom he appointed. Similarly, the laborers on the large farms were essentially under the paternalistic domain of the farm owner.

The relations between Guatemala and the rest of the world under Ubico generally paralleled those of other Central American countries. The major foreign-owned enterprises were the plantations of the United Fruit Company. While not commanding the proportion of the national income that it did in Honduras, the interest of the "Frutera" dominated the International Railways of Central America, controlled the port facilities of Guatemala's only Atlantic port, Puerto Barrios, and owned the Tropical Radio Company. The cosmopolitan Guatemalans had connections in Europe, and some even had (and presumably continue to have) significant European investments. The basic structural relation was that of classic liberal agrarian mercantilism. While most of the population depended upon a subsistence economy, the "national income" was derived primarily from the export of coffee and secondarily from bananas. The income was channeled entirely to the upper sector, and variations in the external market were not reflected in variations in salary levels.

The foreign policy of Guatemala was more or less subservient to that of the United States. During the Second World War, efforts by the local Germans to bring Guatemala into sympathy with their cause were stopped when Ubico allowed the FBI to formulate a black list of Axis sympathizers that led to the intervention of all German-owned properties and the rounding up of many individual Germans for internment in camps in the United States. This was accompanied by the stationing of some thousands of U.S. troops in Guatemala, principally at the airports, for the defense of the Panama Canal. Guatemala was effectively made into a pawn of the United States.

The end of Ubico's regime in Guatemala was paralleled by similar dictatorial collapses in El Salvador, Costa Rica, and elsewhere in Latin America. In Guatemala, however, the United States played a major role. The Second World War literally opened a view to the outside for many people who otherwise would have been little aware of the events beyond their own paternalistic domains. The collapse, it must be emphasized, was not the product of a vast internal upheaval. Rather, it was a revolt of the exiles and the city dwellers. The Indians were quite conservative, and the *campesinos* in general had no particular gains visible in the immediate future. The local upper class had been increasingly bothered by the individual vagaries of the dictator, and his centralization of power was sufficiently felt that his departure caused little sorrow.

The new governmental regime was badly understaffed in experienced bureaucrats and, more particularly, people who were willing to participate in the institution of new offices, organizations, and agencies. This was in part reflected in the fact that they had to find a citizen of another country to take over the presidency. Arévalo, born in Guatemala, was brought back from a professional post in Argentina, and his Guatemalan citizenship reinstated so that he could assume the office.

In understanding the course of Guatemalan social evolution, it is important to see the Ubico period in perspective. It created an ideological revolt, but, at the same time, set the stage for a flourishing nationalism. The structure of the country was increasingly centralized; this direction continued under the domination of the United States, both commercially and politically; and the outcome of the Second World War excited the younger literate Guatemalans to try to formulate a new system of government. At the same time, however, the majority of the population did not participate in the revolution.

The revolutionary period opened with a sympathetic urban population but with a rural hinterland that was essentially unadvised of what was going on. Long dependence on a unitary power structure left few prepared for broad changes. The upper sector, initially in favor of some growth, found itself in little better position to calculate the future than did the lower.

2. *The Period of 1944 to 1954*

The ten years that followed the 1944 revolution comprise the administrations of Juan José Arévalo and Jacobo Arbenz. Since the purpose here is not to recount history, but to identify certain events and processes of importance in understanding the changing national structure, this ten-year period will be dealt with as a whole. While the sequence of events in some instances is important, our concern is also to contrast this decade and those that preceded and followed it.

Arévalo, and the new constitution he was given, began a broad series of social reforms that included a social security program, a government office to foment production, the encouragement of syndicalism, the strengthening of the position of the military, the expansion of rural education, agricultural extension, and public health, and the attempt to promote cooperatives. Of cardinal importance was the reintroduction of open elections, but with the difference that there were serious contenders. The university was granted autonomy, an industrial development law was passed, as well as a law of forced rentals that prohibited sharecropping and profiteering on the rental of agricultural lands to peasants. The *vialidad* law was eliminated, but a new vagrancy law was passed, continuing control over rural labor as previously but without specifying punishment.[14] Indeed, the range of legislation and decrees was astonishingly broad,[15] and it is not surprising that some of the efforts failed to mature. Among the casualties was an effort to develop cooperatives and an attempt to colonize El Petén at Poptún.

Under Arbenz, further measures were taken, but unquestionably the most important was the agrarian reform decree and the dismissal of supreme court judges who contested its constitutionality. Others of relevance in the present context were the efforts to build the highway to the Atlantic and the utilization of the Communists as political support. The issue of communism in Guatemala needs to be treated directly since it has been the specific issue over which the United States has argued its right to internal intervention in the affairs of other countries.

When Arévalo assumed the presidency, there was little experienced bureaucracy to undertake the broad series of governmental and national reforms that were to be introduced. The leaders in the new government were unquestionably Guatemalans, many of whom had been in exile. Of these, some returned to the country with convictions about socialism and communism. It would be difficult to demonstrate, however, that many were more concerned with the flowering of socialism than with the flowering of Guatemala. For the most part, there was a generalized revolutionary, progressive interest that can best be characterized as nationalistic.

In addition to the local people, Arévalo opened the country to help from outsiders. His own experience elsewhere in Latin America led him to especially invite other Latins. Among these were various liberals and socialists, especially from the recently outlawed Communist party of Chile and the underground Aprista party of Peru.

---

[14] Skinner-Klée, *Legislación*, pp. 123–125.

[15] Archer C. Bush, "Organized Labor in Guatemala, 1944–1949," and Leo A. Suslow, "Aspects of Social Reforms in Guatemala, 1944–1949."

The United States, too, had many technical advisers with programs that had begun under the Institute of Interamerican Affairs during the Second World War. During the course of Arévalo's administration, however, certain of the U.S. personnel became offensive to the government, including the ambassador and certain technical personnel. Some of the technical aid missions were terminated.

The split within the Guatemalan political sphere between Arbenz and Arana (see Chapter 4) provided the basis for the championing of the former by the extreme leftists, including the Communists, and of the latter by the more moderate and rightist elements. Arbenz's support by the Communists became increasingly open, along with the equally strong growth of anticommunist sentiment. When the agrarian reform was passed and it was necessary to establish a new agency to operate it, a significant number of those employed in the agency were members of the Partido Guatemalteco de Trabajo (the Communist party); they took an active part not only in administrative affairs, but also in the organization of the agrarian committees in the field and, particularly on the south coast, in field agitation.

Because of rising opposition, both within and outside the revolutionary movement, supporters of the Arbenz government were forced toward active alignment with Communists, who naturally found this expedient. Opposition from U.S. private interests and the U.S. government had already been indicated under the government of Arévalo. Henry Cabot Lodge suggested, in the U.S. Senate, that Arévalo was "Communistically inclined," and strikes against the United Fruit Company were bringing increasing U.S. reaction. Under Arbenz, this began to crystallize with the U.S. government taking an uncritical position in favor of the United Fruit Company's defense against the proposed expropriation under the agrarian reform. The opposition broadened to include various of Arbenz's proposals, such as the importance of the proposed highway to the Atlantic. Since the highway would provide direct and unquestionably successful competition with the International Railway, the American investors in the latter did not want the highway built. As U.S. policy increasingly consolidated around opposition to Arbenz and became generalized against his policies, the Communists concomitantly grew in influence.

This shifting of U.S. official opinion against the government had as its equal and opposite force the emergence of a more conscious Guatemalan group that was able to identify the policies of the United States as being against the reforms felt to be central to the revolutionary movement. It is difficult to estimate the degree to which the concern of the Guatemalans was derived from ideological beliefs and the degree to which it was generated by fury over the attitude of the United States through its diplomatic and commercial agents. Certainly the U.S. concern for its interests in the country long antedated this series of events. The innovation in the Arbenz period was that the Guatemalan government dared to oppose the direct interests of the United States and to air this internationally.

There were other important changes that affected the structure of the country. Without a doubt the single most important one was the institution of electoral procedure. This was no return to the pre-revolutionary plebiscites but, instead, the positive encouragement of party oppositions. This had a special effect in the Indian areas. The naming of young men as candidates for local public offices undermined the position of the elders and the traditional structure of authority of the aged.[16] It had a parallel, though less obvious, effect in Ladino communities. There, the parties chose for their candidates individuals who held no particular loyalty to the local upper class and, in this way, undermined the local power of that group.

Among the most important features of Arévalo's legislation were the law of forced rentals and the labor code. The first had particularly important effects in the *oriente*, where much land was rented out to small-scale cultivators. This law so restricted the possibilities of real profit from such rentals as to severely weaken their local power. The labor code incorporated a number of features that provided protection and support for the laborer. The assumption that the *patrón* knew best was so traditional in Guatemala that many employers were unable to distinguish abuses from favors. The new laws and decrees brought about a crucial shift in organi-

---

[16] See Richard N. Adams, ed., *Political Changes in Guatemalan Indian Communities*; J. L. Arriola, ed., "Ladinización en Guatemala," in *Integración Social en Guatemala*; Manning Nash, "Political Relations in Guatemala," *Social and Economic Studies* 7 (1958): 65–75; Robert Ewald, "San Antonio Sacatepéquez: Culture Change in a Guatemalan Community," *Social Forces* 36 (1957): 160–165.

zational forms. The depth of the effect is illustrated in the article that established the employer as responsible for paying indemnization for fired workers. This allowed the laborer to directly accuse his employer of misconduct and to expect at least to receive government protection, if not active support in the process. Given the attitude of the government in these matters, it is hardly surprising that labor courts were staffed by those favorable to the laborer. The result was that the indemnization clause was utilized as a device whereby laborers could bait employers into firing them in order to force the payment of indemnization. Since most Guatemalan rural employers worked with little cash capital and depended upon annual loans to carry them through until crop time, this was a telling threat on all but the most wealthy. Since indemnization was calculated retroactively, a rash of pressures of this kind from employees could bankrupt smaller farms.

The changes are more evident, however, in the ways in which the reforms were pressed and activated. The most important of these were the *sindicatos*, the *campesino* leagues, the political parties, and, in the last two years of the period, the agrarian committees. In the operation of these new organizations can be seen the manner in which politicization of the *campesinos* was taking place and the way in which the power structure of the country was being pressed to alter substantially.

The 1945 constitution permitted the establishment of unions. At the time of the collapse of the Arbenz regime, there were over 500 such unions in existence, at least 340 of which were on the farms (see Chapter 9). Among the strongest rural unions were those on the United Fruit Company plantations, but the smaller organizations on the coffee farms were extremely active in many areas. Union organizing was often unsuccessful unless the effort could show immediate results. This sometimes led to trumped-up charges against farms as well as the pressing of questionable issues. The purpose of the organizers, however, was to develop organizations that could be counted on not only to challenge the employer, but to deliver votes to the revolutionary parties. The labor code and labor courts gave the Guatemalan worker direct access to the derivative power of the government. The laborer who wished either to press for some benefit for himself or simply to cause the employer trouble could expect better than an even chance of success in the labor courts. For the first time in history, employers found themselves suddenly on the short end of the power relationship.

The spread of *campesino* leagues and the activity of the broad national federation that served to link and bind them were directed more at landed peasants, but included laborers who also were members of rural labor unions. On the basis of a limited study made immediately after the fall of the Arbenz government, the following was noted:

An interesting aspect of the *Unión Campesina* membership is the rather high correlation it offered with membership in religious societies, combined with the fact that it did not have the correlation with low residential continuity which was true of the labor unions and the agrarian committees. These two characteristics suggest that at least the *Unión Campesina* members in our sample were fairly serious, locally rooted, countrymen who found in the *Unión* a means for solving local problems as well as exercising a certain amount of political power. It should not be forgotten that religious societies, in a local Catholic community, are also a means of obtaining and exercising power on the local scene.[17]

The leagues were aimed at providing stimulus to encourage the peasants to seek the rights that were supposed to fall their way under the new constitution and laws of the country. The organization tried to develop local leadership and did serve to help *campesinos* find their way to the centers of power where their cases could be heard. The federation also served the same purpose as did the *sindicatos*, to indoctrinate the individual in politics and gather in his vote for the revolutionary parties. The leagues generally were more successful in the west than in the east.

While political parties had their headquarters in Guatemala City, they did penetrate throughout the rural and provincial population of the republic. There was probably not a single municipal capital that was not somewhat affected by a split over its political affiliation. By 1953 many municipal capitals were political.[18] In the more isolated *cantones* and *aldeas*, the work of the parties may have seemed remote and unimportant, but, looking back from the present vantage point, it is remarkable to note the degree to which political

---

[17] Stokes Newbold, "Receptivity to Communist-Fomented Agitation in Rural Guatemala," *Economic Development and Cultural Change* 5, no. 4 (1957): 360.
[18] Kalman Silvert, *A Study in Government: Guatemala.*

organizers were able to reach even the most isolated areas. The proselytizing was most effective among the younger population, although there were elders everywhere who saw in the new system a way of getting something for themselves. Towns became badly split over elections, and age-old local factions found new issues over which to perpetuate their antagonisms.[19] The parties were a particularly effective politicizing device because, even among themselves, they offered alternatives. If one party did not provide what an individual wanted he could threaten to turn to another. Whereas a person was likely to belong to only one labor union or one league, he could join whichever party seemed to offer him the most promise in getting what he wanted.

The Agrarian Reform Law set up local agrarian committees composed of five members. "These members would be nominated as follows: one by the departmental governor, one by the mayor of the *municipio*, and three by the local peasant organization of the local labor union."[20] The committee's job was to decide which lands should be expropriated and to judge the applications of the local people. Under the Agrarian Reform Decree the committee was responsible only to the president. No court had jurisdiction over their decision except the Supreme Court, and this was packed to prevent decisions favorable to the landholder.

The agrarian committees and agrarian reform best illustrate the structural change that was under way. With the increasing antagonism and threats to his regime, Arbenz found that he was less and less sure of the support of the military. Although a military man himself and confident of such support during the first years of his regime, the growing strength of the Communists within the government left much of the military doubtful about the future. Realizing this, elements in the Arbenz government hoped to arm the agrarian committees in order to neutralize the military just as the work of the agrarian committees had been weakening the local landholders and upper class. Had this been successful, the agrarian committees would have taken over the major position of power in the revolution.

---

[19] Adams, *Political Changes*, case of Magdalena.
[20] Nathan L. Whetten, *Guatemala, The Land and the People*, p. 160. Chapter 8 of this study provides the best summary in English of the agrarian reform.

The role of the military during this decade also changed notably. After the 1944 revolution, the national military academy was subject to some changes, and the officers' corps was increasingly composed of individuals interested in the nature of the government in power. The shift from strong support of Arbenz to essentially no support, when the country was invaded in 1954, marked the emergence of a conservative strength that has continued generally in control until this time.

An important aspect of the lower-sector organizations that developed in this decade is the kind of learning they made possible for the *campesino*. Indians and Ladinos found that it was possible to seek out other authorities and sources of power than those familiar in the unitary patronal system. Whereas before, the *patrón* or the elders had the last word, it was increasingly assumed that not only were they no longer the final authority, but they also could be ignored almost at will. The operation of these new organizations demonstrated that *campesinos* could expect some satisfaction without retribution from the local landowner or the local council of elders. The entire notion that there was a single source of power was effectively breached.

The learning was not, however, confined to the lower sector. As the government increasingly showed its favoritism for the lower sector, the upper sector became more and more hostile. The landowners, businessmen, clergy, and professionals became openly antagonistic to unions, to land reforms, and to the operation of Communists in government. A real fear of the lower sector developed. The agitation in the south coast in 1954 led to burning of sugar-cane fields and the shooting of administrators and *finqueros*. The upper sector, which had traditionally entertained an uncertainty about the potential wildness of the Indian and the *campesino*, became apprehensive of peasant uprisings. In this instance, the 1944 uprising in Patzicía was still clear in the memory, and the specter of more rural people organized for their own ends produced a real state of fear. This was hardly improved by increasing reports of physical violence being carried out to persons captured by the police.

The upper sector had never been very effective at organizing itself. The Guatemalan *finquero* was, above all, an independent operator, with his major concerns revolving around his family. The AGA, the landowners' association, had never effectively acted as a pressure group; it could seldom bring its membership to agree on anything. The AGA published arguments against labor unions and was particularly vocal on the agrarian reform, but it exercised little power because it could, in fact, command no action from its members.

The revolutionary decade saw a systematic weakening of the local and regional power still exercised by the landholders and their access to power at the national level, held in common with the businessmen. At the same time, a complementary series of policies and actions was emerging on the international scene. The United States, as influential as it had been during the Ubico period, became increasingly alarmed over the combination of burgeoning socialism and "anti-American" attitudes. The fact that the United Fruit Company was the largest single landholder in the country and that it was foreign owned made it the obvious target. The quick defense of the United Fruit Company provided by the U.S. government made it appear to many Guatemalans that the two were working as one. The interest of the Arbenz government in opening a highway to their Atlantic port was played down by the United States in favor of developing the east-west roads that would strengthen the Pan American highway system. As the Communists became more important to Arbenz, he came to their defense both within the Central American context and before the Organization of Central American States. Rather than support a statement against communism, the Guatemalan representative voted against the U.S. statement denouncing the operation of communism in the Western Hemisphere at the Tenth Inter-American Conference at Caracas in March, 1954.

Although government officials and sympathizers made trips behind the iron curtain and the arms for the agrarian committees were sent from Poland, the iron curtain countries were entirely unprepared to provide the Arbenz government with even a fraction of the external support that the United States was exercising against it. The Guatemalan government looked to its Latin American neighbors for support, but it received little. Although they identified with Guatemala and hated to see the obvious U.S. intervention, their own economic dependence on the giant to the north completely crippled most of them from taking a stand in favor of Guatemala. More than this, the regimes in Nicaragua and Honduras were particularly antagonistic to the Guatemalan developments and provided the bases and facilities for the Castillo movement that toppled Arbenz. The United States provided funds reportedly in excess of one million dollars for the Castillo movement, and the American ambassador to Guatemala played a direct role in the re-establishment of a new government under Castillo. The Castillo movement put an immediate stop to almost all of the organizational apparatus that had evolved under the Arévalo and Arbenz regimes. Of the revolutionary efforts, there survived few bureaus to threaten U.S. or upper-sector interests.

With some exceptions, the personnel involved in deposing Arbenz was Guatemalan. It was the upper sector's answer to the threat against the traditional power structure. But the change in government, while it did put a sharp halt to the revolutionary change, did not succeed in reversing the direction. As will be seen in the next section, the contemporary situation in Guatemala is in great part due to changes that were actually accomplished during the revolutionary decade. These include the learning that had taken place in the entire population, the "sociological awakening" that could not be forgotten within the generation, the fact that organizing had been learned, and the awareness that the United States had intervened at the international level to stop the organization process. This last could not be easily accepted even by nationalistic Guatemalans antagonistic to Arbenz, and it signaled the operation of legitimate cold war activities at the international level.

Some of the institutions started during the revolution were continued, although with some modifications. Of special importance were the Banco de Guatemala and the labor code and labor courts. The government bank was started under Arévalo and evolved as an important power center. As with other new agencies, it was faced with the shortage of personnel. To correct this, it initiated a system of apprenticeship and fellowships in order to build up a strong staff. The routine was to support selected students in the Faculty of Economics with part-time jobs and then to give the better ones fellowships to take graduate training abroad. In this way, the Banco de Guatemala evolved into what may be considered to be a corporate entity. As such, its mode and preferences were of great importance. Since it developed during the revolutionary decade, the entire staff of the bank was to some degree steeped in a development-oriented viewpoint. With the fall of Arbenz, the new government found it impossible to entirely replace the bank's personnel; it could not have continued at all under these circumstances. As a result, the bank bureaucracy stayed on, and with it a system of producing economists who saw the welfare of the country in rather more progressive terms than did the supporters of the government.

The labor code, labor inspection system, and the labor courts naturally underwent some change with the fall of Arbenz, but much that was initiated in the previous decade continued in some form. Indemnization for laborers survived, and so did the labor inspector system. The inspector system was set up both to seek out infractions of the labor code and to provide a device for the settlement of disputes out of court wherever possible. Labor complaints were first to be brought to the local inspector or regional subinspector. It was his duty to try to resolve the problem between the employer and the laborer. Only if this proved impossible would it then be taken to the labor courts. Although the advent of Castillo severely reduced the enthusiasm with which the labor inspectors sought out infractions of the labor code by employers, the courts tended to keep a rather progressive attitude. Laborers, if they could ever reach the court with adequate legal help, stood a reasonable chance of being granted judicial decisions within the law. Under Arbenz, however, the inspectors were very active, and the *sindicatos* provided guidance and aid in getting access to the courts.

3. *The Period of 1954–1966*

The latest decade of Guatemalan history has been marked by a resurgence of the political dominance of the upper sector, severe restrictions on the political and economic development of the lower sector, and a foreign policy dominated by the presence of the United States. This postrevolutionary decade contrasts so markedly with the previous revolutionary decade that the two provide something of a laboratory case of economic and political development in which the policies and effects of the governments may be compared.

In 1954, profound changes were brought about in the position and policy of the Guatemalan government. Support was entirely withdrawn from all the lower-sector organizations: unions, political parties, agrarian committees, and mass organizations were declared illegal and eliminated. Thousands of the leaders and participants were jailed for varying periods. There began a continuing, if not entirely systematic, promotion of upper-sector interests. The change was in no sense a simple reversion to Ubico-style unitary power structure, but rather a proliferation of upper-sector power foci, together with upper-sector interpenetration of the government overlapping with it. From the point of view of the lower sector, however, one feature reflected the Ubico period: the various, multiple, alternative channels of access to authority and power were reduced in number and severely constricted. In many instances, the restrictions were tantamount to a reestablishment of a unitary power system. The removal of the labor unions and political parties meant that the laborer still had access via the courts, but in practice this was not entirely useful. Similarly, the individual citizen could no longer expect aid through the auspices of mass organizations, such as political parties, or consideration of land needs through an agrarian committee.

Combined with these changes, the military strengthened its general position. It was the explicit lack of military action that had allowed the Castillo forces to win, and, after a brief, open struggle with the "Liberation Army," the military once again closed ranks for its own protection. The role played by the military placed it in an advantageous position to receive increased aid from the United States in materiel and training.

Castillo introduced a major shift in national policy toward the Church by formally opening the country to the entrance of new clergy. Within a few years it was granted *personalidad jurídica* and began to play an important and active role in the rural areas, most specifically among the Indians. In the decade that followed, the number of priests increased fivefold. The overwhelming majority of these were foreigners, and many brought with them a variety of progressive social philosophies. Among the Indians, their major concern was to eliminate certain religious practices surviving from the colonial and pre-Colombian periods. Everywhere, however, activities in social welfare increased.

It was the policy of the major governments of this period to promote the formation of upper-sector interest groups. These groups were of many kinds, and only a few can be explored here. First, and among the most important, were those which were established by law and to which all relevant individuals had to belong. So it was that membership in the ANACAFE was mandatory for any coffee grower who exported coffee. Similar groups concerned with wheat, cotton, and sugar were either created or in the process of creation at the time of the study. Although established under a government mandate, these organizations acted as private interest groups.

Another variety was the privately sponsored *gremial,* such as the many subunits of the Chambers of Commerce and the Chamber of Industries. These were wholly developed by private interests and answered to the government only insofar as they required official recognition in order to have a legal character. In addition to these groups, there emerged a wide variety of other organizations, often pursuing more or less the same interests as those represented by the Chambers of Commerce and Industries.

The farmers also showed that they had learned the virtues of organization. Not only were there the groups now representing different crops and different stages of processing of those crops, but also regional organizations developed, especially in coffee, in order that the growers of a particular region could better compete for their share of the limited international market and have first and surer access to credit facilities.

The growth of these interest groups reflected a number of important changes that differentiated this period from its predecessor. The upper sector was overcoming its earlier organizational ineptitude and mobilizing its own interests against encroachments from whatever source, be it labor, the government, or its own competitors. With respect to labor, particularly, the increased communication that developed between producers and processors of the same crops led to more agile and manipulatory use of migrant labor and avoidance of individuals who had gained particularly bad reputations under the Arbenz government.

Aside from the appearance of new groups of upper-sector interest, another group process occurred with the increased incorporation of certain groups that already existed. Specific among these were the military, the Church, and the government bank. The military had long been a fairly close and self-protective body, but its propensity for cohesion developed to a remarkable extreme during these years. One famous abortive revolt, involving a large number of officers and men against the Ydígoras government (the Thirteenth of November revolt, 1960), led to no prosecution of the guilty officers. A few fled to initiate what developed into the current guerrilla movement. But most who participated were protected by their fellow officers. The corporate nature of the military is enhanced by the fact that future officers are brought into the Politécnica after they finish grammar school at about fourteen years of age. They then receive five years of military training and are commissioned officers at their graduation. This means that military indoctrination of future officers begins in adolescence. The graduate enters a barracks life and a long wait before any hope of a lucrative position. He is provided, however, with special services, such as the Comisariato Militar, where prices are low and taxes are nonexistent. Many can count on especially cheap or free housing, often of a reasonably luxurious variety. The ingroup feeling among the officers is so strong that even those who become *guerrillero* leaders retain personal and informal relations with some of their former fellow officers.

Increasingly evident during this period was the polarization of attitudes within all these groups, with some becoming more positively liberal, progressive, and revolutionary, and others gravitating back toward a conservatism characteristic of the Ubico period. This bifurcation characterizes the entire upper sector, the business and agricultural communities, the Church and the military. While polarization is evident among individuals and groups, it is also reflected in varying attitudes, roles, and specific concerns of individuals. A given individual might, as a farmer, be antagonistic to some form of government control, but, as a new entrepreneur in an industry, he might be seeking stronger government protection and intervention. There are, of course, those who identify themselves almost wholly with one extreme or the other. In general, much of what might be called the old upper class retains a coherent conservative position; and the outcasts of 1954 have, with extremists of a new generation, activated the guerrilla groups that now press for a straightforward and completely socialist government.

The following will briefly characterize some of the social dimensions of this bifurcation. The Church finds itself confronted with socially inclined priests, most of foreign origin, who feel that the older Spanish Catholic conservatism is not only outdated, but also positively dangerous. The military spans the entire political gamut, from the militarily oriented officers of the older Ubico period, who see their role as retaining the social order of the country, to the socialist-oriented extremists who have abandoned the army for the guerrilla movement.

The political parties, naturally enough, have spread themselves across the spectrum, but in some instances have shown the same ambivalence mentioned above. The current party in power, the Partido Revolucionario, tries to identify itself with the revolution, but at the same time looks to the right for permission to survive. The Christian Democrats, who in some other countries become so important, have in Guatemala split into two apparently ununitable extremes. On the right is also the derivative of the party that was initiated under Castillo and set up by the military government; and to the left is the URD, a revolutionary party whose leader was exiled sometime prior to the last election and many of whose members have turned to the PR. At the far left, of course, is the PGT, the Communist party, the oldest Guatemalan political party and currently completely clandestine. The bifurcation marks the business and agricultural community too. Various of the interest groups mentioned earlier are identifiable as being more liberal or conservative.

The end of the revolutionary period, with the suppression of all the lower-sector organizations and the jailing of a large number of people, quieted rural political activity. For many *campesinos,* the retribution for participation was worse than the temporary benefits. The major activists of the revolutionary governments were exiled, and there was an almost complete cessation of revolutionary activity. During the period immediately following 1954, there was a general reluctance to promote revolutionary action. The PGT became ineffective and disorganized, although still in existence. Although most of the extreme revolutionary measures were rescinded (the law of forced rentals and agrarian reform law were annulled), a few major institutional innovations, such as the Banco de Guatemala, the Institute of Social Security, and a reasonably progressive labor code, were continued. To substitute for the agrarian reform, a fairly extensive colonization program was started, principally on the south coast. But almost all the land that had been parcelled out during the Arbenz agrarian reform was restored to its earlier owners.

By 1958, a set of opposition parties had become active. The strongest was the Partido Revolucionario, but its compromises with the conservative governments had led to the emergence of others. Of considerable importance was the clandestine reappearance of the Communist party, working out of Mexican headquarters. From 1958 until 1962, the government promulgated laws that were supposed to promote industrialization, but much of their possible effect was evaded through various forms of graft and privilege. Efforts at colonization were slowed, but internal migration was increasing.

In the rural areas, the situation of the *campesino* retained some of its revolutionary gains. The labor code provided certain basic protections, and the labor courts and inspectors as often as not did act in favor of the laborer. As in much of the Western world, however, the poor have very limited access to the law. The practicing lawyer in Guatemala finds the defense of laborers essentially unprofitable. The system, in an attempt to correct this deficiency, has a series of labor inspectors stationed throughout the republic. These individuals are supposed to review labor complaints and try to mediate them. Should this prove impossible, the case is then taken to the local labor court. The labor inspection and court system in existence generally worked in a fair manner, but it too suffered from facts of local and provincial society. The system was weak not because of its theoretical construction, but because of the ecology in which it found itself. The outcome has been to allow the average rural laborer little or no recourse to the law. In addition to this, the political climate, especially right after 1954 and during the military government that formally took over in 1963, was severely discouraging to the laborer.

Related to this lack of legal access, but also of importance in other connections, was the change in the role of the *comisionado militar*. Under the military government, the *comisionado* in the south coast, and especially in the *oriente*, became a local listening post for the military government. All too often the reports of the *comisionado militar* would lead to the jailing of the organizers. The role of the *comisionado militar* has significant ramifications. Its use by the military as local "spies" provided the military, for the first time, with a communication channel down to the lowest level of the population. Whereas before the *comisionado* was restricted to information derived from strictly military sources, they now had a network that cut into every civilian community. The purposes for which this in-

formation was used during the military government was obviously
determined by the then current perception of what constituted danger to the country as a whole. The future use of the *comisionado* is
uncertain. It seems unlikely that such a useful set of communication
channels will go unused; it is almost certain they will be invoked
to restrict guerrilla activities, but possibly also for other purposes.
Since there is, within the military itself, such a wide range of political interest, much will depend upon the particular character of
the officials responsible in any particular area.

In the latter part of the 1954–1966 period, there began a slow
but ineffectual development of union organizing. A number of farm
unions were established, but at the time of the study their operational status depended almost entirely on the position they held
in the eyes of their employers. In the few cases where the employers
were sympathetic to them, they were reasonably active and enjoyed some successes in gaining improvements for their members.
For the most part, however, employers were not so sympathetic.
Many of the few effective labor leaders found themselves jailed
temporarily because of reports sent in by *comisionados militares* or
employers. Various legal restrictions, some of which have since been
removed, further hampered the activity. Fundamentally, however,
those who had been most active during the revolutionary period
had suffered enough and simply had little stomach for further organizing activity. The ten years since the end of the revolutionary
period had provided no mechanism for the development or emergence of new rural leaders. The result was that few were experienced or willing to guide syndicate organization.

A further problem was complicating the organizational development. While seasonal labor had long been a tradition on the coast,
the continuing explosive growth of the rural population and the
movement from El Salvador of cheap labor were turning the labor
market to the advantage of the employers. Workers who insisted on
unionizing in the face of employer disapproval also faced the realis-
tic fact that labor was cheap. While work could ultimately be obtained, the wages and conditions set were almost entirely in the
hands of the employers.

The latter part of this period saw the reappearance of a cooperative movement. This suffered because of an association of the term
cooperative with *communism* in the minds of some, both in the lower

and upper sectors, even though the movement had been halted in the Arbenz period. And, as with union development, the individuals experienced in organization and administration were next to nonexistent. Nevertheless, the appearance of progressive priests brought to this movement experience and motivation that led to the formulation of a variety of such organizations, especially in the Indian areas of the country. Others were initiated under the sponsorship of Christian Democratic party workers, and yet others were encouraged by the developers of the colonization areas, the rural credit agencies, and the Peace Corps. The cooperatives, especially as they become involved in providing their members with retail services, come into conflict with the local businessmen who are accustomed to profit from most local commercial activity. This has led to the temporary disruption of one particularly successful cooperative in the department of Quiché.

The expansion of Church activity needs special attention, not only because it involved a resurgence of a power center in the upper sector, but also because as an organization it worked directly in the lower sector. Many of the new clergy were North Americans and Europeans who had considerable interest in social development and social welfare among the parishioners. This led not only to innovations in the religious activities, but also to work in schools, clinics, cooperatives, and various other similar programs. This has been particularly notable in the Indian areas where there has been a traditional respect for the clergy but, until 1954, little real leadership. The re-appearance of active priests in the Indian communities has led not only to a reassertion of Catholic orthodoxy, but also to a tendency to favor political conservatism. In this connection, however, it must be remembered that the Indian has always been regarded as politically conservative. The real nature of this conservatism is not entirely clear. In part, it reflects a general vertical allegiance in which the political choices of the elders or caciques are reflected in the votes of the population. Since the local authority of these individuals often rests as much on what they can accomplish with outside authority and power as it does on internal factors, they tend to ally themselves with the traditional sources of power or with the government.

The position of the Guatemalan Indian with respect to the evolving national society and centers of authority has changed. The years of the revolutionary organization penetrated the isolationism of the Indian regions as much as it did the other rural or provincial areas. The Indian, accustomed to the traditional exploitation by the Ladino, is more suspicious of the blandishments of political propaganda. The revolutionary period had telling effects, however. Some *municipios* were deeply politicized, while many others received enough experience to make them respond more easily to future political action. Indians, however, are predominantly small private operators. Such efforts as the agrarian reform and law of forced rental alienated some Indians while winning others to the revolutionary position.

An extreme example of the degree to which Ladino exploitation of the Indian continues today may be seen in the Alta Verapaz. This region, especially around Cobán, Carchá, and Chamelco, includes a number of small Indian farms. The cash crop, coffee, is sold to Ladinos who act as middlemen. The Indian, however, does not have access to a free market. The road system is such that it is impossible for outside truckers to reach the Indian lands except through the lands owned by large-scale Ladino producers. The Indian must therefore bring his crop in for sale. In so doing, he first passes through the lands of the larger owners who buy up his coffee. All buyers are local residents and have an annual agreement as to what price they will pay for the Indians' coffee, thereby eliminating a free market even to local purchasers.

In Jalapa there was another instance of the continued control by the upper sector, here manifested in the conjunction of the Church and government. In the *municipio* of Jalapa are a dozen communities known collectively as the communities of the Gran Montaña de Jalapa. These communities own a great deal of communal land and have succeeded in protecting it in spite of frequent Ladino efforts to gain access to it. Some time ago an active Guatemalan priest began to build a church on the land. Many of the Indians opposed this. They had an agreement that the local bishop could use certain properties they owned in the town of Jalapa, in return for which their community lands would remain unmolested. When their protestations to the young priest failed, they threatened him and killed the mason who was working with him. The response of the government to this was to jail the twenty-four official leaders who represented the community. When new ones were elected and sent to

deal with government officials, they too were jailed. The whole affair
was complicated by various factors that cannot be detailed here,
but the general result was in the classic tradition of the Indian-
Ladino relations.

The overt political activity that came to a complete halt with
the advent of Castillo began to reemerge in a quiet way in the late
1950's. Castillo held a plebiscite, but, following his assassination,
two successive elections were held with competitive candidates.
There tended to be a splintering of factions in the various points of
the political spectrum until the elections of 1966. Prior to that election, the military government, which had actually been in power
for four years, but overtly so for only three, had, for the reasons
mentioned earlier, tended to force underground much leftist political organization. The Communist party was explicitly outlawed,
and the head of a new party, the URD, was in exile. As a result,
politics, even for the open presidential election, became a partially
clandestine affair. Many *campesinos* had developed the practice of
signing up in a number of parties since membership in one or another would serve to appease the various outside demands. To ask
a *campesino* a political question would bring an answer calculated
to fit the listener. The clandestine nature of the political organizing
was both a product of the reprisals and the later military government's state of siege and a condition that was convenient for extremist political activity of whatever color.

The events thus far described were helped in their development
by two external conditions. One was the policy and action of the
United States, and the other was Castro's success in Cuba. With the
success of Castillo Armas' military invasion in 1954, the United
States felt that it should make a special effort to demonstrate that
the revolutionary governments had been wrong in their willingness
to cooperate with Communists. The new government accepted increased amounts of U.S. aid, and foreign private enterprise was
encouraged to come into the country. The position of the United
States in the matter accorded with its policy of economic development. The general thesis was that economic development could
best be had by a combination of private investment with judicial
and encouraging governmental action. This general approach, it
was thought, would bring up the national income most rapidly.

The question of the distribution of the income derived from this

increase was, from the U.S. position, a secondary matter. It was
assumed that when sufficient capital had been introduced into the
top of the system a process affectionately known as the "filter effect" would account for its gradual diffusion throughout the society.
The relatively broad spread of wealth in the United States was attributed to the long-term operation of this process. This position
also accorded well with the interest of U.S. private investors who felt
that, were profits to be made out of U. S. investment, they should
accrue to the U.S. investors and not be channeled from them by
using U.S. tax money in "give-away" programs. The process by
which this policy was to be carried out was obviously one in which
U.S. capital was channeled into those efforts that promised some
reasonably secure profit. This meant large-scale, sometimes speculative, farming, manufacture of consumer goods, commercial export
of U.S. products, and so on. Until the Central American Common
Market was formed, even some of these efforts were not economically feasible.

The success of the U.S. effort to contain and reduce the influence
of communism in the hemisphere had other important effects on
Guatemala. In its confrontation with Castro, the United States
found Ydígoras a cooperative ally. A large farm on the south coast
was converted into a training headquarters for Cuban exiles and
served as one of the major bases for the Bay of Pigs invasion. Guatemala's role in this venture made it a special target of Castro; and
the U.S. attack and failure served to strengthen Castro's general
position in the Caribbean. Guatemalans who were not well disposed
to favor U.S. intervention and were still smarting under the CIA
support of Castillo saw in this an expansion of that agency's efforts
to subvert revolution wherever it might occur. The 1960 military
revolt led directly to the formation of the *guerrillero* bands that
have subsequently served to crystallize the extremist revolutionary
efforts. The United States, having already provided counterinsurgency training for some of the officers of the Guatemalan army (including some of those leading the *guerrilleros*), now stepped up its
military aid to the Guatemalan army to combat the insurgents.
While it consisted mainly of military materials, it also included
promotion of the civilian action program as a device for giving the
army, and the military in general, a better image in the countryside. In the rural population, these insurgency and counterinsurg-

ency efforts served only to heighten the uncertainty and fear already engendered by the reprisals of 1954. Especially in Izabal and the neighboring areas of Zacapa and Alta Verapaz, peasants found themselves subjected to the threats of the *guerrilleros* on the one hand and the reprisals of the army on the other.

The three periods of Guatemalan history here reviewed have seen some important changes in the organization of power. From an essentially unitary system under Ubico, the revolutionary government established a wide sense of lower-sector organizations, a multiple domain, to provide confrontations for the farmers and bring them clearly within the control of the government. The subsequent period found the government attempting to return power to the upper sector, removing it from the lower sector and calling in help from the Church and the United States. The postrevolutionary government needed external derivative power, just as Arbenz had needed it. Arbenz, however, had been unable to get it. He had been unable to lift his confrontation with the United States to the international level of articulation where he could readily call upon other nations to help him.

4. *The 1966 Confrontation in Politics*

Perhaps the greatest impact of the revolutionary decade was the lesson it apparently taught all sections of Guatemalan society, including *campesinos* and laborers, just what alternatives were available. As was reported from a study of peasants jailed following the fall of Arbenz, "An awakening of profound import did take place for many of the members of this sample, but it was not what usually has come under the rubric of 'ideological.' It could better be called a 'sociological awakening,' for it amounted to a realization that certain of the previously accepted roles and statuses within the social system were no longer bounded by the same rules, and that new channels were suddenly opened for the expression of and satisfaction of needs."[21] For some years following the 1954 counterrevolution, the effects of this were not entirely apparent. The suppression of leftist political parties and the operation of an anti-Communist law continued to threaten many individuals. The real impact ultimately became apparent in the voting pattern that

---

[21] Newbold, "Receptivity," p. 361.

finally appeared in 1966 and in the emergence of continuing insurgency. Comparable material is not available from the revolutionary period, but Sloan's study on the postrevolutionary elections is amply revealing in showing that the full effect was some time in coming.[22]

The period immediately following the downfall of the revolutionary government in 1954 found the revolutionary element driven out of the country, sent to jail, and, in a few instances, sentenced to death. Elections began again (not including a plebiscite staged by Castillo) in 1957, at which time the only revolutionary party, the Partido Revolucionario (PR) was not allowed to put up a candidate. This election was declared fraudulent, and, following a brief military regime, another election was held in January of 1958, with two subsequent congressional elections in 1959 and 1961. With the military *golpe* of 1963, there were no subsequent elections until the presidential and congressional elections of 1966 (not counting a single slate elected to a constituent assembly in 1964 to draft a new constitution).

In evaluating these elections, it is possible to deal with a number of variables. There is the classic division between "conservative" and "revolutionary." This differentiation has to be seen also as being between "official" parties, those that are specifically sponsored by the government, and those against the incumbents. As Sloan has pointed out in his study, the shifting alliances between the various parties, including between the PR and conservative parties on occasion, makes it difficult to see consistently just how voters may perceive the bent of a party. Also, during the field work of the present study, it became clear that two important features marked the activities of political parties during the military regime of Peralta Azur-

---

[22] The material concerning these elections is taken in part from John W. Sloan, "The Electoral Game in Guatemala," Ph.D. dissertation, The University of Texas at Austin, 1968, and in part from Map 3–1, which, like the other maps in this volume, was prepared under my direction. An additional source concerning the 1966 election is Kenneth F. Johnson, *The Guatemalan Presidential Election of March 6, 1966: An Analysis.* This last study is useful for some historical materials and census figures, but it also manifests the unfortunate analytical goofs of social scientists who attempt quantitative analyses without a sufficiently intimate knowledge of the area of study. Johnson finds that El Petén is the third most urbanized department of the country and Sololá is the fifth. Escuintla is thirteenth, however, way down the list.

dia. The first, mentioned earlier, was that even the work of legitimate parties had become somewhat clandestine. But with the categorical outlawing of the PGT (Communist) and with the exile of the leaders of the radical URD, it was necessary for many party workers to carry on their activities very quietly in order to avoid being thrown in jail. Second, it became known that on the south coast, and probably in other areas as well, many local people had been approached by so many organizers and promised or threatened so much that it was a common practice to join all parties and to have cards for each. In this way, the individual could adjust to the immediate demands of any party; but by the same token, no party was really sure prior to the 1966 election just who might win. The readiness, described by Roberts, of the *colonia* dwellers to shift party allegiance provides the parallel in the urban setting.

The pattern of voting in terms of general conservative-radical lines was in evidence in the 1958 and 1959 elections. In the first, the PR received the plurality in Escuintla and Izabal; in the second, Guatemala also followed this pattern. In 1961, both Guatemala and Retalhuleu gave PR pluralities, but Escuintla and Izabal failed to. With the exception of a miserable showing in the 1962 Guatemala City municipal election, the PR has generally been strong in the city, but the manner of voting suggests that it is not so much a revolutionary concern as opposition to the government, a pattern that was evident during the revolutionary period as well.

It was not until 1966 that the PR received broad national support, and it did so in a very distinctive way. Map 3–1 has been constructed to show the relative strength of the PR by *municipio* in 1966. It distinguishes those *municipios* that supported both the PR presidential and congressional candidates, those in which the vote was split, and those where non-PR candidates won both elections. The pattern is clear. The vote from the coastal area of Quezaltenango was sufficient to overcome the conservative vote in the highlands and even that of the city of Quezaltenango, so that this department gave its plurality to the PR. Escuintla, Suchitepéquez, Retalhuleu, and San Marcos gave PR majorities. Metropolitan Guatemala also went for the PR, but the eastern and northern *municipios*, Ladino east and Indian west, respectively, were more conservative; the department as a whole, however, gave the PR a plurality. The Ladino east was spotty in its voting, but, with the

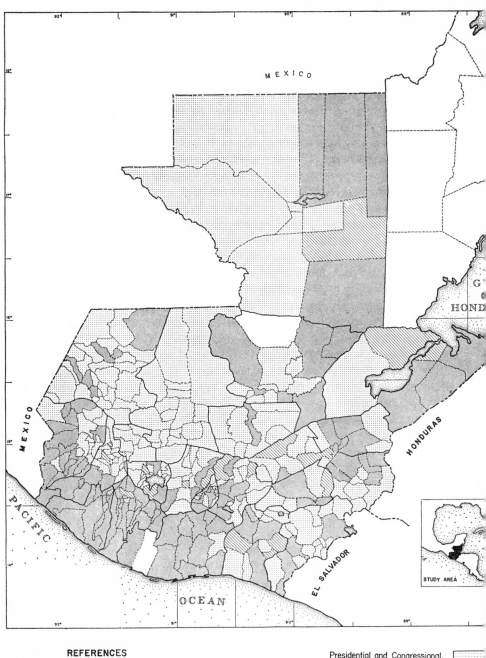

MAP 3–1. PRESIDENTIAL AND CONGRESSIONAL ELECTIONS, MARCH, 1

exception of the department of Jutiapa, all eastern departments gave their pluralities to the PR. Of significance was that, in all except the municipal seat, Jutiapa, the provincial capitals also voted for PR. The Ladino east is irregular in its voting pattern in the same manner that its domain structure varies from small peasant communities to latifundia.

The Indian west displayed a fairly consistent dual pattern. The highland core voted strongly conservative, although there were a few exceptions in San Marcos and Huehuetenango. Aside from these, Alta Verapaz, Sololá, and Chimaltenango followed the pattern of giving the provincial capital to the PR, but the rest of the departments were predominantly conservative. This conservative pattern extended up into the western part of El Petén and to the *municipio* of El Estor. The contrary consistency throughout the entire Indian area was that the coffee piedmont tended to support the PR and did not follow the conservative direction of the highland *municipios*. The *boca costa* areas of Escuintla, most of Suchitepéquez, Retalhuleu, Quezaltenango, and San Marcos, along with the *municipios* of Pochuta, Alotenango, San Miguel Dueñas, all went with the PR although they had heavy proportions of Indians in the populations. It is this kind of shift, of course, that adds special importance to seeing the piedmont as the scene of the first of the great modern migrations. The new areas of the north and northeast gave pluralities to the PR, but the heavy Indian population in both areas weakened the department-wide vote. Except for El Estor, however, the entire area went at least in part for the PR. The basic population, in the area to the south of Izabal, was heavily favorable to the PR (Table 3–1).[23]

The overall pattern of voting generally falls into the area differentiation that the power and growth structure of the country would suggest. The Indian west, excepting the piedmont, was conserva-

---

[23] The data on departmental voting figures for the 1966 election vary slightly between the reports by Sloan ("Electoral Game," p. 250) and Johnson (*Presidential Election*, p. 20). The only case where the figures are sufficiently different to change whether the PR won a plurality or not is in El Petén. Sloan reports the PR as receiving 37.1 percent, and Johnson's figure is 41.6 percent. On the basis of the information in the two sources, it is not possible to know why there is such a divergence. The two sources differ in almost all the figures recorded, but this is the only one that differs for a department as a whole. Table 3–1 gives the data from the two sources.

TABLE 3-1
1966 Presidential Election Vote from Two Sources

Department	Sloan								Johnson							
	PR		PID		MLN		Total		PR		PID		MLN		Total	
	No.	%	No.	%	No.	%	No.	%	No.	%	No.	%	No.	%	No.	%
Metropolitan Zone—Total	69,942	54.2	25,989	20.1	33,052	25.6	128,983	28.4	66,070	54.1	23,377	19.1	32,673	26.8	122,129	28.4
Guatemala	65,977	55.6	22,799	19.2	29,811	25.1	118,587	26.1	62,058	55.1	20,667	18.3	29,997	26.6	112,722	26.2
Sacatepéquez	3,965	38.1	3,190	30.6	3,241	31.1	10,396	2.3	4,012	42.7	2,710	28.9	2,676	28.4	9,398	2.2
The South Coast—Total	67,232	52.7	38,084	29.9	22,202	17.4	127,518	28.0	63,824	52.8	36,137	29.7	21,202	17.5	121,163	28.2
Escuintla	15,679	62.2	4,753	18.8	4,767	18.9	25,199	5.5	14,050	61.8	4,206	18.5	4,476	19.6	22,732	5.3
Suchitepéquez	13,394	56.4	5,728	24.1	4,597	19.3	23,719	5.2	13,251	57.1	5,795	25.1	4,131	17.9	23,177	5.4
Retalhuleu	6,346	53.2	3,893	32.6	1,672	14.0	11,911	2.6	6,109	53.6	3,714	32.6	1,584	13.9	11,407	2.7
Quezaltenango	13,447	42.0	12,738	39.8	5,824	18.1	32,009	7.0	12,927	42.3	12,029	39.5	5,558	18.2	30,514	7.1
San Marcos	18,366	52.9	10,972	31.6	5,342	15.4	34,680	7.6	17,487	52.4	10,393	31.1	5,453	16.3	33,333	7.7
The North Total	6,752	44.9	5,291	35.2	2,987	19.8	15,030	3.3	5,840	43.8	4,730	35.5	2,761	20.7	13,331	3.1
Izabal	5,242	47.7	3,478	31.7	2,249	20.5	10,969	2.4	4,266	44.7	3,183	33.3	2,102	22.1	9,551	2.2
El Petén	1,510	37.1	1,813	44.6	738	18.1	4,061	0.9	1,574	41.6	1,547	21.0	659	17.4	3,780	0.9
The Ladino East—Total	28,748	36.9	25,745	33.1	23,154	29.7	77,647	17.0	27,129	37.0	24,918	34.0	21,277	29.0	73,324	17.0
Zacapa	4,871	45.5	3,596	33.6	2,217	20.7	10,684	2.3	4,136	43.3	3,309	34.7	2,101	22.1	9,546	2.2
El Progreso	2,133	32.5	2,081	31.7	2,234	35.6	6,448	1.4	2,161	34.4	2,057	32.7	2,058	32.8	6,276	1.5

	Sloan								Johnson							
	PR		PID		MLN		Total		PR		PID		MLN		Total	
Department	No.	%	No.	%	No.	%	No.	%	No.	%	No.	%	No.	%	No.	%
Chiquimula	5,932	37.6	3,908	24.7	5,923	37.5	15,763	3.5	5,633	37.3	3,866	25.6	5,627	37.2	15,126	3.5
Jalapa	3,115	40.6	2,895	37.7	1,660	21.6	7,670	1.7	3,085	41.4	2,834	38.0	1,536	20.6	7,455	1.7
Jutiapa	5,945	29.8	7,711	38.7	6,248	31.3	19,904	4.4	5,698	29.5	7,443	38.6	6,136	31.9	19,277	4.5
Santa Rosa	6,752	39.3	5,554	32.3	4,872	28.3	17,178	3.8	6,416	41.0	5,409	34.5	3,819	24.4	15,644	3.6
The Indian West—Total	26,871	25.4	50,754	48.0	27,991	26.5	105,616	23.2	28,036	28.0	47,095	47.0	25,040	25.0	100,171	23.3
Chimaltenango	5,481	33.6	5,898	36.2	4,897	30.0	16,276	3.6	4,927	34.0	5,560	38.3	3,995	27.5	14,482	3.4
Sololá	1,923	20.6	5,080	54.5	2,304	24.7	9,307	2.0	3,766	35.5	5,054	47.7	1,770	16.7	10,590	2.5
Totonicapán	2,248	17.0	8,025	60.9	2,895	21.9	13,168	2.9	2,207	18.3	7,047	58.3	2,831	23.4	12,085	2.8
El Quiché	2,355	17.7	6,821	51.4	4,074	30.7	13,250	2.9	2,288	18.3	6,674	53.2	3,561	28.4	12,523	2.9
Alta Verapaz	5,232	27.3	9,540	49.7	4,392	22.9	19,164	4.2	4,790	27.9	8,418	49.1	3,912	22.9	17,120	4.0
Baja Verapaz	2,880	30.2	4,259	44.7	2,382	25.0	9,521	2.1	2,830	31.2	4,074	44.9	2,178	24.0	9,082	2.1
Huehuetenango	6,752	27.0	11,131	44.6	7,047	28.2	24,930	5.5	7,228	29.7	10,268	42.2	6,793	27.9	24,289	5.6
Totals	199,545	43.9%	145,863	32.1%	109,386	24.0%	454,794	100.0%	190,899	44.4%	136,257	31.7%	102,953	23.9%	430,109	100.0%

SOURCE: John W. Sloan, "The Electoral Game in Guatemala," Ph.D. dissertation, University of Texas at Austin, 1968; Kenneth F. Johnson, *The Guatemalan Presidential Election of March 6, 1966: An Analysis*, Election Analysis No. 5, Institute for the Comparative Study of Political Systems, Washington, n.d.

NOTE: PR, Partido Revolucionario (strongly antimilitarist).
PID, Partido Institucional Democrático (moderately promilitarist).
MLN, Movimiento de Liberación Nacional (strongly promilitarist).

tive. The Ladino east was mixed, but, while a majority voted for the conservative candidates, the plurality consistently (except for Jutiapa) went for the PR. The south coast and the Indian coffee piedmont were strongly PR, as was most of the north and northeast. And, finally, the metropolis was similarly strong for the PR. Sloan makes the point in his analysis that some, if not all, of what has been called "conservative" here may well be "official party," and that this is especially true of the west. The reason behind a conservative vote is probably more closely related to the small domain system of peasant life than it is to some nebulous kind of "Indianism." It is specifically the area of traditional Indians that was conservative, not those who had undergone the experience of working regularly within a coffee finca domain, and who had had the experience of being close to, if not actually involved in, the agitation and politicization of the revolutionary period. In view of this, we may ascribe the conservatism not to being Indian, but to the experiences of living in the restricted domains of the Indian communities and the traditional identification of the government as something to placate.

Sloan (see Table 3–2) has compared a number of independent variables that were prepared by the research project (the distribution of these is shown by various maps in this volume). There is a low but consistent correlation between the proportion of Indians in a *municipio* and its conservative vote. This, however, was also true of literacy, and, for both, the amount of variance explained by the correlation was small. The major correlation that seemed to have real possibilities was with the percentage of individuals who had been born in another *municipio*. This finding conforms with a similar finding of a study carried out after the fall of the revolutionary regimes in 1954: "People of low residential continuity lack ties with a specific locale and have no social continuity in that locale. Lacking social ties to an established social group, they are generally more receptive to innovations for the organization of that group. Their daily relationships are not constant reminders that they are diverging from old ways of doing things . . ."[24]

The variation in voting and other patterns revealed in Table 3–2

[24] Newbold, "Receptivity," p. 358.

TABLE 3–2
Relationship of Certain Variables with a PR vote in the Presidential Election of 1966

Independent Variables	Relationship with Conservative Vote	
	r	r²
Election of January 1958—288 Municipios		
% Indian	.35154	.12
% Effective change	—.26937	.07
% Literate	—.41644	.17
% Effective change	.00243	.00
% Migrant	—.50875	.26
% Population increase	—.34951	.12
Land expropriation	—.18986	.04
BNA and SCICAS Loans per capita	—.24015	.06
Election of December 1959—249 Municipios		
% Indian	.43171	.19
% Effective change	—.29949	.09
% Literate	—.39002	.15
% Effective change	.05396	.00
% Migrant	—.45556	.21
% Population increase	—.29968	.09
Land expropriation	—.27721	.08
BNA and SCICAS Loans per capita	—.25684	.07
Election of December 1961—282 Municipios		
% Indian	.31417	.10
% Effective change	—.21491	.05
% Literate	—.29383	.09
% Effective change	.02562	.00
% Migrant	—.39598	.16
% Population increase	—.23080	.05
Land expropriation	—.12864	.02
BNA and SCICAS Loans per capita	—.27572	.08
Election of March 1966—313 Municipios		
% Indian	.23429	.05
% Effective change	—.15206	.02
% Literate	—.21970	.05
% Effective change	.08247	.01
% Migrant	—.46539	.22
% Population increase	—.26421	.07
Land expropriation	—.17567	.03
BNA and SCICAS Loans per capita	—.17431	.03

SOURCE: John W. Sloan, "The Electoral Game in Guatemala," Ph.D. dissertation, University of Texas at Austin, 1968, Table 8, pp. 213–214.
NOTE: r is the Pearsonian coefficient of correlation.

suggest that radical voting is likely to stem from areas where there are multiple levels of articulation in operation. Given this, voting permits lower levels to attempt to articulate with possibly responsive upper-level units or individuals. However, where there are separate local domains, each of which is seen by its members to relate to the top through a single, unique, or very few vertical channels, then voting is more likely to reflect what the government wishes. Thus, in the Indian highland areas, the government-backed party was not just a plurality in the 1966 elections, but also an absolute majority in El Quiché, Totonicapán, and Sololá and a strong plurality in Alta Verapaz. In view of the distribution of the vote, it seems likely that the government-backed party commands a very strong vote in the highlands of Quezaltenango and San Marcos as well. Indians resident in the coffee piedmont had long since entered other domains, and their exposure led them to vote much more strongly for the nongovernment candidates. Although voting data are treated here as if it were entirely a lower-sector activity, obviously it is not. Not only is it responsive to upper-sector commands in areas of unitary domains, but it is also composed of people at the higher levels of articulation. Nevertheless, votes outside the provincial capitals are probably indicative responses of the lower, rather than the upper-sector.

The most important confrontation within the Guatemalan society today is a step beyond the question of voting within the national regime. True insurgency in Guatemala against the postrevolutionary regimes began after the failure of the Thirteenth of November movement. During the previous five years there had been random acts of terrorism, usually consisting of scattered bombing in Guatemala City. By the time of the present study, in 1965, there were two separate *guerrillero* groups operating in the northeast, one pressing for a more rapid confrontation with the government, and the other following a longer-termed strategy, spending whatever years necessary to build up a loyal base within the *campesino* population, principally within the Sierra de las Minas. Accompanying this would be periodic harassment to try to prevent the government, under whatever party leadership, from making any real success in its own development program.

It is difficult to evaluate the degree to which the clandestine political activity that emerged under the repressive politics of the early Castillo period and the military government of 1963–1966 was articulated with the work of the insurgents. It is clear that there were enclaves of organized groups and that the Fuerzas Armadas Rebeldes (FAR) was systematically trying to develop auxiliary *guerrilleros* among the *campesinos*. This was especially being done in the Zacapa–Alta Verapaz–Chiquimula area and in the central south coast. In the Pacific lowlands, sympathizers worked both directly with the guerrilla forces and as members of radical political groups. The *guerrilleros de la noche* of Escuintla were those *campesinos* and townsmen who would carry on their ordinary activity during the day but at night would carry out activities in favor of the *guerrilleros*. The political stance assumed by the *guerrilleros* was not merely to object to the government's action at lower levels of articulation, but also to publicly challenge the government and its force of arms, thereby requiring that the government recognize that they existed at the same level of articulation as the government itself. This assumption was intentionally ignored by the Peralta government; the *guerrilleros* were publicly classified as bandits and treated as such. News concerning their depredations and successes was kept out of the newspapers. As the two bands became increasingly active, each published newssheets and manifestoes, trying both to bring support to their side and to get wider publicity for their efforts.

The strategy of the *guerrilleros* was that the position of Guatemala (and all other Latin American countries except Cuba) was inevitably under the control of the United States and that anything leading to Guatemala's removal from that domain was legitimate. For its part, the government of Guatemala assumed that it could count on the support of the United States for support against insurgency. The *guerrillero* plan was to gradually create "loyal" units in the countryside, first in the north where they were then operating, then later in the other parts of the country, but especially in the south and east. This activity, not controlled by the government, would bring in the U.S. Marines, whose presence would neutralize the corporateness of the Guatemalan military and contribute to its breakdown as an effective organization and, with it, the collapse of the government. The insurgents would then be in a position to take over the government. Presumably, this would not involve Guatemala alone, but by occurring simultaneously in various places it would find the United States incapable of militarily commandeering so much of Latin America.

In the post-Peralta years, the military has been much more aggressive in suppression of the *guerrilleros*, and the latter have increasingly operated within Guatemala City, where the counterinsurgency devices are less effective. The metropolis had always been part of the *guerrillero* strategy. It served as a source of (1) financing, for example, through kidnappings for ransom, (2) personnel, recruited from the radical students and other upper-sector supporters who could find haven there, and (3) anticipated popular support. The effectiveness of the 1967–1968 military action in the northeast, however, reduced rural activity, and the city became the center of activity. This has been an interesting development from the point of view of the regional structure of the country. The *guerrilleros* have not found the Indian west to be particularly hospitable, and the Ladino east is irregular. The two provincial regions providing support are the new growth zones, and they are linked both physically and structurally by the metropolis.

The fact that the *guerrilleros* exist and have been able to persist since their formulation in the early 1960's is suggestive of the depth of the cleavage that separates Guatemalan society. It is a consequence, in part, of the division that exists at the higher levels and that finds the confrontation and lower levels essential to its success. It is not entirely surprising that conservative interests, also regarding violence as a legitimate tactic, would set in motion units counter to the *guerrilleros*. The Mano Blanca and other right-wing terrorist organizations were bent on the destruction not only of the *guerrilleros*, but also of leftists in general. The strategy being used is not merely to confront the *guerrilleros*, but to at least reduce their level of articulation. By forcing the *guerrilleros* to deal with lower-level groups, their claim of representing a nationalist movement (something that must work at the national level and international level) can be seriously weakened.

The strategy of culture change requires dealing with events on the level at which they occur. The confrontations posed by the *guerrilleros* have occurred at all levels of society—the upper sector and the government itself, principally through attack on military units and public figures, and among *campesinos*. At the time of writing, this had been extended to the archbishop, who, after being kidnapped and threatened, fled the country. The appearance of rightwing terrorist groups brought the *guerrilleros* down to the level of "mere" terrorists and out of the minds of some as serious political contenders. With no more information than is available, it is speculation to discuss what may be the outcome of the tactical situation that holds at the time of writing. There is no question, however, that the confrontations being pressed by the *guerrilleros* are being resisted by the incumbents with all the assistance that the United States thinks is necessary. The area of operation of the *guerrilleros* has been well chosen, being the entire developmental zone from one coast to the other and including the metropolis. It has been within the strategy of socialist planners that some portions of Latin America might become the next Vietnam for the United States. However, the Vietnam experience has been for the United States rather like the Cuban experience has been for much of the Western Hemisphere. Those in power do not want to see it repeated. As a result, it seems far more likely that Guatemala will continue with sufficient derivative power from the various superpowers to keep it in ferment only for as long as the Guatemalans themselves have a stomach for it.

5. *Varieties of Regional Power Organization*

This chapter has thus far dealt with the organization of power as it has varied chronologically. Here the topic will be discussed from a regional point of view, relying on a series of cases that can provide contrast, and that permits the proposal of a construct of the general system.[25]

A geographical region becomes culturally and socially meaningful because of decisions concerning the utilization of human and natural resources; insofar as human adaptation is concerned, there is no such thing as a "natural" region apart from such decisions. It is

[25] The basic data for the descriptions that follow shortly were collected in the summer of 1965 by John Durston for the Department of Jutiapa, Wilford Lawrence for the Department of Alta Verapaz, Larry Grimes for the Department of Chimaltenango, and Theodore Johnson for the department of Escuintla. Although Quezaltenango was included as one of the original departments for the study, it proved too complicated to delineate in the time provided and has been omitted from the present study.

possible to conceive of a continuum of kinds of regions based on the degree of centralization of decision-making. At one end of the continuum are those made by governmental agencies for their convenience: military districts or zones, jurisdictional zones, zones of labor inspectors, zones of responsibility of agricultural agents, civil administration zones of *municipios* and departments, school districts, electoral districts, and so forth. Each branch and office of the central government divides the country geographically so that it can apportion and organize its work. Decisions made for developing commerce are particularly complex. Central offices of national businesses also must think of distributorships in geographical terms. Success or failure, however, provides feedback, and how much effort is expended in any given region is partially a result of an estimate of the market potential in that area. Similarly, the Catholic church, in deciding upon the boundaries of a new diocese, takes into account relevant factors concerning the population insofar as they are known. The same is true in political party organizations. Local organizers draw their regional lines on the basis of estimates of the relative response they may expect, and these, in turn, are based on experience.

At the other end of the scale are regions that are defined not by a single individual or a group or bureaucracy, but by the collective, statistical product of the set of decisions made by a large number of individuals. The choice of one town center rather than another for retail purchases is made individually by many purchasers; this kind of region exists insofar as there is a significant statistical difference among the choices. In this instance, the choice is based principally on transport facilities, services in the town, or economic ability of the individual to make use of each of the first two. The definition of a retail region will necessarily vary with the economic level of the individuals concerned and the relative quality of the services and transport.

To speak of a "cultural" or "social" region, then, is not to consider a single clear-cut geographical entity, but, rather, a whole series of intersecting entities being utilized by the inhabitants for different purposes and being determined by the decisions of human organizations of various scope. In choosing the region defined by power domains as the subject of interest, one avoids dealing with those regions that are the direct product of collective and statistical choice. The quantification and measurement of market variations and of changing choices required a field approach beyond the capacities of the present project.

This brings up an important distinction: there are different regions for the different roles played in the society. For the very wealthy provincial farmer, the retail region always involves Guatemala City, no matter where else he may reside and shop. The retail region for the very poor will be the nearest town; they will occasionally visit other towns or provincial centers, but possibly never visit Guatemala City. Within local populations, there are degrees of cosmopolitan experience. Similarly, domains over which individuals and groups hold power have a geographical dimension, and regions can be defined in terms of the geographical area covered by power domains.

Durston's Jutiapa study distinguished three kinds of "elites," three apparent levels of control by individuals both inside and outside any given territory. These he characterized as local, regional, and supraregional elites.[26] This basic typology will be followed, but it is first necessary to clarify the relation between elites and power. The term *elite* has passed into that jungle of popular terms whose meanings change significantly from one user to another. A recent contribution to Latin American studies uses the term to refer to rulers or dominant people in whatever context anyone happens to be studying. Elites are discussed by institutional affiliation, and there are chapters on the industrial elites, political elites, military elites, labor elites, religious elites, and even cultural elites.[27] In most cases, *elite* refers to that part of an institutional segment that has special decision-making positions with respect to the institution itself and therefore has an especially important role within the society as a whole. In the case of the cultural elites, it is really only

[26] See John Durston, "Power Structure in a Rural Region of Guatemala: The Department of Jutiapa." M.A. thesis, The University of Texas at Austin, 1966. The "local" and "regional" elites referred to by Durston together compose the "local upper class" described by the present writer in "Cultural Components of Central America," *American Anthropologist* 58, no. 5 (October 1956): 890. I now shy away from the term "class" in this context for reasons set forth by Rodolfo Stavenhagen, "Estratificación social y estructura de clases," *Ciencias Politicas y Sociales* 27 (1962): 73–102, but the referent is the same.

[27] Seymour Martin Lipset and Aldo Solari, eds., *Elites in Latin America*.

the second of these features that distinguishes it, whereas in all the others, the question of power is evident.

Here, the concern is less with institutional differentiation between, for example, the military, religious, and political, and more with the formation of the elite in terms of their geographical unity and basis for action. The concept of "power domain" helps in making such distinctions and not only points out the social dimensions of power relationships, but also implicitly permits the delineation of the geography over which these relations range. The various elites that concern us are set apart by differentiating the geographic scope of their power domains.

The *supraregional elite* of Durston, actually part of a larger national elite, is distinguished by the fact that its scope of power may extend to the nation as a whole and may even include international phases. It is supraregional from the point of view of a person in a provincial territory.[28] The individuals who pertain to this elite include those natives of such a provincial area who have followed the basis of their power operations elsewhere. They more often reside in the national capital, although they may maintain a residence in the department, usually on a farm. The national elite also includes those individuals with derived power who have come into the region for a temporary period from the outside, such as the commandant of the military base or the departmental governor (who, in Guatemala, is appointed by the central government and is usually an outsider, often a military man). There are, of course, many members of the national elite who are not part of the many specific supraregional elites.

The *regional elite* includes individuals or groups whose scope of power covers a provincial area larger than a single community or municipal area. While a few are resident in villages or small towns, most live in the major departmental centers, since it is from those places that they can best exercise their controls and see to their interests. Just as the person with national interests cannot operate from the provinces alone, so the individual of province-wide interests lives in an urban center where he has communication and contact with a larger area. The regional elite also includes migrants

[28] Guatemala is subdivided for political-administrative purposes into *departamentos* and *municipios*. Since few of the regions being discussed here coincide completely with specific departmental lines, I am intentionally using the term "provincial" in its generic sense rather than the formal administrative terms.

to the provincial area in pursuit of their occupational, economic, political, or other interests. This includes some who choose to live on their rural holdings, but most find their residences in the provincial centers.

The *local elite* includes residents of smaller communities who have special controls over more limited areas. Their basis of power is local; they cannot afford to be long absent, since they depend on personal contacts. As with the regional elites, the local elite will, from time to time, include such outsiders as the parish priests, extension agents, post office and telegraph officers, or a town secretary. Although often native to other parts of the country, they are resident locally, and their domain is local in scope.

This generalized picture of elites seldom occurs in fact, and it is the variation found in nature that is of special interest. To see how Guatemala looks in this respect, four specific regions will be examined: Jutiapa, Alta Verapaz, Chimaltenango, and Escuintla.

JUTIAPA

The department of Jutiapa has consistently received relatively little attention from the central government and has evolved a full set of elites. Storekeepers and agriculturalists of each local community have tended to take the lead in local government in making decisions for the community as a whole. As is the case in many communities throughout the country, there is usually factionalism, so that there is also a local opposition. In the regional centers of Progreso, Asunción Mita, and the departmental capital, Jutiapa, there are regional power holders of greater wealth and importance than most of those found in the smaller communities. These are large storekeepers who often own a number of stores, agents for major national outlets and industries, regional grain buyers and their credit agents, middle-range farmers who produce for sale, and local doctors, teachers, and lawyers who reside in the provincial centers. The identification of these individuals is made easier by the presence of a Lions Club to which many of them belong and an agency of the Red Cross that finds itself somewhat in competition with the Lions. Some of the components of these groups are rather specialized. Dairy cattle are raised in Asunción Mita by locally resident members of the regional elite. Many have interests besides their dairy business, and all are concerned with national problems as they affect the government's aid to the development of local enterprises. Coffee in Jutiapa is not a major crop, and most of the *finqueros* who grow it for sale belong to this regional elite. Few of them have residences outside the department.

The supraregional elite is composed of those natives of the department of Jutiapa who have chosen for economic, political, or social reasons to live in Guatemala City. They usually have a home in the department, either in one of the major provincial towns or on their farm or both. Locally, they include a number of the cattle raisers, and their business extends from El Salvador and Honduras, where they often purchase cattle, to their farms in Jutiapa, and finally to Escuintla or Guatemala for the sale. A number of these native sons have become professionals, physicians, or lawyers, and some have been consistently interested in national politics, having acted as *diputados* and, occasionally, have had a hopeful eye on the presidency. This part of the supraregional elite pays little attention to the provincial affairs of the major towns and almost none to the events in the small towns. Their interest in the department is closely tied to their economic concerns and the possibilities of political support should they want it. The national elite, of which the supraregional elite is but a small component, is heavily drawn from the natives of the national capital, and for provincials to compete successfully, they cannot allow themselves to be completely occupied with regional issues.

Resident in the region is the chief of the military zone and the governor, both men appointed from the outside and serving indefinite terms of office. During the summer of 1965, when Durston's study was in progress, both were *militares*. The commandant of the military zone was easily recognized as the major power figure locally. At the time, the individual holding that post participated actively in local affairs, belonged to the Lions Club, and was recognized as an important part of the regional social life. Both his job and his bearing marked him clearly as a man from the outside, however, and remarks were as much in admiration of his social participation as they were a quiet criticism of the insufficient local interest manifested by certain of his predecessors.

The rather neat picture of the Jutiapa regional social structure is matched by the fact that the provincial centers act as retail and wholesale centers for the smaller towns of the immediate area.

Townspeople go to Jutiapa in order to buy quality furniture, radios, sewing machines, and bedding, as well as occasionally in search of a doctor, a lawyer, or a place to send the occasional child who is to go to secondary school. The members of the regional elite, who in a sense host these more rural dwellers, in turn make their periodic trips to Guatemala City in order to fulfill certain of their needs. Although patronizing the local stores, they will also make purchases in the city, and may well prefer a Guatemala City lawyer or medical specialist to those available locally.

The Jutiapa regional power organization is balanced. There are power foci at each level, and they each operate to control the *campesino* population and to extract the wealth necessary to maintain their style of life, a style that becomes increasingly luxurious and complex as one moves up the system. There is no question, however, that the supraelite individuals from the outside, the military commandant and the governor, tend to dominate the scene. Next to these, the regional elite was extremely strong, and the local elite naturally played a secondary role to them in commerce as well as in government. The Jutiapa pattern, however, does not hold for the country at large. The other cases will make this evident and will also indicate some of the variables that are relevant in determining the shape that a particular regional structure will take.

ALTA VERAPAZ

The situation in Cobán and neighboring Alta Verapaz towns has a rather unusual recent history. In the nineteenth century, German *finqueros* became important in coffee production and, prior to World War II, maintained a regional society quite distinctive from the rest of the country. To a lesser degree, the German coffee producers of the Guatemalan western piedmont also retained a separate society, operating out of Quezaltenango as the regional center, but this group was much more widespread and less exclusive. The Cobán coffee men shipped their product directly out through Lake Izabal, thereby avoiding much of the red tape of Guatemala City. With the advent of Hitler, a significant portion of the Cobán group became active adherents of Nazism. The non-German Ladino residents of the Alta Verapaz found themselves relegated to a position of second-class citizens. German society in Cobán was the most "dazzling," and they regarded the Ladinos as inferior, finding

Hitler's notion of the master race to be quite congenial. Some towns, such as San Cristóbal, are said to have remained outside the German orbit and still resent the social distinction the Germans marked on the region. Probably related to this is the current attitude of many of the local elite of San Pedro Carchá. Even today, they refuse to share in the social activities of Cobán, although the German remnants are scattered and no longer dominate the social or economic life. The result of this history is that Cobán has a local elite, a population important to itself, but not dominant in the department in the same way that the Jutiapa regional elite is. Similarly, members of the supraregional elite of Alta Verapaz tend to identify themselves with one of the towns rather than with the region as a whole. A person is usually not satisfied to say that he comes from Alta Verapaz, but rather that he comes from Cobán, San Cristóbal, Tactic, or Carchá.

Rather than a regional elite standing over a series of local elites, the Alta Verapaz is composed of a set of somewhat discrete local elites occupying a social spectrum that includes elements of social life ranging from the local to the regional as found in Jutiapa. In Cobán itself, this is signaled by the presence of a Sociedad Beneficiencia, an association that is derived from an older German club and that is today almost exclusively made up of Cobán people. This exclusiveness is due less to a reluctance of the Cobán members to allow others in than it is to the fact that members of the other towns have no real interest in participating in it.

This difference is also reflected in the local power structures. Rather than answering to a general regional elite, each town stands somewhat alone. In San Juan Chamelco, for example, one Ladino acts as a cacique for the Indians of the immediate area. He dominates the local community so successfully that even his local opponents find it difficult to disturb his position of authority. As such, he deals directly with the governor and need not depend upon the support of a Cobán elite.

Only recently, during the summer of 1965, the coffee farmers of the entire region banded together for the first time in their own self-interest and thereby gave evidence of the emergence of a regional elite of the kind found in Jutiapa. This apparently was led by people in Cobán but emerged as a response to the national coffee situation. The other major coffee regions of the country had already formed regional associations in order to assure or improve their proportion of the Guatemalan quota that had been set by international agreement. The Alta Verapaz farmers, because of lack of organization and because their crop usually came in late, were losing out on the world market relative to other Guatemalan producers. It appears that an elite organization is emerging, but at the time of the study, it was not clear whether it would be dominated by a nascent regional elite or by the supraregional elite.

The role of the supraregional elite in Cobán was not sufficiently explored in the present study. There have been important individuals from Alta Verapaz who have regularly occupied prominent positions within the government. One family produced a number of them, including the short-termed chief of state who immediately succeeded Ubico in 1944. None of the Alta Verapaz towns have played a really important role in the national life of Guatemala, however. The reason, presumably, is that the strength of the German elite displaced the local Ladino population for a long time, and when the Germans were themselves displaced, there were few to fill their place.

CHIMALTENANGO

To be contrasted with both Jutiapa and the Alta Verapaz are the departments of Chimaltenango and Escuintla. The population of Chimaltenango, like Alta Verapaz, is made up heavily of Indians. However, the department is divided into two major geographic zones: the central and northern *municipios*, composed of small holdings and fincas that are devoted to subsistence agriculture, rentals, or holding labor, and the Pacific piedmont *municipios*, ecologically part of the Escuintla coastal area. This southern area is a coffee finca zone, and the population is primarily resident labor. In the north and center, however, most individuals are independent agriculturalists, even when they do not own their own land. The description here is only of this northern area.

Chimaltenango borders to the west of the department of Guatemala, and the departmental capital is an easy forty-minute drive by good paved road from the capital city. The combination of a series of locally organized Indian populations, coupled with close proximity to the city, has resulted in the almost complete absence of a regional elite. The few stores in Chimaltenango serve Indians predominantly. Resident Ladinos of any means circulate readily in Antigua or Guatemala City, often spending weekends away. There is relatively little major commerce.

While there is no significant regional elite, the role of the national elite is, if anything, increasing. Entrepreneurs from Guatemala City have found in Chimaltenango a cheap and convenient area to establish an industry. Also, besides the normal departmental government administrative offices, including the governor's office, the national field headquarters of Secretaría de Bienestar Social has been located there, as well as a few agents of banks and extension agencies. For these government agents, however, Chimaltenango is primarily a work locale, and many commute from their permanent homes in Guatemala City. None of the factory owners live in Chimaltenango, nor do they express the slightest interest in doing so. The town of Chimaltenango really serves as a convenient overflow for outsiders from Guatemala City. One factory has gone so far that not only is the ownership absentee, but it also makes use of the cheaper migrant labor from El Salvador rather than local people. The presence of the factory has not had the slightest effect locally on the elite structure.

In the northern part of the department there are a number of fincas of a rather special kind. Some, belonging to one of the country's wealthiest families, hold a special relationship to coffee and sugar farms also owned by the same family on the adjacent piedmont and coast. The highland fincas are not kept as agriculturally productive areas, but as labor-resource fincas. The resident Indian laborers are provided with land to cultivate, and, in exchange for this, they are committed to work as wage labor on the piedmont farms, especially during the harvest time. This *finca de mozos* system, although not widespread, is traditional in Guatemala and grants the *finqueros* control of their seasonal labor. The laborers who have the privilege of using such land are often in better economic circumstances than their peasant neighbors whose private holdings are smaller and not protected by a wealthy *patrón*. A further consequence of the system, however, is that the *finqueros* have little direct interest in the *fincas de mozos*, since they are essentially unproductive.

The southern *municipios* of Chimaltenango, together with the northernmost areas of Escuintla, are composed principally of coffee fincas. This area reaches from Chiapas in Mexico, on the west, into Santa Rosa, with scattered farms in Jutiapa. This great piedmont belt has formed the major source of Guatemalan coffee and, consequently, of the national income since the last century. Most farms have large resident labor forces, many uneconomically large, but unable to be reduced in size under current labor regulations. As coffee growing has expanded, the size of fincas has increased, but, more commonly, the fincas have tended increasingly to use their idle lands. This means that land formerly turned over to laborers for subsistence production has, in some cases, been put into export crop production. Owners of the large farms, or portions of their families, usually live in Guatemala City, but many of the smaller farms are occupied at least part-time by their owners. These farms use Guatemala City as their main supply source, although Antigua (or occasionally Chimaltenango) may provide minor local services. The Indian population has long since adapted to finca living and was one of the targets of union organizing during the revolutionary period. As in the Alta Verapaz area, most local Chimaltenango governments are controlled by the local Ladinos, who form a local elite. Few are of sufficient wealth or importance to form a regional elite.

ESCUINTLA

While similar to Chimaltenango in that it is close to Guatemala City, Escuintla differs in some crucial respects. Whereas Chimaltenango is essentially underdeveloped and numerically dominated by the Indian population, Escuintla is an area of thriving development and is almost completely Ladino. The only characteristically Indian *municipio* is Palín, in the immediately neighboring highlands, and, in the piedmont *municipios*, there is resident Indian labor occupied almost wholly on coffee farms. To a much greater degree than with Chimaltenango, the proximity to Guatemala City has led to Escuintla's being looked upon favorably as a place for industry. The migrant labor that has moved into and through the area over the past twenty years has helped provide a basic labor force for such a development. Yet, with these profound differences, Escuintla and Chimaltenango both lack a clear regional elite. While there are elites in the various local towns, in such new areas as Tiquisate, they are vastly different in composition than in the older communities of Santa Lucía Cotzumalguapa or Siquinalá; in Escuintla and Chimaltenango they are entirely locally oriented.

Escuintla has grown rapidly since 1945, in great part due to migration. The increase has occurred in both the laboring population and the town elite of the departmental capital. A sizable portion of the local elite of the city of Escuintla is composed not of natives of the community but of newcomers from other parts of the republic. A consequence of this is that the Escuintla local elite does not readily form part of a larger regional elite, but stands somewhat apart. Furthermore, this elite fails to act like the regional counterpart in Jutiapa for somewhat the same reason that Chimaltenango has no elite at all. The proximity of Escuintla to Guatemala City means that it actually is not so much a regional center for the surrounding towns and villages as it is a staging poin the city. The major slaughterhouse for the city is located there. Factories are located in and on the margins of the town, but the outlying rural and provincial populations often bypass Escuintla and go directly to Guatemala City for their retail and wholesale needs. Residents of Santa Lucía Cotzumalguapa regard their own town as being a more lively and important center than Escuintla, and for what is lacking there they go directly to the national capital. The same tendency is found among residents of smaller towns of La Gomera, La Democracia, and Nueva Concepción. In Tiquisate, proximity makes Mazatenango more attractive and, again, the town of Escuintla is not used. As might be expected, the *finqueros* of the region generally ignore Escuintla and travel directly to and from their offices and homes in the capital.

Until 1955, the southern central portion of Escuintla was occupied principally by the United Fruit Company plantation of Tiquisate. Following the revolution, the company gave approximately half the land to the government for conversion into a colonization area (see Chapter 8, Table 8–12). This, together with a number of other coastal sections, provided the major basis for the early years of the colonization effort, bringing not only *campesinos* into the area, but also many middle-income people who by hook or by crook obtained titles to some of the parcels. As a result, the area is now composed of *campesino* proprietors, *campesino* renters (the latter working on lands of absentee owners), and some wealthier owners. At the time of the original founding of the colony, it was reported that many of the colonists had been political supporters of the revolutionary regime from the eastern highlands. Later the United

Fruit Company sold off the remaining portions of its Tiquisate lands, except for one small section. These were in large sections for capitalistic development, and the purchasers included fairly wealthy individuals, including a number of foreigners and military officers. It is an important cotton-growing area now, and the town of Tiquisate had grown to over ten thousand by the time of the 1964 census.

It should be clear from these four cases that what at first seemed to be fairly clear-cut and distinctive elites at different levels, encompassing varying scopes of power, actually became somewhat confused and even difficult to distinguish when examined more closely. In Alta Verapaz, the emerging regional association was drawn primarily from the local elites or the supraregional elite. In trying to describe the composition of this group, it developed that it was difficult to distinguish whether there was a regional elite emerging here or not. It seemed evident that if such were the case, it was going to emerge from the expansion of the power base of the members of the local elite. In Escuintla, the local elite of Tiquisate in some part merges with a supraregional elite, since they have come from the outside and presumably have not given up their former interests. It is simply that they currently have a major source of support in the Tiquisate area.

To have a better comparative picture of these regions, we must put typologies aside and deal with process. Let us set up a scale with the small and minimal local elite at one end and the international elite of cartel directors and chiefs of state at the other. Along this continuum may be arrayed the entire population of power holders, each standing in some specific relation to those immediately above and immediately below. The concepts of local, regional, national, or international now become points where power holders may be placed along this continuum (Figure 3–1). Thus, if we impressionistically placed each of the specific sets of elites discussed in this chapter along such a continuum, the position of any one would be unlikely to specifically correspond to another (Figure 3–2).

The elements of Figures 3–2 through 3–4 represent different domains of power, showing how they are at one and the same time regionally distinctive and geographically concentric. In each, the domain of lesser scope pertains to or lies within the control of a more inclusive domain. The national or supraregional elites of Alta

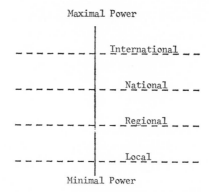

FIGURE 3–1. Continuum of Power Holders

Verapaz and Escuintla play a double role, also operating intermittently at the regional level. In the case of Escuintla, the power
of some members extends to the international level. The local elites
of Chimaltenango and Alta Verapaz (Figure 3–2) are more powerful than are those of Jutiapa and many parts of Escuintla. The Alta
Verapaz and Escuintla varieties operate in both regional and local
capacities; the Jutiapa elites are clearly differentiated at each distinctive level. In the Alta Verapaz, the apparently emergent regional elite is affected by the uncertainty at the moment whether
the new group will be formed more from local people who extend
their power more broadly or by nationally based people who pay
more attention to the Alta Verapaz base or by both.

While the shift from a typology to a scale clarifies the relative

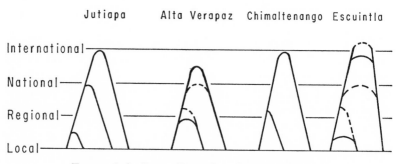

FIGURE 3–2. Power Domains of Regional Elites

positions of the elites along a power dimension, there are still some unanswered questions. In all the cases described here, we are dealing with a single, vertical series of domains. The power organization of each region is technically a *unitary* one, which is to say that all elites tend to be arranged linearly, from the more powerful to the less powerful. The question arises as to why there seems to be no major competition to the elites, and, if there were, how would they be handled within the present scheme.

The answer to the first question is that, at the time of the study, the power structure of the country as a whole was such that the possibly competing elites were completely quieted. Those that were organized were, in fact, powerless. The 1954 government had all but eliminated lower-sector interest groups. Labor unions, mass organizations, and radical opposition political parties were all either unlawful or so weakened that by 1965 they still offered no serious power threat. Succeeding governments allowed a limited political and syndicalistic renaissance, but real opposition parties were forced to work underground or to be inactive, and unions and mass organizations were allowed no political power. While this was the general situation during the Peralta regime (the main period of the present study, summer, 1965), there was an additional restrictive factor. The country was under a "state of siege," with specific rulings that there should be no meetings or political activity of any kind, and special surveillance was kept of union organizers and suspect political organizers.

The result of this was that serious competitive power activity became tactically more clandestine. The *guerrilleros* had been active in the country for at least two years by that time, and they were growing as an active opposition. The situation, as it may be illustrated by the case of the department of Izabal, is indicated in Figure 3–3. There, the local population of the region (*a*) is shown to be simultaneously under the power domains of the *guerrilleros* (*b*) and the Guatemalan government (*c*). The last of these is, at the same time, under the domain of the United States (*d*). The *guerrilleros*, in turn, were to some degree responding to the international level through their relations with the Guatemalan Communist organization in Mexico and contacts with Cuba (*e*).

It will be evident from this that, while the four departments chosen for study were essentially structured as unitary domains,

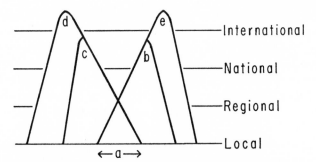

FIGURE 3–3. Power Domains in the Department of Izabal

multiple domains (and hence inherent competition) existed in Izabal. For further contrast, the situation at the time of study can be
compared with a hypothetical case illustrating the situation during
the latter part of the revolutionary decade of 1944–1954. Figure 3–4
shows a rural farm population (*a*) simultaneously under the farm
owner (*c*) and a labor union (*b*) organized by regional organizers (*d*). Both of these were under the domain of the national government (*e*). The union (*b*), under the domain of the national level
union leaders (*d*), received special derivative power from the government and therefore was powerful enough to contest the farmer's
control, which existed mainly at the regional level.

The principal factor that differentiates the elites in each of these
areas is their area of control. It is evident that the structure of
some is changing or has recently changed. The area of control of
any given elite can in part be defined by the region that it covers
geographically. While local elites are dependent primarily on local

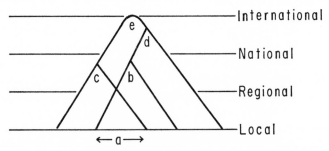

FIGURE 3–4. Power Domains in a Rural Farm Population

power bases, supraregional elites depend not only on the lands and commercial bases within the region, but also on connections and holdings elsewhere, including professions, businesses, or holdings in the national capital or outside Guatemala. They have power independent of their holdings within any specific provincial area. This is reflected in the fact that, unless resident locally, they usually stay out of regional social life, club memberships, and the like. Although such regional associations give a local basis of power, it is a base rejected by the supraregional elite when it conflicts with interests and obligations at the national level. The supraregional elite is likely to participate in the Guatemalan Club in Guatemala City, or even in the American Club. They may be members of the Aero Club, the Club de Caza, Tiro, y Pesca, or one of a number of associations formed around semisocial activities. Their participation in these and other national elite associations varies, of course, with their success at the national level.

This, then, leaves the question of what may be the basis of power of a regional elite. From Figure 3–2, it is evident that there was only one clear-cut regional elite population of the four departments studied, and that was in Jutiapa. Elsewhere, elites that were beginning to behave in regional capacities clearly were composed of individuals who were moving out from the national center or up from the local level. The most telling case is perhaps that of the coffee growers of the Alta Verapaz. These *finqueros*, finding that they were having difficulty in marketing their coffee, finally banded together in order to better their competitive position in the general market. In so doing, they were combining their local power base as coffee producers through organization. The purpose of this organization, however, was to obtain some control at the national level. Their formation into a regional elite organization was then based not on merely a local power base or a national power base, but on both. The regional quality derived from the fact that, collectively, they controlled significant resources of a particular region. They did not become significant, however, until they formed themselves into a group to attempt confrontation at the national level.

A true regional elite is one that controls the resources of a region such that they affect the conditions of life of the remaining regional population. In the contemporary nationalizing and centralizing context of Guatemala, this kind of regional control occurs only when combined with derivative power from the national level. Regional control, without the support from above, could stand in the nineteenth century, when the major competitors were other members of a community of regional controllers. Today, however, unless there is a specific antigovernment force at work, a region can be controlled only with the tacit or manifest consent of the central government.

Although the material at hand does not permit us to formulate the issue clearly, there seems to be an inverse relation among local- and regional-level elites within any set of domains. If there is a strong regional elite, it becomes strong at the expense of the local elite. Since power is finite at any given time—there is only a limited amount that can be controlled—the extension of power from the regional level can, in a sense, draw off the power that was held locally. It can, for example, be assumed that if a regional elite emerged in the Alta Verapaz, it would be at the expense of, among others, the cacique of a town like San Juan Chamelco. Similarly, the access and penetration by agents from the national center generally tend to weaken the local elite, although under some circumstances, local people can tactically utilize the outsiders to their own advantage. It is specifically the older, native regional elite that tends to lose to the new outsiders, since the interests of the former conflict, but the local people do not have the advantage of the derived power available to the outsiders. In general, a national elite, newly arrived on the scene, will come into conflict with the regional and local elite in the specific locales where they have interests, but not throughout an area. There is no question but that the earlier local and possibly regional elite of Escuintla has been all but submerged by the influx of both rural- and urban-dwelling entrepreneurs, just as the countryside has been changed markedly by the appearance of thousands of new laborers and farmers.

The economic development of a region or locality may strengthen any of the elite levels. Most sure to benefit are members of the national elite, as it is usually they who have most ready access to external capital and new knowledge. Second, the regional elite, drawing as it does on the wider resources of the department, channeling products and political controls, tends to have the next call on the new power access. Given the controls available to and exercised by the government on the one hand and by the local and regional elites on the other, widespread development in the provincial areas seems to be under effective restrictions.

"As long as environmental changes affecting power relations in Jutiapa and on the national level are gradual, a small amount of 'progress without change' may be anticipated. There is no reason to expect that the development process and assimilation into a national power structure will lead to a basic reorganization of the regional power structure with its current inequalities in the distribution of power. Rather, those now in control of regional subsystems are well situated to profit from progress, and economic development can only enhance the positions of control held by the regional power elite in Jutiapa."[29] This statement by Durston concerning Jutiapa certainly holds for many other areas of the country—most of the Indian western highlands, most of the *oriente*, and the Verapaces. It could be mildly different in areas of really rapid developmental change, because into those areas migrate not only the poor in search of work, but also the entrepreneurs and wealthy. Escuintla and the southwest coast, and Izabal and the immediately neighboring areas, have seen a great influx of people. In cities like Escuintla, new regional and supraregional elites are emerging. Unlike that of the more traditional areas, these two elites are of national origin; that is, their places of origin are elsewhere in the country, not infrequently the national capital. Their direct knowledge of, and controls over, the local population do not stem from the *patrón-mozo* relationship, nor from the traditional dependence of the subsistence farmer on the local townsman for credit, but from the more purely contractual relation of temporary laborer and temporary employer. The extreme cases of this are evident in the relations that have emerged in the cotton business (see Chapter 7). The entrepreneur does not want a regular labor force of any size. He wants only a temporary force for which he has no special responsibility. The new owners of land parcelled out by the government are often upper-sector individuals who are not seeking subsistence or a farming life, but a source of wealth.

[29] Durston, "Power Structure," p. 149.

The local elite members may, if tactically acute, take advantage of the new sources of power and may even hoist themselves to the regional level of operation. There is one nationally known entrepreneur who started as a local butcher and now is one of the most economically successful individuals in the entire country. In the cases described here, it is clearly the supraregional elite that has benefited principally from the Chimaltenango and Escuintla developments, but, at the same time, a new regional elite may be making its appearance in Escuintla. In Alta Verapaz, a nascent organized group that may work at either the regional or supraregional level (or both) reflects the adjustment of the elite system to external economic realities.

The laborer in Escuintla and Chimaltenango does not seem to be any better off by virtue of this variety of development than he is in Jutiapa. Indeed, labor in a migratory status often suffers in ways that are much more acute than that experienced by local resident labor. There is clearly an expansion of the upper-sector, however. Not only are the residual upper-sector members benefiting, but there is a physical expansion in the number of people who are enjoying the benefits. The local and regional elite has been enlarged, restructured, and is materially more successful. Development in the provinces is, then, beneficial for those who are in the position to make the best of it. But rapid development finds some areas without a local and regional elite ready to do this, so that additional people "in the position to make the best of it" import themselves. Frequently, their better access to credit, influence, and power permits them to do much better than the locals, and the locals find themselves relegated to and restricted to a limited number of income sources. The community of Poptún in El Petén illustrates this. The older inhabitants, of whom there are very few, find themselves not as ready to take advantage of the influx of new people and new sources of funds as are some of the newcomers themselves.

In Guatemala, provincial and regional development is marked by migration. Population movement out of an area, whether permanent or seasonal, is usually the index of slow growth if any. Such changes in population affect the power structure, but not radically. The kinds of networks described for Jutiapa extend themselves; the kinds of new elites described for Escuintla appear. But networks are still closely tied to governmental control devices, and the new elites occupy essentially the same place in the total structure as did the old. What is lost is "regionalism," the flavor or differentiation because of different places of origin. The culture changes, but the structure remains essentially the same.

4 | The Development of the Military

It is unfortunate that there is implanted in the Western scholarly and political communities the idea that Latin American nations have been intermittently under military governments since the time of independence. It is unfortunate because, first, it is of dubious truth, and, second, it has obscured the fact that the military has in fact grown in strength over most of the area in recent years. An examination of the comparative power structure of Guatemala since the Ubico period makes it quite clear that just because there was a dictatorship during the 1930's did not mean that it was a military government. Furthermore, the military since that period has had its own very significant history, the structure of which particularly involves the United States, and has allowed it to emerge in a new role within the country.

Three processes are currently evident in the activities of the military: professionalization, incorporation, and an assumption of regnancy. In a study of this scope it is impossible to explore the historical roots of these processes, but the current performance can be seen in the light of concomitant structural changes. The underlying trend is an increasing assumption of power and exercise of controls for various purposes, a trend in which the efforts of the military

Note: This chapter is based on materials collected by Jerrold Buttrey.

parallel those of the nation itself. Each of the three processes chosen for discussion here reflects an aspect of this increasing control.

1. *Professionalization*

The military was first seriously nationalized under García Granados and Justo Rufino Barrios in the nineteenth century. In addition to the initiation of the Escuela Politécnica in 1873, a reform of the armed forces was started. Earlier in the century it was not impossible for officers of garrisons to ignore orders from the central government with impunity. Zamora Castellanos cites two cases where commandants who were to be replaced simply took over the garrisons and refused to leave.[1] One, Rafael Ariza y Torres, gave himself a colonelcy and declared himself *comandante general de las armas*, and the government finally recognized both! The Escuela Politécnica was originally set up and run by Spanish officers and by the turn of the century had developed a strong esprit de corps. Presumably, some were finding it possible to have a career in the military service.

The identification of the military with the nation and the creation of a career for officers have produced an increasingly professional officer. A professional, in this sense, refers to the identification of one's primary interest in his own occupation. It means devoting most of one's efforts and attention to the chosen line of work and a motivation to maintain or improve his status among his professional colleagues. There is no question that being an officer in the Guatemalan army or air force may constitute a career; and it is equally clear that it is increasingly being seen as a profession. The concept of "professional" in this sense should not be confused with nonpolitical. The tendency of some contemporary writers on the military in Latin America to equate professionalism with non-political concern is misleading in Guatemala. As can readily be seen if we were to follow this line of thought, the most "professional" army in recent years would have been that of Ubico. The position taken here is that men of any profession may also be political; their political action may or may not interfere with, obstruct, or enhance their professional work.

The major obstacle to professional identification in the Guate-

---

[1] P. Zamora Castellanos, *El grito de independencia*, cited in Jean Henry, "The Guatemalan Military, 1820–Present," MS, 1965 (in author's possession).

malan military is not politics, but the fact that the economic organization of the armed forces makes it difficult, if not impossible, for an officer to be entirely professional. While emphasis is placed on advanced training, the salary system makes it almost impossible for an officer to be satisfied with the income he receives and forces the more ambitious individuals to spend a great deal of time in trying to gain a better position. The new second lieutenant receives a base pay of some seventy-five dollars a month, with a fifty-dollar mess allowance, twenty-five dollars for a wife, and five dollars for each child. Each increase in rank brings a twenty-five–dollar per month increase in salary, and regular promotions are scaled to occur about once every three years. No one in the army holds that these salaries are sufficient. It is expected that an officer will seek additional income. The question then becomes one of how it will be obtained and what effect this will have on the professional role of the officer.

An officer may obtain extra income by two principal methods. One is to obtain within the government a military position that has a *sobresueldo*, an additional stipend that accompanies certain posts. Most major positions have such salary additives, and they vary from one post to another. The fact that the major official fund sources are attached to the limited number of such positions means that a high value is placed on obtaining them. This is the specific economic mechanism that promotes power seeking within the army. Merely to survive on the official income, one must strive to obtain and keep the higher-paying posts.[2]

The other source of income is private enterprise outside the army. Officers are allowed to initiate and carry on almost any kind of private venture they wish, with certain exceptions. They are not allowed to own liquor factories or to run cabarets. As is the case generally in the cultural traditions of the Guatemalan upper sector, however, the ownership of land is given a particularly high priority.

---

[2] There are reports of using military positions to enhance one's private income. Most-favored jobs within the armed forces include those related to the handling of supplies and running the commissaries. There is no reason to imagine that the Guatemalan officers are any less subject to temptation than those in other armed forces in this regard. The present study did not concern itself with this subject, however, and, in the present context, it can only be assumed that the level of dishonesty within the military is no different from that in the population at large.

Officers who can obtain fincas through one means or another will almost inevitably do so. One of the complaints of *campesinos* in the colonization areas has been the surprisingly high number of officers who have been granted land.[3] There are fairly well-known cases, such as that of the former national finca of Santo Tomás in Escuintla, which was repartitioned among some sixteen officers, including some of the leading colonels, with each receiving sixty-four manzanas or more of land. A very few officers work the land themselves, usually with the help of laborers; most simply collect rent.

The problem of income for officers is a serious one. Training in the Escuela Politécnica, together with upper-sector aspirations and tastes, gives the young officer graduate a view into the prerequisites of good living but almost no means of access to them. The two channels available to him have inevitable consequences. If he opts for seeking positions with *sobresueldos*, he must inevitably become involved in political action, usually both within and outside the military service. If he opts for private ventures, he must obtain capital, and the most readily available sources are those that are open to him by virtue of his military position. Of course, the higher the position, the easier it is to obtain capital, and vice versa. Both avenues (and they are often used together rather than separately) may lead to conflicts with professionalism. The individual seeking politically powerful positions must inevitably compromise his professional attitudes, and the individual engaging in private enterprise obviously will have demands on his time and privileges that conflict with military responsibilities.

Although low salaries pose serious problems to professional development, there are contrastive factors that are building a more professional situation within the army. The most important of these is the postgraduate training that the officer is expected to undergo. Although it was not possible to obtain data on the amount of additional military training that officers have had available to them, Table 4–1 shows that following the 1944 revolution, there was a severe deemphasis on the officer graduate taking additional work

[3] The newspaper, *El Imparcial*, of November 24, 1960, reported that President Ydígoras announced that two national fincas would be divided among deserving members of the military. It seems likely that "deserving" in this context refers to the role the officers played in the November 13 attempted military coup against the Ydígoras government.

outside the military service. While it was previously customary for a small proportion of the officers to seek such additional education, the post-1944 military establishment discouraged an officer from seeking additional extramilitary education and provided neither effective opportunity nor any regular program for him to attend one of the nation's universities. Emphasis was placed, instead, on additional professional training. It is fairly obvious to the younger officer that training, especially in foreign countries and currently in the United States, provides the individual with both skills and contacts that are to his benefit, as well as contributing positively toward his possibilities for advancement. This training, which dates back well into the prerevolutionary era, has increasingly become one of the features that distinguish the new younger officers from the older, separating them in experience and sympathies.

In recent years, the most important army elite training has been that related to ranger and counterinsurgency work. The appearance of *guerrilleros* has provided the Guatemalan army with a real enemy for possibly the first time since Justo Rufino Barrios led Guatemalan forces to El Salvador in the name of Central American union. The traditional military training, however, is obviously entirely inept for this kind of war, and the protracted war in Vietnam has made some Central Americans aware of the potentials of guerrilla warfare.[4] With the initiation of the guerrilla activity following the failure of the November 13 revolt in 1960, the importance of counterinsurgency training became increasingly evident.

The training in counterinsurgency has been provided by the United States. Fearing a Latin American insurgency movement comparable to that of Vietnam, the military establishment a few years before had initiated a program of training Latin American officers in methods of warfare appropriate to guerrilla activity. Among their students were some young Guatemalan officers who were involved in the November 13 movement. With the failure of this coup, a few of these fled to the interior and began what was to

---

[4] The writer recalls a discussion he had with a member of Panama's oligarchy in the Union Club in Panama City in 1953. His host explained a fairly involved but well-thought-out exposition of how the various "forces" or "interests" in Panama could and, according to the speaker, would undertake a guerrilla war to eliminate the oligarchy and eventually U.S. control in the country. Vietnam's struggle against the French was the explicit case in point at that time.

erupt a few years later as a full-scale guerrilla operation. In a very real way, the guerrilla activity in Guatemala, while ideologically aided by Fidel Castro's success, has been directly helped technically by the United States. In its enthusiasm for developing counterinsurgency skills in the Latin American armies, the United States provided the basic training of the leaders of the first years of the movement. These leaders, in turn, were at that time reacting in part to U.S. dominance in Guatemalan affairs, especially the activities of the U.S. military and those related to the training of anti-Castro, Bay of Pigs forces in the Finca Helvetia on the Pacific Coast. While there may be dissension within the army itself over the role of *guerrilleros* in the country, the presence of an active enemy and the opportunity for counterinsurgency training seem to have been playing a relatively positive role in the increasing professionalism of the service.

A final consideration is the relatively minor role played by family in the overall military establishment. In estimating the relative importance of criteria in selecting individuals as colleagues within the service, one observer felt that both political considerations and individual ability came before family. While there are sets of siblings and obvious cases of relationships among officers, there seem to be no "old military" families in Guatemala. Furthermore, while the sons of some officers do follow their fathers' careers (admission to the Escuela Politécnica encourages this by providing preference for such candidates), informants generally agreed that the much more common pattern was for the children of officers to go to the university.

Familialism in Guatemala could work both for and against professionalization. On the one hand, it could enhance professionalization if various generations consistently went into the service, thereby passing down through the home the traditions of the service. But in many Latin American situations, obligations that attach themselves to familial relationships frequently come into direct conflict with professional duties and requirements. The apparent lack of traditional military families in Guatemala is probably indicative of greater professionalization, rather than the reverse. However, relative absence of the influence of family relationships is not necessarily due to any conscious effort to achieve a more professional service. It may be that the low salaries paid most officers discourage young men, and the sheer antagonism that is manifest among young people in the secondary schools about cadets and militarism probably is enough to discourage the sons of some officers from pursuing their fathers' career. If the father has been especially successful, the child probably has enough advantages so that the special privileges of the service mean relatively little. He can find better advantages outside. If the father has been unsuccessful, the life experienced by the son probably affords little that is sufficiently attractive to recommend itself. Whatever the reasons may be, the attrition among students entering the Politécnica is extraordinarily high and suggests that a serious career is not yet as fully attractive as it might be.

2. *Incorporation*

The officers' corps of the Guatemalan military has developed into a corporate group. The establishment of the Escuela Politécnica in 1873 laid a necessary base for this, but it was not until the post-1944 revolutionary period that the protective devices and perquisites became so evident that there were positive advantages to staying in the military. To say that the military protects its own does not mean that there are no factions, that officers will not oppose or even, under some circumstances, kill one of their own. The comparison may be made with any other profession in Guatemala. To be a physician or dentist does not obligate the individual to give special allowance for his fellow professionals. Professional associations exist for various purposes, but there is no effort to live in a society of physicians or dentists. In contrast, the corporate quality of the military establishment is such that it encourages its members to seek their rewards almost entirely from within the establishment.

One of the most important characteristics of the military is that, except in extraordinary circumstances, the military is most reluctant to ostracize or seriously punish one of its members for misconduct. An outstanding example of this is the retribution allotted to the perpetrators of the November 13 movement. While many officers were involved in this, almost none were punished. The most common way to get rid of an officer is to retire him or to send him off on a diplomatic mission, usually as military attaché in a foreign embassy. Retirement, however, is heavier punishment than assignment abroad, because it removes the individual from some of the privileges available to those on active duty.

The circumstances under which an officer may be more severely punished most commonly stem from outside the military. A major example here is what happened to Arbenz and the few officers most closely associated with the excesses of the Arbenz regime—Rosenberg, Cruz Wer, Alfonso Martínez, and Weyman Guzmán. All of these officers fled the country when Arbenz went into exile. They did so, however, less because their fellow officers were against them than because they had achieved a public notoriety such that they might have been subject to severe treatment at the hands of the new government in the months immediately following the fall of their government. Individuals are also punished when they have become the object of concern of a particular chief of state. Under Ydígoras, for example, imprisonment and even torture were inflicted on an officer whom Ydígoras particularly disliked. Here again, however, it was not the military establishment that was involved, but rather the police who were used against individual members of the military.

In recent years, the military has taken steps to provide means of support for its retired officers beyond what individuals may derive from their own private business or farming ventures. Among the training courses available to officers are some in public administration. It was argued by one informant that these were felt to be especially important, since officers, upon retiring, could then take up positions as departmental governors or in the various ministries of state. This both provided for the individual's future and helped to supply the nation with trained public administrators.

Perhaps the most important innovations in recent years to contribute to the corporate quality of the military officers' establishment have been the increased perquisites made available to the officers and the requirement of Escuela Politécnica training. The Military Commissary was established after the 1944 revolution so that officers could buy, at reduced prices, food, appliances, and other items generally available at department stores. This was of particular importance for such items as imported liquors, which could be sold tax free. The commissary not only provided the officers themselves with needed items at reduced prices, but it was also used by some to obtain goods for resale, thus providing the individuals concerned with extra income.

The military hospital provided free service for active-duty officers and their entire families, including parents. In a society where responsibility for one's family extends both upward and downward, this extended family care is an important service. In recent years, the army has purchased finca land in and around Guatemala City and has undertaken the expense of subdividing it into housing lots. These have been made available to the officers at a cost proportional to the original purchase price and at low rates of interest, thereby reducing materially the investment necessary by the individual officer. Here again, the opportunity presents itself for the officer to rent out the lot or house, thereby turning the matter to direct financial advantage. Finally, the Fondo de Previsión Militar acts as a credit union for the military, a credit facility still relatively unavailable to other segments of the population.

Unquestionably one of the central mechanisms conducive to the corporate quality of the army has been the Escuela Politécnica. Since the school picks up youths shortly after they have finished primary school, they are still highly impressionable. Free matriculation at the Politécnica involves a commitment to remain in the service for six years thereafter. This means that the day-to-day associations of the individual are severely restricted to his colleagues in the service from the middle teens to the middle twenties, the entire early adult life. This period, during which the individual in Guatemala generally becomes politicized, is spent in a restricted military society. From the point of view of creating a cohesive corps, this could hardly be bettered.

As may be expected, however, an inevitable characteristic of large corporate organizations is internal factionalism. Within the military, the major rewards of power and income are limited and consequently a significant amount of competition occurs. Furthermore, although the organization may be corporate, it is completely Guatemalan, and its members of necessity are concerned with the state of the national society as well as their own microcosm. The social cleavages in the military organization are of two types: those distinguishing officers from enlisted men and those defining factions or differentiations within the officer corps. The present study unfortunately touched only in passing on the situation of the enlisted man and the noncommissioned officer in the army. It is a subject that needs real study, and certainly an adequate understanding of the full role of the army in the country at large will not be had until such a study is made.[5] An indication of the gulf that separates the officers from their enlisted troops may be had by figures made available on the language and literacy situation. One report states that "of the total of individuals who enter the service [permanent force and military reserves], 62.50 percent is illiterate and 57.13 percent belongs to the Indian race, and of these, 13.71 percent speak no Spanish when entering and only 30.63 percent have Spanish as their maternal tongue."[6] The quality of the differentiation between an officers' corps, all the members of which have at least secondary school education, and an enlisted population, in which less than a third even have Spanish as a native language, is patent.

It has always been the practice, and continues so today, to recruit, or conscript, enlisted men from the ranks of the Indian and rural Ladino population. To be liable for conscription is a good index to one's lack of power to avoid it. The Ladino town dwellers of the western Indian region are generally not subject to recruitment, although the poorer ones may be enlisted in the local reserve units and be subject to training on a weekly basis. The distinction between officers and enlisted men, being a thoroughgoing caste line, is more than just similar to the national scene; it is a caricature of it. One officer distinguished Indian from *oriente* Ladino conscripts by indicating a preference for the former. Once you broke his customs, he explained, the Indian was much easier to change and discipline than was the Ladino.

That the Indians receive somewhat different treatment was also

---

[5] While cooperation was offered to the study by a number of elements of the officers' corps, a more common reaction to inquiries or requests for permission to obtain information was one of distrust. It was not possible in the time available to obtain contemporary data on the enlisted forces or on details of the sociological background of the members of the officer's corps. It is perhaps an indication of the very corporate quality here under discussion that a perceived threat to any part of the military establishment is seen as a threat to the entire organization.

[6] El Servicio de Analfabetización del Ejército, "La alfabetización en el Ejército: Estudio sobre la contribución del Ejército en la lucha contra el analfabetismo en Guatemala"; author's translation.

illustrated by one of our informants. He held that there was some sort of difference between the military who worked in the eastern and western parts of the country. In trying to clarify what this difference might be, another informant explained that officers who, upon leaving the Escuela Politécnica, were sent to the western region for their first tour of duty, dealt entirely with Indian soldiers. The pattern of treatment of the Indian soldiers was rather harsh; many understood little Spanish when they were conscripted, and they tended to accept some degree of humiliation without reacting. Young officers who, in a sense, learned how to treat soldiers in the Indian areas would, upon occasion, be transferred to the *oriente*. There, the patterns of behavior learned in the west not only did not work, but actually caused violent reactions. The *oriente* Ladinos, regarding themselves as individualistic as the young officers, refused to carry out orders under humiliating terms and, in a few instances, physically attacked the officers.

While no study has been made, nor does it appear likely that an objective one may be made in the near future, there is little evidence that what may be described for the officers also holds true for the Indians. The degree of professionalization among noncommissioned personnel is so slight that the turnover of enlisted men every two years is almost 50 percent. There are few benefits that make it attractive for them to identify strongly with the institution. The area in which they may be said to gain something is in language, literacy, and a mild degree of politicization. The army has, with some consistency, supported a program of literacy for its recruits, as well as produced materials for civilian programs. Similarly, the participation in the anti-*guerrillero* campaigns must have some side effects upon those soldiers who are curious as to what they are doing. Finally, conscripted monolingual Indians are taught Spanish during their two-year period. Taken together, these, and possibly other less-evident features, serve to ladinize. Since most recruits are either kept in the region in which they are recruited or sent to Guatemala City, they generally have little opportunity to become familiar with the country at large. Taken as a whole, there are few areas of Guatemalan life that are less known than the life of the enlisted man. What the army does to him and what he contributes to the army have never been systematically studied.

Aside from the officer-enlisted man differentiation, the major factional lines within the military have formed around the following differences: army–air force, line officer-Politécnica graduate, young-old, liberal-conservative, and vertical divisions or loyalty, coupled with specific ties of common graduating class and the *centenario* relation.

The army–air force split is unquestionably the most recent of these. Originally the flyers were army officers with flight training. After the Second World War, however, when the air force received some planes and clearly had its own barracks and bases, the differentiation between the two became increasingly evident. Among the gifts showered on Guatemala by the United States after the fall of Arbenz were some World War II Mustang fighters. The final turning point can probably be dated from the Thirteenth of November movement. Ydígoras, in order to keep the air force loyal at that time, promised new equipment, distinctive blue uniforms, better flight pay, and license to earn money on the side by flying. Since that time the split between the army and the air force has widened appreciably. The position of unique power held formerly by the army has been sharply disturbed by this division, and Guatemala has now entered the ranks of those countries in which different branches of the armed forces may take different sides in the national political scene.

The distinction between the line officer and the Escuela Politécnica graduate is one of the oldest of the cleavages, but one that is gradually becoming less important. The most famous relation in which it played a role in recent history was the fact that Arana was a line officer and Arbenz was a Politécnica graduate. The general history of this affair is fairly well known, and the details are not relevant to the present analysis. It was a case, however, in which the distinction contributed directly to the entire national political process. The castelike distance that separates officers from men was described earlier. In past years, there were many line officers who never went to the Escuela Politécnica. Of these, some were named out of the ranks, and during the nineteenth and early part of this century, there were cases of individuals of humble origin who reached positions of extraordinary power. The most famous of these in recent years was Ubico's secretary of war, General José Reyes.

Table 4–1
Military School (Politécnica) Entering Classes and Graduates

Year (Promotion)	Entering Students			Graduates			Colonel in 1964					Taken Additional Degree	
	Total	New	Line	Total	New	Line	Total	New		Line		No.	%
								No.	%	No.	%		
1920 (1 & 2)	31	31	0	22	22	0	16	16	72.7	0	0	2	9.0
1921 (3 & 4)	32	32	0	21	21	0	14	14	66.6	0	0	2	9.5
1922 (5 & 6)	43	43	0	31	31	0	22	22	70.9	0	0	1	3.2
1923 (7 & 8)	19	19	0	10	10	0	6	6	60.0	0	0	0	—
1924 (9 & 10)	36	36	0	18	18	0	15	15	83.3	0	0	0	—
1925 (11 & 12)	23	23	0	14	14	0	8	8	57.1	0	0	2	14.2
1926 (13 & 14)	22	22	0	6	6	0	3	3	50.0	0	0	2	33.3
1927 (15 & 16)	62	62	0	21	21	0	16	16	76.1	0	0	1	4.7
1928 (17 & 18)	27	27	0	18	18	0	10	10	55.5	0	0	1	5.5
1929 (19 & 20)	36	36	0	13	13	0	7	7	53.8	0	0	1	7.6
1930 (21)	33	33	0	17	17	0	16	16	94.1	0	0	1	5.8
1930 (22)	32	32	0	18	18	0	15	15	83.3	0	0	1	5.5
1931 (23 & 24)	81	81	0	48	48	0	38	38	79.1	0	0	4	8.3
1932 (25 & 26)	34	34	0	28	28	0	21	21	75.0	0	0	4	14.2
1933 (27 & 28)	38	38	0	23	23	0	20	20	86.9	0	0	0	—

(Table 4–1, continued)

Year (romotion)	Entering Students			Graduates			Colonel in 1964					Taken Additional Degrees	
	Total	New	Line	Total	New	Line	Total	New		Line		No.	%
								No.	%	No.	%		
1934 (29)	33	33	0	19	19	0	11	11	57.8	0	0	1	5.2
1935 (30 & 31)	40	40	0	24	24	0	15	15	62.5	0	0	4	16.6
1936 (32 & 33)	39	39	0	21	21	0	17	17	80.9	0	0	1	4.7
1937 (34 & 35)	24	24	0	17	17	0	7	7	41.1	0	0	2	11.7
1938 (36 & 37)	26	26	0	20	20	0	15	15	75.0	0	0	1	5.0
1939 (38 & 39)	53	53	0	43	43	0	27	27	62.2	0	0	9	20.9
1940 (40 & 41)	28	28	0	21	21	0	10	10	47.6	0	0	1	4.7
1941 (42)	8	8	0	8	8	0	6	6	75.0	0	0	1	12.5
1942 (43)	41	41	0	28	28	0	5	5	17.8	0	0	8	32.1
1943 (44)	29	29	0	25	25	0	10	10	40.0	0	0	7	28.0
1944 (45)	36	36	0	24	24	0	11	11	45.8	0	0	3	12.5
1945 (46)	35	21	14	27	13	14	18	6	40.0	12	85.7	1	3.7
1946 (47)	63	50	13	43	31	12	31	19	61.3	12	100	2	4.6
1947 (48)	76	48	28	49	26	23	17	0	0	17	74.0	2	4.0
1948 (49)	59	35	24	32	10	21	16	0	0	16	76.2	0	0

(Table 4–1, continued)

Year (Promotion)	Entering Students			Graduates			Colonel in 1964					Taken Additional Degree	
	Total	New	Line	Total	New	Line	Total	New		Line		No.	%
								No.	%	No.	%		
1949 (50)	50	31	19	24	7	17	16	0	0	16	94.0	0	0
1950 (51)	42	32	10	16	8	8	6	0	0	6	75.0	0	0
1951 (52)	56	36	20	31	12	19	18	0	0	18	99.7	0	0
1952 (53)	54	38	16	29	17	12	10	0	0	10	83.2	0	0
1953 (54)	65	57	8	14	8	6	6	0	0	6	100	0	0
1954 (55)	44	40	4	12	9	3	3	0	0	3	100	0	0
1955 (56)	47	47	0	22	22	0	0	0	0	0	0	0	0
1956 (57)	60	35	25	41	23	18	15	0	0	15	83.3	0	0
1956 (58)	11	11	0	5	5	0	0	0	0	0	0	0	0
1957 (59)	45	45	0	19	19	0	0	0	0	0	0	0	0
1958 (60)	87	87	0	45	45	0	0	0	0	0	0	0	0
1959 (61 & 62)	68	68	0	32	32	0	0	0	0	0	0	0	0
1960 (63 & 64)	33	33	0	9	9	0	0	0	0	0	0	0	0
1961 (65)	14	14	0	8	8	0	0	0	0	0	0	0	0
1961 (66)	14	14	0	—	—	—	0	0	0	0	0	0	0

(Table 4-1, continued)

Year (Promotion)	Entering Students			Graduates			Colonel in 1964					Taken Additional Degrees	
	Total	New	Line	Total	New	Line	Total	New		Line		No.	%
								No.	%	No.	%		
1962 (67)	33	33	0	—	—	—	0	0	0	0	0	0	0
1962 (68)	22	22	0	—	—	—	0	0	0	0	0	0	0
1963 (69 & 70)	69	69	0	—	—	—	0	0	0	0	0	0	0

SOURCE: Data from Francisco A. Samayoa, *La Escuela Politécnica a través de su historia,* Vol. , Guatemala, 1964. This table was prepared by Jerrold Buttrey.

Today it would be almost impossible for a person to reach such a position in the service without a Politécnica background.

One of the devices used to strengthen the officer corps following the 1944 revolution was to pressure line officers to go to the Escuela Politécnica and take a degree. Table 4–1 shows the beginning of matriculation of such line-officer students in 1945. A number of interesting features should be noted here. In the first place, if one compares the attrition of the line officers in the 1945–1954 decade with that of the newly matriculating students, it is clear that the line officers were committed to the military profession to a much greater degree than were new candidates. It will also be noted, however, that all of the colonelships given after the 1944 revolution were to line officers; none were given (as of the cutoff date of these data, 1963) to any newly matriculating candidates who entered the Politécnica after 1944. While the government tended to follow the policy of naming no more line officers directly from civilian life after the 1944 revolution (except special instances, such as medical officers), it seems to be the case that the officers who had been in the service prior to 1944 were able to obtain the army's highest rank by 1965. Whether matriculation at the Politécnica was an effective prerequisite to this rank is not clear, but the data in Table 4–1 indicate that 73 percent of the line officers who did matriculate achieved the rank of colonel.[7] The line officers who attended the Politécnica did not necessarily regard it as a privilege, nor did it make them feel closer to the society of regular Politécnica graduates. Many of them refused to wear the special insignia allowed only to graduates of the school.

The features that characterized the line officer–Politécnica distinction are, today, increasingly characterizing the distinction between older and younger officers. "Young" here refers primarily to the post-1944 graduates. With the advent of the revolution and the role played by the Escuela Politécnica in it, greater emphasis has been placed on equipping the officer candidate for participation in national political life. The process of politicization is specifically relevant in the younger officers. Under Ubico, officers were supposed to be strictly military men and answerable to the military. Ubico allowed no politicking among his officers. Older officers today criticize their younger colleagues for being too concerned with a comfortable life and perquisites than with the real responsibilities of military service. Younger officers, however, have tended to participate more in the foreign training, especially in the counterinsurgency. The older accuse the younger of being "leftists" or "Communists," whereas the younger regard the older as conservative and old-fashioned. In 1950, Monteforte Toledo submitted a questionnaire to thirty students of the Escuela Politécnica and thirty graduates aged twenty-nine and thirty.[8] While there is no evidence that the selection of persons interviewed was in any sense random, the reported differences do not seem to show a consistent conservative bias by the older officers. For example, responses that could be interpreted as showing a conservative bias for the graduates are shown in Table 4–2.

On the other hand, there were a number of questions which could have shown such conservatism but did not do so, as shown in Table 4–3.

Although technically defective and out of date, these data are re-

---

[7] With the downfall of Ubico and the institution of the revolutionary regime, all ranks above that of colonel in the Guatemalan army were abolished. Colonels have, then, achieved the highest rank the army has to offer.

[8] Mario Monteforte Toledo, *Guatemala: Monografía Sociología*, pp. 364–369.

TABLE 4–2
Conservative Opinions of Politécnica Graduates

Issue		Students	Graduates
Labor unions	In favor	7	6
	Against	17	19
	Indifferent	6	4
Political parties	In favor	14	8
	Against	12	20
	Indifferent	4	2
Treat Indians as equals*	Yes	11	6
	No	16	20
Strong friendship with	In favor	1	9
the United States	Against	16	14
	Indifferent	3	7

* Apparently the question refers to how the subject thinks the Indians *ought* to be treated, but this was not clear in Monteforte's text.

produced here because they are the only actual questionnaire materials that are available on the military officer population. The Escuela Politécnica now generally refuses to allow any sociological inquiry to be carried on, and it has proved equally impossible to obtain permission of the officers in charge to allow such questions and interviews of soldiers or officers on active duty. Of greatest interest here, if these data are at all valid, is that the old-young distinction at that time did not conform to a simplistic political dichotomy. The features of the older graduates do, however, seem to conform to what one might predict if he were to relate them to the Ubico period—strong friendship with the United States, a civil government with no political parties, a somewhat directed economy with no labor unions, a general disinterest in the Church, and a strong hand with the Indians.

This brings us to the fourth of the dichotomies within the corporate officer groups, that based on political predilections. A clear division may not really exist, but there are various references to it in the literature, especially during the Arbenz regime. Schneider refers to "a new force . . . coming into control of Guatemala, an al-

TABLE 4–3
Nonconservative Opinions of Politécnica Graduates

Issue		Students	Graduates
Religion	Practicing Catholic	4	4
	Nonpracticing Catholic	20	13
	Protestant	2	1
	No religion	4	12
Political preference	With liberals	9	8
	With conservatives	3	1
	With October 1944 revolutionary movement	12	9
	None	6	12
The best government of the country would be:	Civil	13	14
	Military	17	12
	Mixed*	—	4
Socioeconomic preference	Free economy	19	16
	Directed economy	5	9
	Indifferent	6	6

* "Mixed" category not included on student questionnaire.

liance of the young 'school' officers of the army with the extremist leaders of organized labor."[9] Although Schneider reports this as established fact, there is serious doubt that any such alliance ever existed. Baker contends: "It must be stressed that Arbenz' favoritism created serious conflict within the armed forces. He had created a privileged class of junior officers who received rapid promotion, special favors, and choice of assignments."[10] This, however, merely states that there was an intentional effort to split young from old, a factionalism already noted. Moreover, Baker notes that, "the Communists [*sic*] had not launched a major organizing campaign in

[9] Ronald Schneider, *Communism in Guatemala, 1944–54*, p. 31. The question as to this alliance was brought to my attention by Jerrold Buttrey.

[10] Ross K. Baker, *A Study of Military Status and Status Deprivation in Three Latin American Armies*, p. 72.

the armed forces. (Nonetheless, they had attracted a few converts among junior officers and cadets.) Instead, they chose to infiltrate the ranks of the judicial and civil guards—the national police forces of Guatemala.[11] Although Baker refers to the younger group as if they were politically loyal to Arbenz, he mentions only two by name and fails to explain the lack of support from the alleged "group" when the army abandoned Arbenz in 1954. He does note, however, that "most officers were probably neutral or undecided."[12]

Indeed, while there were certainly officers loyal to Arbenz, that some kind of "alliance" existed was probably more a figment of anti-Arbenz or anticommunist paranoia than of systematic connivance between the two sectors. It is not clear at present that there is any real political "split" within the officer corps, although there are surely various shades of political interests and commitments. While there is little question but that the military is generally predisposed to find its interests closely allied to those of landholders and the upper sector in general, individual members are perfectly capable of learning alternative philosophies or identifying their interests with elements of the lower sector or with international interests antagonistic to that group. Since the first *guerrillero* bands were led by Politécnica graduates, there is ample evidence of this.

The internal organization of the officer corps is not easy to delineate, except by hearsay. Two features that were mentioned by many informants as being of particular importance: the bond of being in the same graduating class, or *promoción*; and the *centenario* relation. As is the case in most Western educational institutions, students entering at the same time and living through the years of training together form an especially important bond. Within the corporate life of the officer corps, the graduates of the same *promoción* continue through their professional life to recognize a special loyalty to each other and to make allowances that would not occur otherwise. An officer who finds himself in a position of particular power tends to seek at least some of his supporters from among those of the same *promoción*.

The *centenario* relation is similar, except that it exists between two individuals rather than within a group. Upon entering the

[11] Ibid., p. 43.
[12] Ibid., p. 72.

Politécnica, each new candidate is given a consecutive number. The special relationship occurs between individuals with the same last two digits in their numbers. An individual who has (picking a number at random) Number 421 will have a special responsibility for Number 521 when he enters. The elder is particularly responsible for the welfare of his younger *centenario* during his years at school and through the rest of his military career. If a person reaches power, then his *centenario* will generally be on the scene too.

The *promoción* and *centenario* relations are of importance because they obviously serve to crosscut certain faction lines that have already been described. Older men thus have special responsibility for certain younger men, and political preferences can often be laid aside through the necessity of recognizing the loyalty expected of the members of one's own *promoción*. There is a story to the effect that an evening party was held a few years ago by members of a particular *promoción*, and in attendance was Yon Sosa, the guerrilla leader. The fact that in the regular line of duty he was the official enemy of the officers present was put aside for an evening in recognition of the fact that he was also of the same *promoción*. While the story is unsubstantiated, the mere fact that it has been rumored suggests the importance generally attached to the relationship involved.

Even with the internal organization, loyalty within the service also varies with political affiliation outside. One informant specified that the politics of the individual was the prime consideration determining who would be a loyal follower. This means that loyalty and politics within the service are intrinsic parts of the politics of the national and international scene. While this has obvious consequences for the professional quality of work, it also means that the power structure of the military not only is similar to that of the upper sector as a whole, but also is an intrinsic part of it. Since major benefits are derived from appointments to posts and these are granted by individuals in power, the vertical structure of military appointments is conducive to an apparent "personalism," which is perhaps better seen as a mobility device. The officer ambitious for success in the service must seek certain kinds of positions. To do so, he must profess a politics that will enable him to be granted the desired appointment. Which politics are most indicated depends upon who happens to be in control at the moment. Politics and personal loyalties are a latticework woven against the framework of the general power structure.

The officer corps, while clearly part of the upper sector, has developed rather specific relations with certain other elements of that sector. Of particular importance are those with the landholders, the Church, the United States, and the university students. The general political position of the military is indicated by the kinds of relations that hold with certain other sectors of the population. Until the Second World War, the military and the landholders had a running feud over the allocation of labor. The army wanted to conscript men, and these men could be most readily obtained from the rural labor force. Until that time, however, labor was generally short, and the landholders were defensive about trying to protect their own laborers from military service so that they would be available for agricultural work. The landholders saw the military as a parasite. The army, for its part, complained publicly during the 1920's that the *finqueros* were hiding their laborers. This antagonistic relation was vitiated by two things. The general increase in the laboring population made the landholders, by 1950, less sensitive to the loss of labor and, in some instances, glad of it. And events in the world power structure were making nations like Guatemala the scene of cold-war conflict. Since the shortage of manpower for cannons and coffee as an issue has been replaced by the common threat of world-wide socialism, the landholders and military have banded together. One still hears complaints by landholders that the military is parasitic and by the more liberal military that the large landholders are rapacious. But of much greater importance is that politically inclined landholders have no hesitation in seeking military action and military controls in order to defend themselves against what they see to be a Communist threat.

A similar change has occurred between the military and the Church. With the installation of the liberal regime in 1871, Guatemala's official and emotional position was extreme anticlericism under the liberal political banner. This continued through the revolutionary period of 1944–1954. The same concern that brought landholders and military together, however, also brought the Church increasingly to the side of the army. Although they were given no public promotion, the Jesuits under Ubico were encouraged to start schools in Guatemala City. When the public issue became communism in the early 1950's, the military found in the Church an ally it needed for closer contact and control over the rural population. First Castillo Armas, then Ydígoras, opened the society again to active Church work. Both regarded themselves as military men of liberal persuasion and realized that such cooperation was necessary to keep socialism out.

A final and crucial ally of the military is the United States, specifically its military, diplomatic, and commercial community. The relationship has long been an active one, but it has seen some problems in recent years. Prior to the "Good Neighbor" era, the role of the United States in Guatemala was not unlike that elsewhere in Central America. The United States operated semiopenly in governmental affairs, helped keep Cabrera in power, and, by the early 1930's, the Politécnica was under the directorship of an American military officer. American marines were accused of funneling arms to the anti-Unionist party in the early 1920's.[13] During the Second World War, the U. S. military had a large contingent in Guatemala for purposes of Panama Canal defense. Since that time, including the entire revolutionary decade, there have usually been U.S. military attaché and mission officers in the country.

Beginning particularly with the U.S. role in the fall of Arbenz, there has been an increasing ambivalence on the part of the Guatemalan military toward the United States. On the one hand, there is heavy dependence on the United States for a continuing supply of arms and training. Specifically in the *guerrillero* work, the U.S. sources have been of primary importance. On the other hand, while the Guatemalan military will not publicly take a political position against the United States, this dependence is a constant source of irritation to the nationalistic pride of the Guatemalan officers.

The specific set of events that inflamed this antagonism had to do with the succession of Castillo Armas. Since the military's refusal to take to the field in defense of Arbenz played a major role in the collapse of his regime, many officers felt that they had a right to determine the succession to the presidency. However, through diplomatic moves, the United States succeeded in gaining the position for Castillo Armas. Military feeling against the Liberation

[13] *Relatos del Normalista y Soldado, Verdaderos Causas de la Caída del Poder Público del Sr. Lic. Manuel Estrada Cabrera.*

Army was particularly strong, and when Castillo demanded that they receive special recognition by leading the victory parade, the military was enraged. One result was an attack by the cadets of the Escuela Politécnica on a small contingent of Liberation Army forces billeted in the Roosevelt Hospital. The cadets were relatively successful and had to be called off with guarantees that they would not be punished. Castillo then sent some students home and others abroad on scholarships. With no students left, he closed down the Escuela Politécnica for two years. Since most of the military officers were Politécnica graduates and looked at the cadets' action as little less than heroic, they saw the United States looming behind Castillo as the real cause of what was interpreted as an insult to their alma mater.

When Ydígoras arranged that Cuban anti-Castro forces should be trained at a private finca on the south coast, the military again saw the United States as using Guatemalan soil for foreign forces without the national military's consent. This was regarded as being of dubious value to Guatemala, and whatever payoff was to be had was clearly being received solely by Ydígoras and the owner of the farm, Alejos; the Guatemalan military was not benefiting from it. This issue was a principal rationale behind the Thirteenth of November military revolt, and when that uprising failed, the government was accused of using planes flown by foreign pilots from the training camp against Guatemalan military units. It has been suggested that Ydígoras' flight to Quezaltenango during the revolt was due in part to the fact that he felt he could rely on the foreign forces at Helvetia to protect him should the revolt prove difficult to contain.[14]

The consequence of all this is that while the military depends on the United States as a source of aid, the anti-U.S. feeling is not limited to some alleged "left wing" segment of the Guatemalan military establishment. It was manifest through much of the Peralta administration, when the top positions in the Guatemalan government were manned almost entirely by military men, and they refused to accept most efforts to provide U.S. aid in economic development. It seems that it was not only the younger contingent

[14] Jerrold Buttrey, "The Guatemalan Military, 1944–1963: An Interpretive Essay."

of the military that was mainly active in this; many of the older and more conservative members were delighted to see the frustration of the U.S. officials.

This relationship also reflects the increased incorporation of the Guatemalan military. While the United States provides materials and training, the Guatemalan officers are careful not to reveal specific statistics and figures about their own condition. They feel that the integrity of their own service is threatened by the larger power and bring their corporate quality into play as protection. Even strongly conservative officers in the Guatemalan military go to considerable lengths to make it clear that the United States is not supposed to be running the Guatemalan army.

In contrast to the three relationships of the military so far described—with the landholders, the Church, and the United States—that between the military and the university students has been consistently antagonistic. Students have a long tradition of categorical opposition to the military. They fought the army in 1870 and did so against Ponce in 1944. The military has always been a principal target in the annual Huelga de Dolores, the burlesque spoof that the students (when permitted) stage annually to criticize current events. Until 1950 or 1951, an open fight between students and cadets was a regular part of this annual affair. At that time, the cadets were sent out of the city on maneuvers so that there would be no contact. The reason today for this antagonism is, if anything, greater than in the past. The interest of the military in government now makes them a greater threat than ever before to the civilian students. The corporate quality of the army, discouraging its officers from even taking university work, helps to promote the separatism. Since the students in no way comprise a corporate entity themselves, the conflict between the two is a peculiar one. It will presumably continue as long as the military manifest any continuing interest in governing.

3. *An Assumption of Regnancy*

The "assumption of regnancy" refers to what appears to be an increasing trend in the Guatemalan military for which there is no ready term in English. There is evidence from various events that the military, as a part of its increasing corporateness and continuing politicization, has been moving toward a regulating position in governmental affairs. It is, in a sense, taking over the ruling of the country.

In the first place, in recent years the elements of the military have been regularly involved in governing Guatemala one way or another. For thirty-seven years between 1900 and 1966, the Guatemalan chief of state was a military man.[15] Three of the last five took power by other than constitutional means. Second, the armed forces themselves have been used almost exclusively for purposes of internal control. Even José Rufino Barrios' attempt to recreate a united Central American union was aimed at expanding regional controls. As other observers have noted, this is characteristic of Latin America in general.[16] In Guatemala, the army has been used to supplement the policing activities of other agencies and sometimes to substitute for them.

It can be argued that the responsibility of the military for fighting external wars has, for practical purposes, atrophied. One of the structural consequences of the establishment of the United Nations and the Organization of American States, each under the domination of one or more of the major world powers, is that the possibility for small and underdeveloped nations to carry on small wars is very much reduced. When Peru and Ecuador, or Costa Rica and Nicaragua, or another set of lesser powers get close to armed conflict, the peace-making mechanisms of the large powers go to work to put a stop to it. War has increasingly become a prerogative of major powers and insurgents, and the government of Guatemala probably has lost any initiative to wage war it may have had. The obvious consequence of this is that while Guatemala has had no real outside wars since the last century, it would now find it difficult to initiate one. It does not follow from this, however, that the military has no function. It is not that wars have disappeared; merely that the right to initiate them has changed hands.

It is clear that the Guatemalan military has played an important role in ruling in the recent past and that the scope of its interest in

[15] J. M. Orellana, 1922–1927; Lazaro Chacón, 1927–1931; Jorge Ubico, 1931–1944; Federico Ponce, 1944; Jacobo Arbenz, 1950–1954; Carlos Castillo Armas, 1954–1956; Miguel Ydígoras Fuentes, 1958–1963; Peralta Azurdia, 1963–1966.

[16] John J. Johnson, *The Military and Society in Latin America*, 1964, pp. 47–48; Irving Louis Horowitz, "The Military Elite," in Seymour Martin Lipset and A. Solari, eds., *Elites in Latin America*, pp. 146–148.

this activity has expanded since 1944. The overt rationale for this has been the internal threats of armed insurgents and "communism." Two conditions, however, lie behind this increase: the technical and material aid from the U.S. military, and the gradual increase in power of the central government. During the Second World War, and years preceding the fall of Arbenz in 1954, the United States contributed relatively little to the Guatemalan military establishment. Beginning in 1956, the United States Department of Defense cites the following as the annual deliveries, chargeable to appropriations: [17]

(in millions of dollars)

1956	0.3	1960	0.2
1957	0.3	1961	0.4
1958	0.1	1962	1.3
1959	<.05	1963	2.6
		1964	1.4

In comparison with the rest of the Middle American countries, Guatemala received more than any except the Dominican Republic. These figures show that the input of U.S. aid began in 1956, but that it remained relatively low until fiscal year 1962, at which time it tripled in one year, then doubled again the next.

No matter what other factors may have been involved, it can hardly be a coincidence that the first time in recent Guatemalan history a military government has taken over the entire control of the country occurred after it had received some millions of dollars worth of equipment from the United States. "As if" history is unsatisfactory for facts, but one must certainly speculate whether the military would have been equipped to undertake so vast a job a few years earlier.[18] The other, and more profound, factor that contrib-

[17] U.S. Department of Defense, *Military Assistance Facts, 15 February 1965* (unclassified, no date or place of publication).

[18] Willard F. Barber and C. Neale Ronning report that in 1959 the United States Congress amended the Mutual Security Act to provide that "internal security requirements shall not, unless the President determines otherwise, be the basis for military assistance programs to American republics" (*Internal Security and Military Power: Counterinsurgency and Civic Action in Latin America*, p. 45). In a State Department Bulletin of March 11, 1963, Assistant Secretary of State Martin stated that the improvement of Latin American national internal security was one of the ways that the United States was taking

uted to the movement toward military regnancy has been the gradual increase in power and controls of the central government through the continuing nationalization of the country as a whole. In the early days of the republic, the military could not have played such a role because it was not sufficiently cohesive. At the end of the nineteenth century it still could not have done so because the country was essentially regionally separated, and sheer military force could not have assured continuing government over such a long period of time. By 1960, fifteen years of politicization had followed the revolution. *Finqueros* no longer expected to treat their farms as isolated domains. For the most part, they wanted better communication and transportation facilities, not worse, and, by so doing, signaled the emergence of Guatemala from the era when a region could even consider political succession. The kind of power exercised by Ubico relied on a scattered population, lack of communication, and lack of knowledge of political activities. When the Peralta government took over in 1963, a larger segment of the population had tasted political power, the population was increasingly concentrated in Guatemala City, and the country had shrunk under extending telegraph, telephone, radio, and road systems. With this shrinkage, the government had grown so that it was actually exercising much more control than had been the case under Ubico, although the manner of that control was not so subject to the whims and tastes of a single individual.

This expansion of the power of the central government cannot be explained here except in most general terms. Similarly, its style of expression, at once a matter of Guatemalan culture history and response to outside pressures, is a complexly interwoven product that requires an inquiry far beyond the scope of the present one. Given the expansion, however, it became possible for whoever took control

---

to combat the spread of Communist subversion in the hemisphere. A year later, it was expressed as a matter-of-fact doctrine in the State Department memorandum entitled *Points in Explanation of U.S. Military Assistance Program for Latin America*: ". . . this administration is seeking to orient the military assistance program in Latin America away from the outmoded concept of hemispheric defense toward greater emphasis on meeting the internal subversive threat." Two years before, in its joint resolution of October 3, 1962, Congress had already called for immediate steps "by whatever means may be necessary, including the use of arms" to prevent Cuba from extending communism in the hemisphere.

of Guatemala to exercise that control more broadly than had been the case earlier. This, as described in Chapter 2, involved a change in the basic power structure and the emergence of more complex governing arrangements than had previously been the case. When the military reached the position that it could handle such a complex situation, it could—in fact did—undertake to establish such a rule.

Besides these two general changes in basic conditions, there were two specific threats that caused the military to react as a corporate entity to defend itself. The first of these were the periodic attempts, both successful and unsuccessful, to arm other segments of the population to bring a counterforce to bear on the military's power. The second was the emergence of the *guerrillero* forces following the Thirteenth of November movement.

Prior to the revolution of 1944, it was standard practice for upper-sector citizens, especially in the rural areas, to have arms in their homes. These were used both for hunting and for personal protection. In the lower sector, the possession of arms was more sporadic, but, especially among Ladinos, it was usually desirable to have them around for the same reasons. Beginning in 1944, there occurred a set of events nationally that served to spread the possession of arms. The first was the abortive Caribbean Legion, established to promote democracy elsewhere in the Caribbean. While this effort never proved conclusive in its original design, it did serve to introduce arms to its adherents in the country.

In 1954, a much more famous case occurred. Prior to the Liberation, and surely one of the triggers of that event, a shipment of arms from Eastern Europe arrived at Puerto Barrios on the *Alfhelm*. These had been contracted for by Arbenz with the goal of arming the agrarian committees, those countryside cadres entrusted with the process of agrarian reform in the provincial areas. Arbenz, aware that the army was becoming increasingly suspicious of the political flavor of his government, thought to circumvent its power by this means. The army intercepted the shipment at the dock, however, and did not allow it to diffuse into the countryside. In spite of this, the political parties and mass organizations of the period facilitated the irregular spread of arms to leaders and members, so that while there was neither a consistent concentration nor an orderly distribution, the possession of arms became more widespread. Finally, the 1954 Liberation movement itself was an entirely new source of arms, both in the urban areas and in certain parts of the countryside. Much of the U.S.-supplied funds for that movement went into the purchase of weapons that are still abroad in the population, especially in the hands of politically conservative and reactionary elements.

The most recent formal distribution reported to the research team occurred under Ydígoras Fuentes. In 1959, his supporters organized, particularly in the *oriente,* a series of vigilante groups whose principal function was to intimidate those *campesinos* who would not support him. They distributed arms, including machine guns. With the fall of Ydígoras, these groups quickly evaporated, but the arms they received presumably have remained in the rural areas. The military has been increasingly aware of the buildup in civilian armament, and it certainly must weigh in their concern with the balance of power in the country at large.

The other threat, the appearance of the *guerrillero* forces, has naturally been of much greater recent concern. The first two years of *guerrillero* activity, during the Ydígoras administration, saw little effective counteraction. It was a period during which Yon Sosa, Turcios, and the other Thirteenth of November escapees were formulating and developing their philosophies and plans of action. During the period they were not taken entirely seriously and spent some of their time outside the country. According to Yon Sosa's description of his conversion into a *guerrillero* leader, he had not been aware of the real discontent that was latent in the *campesino* population. Upon discovering this in his attempt to formulate a successful coup during the Thirteenth of November, he then turned to the *campesino* population entirely and withdrew from any further attempt to steer the military into a significant revolt.

Following the assumption of power by Peralta Azurdia, the *guerrillero* forces became clearly differentiated. Both leaders spent time outside of the country, reportedly in Mexico and Cuba: Yon Sosa, operating primarily in Izabal and Alta Verapaz, carried on sporadic attacks both in that area and occasionally in the capital city. Turcios developed his work in the Sierra de las Minas on a somewhat different, and probably sounder, operational philosophy. He spent more time in the indoctrination of peasants and in assuring himself of a firm *campesino* base in the mountains, venturing forth somewhat less and showing himself to be less flamboyant than Yon Sosa. Both were for an immediate socialist revolution, but Turcios became much more closely allied with the Partido Guatemalteco de Trabajo. The Communists, at that time, regarded Yon Sosa as relatively unreliable, both militarily and ideologically. During the period of the study in 1965, the Yon Sosa band was losing its effectiveness, apparently from the failure to secure its *campesino* foundation. Turcios' group, on the other hand, had made it public that they were working on a strategy that allowed for fifteen or twenty years of conflict.

Although both groups had succeeded in issuing mimeographed newspapers, and newspapermen and even American television reporters carried out extensive interviews with the leaders, the government under Peralta publicly regarded the *guerrillero* forces as bandits. In the course of informal conversations during the summer of 1965, it was found that urban government and private individuals alike spoke of the *guerrilleros* as being more of a bother than a menace. In subsequent months, however, this attitude began to change. Through kidnapping wealthy individuals for ransom in 1965–1966, the *guerrilleros* built up what conservatively can be estimated as $500,000 in cash. They continued to obtain most of their arms from the military, usually through raids, or through killing individuals. They began systematically to kill private citizens whom they felt were harmful to their safety. Even though the Peralta government kept almost all information of their activities out of the newspapers, the military presumably became increasingly aware of their danger. The government also began to receive increasing kinds and amounts of U.S. military aid. When the government was taken over by Julio César Méndez Montenegro in 1966, it was with the reported understanding that the military would be free of civilian government controls insofar as the pursuit of the *guerrilleros* was concerned.

It is neither possible nor appropriate here to attempt to outline the recent history of *guerrillero* activities. They have received amazingly, although episodic, wide coverage in the press, both in Mexico and in the United States, although presumably information of immediate tactical value is missing from most accounts.[19] Of importance from the point of view of understanding the military, however, are the following points: (1) The *guerrillero* leaders in the earlier phases were Escuela Politécnica graduates who claimed they were rebelling against those elements of Guatemalan society that were inhibiting the national destiny. By virtue of these two facts, they had wide-ranging relationships within the Guatemalan military, and this surely made it difficult for some officers to seek them out to kill them at the outset. Their challenge to the United States was subtly appreciated in military circles, and the corporate quality of the military gave them an initial degree of protection. (2) The early *guerrillero* leaders were trained in counterinsurgency by the United States and so were more than mere amateurs, even though they varied in their strategic skill in applying their learning. (3) They had adopted a political position in favor of extreme socialist revolution and refused to be involved in any democratic processes of elections or compromises with the government. They thereby placed themselves in direct opposition to the entire established regime. (4) They called upon and received a continuous, although quantitatively unknown, support in men and materiel from urban dwellers, especially sympathetic university students. Their operation was by no means a rural one, but was geared to the urban-rural axis upon which the country as a whole was based. They also, at

[19] Alejandro Rivera, "Llamamos a lo toma del poder, dicen las guerrillas," *Economía* 2, no. 3 (March–April 1965): 29–33; Daniel James, "Subversive Document Revealed," *Latin American Times* 1:18; Alan Howard, "With the Guerrillas in Guatemala," *New York Times Magazine*, June 26, 1966; Joseph G. Goulden, "Guatemala: A Democracy Falters," Alicia Patterson Fund, Report JCG-10, 1966; *Revolución Socialista, Organo Divulgativo del Movimiento Revolucionario 13 de Noviembre*; Georgie Ann Geyer, twelve-article series on the guerrillas in Guatemala, *San Antonio News* (final article appeared on December 31, 1966); *Carta de Guatemala, Organo de las Fuerzas Armadas Rebeldes; FAR*, sección de propaganda de las fuerzas armadas rebeldes; Adolfo Gilly, "The Guerrilla Movement in Guatemala," *Monthly Review* 17 (1965): 7–41; Mario Menendez Rodríguez, "Guatemala: Vietnam de las Américas," February 19, 1966, "Un Pueblo Sojuzgado," February 26, 1966, "La Lucha de Los Guerrilleros," March 19, 1966, "Las Fantasmas de la Sierra," March 12, 1966, "Fusilén a los Asesinos," March 26, 1966, "Ingresamos a las Guerrillas," April 2, 1966, "La Guerrilla Urbana," April 9, 1966, "En la Sierra de las Minas, Guatemala: Libertad!" June 18, 1966 (all from *Sucesos*, Mexico City).

least in the early period, had irregular contacts and temporary understandings with some national political figures. And finally, (5) at least one of the organizations was operating on a long-term plan that involved a strategy of placing the Guatemalan military in such an awkward position that it would be necessary to bring in the United States Marines. Reflecting possibly on the fact that Sandino in Nicaragua was never beaten by the marines and that the position of the U.S. forces in the Dominican Republic at that time was becoming an increasing embarrassment, they felt that the U.S. presence would effectively neutralize the Guatemalan army, help to shatter its corporate quality, and prove it to be so ineffectual that its more revolutionarily inclined officers would abandon it.

Given that the military was faced with these threats within the nation, the final question leads us to explore just what some of the processes have been whereby the military has gradually moved toward regnancy. These have consisted of two major paths: (1) the increasing spread of a network of contact with the general population and (2) an experiment at government.

The network of contacts has been of two kinds. The first has already been alluded to and consisted of the identification of interests with certain other segments of the population. The landowners and the Church have both become specific allies, and the older conflicts with these sectors have generally disappeared. The second kind of contact has been an attempt to extend controls more directly by the military over the *campesino* and provincial population. The prerevolutionary military consisted of a few officers and small garrisons, with the officers keeping rather more to themselves and treating *campesinos* as the inferiors they were thought to be. The Monteforte study showed that twenty out of thirty of the older graduates of the Escuela Politécnica in 1950 apparently thought Indians ought to be treated as inferiors (see note 8). The only contact that the *campesinos* had with soldiers, aside from being conscripted, was to be rounded up and taken to vote, or to see the army in its role of policeman. Because of this general picture, the military neither had any idea of what was going on in the rural population, nor was it appreciated by that population.

In the years following the Thirteenth of November movement, two steps were taken to rectify this situation. To gain more knowledge about the political and other affairs of interest, the army revised the role of the *comisionado militar*, and civic action programs were initiated. Until this time, the *comisionado* was an army reserve appointee in each *municipio* and large farm, whose principal responsibility was to round up the conscripts, deliver them to the army, and occasionally report matters of interest to the military. They had aides in the smaller settlements. They were usually ex-soldiers, often noncommissioned officers, and were responsible to the chief of reserves, an officer located in the capital city of the province. The chief of reserves, in turn, was responsible to the chief of the military zone.[20]

During the revolutionary period, the *comisionados* were already perceived by the emerging *campesino* organizations as real or potential threats. Baker reports that the "Communists" tried "to effect changes in the *comisionados militares*, the local military auxiliary units stationed in the rural areas which came under the ultimate control of the chief of the armed forces. Officers of the local branches of the CNCG [the National Confederation of Campesinos] flooded the offices of armed forces chief Díaz with requests for the transfer of *comisionados* who opposed agrarian reform or resisted CNCG officials."[21] Baker cites these requests as beginning in 1951, but as becoming especially heavy toward the fall of the Arbenz government in 1954. There were apparently about two dozen such cases altogether in the records he inspected.[22] This material does indicate that the revolutionary activities, specifically the CNCG, saw this

[20] See G. A. Moore, "Social and Ritual Change in a Guatemalan Town," Ph.D. dissertation, Columbia University, 1966, p. 359:
". . . the *comisionado militar* . . . has been present in the village for the last generation, and he acts to intervene as a direct arm of the Army whenever that institution seeks to influence action on a local level. Thus, on the one hand, he and his four assistants act as a police force during an official state of seige, and also act as an information agency. *When for example, the military regime sought to change the municipal corporation in 1963, this was the Army's means of penetrating this particular village* [emphasis added]. The commissioner's role itself is given no particular ideologic content save that which accompanies any military training. The commissioner retains his army rating and owes obedience and loyalty like any good soldier. Complaints directed against him by the villagers stress his overemphasis of military duties at the expense of local etiquette."
[21] Ross K. Baker, *A Study of Military Status and Status Deprivation in Three Latin American Armies*, pp. 43–44.
[22] Ibid., pp. 101, 117.

arm of the military as a potentially dangerous threat to the efforts
to alter the social structure of the country.

The innovation in the *comisionado* system was to convert what
had been a device for local control into a widespread, active spy
network. It was the duty of the *comisionado* to report on the activities of the local people. Incidents that seemed to have any interest
for the military, and this included activities of a political nature,
were reported. This became especially active under the intermittent
periods of martial law. The procedure was changed under the
Peralta regime so that the information came directly to the chief
of state's general staff. While the change in activity of the *comisionado* succeeded in establishing a network of information and control
over much of the nation, it did operate differently from one region
to another. In the manner here described, it was particularly important in the south coast and the *oriente*. The research team found
little evidence of this kind of activity in the western departments. In
the northeast where *guerrillero* activity was overt, the term *comisionado militar* applied to a rather different type of individual. There,
he was a one-man army who moved from one settlement to another, on the lookout for evidence of *guerrillero* activity. In this case,
the *comisionados* were occupied full time in their task and were paid
for it.

The response to the *comisionado*-turned-spy was, as might be
expected, suspicion. Known in Guatemala as *orejas* ("ears"), these
domestic spies are quite familiar, and every government within living memory has had some. With the increasing antagonism that
accompanied the expanded role of the *comisionados*, the *campesinos*
were encouraged by their more revolutionary or radical friends to
do away with particularly obnoxious *comisionados*. The *guerrillero*
bands took to reporting that they had killed specific *comisionados*
as a service to the *campesinos*. In some instances, however, the
comisionados were themselves sympathetic to the political concerns
of the *campesinos* and presumably provided the military with little
useful information.

The other major step taken by the army, the civic action program, was designed to gather intelligence about provincial areas
where there was little current control and, simultaneously, to provide a better image for the military in the eyes of the civilian popu-

lation. The civic action programs and counterinsurgency were closely coupled activities, the former being one rather specialized phase of the latter. While military civic action was used much earlier in the Philippines to control the Huks, Guatemala was the first country in Latin America to actively undertake such a program.[23] The Guatemalan army had for years participated in limited civic functions. The most important were road building and the extension of the telegraph service. During the 1930's, such emphasis was placed on this that for a time a special alternative degree was offered in road engineering in the Escuela Politécnica. One of the outstanding features of Ubico's administration was the extension of the road system to many formerly inaccessible corners of the country. These were done in large part under the direction of army officers.

The expansion of civilian ministries under the post-1944 governments led to a reduction of army participation in much of this kind of work. In 1960, however, the Inter-American Defense Board approved a resolution to use military personnel and equipment for purposes of economic development, education, and highway settlement work, insofar as such work did not interfere with the civilian agencies and the regular military tasks.[24] While this resolution was approved on December 1, 1960, in the previous month of the same year the United States had already sent a civic action team to Guatemala at the request of Ydígoras. Ydígoras openly supported its development. In 1964, a committee in each locality was set up to be responsible for determining what projects would be carried out. For the most part, the some 240 committees that were set up were inoperative by 1966.

Reportedly the most active and probably the most successful of the various attempts were in inoculation, school lunches, and literacy.[25] The inoculation program is supposed to have reached some

[23] Harry F. Walterhouse, "A Time to Build: Military Civic Action—Medium for Economic Development and Social Reform."

[24] The data on the background of civil action in Guatemala are taken from Barber and Ronning, *Internal Security*.

[25] Most of the data on current activities of the civic action program are taken from the University of Pittsburgh doctoral dissertation, in preparation, of Jerry Weaver. Quotations are from that manuscript source.

thirty thousand people in the department of Izabal in 1964. Mobile medical teams reached various places irregularly. The medical program, started much earlier, had proved so successful that it had run into objections from the Ministry of Public Health and had to slow down. From 1963 until 1966, the school lunch project expanded from "740 schools and 78,000 children to 3,320 schools and 338,775 children." The *memoria* of the Dirección de Desarrollo Socio-Educativo Rural for 1965 states that approximately 75 percent of the rural school population received hot lunches. But only 26 percent of all rural children, ages seven through fourteen, were enrolled in school.

Perhaps the strongest arm of the civic action program has been literacy. The army printing plant (with strong support from AID) turned out two million sets of a first reader series, together with workbooks, teaching aids, charts, and other material during the 1963–1965 period. In an analysis of the total national literacy effort for the month of January, 1965, it develops that, of the 64,589 students recorded, 13,631 were receiving instruction from military personnel in the civic action program. The greatest number of these were in Sololá, Huehuetenango, and Alta Verapaz, only the last of which is an area of particular concern in the efforts of the insurgents. The total effort, however, was reaching only 2 percent of the illiterate population, and, of those enrolled, between 30 and 40 percent passed the program successfully.

Evaluation of the civic action programs is as difficult as is evaluation of any military action. Most of the information is hard to come by, and, even though civic action officers of both the Guatemalan and U.S. military were cooperative to the research team, some crucial information is simply unavailable. There is little question, however, that such activity has been carried on and that it could not help but have had some effect of the kind for which it was designed. Whether it profoundly changes the traditional suspicion of the *campesino* toward the military is an open question.

Given the growth in strength of the military, their increased incorporation and professionalization, and the threats that they perceived due to the cumulation of arms in the provincial areas and the advent of the *guerrilleros*, one further factor has contributed to the tendency toward regnancy. This was the first year of practice rule that they had from 1962 to 1963, and then the three years of overt rule, from 1963 to 1966.[26] Following the public disturbances in March, 1962, the Ydígoras government was all but taken over by military officers. Cabinet and other central posts were occupied by officers, and the president was allowed to play only a superficial, essentially vocal role. Finding that they were able to handle matters at least as well as, if not considerably better than, Ydígoras had, the officers then took over completely in 1963. In a real sense, the take-over was not merely military, since it had the strong support, if not the overt cooperation, of many segments of the population. But that it was militarily led and that the government continued to be militarily staffed meant that it was a reasonable approximation of what a military government would look like. The three years of open rule confirmed what the military had learned in the previous year of covert control. They could handle it just as well as their civilian predecessors. The fact that a good many steps in development were not taken was explained as an attempt to avoid the impression that the military government wished to remain in power. The chief of state, Enrique Peralta, refused for this reason to take the title of president, and, being assured of the elimination of the really un-desirable candidates (from the military point of view these included Juan José Arévalo, Francisco Villagrán Kramer, and, possibly, Mario Méndez Montenegro), the election of a civilian government was overseen in a traditionally democratic manner.

If there is a tendency toward regnancy, as is proposed here, why did the military permit a civilian government to resume power? Answers lie in at least five areas. First, the military did not give up some crucial powers, such as the freedom to continue to handle the *guerrilleros* as they pleased and to name the minister of defense. Second, it was public knowledge that a sizable portion of the con-servative officers was deeply suspicious of a "leftist" civilian ad-ministration and was constantly threatening, along with conserva-tive civilians, to topple it. Third, since the time that the Guate-malan military committed itself to act sheerly as an interim gov-ernment, two other major Latin American countries were taken over in such a way as to leave no doubt that a military regime might continue to exist indefinitely. In Argentina and Brazil, military

26 Cf., Buttrey, "The Guatemalan Military."

governments had made it clear that they did not regard the immediate return of a civilian democratic government to be at all desirable for the welfare of the country as a whole. Fourth, the personality of Enrique Peralta Azurdia must be considered a factor. This officer had, on previous occasions, ample opportunity to become chief of state but actually avoided it. His first opportunity followed the 1944 revolution, at which time he was favored for the new presidency. He rejected the offer, however, and consistently showed himself to be unwilling to assume such a permanent position thereafter. When Peralta was placed in the temporary seat of power, his subsequent actions seemed to be consistent with his earlier predisposition.

Finally, the position of the United States, especially influential in Caribbean politics and relatively less so in Brazil and Argentina, was that it did not wish to support a military dictatorial government. While not wanting to appear as if it were influencing the Guatemalan political situation, neither did it want to be accused of supporting military dictatorships. Presumably in good faith, the United States took the policy position that a civilian, democratically elected government would be better in the long run, especially if the military kept to their task of running down the *guerrilleros*. Following the resumption of civil government in 1966, the United States made every effort to discourage another military coup.

It is not possible to evaluate these five factors relatively. We can, however, ask what would happen were they different. In the first place, given its current power, the military is not likely to give up its ability to control its own position. Secondly, it is quite possible for the conservative element of the military to take over the direction of the whole, particularly if the civilian government proves ineffective. Third, Brazil and Argentina now stand as models of what a military government may attempt should it so wish. Fourth, there is absolutely no reason to think that the next military leader will be reluctant, as was Peralta Azurdia, to assume dictatorial powers. And finally, the United States, if it is sufficiently afraid of the "Communist" *guerrilleros*, and if it is true to form, will automatically opt for an incumbent government that promises to "achieve stability and democracy."

In terms of the total power structure of Guatemala, it is erroneous to think that the military acts merely in some predestined, cyclical manner. The role of the military in Guatemalan public affairs has changed steadily, and the change has been in one direction. While it has broadened its position in the society at large, it has consistently consolidated its mechanisms and bases of control. It is in the position to take over the government whenever conditions indicate that it should, and it is capable of ruling for an indefinite period. That is, it is capable of this if the population's interest, motivation, and bases and mechanisms for political action do not grow. In this era of world history, these *if*'s warrant serious attention.

5 | The Renaissance of the Guatemalan Church

1. *The Expansion of the Church*

PERHAPS THE LONGEST and most severe restriction that the Catholic church has suffered in Latin America has been the repression begun by Guatemalan liberals in 1871. Under the liberal regime, almost all foreign clergy was sent from the country, and a total of 119 survived, a figure that remained essentially unchanged until the revolution.[1] All Church properties were confiscated, and the *personalidad jurídica* was revoked. Indeed, if a crucial case is needed to counter the die-hard stereotype that blames all Latin American ills on the Church, Guatemala is that case. For, in the some eighty years of liberal suppression, the Church could hardly be accused of being the major offender in keeping Guatemala underdeveloped;

NOTE: This chapter is not concerned with religion in general or with the various sects in Guatemala, but only with the Catholic church as an institution, and specifically with the Church hierarchy or clergy within that institution. The lay elements within the Catholic church and other phases of religious activity need to be studied in much greater detail than was possible in the present investigation. This chapter was written with major dependence on the field notes of Bruce Calder. He has now prepared a thesis on the basis of the same materials: "Growth and Change in the Guatemalan Catholic Church, 1944–1966," M.A. thesis, The University of Texas at Austin, 1968.

[1] Mary P. Holleran, *Church and State in Guatemala*, p. 236. This source provides a good historical background on state-church relations.

and yet during those eighty years Guatemala was one of the most underdeveloped of all Latin American countries. The implicit assumption of this chapter is that the Church is a part of underdevelopment, not a cause of it. The chapter will go some distance in demonstrating that the renaissance the Church in Guatemala is now experiencing is a part of the kind of development that Guatemala itself is undergoing. It is growing, consciously, as a part of the growth of the upper sector, and its health is inextricably involved in the health of that sector. The basic argument here is that the Church, in itself, has almost no significant power base. What it had in the nineteenth century it lost under the liberals. Its power today is seen to rest principally in its dependence upon, and the derivative power it receives from, the upper sector and the government. Since both are important and for the moment are in general agreement with each other, the Church's best line of action is to try to keep good relations with both.

While the weakness of the Church and clergy for three quarters of a century might be expected to have inhibited popular interest in the Church, it seems that the Ladinos of Guatemala differ little from the population of most of Latin America in this regard. And the Indians, to the contrary, have maintained a strong societal integration with Church affairs. The general patterns in evidence elsewhere hold also for Guatemala: interest is stronger among women than men and stronger among wealthy conservatives than among the poor.

The fact that a weak clergy is not necessarily going to result in weak ritual is best illustrated by the Indian population. The reaction of the Indians to the shortage of priests was to become independent for most of the sacraments and rituals and to crystallize a series of customs that combine colonial Catholic practices with aboriginal Mayan survivals. Ritualism was probably, if anything, strengthened, but it was also transformed and became autonomous at the community level. From the point of view of religious organization, what was weakened was the participation of the clergy and the Indian's need for clerical services. The colonial Church played a strong role in Indian life and continued in some degree to do so until the advent of liberalism in the 1870's. The consequence of the subsequent years of liberal rejection of the Church was to weaken the general interest of the Ladino in the entire religious organization. In the Indian population, however, the result was to separate the community religious practices from dependence on the Church. Religious activity among the Indians flourished, but was increasingly free of the direct administration of the clergy.

The residual native clergy during these years found its security in keeping allegiance to the interests of the upper-class conservatives and serving their religious needs. It was predominantly oriented toward the capital city, and relatively few priests operated in the provincial areas and almost none in the outlying rural sectors. As the population grew, the fact that the Church could own no wealth meant that a minimum amount of support would keep it going in a minimal way. Most of the middle and upper economic strata were liberal in their general attitude and felt little obligation to support the Church. Under such circumstances, the Church remained poor, a very limited native clergy developed, and there was no effective accumulation of popular support.

Although the initial signs were slight, there was a gradual regrowth of the Church's role on the national scene. Under the last of the prerevolutionary liberal chiefs of state, Jorge Ubico, the first appointment of a papal nuncio was made in 1936. The archbishop was granted quiet permission for a few priests to enter the country. In 1937, some Jesuits came to teach in the archbishop's seminary in order that more national clergymen could be prepared. The Jesuits and the archbishop parted ways in 1951, but by then the former had been given the La Merced Church in Guatemala City as their responsibility. Ubico also allowed the opening of secondary education under direction of priests for the upper sector.

In 1943, two Maryknoll priests, exchange prisoners who had been working in China at the outbreak of the war, came to Guatemala. They were gradually followed by others. Archbishop Rossell also brought in other orders, including Maristas and Salesians. Ubico's regime was the first liberal regime to show some tolerance toward the Church. Since there was little political action in the country under Ubico, the Church's main interest was in surviving and working toward the day when it might regain legal status and expand its operations in order to carry out its responsibility as perceived by the clergy.

The 1944 revolution and the following decade saw no official change in government policy toward the Church, but apparently some clergy were tacitly permitted to enter the country. During the Arbenz years, Rossell took particular interest in the clandestine political development of the Church. A major element in this was the initiation of the Movimiento de Afirmación Nacional de Cristianidad (MANC), an organization that was the forerunner of the Christian Democratic party. Particularly important was the fact that the schools which had been initiated under Ubico had turned out Church-oriented upper-sector individuals. These men took the lead in the clandestine political developments and were destined to play a central role in the Congress of 1956 and the restrengthening of the Church.

Under Arbenz, Archbishop Rossell took an open position against what he regarded as the government's dangerous drift toward communism. At the same time, he saw himself as the leader of the Guatemalan Church's return to power and, as such, resented activities by other Church members when he felt they infringed on his prerogatives. During the Ubico and Arévalo governments, although decreasingly so, the relation between Church and state reflected the specific relation that held between the chief of state and the archbishop. Rossell wanted to keep it this way, but certain conditions were making this increasingly impossible. The very growth of foreign clergy in the country was bringing divergent interests and orientations within the clerical hierarchy, and world events were focusing the attention of the Church elsewhere in Latin America.

Since the Church was still essentially weak, Rossell was still dependent upon his close ties with a small portion of the upper sector. He recognized the responsibility the Church had toward the lower sector, especially the Indian, and initiated two schools for Indian children in Guatemala City. In 1945, he started the Colegio Santiago for boys and, in 1949, a girls' school. The reason behind the Church's action in this area was also somewhat political, because Rossell saw the underprivileged Indian mass as a potentially revolutionary force; to him the Church was an institution that could forestall this radical possibility.

The condition that led to the improved position of the Church emerged from four areas, two internal to Guatemala and two external. Inside Guatemala, there was the growth of a stronger and more politically Church-oriented group in the population, and the number of foreign clergy increased, bringing in progressive ideas about Church action. Outside, the Vatican was becoming increasingly concerned about the apostolic state of Latin America, the continent with the largest single number of Catholics in the world and with unquestionably the most underdeveloped clergy and Church structure. In addition to this, the United States brought its power to strengthen any political entity that could be mobilized in the resistance and fight against the Communist threat. In so doing, it supported the movement of Castillo Armas, as well as subsequent governments. These governments, in turn, found in the Church an important ally to enhance their own control over the expanding population and far-left groups, and so were willing to grant the Church some of the legal rights it held prior to the liberal repression.

Rome acted through the papal nuncio. Rossell's central position disturbed the Vatican, because he gave little evidence of wishing the hierarchy to expand. Theoretically, the bishops of Guatemala are equally autonomous, and the archbishop, unlike his colonial predecessors, is not superordinate to them. Rather, the archbishop is merely one of the bishops, specifically responsible for his own diocese but with no authority over the others. The bishops are directly responsible to Rome, and Rome's representative in Guatemala was, of course, the nuncio. When Rossell was made archbishop in 1939, there were only three dioceses in Guatemala. To cut into what apparently was a hard crust of Church conservatism, the nuncio recommended, and the Vatican acted upon, the naming of three new bishops, all foreigners. The new bishops were men who had little or no hard ties with the traditionally conservative Guatemalan upper sector. The reaction of Rossell and the Church establishment in Guatemala was so violent that it resulted in the recall of the nuncio; but the appointments held, and the break had been made. The Vatican's concern apparently went further than the mere question of making the Guatemalan Church somewhat more progressive. It was also concerned with the specific political identification that Rossell seemed to have made with Castillo Armas.

The "Liberation Movement," led by Castillo Armas and financed by the United States, found a tacit ally in the Guatemalan military, but Rossell was much more vocal in his approval. It was clear shortly after the downfall of Arbenz that the Church was in for a "new deal" from the state. Though the Castillo government claimed to carry on certain of traditional liberal ideals, hostility to the Church was not one of them. Castillo specifically allowed and encouraged the Church to import clergymen, and the laws enacted three quarters of a century earlier began to crumble. In essence, the state began to treat the Church as a special friend rather than as a special enemy.

The immigrant foreign clergy grew rapidly and soon far outnumbered the native clergy. They were by no means all progressive; in fact, few probably had any serious interest in the enlightened principles that were to be enunciated later at the Second Vatican Council. Combined with the political activities that were generating the Christian Democratic party and the congressional action and lobbying that led to the improvement of the Church's legal position, they served to give the Church a totally new shape in the country at large.

Based on the changes of the Ubico and revolutionary periods, the Church began an overt and important expansion following the fall of the revolutionary government in 1954. The prerequisites for this were the increased contact with Rome (begun with the residence of the papal nuncio) and other Catholic centers, the slow emergence of a Guatemalan lay public that could support the Church in bettering its position with respect to the state, and the public position taken by the archbishop against the Arbenz government and in support of the "Liberation." When asked where the new clergy (usually foreigners) were most needed, the Church leaders in the city suggested the isolated Indian areas. With this, attention began to focus on the Indians, and problems of development began to come into view. The increase in numbers brought with it the segmentation of the dioceses. The new emphasis on the provinces, together with the proliferation of dioceses responsible directly to Rome, resulted in decentralizing the national Church organization. And this decentralization in Guatemala accompanied an increase in exercise of power from Rome, which made its first broadly public appearance during the Second Vatican Council. In keeping with the usual workings of power structures, then, the changing external relationships were accompanied by changing internal organization. The Guatemalan Church began to expand, decentralize, and become more dependent upon Rome and other external Catholic sources.

It is not possible to be precise about the number of priests and other religious personnel in Guatemala, but precision may not be necessary, since the number is constantly increasing. During one phase of the present study, in the summer of 1965, the number of priests was placed at about 470 and that of nuns at about 775. In February of that year, the same source stated that there were 472 priests and brothers, 739 nuns, and 102 students.[2] In July, 1966, it reported that there were 531 priests in the country, of which 434 were foreigners. At this time, there were 805 sisters and 96 brothers. Of the priests, 97 were Guatemalan, whereas only about 100 of the sisters were native. All brothers were foreign. This is a significant increase over the reported 120 of the middle 1940's, involving new orders and congregations, and composed almost entirely of foreigners. Support for the Church is still so slight in Guatemala that it is most advantageous for priests to come from religious orders or dioceses to which they can look for continuing support. Secular clergy, often from dioceses in the United States, also continue to receive some help, as well as direction. The newcomers in each case are requested and approved by the local resident bishop.

The increase in religious orders is significant, although it was not possible to identify the rate of increase during the course of research. In 1965, there were thirty-six feminine and twenty-seven masculine orders, congregations, and secular institutes coming from, among other places, Ireland, Spain, Mexico, Belgium, Canada, Italy, Colombia, and the United States. The markedly different outlooks and goals of the different groups are apparent in their actions. The most welfare oriented, in the sense of caring for the problems of the society as well as the spirit, have been certain North American and European orders. In general, the Latin American groups are as conservative as the older native Guatemalan clergy. The missionary groups, such as the Maryknoll, have been especially active. Since there are relatively few priests in the country, contact between groups is limited, and there is, therefore, little evidence of competition between them as yet. The only clear instance of serious rivalry concerns the conflict stemming from the fact that the Opus Dei is operating in an area of traditional concern to the Jesuits.

The growth in the number of dioceses, as was suggested earlier, was not a response to the increase in clergy, but was aimed at encouraging diversification and decentralization within the clergy. Archbishop Rossell, while early condoning the entrance of foreign

---

[2] Provided by the Conferencia Nacional de Religiosos y Religiosas de Guatemala, *Boletín Informativo y Tercer Informe General* 2, no. 3 (March, 1965).

clergy, became increasingly hostile and nationalistic during his later years in office. It was partly because of this that the new dioceses were established under the recommendation of the nuncio. Since bishops act with considerable autonomy, it was only necessary to place more bishops with a propensity to enlarge the number of priests. In recent years, even bishops of recognized conservative and nationalistic inclinations have begun to seek out foreign clergy, recognizing that it is impossible to carry on their tasks without such help.

Under Rossell, the organization of the Church in Guatemala was minimal. Everything that he was able to control himself, he did. Since there were few dioceses during the first part of his career, his own archdiocese covered a large territory. The establishment of new dioceses and the increase in the number of bishops decreased the direct responsibility of the archbishop and left the organization of the rest of the country to the respective bishops. There was not, nor had there ever been, coordination between these Church leaders. The archbishop was a leader only in the sense that he spoke for the bishops to the government; he had no authority over them.

Prior to 1951, there were both a major and a minor seminary in Guatemala, pertaining specifically to the archdiocese. These had been run by the Jesuits since 1937. In 1951, the major seminary was closed,[3] and the residual student body was sent to complete their work in other countries. In 1960, Rossell invited the Sulpicians of Canada to take over a newly constructed major seminary. The minor seminary, then in a very old building downtown, was also moved to a new building on the outskirts of the city.

The importance of the seminary cannot be underestimated. The very limited available native clergy is a major problem for the Church. Since priests must be recruited among young men and older adolescents, the quality of the seminary influences who applies. According to one informant, the educational quality of the older seminary was as good as any in neighboring countries, but the upper class was prejudiced against sending their sons to it. This has meant that in the past much of the native clergy had come from homes of relatively little education. The seminary currently, as with the rest of the Church, is badly understaffed. The quality of the edu-

---

[3] It was reported that the Jesuits concerned were sent out of the country at that time, but no details concerning this were ascertained.

cation, however, is improving. A Serra Club, composed of laymen of the wealthier socioeconomic strata, has been started in an effort to obtain better support from the community. The major seminary has been made the national seminary; a minor seminary exists in Quezaltenango, another is now operating in Sololá, and the minor one in Guatemala City continues. Among the innovations in the preparation of the students has been the substitution of Cakchiquel, a Guatemalan Indian language, for French as an additional language requirement. The problems confronting the seminary today suggest how long it will be before a strong native clergy will be operative in Guatemala. These include a deficiency of qualified or likely candidates, of funds to expand the establishment, and of both laymen and priests as teachers. There seems to be no rapid solution to the problem of recruitment.

The Conferencia Episcopal de Guatemala is a national organization of bishops. Early in the 1960's it was recognized that the lack of coordination between the various dioceses was seriously inhibiting the development of the Church throughout Guatemala. It seems likely that this realization was enhanced with the organizing of the Latin American bishops of the Consejo Episcopal Latinoamericano (CELAM) in Río de Janeiro in 1955. The Guatemalans began their organization with an entity called the Secretariado Católico Nacional to act as a center of information and services for all the dioceses. The objectives were explicit in the regulations approved by Rome: "(a) to coordinate and organize the Guatemalan Catholics in order to achieve the social and educative mission of the Church in the reconstruction of Christian living; (b) to lend orientation and assistance to the Catholic regional and parish associations that solicit it, and (c) to develop all activities that will tend to increase the active participation of laymen in affairs of the Church."[4] At the time of the study, the only activity initiated by the secretariat was an office of press and communications, established to get better news coverage on activities and events relating to the Church anywhere in Guatemala. Personnel to man the other offices has not yet been arranged. The involvement of the bishops in the Second Vatican Council evidently slowed the organizational work. The development of the secretariat, as well as the degree of communication be-

---

[4] Statement provided by the office of the Secretariado Católico Nacional.

tween the bishops, suggests that it is a significant advance over the earlier absence of organization.

The roots of the problem of organization of the Guatemalan Church lie in its relationship with Rome. Since the archbishop no longer has the superior role permitted him from the colonial period until 1921, when the entire country was a single diocese, the center of power now lies in Rome. The archbishop is the public figure for Guatemala and therefore holds a special place in the public's mind. The papal nuncio, however, has a much more direct relationship to the pope. Theoretically, all bishops are directly responsible to the pope and may communicate directly with him. In fact, of course, they cannot attempt this, and the papal nuncio is the intermediary. The nuncio is also the bearer of news and advice from the pope and therefore stands in a position of apparent derivative power. Since the bishops are all under somewhat similar pressures and all face somewhat similar problems in their dioceses, there are good reasons for them to organize. When the Guatemalan bishops were in Rome at the Second Vatican Council, they voted as a conservative bloc. Given the usual public emphasis on national figures, there is a natural ambiguity of power in the positions of the archbishop and the nuncio, but such ambiguity must necessarily be present if there is to be local autonomy of action by bishops on the one hand and strong central authority of the distant Roman Curia on the other.

The problems of Church organization existed in equal measure at the lower levels, within the dioceses. In the Indian areas, the independence of the Indian organizations, especially as manifest in the colonially inspired *cofradía* system, challenged the responsibility of the new priests. As will be related later, the mode of attack on this problem has been, in part, to try to form a competing group, primarily of younger people. The success of this has varied, but it has been rather more notable in those areas where the priests were willing to promote social welfare measures. The Indians, however, while posing serious organizational problems for the new generation of missionary priests, at least provide a base of people interested in and committed to the Catholic church. The Ladino population in this matter, like the Indian, has been without an intensive dependence on the clergy for so long and has so successfully survived the lack of clerical ministrations for all but the minimal sacramental needs that the resurgence of an active clergy finds in them little or no response. Unlike the Indian, however, and like the culturally mestizo population elsewhere in Latin America, the Ladino has simply not found the Church to answer any real need. In the long conservative period that preceded the liberal takeover in 1871, the Church was an intrinsic ally of the powerful in Guatemala. It played the same role there that it has generally in the history of Christian Latin America: it has lived in something of a symbiotic relationship with the wealthy, oligarchic upper sector.

Today, Rome has given evidence in both actions and words that it is again concerned with its New World faithful. What may come of this expression at this late date, however, remains to be seen. The "faithful" today are as calculating in their relations to the Church as the Church must be to them. They judge whether the Church is of value to them more in temporal than spiritual terms. In facing the problem of extending its influence once again over the large nominally Catholic population, the Church now finds itself in the position of having to demonstrate that what it has to offer is of material use in the evolving goals of the Guatemalan population. While this oversimplifies the case, it helps to keep in mind that the goals are different in the two sectors. In some instances, such as the famous case of Quiché to be described later, the parish priest who develops a cooperative in the interest of the Indians comes into direct conflict with the interests of the local Ladino storekeepers and moneylenders. The problem in organizing lower-sector Ladinos, however, is even different from the two sets of interests represented in the Quiché case. The poor rural Ladino has neither the Indian's defensive commitment to the Church and the religion nor the wealthier Ladino's developed interest in augmenting his own position of control. To involve this Ladino and the growing number of his urbanizing cousins, the Church can only expect success through the medium of works of demonstrated relevance to their values. The evidence to date suggests that the Church has not successfully identified these values, nor found a way to minister to them.

The organization of the Guatemalan Church, while perhaps appearing monolithic to the outsider and those in the lower ranks, appears weak and disoriented to its leaders. The lack of administrative development under Archbishop Rossell is one historical antecedent to this, and the opinion is confirmed by the ambiguities resulting from the concentration of power in Rome and in the hands of the bishops. The presence of an archbishop of Guatemala is, in a very real sense, a compromise with the fact of national governments. The Church in Rome apparently cannot allow a concentration of power at the national level that is sustained by both independent and derivative power. Given this policy, whether overt or covert, the Church organization on the international level becomes more important than it is at the national level. And given the facts of nationalism, this inevitably leads to the problem of conflict between national clergy and foreigners.

It comes as no surprise, then, that the major immediate structural consequence of the expansion of the Church in Guatemala has been the schism between the native and the foreign clergy. Currently only a little over 15 percent of the clergy is Guatemalan, and the proportion promises to become less before it increases. The issue became pronounced at the time of the appointment of the three foreign bishops over the objection of the archbishop. This act served to emphasize that conservatism and nationalism are strongly linked in the Guatemalan Church. Over the past two decades most (but, very significantly, not all) of the progressive priests have been foreigners. The native clergy has become sensitive to the issue, which has also been brought to public attention through newspapers. In April of 1966, the traditional gadfly of Guatemalan journalism, and then also vice-president–elect of the Republic, wrote: "When we read of those actions by the government [the exile of the foreign clergy in the 1870's] we are repelled. But now, seeing the steady rise in power of today's foreign clergy, we think they [the government] did well."[5] The problem faced by the Guatemalan Church is a frustrating one. To be strong, the clergy in the country must increase. But the only way to assure this over the next few decades is to import foreigners.

Although the cause of nationalism is recognized by the governments clearly, the postrevolutionary governments have all been sympathetic to the Church. While individual foreign priests may be expelled from the country, there is no suggestion of any wholesale expulsion. One of the devices that the foreign priests are using to operate more effectively and to minimize their visibility is adoption of Guatemalan citizenship. To be named a bishop in a country, one

[5] *La Hora*, April 5, 1966.

must accept citizenship of that country; consequently, the three bishops are currently becoming or have become Guatemalans and are no longer technically foreigners. Following the expulsion of a progressive Spanish priest from the department of Quiché, others among the remaining Spanish priests in the country applied for citizenship, thereby avoiding such a problem in their future. This does not, however, cover all aspects of the problem, since the outsiders cannot so easily adopt Guatemalan culture.

Currently the Church readily accepts foreign help. Archbishop Rossell was strongly opposed to it but apparently gave up the fight before his death. The incumbent archbishop seems to have no strong objections. It is of interest that it is not merely missionary priests who have come to Guatemala, but other dioceses, especially in the United States, have sent men to work in special areas under the auspices of local bishops.[6] The foreign clergy, however, brings problems as well as solutions. As is true of foreigners of whatever calling, they come with usually well-developed, misleading preconceptions. The easily developed antipathy that occurs between foreigners and provincial Ladinos is reinforced in the Indian areas by the sympathy the priests feel for the Indian, and in the Ladino areas by the general lack of interest by the local population. The foreign clergy tends to look down on much of the local clergy as ill trained and self-interested. It is recognized that there are outstanding exceptions, just as there are among the foreign clergy. But in general, the opportunity for real communication is slight, and each continues with the stereotypes concerning the other.

Priests bring their own special problems, as well as those of merely being foreign. Spanish priests tend especially to look down on the local clergy, following the 450-year tradition of superiority of the peninsular Spaniard over the mestizo. The United States priests are as likely as not to carry U.S.-inspired concepts of race and class, neither of which is congenial or appropriate to the social organiza-

---

[6] Stahlke reports, on material provided by the Secretariado Católico Nacional, that priests from six U.S. dioceses have come to work in rural or provincial areas. The U.S. dioceses are Belleville, Illinois; Helena, Montana; New Ulm, Minnesota; Oklahoma; Spokane, Washington; and Wheeling, West Virginia. Almost all these priests are working in Indian areas (Leonardo E. Stahlke, *Estadística Religiosa Cristiana de Guatemala*, p. 83).

tions of Guatemala or the rest of Latin America. The Spaniard's unreal view of intrinsic superiority is paralleled by the North American's unreal view of intrinsic democracy. It is hardly unnatural that such conflicts born at home are carried into the next context, even when extending to the differences reported between two Belgian priests, one Flemish, the other Walloon.

The importance of the foreigner lies not merely in the fact that he is active in an area where priests are few, but also in the fact that he often brings financing from home. The Church in Guatemala has never recovered from the disappearance of imperial support that accompanied independence. The production of new national clergy brings with it the necessity to open up new sources of national support. Stahlke reports that in 1966 there were 225 *seminaristas*.[7] This is almost three times the number of native-born priests currently working in the country. Clearly, should any sizable proportion of them ever reach the priesthood, they will have to extract a good deal more financial backing than is available currently. It should be noted that the problems in financing the Church parallel those appearing in other aspects of development. Local communities that support a priest may face real hardships; the priests must then be willing to face hardships themselves. Major financial support must come from members of the upper sector, and they are presumably influenced in this expenditure as they are in any investment in the development of the country. They must be convinced that it will pay off in terms that are meaningful to them.

Foreign support has not come, incidentally, merely in the form of support for individual priests. It was reported by a number of sources, although not confirmed, that both the Vatican and the German bishops' fund, Miserior, provided support of the development of the Church. Presumably, like all such sums, no measure can be made of their real effect in an area where there is so much that could be done.

The problem of foreigner and national in the Guatemalan Catholic church is not made any simpler by the fact that the foreign priests, especially the North Americans, receive both overt and covert support from agencies of the United States government. The

[7] Ibid., p. 85.

Agency for International Development has seen the priests as particularly appropriate devices for promoting development at the local
level, especially in the Indian areas. Similarly, the government under Peralta Azurdia, with the same goal in mind, encouraged the
Maryknoll priests in Huehuetenango to play a special role in certain
development matters concerning migrants. This kind of backing
from official governmental agencies, especially those of the United
States, does not endear the foreigners to the native clergy. Moreover,
since it is reflected at the upper levels of the agencies concerned, it
is met by concern at the upper levels of the Church hierarchy. The
Guatemalan bishops act after their own judgment of the situation,
and this leads to increased dissension within the bishops' council.
The archbishop, presuming to represent, as he must, the general
national interest of the Church in Guatemala, inevitably takes a
dim view of excessive meddling by the foreign agencies, regardless of
their motivations. The participation by U.S. government agencies
in Church activities obviously supports accusations by those hostile
to both that the two are in alliance. The fact is that to some degree
they are. While hardly in national alliance, the U.S. government
does find common cause with the Vatican's concern with the development of Latin America and the resurgence of the Church as a
controlling factor in Latin American populations.

The structural problem, then, combines the intricacies of nationalism, international Catholicism, and interests of the United States
in maintaining its position of general control in the affairs of the
country. Guatemalans find themselves faced by an almost unsolv-
able dilemma; and, as is usually the case, they prefer to avoid dealing with it until circumstances require periodic showdowns.

2. *Promotional Activities of the Church*

Only by the most brutal kind of analytical blustering is it possible to deal with the various activities of the Catholic church in
such a way as to ignore their ecclesiastical aspects. To treat the
efforts at social justice, organizing cooperatives, planting corn, or
teaching literacy as apart from the role that these activities are seen
by the Church to play in its own development makes it quite impossible to understand why the clergy acts as it does. It is, therefore, necessary in any discussion of these activities to make clear

at the outset that certain principles guide the Church's action. While possibly not expressed in these terms, the following points are clear to Church members:

(1) Activities must be at once both theological and political.

(2) The political aspects of any act are to strengthen the Church, as concerns its internal organization and/or its place in the world at large.

(3) The activities must conform to some degree to the dogma and instructions issued by the Church and, at the same time, to the practical media in which they are to occur.[8]

Lest there be misunderstanding, I must emphasize that the term

---

[8] The points as stated here must necessarily represent the mission and activity of the Church as seen by an outsider in the context of the present sociological discussion. Our emphasis is on the structural position and consequent activity. To see the same mission in terms more meaningful to the contemporary Church itself, however, the following quotations taken from the Second Vatican Council documentation may prove helpful. I am indebted to Fr. Ricardo Falla for calling these statements to my attention:

"While helping the world and receiving many benefits from it, the Church has a single intention: that God's kingdom may arrive and that the salvation of the whole human race may come to pass" (G.Sp. 45). Her mission from Christ is therefore "to shed on the whole world the radiance of the gospel message, and to unify under one Spirit all men of whatever nation, race and culture . . ." (G.Sp. 45, 92).

This mission is carried on throughout the world by the bishops, whose duties are, directly or indirectly, (a) to preach the gospel (L.G. 25), (b) to function as priests especially in the Eucharist (L.G. 26), and (c) to govern with their authority the particular churches entrusted to them (L.G. 27). Thus, "bishops have been made true and authentic teachers of the faith, pontiffs, and shepherds" (Ch.D. 2).

The priests are "prudent cooperators with the episcopal order, as well as its aids and instruments" (L.G. 28). Their concrete tasks can be various, for they can be "engaged in a parochial or supraparochial ministry; devoted to scientific research or to teaching; or they can be sharing by manual labor in the lot of the workers themselves . . ." (P.O. 8).

Finally, the Church suffers a tension between two extremes:

". . . although the Church needs human resources to carry out her mission, she is not set up to seek earthly glory, but to proclaim, by her own example too, humility and self-sacrifice" (L.G. 8). "Christ, to be sure, gave His Church no proper mission in the political, economic, or social order. The purpose which He set before her is a religious one. But out of this religious mission itself comes a function, a light, and an energy which can serve to structure and consolidate the human community according to the divine law. As a matter of fact, when *political* here is not used in its narrow referent of civic government or political parties, but in its broader generic and structural sense of the condition of competition between social entities. The point is that the Church-sponsored activities must help to strengthen the Church and that this should be done in a state of mind to indicate reverence for the dogma of the Church.

Since it is senseless to classify Catholic activities as being either political or religious, we will take up certain of the Guatemalan activities here in terms of the actual problem on which they focus. In this way, we avoid trying to analyze motivations and look instead to the form the activity takes, the rationale given it, and the place it occupies in the structure of the Church in the contemporary world. An additional note of caution is necessary here. Since this discussion is framed simultaneously in religious and political terms, the question of whether a given set of activities should be interpreted as more or less "progressive" will obviously have to answer to other criteria. The concern here is less with whether a "modernization" process is under way (an issue that is of great concern to many contemporary political scientists and sociologists) and more with changes in Church activity that reflect adaptation to the contemporary world, the causes behind these changes, and the desired adaptation toward which they are directed. That some of these activities may be seen as "progressive" and others not is an important observation, but not one necessarily central to our analysis.

Aside from the normal duties required of pastoral work, the broadest single organizational activity of the Church in Guatemala comes under the rubric of Acción Católica. Varying from one place to another, the way Acción Católica is organized illustrates a number of things about the functioning of the Church. Formally, it is a mode of

---

circumstances of time and place create the need, she can and indeed should initiate activities on behalf of all men" (G.Sp. 42).

Sources:

L.G.: *Lumen Gentium*, the Dogmatic Constitution of the Church; Vatican II.

G.Sp.: *Gaudium et Spes*, Pastoral Constitution of the Church in the Modern World; Vatican II.

Ch.D.: *Christus Dominus*, Decree on the Bishops' Pastoral Office in the Church; Vatican II.

P.O.: *Presbyterorum Ordinis*, Decree on the Ministry and Life of Priests; Vatican II.

involving laymen more profoundly in the work of the Church and against the ideas stemming from humanism, Protestantism, rationalism, autorevelation, historical materialism, and laicism.[9] It is open to all, holds strongly for obedience to the hierarchy, permits political action through political parties, and is a union of pure doctrine and "legitimately constituted social activity." Each center of Acción Católica has an ecclesiastical adviser who exercises control over the activities and thus provides the "support and authority of the bishops." The organization is formally instituted from the top of the hierarchy, with the major figures named by the archbishop or the bishops; but the various active groups are, of course, scattered over the country under the direct supervision of the local priest.

At the national level there is a president and vice-president of men, a vice-president of women, and an adviser. These, together with a treasurer and governing members, make up the Presidencia General. Below this is a larger council, composed of the Presidencia General members plus such further officers as the parochial presidents, the presidents of the various branches of Acción Católica (including men, women, girls, and boys), the president of Acción Católica Rural, the president of the Secretariado Católico Nacional, and others. There are, then, below this council the actual parish groups, theoretically four in each parish (men, women, boys, girls). There are different kinds of membership, ranked in terms of the degree of participation.

In actual operation, the way the Acción Católica groups are organized depends heavily on the enthusiasm of the individual priest and the nature of the situation in which he finds himself. The most numerous subsegment of the organization is the Acción Católica Rural, established separately in each rural and provincial parish. One of the major concerns of this branch is to teach the catechism and to prepare the population to take the sacraments. Emphasis is laid on getting at the leaders or potential leaders in the community, especially among the younger people, and encouraging them, in

---

[9] As well as depending on Mr. Calder's interviews, these notes draw heavily on two volumes: *La Acción Católica*, Impreso en Iberia-Gutenberg, 6ª Avd. 15–70, Z. 1, n.d.; and *Estatutos Generales de la Acción Católica de la Arquidiócesis de Santiago de Guatemala*, Tipografía Sánchez y de Guise, 8ª Avd. S. No. 30, n.d., signed by Rossell y Arellano. Both published in Guatemala.

turn, to pass the word on. The *catequistas* thus trained have the responsibility of training others. Once the groups are formed, however, the priest may take the opportunity to use them for other educational, social, or moral purposes, such as marriage counseling.

The *catequistas* have been the spearhead of the Church's effort to reconquer the Indians for Catholicism. The Indian religious organization, as it developed in most of Guatemala, has evolved around the special role of the *cofradía* organization and the place these organizations had in the general social and political life of the community. In general, the *cofradías* were structured along a form of age grading, whereby older individuals achieved higher positions or dropped out of the running. This resulted in the governing of *cofradías* being the prerogative of successful middle-aged and older men; and the positions themselves, being of great local prestige, led to the society placing special confidence in their occupants. The appearance of priests from a non-Latin cultural tradition (possibly the first in any quantity in Guatemala being the Maryknolls) brought an immediate conflict on the local level. The affairs of the community, intimately bound up in the affairs of the religion, suddenly became the target of special interest to the new priest. In an attempt to eliminate antiquated colonial and precolonial pagan practices, the very structure of the political organization of the community was being attacked. Almost everywhere the new priests went in the Indian area they found themselves faced with the problem of dealing with the *cofradías*. In some, the older organizations were already under structural pressure from other events in the country, such as the imposition of *intendentes* under Ubico instead of local alcaldes, or the use of political parties under Arévalo and Arbenz. In many, however, the Indian organization was strong, and the priests were unable to make any significant inroads on the Indians' area of authority and power.

Where the priests were not actually driven out, the Acción Católica provided a convenient tool to combat the older system. By concentrating on younger people and training them as *catequistas*, it was possible to bring factionalism into the community, separating the new from the old. The priests, while not impregnable, did have certain weapons to reinforce the *catequista* work. They could refuse to give mass or, even more important, to baptize. Basically, however, it depended upon the building up of what amounted to a new kind of convert, the individual who converted from Guatemalan Indian Catholicism to modern Roman Catholicism.[10]

The success of Acción Católica Rural has, of course, also varied with the nature of the population, and a lack of general success has been evident in Ladino areas. In some instances it may be due to lack of interest by the priest, but there are no systematic data on the subject. Where Acción Católica Rural has been successful, however, it has not necessarily followed the plan of having four different parish organizations. Rather, a given local priest may regard himself as lucky if he has formed even a reasonably solid adult male group.

In the city, the greatest Catholic effort at "conversion" is not directed at the poor, but rather at the upper sector. The Church is concerned not only with expanding its area of influence here, but also with protecting that which it has gained to date. There have been a number of approaches. Among them are the work of branches of the Acción Católica in the universities, professional groups, and married couples; a set of retreats for leaders; and the particular efforts of the Opus Dei. Common to the work of all of these is the notion that to be a good Catholic one must manifest responsibility in all phases of daily life, including his professional work. The emphasis varies with the particular organization and probably varies somewhat within each as they operate in different countries.

Of the four, the two Acción Católicas are, of course, branches of the larger organization described above. The more developed is that of the Acción Católica Universitaria. Although still rather small, it is specifically directed at students in the national University of San Carlos. It is composed of teams of about ten students in each of the faculties of each university who gather to discuss a variety of subjects, some theological, some to do with problems of the university and student life. As with the rural branch, it is concerned with the promotion of doctrinal matters as well as imbuing the ongoing daily life of the individual with religious qualities. The goal of the priest now in charge of advising the teams is to create teams of high

[10] There have been cases reported on this kind of conflict. See Ruben E. Reina, *The Law of the Saints: A Pokoman Corporate Community and Its Culture*; E. Michael Mendelson, *Los Escándolos de Maximón*. For more general background, see Richard N. Adams, ed., *Political Changes in Guatemalan Indian Communities*.

quality people who will then effectively penetrate the student society and exert their influence. He specifically is not so interested in numbers as he is in the quality of the individuals. The goal is to establish a whole series of such teams, as many within each faculty as can be successfully established. While the Acción Católica is distinct from the Opus Dei, some students are members of both. There is considerable emphasis on social justice, however, in the Acción Católica, a feature less central to the Opus Dei. Students are supposed to be aware of the social injustices and to be willing to attempt to take some action about them.

Students graduating from the university are supposed to move into the Acción Católica Profesional. As with the other branches, they are to continue to evangelize, as well as to act responsibly and to carry out their daily tasks with dedication. This is still a very weak organization, and little was learned of it in the course of research.

Another organization that is technically a part of Acción Católica, but which is autonomous in its operation, is the Movimiento Familiar Cristiana de Guatemala. This is patterned after similar organizations that have been operating elsewhere in Latin America and participates with them in periodic international conferences. The organization consists of sets of eight couples, each of which meets every two weeks to discuss how to carry on a better family life. At the time of the present study (1966), there were reported to be six hundred couples participating. No investigation was made of this organization, however, and it is mentioned here only as a note that in this area, too, Catholic organization has been at work.

The Cursillos de Cristiandad that have been started for leaders in Guatemala are evidently not related to any particular institution. The organization of the first is ascribed to a Maryknoll priest. A *cursillo* consists of a three-day retreat for individuals who are selected as leaders within professional fields and the community. It was described by more than one informant as starting with a "shock treatment" designed to bring individuals into active participation as Catholics. It is quite overtly aimed at building a "superelite" of lay Catholics, men with power to protect the Church, as well as to build a Christian society. The retreats are carefully planned so as to provide the right environment and atmosphere to involve the participant. It begins with confession and communion and then consists of periods of meditation and prayer, classes, and talks given by laymen, at least some of whom were participants in earlier *cursillos*. Each of these is followed up by weekly meetings during which problems are discussed. One description of the *cursillo* indicated that the participants numbered about 35 and consisted ideally of 10 each from the upper and lower classes and 15 from the middle class. Whether any or all of the *cursillos* conform to this pattern was not ascertained. As of the time of study, between 450 and 580 individuals were reported to have gone through *cursillos*. In 1966, at Santa Tecla, El Salvador, there was an "Ultreya," a large congress intended to include all those who had undergone the experience, in order to help reinforce it.

The *cursillo* parallels the purposes of Acción Católica in many respects but, obviously, is specifically concerned with mobilizing the leadership of the society to strengthen lay interest in the Church. In Guatemala, where the upper sector has been more interested in the Church for its political utility than its spiritual qualities, this effort takes on special importance. Not having a widespread and deep upper-sector commitment, the Church has turned to this particular device, old in practice but new in appearance, to elicit from the society greater support.

The last of the four modes for promoting the Church is that sponsored by the religious secular institute, the Opus Dei. While a *cursillo* is organized specifically by a given priest and the Acción Católica is sponsored from the diocesan level, the Opus Dei is an international religious organization of priests and laymen. The explicit mission of Opus Dei, as stated by its founder, Msgr. Escrivá de Balaguer, was to seek God in one's daily affairs. "The ways of God on earth are many. More than that, all the ways of this earth are God's. Any state, any profession in this world, as long as it is honest and is lived with a right intention, can be an encounter with God . . . and this is why, since October 12, 1928, we are trying to tell all souls, through example and with words—with doctrine—that the divine ways of the earth have been opened up." The overt activity of Opus Dei is to enlist laymen as active participants. While there are priests who are the guiding members, they act as secular priests and "live and act essentially as do other diocesan priests in whatever diocese they carry on their spiritual ministry." In addition to both the priestly and laical membership, there are "cooperators," individuals who favor the works of Opus Dei and who help without becoming members. Opus Dei is reported to be the first of the Catholic organizations that includes non-Catholics as "cooperators."

Opus Dei is an outstanding example of the Catholic Church's adaptability to the contemporary world. It says essentially that any individual in any honest professional work may participate; this participation in turn sanctifies the particular work that one is doing, such that the very carrying on of the profession becomes a work of God. In a letter to Escrivá, Paul VI wrote: "Opus Dei has arisen in our time as a living expression of the perennial youth of the Church, fully alert to the demands of a modern apostolate, ever more active, organized and far reaching."[11]

Opus Dei started operating in Guatemala in 1953 at the invitation of the archbishop.[12] According to one informant, some of the major activists came directly from the organization's work in Mexico. It claims to be unindentified with any social class and substantiates this by showing that it has established day nurseries for children of market women, a school for domestic servants, residence halls for university students, a school for social work, and a workers' club. These efforts, however, are supported by an increasingly broad wealthy and generally conservative membership.

The role of Opus Dei is, however, only partially indicated by these activities. It places a strong emphasis on lay membership and encourages the individual to do whatever he wants with the blessings of the Church. The public pronouncements of the founder of the order place emphasis on the fact that the Opus Dei is a spiritual association and that it is highly decentralized; that it is concerned with improving each individual's own work in the world and that it is not concerned with public policies. There is no central directorate, but each national association works independently. It is an organization to make man more spiritual by introducing spiritual values into his daily work whatever it may be.[13]

When one turns elsewhere to evaluate Opus Dei, the task becomes complicated. It has achieved a reputation of being a powerful, cen-

[11] Both quotes from John F. Coverdale, "Opus Dei," *St. Joseph's Magazine* (October 1965).

[12] Msgr. Mario Casariego, Archbishop of Guatemala, in the *Boletín Eclesiástico de la Arquidiocesis de Guatemala* 7 (July–Sept. 1967).

[13] Interview with Msgr. Escrivá de Balaguer in *Le Figaro*, May 16, 1966.

tralized, conservative, secret organization, subtly infiltrating national societies. The Jesuits, historically reputed to be particularly clever and intellectually astute, find the Opus Dei to be a severe threat to their importance in the Catholic intellectual and professional world. The Opus Dei influence in Franco's Spain is cited as the way that the organization has "moved in" and "taken over" both civil and religious posts. Catholics and non-Catholics find it difficult to pin down the exact organization of Opus Dei. The members say this is the case because it is disorganized; its critics say it is secretly organized and therefore may be up to no good. The Opus Dei has already gained in Guatemala the reputation that it carries in Spain, France, and elsewhere in the Catholic world. That is, it is regarded suspiciously, although the suspicion is based more on lack of knowledge about it than on specific knowledge of its activities. If one sees it as an ever-growing network of professional and public men, then it takes on the aspect of a Masonic order, except that it is freer in terms of what it offers its members.

Taken as a whole, the Acción Católica, *cursillos*, and the Opus Dei all form part of the expression of the Church's broad effort to extend its power and influence. Whether working at the parish, diocesan, or world level, whether concerned with upper-class elite or lower-class Indians, the Church is adapting its traditional methods to grapple with the nature of contemporary societies. The new formal quality in the work is the emphasis or permissiveness in one's daily life. The degree of permissiveness varies with the particular social group at which the effort is directed. It seems likely, for example, that the three-year Opus Dei school for domestic servants demands a different kind of formalized, normative, and rigid behavior than is expected from wealthy, upper-class, conservative Opus Dei members in their financial operations. Similarly, the degree of social consciousness and its expression in all these efforts is guided by what seems to be the most expedient for survival of the Church in the society as it is currently constructed, rather than by any set of principles concerning social justice or human rights.

Novelty in the operations of the Church, however, is not limited to the broad scale of operations, but has also been evident in the techniques brought to bear on local and specific issues. Two problems that have placed themselves directly in the way of the Church's efforts are the fact of the ever-expanding population and the accompanying problems of communication, and the fact that much of the population is becoming increasingly aware of its own relative social and economic deprivation. These combine in the rural areas to make it especially difficult for the newly arrived priests to get around to the parishioners and to find ways of solving their economic problems. Toward a solution of the first problem, United States priests in Huehuetenango and Sololá have established radio schools whereby receivers are used in a number of places to receive educational programs beamed from the parish center. The effects of these schools have not yet been measured, but, as of 1966, there were forty-two in operation in Sololá and two in Huehuetenango. The Belgian priests in Chiquimula have set up a radio station that is not used for formal schooling, but over which educational programs, local news, music, and notices of cooperative classes and programs are announced. One progressive Guatemalan priest has argued vehemently for the United States to set up a strong broadcasting station to compete with the Radio Havana. Since most of the Voice of America is beamed at the middle class, *campesinos* and workers listen more to the Cuban station than to North American programs. It is unlikely, of course, that such a United States station could offer the heady fare that stems from Havana.

Of great importance in the long run have been the efforts by a number of priests to establish cooperatives and credit unions within rural population centers. Some have been established by men who were inexperienced in the ways of cooperatives and, as a result, there have been severe failures, as well as some rewarding successes. Primary among the deficiencies in these efforts has been the lack of appreciation of how economic factors operate and, in some instances, that they operate at all. The foreign priests bring with them the enthusiasm necessary to involve their followers in such efforts, but they often fail in an understanding of the broad principles under which cooperatives and other businesses must operate. Nevertheless, there have been enough successful cases that the indicated remedy is to train priests better and not to avoid cooperatives. These and other similar matters bring into question the time-worn assumption that seminary training, the favor of God, and the bishop equip a priest to undertake any task that motivates him. It is, of course, an indictment of the Church that a few priests are depended upon so heavily for such activities.

Another important aspect of the work of priests has been brought into focus by the adventures suffered by the cooperative in Quiché. The case here concerns an apparently successful effort involving some thousands of Indians. The priest was a progressive Spaniard who had established a series of cooperative organizations, including a store and agricultural, weaving, and credit co-ops. He had done this with considerable vigor and was so successful that the cooperatives cut severely into the usurious money-lending patterns and credit operations of the local Ladino storekeepers. The governor of the department at the time was a military man who had little patience with either priests or foreigners, and the local Ladinos complained bitterly to him of the fruits of Indian progress. The governor received support from the central government, at that time under Peralta Azurdia, and the priest was ordered by the papal nuncio to leave the country. He was replaced by another who was much more moderate, less progressive, and less interested in this aspect of Indian development. This story received currency at the time in Guatemala to show that the military and the Church were allied against the poor. It is possible, however, that it is more an illustration of the decision of the Church hierarchy to avoid issues that will bring it into conflict with the government. Later, under another government, the priest was returned to his original post. The Peralta government, as did the preceding and following governments, supported warm relations with the Church but could not have done so if priests were involved in conflicts that involved the civil administration. The Church, in this instance, demonstrated its political awareness by subordinating interest in social and economic development when faced with the prospect of offending the government. Following the petitioning in person by two hundred credit and cooperative members for the removal of the military governor, the government also acceded and replaced him. The government did this less to help recreate the successful cooperative than to avoid a more violent scene.

The clergy has not proved to be so innovative in economic and social problems facing the growing urban population. Mention has been made of a Guatemalan priest who has recommended the use of a strong United States broadcast to reach the *campesinos* of Latin America. This priest has run his own broadcast in Guatemala City but has received very little support and no encouragement from the

Church establishment. Another urban-based priest, like the previous one, a native Guatemalan, has the responsibility for the parish located in La Limonada, one of the major rapidly growing slum areas of the city. He, too, uses both the radio and television. The two priests are among the very few effective progressive Guatemalan priests who work in the city. The problems they face are overwhelming, and the disposition of the Church toward them is to allow them to continue until their activities prove too threatening to the rapprochement of the Church with the upper sector. Presumably, it does no damage to have one priest who is referred to as the "Communist," providing he is not too successful.[14]

A rather different urban parish is the one administered by the Maryknoll missionaries. Urban work is essentially something new for this order, but the Villa de Guadalupe to which they were assigned includes everything from the most miserable shacks to the mansions like the United States Embassy residence. The population of some thirty thousand is somewhat smaller than that falling within the responsibility of the Guatemalan priest in La Limonada, but the Maryknoll have a handsome new headquarters for their work in Guatemala City and four priests to serve the parish. Even with this fourfold advantage and the financial backing they enjoy, the Maryknoll regard their task as quite impossible. It is here, faced with the problem of reaching such an extensive parish, that the Maryknoll priests have initiated the *cursillo*. Their purpose is to try first to identify individuals who can be so influenced by the *cursillos* that they will, in turn, act as centers of dispersion of doctrine and religious interest.

Another parish, illustrating a more traditional approach, is of La Merced in the north of the city. Here a Jesuit priest started a large school, and this was followed by medical and dental clinics. All of the institutions charge minimal fees for their services, mainly because there is no other way to get support. Some four years after beginning the first school, the priest started yet another. This time he was able to get the building subsidized by the owners of the large nearby brewery. This priest, a Spaniard born of a Guatemalan

---

[14] Subsequent to the period of field study, the second of these priests was proving to be so threatening to the government that the Church sent him out of the country.

mother, illustrates the very active work possible by a more tradi-tionally oriented priest. While well aware of many of the develop-mental needs of Guatemala, he finds that he can make the best con-tribution by following the traditional mode of his order, teaching. There was no evidence that any special note has yet been taken by the Church hierarchy that urbanism presents very special problems. The La Limonada priest started a small cooperative of dressmakers, but as yet there seems to have been no very serious experimenting with this kind of endeavor in the city. His attempts to obtain finan-cial help from the outside received no assistance from the establish-ment, and there was some feeling that they actually hindered his work.

The Church still places its major interest and confidence in more traditional activities. This is true of both foreign and national priests. The locus of the traditional interest and concentration of the Church has been the city, however, as is illustrated by the approximate dis-tribution of schools. While figures from different sources do not entirely agree, the burden of their distribution is the same. Table 5–1 shows that 41.5 percent of all the schools and 55.0 percent of the secondary schools sponsored by the Catholic Church are lo-cated in the city of Guatemala. The burden of the remainder, 33.5 percent, is located in the four dioceses heavily populated with In-dians (Verapaces, Quezaltenango, Sololá, and Huehuetenango), or elsewhere in the archdiocese (13.1 percent). Of those in the Indian departments, Huehuetenango and Quezaltenango together account for 21.7 percent of the total. This reflects the fact that Quezaltenango is the second city of the republic, and one-fourth of the provincial schools are located there. Huehuetenango may be a special case, as it has been the particular target of the Maryknoll priests, who have worked in the area for over twenty years.

Another aspect of the educational emphasis is seen in Table 5–2: While the Catholic schools account for only 7.4 percent of the pri-mary school students of the country, they include 21.1 percent of the secondary students. This compares with 33.9 percent for all other private schools and 45 percent for public schools. Table 5–3 indicates that one-third of all the private secondary and normal schools of the country are run by the Church. In a country where the immigration of foreign priests was slight until a decade ago, this is a profound influence. It is clear that this is an area of major emphasis by the

TABLE 5–1
Schools Sponsored by the Catholic Church

Diocese	Primary		Secondary		Normal		Technical		Total	
	No.	%	No.	%	No.	%	No.	%	No.	%
Esquipulas	3	2.0	1	1.7	0	0.0	0	0.0	3	2.0
El Petén	1	0.7	0	0.0	0	0.0	0	0.0	1	0.7
Jalapa	3	2.0	3	5.0	0	0.0	0	0.0	3	2.0
Zacapa	6	4.0	2	3.3	1	4.3	0	0.0	7	4.6
San Marcos	4	2.7	1	1.7	1	4.3	1	7.1	4	2.6
Verapaces	9	6.1	3	5.0	1	4.3	0	0.0	9	5.9
Quezaltenango	18	12.1	9	15.0	3	13.1	2	14.3	19	12.5
Sololá	9	6.0	1	1.7	1	4.3	0	0.0	9	5.9
Huehuetenango	13	8.7	4	6.7	1	4.3	0	0.0	14	9.2
Guatemala Total	83	55.6	36	60.0	15	65.3	11	78.6	83	54.6
(Guatemala City)	(63)	42.2	(33)	55.0	(15)	65.3	(10)	71.4	(63)	41.5
(Guatemala Outside City)	(20)	13.4	(3)	5.0	(0)	. . .	(1)	7.1	(20)	13.1
Total	149	99.9	60	100.1	23	99.9	14	100.0	152	100.0

SOURCE: *Boletín Informativo*, No. 7, IX Congreso Interamericano de Educación Católica, Mim ographed, San Salvador, El Salvador, n.d., Table 1.
NOTE: The total is of named schools; in all but a few instances, primary schools are connecte to higher schools, and the combination is counted as a single school in this table.

TABLE 5–2
Students in Guatemalan Schools, 1966

Level	Official Government Schools		Private Schools		Catholic Schools		Total	
	No.	%	No.	%	No.	%	No.	%
Primary	357,953	80.8	52,579	11.9	32,620	7.4	443,152	100.1
Secondary	16,346	45.0	12,316	33.9	7,647	21.1	36,309	100.0
Normal	3,625	53.6	1,933	28.6	1,198	17.8	6,756	100.0
Technical	4,125	62.4	1,864	28.2	629	9.5	6,618	100.1
Superior	7,547	93.4	—	—	533	6.6	8,080	100.0
Total	389,596		68,692		42,627		500,915	

SOURCE: See Table 5–1.

TABLE 5–3
Private Schools in Guatemala, 1966

vel	Private School		Catholic		Total	
	No.	%	No.	%	No.	%
Primary	1,019	87.2	149	12.8	1,168	100.0
Secondary	223	66.0	88	34.0	311	100.0
Normal	51	66.2	26	33.8	77	100.0
Technical	48	76.2	15	24.8	63	100.0
Total	1,341		278		1,619	

URCE: See Table 5–1.
OTE: Secondary schools are counted separately whether or not they are administratively related to primary schools.

Church, and it reflects its emphasis on the upper sector rather than the lower. It sponsors almost as many secondary and normal schools in the whole country (eighty-three) as it does primary schools outside the capital city (eighty-six).

Figures that are less clear suggest that the allocation of hospitals and clinics follows the concern with the Indian population. According to Stahlke,[15] twelve of the eighteen dental clinics and 65 percent of the sixty dispensaries are located in the dioceses of Quezaltenango, Sololá, and Huehuetenango. This distribution coincides with that of the agricultural cooperatives reported by Stahlke (all eighteen are in these departments), and surely the greater enterprise of the priests in these dioceses is reflected in both. The interesting fact is, however, that even where such new efforts as cooperatives are introduced, they accompany the older, more traditional service devices that have characterized Catholic "civic action" since the colonial period.

In the field of education, the establishment of Rafael Landívar University follows the earlier practice of carrying Catholic control in education through the university level. Started in 1961 under the academic control of the national university, it was granted autonomy with the new constitution of 1966. As is the case with Catholic universities elsewhere in the hemisphere, the students have no active role in political life and are expected to be more constant in

[15] Stahlke, *Estadística Religiosa*, pp. 85–86.

their attendance than is the case at the national university. Similarly, the faculty is paid for the actual lecturing, not for formally offering a course. The university is controlled by a directive council, composed of both Jesuits and laymen. Originally much of the faculty also worked at San Carlos, but, under the military government, the San Carlos law students forced out all those who did not oppose the Peralta government so that there is less overlap than was the case formerly. Tuition at thirty dollars a month is fairly high, but about half of the approximately one thousand students (1966) were on scholarships. Scholarship holders still pay a minimal tuition, but it is reduced for some to as little as two dollars a month. The school received an original governmental subvention of $300,000 to construct the first buildings and is supported by the tuitions plus the donations of interested individuals. The control of the university is firmly in the hands of elements of the conservative upper sector and the Jesuits.

The traditional quality of much of the Church work is also illustrated by the activities of the Franciscans who are generally responsible for Jutiapa. The eight individuals working there in 1965 were all supported financially from the United States; all had "jeeps, electric generators, comfortable houses, and other symbols considered to indicate membership in the regional elite."[16] They found the Ladinos of the towns to harbor a "fanatic anticlericism," and some felt that working there required that they live in a "lower culture" than their own. They saw their role as being entirely traditional. Religious proselytizing was the major issue, and the operation of schools, youths' and women's groups, and charitable activities were the acceptable ways to implement it.

The promotional activities of the Church constantly have at their core the issue of expanding and consolidating the position of the Church as an institution and the Catholic religion and ideology as an integrating element in the total society. It is the only corporate institution that claims such broad interests and responsibilities. Today in Guatemala, the Church is applying many old formulae to obtain this end, as well as experimenting with various newer approaches. In general, even with the large proportion of foreign clergy

---

[16] John Durston, "Power Structure in a Rural Region of Guatemala: The Department of Jutiapa," M.A. thesis, The University of Texas at Austin, 1966, pp. 100–101.

and new dioceses, both the hierarchy and the parish priests tend to
follow a strongly traditional, conservative, and spiritually oriented
line. Schools, dispensaries, and teaching doctrine take precedence
over newer devices. From the outside, however, has come a series of
approaches that are putting some pressure on the total structure of
the Guatemalan Church to adapt it to the contemporary realities.
In part, these have come through open concern with problems of social justice and of general welfare, but they also have come through
the institution of efforts that are best illustrated by Acción Católica
and Opus Dei, organizations overtly designed to permeate the body
politic and establish the religion and the Church as an influential
aspect of every human being. Of these, the Opus Dei may reflect
external controls, whereas Acción Católica is fundamentally based
within the dioceses. Whether the context is national or international
in scope, the principles of operation are consistent. The differences
arise in terms of who is perceiving the relation between the means
and the ends. Most clerics in Guatemala still see the welfare of the
Church in terms of the old order; a few see political danger in that
direction and are making an effort to rescue both the prestige of the
Church and its position of influence and power by carrying its work
into more developmental activities and enterprises directed toward
gaining social justice. A very few, mainly native Guatemalan, talk
of revolutionary reforms. They have neither influence nor real effect, but serve to give the Church the appearance of being the pro-
tector of all doctrines.[17]

3. *Politics, Power, and the Guatemalan Church*

The Catholic Church in Guatemala is expanding and carrying out its activities within a context of power that sets some rigid
restrictions. Locally, the degree of interest of the population in
spiritual issues, the government, the political situation, the growth
of other churches, and nationalism are all factors to be confronted.
Beyond the borders of Guatemala lie Rome, the United States, and
others who place demands on it.

[17] The recent expelling of three members of the Maryknoll order from the
country on the basis of their announced intention to support revolution is the
first open break of clerics in Guatemala with the Church and state association.
The fact that they are North Americans makes them somewhat more visible,
but they have Latin American counterparts in other countries.

Of central importance in the expansion of the Church has been
the change in its legal status. While various rights were restored to
it under the postrevolutionary governments of Castillo Armas and
Ydígoras Fuentes, the essential reinstatement of the Church to a
legal situation it had enjoyed prior to 1871 was accomplished with
four articles of the 1966 constitution. Article 67 confirmed and extended the rights to hold property that had been granted in the 1955
constitution. Prior to this time, the Church had "held" properties
for which it had no legal title. The La Merced Church, for example,
which was "given" to the Jesuits in 1950, was not legally held by
them. This article not only granted the Church tax exemption on
properties that it held for religious and educational purposes, but
it also made a provision for granting to the Church titles for the
properties that it had held and even those that the government had
seized in the past.

Another matter in which the Church had made some gains in the
1955 constitution was permission to include religious education in
the regular schools. Under Article 93 of the new constitution, this
constitutional provision was extended so that it openly declared it
to be in the national interest that religion be taught in the schools,
thereby establishing a place for religious education in the national
curriculum. Previously, the Ministry of Education had appended
such education as an after-school, optional subject, so that few took
it.

Article 85 of the 1966 constitution reintroduced the Church as a
legal agent for marriage. Under the previous liberal constitutions,
a marriage was legal only after it had been performed in the local
municipality office. The new article made Church marriages legal
also. The additional rationale behind this was to encourage people
in common law union to get married, arguing that if they could do
it either civilly or religiously, it would be more likely to happen.
This rationale is meaningful only where there are priests available
to promote marriages. For many, especially Indians, the reason to
avoid formal marriage previously was to avoid the costly celebration
that had to accompany the ceremony when it was performed by the
municipality and the Church. Finally, as was mentioned earlier,
Article 102 granted autonomy to private universities. This specifically allowed Landívar to be released from the academic controls
held by the national university.

The years following the revolutionary decade saw, then, the gradual legal reestablishment of the Church. The increasing position of strength and power gained first from the 1955, then from the 1966, constitution meant that the government was once again inviting the Church to share with it the responsibilities for social control within the country. Certain elements of the upper sector found this to their advantage, but enthusiasm for it was far from being shared by all the populace. While the Indians found the return of the priests generally advantageous, although there were serious reservations on the part of the more traditional communities, the provincial Ladinos were much less interested. One particular case that suggested that the pre-1871 stance of the Church was going to be repeated in practice as well as in law occurred in the early summer of 1965 in Jalapa.

The Montaña de Jalapa is a region of some thirty thousand *campesinos* who live on a series of lands held in communal property. The communal owners of these lands have long since acted as a corporate community to protect the lands from being subdivided and sold to outsiders. Although culturally Ladino in most respects, the individuals involved have retained the designation *indígena* to suggest that they hold these lands through age-old rights and because they think of themselves as being somewhat apart from the general neighboring Ladinos. Among the lands they hold are those on which are located the major church of the departmental capital of Jalapa and the residence of the bishop. The bishop, in what was a new diocese, originally established good relations with the *comuneros* but later insisted on sending to them a priest whom they found offensive. Specifically, the priest insisted on building a church on the community land, a thing the *comuneros* did not want. After various preliminary incidents, about 450 *comuneros* tried to tear down the partially built church and in so doing killed the mason and roughed up some of the others involved, including the priest. The local military reservists from the provincial capital arrested the entire group, bound them, and paraded them through the streets of Jalapa. Soldiers were sent in to keep the peace, and the entire group of twenty-four governors of the community lands were jailed. Subsequently, others were jailed. The whole performance was taken locally, and probably correctly, as a continuation of the traditional links between the local Ladinos, the government, and the Church establishment, essentially the same situation that resulted from the Quiché incident described earlier. It received fairly good coverage in the national press, and, while some editorial opinion was expressed against the government's and the Church's roles, it evidently had no beneficial effect for the Jalapa *indígenas*.[18]

To enjoy the government's protection is a matter that cannot entirely be left to chance, however, and the Church readily remembers its past history in Guatemala. The years of liberal repression and the outright antagonism that existed during the latter days of the revolutionary period have not been forgotten. As was mentioned earlier in this chapter, the beginnings of the Guatemalan Christian Democratic party (DCG)[19] were to be found in an organization that began in the revolutionary period with the approval of the archbishop. In 1955, the new party was allotted five congressional seats, but it never succeeded in manifesting very great success and usually gained position only by combining with other parties. Finally, in the early 1960's, the left and right wings of the party split. Perhaps such a split was inevitable when the issues were removed from the protective and diluting influence of direct Church participation. The political differences were too raw to permit party unity. Although it mustered a sufficient number of signatures (fifty thousand were required) to officially place a candidate in the 1966 elections, the electoral officials refused to allow the registry until after the election.

At its inception, the party was unquestionably looked upon fondly by the conservative members of the Church, but it was also a political nonentity. As the decade of the 1950's drew to a close, formal ties between the Church and the DCG ended. By the time of the split within the party in the 1960's, the left wing was violently denying any relationship with the Church at all and today even claims that there never was such a link. There are, as far as can be determined, no formal links between the Church and any political party in Guatemala. The more moderate and conservative supporters of the right wing of the DCG do recognize a strong identification with the interests of the Church. This, however, is by no

[18] Of particular interest is the editorial by Clemente Marroquín Rojas in *La Hora*, July 17, 1965, and the petition presented to the government by the people of the Montaña, *La Hora*, July 8, 1965.

[19] Democracia Cristiana Guatemalteca.

means limited to DCG affiliates; supporters of other conservative political groups equally identify with the Church. It is not beyond the individual operators in both the Church and the DCG, however, to take advantage of the possible link. Some DCG party workers have tried to use the membership in Acción Católica as a means of extending their influence in the Indian areas.

It is not really clear whether the overt separation of the Church from any party support or affiliation is more a product of the left wing of the party wishing to avoid such a public relation or whether the Church decided that the party was doing so badly that an alliance would do it more harm than good. In any case, it is clear that the Church regards any such clear-cut political affiliation as a limitation to its ability to work with all parties. During the late 1950's, members of the parties deriving from Castillo Armas' Liberation Movement were more powerful and more helpful than the DCG was. The Church basically defines its political interests in the light of the pervading powers within the total governmental structure, as long as they are reasonably congenial to the Church establishment.

A corollary of the Church's preference of cooperation with a supportive government is a policy of not pursuing changes in that system. Efforts by foreign priests and by the outside agencies toward changing the activities and performance of the government hold little interest for the Church establishment. Coupled with this is nationalist pride among the native clergy against attempts by foreigners, be they clerical or not, to control affairs in Guatemala. Nationalism within the Church has changed perceptibly since the early days of Archbishop Rossell's reluctance to admit foreign priests to the country. The papal nuncio's naming of three bishops confirmed change in the official attitude already apparent in Rossell's changing policy. And more recently, when an ultranationalistic paper called *El Católico* was extreme in its denunciation of foreign influence, the current archbishop requested that it stop publication.

Even with this change, however, the Guatemalan clergy continues to combine conservatism with nationalism. The nationalism is not one that promotes innovation in the country, but rather one that is reactive to what can be regarded as criticism from the outside. It is expressed in the question "Who do they think they are, coming in here and telling us how to do things in our own country?"

The question has been asked particularly of the Agency for International Development of the United States government. It has been expressed by Guatemalan clergy, both priests and bishops. Efforts by U.S. officials and technicians to introduce changes are regarded as merely efforts to consolidate and shore up U.S. commercial and investment interests. The fact that the agency officials can seldom demonstrate the contrary does little to lessen the opinion.

Clerical nationalism is, however, strongly tempered by the fact that the clergy is identified with the international Catholic order. When the government became irritated, particularly with priests of Spanish origin following the Quiché co-op incident, most of the Spanish priests in the country immediately took out Guatemalan citizenship papers. When the chief of state called in the "Spaniards" to advise them of their proper roles, very few showed up because most had technically become Guatemalans. The simple switching of citizenship does not, of course, make the native Guatemalan clergy any happier with the influx and activities of the clergy of foreign origin. It does, however, take some of the sting out of the effort.

The conservatism of the clergy is illustrated by the reaction that was recorded a number of times concerning the new ecumenical movement and the directions sent down from Rome concerning the proper efforts of the clergy toward this goal. A number of priests in all seriousness responded that ecumenism made great sense: all that was necessary was for the Protestant churches to recognize the authority and infallibility of the pope, and there would be no bars to cooperation.

Just as the Church is placing little or no pressure on the government to change, so the government has made no vehement suggestion that the Church change its approach. The two are under pressure from other quarters, and the Church is particularly under tension from factors deriving from outside the country. The two most active sources are Rome and the United States. The pressure from Rome has come through the ways already mentioned at the beginning of the chapter and through direct dealing with the bishops. Rome, in a way, is trying to infiltrate the Guatemalan Church in much the same way that the Guatemalan Church is trying to infiltrate the Guatemalan society. The influence of U.S. agencies is both direct and indirect. The primary medium of influence is money. Both the government and the private Catholic sources in the United States channel funds to the clergy in Guatemala but, in so doing, make certain requirements. Such influences may come from American diocese bishops who are sending priests with support to work in Guatemala, or from the Agency for International Development that wants to encourage priests to be more enterprising in social welfare and development work.

One case that exposes many of the problems involved is that of the Guatemalan agency Caritas and its relations with the Catholic Relief Service (CRS). This history began in 1959 when the Catholic Relief Service started sending food made available in the United States through Public Law 480 to the Guatemalan agency Caritas for distribution. Caritas was an organization of Guatemalan bishops set up for this purpose, just as the CRS was a similar organization of United States bishops. The program reached its peak in the middle 1960's when the food program alone amounted to over $200,000. The CRS acted as a channel for more than surplus food, however. It also provided medical supplies to clinics and hospitals and dispensaries, identified posts for medical personnel who volunteer their services through the Catholic Medical Mission Board, sent clothing for distribution through the same channels as the food, and sponsored various other efforts, including some in "socioeconomic" development.

Over the years of work between Caritas and CRS, it developed that the Caritas was keeping few records, and the CRS was unable to provide the necessary reports to the United States government as to the disposition of the surplus material. This further complicated the situation for the CRS in Guatemala, since it could not well estimate the appropriate size of future shipments. In early 1966, a new North American director of the CRS in Guatemala, backed by individuals in the Agency for International Development, demanded of the bishops that they reform their organization to eliminate certain food disposition that did not come under the law of the United States and that they institute more orderly bookkeeping and reporting arrangements. These demands resulted in some clashes between the clerics and the United States CRS officials. The latter felt that the Guatemalans were abusing U.S. funds, and the former that the U.S. officials were forcing their ways on the Guatemalans.

By the time the uproar reached a peak, the actual amount of surplus food had diminished considerably. CRS, however, had long since entered into other supportive ventures and had started to act as a middleman for the clerics in getting funds from extranational agencies, both in the United States and elsewhere. In this way they became the intermediary funding agent for getting tools and other aid for co-ops, aiding colonization projects in the northwest, sponsoring irrigation projects, and in general, searching out worthwhile projects being promoted by the clergy. In doing this, they bypassed the Caritas organization and dealt directly with the soliciting groups. The result of all this was that Caritas found it almost impossible to do without the funding that CRS mediated and was unable to solicit alternative support from Guatemalan sources, apart from an annual subvention from the government. Caritas and the bishops had to undertake a reorganization of their effort more in accord with the demands made by the North Americans. They did this in preference to stopping the funds, since this not only would entail a decrease in the final product, but would also essentially sound the death knell for their organization.

The direction of North American influences varies all the way from demands for greater efficiency, such as was the case of the CRS-Caritas venture, to conservative slowdowns. A case of the latter variety occurred in the work of a priest sent out from the United States diocese. His Guatemalan bishop, who had arranged for his local work with his home bishop, was generally encouraging in matters pertaining to socioeconomic development. His home bishop, however, felt that the real reason for his presence in Guatemala was to evangelize and that he should not dilute his efforts with mundane matters. He held up funds, was slow in granting permissions, and in general tried to discourage the priest's nonevangelical work. However, the best influence of the U.S. agencies is toward a greater amount of welfare and social development work. It falls far short of promoting fundamental reforms in the agrarian or marketing system and emphasizes things that a priest can do within his own parish with only a limited amount of outside help. The economic product is necessarily marginal to general development.

The Church in Guatemala is reforming its approach to its members and to the process of conversion almost entirely in response to external stimuli. Rome, foreign priests, foreign orders, and foreign governments (most especially the United States) are all pressing the Guatemalan Church to adapt its methods to the contemporary scene, assuming that this will enable it to more successfully pursue its ancient goals of theological dominance, social control, and political influence. Although to its activists the Church in Guatemala seems weak and poorly supported and to its enemies it seems monolithic and demonic in its goals, there is little doubt that it is playing the role of the conservator of contemporary regimes, and no matter what its individual agents may profess, its actions will be gauged not to threaten its good standing with that order. The goal of the Guatemalan Church is its own renaissance, and the development of Guatemala is relevant insofar as it is seen to contribute to that end. The principal reason for this position was suggested in the opening section of this chapter when it was pointed out that the Guatemalan Church has almost no independent power base. Perhaps it will venture into more independent action if, and when, it feels more secure in its own realm. As long as it seeks an independent base within the upper sector, however, and not within the larger population, there is little reason to expect that its major orientations will change.

6 The Expansion of Upper-Sector Interest Groups

CONTROL OVER THE PRODUCTION and distribution of natural resources has always been, and presumably will continue to be, the single most important independent power base of any society. To say this, however, is to point a discussion in the direction of economics, a topic which, in the present context, tends to cloud the issues. To focus on the resources themselves leads to the differentiation of the economic from the political and to the kind of argument holding that political actions are irrational within the area of economic choice. Since it is an underlying assumption of this study that choice is basically rational and that political choice is no dif-

NOTE: The material on which this chapter is based is derived entirely from the work of Mavis Ann Bryant. During the summer of 1965 and in a few short subsequent visits, Miss Bryant compiled a large collection of source materials, now in the Latin American Collection of The University of Texas at Austin. From the interviews and source material, she prepared a master's thesis, "Agricultural Interest Groups in Guatemala," The University of Texas at Austin, 1967 (Bryant, 1967a), and a first-draft manuscript, "Industrial and Commercial Associations in Guatemala" (Bryant, 1967b). Both manuscripts are on deposit at The University of Texas at Austin and at the Seminario de Integración Social Guatemalteca, Guatemala City. The present chapter is a reanalysis of Miss Bryant's materials, specifically those found in the two manuscripts. So many of the ideas used herein originate in one or another part of Miss Bryant's work that I can claim no originality for this chapter except for emphasis and the form of analysis. As in the other chapters in this volume, this can only be an exploration into the subject, not a final study.

ferent from the economic in this respect, our focus will not be on the resources themselves, but on the systems of control that are exercised over them. Here, attention is directed to an area of traditional economic interest, that of productive and distributive enterprise, and how the systems of control of these enterprises have varied over the period of Guatemalan history under discussion.

There is much more to be said, both fundamentally and marginally, about the control of goods and values than we will be able to discuss here. As with other sectors of the society, however, we have chosen to look into the subject by focusing on one aspect. In this case, it is the manner in which individuals and groups have tried to retain and improve their control over the production and distribution of resources through organizing into networks and groups of control. It will not deal with the parameters of this control, the legal systems that operate behind it, or the vast set of economic mechanisms that accompany it. Interest groups, or the articulation of interests, will be used as a means to examine how members of the upper sector have used each other, their government, their lower sector, and outside elements in an attempt to gain or hold power.

1. *The Nature of Interest Groups*

"Interest group" refers to an organization that articulates and differentiates individuals on the basis of activities designed to promote their own perceived individual well-being. In the general jargon of social science, the term is usually used to refer to networks or groupings formed to better economic circumstances, most specifically to enhance the individual's income and profit. Interest groups also form around noneconomic issues; such things as sewing circles and faculty clubs are examples. Here, however, we are by definition concerned with the coming together of people in order to enhance their economic and political well-being.

Further distinction must be drawn, however, for any complex business or industrial enterprise is, in a sense, an economic interest group. Interest groups are made up of discrete parts, and these parts are combined to promote the economic situation of each of the individual members, not the combination of such parts. So it is that the chain of farms owned by a single individual is formed to enhance the well-being of that individual, not of each of the farms in itself. The organizations that concern us here are those formed when discrete enterprises come together to enhance their individual well-being, and not to enhance the organization that is formed thereby. A man joins or resigns from the Chamber of Commerce because it helps him, not because it helps the Chamber of Commerce.

There are two other features associated with interest groups that are generally applicable here but do not serve as definitive characteristics: the qualities of being nonprofit and voluntary. Since interest groups are not formed to produce income for themselves, they are generally nonprofit. In some instances, however, sets of individuals join together and take on the form of what are usually recognized to be profit organizations. The Algodonera Guatemalteca, S.A. (AGSA) is such a case. This organization was actually formed in most respects like an interest group, but the fact that it has taken a corporate form as a *sociedad anónima* technically makes it profit making. The evidence in this instance, however, suggests that the formation of AGSA in almost all respects conforms to that of other nonprofit groups and therefore can be included within the present discussion. It was formed in order that the individual cotton growers could be assured of satisfactory ginning facilities. In 1953, when it was started, the gins of Guatemala were small and obsolete, and, to improve the situation, most of the growers of that period joined together in the AGSA. By 1965, AGSA had 160 stockholders, possessed six gins, exported its cotton, maintained an oil factory that supplied a wholly owned vegetable shortening factory, and produced for export construction board of pressed cottonseed hulls. Since the stockholders were almost entirely the cotton growers themselves, the organization also acted as an interest group.

The question of whether or not interest groups are voluntary associations is also a little problematical. Almost all of them are voluntary in that a given individual may choose not to belong. Nevertheless, there are some in which, because of the regulatory and control functions assigned them by the government, membership becomes a prerequisite to effective economic action. Since the Asociación Nacional de Café, for example, has complete control over export marketing of coffee, any coffee grower of any size who fails to join is almost guaranteed to be unable to market his crop. The question of the quality of being "voluntary" has not come up only in recent years, but was inherent in the very emergence of some organizations. In general, in those areas concerned with agricultural export, the interest organizations have tended (or are tending) to take on regulatory powers, and therefore individuals wishing to participate find they must be members in order to export their crops.

All economic interest groups are concerned with control. In every case for which we have any data, if an organization is actually operating and does not exist merely on paper, the functions and goals are multiple. None exists with only one purpose. It is recognized in the culture, currently, that such an organization can potentially serve a number of purposes. Not infrequently, the purpose that motivates the initiation of such a group is quickly replaced by another as new problems arise. It is, then, quite impossible to classify the groups in terms of their purposes or goals, although it is quite possible at a given point to infer that at that point in its history, a given group is more concerned with one than another of a repertory of activities and goals.

In the groups studied, it was possible to distinguish at least eight aspects of the environment that were regarded as significant matters of control. (The number eight is meaningless, since each of these can be analyzed into components.) Perhaps the most obvious, control over the raw materials or resource base itself, was seldom a basis for the formation of a group. Where it was, it did not have to do with resources in the natural environment, but with control over the import of elements for elaboration within the country. Where this was the case, such as when Gremial de Fabricantes de Acumuladores of the Cámara de Industria successfully stopped three automobile dealers from starting their own battery factory, it can also be seen as a matter of defending oneself against local competition.

The major areas of control in evidence are local competition, foreign competition, marketing, production, processing, credit, labor, and government taxation and regulation. Of these, the last is the most pervasive. Almost all organizations in this area have found themselves trying to apply pressure on some agency of the government, if not on the president himself, to do, or to stop doing, something. The organizations most commonly involved in this are the various *gremiales* of the Cámara de Industria and the large organizations of major producers of coffee, cotton, and sugar. More limited, but very important for those so involved, are local and foreign competition and the facilitation of production processing, or marketing. Some associations, as will be seen in more detail later, are quite concerned with competition from foreign sources. They usually take on a nationalistic tinge and frame their demands in terms of what is best for or is hurting the country. Foreigners, especially North American investors, are cast as evil, destined to destroy the native fabric of the nation. Local competition is usually concerned either with restricting the number of enterprises, as in the case of the battery group just described, or with assuring the local producers of a sufficient share of a restricted market. In this regard the various regional coffee groups are very much concerned with the latter as, under the international coffee agreement, Guatemala is limited to a quota smaller than its annual production.

The facilitation of production, processing, or marketing is taken care of both by major organizations as a part of their broader responsibilities and by special organizations established to carry on research into such matters. Their basic reference point is the government, which either allows such groups to form or refuses such permission. If formation is allowed, the government may encourage and facilitate the process or inhibit it through any one of a multitude of ways. In matters having to do with competition, both domestic and foreign, the major target of influence is the government and the regulations and licenses that it controls. Even in research, government assent is basically necessary, since the import of personnel and materials is crucial.

Over the years, the government has increasingly used the associations for regulative functions and, in so doing, has brought the associations more closely under its own control. It not only continues to hold the position of being the major recipient of petitions, but also is the major judge of petitions concerning third parties. With few exceptions, the associations exist within the unique domain of the government and have no other channel to which to turn for authority and derived power. They do, of course, through their collective coordination of common interests, have the possibility of manipulating the resources or products that they control. They have, at least theoretically, an independent power base, although it may be a very weak one.

2. *Internal Organization*

Not all interest groups are formally organized. Indeed, there is good reason to suppose that among the most important are some that are fairly informal organizations. A good example of this is to be found in the area of coffee production. The coffee sector is broadly organized within the Asociación Nacional de Café (ANACAFE), which exclusively controls the export marketing of the coffee as well as providing many services to its members. Within the country, however, there are regional coffee associations, one each for the east, the west, and the north. Over the years of its existence, however, the ANACAFE has generally not been controlled dominantly by the growers from any of the three areas represented by the separate associations, but by those from the central part of the country. Aside from an Asociación Experimental Cafetalera, a small group interested in coffee research with members from the central region, they are represented by no formal organization. Although individuals from other areas played important roles, from 1961 through 1967 the Junta Directiva of the ANACAFE was dominated by a limited number of individuals from the central region and/or from the experimental association.[1]

[1] Bryant, 1967a, pp. 141–144 states:

"It is important to compare the total number of positions held by the representatives of the four interest groups in the 1961–67 period; also relevant is the average number of years such groups' representatives served. The longer an individual served, the more powerful he would likely be, not only because re-election would signify a powerful position, but also because tenure in office would give him access to resources of knowledge not available to others. The Asociación Experimental Cafetalera, counting Franz Pieters, had held office for 18.5 years, for an average of 3.7 per person. If Pieters is dropped from this total, the association had 18 positions, for an average of 4.5. The Central group had served 18 years for an average of 4.5 as well. The men from the East had had 15 positions, for an average of 2.5 per man. From the West, twelve men averaging 1.5 each had served 17.5 years. Finally, the remaining men, composed of two government representatives, one from Alta Verapaz, and six of unknown affiliation, held twelve positions for an average of 1.3 each. The low average for the unknown makes it less likely that the picture presented here will miss important members of one of the four interest groups under discussion.

"The Asociación Experimental Cafetalera and the Center group had the most representatives and the highest average length of tenure, followed by the East and then the West. The Asociación Experimental and the Center group both represented the Center region and cooperated closely in coffee politics. The two groups together held 36 of the 81 total positions in the 1961–67 period. From them came eight of the twelve men with indexes of participation of .50 or more; the other four were all from the East. Every indication was that the Center was dominating the ANACAFE's direction."

In the area of cotton production, Bryant learned of six distinctive interest groups, but of these, only two are formally organized. Without a separate study specifically of that subject, it would not even be possible to know who the members of these other four groups were. In her analysis of the participation of various growers on national and international commissions and on the recently formed Consejo Nacional de Algodón, it develops that all six groups were almost always represented, and the particular individuals involved did not vary greatly. It was less important for any one of the groups to dominate in cotton than in coffee, since in the latter the market was limited, whereas in the former, there was still essentially an open market. It was not practically possible, however, to pursue study of the informal groupings throughout the nation, and the present investigation focused instead on the formal organizations. It should be reiterated, however, that this focus does not suggest that the other kinds of organizations are unimportant, but merely that study of them requires additional research.

The formal interest groups followed a fairly basic pattern of organization. Bryant describes it as follows:

A non-profit association had a characteristic type of organization. The *Junta General* of the association was the entire body of members meeting in conjunction; this took place usually once or twice a year, but special meetings might be called by the *Junta Directiva* or upon request of a certain number of members to deal with special problems. This body generally elected the *Junta Directiva*, approved the budget, and decided other matters of importance submitted for its consideration by the *Junta Directiva*. Voting in the *Junta General* might be unitary or proportional to production. Individuals might, when authorized, exercise *representation* on behalf of a person not present; this meant that the latter's votes might be cast by the authorized representative. The *Junta Directiva* corresponded to a Board of Directors, its President serving as President of the Association. The number and titles of members of the *Junta Directiva* varied: a President and Secretary were frequently joined by one or more Vice-Presidents, a Treasurer, and several *Vocales* or *Directores*. These latter could be *Propietarios* and optionally, in addition, *Suplentes* (alternates).

Many associations had a professional staff headed by a *gerente* (manager) or a *secretario ejecutivo* (executive secretary) who also frequently served without vote as Secretary of the *Junta Directiva*. The Asociación General de Agricultores (AGA) had an auxiliary body called the *Consejo Consultivo* which was appointed by the *Junta Directiva* and was called upon for advice in specific matters. This same association had subdivisions based on specific occupational groupings, called *gremiales*, several of which had their own *Juntas Directivas*; the Presidents of *gremiales* were *ex-oficio* members of the *Junta Directiva* of the parent association. The Asociación Nacional del Café (ANACAFE) had internal groupings along regional lines called *regionales*, again with their own *Juntas Directivas*.

Before an association might deal officially with the government, celebrate contracts, etc., it had to have had its *estatutos* (statutes) approved by the appropriate government ministers and published in the official newspaper, *El Guatemalteco*. The statutes contained statements of purpose, structure, rights and duties of members, and so on. Some associations had further *reglamentos* which detailed their internal functioning.

The non-profit association was barred by law from participating directly in politics, and the apolitical status of such associations was frequently emphasized in their statutes.[2]

Variations in this basic pattern occurred with size and whether or not the organization was affiliated as a *gremial* in the Cámara de Comercio or Cámara de Industria. When the two Cámaras were concerned, any action in the public area, any relations with the government or other organizations, had to be carried out through the Junta Directiva of the Cámara. The major consequence of increased size led to undertaking additional activities, the formation of special committees and special commissions, and the proliferation of offices. With few exceptions, the *gremiales* pertaining to the Cámaras had between five and twenty members.

The independent organizations might number up to two or three hundred except for some organizations of small operators, such as the Gremial de Trigueros with approximately six thousand members, and the Asociación Guatemalteca de Transportes with some fifteen hundred members. In most instances where membership was not effectively mandatory for successful operation of the enterprise, membership usually was considerably less than the total number theoretically possible. Although growing size generally increased effectiveness, an equally important index was the income that the association could depend on to carry out its functions.

[2] Bryant, 1967a, pp. 6–8.

Those associations that were given regulatory functions by the government, or that provided marketing services for their members and therefore could extract a given sum for each unit quantity marketed, had the advantage since they could anticipate a guaranteed income. Aside from this, the best supported associations were those experimental groups to which the members looked for basic developments and which they were therefore willing to support as necessary. The Gremial de Trigueros, Asociación de Productores de Aceites Esenciales, ANACAFE, the AGSA, and AGUAPA (Asociación Guatemalteca de Productores de Algodón) benefited from the first circumstance, whereas the research groups in essential oils and coffee were well supported by the second. Permanent financing at any significant level, however, also reflected a need for expenditures. Even though a major purpose of most interest groups was to deal with the government, and this required minimum clerical help and the time of the officers of the association, many groups worked on slender budgets.

As was suggested by Bryant's description of the internal organization of the groups, the actual control over day-to-day policy and general activity was held by the Junta Directiva, and, where there was one, with the *gerente* and/or the Consejo Consultivo. The real control, however, was determined by the voting arrangements and this, in turn, hinged on whether leadership in the organization was of interest to particular individuals. Voting was usually established on one of two bases: either one vote was assigned to each member, or votes were allocated in some proportion to the size of the crop of the member. The former system was most common in smaller associations or in associations started with the express purpose of taking issue with actions by the government. Under these circumstances, the issue was to obtain the common expression of all relevant individuals. When, however, the association had to do with setting policy on marketing, purchasing, or services to the members, then the large producers felt that their interests should be represented more proportionally to the financial input they supplied to the association. Since financing was usually based on some proportion of production, usually a small tax on each hundredweight of delivered produce, the large producers in fact provided substantially more support than could the small ones.

An example of where the difference counts occurred in 1959 in the AGUAPA. Much of the cotton ginning until that time had been handled by the AGSA. According to Bryant:

> In 1959 a number of smaller growers within the AGUAPA decided that cotton could be ginned for less than the fee charged by AGSA. In a tense meeting, because voting in AGUAPA was individual and not in accord with production, the small producers were able to vote that AGUAPA should install a gin. Thirteen men, the largest AGSA stockholders, left the association. [Three AGSA members remained, and one of these was elected President.] Shortly, as it became clear that AGUAPA could get financing for the proposed gin from the recently formed Banco del Agro, and for other reasons which are not clear, those three men also left the association. The impact of this split may be inferred from the fact that between 1954 and 1960, the lowest annual portion of the national cotton crop produced by AGUAPA was 53%, whereas in 1962–63 the portion was only 13%.[3]

In this instance, the AGUAPA, which had formerly been the largest of the cotton interest groups, both in members and proportion of production, was reduced to merely one of six such interest groups.

One aspect of group control that is subtly changing and that can only be inferred currently from slight indicators is the increase of direct government control. From the beginning of the revolutionary decade, when regulatory powers were allowed to certain of the organizations, such as the Asociación de Productores de Aceites Esenciales and the Asociación Nacional de Productores de Harina and later the Coffee Association's complete control, the government has naturally been concerned with the policies of the organizations. At times, control offices have been set up within the government, such as the Oficina Central de Café, which Ubico placed within the Ministry of Agriculture. In recent years, however, the government has proposed and attempted from time to time to establish commissions that were composed jointly of government and private interests to handle the problems of the various economic sectors, but, almost without exception, such efforts have been spurned by the private sector or have failed because the government retained veto power.

The most recent effort in this direction was the 1965–1966 effort by the government to take over the control of the ANACAFE. During the previous coffee year, rumors were rife that coffee had been

---

[3] Ibid., pp. 83–84, and citations therein.

smuggled in from El Salvador to cover an expected deficit in meeting Guatemala's international coffee quota. When the Guatemalan crop turned out to be more than adequate, many Guatemalan growers and exporters found themselves with unsalable coffee on their hands. It was also rumored that the ANACAFE had a million dollars in reserve funds. The government, under complaints from both growers and exporters, with the alleged treasure of a million dollars in sight, decided to reform the statutes of the association in such a way that it would be essentially controlled by the government. This brought about a concerted reaction from all parts of the coffee private sector to oppose the plan, and even though it had been decreed, a second decree was then issued modifying the change. Nevertheless, the government was definitely expressing its intent to exercise more direct control over the workings of the association.

An interesting feature of this event is that it shows the vulnerability of the associations by virtue of their position within the domain of the government. Since such associations must have governmental approval to exist, and since some of them were formed in part at the behest of the government, many private participants pursued their activities as if they were safe from governmental interference. Quite clearly, however, if the control for establishing such organizations lies within the domain of the government, then it is equally possible that the government will use them to its own ends. In this, the relation upper-sector associations have with the government parallels that which the lower-sector organizations had under Arévalo and and Arbenz. During the revolutionary decade, it was quite clear that the formation of labor unions, mass organizations, *campesino* leagues, and the like was to mobilize political support for the incumbent government and to permit the government to manipulate the activities of each of them in power contests with other sectors of the society. The direction being taken by the government during the mid-1960's suggests that the upper-sector organizations may be increasingly utilized in the same manner. Although clearly under many influences and pressures from upper-sector members, the government has basic power over the associations through statutory control. It is not clear at present writing just what the government may intend to do with this control, aside from satisfying personal interests of certain of its members. It does mean that the issue of who controls the government policies would, with this turn of events, become even a greater issue, and the possibilities of the upper sector being satisfied with a mildly socialistic government would be even less than it was in 1965.

In general, with the exception of those groups with regulatory powers, most interest groups act by fits and starts, reacting to measures that they see as harmful to their well-being, but otherwise lying dormant. Their internal organizations obviously must reflect the degree to which they are active, viable, and dynamic, and whether they are capable of effecting the influences and changes that they deem necessary.

3. *The Prerevolutionary and Revolutionary Periods*

The most significant feature of the recent interest-group history has been the great proliferation of these groups' numbers. In the course of Miss Bryant's study, it was quite impossible for her to explore all the groups that have been initiated during the past forty years and equally impossible for her to exhaustively investigate each one about which she did obtain data. Of the some seventy-seven that turned up, it was possible to substantiate the impression that there has been in recent years a very significant increase in numbers and that this increase has been mainly in the commercial and industrial sectors.

Table 6–1 provides a list of all the associations and *gremiales* that appear in Miss Bryant's studies, in accord with the political regime under which they were founded (where such data were available) and in terms of the three major sectors to which they pertained. Prior to the 1944 revolution, there was very little development of such associations. While the Cámara de Comercio was founded in 1894 by a decree of José María Reyna Barrios, the first formal Junta Directiva was not elected until 1921. In 1920, the Asociación General de Agricultores (AGA) had statutes approved, and in 1928 an Oficina Central del Café was set up. In 1931 the Consorcio Azucarero was organized among the sugar mills in order to limit production and assure that each mill received a part of the much reduced depression market. Under the government of Ubico, the AGA was closed down entirely, and the Oficina Central de Café was placed directly under the Ministerio de Agricultura. The Consorcio Azucarero apparently continued to operate until 1948, and the Cámara de Comercio, with some slight interruptions, continues today. The

Cámara included both commercial and manufacturing interests, since the latter were of little importance.

The revolution brought about the first of a series of important changes in the advent and activities of interest groups. Ubico's long policy that only he could make politics was ended, and private citizens were beginning to look openly to other means of influencing the political process. In addition, the various families and individuals who had traditionally received Ubico's favor were now, in a sense, on their own and could no longer depend upon the exclusive favor they had previously enjoyed. Just as a new order of politics was to be anticipated, so a whole new set of possible entrepreneurs could anticipate finding favor with the government. The end of the Second World War and the advent of the revolution literally created an entirely new environment for Guatemala, and that environment promised many new facets over which individuals could seek control. One major innovation was the encouragement to begin or expand new crops to make Guatemala less dependent upon the dominant coffee export and the less important banana trade. Another was a general attitude of nationalism that encouraged individuals to enter into and take over the commerce and industries that had heretofore been dominated in great part by selected foreign concerns and agents.

Under the new regime, interest groups were organized in all major economic sectors, as may be seen on Table 6–1. Of special interest is the Asociación de Productores de Aceites Esenciales. This group was organized, with the encouragement of the government, to pick up the production of vegetable oils, primarily from citronella and lemon grass, which had received a tremendous impetus during the war years. The basic pattern of this organization was influential in the later establishment of other agricultural associations, and many of the individuals who became leaders in the formation of other specialized groups received their indoctrination in this association. One of the first outgrowths of the association was a subgroup interested in developing new products in the area of essential oils. Twenty-five members formed the Consorcio Experimental Agrícola to contract with a French perfume firm to provide technical aid in diversifying, expanding, and improving the output. A subsequent group of entrepreneurs who had formed a corporation to extract chlorophyll on the basis of the Consorcio work later

Founding of Interest Groups by Era

Political Regime	Agriculture	Commerce	Industry	Other	Total; average per year
Pre-1944 revolution	Asociación General de Agricultura AGA (1920) [Oficina Central de Café (1928)] Consorcio Azucarero (1931–48)	Cámara de Comercio (CC) (1894; stopped under Ubico, started again in 1944)			4
Revolution-ary decade 1944–1954	Asociación de Productores de Aceites Esenciales (1948) Consorcio Experimental Agrícola (1951–) [Algodonera Guatemalteca—AGSA (1953)]	CC: Gremial de Productos Farmacéuticos y Anexos (1947) Asociación Guatemalteca de Instituciones de Seguros (1954) Asociación General de Comerciantes Guatemaltecas (1954)	Asociación General de Industriales (merged in 1959 with Cámara de Industrias) Asociación Nacional de Fabricantes de Alcohol y Liquores ANFAL (1947) [An organization of sawmill owners] Asociación Nacional de Productores de Harina (1949)		9 or .9/year
Castillo and successors 1955–1957	Asociación Guatemalteca de Productores de Algodón-AGUAPA (1955) Asociación de Azucareros (1957) Asociación Experimental de Café (1957)			Comité Coordinador de Asociaciones Agrícolas, Comerciales, Industriales, y Financieras CACIF (1957)	4 or 1.3/year

(Table continued)

(Table 6–1, continued)

Political Regime	Agriculture	Commerce	Industry	Other	Total; average per year
Ydígoras-Alejos period 1958–1962	Asociación Gremial Paneleros (1958) Asociación Nacional de Cañeros Asociación de Caficultores del Oriente de Guatemala-ACOGUA (1958) Asociación Nacional de Café-ANACAFE (1960) Gremial de Trigueros (1961) Asociación de Productores de Hule (1962)	Asociación de Distribuidores de Vehículos Automotrices de Guatemala (1959) CC: Gremial de Representantes de Casas Extranjeras CC: Gremial de Compradores y Exportadores de Café Asociación Guatemalteca de Transportes (1960) CC: Gremial de Abarroteros (1961) CC: Gremial de Transportes Marítimos (1961) CC: Gremial de Agencias de Viajes y Turismo (1962) CC: Gremial de Proveedores (1961)	Cámara de Industrias (CI) separate from CC (1959) CI: Gremiales in existence: de Curtidores de Fabricantes de Farmacéuticos de Aserraderos de Metalurgia de Textiles CI: Gremial de Artes Gráficos (1960–62) CI: Gremial de Fabricantes de Alcoholes y Liquores (1960–62) CI: Gremiales reorganized-Textiles became Gremio de Hilados, Tejidos Planos y Acabados (1962–63) CI: Gremial de Confección de Ropa (1959–60)	Centro de Estudios Económico-Sociales CEES (1959) Asociación de Gerentes (1959) Asociación de Banqueros de Guatemala (1962)	20 or 4/year
Peralta period 1963–1966	(Federación Nacional de Cañeros proposed (1964)) Asociación Coordinadora de Asociaciones Regionales de Caficultores del Occidente de la República CARCOR (1964)	CC: Gremial de Agentes de Aduana (1963) CC: Gremial de Distribuidores de Aparatos Eléctricos y Electrónicos (1963) CC: Gremial de Comerciantes en Artículos de	CI: Gremial de Fabricantes de Acumuladores (1963–64) CI: Gremial de Fabricantes de Artículos de Perfumería y Cosméticos (1963–64) CI:Gremio de Trans-	Carnera Guatemalteca Alemana de Comercio e Industria (1965) Asociación de Abogados Bancarios (1965?)	

(Table 6–1, continued)

Political Regime	Agriculture	Commerce	Industry	Other	Total; average per year
Peralta period 1963–1966	Asociación de Cañicultores Retaltecas (1965) Consejo Nacional de Algodón (1965) Asociación de Cañicultores de Alta Verapaz (1965) [Instituto Agrícola Industrial de la Caña—proposed (1965)] [Gremial de Cañeros de Escuintla of AGA seeks separate legal status]	CC: Gremial de Distribuidores de Vehículos Automores (1963) Unión de Propietarios de Farmacias de Guatemala (1963) CC: Gremial de Compañía de Seguros (1964) CC: Gremial de Ferreteros (1964) CC: Gremial de Proveedores de Productos para la Agricultura (1964) Asociación Guatemalteca de Hotelero (1964) Asociación de Propietarios de Droguerías (1965) Asociación de Exportadores de Café (proposed—1966)	CI: Gremio de Confites, Chocolates, y Similares (1963–64) CI: Gremio de Industrias Electromecánicas y Similares (1963–64) CI: Gremio de Fabricantes de Calcetería (1963–64) CI: Gremial de Industrias en Jabón (1964–65) CI: Gremial de Industrias Automotrices (1964–65) CI: Gremial de Fabricantes de Helados (1964–65) CI: Gremial de Fabricantes de Vinos (1964–65) CI: Gremial de Fabricantes de Artículos Plásticos (1964–65) CI: Gremial de Embotelladores (1964–65) CI: Gremial de Medias, Calcetería, y Tejido de Punto (1964–65) CI: Gremial de la Industria del Vestido (1964–65)		31, or 10.3/year

SOURCE: Mavis Ann Bryant, "Industrial and Commercial Associations in Gautemala," manuscript, 1967.

(1955) formed the Algodonera Retalteca, S.A., which became one of the six major cotton interest groups.

It was mentioned earlier that the first of the major cotton associations, the AGSA, began in 1953. Cotton was basically a new export crop in Guatemala, and among those interested in its development was Jacobo Arbenz, who undertook to plant some himself. This may explain in part why the AGSA was started with relative ease. Sugar, however, followed a somewhat different history. The Consorcio Azucarero that had been started in 1931 was composed of the sugar refinery owners, and they had retained tight control over the market within the country, both purchasing cane from other growers and setting the price of sugar for sale. The government apparently found their mode of handling this unsatisfactory and, at some point, intervened in order to administer sales and prices. Arbenz then enacted legislation that guaranteed the cane producers a fixed price for their product. There was a strong antipathy between the revolutionary governments and the sugar refiners. The latter had for years exercised an oligopoly over the local market, and evidently the government was determined to break it, but they succeeded only in part. While the Consorcio Azucarero did stop formal operation in 1948, the owners continued with a gentleman's agreement until after the fall of Arbenz, at which time they formed again as the Asociación de Azucareros. As in the case of cotton, the interest of the government on the side of the cane grower was not entirely a matter of concern for diversification of production. One of the leading (and still leading) cane producers was Guillermo Torriello, the local foreign minister under Arbenz. As will be seen shortly, the problems between the cane growers and the refinery owners were still unresolved at the time of this study.

In the industrial sector, the Asociación Nacional de Fabricantes de Alcohol y Licores (ANFAL) started under the express push of the government, with notice that it was not to intervene in labor matters. It was directed to participate in the drawing up of a new law under which liquors were to be produced. Another product that evidently received positive support from the government was flour. It is reported that generous government-backed credits were made available to mill owners. It backed the formation of the Asociación Nacional de Productores de Harina, which, among its other privileges, was able to set prices for the purchase of wheat. As in supporting the sugar producers, the Arbenz government also had a Ministro de Relaciones Exteriores who had a personal stake in the flour-milling business, Roberto Fanjul. In 1965, ten of the some twenty-two mills still belonged to the Asociación and accounted for 61.4 percent of the flour milled that year. It seems evident that the revolutionary governments, irrespective of their interests in the development of a better laboring situation, were not blind to the profitable benefits of government support of enterprise, especially when that enterprise included sectors in which important politicians had their own interests.

Also during the revolutionary decade the first signs of dissension occurred between the industrialists and the commercially oriented members of the Cámara de Comercio and among other entrepreneurs. In 1947 the Cámara de Comercio changed its name to the Cámara de Comercio e Industria in recognition of the increasing importance of the latter members. This proved insufficient for some of the new industrialists who were sympathetic toward policies being introduced by the revolutionary government, and they broke away in the early 1950's to form the Asociación General de Industriales. A parallel splinter group emerged in the business area, the Asociación General de Comerciantes Guatemaltecos. It was made up primarily of small businessmen and continued to exist at the time of the study. Its membership had never intersected to any significant degree with the other major business interest groups. The splinter industrial association ceased to exist with the formation of an independent Cámara de Industria in 1959.

While the evidence from the study suggests that most of the new organizations evolving during the revolutionary decade were products of government encouragement, apparently there was also an organization of sawmill owners that formed in order to defend themselves against certain of the new labor laws. In general, however, employers of the period seemed unable or unready to organize themselves to meet the new demands that were evolving out of the new labor legislation. Perhaps the outstanding example of this is the performance of the Asociación General de Agricultores. While this had been dissolved by Ubico, it was started again in 1944 under the new regime. Generations of dependence on government fiat and on handling their own local affairs left the great majority of the owners of Guatemala's large farms completely unprepared to organize in what might seem to be their own defense. When the new labor code was issued under Arévalo, the AGA did prepare and publish a polemic against the dangers of labor unions, but it apparently had little influence. It was not until the publication of the Agrarian Reform in 1952 under Arbenz that the members of the AGA were shaken into a realization that they were faced with some fairly profound changes. The AGA leadership at the time did make strong protestations to the government concerning the law, but they had almost no effect. Among the products of its concern was the refusal to cooperate in the execution of the law. The law allowed for a minor representation of a member of the local community on each of local agrarian committees that was destined to make the decisions as to the reallocation of land. Under the urging of the AGA, the employers refused to sit in these committees since they were clearly in a minority position and could hardly be expected to exercise any influence on the decisions made therein.

Although it is not clear just why it was initiated, the Gremial de Productos Farmacéuticos y Anexos of the Cámara de Comercio was started in 1947 and included as its members both foreign and domestic drug importers, wholesalers, and retailers. There was in existence at the time a Comité de Control de Precios de Medicina, and it seems likely that one of their chief concerns was to try to influence this group. According to one informant, the Gremial had over two hundred members early in its history and did, in fact, successfully influence the work of the committee. Over the years, however, dissension between members with local interests and those with import interests and representatives of foreign-owned concerns grew, and by the time of the study, there were four different organizations representing various aspects and interests in the pharmaceutical area.

One group that formalized itself during the Arbenz period had an explicit nationalistic position. This was the Asociación Guatemalteca de Instituciones de Seguros. Since most insurance at that time was handled by foreign companies, the local firms joined together in the hopes of gradually eliminating foreign companies from the area, as happened in Mexico.

In general, the revolutionary decade was an important one in the history of interest groups. Beginning, as it did, with almost no groups that played any significant role in influencing the government, the ten-year period saw the evolution of a very clear notion that the government could encourage the formation of groups to promote both the economic development of the country and the special sectors that needed help in competing with the more traditional interest areas. The dominant tone of the period was, as in the case of the lower-sector groups that were being created, the formation of groups that would be helpful to the government's evolving programs of diversifying agriculture, bringing in more entrepreneurs from the national scene and encouraging them as over and against foreign operators. The use of these associations as devices to influence the government was nascent. The AGA made some attempts, and the Cámara de Comercio presumably made representations from time to time. The major economic sector of the country was not ready, however, to use the interest group effectively. The large-scale farmers were unable to cooperate; they were still dominated by an individualistic perspective that saw each neighboring farmer to be almost as much of a threat as were the new measures of the government and the expanding demands of labor.

One additional aspect of the environment was changing during this period, although its importance became clearer later. This was the expansion of agriculture, especially in sugar and cotton, on the coast. Earlier, the coastal area had been relatively unoccupied and was used principally for small-scale cattle production. The revolutionary decade saw the beginnings of widespread public health efforts to reduce the threat of malaria, together with the introduction of drugs developed during and after the Second World War. The demand for citronella and lemon grass was followed shortly by the increased demand for cotton on the world market. Without any question, this geographical area became a major element in the economic and political processes that followed. The growth of agriculture during the decade, together with the pressure for land in the highlands, began to bring an increasing number of people to the coastal areas. It was among these people that the greatest public agitation for land reform occurred and the greatest political success of the revolutionary regime was to be found.

Control over the coast, both economically and politically, was an accomplishment of the revolutionary governments that was to last far beyond the governments themselves.

In the years prior to the revolution, very few interest groups were formed, and some that had existed were severely restricted in their activities or were eliminated. The revolutionary period ushered in a whole new role for such groups, as well as setting forth vast new areas of the environment for control. While we could account for only three such groups prior to 1944, there were as least nine during the subsequent decade, as well as unquestionably renewed activity on the part of the Cámara de Comercio e Industria. Interestingly enough, the new groups appeared in about equal numbers in the agricultural, commercial, and industrial sectors.

4. *The Postrevolutionary Period*

The period from the fall of Arbenz until 1958 when Ydígoras finally became president was in every sense transitional. Little happened in the commercial or industrial sectors in the formation of new groups. Castillo Armas and his successors apparently had no clear policy as to how interest groups might be used and did little to either discourage or encourage them. In 1955 he removed some protective legislation in the cotton area, and, for the first time, there was an almost united reaction from the growers: they joined together to form a new association, the Asociación Guatemalteca de Productores de Algodón (AGUAPA). Unlike the other association that represented all the possible members of the sector, however, this one had no government encouragement and was obviously granted no regulatory powers. It was, in the purest and simplest sense, a voluntary association formed on a nonprofit basis to defend some common interests. When the immediate emergency passed, however, there was evidently little else of common interest to hold it together, and the competition among growers and ginners for the international market divided the group, with the result that in 1965, there were six identifiable groups.

The special support for the sugar growers stopped with the fall of the Arbenz government, and the owners of the refineries formed the Asociación de Azucareros to continue their control over the price of raw cane. Since all mill owners were also growers of cane, they had their own source of raw materials, as well as having to depend upon other growers. There was (possibly during this period, but the records are not clear) a Gremial de Cañeros within the AGA, but, as such, there was little that it could do through the AGA that would be contrary to the interests of the co-members who were refinery owners. The strength that the cane growers may have been gathering under their politically influential members with the revolutionary regime clearly carried little weight with the immediately postrevolutionary governments.

The two events of most interest during this period were the formation of the Asociación Experimental Cafetalera and the establishment of the Comité Coordinador de Asociaciones Agrícolas, Comerciales, Industriales, y Financieras (CACIF) in 1957. The coffee group was composed predominantly of coffee growers of northern European extraction; there were, of the some fifteen members, only two with Spanish surnames. Of greater importance, it was a set of individuals who had experience in the essential oils venture and had participated in the Consorcio Experimental Agrícola of that organization. For this group, essential oils had always been a secondary pursuit. It made sense to apply similar efforts to development of their major interest, coffee. During the previous years a few foreign coffee specialists had been working in Guatemala. Since Guatemalan coffee had never been subject to scientific development, the traditional practices of the Guatemalan growers were extremely primitive to the eyes of the specialists. The experimental association was of particular importance because it provided one of the first occasions on which coffee growers themselves contributed voluntarily for a continuing research organization. Later, as the international coffee market was being glutted by overproduction and the ANACAFE itself developed research facilities, this small organization naturally declined.

While the organizations started by the cotton growers and the sugar refiners reflected to some degree the policies of the Castillo government, the CACIF was the one organization that emerged in this transition period that clearly reflected the tenor of the times, and that presaged the developments to come. Bryant describes the process as follows:

After the "Liberation," Castillo Armas conferred with leaders of private enterprise and created an advisory body, the Consejo de Iniciativa Privada, providing it with government-appointed *Secretario Ejecutivo*. During the talks it had been understood that the group would be strictly private. Differences of opinion arose between members of the Consejo and the government; in the last meeting there was a great argument about the just level of profits. Either before or after the formation of the Consejo, an Asociación de Iniciativa Privada existed; no further information concerning it was collected, however. For 1956–58, Castillo Armas appointed a *Junta Provisional* to oversee the formation of a new Banco del Agro; it might be presumed that he chose men willing to support him and his policies. Castillo Armas was killed in July, 1957.

One participant stated that many of the members of the Consejo de Iniciativa Privada were founders of the CACIF. The latter organization was founded in January, 1957, to conciliate the interests of member groups and to allow all of private enterprise to cooperate when necessary. The government had begun to create mixed bodies with government and private enterprise represented at a time when the only associations extant were the Cámara de Comercio e Industria and the AGA; by 1957 the situation had changed, and the more specialized associations were clamoring for representation. As the usefulness of the Consejo de Iniciativa Privada declined, the CACIF increasingly served as a forum for the former's members. The Consejo ceased to function after Castillo Armas' death, but the CACIF continued. The members of the CACIF were various associations, each of which was allowed two representatives.[4]

While the original members of CACIF were only the Cámaras de Industria and Comercio, the Asociación General de Industriales, and the AGA, they were soon joined by other groups and, by 1965, had as members an array of organizations that were not at all equally conservative. The general position of CACIF was conservative, however, and it did not hesitate to ridicule organizations that reflected a pre-1954 nationalism, such as the Asociación General de Comerciantes and the Asociación Guatemalteca de Instituciones de Seguros.

In all, during the three years between the fall of Arbenz and the assumption of Ydígoras, there were at least four new organizations. This is not a significant increase over the previous decade. Of particular importance, however, is that in great part they were reactionary political organizations. The CACIF was clearly a gen-

[4] Ibid., pp. 187–188.

eral conservative attempt to promote general business and liberal economic interests; the AGUAPA formed to contest Castillo's removal of protective legislation; and the Azucareros were organized to reassert their former hegemony over the local sugar market. In a way, even the experimental coffee organization reflected a reaction to the fall of Arbenz, since the members of that group had clearly felt little motivation to invest their money in coffee research under the Arbenz government, which had made it clear that it was uninterested in helping the traditional coffee sector.

The first major acceleration in the formation of associations occurred during the presidency of Ydígoras. While it is technically correct to think of this as the Ydígoras period, it probably would be historically more accurate to include in consideration the name of Roberto Alejos, for he seems to have been as deeply involved as Ydígoras in the policies followed during the period. The policies of diversification of agriculture and of industrialization that were initiated during the revolutionary decade took on a much stronger impulse during the Ydígoras regime. In spite of graft that tended to modify many serious efforts and the emergence of serious new revolutionary activities by *guerrillero* groups, this period saw the maturation of the interest group as a device whereby the entrepreneur could operate both in putting pressure on the government and in extending his controls over his sector to approximate at least an oligopolistic control. This did happen, and probably only could have happened, in a period of expansion of industries and of a continuing world market generally receptive to Guatemalan exports.

Aside from encouraging foreign petroleum companies to seek oil, the government made no radical innovations in exploiting the environment. Those areas which had opened up under Arévalo and Arbenz were more fully exploited. The use of insecticides and herbicides increased in the coastal areas and was extended into the highlands. El Petén, where Arévalo had unsuccessfully tried colonization in the late 1940's, became the scene of increased activity, with both Kekchí Indians from the Alta Verapaz and Ladinos from the *oriente* forming part of the immigrant groups. On the south coast, Escuintla and the neighboring southwestern departments received increasing numbers of migrants, both seasonal and permanent, and the United Fruit Company began to sell its holdings in Tiquisate, thereby bringing a new generation of agricultural entrepreneurs to the south coast. Ydígoras passed a law to encourage the establishment of new industries, and Guatemala became deeply involved in the development of the Central American Common Market, with all the regulatory controls for importation and local development involved therein.

Certain patterns emerged during this period: a number of organizations came into being to pressure the government to change circumstances to their advantage; political ambitions of Alejos led him to promote the formation of a number of large membership groups of small operators; the Cámara de Comercio e Industria split into two separate Cámaras; the coffee growers finally achieved both regional and national organization; the bankers organized, and a conservative propaganda organization came into being. Organizing was beginning to become a fad, and, in addition, a number of groups formed with little purpose other than to look at themselves.

The single most common purpose for the formation of interest groups has become influencing the government in favor of one's own interests. The Cámara de Industria formed a number of *gremiales* during this period that were primarily concerned with this activity. Printers (Artes Gráficos) were having problems getting paper out of customs, and makers of clothing and weavers of cloth were afraid of the consequences of new tariffs enacted in Honduras and Nicaragua. In one case, the government itself was responsible for the problem. Through the initiation of a requirement for liquor manufacturers to use a special imported bottle cap to which there was attached a graft-laden scandal, the manufacturers found themselves floundering in bottle caps that either were not available when needed or did not work when they finally arrived.

A development that was unique to the Ydígoras period was the effort by Ydígoras' supporter, Roberto Alejos, to organize a number of large groups of small producers and operators. This move has been ascribed to Alejos' ambition to become Ydígoras' successor in the presidency. It was assumed that such organizations would provide additional political support. Three of these were the Gremial de Trigueros, the Asociación Guatemalteca de Transportes, and the Gremial de Paneleros. Organization had a distinct advantage for each of these groups. The wheat growers of Guatemala were principally small producers, mainly Indians in the western highlands. The small growers were entirely at the mercy of the market controlled by the millers. The Gremial de Trigueros was established as a universal organization; all growers were supposed to belong to it, and each hundredweight of wheat produced provided ten cents for the treasury of the Gremial. A most important feature was that the government also fixed the price of flour at a level well above the world market. Millers, in turn, were required by law to buy the national wheat at the fixed price before importing foreign wheat at a lower price. The millers, formerly in control through the favoritism shown them in the revolutionary period, were now controlled by governmental regulation and were forced to work with a price level that did not answer to world market conditions. A unique aspect of the Trigueros association was that the membership was predominantly Indian, and at the time of the study the Junta Directiva was composed of Indians. Unfortunately, shortly thereafter, the Junta was found to have mishandled a significant portion of the gremial funds, and some of the officers were arrested.

Another group formed under the encouragement of Alejos was that of the small sugar-cane producers who supplied the liquor and alcohol factories. The Gremial de Paneleros was formed and again given special rights by the government. In this instance, the producers were given the exclusive right to sell crude sugar to the factories, thereby excluding the large refineries from disposing of their surplus syrups in this manner. The guarantee provided in this manner was an obvious economic advantage to the small producers and clearly could have political advantages for Alejos.

The Asociación Guatemalteca de Transportes was the third such large membership group. It was composed of the companies and individuals involved in automotive land transport. Their concern was with control of the trade in Guatemala, but, as the Common Market opened up, they pushed for and obtained exclusive rights for home fleets to carry freight between two points within their own country. Had events not overtaken Ydígoras and Alejos, these associations, whose members numbered in the thousands, would have provided significant political support.

It was mentioned earlier that during the revolutionary period the diverse interests of the businessman and the industrialist were recognized in their common representation in the Cámara. In 1954, following the overthrow of Arbenz, new statutes were issued under which the organization took the name of the Cámaras Unidas de

Comercio e Industria de Guatemala. It continued in this form until 1959, when the industrialists split off, formed their own separate group, and were joined by the Asociación General de Industriales. In retrospect, it seems strange that the two sectors could have remained so long together, for their interests in many instances were in opposition. The commercial sector, in previous years, had been closely tied to foreign interests. The increase in imports following 1944 led the commercial sector to seek to retain control over the external sources and the local market. The push to develop national industries, however, obviously conflicted directly with the market interests of the importers. Each time a new industry started, it was said, an old business died. Importers and retailers of imported goods found little advantage in the emergence of industries that would replace their activities.

The nature of the conflict was such that interests not necessarily industrial in themselves, but which were opposed to the position taken by the Cámara de Comercio, began to gravitate to the new Cámara de Industria. One example of this was in the transport area. The Asociación Guatemalteca de Transportes was paralleled in the Cámara de Industria by a Gremial de Transportes (started in 1963–1964). The Gremial had the same goals as did the association but was composed of the major carriers. They wanted to keep foreign trucking lines from coming through Central America and to prevent foreigners from starting trucking lines in the country. They were successful in stopping a North American entrepreneur from doing this and were able to force the large foreign oil companies to negotiate over whether they could bring in their own fleets of oil trucks. Quite naturally, the orientation of both these associations was toward internal markets.

In contrast, the Cámara de Comercio had a Gremial de Transportes Marítimos composed of representatives of the major steamship lines. Their interest was clearly in foreign suppliers and markets, in imports and exports. Their concern was over the improvement of port facilities. When they complained about the inadequate facilities of the port at Matías de Gálvez, the Asociación Guatemalteca de Transportes trumpeted that foreigners had no right to criticize the national facilities of Guatemala. When the ship company representatives tried to have railroad facilities extended to Matías de Gálvez, the trucking industry took the contrary stand, thereby hoping to keep the transport needs of that port firmly within their control.

In the same way, it was the Cámara de Industria that became especially involved in the developments entailed by the Central American Common Market. In 1965 it set up an Oficina de Integración and a three-man Consejo Consultivo de Asuntos de Integración to guide it. Various *gremiales* of the Cámara de Industria individually entered into agreements and established organizations of a Pan–Central American nature. A Federación de Cámaras de Industrias de Centro América began to spawn its own *gremiales*, such as the Gremial de Fabricantes y Convertidores de Papel Centroamericano.

While the proponents of the general position of the Cámara de Industria were generally more successful in their contests with the Cámara de Comercio, such was not always the case. The Asociación de Distribuidores de Vehículos Automotrices de Guatemala, with its corresponding Gremial de Distribuidores de Vehículos Automotores (founded 1963), was naturally concerned with the threat of establishing elsewhere in the isthmus assembly factories of major automobile manufacturers. On the one hand, its members did not want such plants to be established, but, on the other, they would not mind if they happened to be the local entrepreneurs to undertake such an effort. The position of the distributors, then, was to hold off new entrepreneurs from undertaking such installations until the various Common Market agreements should become clear, at which time they themselves might try to handle the new enterprise.

The Ydígoras period marked the beginning of real expansion of both the Cámaras, and it is interesting to note that the creation of *gremiales* in these organizations did not exclude the organization of the same interest outside the Cámara. There were a number of cases where the very same individuals would be organized as a *gremial* within a Cámara and at the same time form a separate organization outside. There were, for example, *gremiales* and separate associations of coffee exporters, owners of drug houses, and hotel keepers. In these cases, the *gremiales* existed first and were followed by the association. The major reason for the double organization is that *gremiales* had to carry out all petitioning and external relations through the Junta Directiva of the Cámara. They could not operate independently. Since there was inevitably a clash of interests between the *gremiales* of a Cámara, it was often the case that a specific *gremial* could not expect the Junta to press its case. Therefore, the formation of a separate organization gave the interested individuals the freedom to act outside the Cámara organization. The separate organizations were not limited to those representing solely the interests of Guatemalan enterprises. The textile mills found in some instances that they could be more effective through the Asociación Centroamericana de Industrias Textiles than through the Gremial of the Cámara de Industria of Guatemala.

In some cases the reverse situation prevailed, and the members of independent associations duplicated their organizations in parallel *gremiales*. As a *gremial*, they could get the influence of the entire Cámara behind them. Such was the case with the automobile distributors, the automotive assembly industries, and the manufacturers of alcohol and liquor. In all cases, a *gremial* was created later in order to put additional pressure on the government. Most useful were the cases in which the government, when considering some new measure, would send the proposal to the appropriate Cámara (most commonly the Cámara de Industria), and it would then be referred to the relevant *gremial* for an opinion. While the government did not always pay attention to the recommendation that the Cámara would make on the basis of the *gremial*'s opinion, in many cases it did. This became extremely important as the Central American Common Market evolved, and the question of the removal or setting of tariffs was constantly under discussion.

Perhaps the most important single organization to emerge in this period was the Asociación Nacional de Café (ANACAFE). Prior to this time, coffee growers had been organized only through the AGA and had never been able to exercise any significant concerted action. The first evidence of real cooperation among the growers was the experimental group described earlier, and this was obviously limited. Of greater organizational significance was the appearance a year later of the Asociación de Cafecultores del Oriente de Guatemala (ACOGUA). That this was the first major voluntary association of coffee growers is of considerable interest. Taken all in all, the *oriente* departments probably account for somewhat less than 20 percent of the national production, and fully one-half of that is concentrated in the department of Santa Rosa. The farmers of the area, in considerable part, are provincial residents who prefer living on their farms. There are among them very few individuals of northern European ancestry; most are old Spanish-surnamed Guatemalan families. As far as can be determined, the group was formed out of a realization that the *oriente* producers were not receiving the attention from the national government that they felt they should. Among the benefits they could offer was to assure their members of credit. Under Castillo Armas, the Banco del Agro had been started to provide credit specifically for large-scale farming. The ACOGUA made sure that one or more of its members served on every board of directors of the bank, thus assuring its members that their requests would be reviewed by a board on which sympathetic members would be found.

At a higher level, the impulse that led to the formation of the ACOGUA also set in motion the ANACAFE; both were products of stimulation from the outside. In 1959 the International Coffee Agreement was signed by most coffee-producing and consuming countries. A consequence of Guatemala's participation in this was that a quota was assigned the country's coffee export. The growers in Guatemala, afraid of the mismanagement that might occur were the decisions on such matters left in the hands of the government, were able to persuade Ydígoras, through Roberto Alejos, to support the formation of a private office to handle this problem. The Gremial de Cafecultores of AGA set up an Oficina Controlora Cafetalera, which sponsored the statutes of the association. The ANACAFE was then created through an act of Congress, and the internal structure was approved and went into operation in 1961. The ANACAFE received a total of thirty-nine cents on every bag of coffee exported and thereby had an assured financial backing. Since it was granted the entire regulatory authority for issuing export licenses, exporters as well as growers were members. The internal organization of ANACAFE was complex and involved a staff of some eighty people. It was not only concerned with matters directly affecting coffee, but also brought in food and agricultural organizational experts to aid in the importation of new marketable crops, which then would encourage local growers to eliminate heavy coffee production. It kept extensive records on matters pertaining to national production and, of course, represented the country at the international coffee meetings.

Since coffee continues to be the major export, and therefore the major single source of income for Guatemala, the control of the production and sale of the crop is a matter of prime national concern. To a government oriented toward increasing nationalization, a single private group that exercises the extensive controls possible under the ANACAFE can clearly be seen as a threat. The threat would appear especially obvious to other interest group contenders for national hegemony. This seems to have been the case under the Peralta government. Although Peralta had been Minister of Agriculture at the time that ANACAFE was created, it was pushed through by Ydígoras and Alejos over Peralta's clear lack of enthusiasm. When he became chief of state, a concerted effort was made to bring the ANACAFE under the control of the government. The process was still underway at the time of writing. Irrespective of the specific outcome, however, if the ANACAFE continues to hold the extensive powers first accorded it, it will, like the Church and military, inevitably be seen as a threat by a nationalistic government, since it allows extreme powers to rest in the hands of a group with particular private interests.

Two other associations that appeared in this period were the Asociación de Banqueros and the Centro de Estudios Económico-Sociales (CEES). Under the early revolutionary government, a national bank of Guatemala had been established, and later the Banco Nacional Agrario was set up to provide credit for people receiving land under the agrarian reform. Apart from these efforts, however, the banking structure of the country remained fairly simple. When Castillo took office in 1954, he established the Banco del Agro to provide the large planter with a specific source of credit and then encouraged foreign banks, specifically the Bank of America and the Banco de Londres y Montreal, to go into business. Under Ydígoras, and later Peralta, a number of other local banks were started, so that banking had in fact become a business with some variety and competition. In 1965, of the fourteen banks operating, eight were nationally owned private banks, two were branches of foreign banks, three were government-owned development banks, and one was the Bank of Guatemala, which acted as the bank for the government and for the other banks but did no private business itself. There were, also, two credit institutions that were members. The purposes of the association were mainly for obtaining a degree of internal order in the banking community and in proposing changes to banking laws to improve the structure as a whole. It cooperated closely with the ANACAFE by granting larger credits during some difficult years and by having the ANACAFE refuse export licenses for coffee still mortgaged to one of the banks.

The CEES can best be described by quoting Bryant:

> In 1957 several Guatemalan businessmen participated in a U.S. government-sponsored trip to study labor-management relations in the U.S. At the end of the trip several of them decided to found a center to educate upper sector members about the dangers of state intervention in private enterprise, such as they had witnessed in the U.S. Generally basing its economic viewpoints on the doctrines of the English "liberal" school, the Centro de Estudios Económico-Sociales distributed materials published by the Nathaniel Branden Institute in the U.S., the Instituto de Investigaciones Sociales y Económicas in Mexico, and the Asociación Nacional de Fomento Económico in Costa Rica. It held conferences, translated books, and published articles and small notes in local newspapers and magazines. Many of these articles were written by members of the *Consejo Directivo* of the Centro. At the time of the study 80% of the finances of the Centro were contributed by the Friedrich Naumann Stiftung, a German foundation which attempted to increase the cultural influence of Germany. In return for the funds the CEES provided the foundation with office space and administrative help. Despite the announced desire of some of the directors of the Centro to prevent Guatemala from copying the U.S. in labor relations, several of them had strong ties with the U.S. besides the connection with the Nathaniel Branden Institute. At least five of the eight were educated there, one was a former employee of the United Fruit Company, one worked for the U.S.-controlled Empresa Eléctrica, and one was a corporate member of the American Club.[5]

During the five years of Ydígoras' presidency, the rate of appearance of interest groups increased about fourfold. Interestingly, groups continued to appear in about equal numbers in all the major sectors. In addition, the financial community had so expanded that it too organized and, above all, the general needs of the upper sector began to be published through a specialized organization of propaganda. It turned out, however, that the Ydígoras years were merely the beginning of an expansion that flourished under the military government of Peralta Azurdia. While new associations appeared

[5] Ibid., pp. 191–192.

at a rate of about four a year under Ydígoras, under Peralta this increased to over ten. Also, for the first time since the revolution, there was a distinctive change in the pattern. While there were twelve new commercial associations and fourteen new industrial ones, only four new groups formed in the agricultural sector.

While there was relatively less activity among the agricultural enterprises, it is hard to discern patterns in the three years of the Peralta administration. Under the Ydígoras government, it was already beginning to look as if some of the new associations were in response to a fad rather than to any clearly perceived need for organization. It was not clear in the study what was gained by the associations having to do with tourism, rubber growers, and food retail stores. Most of the expansion in numbers was in *gremiales* of the two Cámaras, and, as such, their needs were specific issues that could be handled through the presence of the parent organization. There were no new independent industrial associations recorded by Bryant for the Peralta period, and only four of the eleven new commercial organizations were not *gremiales* of the Cámara de Comercio.

In the agricultural sector there were two clearly discernible patterns. One was reflected in the creation of a Consejo Nacional de Algodón, which was, in some part, supposed to be a parallel organization to coffee's ANACAFE, but its role was not entirely clear. There was also being proposed at the time of the study a Federación Nacional de Cañeros to be a comparable organization for that set of growers and an Instituto Agrícola-Industrial de la Caña to act as the bargaining agency between the cane growers and the sugar mills. The sugar associations were being proposed by the cane growers in order to better their position with respect to the refineries, but the government was not acting rapidly on their plans. The other evident agricultural pattern was the appearance of active regional associations. The Asociación de Cañicultores Retaltecas was officially recognized in 1965, and the Gremial de Cañeros de Escuintla of the AGA had for some time been seeking separate legal status. Like the innovations advanced by the leaders of the cane-growing community, the Escuintla group was not receiving rapid action on its proposal.

Insofar as coffee production is concerned, the most important area is western Guatemala. The departments of San Marcos, Quezaltenango, and Suchitepéquez alone account for one-half of Guatemala's coffee export production. While there had been local groups in existence throughout the western area, they were brought together in 1964 under a single regional organization, the Asociación Coordinadora de Asociaciones Regionales de Cafecultores del Occidente (CARCOR). Immediately the westerners began to be better represented on the Junta Directiva of the ANACAFE. During the period 1961–1964, they had only four posts on the board; from 1964 to 1967, they occupied fourteen. Concomitantly, the representation during those two periods for the eastern growers dropped from nine to six, and that of the Asociación Experimental Cafetalera dropped from twelve to six. The other distinctive coffee-growing areas of the country, accounting for less than 10 percent of the national production, is the Alta Verapaz. This region had, until 1965, received no special representation in the national coffee circles, and during that year they formed an organization. Their problem, as with other growers, was to get a larger share of the restricted coffee market.

In general, the evolution of interest groups during the recent history of Guatemala has seen a very sharp increase in numbers under recent regimes, clearly reflecting that the upper sector of Guatemala has learned well that such organizations can be of considerable help. It also reflects an increase of activity in these areas, especially in the industrial and commercial areas. Organizations have been formed both within parent organizations, such as the AGA, the Cámara de Comercio, and the Cámara de Industria, and independently. While each specialty is pursuing its own welfare, resulting in a proliferation of specific organizations, the regulatory responsibilities and powers that have begun to devolve into the hands of some of the associations have led to the appearance of organizations representing entire sectors. This has occurred thus far in coffee and cotton and may take place in other areas as well.

The expansion is not only occurring in terms of bringing together separate subgroups or heretofore unorganized individuals, but is also reaching out into international networks. The advent of the Common Market has led to the appearance of a series of Pan–Central American associations. The Asociación de Azucareros is, for example, not merely a member of the Cámara de Industrias, but also belongs to the Federación de Azucareros de Centro América; in addition to this, it pertains to the Consejo Latinoamericano del Azúcar.

Presumably to be evaluated in each case is to what degree these ties and connections represent active and substantial bonds that are improving the position of the Guatemalan members, and to what degree they are merely paper structures that use time and money but produce little. This is clearly far beyond the scope of the present study.

A further characteristic that needs more investigation is the question of the degree to which the economic life of the country lies within an oligopolic control. It is clear in Bryant's study that each of the associations tends to be controlled by a relatively small set of individuals. There is also some overlap within the membership of the various groups. Two factors tend to obscure the control situation, however. One is that the real control behind these associations is the ownership and regulatory control over the resources and market and not merely the associations used as a means; and the other is that the offices of the various associations are necessarily held by individuals strongly interested in the particular association and not therefore necessarily interested in being active in more than one association or sector.

While it is obviously the case that the real owners, and therefore centrally interested persons, play a dominant role in the interest groups, they do not necessarily play a role proportionate to their real control. There were various indications in the study that informal alliances and common interests that never formalized into open interest organizations often governed the action taken by these organizations. The present study of interest groups, then, can be only suggestive about what is really happening in the power picture.

The course of development of upper-sector interest groups has concentrated first in economic matters. However, this concentration should not be misunderstood. The economic controls that are achieved in this way are fundamental elements of power within the Guatemalan society, and their aggregation in the upper sector provides that part of the society with a continuing and cumulative increase of its power. The steady growth suggests that, in this aspect of the system, we are dealing with a structural feature that is somewhat independent of the specific government in power, even though governmental policies can slow or hasten the process.

7 The Costs of Growth: Expansion in Cotton

THE STUDIES OF THE MILITARY, Church, and upper-sector interest groups provide insights through certain kinds of institutions as to how the upper-sector expansion has taken place and what the role of power both within and outside the nation has been in the process. Implications as to some of the ramifications elsewhere in the society and on matters pertinent to the nation are both explicit and implicit in those chapters. Perhaps the most important area of economic expansion, however, is the continuing growth of export agriculture. A full study of this subject was not undertaken, but the growth of cotton was investigated. Cotton was chosen because it has seen the most meteoric and significant growth in the period under study of any of the export crops or, probably, of any specific industry or type of enterprise. This growth occurred in the area of traditional upper-sector economic dependence, the agrarian export economy. It reflects the relationship that holds between this sector and the government and the interrelations of the entire structure

NOTE: This chapter and much of its argument are based primarily on material collected by Julio M. Jiménez and analyzed in his M.A. thesis, "A Critique of the Policies and Attitudes Affecting Cotton Agriculture in Guatemala through a Study of Its Development," The University of Texas at Austin, 1967. The reader is referred to that source for substantiating materials and further data not included herein. Additional data come from the thesis of Mavis Bryant.

with the world market; and, perhaps of greatest interest, such growth shows how an area often looked at as developmental is in fact often not only less developmental than claimed, but can also be argued to be antidevelopmental in significant respects. The ultimate basis of power is in the control of the environment and its products; the expansion of these products, as has been the case with cotton, provides a basis for the expansion in power. Who gains from such expansion is important in understanding the relationship between power and development.

1. *Conditions and Constants in Cotton Expansion*

Since late in the last century, the Guatemalan economy has been dominated by coffee. This crop, promoted by the early liberal government of Barrios, became the major source of national income, the major financial prop of all governments, and the dominant source of cash income for an increasing number of the national Indians and subsistence farmers. Coffee grew in importance because of the special attention given it by foreign-born entrepreneurs, particularly Germans. During the early part of the century, most of the coffee was produced under the direction of the newcomers. Even when, as during the Depression, prices dropped to a low that could not support production, coffee continued to be the major source of income. During the present century, banana production, even more directly in the hands of foreigners, became the export of second value to the nation. The Second World War, with the intervention of the German interests in Guatemala, brought a sharp halt to the dominance of the German colony in the country. The fall of Ubico and the installation of a revolutionary regime opened the doors of Guatemala to its own citizens to try their hand at the enterprises that had heretofore been the dominant interest of foreigners or a subsociety of foreign descent. By this time, an increasing amount of coffee was being grown by native Guatemalans, but the basic marketing and growing patterns had long since been established. Bananas required either alignment of the grower with specific exporters or equipment and an establishment of the order of a United Fruit Company. At this point in time, cotton appeared as a crop that could be grown rapidly and could offer a source of enterprise.

Guatemala had grown cotton previously, but it had never become a crop of continuing importance. It was grown when, during the Civil War in the United States, prices reached an historic level of one dollar per pound. With the drop of prices after the war, Guatemala's production declined. It saw a brief growth during the Second World War but again declined. In the postwar period, however, cotton began to be grown for the world market in El Salvador and Nicaragua, and during the 1944/45 to 1950/51 period, Guatemala was the only Central American nation that found it necessary to import raw cotton for local needs. With the Korean War, the world price for cotton reached a new high. This was not due to a simple expansion in demand, but to a complex reduction of production of cotton in the United States and the stockpiling of cotton reserves with a view to possible world consequences of the Korean conflict.

In addition to the need for local production for national needs and the tempting prices of the world market, Guatemala was also like El Salvador and Nicaragua in that it had on the Pacific coast an appropriate environment for cotton production. This area had been vastly underexploited agriculturally for hundreds of years. In recent decades, it was the scene of very small subsistence settlements, one large concentration of the United Fruit Company, and dispersed and low-grade cattle operations. The control of malaria and insects provided by drugs and chemicals stemming from the work stimulated by the Second World War opened the coast to much more intensive human agricultural efforts than had previously been possible. While the south coast rainfall was greater than was common in other cotton areas, this did not prove to be a critical obstacle to development of cotton as a crop. The diseases that had discouraged intensive human exploitation were seemingly conquered, or at least controlled, and the new insecticides promised to control any dangers to the cotton itself.

Finally, the general agricultural economy of the country seemed to be stagnating at the very time a new revolutionary government was trying to institute many innovations in the social and economic life of the nation. In its annual report for 1949 (published 1950), the Instituto Nacional de Fomento a la Producción (INFOP) reported the following: "Excepting some few new activities of which the most important are the growing of citronella, lemon tea, abaca, and the elaboration of vegetable grease and oil, it can be said that the national economy has suffered in the last decade an alarming grade of paralysis."[1] Into this scene, then, stepped the revolutionary government, with its new development office, the INFOP, and with some specially significant private interests among those who were involved in the government. Specifically, Jacobo Arbenz, destined in a few years to become president, was one of a set who saw in cotton the promise of combining rapid national development with an equally rapid increase in private fortune.

2. *The Growth of Cotton and Governmental Action*

The Guatemalan government promoted the establishment of cotton as an important crop to improve the national balance of payments, as a device to diversify agriculture, and as a means to meet the local needs for the crop. INFOP took the lead through extending credit on relatively easy terms for planting cotton. It also, however, took two more direct steps in the development. It made some direct investments in private companies in order to encourage private entrepreneurs, and it undertook research concerning the best conditions for growing cotton in the country. There are not sufficient data on the first of these to pursue it here.

The experimentation, however, was successful. It rapidly suggested which strains of cotton would be most likely to produce well under Guatemalan conditions, what control of insects was possible, and what would be the best timing for planting and harvest. With the 1953–1954 season, experimentation stopped, "with the excuse that cotton was an established crop, and that further experimentation should be left to private interest."[2] This rash end to what could, under the circumstances, only have been the beginning of serious agricultural research indicates that the motivations behind those in the government were not the establishment of a dependable and well-thought-out agricultural enterprise designed to meet carefully estimated national needs, but, rather, a hasty entrance into a hopefully lucrative market. While it is not possible to be certain at this time of the rationale that led to the end of the INFOP research, its

---

[1] Jiménez, "Critique," p. 3.
[2]. Ibid., p. 19.

timing certainly coincided with the success of cotton on both the local and the international market.

The indicators that things were going so well that the government could drop research were that the local market was now almost completely free of cotton imports, and that significant cotton exports had begun. Table 7–1 shows that the 1952–1953 season saw the first yield that exceeded the local consumption and the first sizable export in the following year. The cessation of cotton research at this time, from the standpoint of the serious development of the field, was about as rational as it would have been to stop heart transplant research with the first surviving patient.

INFOP's participation in matters pertaining to cotton did not stop entirely, however, since there were certain other aspects that growers still might feel to be of special benefit to them. Specifically, INFOP continued to be the major credit agency. From the 1949–

TABLE 7–1
Production and Marketing of Guatemalan Cotton, 1949–1964

ar	Area Cultivated (manzanas)	Yield (100 lbs. *oro*)	Yield per Manzana	Exports (100 lbs. *oro*)	Internal Consumption (100 lbs. *oro*)
1949/50	—	13,140	—	—	43,745
1950/51	—	19,858	—	—	34,401
1951/52	11,712	42,703	3.6	—	44,347
1952/53	13,000	74,954	5.7	—	39,818
1953/54	16,031	132,194	8.2	113,324	48,389
1954/55	22,840	175,341	7.6	140,672	55,857
1955/56	30,374	208,032	6.9	169,706	60,000
1956/57	18,519	218,524	11.0	145,190	78,334
1957/58	25,135	286,770	11.0	208,630	78,140
1958/59	39,652	352,513	8.8	237,856	No. inf.
1959/60	25,291	323,457	12.7	249,194	No. inf.
1960/61	36,835	446,087	12.1	392,694	No. inf.
1961/62	64,177	557,179	8.7	No. inf.	No. inf.
1962/63	102,716	1,145,189	9.9	No. inf.	No. inf.
1963/64	130,233	No. inf.	No. inf	No. inf.	No. inf.

URCE: Mavis Ann Bryant, "Agricultural Interest Groups in Guatemala," M.A. thesis, University of Texas at Austin, 1967, Table 13, p. 78. Data from Asociación Guatemalteca de Productores de Algodón (AGUAPA), *Informativo Algodonero*, Nos. 7–8, February, 1960; and ibid., o. 10, January, 1964.

OTE: A manzana equals approximately 1.72 acres. *Oro* refers to the processed product.

1950 to the 1954–1955 growing seasons, the number of loans made by INFOP to cotton producers grew from 11 to 104, and the funds involved increased from $149,103 to $1,342,276, an increase of almost tenfold in both sets of figures.[3] Relative to other possible areas for development, the loans made to cotton in 1951–1952 constituted 51.7 percent of all agricultural loans made by INFOP that year and one-fifth of all loans made for whatever purpose. By 1953–1954, these figures had risen to 68.2 percent and 39.1 percent respectively. In a nation that was attempting to diversify in agriculture and to expand its economy, this concentration of funds in the development of one crop—to be used only as working capital—is little short of amazing. The possibility that people in the government were overly interested in their own financial advance can hardly be laid aside as idle speculation. The revolutionary government was clearly concentrating growth in a new sector that was going to be especially profitable to its own people. This activity of INFOP continued until after the change in government in 1954, at which time INFOP was taken out of the cotton-support business.

INFOP did one further favor to the growers in order to encourage them. In 1952 the government prohibited the further importation of raw cotton, and INFOP was instructed to act as the purchasing agent of the country to achieve a local stabilized price. It offered prices in excess of those being offered on the world market, and the growers were delighted. The next year, INFOP placed this stored cotton on the world market at a price below that which it paid, and this began the export of Guatemalan cotton with a direct loss to the government of over one million dollars. While the government stood the loss, the growers willingly took the profits from the amount paid by INFOP. As Jiménez points out repeatedly in his study, one can hardly be surprised at the joy with which cotton growers launched into their new-found enterprises.

The fall of Arbenz' revolutionary government led to some important changes in the social structure of cotton development, but none that seriously threatened it. The major shifts consisted of the removal of government protection policies, the elimination of INFOP as the principal credit source, the availability of new lands on the Pacific coast, and the organization of the growers. Castillo

[3] Ibid., Table 2–5, Part B, p. 23.

Armas came into Guatemala in July of 1954 after the beginning of planting for the 1954–1955 season. His assumption of power marked the end of the revolutionary period, a return to a modified form of nineteenth-century liberalism, the temporary end of all syndicalist and trade-union activities, the end of lower-sector interest group support by the government, and the exiling of all individuals closely identified with the Arbenz government (including a few important cotton growers). One thing that did not basically change, however, was the desire of the government that cotton continue to grow, since it held potential for the nation. Some important changes did take place in the government's handling of cotton, however. As described by Jiménez:

> The direction of the government policy changed during this period of fluctuation from the INFOP to the central bank of the Republic, the Banco de Guatemala. The end of the stabilization program brought the end to the INFOP's contributions. Although since the beginning the central bank had had an important role, it had been secondary to the INFOP, which had carried on the experimentation, the feasibility studies, and the actual management of the program. The central bank had acted as a banker for the INFOP, rediscounting loans made to cotton growers and lending the money used by the INFOP to buy and store cotton during its stabilization program. However, although the central bank had the power to stop or curb the investment in cotton, it always played a passive, secondary role in the period in which cotton was introduced into Guatemala. From the end of the 1954 season the roles were reversed. All of the INFOP's incentive programs ended as it was believed that cotton was an established product which should be left for private enterprise. From that time onward the INFOP's only action was to serve as a lending agency, in response to the central bank's wishes that easy credit should be made available to the cotton growers. In order to carry out this goal, the central bank rediscounted a fixed percentage of all loans made to cotton by any of the banks in the system, including the INFOP which is also legally a bank. Depending on the push the central bank has wanted to give cotton, it has varied the amount of the loans which it has rediscounted. In no instance has this been less than 50 per cent. Nevertheless, due to its previous important position the INFOP continued for several years to be the chief lending agency for cotton.[4]

4 Ibid., pp. 34–35.

In short, the Castillo government did not want to stop the lucrative business that was cotton, but neither did it want to take any risks beyond agricultural loans. The price stabilization program was stopped. World prices were adequate, and yield high enough that further support was unnecessary; and the new government probably was uninterested in continuing support on personalistic grounds, since it did not have many direct friends deeply involved in the venture. The government therefore returned to a more straightforward, liberal, economic policy of letting the growers work directly with the world market. One might suppose, under this kind of change, that the total government support of loans to the growers would have been reduced, but this does not seem to have happened. The loans were continued, but the basic support was shifted from the INFOP directly to the Banco de Guatemala. Probably the principal reason for this lay in a combination of circumstances. Since cotton was successfully started, it could be argued that it was no longer in the province of a development agency like INFOP to handle the loans. Also, however, INFOP was almost bankrupt and had been developing a bad reputation for inefficiency and corruption under the Arbenz government. Aside from these, however, the most important factor lay in the character of the Banco de Guatemala itself.

The Banco de Guatemala was originated by the first revolutionary regime under Arévalo. Prior to this time, there had been no wholly government-owned bank; the nation used a private bank that belonged to a group of upper-class citizens. The Banco de Guatemala grew under a progressive regime and evolved with an ideology generally congruent to progressive political policies. It was not socialistic, but the directors were sympathetic to the reform-oriented government. The Banco began early to develop a means of recruitment of personnel that was to convert it into an organization with almost corporate qualities. There were, at the outset of the revolutionary period, almost no economists in Guatemala. The faculty of economics of the university was just getting under way, and the Banco desperately needed trained personnel. It began the practice of hiring students, a custom followed by other agencies of the government, as well as the private sector. The most promising of these students were then given fellowships to take advanced degrees in Europe or the United States. Upon their return, they were given posts within the Banco. Over the ensuing years, this system served to bring a consistency in manner of thought to the Banco's personnel. In something of the same manner that the military service began to indoctrinate its personnel in school and to continue this indoctrination into the professional career, so the Banco initiated the indoctrination while the student was still in college. It may be assumed, then, that if any important organization in Guatemala could find a good reason for continuing the support of cotton after the fall of the revolutionary government, it would be an organization whose origin lay in that revolution, but which was firm enough to withstand the change of regime.

The Banco de Guatemala was such an organization. Furthermore, it had three very good reasons to continue support for cotton, apart from any personal interests that might have been felt by the members of its staff. One of these was that cotton continued to be attractive because it was a promising source of foreign exchange. The fluctuations of the coffee market were well known, and world production was increasing, threatening to send prices down. Cotton, still new to Guatemala, seemed like a good alternative. World market prices, while dropping, continued relatively high. Cotton could also supply a national industry and therefore could be said to contribute to the balance of payments, as well as to nationalistic pride. The other aspect of cotton that would have been attractive to the Banco was the fact that coffee was still predominantly grown by farmers of an older tradition, individuals who had, during the revolutionary period, generally turned against Arbenz. Cotton was a part of the diversification of crops that was bringing new entrepreneurs, new attitudes, and new interests into the open. The promotion of diversification in both crops and personnel would have been congenial to the Banco's policy makers.

Thus it may have been that the continued support of cotton by the Banco de Guatemala was one of the inheritances bequeathed by the revolution to succeeding governments. "In 1964," reports Jiménez, ". . . the Banco de Guatemala, the nation's central bank, gave 40.4% of its rediscounts, or about Q9,000,000, to be used for loans made to cotton. As large as this figure is, it does not in fact represent the actual amount of central bank resources which were made available to the cotton growers, for it does not include rediscounts made the previous year which were extended in time and

rediscounts assigned to cotton in foreign currencies."[5] Jiménez then
estimates that the minimum rediscount in national currency alone
was probably really above Ø14,000,000, although it is impossible
to arrive at an accurate figure based on available data. In all, the
change in government not only did not reduce the government's
interest in cotton, but, rather, signaled a new kind of interest. The
successful beginning in cotton was enough to demonstrate that cotton was providing a new basis of power.

In the years following the fall of the revolutionary government,
a subtle but structurally important change evolved in the relationship between the cotton-growing sector and the government. Whereas the revolutionary government took the lead in determining the
role it was to play in cotton development (not forgetting that there
were important growers in government), beginning about 1953
the first signs appeared that the growers were capable of some independent organization themselves. By the 1960's, the growers were
making demands parallel to those of other interest sectors, and the
government's role had become that of a reactor.

The first major organization of cotton growers was the Algodonera
Guatemalteca, S.A. (AGSA), formed in 1953 to rent a gin for their
own use. Ginning costs had long been irksome, and over most of the
recent history of cotton in Guatemala, growers have tried to free
themselves of what they have considered to be excessive ginning
costs. At the time that Castillo Armas rescinded the protective legislation, there were about eighty growers and three gins in Guatemala.
The growers then again united in January of 1955 in the Asociación
Guatemalteca de Productores de Algodón (AGUAPA). Having
weathered the immediate emergency posed by the government's
action, splinter groups appeared, and in 1959 a major exodus occurred when some of the major (and original AGSA) member abandoned the AGUAPA, disagreeing over a new ginning project. At
the time of her study in 1965, Bryant felt that six distinctive interest
groups could be identified among the cotton growers. All, she held,
participated in the various kinds of activities that such interest
groups promoted. All were represented in one way or another on
the major delegations to international and national bodies, in representations before the Guatemalan government, in the founding of

[5] Ibid., p. 93.

the Centro Experimental Algodonero, and in the ultimate formulation of the Consejo Nacional del Algodón.[6]

From the fall of Arbenz until well into the government of Peralta Azurdia, the growers were expanding their exercise of power with respect to the government. Evidence for this may be seen in the fact that they were able to hold off the imposition of a tax on cotton attempted in 1962 by the Ydígoras government until 1964.[7] Jiménez further reports that they were also able to divert a governmental attempt to preserve the quality of the land by imposing legal requirements for crop rotation and, similarly, a law controlling the use of insecticides.

The IGSS (Instituto Guatemalteco de Seguridad Social), complaining that the insecticides are being used without any health protections for the workers involved or the people in the surrounding areas, asked that the government suspend use of the very toxic insecticides and that laws regulating their use be written up before their use was permitted again. However, the power of the growers was brought to the test in this case, and by a massive propaganda campaign and political pressures brought to bear by them, the government, despite the objections of the IGSS, granted the growers permission to continue using the dangerously toxic insecticides at their discretion without the acceptance of any legal regulation of their use.[8]

The change from a revolutionary government to a liberal regime did not essentially divert the interest in cotton; it merely served to take the leadership and control from those in the government to those who were directly involved in making a profit out of growing and ginning. By the time of Jiménez's study, a further major step had been taken in this direction. In 1965, the various growing interests collaborated in the formation of the Consejo Nacional de Algodón, an organization to which all cotton growers belonged. The statutes were reportedly written by members of the six major interest groups and, in July of that year, were approved by the government. The statutes were followed by an effort to get the government to approve a decree to give the Consejo five cents on every

---

[6] Mavis Ann Bryant, "Agricultural Interest Groups in Guatemala," M.A. thesis, The University of Texas at Austin, 1967, Chapter 5.

[7] Ibid.

[8] Jiménez, "Critique," p. 110.

quintal of cotton exported. Bryant reported that various reasons were given by the growers for the formation of the Consejo:

Internal problems included fighting government taxation, promoting agricultural research as world prices declined and costs of production rose, and defending the growers against a group of bee-keepers protesting the effects of fumigation. Problems cited on the international scene involved threats by the U.S. to "dump" the Commodity Credit Corporation's surplus stores of cotton on the world market, feelers being sent out by the U.S. concerning the possibility of forming an International Cotton Agreement similar to that in effect for coffee, and the question of Guatemala's dues and representation in international cotton producers' associations assuming increased importance in view of the foregoing factors.[9]

The case of growth of the upper-sector interest groups in cotton (related in the last chapter to the growth of such groups across the agricultural, commercial, industrial, and financial spectrum) here can be seen also to be related to a gradual increase in power outside the government. If the mere numbers of such groups are any index of the real distribution of power across the upper sector and outside the government, then the postrevolutionary period has been one of extreme importance for the general power structure of the country. It is not possible to estimate from these data on cotton development the degree to which decentralization of power has actually been occurring throughout the entire upper sector. Similarly, in considering the whole, the relative growth of the military as a paragovernment body can also be seen as decentralizing power within the government itself; but, again, it is difficult to estimate the relative amount of power involved. Cotton illustrates how the governmental interests, whether under revolutionary or postrevolutionary regimes, have contributed to the growth of a new base of power within the country and how this new base, once formed, has separated from governmental controls that spawned it and has proceeded to act solely in its own interests.

3. *Growth, Profits, and Development*

The major stimulus to the regular growth of cotton production has obviously been the fact that the crop has been profitable. Table

[9] Bryant, "Interest Groups," p. 228.

7–2 shows the general course of growth of cotton production in the country. While somewhat irregular, the yield clearly increased over the first seven years of production and then leveled off at about thirteen quintales per manzana. The major significant production growth began in 1960 and probably reflects the full entrance into the market of major Guatemalan investors, an increase in foreign investors, and a sharp expansion of the area under cultivation by the successful producers. Cotton had proved that it could be expected to produce well in the Guatemalan environment, early speculators

TABLE 7–2
Cultivation and Production of Cotton, 1949–1966

Year	Area Cultivated (in manzanas)	Production of Ginned Cotton (in quintales)	Average Yields per Manzana (in quintales)
1949/50	—	13,140	2.93
1950/51	—	19,140	5.70
1951/52	10,530	42,703	4.06
1952/53	11,700	74,954	6.41
1953/54	14,428	132,194	9.16
1954/55	20,556	175,341	8.53
1955/56	27,337	209,032	7.65
1956/57	16,667	218,638	13.12
1957/58	22,621	301,741	13.34
1958/59	35,606	352,513	9.90
1959/60	22,762	322,457	14.17
1960/61	33,151	446,087	13.46
1961/62	60,904	791,895	13.00
1962/63	92,934	1,301,076	14.00
1963/64	117,210	1,600,176	13.65
1964/65	128,086	1,633,008	12.75
1965/66	134,201	1,730,507	12.89

SOURCE: Julio M. Jiménez, "A Critique of the Policies and Attitudes Affecting Cotton Agriculture Guatemala through a Study of Its Development," M.A. thesis, University of Texas at Austin, 57, pp. 32, 39.

NOTE: These figures vary considerably from those cited from AGUAPA sources by Bryant (Table 1). The differences are not important in the present context; the reader is referred to the two ginal sources for the causes of the discrepancy. Jiménez, *Memorias del INFOP, 1949–1954,* and inisterio de Agricultura, Dirección de Mercadeo-Agropecuario. Bryant, *Informativo Algonero,* Nos. 7–8, February 1960, and ibid., No. 10, January 1964.

TABLE 7–3
Number and Size of Cotton Farms

Growing Season	Number of Farms	Average Farm Size	Average Size of Farms over 100 Manzanas	% of Farms over 100 Manzanas
1957/58	88	285	299	87.5
1960/61	120	305	334	89.0
1963/64	357	360	396	95.0
1965/66	367	399	423	93.0

SOURCE: Jiménez, "Critique," p. 41.
NOTE: "Based on information concerning planting permits granted by the Dirección General de Investigación y Control of the Ministerio de Agricultura. From these figures I subtracted all the registered farms of less than fifty manzanas, for the Banco Nacional Agrario informed me that it had proven that most plots of that size were rented out to nearby large owners. This was especially true of all plots of land acquired through the land reform program" (Jiménez, "Critique," p. 129).

had undergone the testing period, and the world market still promised profit.

Growth is not reflected merely in the total output, however. Of equal importance from the point of view of understanding the role cotton played in the drama of shifting power is that the average farm size significantly increased. Table 7–3 shows that the average increased and also that those of a hundred manzanas and more also increased. A hundred-manzana farm is deemed to be the "smallest efficient farm size because it most effectively uses the smallest bulk of capital equipment which can be bought."[10]

It has also been possible to calculate something of the nature of the profits that have accrued to the investors over these years. During the early 1950's, costs were still low. The future cost increases in insecticides, spraying, and fertilizers were ignored at the outset. Jiménez cites a cost figure of approximately Ø180 per manzana for 1952. Since production per manzana over this period was increasing, even the fluctuations and decline in the world price did not prevent the Guatemalan grower from making a profit. Also, it must be recalled that INFOP bought up the early cotton at a price of Ø46

[10] Jiménez, "Critique," p. 41.

per quintal, and sold it at Ø32, giving the farmer a Ø14-per-quintal subsidy. Calculated in terms of total costs and the price paid, the Guatemalan farmer in cotton cleared at least Ø200 per manzana in 1954. Subsidization stopped in 1954, however, and costs began to rise significantly. By 1959 they were estimated to be Ø220 per manzana, and by 1965 the figure had reached a point somewhere between Ø250 and Ø300. If we can assume that for the first decade and a half of effort profits were sufficient to encourage an increase in area from 10,000 to over 134,000 manzanas, the only question might be what the general order of magnitude of the profits is.

Jiménez estimates that the average price of Ø27.03 per quintal brought by cotton in 1965 would yield a gross revenue of Ø344 per manzana. The highest cost estimate Jiménez received was Ø310 per manzana, and other estimates range from Ø250 to Ø300. Calculating the owner's rent at Ø30 and salary for administration at Ø6, the revenue that an owner received varied from Ø70 to Ø105 per manzana, with the only variation being due to net profit. On this basis, a farm of 75 manzanas made between Ø5,250 and Ø7,875; one of 150 manzanas made between Ø10,500 and Ø15,750. Since 55 percent of the cotton farms in Guatemala are larger than 200 manzanas, it can be assumed that their revenue is, in general, a stimulus to investors.

Since risk is an important part of investment and the world cotton market is notoriously unpredictable, it may be argued that such high revenues are well deserved. However, the fact of the matter is that cotton demands and gets such a great amount of working capital through loans that the risk to many investors is actually very small, as was indicated earlier in discussing the relative support the government provides to back up loans to cotton growers. Also, there is some indication that the growers have been somewhat remiss in maintaining their credit. Jiménez reports that during the summer of 1966 there existed a defaulted debt of over ten million quetzales to agricultural supply growers. "Reportedly the agricultural suppliers were forced to form a credit union to keep the same growers from opening accounts with all of the supply houses. Only five growers of the over 350 in Guatemala were qualified by the credit union as recipients of future credit!" Jiménez goes on to suggest that "this is not a sign of the high risk and the low profitability of cotton, as the

growers would like everyone to believe. It is in fact a sign of the
financial irresponsibility of the majority of the growers."[11]

In short, even with rising costs and rising risks in terms of world
market fluctuation, cotton continues to be a very profitable business.
Whether the slight deceleration in growth indicated by Table 7–2
is due more to the threat of an undependable market or to other
factors is probably less significant than the fact that expansion
of cotton has reached such extraordinary proportions. All the profits
made by growers are not merely on the raw cotton, however, since
a large proportion of growers have banded together to invest in and
utilize their own cotton gins. Jiménez draws a picture of the financial operations of one such combine, showing at the same time how
the risks of investment are minimized through heavy dependence on
loans.

The type of industry generated by cotton agriculture can best be
seen by an analysis of one such organization, hence a brief look at a
ginning and cottonseed producing company. Its ownership is almost
exclusively by cotton growers. Profits as reported in the annual reports
of the company are not very large. In 1961–62 they reported a 5.4 per
cent return on the equity of the company. In 1963–64 they reported an
increase to 7.3 per cent. This return seems good but not outstanding.
However, during the same time period, the company was able to
depreciate[12] about 44 per cent of the increased value of its fixed investment since 1961–62 as calculated from the stated value of the 1963–64
report. At the same time, the value of fixed investment was increasing
by about 47 per cent with reference to fixed investment in 1961–62.
All of the capital for the investment of the company, except for the original equity, has come from borrowed funds. In 1961–62 the company
has loans outstanding equal to 63 per cent of the net worth[13] of the
company. By 1962–63 total loans outstanding equalled 81 per cent of the
net worth of the company. By 1964 the original value in just fixed investment was over 2.5 times the value of the original investment by the
stockholders. The growth of the company has been tremendous and in
a sense reflects the growth of cotton production. What is so exceptional

---

[11] Ibid., p. 101.

[12] Although depreciation is merely an accounting convention, the income
profit and loss statements of the company show that the value of depreciation
was actually retired from the company's income.

[13] Net worth defined as all assets minus all liabilities not including capital or
surplus accounts.

about the growth of the company is that all of its growth has been brought about by borrowed capital without the need of the company to reinvest its earnings. Not only that, but the bulk of the credit outstanding is of relative short term. Thus as an example, in 1963–64 the company invested Q106,712 in fixed capital, but in the same year, the company borrowed Q1,312,317, a sum greater than the value of all its issued stocks, in an effort not only to pay for the year's investment but also to refinance the portion of their debt due that year. What is most astonishing is that they have not needed to use their accumulated depreciations for anything. In fact, there is no record of what is done with this money. As far as the company is concerned, the money could have been paid out to the stockholders. This company is by no means an exception to the rule. It demonstrates the profitability of this type of industry, the great amount of loanable funds which they have had available. This type of activity carried out by many companies at the same time makes one wonder whether there is actually a capital shortage in underdeveloped countries.[14]

The only detailed study of cotton farms from the standpoint of the laborer is that by Schmid on migratory labor in Guatemala.[15] Cotton cultivation has been an important source of labor for the expanding population of the Indian highlands. Schmid cites data collected by the National Service for the Eradication of Malaria for the 1965/66 harvest period, on the basis of information from 33,802 cotton-farm migrants. Of these, 78 percent came from the highlands departments of Quiché (17.3 percent), Huehuetenango (17.1 percent), Baja Verapaz (11.9 percent), Sololá (10.3 percent), Totonicapán (9.7 percent), Quezaltenango (4.6 percent), San Marcos (4.0 percent), and Alta Verapaz (3.4 percent). Jutiapa was the only eastern department of any consequence and accounted for 10.6 percent of the total. Additional data collected in Schmid's own study indicated that Chimaltenango and Jalapa were important too. The total number of migrant laborers was estimated to be between 118,-000 and 150,000 in cotton, 167,000 and 237,000 in coffee, and 17,500 to 21,000 in sugar cane. In addition to this, there are an estimated 4,700 permanent employees and laborers on the cotton farms.

[14] Jiménez, "Critique," pp. 49–50. [Author's corrections have been included in this version.]

[15] Lester Schmid, "The Role of Migratory Labor in the Economic Development of Guatemala," Ph.D. dissertation, University of Wisconsin, Madison, 1967.

Wages for the migrants are better in cotton than in the other two major harvests, but living conditions are considerably worse. Daily wage estimates ranged between Ø0.93 to Ø1.30 for cotton, while the range in coffee was Ø0.57 to Ø0.75, and in sugar cane was Ø0.65 to Ø1.00. The annual wage received for average number of days worked on each type of farm was Ø95.78 for seventy-four days in the cotton farms, Ø70.62 for seventy-three days in coffee, and Ø92.70 for ninety-nine days in sugar cane. For the permanent labor, the average annual value of wages and perquisites for cotton farms was Ø535.88, for coffee Ø258.58, and for sugar cane, Ø430.30.

Working conditions showed a different side, however. The best housing was found on the sugar-cane farms, and the worst on cotton farms. Fully 50 percent of the cotton farms provided no corn ration at all, whereas only 6.5 percent of the coffee farms and 16.7 percent of the sugar-cane farms did not provide corn. Concerning the climate in which they worked, 27 percent of the cotton workers regarded it as injurious, whereas only 12 percent of those in sugar cane and 5 percent of those in coffee found their locales dangerous. Free medicine was reported to be received by 20 percent of the migrants on cotton farms, 54 percent of coffee fincas, and 70 percent on sugar-cane farms. Payment was not given to laborers when ill in 80 percent of the cotton farms, and about 59 percent of the coffee and sugar-cane farms. The ruling in Guatemala that a farm should give a seventh-day salary when a worker has worked six days was observed on 100 percent of the coffee fincas, on 75 percent of the sugar-cane farms, but only on 26 percent of the cotton farms. Even regarding the right to pick fruit on the farm, cotton came out last: permission was granted to 8 percent of cotton workers, 65.2 percent of the coffee workers, and 20.8 percent of the sugar workers. In Schmid's sample, fifteen of the sixteen cotton farms had no service by a medical doctor whatsoever; five of the eighteen coffee fincas and three of the seven sugar-cane farms had no service.

Indeed, for almost every subject on which Schmid collected data, except base salary, the cotton farms provided a lean and callous profile. But, since many benefits had to be purchased by the laborer in cotton, whereas his counterparts on other types of farms had a greater chance of receiving them as services, it is doubtful if the absolute income can be regarded as really that advantageous. Nevertheless, many migrants preferred the cotton harvest, presumably because of the better wages. Probably the most favorable feature about the cotton-farm labor opportunities is that they were there. As miserable as their conditions were, and with as little actual funds that they were able to take home, the migrants at least found a means to survive through that period of the year.

Profits to individual investors, while not widely disseminated, cannot be argued to be the sole objective in the introduction and support of a new crop like cotton. Of equal, if not greater, importance are the benefits to the nation as a whole in such matters as foreign exchange, the stimulus to other industrial and commercial growth, the contribution to basic wealth of the country, and the enhancement of science and knowledge. These are contributions to the national development of the country, and the importance of cotton must be evaluated with these in mind.

One of the major original reasons for the promotion of cotton by the Guatemalan government was that it would contribute to the balance of payments by bringing in foreign exchange. As coffee income began to wane in 1955, this need for other sources of foreign exchange became even more pressing. The impressive growth of cotton, especially from 1961 on, seemed to prove that the government's original faith in cotton as a substitute enterprise was well founded. Table 7–4 shows both the growth of these earnings and their importance in the total foreign earnings of the country. The final sum of Q154,030,238 is impressive. Jiménez, however, has some severe reservations about taking this figure at its face value. If one takes into account the costs of imports occasioned by cotton (including the cost of gasoline, oils, lubricants, fertilizers, insecticides, depreciation of equipment, maintenance in terms of spare parts, tractors, trailers, farm equipment, planes, trucks, fumigation equipment, and the gins), Jiménez calculates that the cotton industry has spent Q87,130,480 in imports during the period of 1954 through 1965. Thus, instead of over Q150,000,000, Jiménez finds the real contribution to Guatemala's foreign exchange to be more on the order of Q67,000,000 for the period in question. This is a sizable figure, but far from that claimed by the cotton growers and their supporters in the government. It might be further added that aside from the fact that a great proportion of the import costs are in expendable goods, much of the capital equipment, such as gins, are highly specialized and, should the cotton market break, cannot

TABLE 7–4

Foreign Exchange Earned by Cotton Agriculture in Guatemala, 1954–1965

Year	Cotton	Cotton Seed	Other By-Products	Total	Percentage of Foreign Earnings
1954	Ø 3,655,653	Ø 242,986	Ø 220	Ø 3,905,859	4.1%
1955	4,485,578	483,485	20,672	4,989,742	5.0
1956	4,919,357	205,095	33,324	5,157,776	4.4
1957	4,144,596	116,309	72,350	4,333,255	3.9
1958	5,414,828	140,384	68,580	5,623,729	5.4
1959	4,031,629	80,449	109,625	4,221,703	4.1
1960	5,765,692	631,726	76,927	6,474,345	5.7
1961	10,116,249	246,398	117,671	10,480,318	9.5
1962	15,157,865	151,881	205,022	15,514,768	13.5
1963	24,291,780	897,125	454,473	25,643,378	16.9
1964	31,907,450	401,117	157,443	32,466,010	20.0
1965	33,893,871	754,891	553,391	35,202,153	18.9
			Grand Total	Ø154,030,238	

SOURCE: Dirección General de Estadísticas; Jiménez, "Critique," p. 44.

readily be adapted to other uses. None of this, of course, includes the portion of profits paid out for imported luxury goods.

Another national benefit that cotton production induces is the development of secondary and related industries and commercial activities. The development of the ginning industry can be mentioned here, but it should be pointed out that many of the gins are owned by the growers and cannot really be considered as entirely separate enterprises. Jiménez estimates that while the cost of gins is initially high, running about Ø400,000, they usually pay for themselves within five years of operation, particularly if they can gin more cotton than that produced by the owners. At the time of the study, there were twenty-three gins in the country. The increase in cottonseed production has generally paralleled that of ginned cotton. Apparently most production is used within the country, although there have been significant exports and even some imported. While much of the internal use was long under monopolistic control, there are now a number of competing plants, and the industry promises continued growth.

The industry for which cotton production promised the most was the textile industry. National self-sufficiency for textiles was one of the two major reasons for promoting cotton in the first place. It will be remembered that the importation of raw cotton ceased in 1953, and the local textile industries have been utilizing domestic production predominantly since that time. In this sense, the substitution of local production for import cotton has been successful. There has been, however, no evidence that the textile industry has grown at a pace significantly higher than that of the general population. From a base index of 100 for production in 1946, the textile industry index remained below 100 from 1950 until 1957 and then rose slowly to 182 in 1965 (see Table 7–5). The availability of local cotton did not, it seems, in itself provide much of a stimulus for the expansion of this industry. Indirectly, however, the availability of local cotton, coupled with the pressure growing out of the Common Market, has probably led to the growth of textile production. The Guatemalan government has not undertaken any such promotion of the textile industry or any combined strategy of development of the cotton and textile industry together.

TABLE 7–5
Indexes of Clothing and Textile Production

Year	Clothing	Textiles
1950	91.2	85.1
1951	79.3	66.9
1952	90.5	86.9
1953	95.1	77.5
1954	92.3	86.0
1955	105.1	81.8
1956	111.0	90.5
1957	144.4	99.1
1958	225.7	114.6
1959	219.6	101.9
1960	213.8	108.2
1961	191.4	124.0
1962	167.6	131.4
1963	182.9	152.4
1964	228.0	154.9
1965	279.8	182.0

SOURCE: *Boletín Estadístico*, 1958–1966; Jiménez, "Critique," pp. 55, 81.
NOTE: Base 1946 = 100.

One of the consequences of this lack of articulation among policies for development is that while the textile industry grows slowly, depending upon nationally produced cotton and thereby saving on foreign exchange, the clothing industry has been growing very rapidly, although somewhat erratically (see Table 7–5). This growth is not directly related to the textile industry growth, since most of the textile growth is in finished flat goods, whereas much of the clothing growth depends upon the importation of cloth. Thus, while cotton is promoted to produce foreign exchange and make textiles nationally self-sufficient, one of the major outlets for textiles, clothing, continues to use foreign exchange in order to import basic materials, ignoring the textile industry and presumably being ignored by it. The market for textiles has increased only slightly, whereas the clothing market has increased pronouncedly.

While cotton's effective stimulation of other industrial development in Guatemala has been spotty, in one commercial area there is no doubt of its warm reception. Jiménez points out that investment in cotton has provided gratifying returns for private bankers.

As a by-product of the finance of cotton, the banking system in Guatemala has been reaping unwarranted profits. Lending for cotton production is one of the most profitable loans that a bank in Guatemala can make, due to the large amounts of central bank rediscounts assigned for this purpose. On the average in the last few years banks in Guatemala have lending about Q175 per *manzana* to the cotton growers, about 60 per cent of estimated costs. The rediscount rate for loans for cotton is 3 per cent, the preferential rate. However, since all loans made by the banking system are made at 8 per cent, the maximum allowed by law, the commercial bank is receiving as a gift from the government 5 per cent on the money that was rediscounted per *manzana*. At the same time the bank is earning 8 per cent per annum on the Q75 of its own funds per *manzana*, or Q6. This operation gives the commercial bank a gross return of Q11 per Q75 lent, or a return of 14.6 per cent. If one were to suppose that the commercial banks had high costs of lending of about 3 per cent, and that it paid its depositors the going rate of 5 per cent, this would leave the bank with a net return on its loans of 6.6 per cent. The larger the rediscounts have been, the larger the net return for the banks has been. It is obvious that the banks would want to lend to cotton under the above profit conditions.[16]

[16] Jiménez, "Critique," pp. 96–97.

Here, at least, there seems to be little doubt that business has been stimulated by the development of cotton. As with the grower's benefits, this provides more money for the upper sector.

When we turn from the question of stimulation of growth in commerce and industry to the question of the contribution that cotton growing makes to the basic wealth of the nation, we move from the spottily positive to the darkly negative. One of the unfortunate aspects of cotton development in Guatemala is that the general set of attitudes and interests under which it is done is leading to serious damage of the environment in short- and long-range terms. One of the conclusions of Jiménez' study is that Guatemalan cotton investors, beginning in the revolutionary period, have primarily operated on the basis of short-term investment for quick profits. While indicated by the credit situation in which the suppliers found themselves, the desire for quick profits is nowhere clearer than in the effects that the development is having on the natural environment.

Cotton production has introduced two destructive devices: the variety of toxic poisons that are killing animals and human beings as well as insects for which they are intended; and the intensive overexploitation of the soils without allowing opportunity for the nutrients to rebuild. The problem with the use of insecticides seems to involve both the uncontrolled use of the poisons and the fact that usually not even minimal safety precautions are observed. The Guatemalan Social Security Institute complained strongly to the government concerning the use of insecticides without any health precautions, but the growers were able to keep the complaint from leading to any legislation or decrees that would in any way restrict their laissez-faire methods. In 1964 the IGSS "had treated 548 cases of confirmed poisoning resulting from insecticides and had confirmed five deaths from the same cause."[17] Another source, citing IGSS information for 1965, stated:

According to the Instituto Guatemalteco de Seguridad Social (IGSS) over 1,500 persons were clinically ill with insecticides last year (1965), with about 10 deaths having occurred. According to Dr. Gustavo Cordero of IGSS, most poisonings occur on cotton farms, lesser numbers on coffee farms, and few on sugar cane farms and vegetable crop farms. Dr. Cordero has reported that from June to October, 1966, 300 persons

---

[17] Ibid., p. 109.

had been treated for poisoning and seven deaths had occurred. . . . About 1300 cases of poisoning and about 12 deaths had been reported to IGSS from June of 1966 to March of 1967.[18]

Conversations with farmers in the coffee piedmont suggest that the number of poisonings and deaths probably far exceeds that suggested by the IGSS report. Many are never reported to the IGSS, and, in many instances, it is quite impossible for doctors to be sure whether poisoning is involved.

Most farmers evidently do not know enough about the cycle of growth of insects and the conditions under which they survive and can best be eliminated. As a consequence, insecticides are used in proportions which are often either much too large or otherwise inappropriate for the specific conditions at the time of use. The FAO reported that "farms that have carefully kept track of insects reported a saving of about 30 per cent on budgeted insecticide expenditures."[19] The consequence of this unreasonable use of the poisons has been not only the direct killing of human beings, but also the reported elimination of much of the wildlife in the area. Conservation is not a strong philosophy in Guatemala, and the loss of wildlife tends to be of little interest to most of the growers, just as it is to those who seek a profit out of the environment all over the world. The order of magnitude of the destruction in Guatemala presently is totally unknown, and, as a result, the effects on the total ecological balance of the areas affected are also unknown.

Of more immediate importance, and of much clearer consequence, has been the systematic destruction of the soils. The lowland areas that have provided the environmental basis for the growth of cotton production lie principally in the adjacent departments of Escuintla, Suchitepéquez, and Retahuleu, with the major portion being in Escuintla. Prior to the advent of the cotton boom, much of the land was in tropical growth, small areas being used by subsistence farmers, and occasionally larger areas being used for nonintensive creole cattle production. The only intensive farming in the area was that in Tiquisate, then one of the two major banana plantations of the

[18] Schmid, "Migratory Labor," p. 229.

[19] F. S. Parsons and Angelo de Tuddo, *Informe Sobre los Aspectos Agrícolas, Técnicos y Económicos de la Producción de Algodón en Centroamérica* (Rome, FAO, March, 1959, p. 190). Cited in Jiménez, "Critique," p. 108.

United Fruit Company. Following on the combination of increased costs, labor troubles, and storm damage, the United Fruit Company gave a large unused section to the nation following the fall of the revolutionary government and sold most of the larger sections of land that were planted in bananas. Since much of this land was already cleared of forest growth, it was readily accessible for cotton planting and contributed to the rapid later growth of production.

Tropical conditions like those on the Guatemalan south coast, involving heavy rainfalls, produce depletion of the soils and the ready loss of topsoils through wind erosion during the dry season. No matter what is planted in this area, there is likely to be serious loss of soil nutrients if care is not taken to see that organic materials are replaced and supplemented with fertilization. The rapid growth of cotton farming in this zone has in no way brought any special attention to the preservation or reconstruction of these soils. In the middle 1950's, it was already evident that the cotton entrepreneurs included many who had no interest whatsoever in long-term farming. LeBeau termed their efforts "speculative agriculture" because it was, in most respects, like speculation elsewhere.[20] The general pattern was to rent land for a year at a time to be able to leave if the market became dangerous. Under these circumstances, it is obvious that the major motivation was to get the crop out of the land and the cash out of the crop as quickly and as neatly as possible, with no interest being shown in the future of the land itself. By 1965 renting was more commonly done for three to five years. Observation in Guatemala has shown that these lands significantly decline in fertility after five or six years of continuing cultivation in cotton. Cotton has been expanding so rapidly, however, that much of the land is still producing very well, and the decline in the quality of the older lands is masked by the total figures.

Studies by FAO cotton experts in Guatemala have made it clear that the loss in good soils can be avoided. It requires, however, not merely the use of fertilizers, for they can only be of declining help over the years; it also needs the actual restitution of nutrients to the topsoil, saving that soil. Thus, there must be crop rotation and the soil must be under regular cultivation. Wind erosion can be avoided,

[20] Frances LeBeau, "Agricultura de Guatemala," *Integración Social en Guatemala*, vol. 3, pp. 267–312.

and the organic materials can be replaced only through the systematic resting of the land and replanting in complementary crops.

Jiménez estimates that no less (and probably much more) than 40 percent of the cotton land in Guatemala is rented, and much of this is in small pieces of fifty manzanas or less, which are not economical to cultivate except as a part of a larger operation.[21] Obviously a renter will have only a dim interest in whether or not he ruins someone else's land and will probably look upon the rotation of crops with little or no market as being a positive investment loss. It is much easier to use up a piece of land and, as Jiménez expresses it, calculate depreciation as being equivalent to selling the land for scrap. In many instances the land is owned by people who have only recently come into it through government grants under the colonization program or through purchase. Many of these individuals, too, have little interest in the land except for what they can rapidly derive from it.

The result of this set of factors is that an area that is perhaps the most promising for general agricultural development in Guatemala and that should be treated rationally for long-term production is under systematic destruction. This destruction is not something that *may* happen if steps are not taken; it is already happening and will continue as long as there is a satisfactory international cotton market and there is still land left to destroy. Unfortunately, it cannot even be argued that the loss of this national resource is in the interest of some significant part of the nation. The cotton growers, the land owners who rent to them, and the agricultural suppliers who get the actual profits from this cultivation probably number less than two thousand and possibly not much more than one thousand. Guatemala is not a country of endless resources either in quantity or quality. The investment in cotton is proving to be damaging to the natural environment, and its major returns are limited to a very few.

Given that cotton has proved to be a lucrative venture for a few but generally of sporadic help to the country as a whole, it would be nice if there were at least some by-product of scientific knowledge that could be marked up as a gain. Even this is lacking. As noted, the government stopped all experimentation before the fall of the

[21] Jiménez, "Critique," p. 73.

revolutionary government. Somewhat later, a private group did initiate a Centro Experimental Algodonero, which received contributions from INFOP, AGUAPA, and the FAO. According to Bryant, however, ". . . after a somewhat stormy career it collapsed. Partially as a result of this experience, a difference of opinion existed among cotton growers as to the place of research in cotton politics. Some . . . felt that conditions for cultivation varied greatly inside the country and demanded separate investigation on a scale feasible only with government support and direction. Others . . . felt that a private association of cotton growers could finance the necessary research, much as ANACAFE (the national coffee association) had done with coffee."[22]

Taken together, then, cotton has brought rapid profits to a small segment of the Guatemalan population, is currently bringing important agricultural lands to a state of ruin, has proved of little stimulus to Guatemalan industry, and has contributed in a small, but surely not insignificant, way to foreign exchange and to improving the balance of payments. It is not the purpose of the present study to brand this sequence of events as "good" or "bad,"[23] but to indicate how economic investment under the guise of being advantageous to the national development is, in fact, determined not by developmental goals, but by the rational seeking and manipulation of new power bases by members of the upper sector. It is important to see that what superficially may appear to be a healthy sign of growth is also a manifestation of a continuing tendency to lay waste to the environment for the profit of a very small segment of the society. Such growth is illusory, since there is hardly any cumulative product for the nation aside from the loss of good land.[24]

[22] Bryant, "Interest Groups," p. 102.

[23] Although there is no question in Jiménez' study that he regards both the role of the government and the growers as being extraordinarily irresponsible and negligent.

[24] Jiménez carries the argument much further than I have in this chapter. He indicates that, in addition to the features related here, one should also consider that the promising decline in world cotton prices will necessarily bring a decline, if not a bust, to the Guatemalan market. Guatemalan cotton has been of generally low quality, and there has been little interest in improving it in order to be surer of a market. Also, the emphasis on cotton has diverted continuing agricultural attention away from the development of food crops.

8 The Problem of Access

IT IS THE THESIS of this volume that Guatemala is expanding its general wealth, both proportionally and absolutely, but that the nature of the power structure is such that this increase is not widely distributed in the total population. While development is occurring in a North American sense, this failure of distribution means that it is not really occurring in the sense of the term that many Latin Americans recognize. The four preceding chapters have shown how certain sectors of the society have expanded, how they have grown in power and control. The question remains as to how and why other portions of the society do not participate in this growth.

From the standpoint of the individual of the lower sector and from the aspirant within the upper sector, the problem is one of access. Among those of the lower sector, the question is less one of whether they may have access to the power that is implicit in a great accumulation of wealth and more one of getting sufficient resources for survival and endurance. Some members of this lower sector, however, have been affected by the value system of the upper sector and wealth alone is not the issue; for them, some access to power and upper-sector prestige symbols have become additional goals.

In traditional anthropological terminology, one of the processes at work here is acculturation or, specifically, what Eric Wolf has called "internal acculturation." The lower sector, in long and continuing contact with the upper sector, structurally having been part of a single interrelated society, is not separated by an impermeable membrane. There is mobility between the two and between one generation and the next: parents who were Indian produce children who are known as Ladino, and peasants and laborers of the countryside produce urban-oriented offspring. The structure of power between the upper and lower sector does not change, but some individuals move from one to the other.

It has been suggested that the only major attempt toward altering this structure, during the period of the revolutionary decade, was doomed to failure. The older power structure, acting through both national and international channels, reasserted itself and had become stronger. The revolutionary power structure, the establishment of a widespread network of multiple channels to power, was not entirely destroyed with the overthrow of the revolutionary regime, but it was severely restrained. From the standpoint of the lower sector and many upwardly mobile of the upper sector who were being successful under the revolutionary regime, the reassertion of the older structure was obviously a closing off of access to power through these newer channels. Wealth, in the form of significantly increased wages and in terms of land, was as distant as ever; and power, in terms of access through channels of organization, education, or the law, was also restricted.

It is the purpose of this and the next two chapters to look into some aspects of this problem of access. In the present chapter, there is a brief review of what seems to have happened in terms of increased wages, access to land, and access to justice. In Chapter 9, Brian Murphy describes how the organization of the rural population has undergone first expansion under the revolutionary government and then restriction in the postrevolutionary years. In Chapter 10 Bryan Roberts looks to the readaptation of the population to the urban scene, how within the modern society power seeking has, at times, become niche seeking. In all, we are concerned here with the fact that the lower sector's position within the power structure has changed very slightly, and that it is possible to examine the mechanisms whereby this structure is kept intact. It is neither the purpose nor within the scope of this book to try to answer the question of whether new changes may successfully bring about significant alterations of the power structure. This has happened with varying degrees elsewhere in Latin America—in Cuba, Bolivia, and, in its earlier years, Mexico. To describe the current (as of 1965) state of affairs in Guatemala is not to predict its condition in some later period. We are here dealing with description, ethnography, or, if you will, natural history.

1. *Access to Wealth: Wages*

What follows here is not the product of a systematic investigation, but rather a collection of fragmentary data from already published sources. No claim can be made for comparability of the material; each piece of information is an indicator of a condition or state of affairs, and none in itself is conclusive. With regard to "wealth," I arbitrarily chose two topics for discussion: income and land.

The National Economic Planning Council has stated that the "distribution of the national income has become increasingly concentrated, to the point that the average annual income for an individual in the rural sector has declined from 87.00 *quetzales* per year in 1950 to 83.00 *quetzales* in the most recent year (1964), a decrease of 4.6%."[1] Another statement from the council gives us the data that appear in Table 8–1. These data indicate that the proportion of the total population which may be considered to be in the lower sector has increased slightly in the years between 1950 and 1962. The subsistence economy population grew from 71.3 percent of the population to 72.7 percent, while the low-income commercial sector decreased from 21.1 to 20.0 percent. This slightly increased proportion of the population that comprises the lower sector received proportionately less of the gross national product in 1964 than it did twelve years previously. The proportion so allocated dropped from 48.2 to 42.8 percent.

Although these two statements are disturbing, there is evidence that suggests Guatemala has not suffered extensive inflation during this period. Tables 8–2 and 8–3 give slightly varying data on the trend in cost of living during the period. Table 8–2 is included because it indicates that there was a sharp increase in food costs following the fall of the revolutionary government, although there was

---

[1] General Secretariat of the National Economic Planning Council, *La Situación del Desarrollo Económico y Social de Guatemala*.

TABLE 8–1
Distribution of Income

Kind of Activity	1950		1962	
	Percentage of Population	GNP %	Percentage of Population	GNP %
Subsistence economy	71.3	24.0	72.7	21.9
Commercial economy	28.7	76.0	27.3	78.1
a. Low income	21.1	24.2	20.0	20.9
b. Medium & high income	7.6	51.8	7.3	57.2
Total (1 & 2a)	92.4	48.2	92.7	42.8

SOURCE: General Secretariat of the National Economic Planning Council.

NOTE: I have been unable to locate the materials on which this table is based. The only formal reference is a statement in *Aspectos generales del plan de desarrollo económico y social de Guatemala, 1965–1969,* issued by the General Secretariat, dated August 1965 (p. 5 of Chapter II): "El sector que se desenvuelve en una economía de subsistencia, que en 1950 abarcaba el 71% de la población, pasó a representar en 1962, el 73% del total."

TABLE 8–2
Cost of Living Index

Year	Total Wealth	Food	Fuel	Housing	Apparel	Other
1953	130.6	130.6	106.8	110.8	181.6	110.1
1954	134.2	134.2	107.4	110.8	126.1	111.5
1955	136.5	152.7	100.1	110.8	135.4	112.5
1956	137.8	155.7	103.4	110.8	122.6	116.8
1957	136.3	153.2	102.6	110.8	121.6	117.2
1958	137.8	155.6	100.3	110.8	124.6	117.2
1959	137.2	152.6	101.4	110.8	133.5	119.1
1960	135.5	148.5	102.9	110.8	134.9	123.2
1961	134.8	146.8	101.6	110.8	135.4	125.2
1962	137.6	149.6	103.2	110.8	139.5	130.6

SOURCE: Comisión Nacional del Salario, *Estudio Económico para la Determinación del Salario Mínimo en la Industria de Comercio,* Guatemala, 1964, p. 98.

NOTE: Base 1946 = 100.

a decline in fuel and apparel costs. Otherwise, the two tables generally agree that there was little important subsequent change. While the average individual in the lower sector probably had no more to spend, neither did he have to spend a great deal more.

Wages in Guatemala, however, are not consistent or constant in

TABLE 8–3

Consumer Price Index for Wage Earners in Guatemala City

| Monthly Averages | Indexes of the Indicated Groups | | | | |
	General	Food	Housing	Apparel	Other Expenses
1955	100.0	100.0	100.0	100.0	100.0
1956	100.9	102.0	100.9	90.5	103.8
1957	99.8	100.4	100.7	89.8	104.2
1958	100.9	101.9	100.1	92.0	104.2
1959	100.5	99.9	100.4	98.6	105.9
1960	99.3	97.2	100.8	99.6	109.5
1961	98.7	96.1	100.4	100.0	111.3
1962	100.8	98.0	100.9	103.0	116.1
1963	100.9	98.2	101.1	104.0	114.9
1964	100.7	97.7	101.6	101.8	117.0
1965	99.9	97.7	102.0	95.3	114.7

| Monthly Averages | Percentage Change with Relation to the Period Immediately Preceding | | | | |
	General	Food	Housing	Apparel	Other Expenses
1955	—	—	—	—	—
1956	0.9	2.0	0.9	—9.5	3.8
1957	—1.1	—1.6	—0.2	—0.7	0.4
1958	1.1	1.5	—0.6	2.2	0.0
1959	—0.4	—2.0	0.3	6.6	1.7
1960	—1.2	—2.7	0.4	1.0	3.6
1961	—0.6	—1.1	—0.4	0.4	1.8
1962	2.1	1.9	0.5	3.0	4.8
1963	0.1	0.2	0.2	1.0	—1.2
1964	—0.2	—0.5	0.5	—2.2	2.1
1965	—0.8	0.0	0.4	—6.5	—2.3
Overall	—0.1	—2.3	2.0	—4.7	14.7

SOURCE: *Boletín Estadístico*, No. 13, Instituto Interamericano de Estadística, Pan American Union, Washington, D.C., July 1966.

any respect except that they are extraordinarily low. A study by the Inter-American Committee on Agricultural Development collected information from twelve large farms in western and southern Guatemala. The thesis of that study was that there was no relation between the wages paid and the amount of production, either by land area or in terms of man-hours. While the study obviously suffers from having few cases and from not being representative, the results (Table 8–4) are nonetheless suggestive and indicative. The data clearly indicate that there is no relationship between the gross value of production per man-day, nor the per unit land area, and the annual wage received by the laborer. There is also great irregularity in the relative amount of the total wages that are received in food and services (see Table 8–4).

Wages have increased over the years since 1944, but, as the annual incomes suggested in Table 8–4 indicate, they still fall far below that which might be expected of a developing country. Here again, data are fragmentary, but the following may be indicative. In 1945 a study was made of wages in Guatemala City (Table 8–5), and the incomplete results indicated an hourly wage of about twelve cents. Dependable wage data on the Ubico period seem all but ab-

TABLE 8–4

Productivity and Annual Remuneration on Multifamily Farms

	Gross Value of Production (quetzales)		Gross Annual Income of the Workers (in quetzales)	
Farm Number	Per Man-Day	Per Hectare	Total Income Per Capita	Percent of Total Not Received in Cash
1	1.2	205	326	38.0%
8	1.3	275	295	0.0
6	1.3	335	362	20.7
3	1.4	113	328	30.7
2	1.5	138	664	15.4
4	2.6	55	262	48.5
11	2.7	50	366	30.4
9	3.7	514	329	24.0
12	4.3	148	503	19.0
10	4.4	333	310	21.0
5	6.4	202	295	18.0
7	15.0	1,172	360	8.1

Source: Comité Interamericano de Desarrollo Agrícola, *Tenencia de la Tierra y Desarrollo Socio-económico del Sector Agrícola, Guatemala,* Pan American Union, Washington, D.C., 1965, Table II-10, p. 76.

TABLE 8–5
Average Hourly Wage, 1945

Industry	Average Hourly Wage in Centavos		
	Both Sexes	Male	Female
Foods	12.3	13.1	10.4
Medicines	11.4	11.4	7.5
Tobacco	16.0	16.1	15.9
Chemical industries	9.3	9.9	8.1
Wood	12.8	12.8	—
Skins & leather	13.0	13.0	13.4
Textiles	11.1	12.8	9.5
Clothing	10.8	14.1	10.3
Construction materials	13.6	13.6	11.2
Metals	13.5	13.5	—
Average	12.1	12.4	10.3

SOURCE: Romeo Manuel Hernández Cardona, *El Salario Mínimo en Guatemala,* Guatemala, 1963, p. 220. Data from Dirección General de Estadística, Boletín Número 5, Guatemala, January 1947, p. 7.

sent. *Finqueros* claim that in the 1930's they were paying ten or fifteen cents a day and finding that difficult. Beginning with the revolutionary period, some material is available on urban wages (Table 8–5). Data on agricultural wages are cited by Monteforte from Banco de Guatemala sources for the period of 1950 to 1955 and are reproduced directly from his text in Table 8–6.

It is difficult to know whether the figure for 1950 is relatively more inaccurate than the subsequent ones or whether there was, in fact, such a severe drop between 1950 and 1951. In any case, the best that can be said is that, by 1955, the figure was eighty-six cents per day. Ministry of Labor figures for 1963 indicate that the national average of agricultural labor (probably including white collar and skilled labor) for the country as a whole was Q1.07. However, as is evident in Table 8–7, the regional variation is great. In ten of the departments, the average wage is under the 1955 figure; in only four has it risen more than 10 percent over the earlier figure. It should be noted that these figures are based on very small numbers in some departments, especially in the *oriente*, and therefore can be expected to be in error. Nevertheless, there is the case of the

TABLE 8–6

Average Annual and Daily Salaries in Four Economic Activities

	1950			1951			1952		
	Annual	Daily	%	Annual	Daily	%	Annual	Daily	%
A	296	0.81	100	253	0.69	85	246	0.67	82
B	557	1.52	100	574	1.57	103	598	1.63	111
C	915	2.50	100	950	2.60	104	998	2.73	109
D	541	1.48	100	555	1.52	102	600	1.64	110
	1953			1954			1955		
	Annual	Daily	%	Annual	Daily	%	Annual	Daily	%
A	267	0.73	90	290	0.79	97	316	0.86	106
B	668	1.83	120	710	1.94	127	755	2.06	135
C	1,049	2.87	114	1,098	3.00	120	1,150	3.15	126
D	729	1.99	134	807	2.21	149	894	2.44	164

SOURCE: Mario Monteforte Toledo, *Guatemala: Monografía Sociológica*, second edition, Instituto de Investigaciones Sociales, UNAM, Mexico, 1965, p. 474.

NOTE: *A*: agriculture, forestry, hunting, and fishing; *B*: extractive and manufacturing industries, building and construction, transportation and communication, hotels and personal services; *C*: commerce; *D*: public services and other general types (medical and religious services, education, arts and sciences). The agricultural salaries include payment in kind.

Alta Verapaz where the average for over 17,000 laborers is just under fifty cents a day. It is not possible to know to what degree these figures represent departmental capital figures and to what degree rural data. It seems likely that there probably was increase in the urban areas, as the figures for business cited in Table 8–8 suggest that in 1959 they were everywhere higher than those cited for 1945 (see Table 8–5).

Wage and income situations vary among rural peoples. The *campesino* may be a full-time subsistence agriculturalist; he may supplement his own subsistence work by working occasionally or for limited periods locally for other *campesinos*; he may engage periodically in seasonal migration to coffee, cotton, or sugar-cane harvests; he may migrate seasonally to rent land for additional cultivations; or he may be a full-time laborer, sometimes migrant, but more usually a full-time employee. Due to studies by the Wisconsin

TABLE 8–7
Guatemalan Agricultural Enterprise, 1963

Department	Number of Enterprises	Number of Workers	Days Worked	Average Daily Wage
Guatemala	67	10,894	1,711,433	Ø2.28
El Progreso	—	—	—	—
Sacatepéquez	39	4,445	383,092	0.93
Chimaltenango	81	8,051	1,173,565	0.97
Escuintla	125	61,430	3,912,502	1.40
Santa Rosa	60	16,079	1,123,219	0.90
Sololá	27	2,256	266,516	0.85
Totonicapán	2	4	50	0.50
Quezaltenango	183	26,273	2,945,234	0.95
Suchitepéquez	212	38,554	3,447,261	0.93
Retalhuleu	118	26,390	1,591,975	0.96
San Marcos	226	45,405	4,403,863	0.87
Huehuetenango	83	1,250	97,389	0.50
El Quiché	53	3,507	174,086	0.63
Baja Verapaz	29	916	59,462	0.54
Alta Verapaz	156	17,286	1,439,779	0.49
El Petén	2	15	1,155	0.75
Izabal	2	15	2,759	0.60
Zacapa	10	887	86,503	0.80
Chiquimula	2	12	139	0.25
Jalapa	3	34	5,506	0.42
Jutiapa	12	459	39,338	0.92
Total	1,491	264,162	22,891,826	Ø1.07

Source: Ministerio de Trabajo, 1965; information submitted voluntarily by *patrones* in 1963.

Land Tenure group, we fortunately have some income data on at least a few of these situations.[2]

Comparing the *campesinos* who do not have to migrate annually for seasonal labor (but with no data on those who may migrate for

[2] The materials cited herein are taken from Lester Schmid, "The Role of Migratory Labor in the Economic Development of Guatemala," Ph.D. dissertation, University of Wisconsin, Madison, 1967. Some of it is cited from an unpublished study by George W. Hill and Manuel Gollás on the Indian population and agriculture of the western highlands of Guatemala, 1964; the rest comes from Schmid's own field work. The former will be cited here as Hill-Gollás.

TABLE 8–8
Hourly Salaries

Department	Total			Wholesale Business			Retail Business		
	Number of Workers	Total (quetzales)	Average (centavos)	Number of Workers	Total (quetzales)	Average (centavos)	Number of Workers	Total (quetzales)	Average (centavos)
Guatemala	8,126	4,017.11	49	796	719.29	90	7,330	3,297.82	45
El Progreso	44	6.67	15	—	—	—	44	6.67	15
Sacatepéquez	158	31.32	20	3	0.24	8	155	30.68	20
Chimaltenango	33	4.23	13	—	—	—	33	4.23	13
Escuintla	268	76.27	28	26	16.71	64	242	59.56	25
Santa Rosa	66	10.36	16	—	—	—	66	10.36	16
Sololá	16	2.62	16	—	—	—	16	2.62	16
Totonicapán	140	24.20	17	—	—	—	140	24.20	17
Quezaltenango	562	176.22	31	5	2.17	43	557	174.05	31
Suchitepéquez	269	70.80	26	—	—	—	269	70.60	26
Retalhuleu	129	44.31	34	22	17.43	79	107	26.88	25
San Marcos	10	1.98	20	—	—	—	10	1.98	20
Huehuetenango	41	12.18	30	—	—	—	41	12.18	30
Quiché	66	10.91	16	—	—	—	66	10.91	16
Baja Verapaz	17	5.40	32	—	—	—	17	5.40	32
Alta Verapaz	146	28.38	19	4	1.04	26	142	27.34	19
El Petén	12	2.51	21	—	—	—	12	2.51	21
Izabal	136	35.90	26	—	—	—	136	35.90	26
Zacapa	41	10.32	25	—	—	—	41	10.32	25
Chiquimula	73	16.54	23	—	—	—	73	16.54	23
Jalapa	36	6.94	19	—	—	—	36	6.94	19
Jutiapa	136	27.21	20	—	—	—	136	27.21	20
Undetermined	2	0.18	9	—	—	—	2	0.18	9
Total	10,527	4,622.36	44	856	756.88	88	9,671	3,865.48	40

Source: Comisión Nacional del Salario, *Estudio Económico para la Determinación del Salario Mínimo en la Industria de Comercio*, Guatemala, 1964, p. 84.

additional seasonal cultivation), Hill-Gollás provide comparative figures from the seven western Indian departments that show consistently better annual family incomes for the nonmigrants than for migrants. On the average, the migrants receive only 60 percent of the income of the nonmigrants, although it is closer to 66 percent on a per capita basis (see Table 8–9). The salaries paid on the farms to permanent employees are suggested from data provided by Schmid (see Table 8–10). Although these data are casual, they conform generally to the experience I have had over the years in Guatemala. Other material from Schmid was cited in Chapter 7, comparing the relative wages between coffee, cotton, and sugar-cane farms.

Just as wages in the western highlands are generally lower than

TABLE 8–9
Annual Incomes of Migratory and Nonmigratory Workers

Department	Cases	Income in Community		Income from Work on Fincas		Total Income	
		Family	Per Capita	Family	Per Capita	Family	Per Capi
Chimaltenango							
Migratory	31	$136.14	$24.80	$ 22.47	$ 4.00	$158.61	$28.88
Nonmigratory	69	265.50	42.14	—	—	265.50	42.14
Totonicapán							
Migratory	7	100.28	20.05	46.83	9.43	147.11	29.48
Nonmigratory	37	199.94	31.24	—	—	199.94	31.24
Huehuetenango							
Migratory	11	85.13	13.95	38.35	6.30	123.48	20.25
Nonmigratory	16	161.23	23.03	—	—	161.23	23.03
Quiché							
Migratory	7	91.26	19.84	40.35	8.35	131.61	28.19
Nonmigratory	58	235.21	41.27	—	—	235.21	41.27
Sololá							
Migratory	8	153.86	22.96	30.00	4.39	183.86	27.35
Nonmigratory	62	349.34	58.19	—	—	349.34	58.19
San Marcos							
Migratory	7	218.62	41.25	51.31	9.56	269.93	50.81
Nonmigratory	13	328.03	52.11	—	—	328.03	52.07
Quezaltenango							
Migratory	—	—	—	—	—	—	—
Nonmigratory	22	301.86	42.51	—	—	301.86	59.18
Average Totals							
Migratory	71	127.56	22.76	32.82	5.88	160.38	28.64
Nonmigratory	277	268.71	43.34	—	—	268.71	43.34

SOURCE: Hill-Gollás Study; Lester Schmid, "The Role of Migratory Labor in the Economi Development of Guatemala," Ph.D. dissertation, University of Wisconsin, 1967, pp. 259–260.

TABLE 8–10
Average Monthly Wages

Type of Worker	Cotton		Coffee		Sugar Cane	
	No.	Average	No.	Average	No.	Average
Peon	6	$28.33	28	$20.48	5	$20.44
Electrician	—	—	1	36.00	—	—
Mechanic	2	85.00	—	—	—	—
Tractor driver	2	36.50	—	—	2	74.00
Caporal (foreman)	2	44.00	2	29.25	3	47.03
Moledor (miller)	—	—	—	—	1	12.00
Guardian of warehouse*	1	90.00	—	—	—	—
Plaqueros†	2	45.00	—	—	—	—
Carpenter's helper	—	—	—	—	1	27.00
Mechanic's helper	1	33.60	—	—	—	—
Total	16	44.66	31	21.55	12	35.86

SOURCE: Lester Schmid, "The Role of Migratory Labor in the Economic Development of Guatemala," Ph.D. dissertation, University of Wisconsin, 1967, pp. 259–260.
* The job consisted of keeping an account of the contents of the warehouse.
† *Plaqueros* work in the spraying operations.

in the more developing areas, so wages paid by lower-sector employers are lower than those usually paid by export-oriented enterprises. Table 8–11 shows a set of data on local community wages reported by migratory workers to Schmid. The mean agricultural wage is around forty cents a day, and for nonagricultural employment, the wage is in the fifty to fifty-five cent category. It will be noted that the wages in the west are, again, generally lower than those elsewhere. In terms of the income from migratory labor wages, perhaps the most telling statistic Schmid cites is that from the total wages the migrants obtain during their months of labor: they take home only about Ø18, or 20 percent.[3] Therefore, the migratory labor does not provide additional income to get the laborer through a lean period at home, but it merely takes him to where the income is during the lean period. There are no significant savings or accumulation of capital from this outside work; it is merely part of the survival system. In calculating the total annual incomes and living

[3] Schmid, "Migratory Labor," p. 252.

TABLE 8–11

Wages Reported by Migratory Workers for Agricultural and Nonagricultural Work

Region				Wages in Cents per Day				
Agricultural Work:	15	20–25	30–35	40–45	50–55	60–75	Over 80	Total
West	1	26	15	5	13	3	1	64
South Central	—	—	3	—	5	2	1	11
Southeast	—	—	1	2	8	1	—	12
North Central	—	1	2	—	4	1	—	8
Total	1	27	21	7	30	7	2	95
Nonagricultural Work:								
West	5	3	3	3	—	1	2	17
South Central	—	1	—	—	2	1	2	6
Southeast	—	—	—	3	—	1	—	4
North Central	—	—	—	1	1	—	—	2
Total	5	4	3	7	3	3	4	29

SOURCE: Lester Schmid, "The Role of Migratory Labor in the Economic Development of Guatemala," Ph.D. dissertation, University of Wisconsin, 1967, pp. 161–162.

expenses for migratory workers, Schmid concludes that those who are married have an average income of between Ǫ161 and Ǫ219 per year, but end up with a deficit of between Ǫ26 to Ǫ53; for single men, the average income varies between Ǫ191 and Ǫ171, but they end up with a slight surplus, varying from Ǫ21 to Ǫ27 for the entire year.[4] For the single man, this surplus is probably long since used up when the year ends.

In general, the full-time farm employee and the peasant are better off than the migratory laborer. It is disturbing, then, to find that there is a large increase in migratory labor. Schmid cites Coffee Association data that "there were 74,474 permanent workers and 151,886 seasonal employees on coffee fincas during 1960, compared to 80,385 permanent workers and 99,046 seasonal workers in 1950.[5] The decline in full-time finca labor can probably be attributed

[4] Ibid., p. 256.
[5] Ibid., p. 21, citing Klaus Berg, "Agricultural Structure of Guatemala."

most directly to the reaction of the farm owners to the events of the revolutionary period. Those who had large numbers of employees under the revolution's labor laws found themselves in a very vulnerable position. They reacted to rid themselves of as many formally inscribed laborers as they could following the revolution. Many took advantage of the temporary breakdown in the labor law operations to scare "troublemakers" off the farms; others did it through legal means, systematically firing a few people each year until their lists were at a point that was economically viable for the farm. The increase in migrants is partly due, presumably, to the movement of some of these individuals from the permanent labor forces; but the greater number is doubtless due to the natural increase of the Indian population and the traditional use of seasonal migration for survival. The fact that the cotton harvest, a phenomenon essentially new to Guatemala, is predominantly worked by Indians shows this new cultivation merely served to handle a migratory overflow that coffee could not have absorbed.

It is hard to avoid the conclusion that the Guatemalan *campesino* receives an extraordinarily low income and that it is probable this income has decreased during the past fifteen years. The Inter-American Commission holds that "the rural workers are in a social and economic situation that imposes apparently insuperable restrictions. Furthermore, it is confirmed that the situation of agricultural laborers has worsened in recent years."[6] In 1961 Nathan Whetten wrote, "As of 1959, most of the farm workers were probably worse off than when the agrarian laws were instituted in 1952. For instance, the Guatemalan Minister of Labor announced in 1957 that wages had recently been reduced on about 75 percent of the large plantations (Source: *New York Times*, April 7, 1957, p. 11). . . . [some landlords] refused to give their former workers plots of land to till for their own use, as they were formerly accustomed to do, for fear that these workers might again demand permanent possession of these plots."[7] While it is certainly the case that a much more profound study of the subject needs to be made, such further investigation is unlikely to produce findings very different from those reviewed here. The Guatemalan *campesino*'s access to the economic wealth

---

[6] Ibid., p. 90.
[7] Nathan L. Whetten, *Guatemala: The Land and the People.*

of his country has not changed significantly in spite of a registered per capita development of the economy and a significant increase in investment by the upper sector.

2. *Access to Wealth: Land*

One need not resort to statements about mystical ties between the Indian or *campesino* and the land to confirm that agriculture is of central importance to most of the Guatemalan population. Whether one is a subsistence farmer on his own or rented land, an agricultural laborer on a coffee or cotton farm, or an upper-sector entrepreneur looking for a prestigious and profitable investment, land is the base. One of the major problems of access to wealth is simply getting access to land. There have been up until now no credit facilities readily accessible for the purchase of land. The major banks will give credit on annual crops, but not on the loans that would be paid over a long period of time. Long-term credit is hardly available, and, for the subsistence farmer, it is absolutely out of the question.

The only way that one can get land, therefore, is to rent it, arrange for some other kind of usufruct (such as through the *colono* system), receive it under a colonization scheme, settle on unclaimed land, or somehow accumulate enough capital to pay cash. This system means that even if a large landholder is inclined to sell his property to small holders, he is discouraged from doing this because he must also stand as the credit agent to cover the transaction.

There are two great migratory movements under way in Guatemala. The areas supplying the migrants are those where land is in relatively short supply, where it is either poor or in such large unproductive holdings that there is neither labor nor land available. The migrants split. Some move to the larger towns and ultimately to the capital city; people from the countryside, however, tend to seek other rural areas where there may be land or work. During the revolutionary period, the movement was strongest to the south coast where the initiation of cotton and the opening up of the coast gave promise of land. In recent years, there has been further movement into El Petén, particularly the southern portions. The effort to find land on the south coast was successful mainly for those who came in at the time that the colonization programs were in effect; El Petén is the major area that still has land open for the migrant.

In the matter of land, the three periods of Guatemalan history here under consideration provide a sharp contrast. Under the Ubico regime, land was still regarded as a proper, liberal, exploitation base. Ubico's version of the encomienda system was that the Indian did not belong to a private farmer's land, but that his labor did belong to the *patria*, and the government had the right to expropriate it if it was not being used well by its owner. The wealth of the country lay in its coffee, and coffee had to be picked by Indians. However, there was mobility, even though it was made effectively unpleasant. The *campesino* himself lived in a state of peasant semi-isolation, participating in annual harvests of coffee, available for road and finca labor drafts, unfamiliar with urbanism in any but its provincial aspects.

The revolutionary regime, under the Arbenz government, launched an agrarian reform. Decree 900 provided for a series of ways for *campesinos* to get land and placed the governmental responsibility and authority directly in the executive office. The regular courts were not allowed jurisdiction over cases rising out of the implementation of the law. As written, the law was not excessive. One can always argue that bonds promised under such a widespread reform system are unlikely to be paid, but one can equally argue that the land designated for expropriation was itself mainly unproductive. The postrevolutionary governments took back most of the land given out under the agrarian reform (see below) and started, in its place, a series of colonization programs that helped to some extent; but this move got to the heart of neither the problem of the quantity of people needing land, nor the structure of relations that permitted land to continue unused.

There is an important distinction between an agrarian reform of the type sponsored by Arbenz and the colonization projects of the postrevolutionary period.[8] An agrarian reform requires an actual legal reform in the system of tenure. This usually calls for the establishment of some new tenurial arrangements and, in current usage, is specifically used to refer to collectivization or governmental determination of the nature and amount of land that may be held by individuals. Colonization refers to any of the various processes whereby land is formally obtained by some agent (in the present

---

[8] See Oscar Delgado, ed., *Reforma en la América Latina,* especially Part IV.

case, by the government) and distributed to individual holders. It does not change the tenurial system and therefore is, properly speaking, a colonization program.

The agrarian reform of Arbenz was a reform under this definition. It allowed the government to expropriate lands, and the holder was denied the usual recourse to the rights and privileges of private property. The postrevolutionary period saw the establishment of colonization programs. The Castillo Decreto Agrario and the subsequent decrees and laws all have had to do with the acquisition of lands and their distribution without challenging the standing tenurial system.

→ The distribution of land in Guatemala is in the classic latifundia-minifundia mode. Modern agricultural technology has finally begun to make itself known on some of the larger farms, bringing with it the beginnings of social reorganization of the farm system. The 1950 Agropecuario census and numerous other sources have demonstrated that Guatemalan lands are predominantly held by a very few people and that much of this land is not under cultivation. They have also shown the complementary pattern in the fact that the greater majority of Guatemalans are rural *campesinos*, either small operators or wage earners or both, and that the amount of land available to them is a minute part of the total. For reference, four tables from the Inter-American Commission's study are given here to indicate the approximate pattern of distribution and the approximate amount of unused land involved (Tables 8–12, 8–13, 8–14, and 8–15).

The agrarian reform under Arbenz claimed to have expropriated, over a period of one and a half years (January, 1953, through June, 1954), slightly over 600,000 hectares of land. The records of the Departamento Agrario Nacional (DAN) were evidently destroyed by the Castillo government, but the Instituto de Investigaciones Económicas of the University of San Carlos has laboriously compiled the data from the materials published in the official government paper, *El Guatemalteco*.[9] On the basis of these figures, it has been possible to calculate the approximate amount of land expropriated per *municipio* and, by using the 1950 census figures, to provide

[9] José Luis Paredes Moreira, *Estudios sobre Reforma Agraria en Guatemala: Aplicación del Decreto 900, Cuadro No. 1, Compilación de los 1012 acuerdos de expropiación.*

TABLE 8–12

Distribution of Agricultural Holdings

Type of Holding	Number of Fincas		Area of Fincas		
	Number	Percent	Total Area (Hectares)	Percent	Average Size (Hectares)
Microfincas	74,270	21.3	28,600	0.8	0.4
Subfamilial	23,800	67.1	504,600	13.5	2.2
Familial	33,040	9.5	500,800	13.5	13.2
Medium multifamilial	7,060	2.0	1,167,500	31.4	165.4
Large multifamilial	520	0.1	1,519,300	40.8	2,921.9
Total	348,690	100.0	3,720,800	100.0	

SOURCE: Comité Interamericano de Desarrollo Agrícola, *Tenencia de la Tierra y Desarrollo socio-económico del Sector Agrícola, Guatemala,* Pan American Union, Washington, D.C., 1964, p. 58.

TABLE 8–13

Land Use by Conventional Size of Farms

Conventional Size	Total Area	Cultivated	Uncultivated	Uncultivable
Microfincas	28,575	27,125	—	1,450
Subfamilial	504,556	400,503	74,010	30,043
Familial	500,830	250,498	205,647	44,685
Medium multifamilial	1,167,532	574,996	502,701	89,835
Large multifamilial	1,519,339	433,239	922,175	163,925
Total (approx.)	3,720,832	1,686,361	1,704,533	329,938

SOURCE: See Table 8–12.

NOTE: The size of the fincas, in general, is directly related to the quantity of labor employed. Therefore, the four groups have been classified according to labor force and consequently to the number of families that the fincas can sustain. They range from the "subfamilial" plot, too small to sustain a family (less than two man-laborers per year), to the "multifamilial," where more than four workers are employed during the year. Since the census does not present facts that directly relate the size of the fincas to the labor force, this study employs the same classification used by Maturana. The "subfamilial" finca is less than 10 manzanas; the "familial" covers from 10 to 64 manzanas; the "medium multifamilial," between 64 and 1,280 manzanas; and the "large multifamilial," more than 1,280 manzanas.

"Cultivated land" comprises cultivated land area, coffee plantations, fruit trees and vineyards, and uncultivated pastures. "Uncultivated land" refers to lands lying fallow, forests, mountains, and rough regions.

Crucifixion by Power

TABLE 8–14
Land Use by Conventional Size of Farms:
Percentage Distribution by Use

Conventional Size	Total Area	Cultivated	Uncultivated	Uncultivable
Microfincas	100.0	94.9	—	5.1
Subfamilial	100.0	79.4	14.7	5.9
Familial	100.0	50.0	41.1	8.9
Medium multifamilial	100.0	49.2	43.1	7.7
Large multifamilial	100.0	28.5	60.7	10.8
Total	100.0	45.3	45.8	8.9

SOURCE: Table 8–13.

TABLE 8–15
Land Use by Conventional Size of Farms: Percentage of
Each Size with Respect to Total

Conventional Size	Total Area	Cultivated	Uncultivated	Uncultivable
Microfincas	0.8	1.6	—	0.4
Subfamilial	13.5	23.8	4.3	9.1
Familial	13.5	14.8	12.1	13.6
Medium multifamilial	31.4	34.1	29.5	27.2
Large multifamilial	40.8	25.7	54.1	49.7
Total	100.0	100.0	100.0	100.0

SOURCE: Table 8–13.

an estimate of the amount of land expropriated per capita. The lack of records makes it impossible to know how much of this land had actually been distributed and in what form it was distributed. Also, the exact number of beneficiaries is not known.

On the basis of these calculations, Map 8–1 has been prepared. It gives the amount of land per capita (1950) *per municipio* that was expropriated under the Arbenz reform. If we may assume that the land was distributed in more or less equal parcels, then these figures do provide some notion of the relative number of people who were recipients of land under Arbenz' Decree 900. The larger the number of hectares per capita, the greater the number of people who may

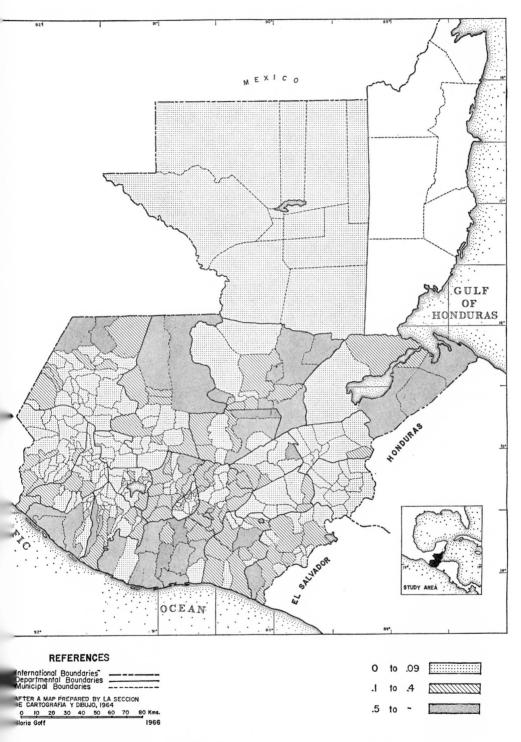

MAP 8–1. LAND AREA EXPROPRIATED PER CAPITA, 1952–1954 (Hectares)

be assumed to have received land under the reform. The Inter-American Commission cites two sources, one stating that 100,000 *campesinos* benefited from the reform, another that the figure was 88,000.[10] Monteforte Toledo also cites two different figures: 54,000 and 71,000.[11] Because of the lack of data on this matter, the present study will use the relative figures (see Map 8–1) rather than absolute numbers of people.

As might be expected, the major areas affected by the reform were those of the United Fruit Company and the large unused lands of the south coast and the northeast. However, of particular interest is that some significant expropriations within the Indian areas did take place, especially in Chimaltenango. As with the number of people affected, so there is also lack of hard data on the amount of land that was returned to original owners after the entrance of Castillo Armas. The Inter-American Committee cites local information to the effect that only 0.4 percent of the beneficiaries remained on the lands by the end of 1956. Monteforte Toledo states that 90 percent of the land was repossessed, and 60 percent of the beneficiaries were dispossessed.[12] There is no way to be sure of any of these figures, but it seems to be a safe assumption that almost all, if not all, the land expropriated under Decree 900 was taken back, and that for practical purposes most beneficiaries were dispossessed. Certainly no one is making boisterous claims that the recipients in 1953 and 1954 still hold the land.

There can be no doubt that the events of 1953 and 1954 were the cause of intense frustration, both to the *finqueros* and to the later dispossessed beneficiaries of the agrarian reform. The reform brought to the attention of a wide *campesino* public that it was actually possible to have land and that this land could, under some circumstances, be taken from other landholders. The readiness to invade lands that were not formally expropriated during the latter Arbenz years is indicative of the readiness to receive lands should

[10] Ibid., p. 42.

[11] Mario Monteforte Toledo, *Guatemala: Monografía Sociología*, pp. 434, 442–443. Monteforte gives no source for these figures.

[12] Comité Interamericano de Desarrollo Agrícola, *Tenencia de la Tierra y Desarrollo Socio-económico del Sector Agrícola, Guatemala*, p. 45; and Monteforte Toledo, *Guatemala*, pp. 442 and 444. Monteforte gives no source for his data.

they be made available in the future. There can be little question that the growing populations of those areas where the agrarian reform hit the hardest were severely embittered by the postrevolutionary events.

In the years following the fall of Arbenz, a new series of colonization projects was undertaken. Tables 8–16 and 8–17 indicate the form and relative number of people affected by these programs. The number of beneficiaries recorded by this government study for the colonization efforts between 1955 and 1963 was 24,496; of these, however, 20,708 received agrarian parcels of land. If we take an absolute maximum family size of six persons per family, this means that a maximum of 125,000 individuals benefited from land received. During this period, however, the population of Guatemala increased by about 1,000,000 people. If we estimate that approximately 650,000 of these could be classed as "rural," it then emerges that during the period the government was distributing the colonization lands, the population was increasing over five times as fast as people were benefiting from the land being distributed. Not only did the land distribution programs not make a dent in the population of 1955, but there were about 500,000 people worse off in 1963 than when they started in 1955.

Even the above estimation of the benefits of colonization may be unrealistically optimistic about what has actually happened. Schmid cites a report in which it is estimated that up until 1964, 5,000 farm units had been established.[13] (This probably refers to the parcels of the Agricultural Development Zones, which total 4,964 in Table 8–16.) It was estimated that these cost four thousand dollars per farm and that studies in two of the areas indicated that 25 percent of the parcels were being leased out and not cultivated by the official *parcelarios*. Finally, the report concludes that perhaps five thousand families have improved their economic condition substantially, and another five thousand have benefited slightly.

It is quite apparent that the colonization program has benefited too few people, has been carried out too slowly, and has been too expensive. Because of problems of measurement, bureaucratic delays, disagreements in planning, and in general no great sense of

[13] Schmid, "Migratory Labor," pp. 383–384, citing a mimeographed report by Leonard Rhodes, "Colonization and Land Reform," May, 1964. Rhodes was an AID adviser.

TABLE 8-16
Land Distributed by Colonization Program (in Hectares)

Year	Agricultural Development Zone		Microparcels		Agrarian Communities		Urban Lots		Total	
	Parcels	Area	Number	Area	Beneficiaries	Area	Beneficiaries	Area	No.	Area
1955	153	1,070	1,663	3,280	251	670	—	—	2,067	5,020
1956	1,250	24,362	1,838	3,627	1,972	5,467	402	42	5,462	33,498
1957	1,356	28,067	454	3,676	5,890	32,968	226	23	7,926	64,734
1958	188	4,191	—	—	277	726	108	5	573	4,922
1959	757	14,365	—	—	1,990	4,952	648	54	3,395	19,371
1960	141	4,834	—	—	1,631	2,351	244	18	2,016	7,203
1961	825	9,355	57	196	—	—	1,055	93	1,937	9,644
1962	280	11,926	573	839	86	38	229	18	1,168	12,821
1963	14	760	40	63	—	—	876	26	930	849

SOURCE: Rony S. Alvarado Pinetta, *La Transformación Agraria en Guatemala*, n.d. Census data from Departamento del Censo, Dirección General de Estadística, Ministerio de Economía, Guatemala, C.A.

TABLE 8-17
Land Distributed by Colonization Program, 1955–1963, by Department (in Hectares)

Department	Agricultural Development Zone		Microparcels		Agrarian Communities		Urban Lots		Total	
	Parcels	Area	Number	Area	Beneficiaries	Area	Beneficiaries	Area	No.	Area
Guatemala	—	—	725	1,657	618	4,614	883	27	2,226	6,298
Sacatepéquez	—	—	85	105	671	1,529	139	11	895	1,645
Chimaltenango	—	—	731	518	1,184	2,873	—	—	1,915	3,391
Escuintla	2,106	37,081	1,478	5,485	196	278	1,655	137	5,435	42,981
Santa Rosa	—	—	318	515	1,211	1,562	292	42	1,821	2,119
Quezaltenango	141	2,819	261	403	208	773	244	18	854	4,013
Suchitepéquez	1,407	31,514	176	1,197	777	1,405	325	20	2,685	34,136
Retalhuleu	255	5,339	—	—	331	1,021	66	10	652	6,370
San Marcos	129	2,071	81	190	2,385	5,148	—	—	2,595	7,409
Huehuetenango	—	—	—	—	1,274	11,873	—	—	1,274	11,873
Quiché	—	—	—	—	1,074	7,381	—	—	1,074	7,381
Baja Verapaz	—	—	—	—	454	1,928	—	—	454	1,928
Alta Verapaz	—	—	—	—	1,204	4,550	184	8	1,388	4,558
Izabal	448	16,169	—	—	32	225	—	—	480	16,394
Zacapa	—	—	—	—	45	676	—	—	45	676
Jutiapa	178	3,931	60	215	122	406	—	—	360	4,552
Chiquimula	—	—	—	—	36	225	—	—	36	225
El Progreso	—	—	—	—	307	1,227	—	—	307	1,227
Totals	4,664	98,924	3,915	10,285	12,129	47,694	3,788	273	24,496	157,176

SOURCE: Rony S. Alvarado Pinetta, *La Transformación Agraria en Guatemala*, n.d. Census data from Departamento del Censo, Dirección General de Estadística, Ministerio de Economía, Guatemala, C.A.

dispatch, the colonization effort has gone much more slowly than did the agrarian reform. Similarly, due to reasonable concerns that enough land be given so that the individual can make an income superior to that of the *minifundista*, the total number of people are necessarily fewer. Here, however, the slowness of the entire operation is also a factor, since there are still great areas to be colonized, and they are being prepared slowly.

Although almost no published data are available concerning the matter, certainly a major defect of the colonization program has been the degree to which it has been infested or penetrated by non-*campesinos*. One cannot visit a colonization area without coming across many cases of land parcels that are being controlled by absentee holders, usually people living in coastal towns or the capital city. Cases are legion of possession by military officers and cited frequently are instances of *parcelarios* renting out lands (illegally) to other *campesinos* who have not been so fortunate as to receive them.

The position of the small-scale, illegal renter is particularly difficult. Since renting parcels is illegal, high rents and bad treatment at the hands of the parcel owner cannot be effectively taken to law. There are still so many *campesinos* in Guatemala who need land that many will submit to this situation in order to obtain it. It is quite obvious that it is to almost no one's advantage to reveal knowledge of these matters in detail. Since some of the landowners of this type are in positions of some power, either locally or nationally, the local person who is responsible for reporting is very likely going to suffer. Certainly, the illegal renter will not mention it, nor will the government officials who have been responsible for so allocating the land. Even the credit agencies, among whose employees are the friends that provide the credit for such ventures, have nothing to gain by exposing their clients. It is the *campesino* without land who is the loser, and it is he who has thus far had no spokesman with both the power and the motivation to act in the matter.

While the beneficiaries of the colonization programs include many who can only be pleased by the event, since they gain through absenteeism, the legitimate *parcelarios* also have some difficulties to overcome. For the most part, much of the land is uncleared, and efforts to establish effective cooperatives have been plagued with problems. Credit agencies have proved unable to meet the numerous and varied demands that must inevitably accompany an operation as complex as colonization. Bureaucratic competition between the Agrarian Transformation Institute and other agencies has led to inadequate educational facilities being established, as well as other services and facilities that need the support of other branches of the government.

Although far from perfect, two agencies have provided credit for the annual work of *campesinos*. The Banco Nacional Agrario, inherited from the Arbenz government, and the Servicio Cooperativo Interamericano de Crédito Agrícola Supervisada (SCICAS), started in the postrevolutionary period, have both served to make funds available to limited numbers of *campesinos*. As is so often the case when two bureaucratic agencies seem to be working in the same area, these two have seen themselves in competition. Rather than each trying to make its own service superior, some of the competitive action has been in trying to block or undercut the other. Nevertheless, while there is inevitably such waste motion, there is an important product. Map 8–2 gives some indication of the distribution of the services of these two agencies together. The availability of figures on a municipal basis has made it possible to give this information only for some of the years of service. It should be noted that SCICAS does not work in all the departments, although it is planning to expand its services. Effective credit is obviously one of the services that *campesinos* desperately need and one that can serve them most directly in the adequate development of their own resources.

The experiences of many *campesinos*, both those who have received land and those who have not, in the colonization areas have been such as to increase their frustrations and awareness of their inability to be able to depend upon support from the authorities. In addition to this, they are exposed daily to the open control of many parcels of land that, under the spirit of the colonization program, should be available to *campesinos* but are in fact held and exploited by townspeople and fairly wealthy individuals in the national capital.

In summary, efforts at agrarian reform and colonization to date have been far from ideal. Colonization efforts, plagued as they are, have in no way substituted for the projections of Decree 900. The entire series of experiences has served to make those *campesinos* so

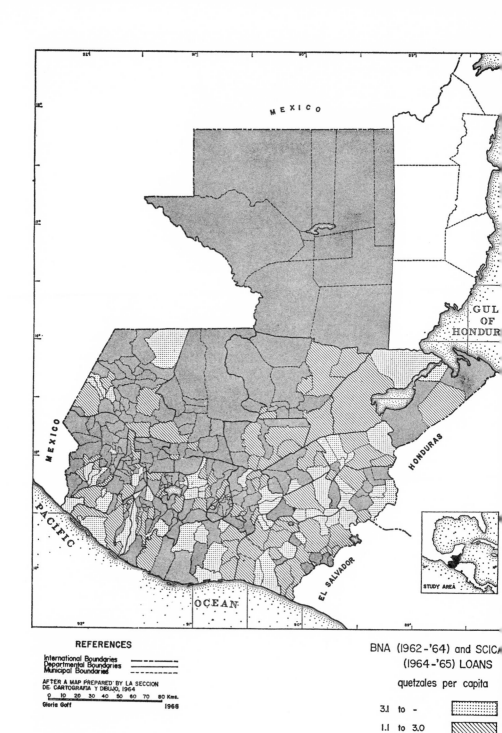

MAP 8–2. DISTRIBUTION OF BNA AND SCICAS SERVICES

involved much more aware of the nature of the economic and political processes involved but without having served to satisfy the needs that they unquestionably have. The participation of the rural lower sector in the acquisition and control of land is, therefore, still such as to exclude the *campesino* from participation in the decision processes that have to do with his control and to inhibit access to the only means of production with which he is familiar.

3. *Access to Law: The Role of Lawyers*

Money and land are direct sources of power; they are power bases, although operating within culturally defined contexts. Most members of modern society, however, do not have direct control of power bases. They depend, instead, on derivative power, the control that is allowed to them through the established power and authority systems of the society. In modern Western society, a major mode of access for individuals to derivative power is through the devices known collectively as justice. As elsewhere, we cannot fully explore this critical area here, but we can look into some of its facets. Since the lawyer plays a particular role in articulating the citizen with the sources of derivative power, we will first look to him to see how this articulation is accomplished.[14]

Lawyers occupy a unique position within Guatemalan society. Collectively they exercise extraordinary controls over the lives of individuals and the operation of institutions, but their power is almost entirely derivative. They are part of the networks that link the members of Guatemalan society but that primarily benefit the upper sector. It is not our concern here to examine the role of the lawyer as an intellectual, or part of what Bonilla has referred to as the "cultural elite,"[15] but to examine them as articulators of Guatemalan social organization and to understand their role in the power structure. The discussion will concern itself with two phases of the profession: the lawyer as power seeker and broker, and the formal organization of the law profession.

Until 1935 there were only two university-level faculties in

---

[14] Almost all the material in this section is derived from field work and reports prepared by Fredda Bullard.

[15] Frank Bonilla, "Cultural Elites" in Seymour Martin Lipset and A. Solari, *Elites in Latin America*, pp. 233–255.

Guatemala, those of law and medicine. Together, they provided the only higher education available in the country and reflected the restrictive and limited access to education in the society generally. Following the beginning of the engineering curriculum in 1935, the entire university experienced a continuing growth. Even with the loss of many of its curricular areas to the new faculties of humanities and the strong competition for motivated students by the faculties of economics, architecture, and engineering, the law faculty grew more rapidly than did the university as a whole. The overall university increase from 1945 to 1963 was about 300 percent; the law student registration increased by almost 500 percent. The popularity of the law school is due in part to the fact that it promises a professional future. Of possibly greater importance, however, is that the law is a recognized means for the manipulation and achievement of power. Lawyers are trained in knowledge that allows them access to many of the controlling devices of their society.

The lawyer's position with respect to power, however, is basically manipulative, not productive. He can devise and elaborate controls, but his abilities are limited to the organizational and ideological. In being a necessary adjunct to the other kinds of power seekers, he operates for his own ends as well. He must turn to the sources where the power lies, and he generally looks to those areas where he may expect success. As a result, the lawyers of Guatemala operate within the upper sector whenever possible. It is this area that has the financing and contacts; in it the lawyer hopes to benefit from relationships with individuals of greater power than himself.

The career of the young lawyer in Guatemala is strongly influenced by his initial contacts and relationships. Those from better-connected families can expect to find their services wanted by industries, wealthier farmers, and businessmen. These graduates usually have an urban background and no intent of living in the provinces. Students from poorer backgrounds, and particularly those who come from the regional elites and who lack connections within the city, can seldom expect work with important established legal offices. Their main opening is to be found in minor positions in the judiciary or other branches of the government. The amount of law practice possible in Guatemala is finite. There are relatively few big businesses, and these depend upon lawyers who can be expected to have good connections and, preferably, have already demonstrated their ability to be successful. Since jobs of all kinds are limited, and the law school produces more lawyers than can be used formally, the poor student in law school spends much of his time establishing connections that may serve him when he finally becomes licensed. Classes are generally held in the late afternoon and evening, allowing the student to work outside full time.

Among the three faculties—humanities, economics, and law—that are the principal loci of student political activities, the law faculty is the most prestigious and traditionally the leader. The Asociación de Estudiantes de Derecho (Association of Law Students), or AED, is the largest of the student organizations, and, within the student body, political concerns are aired more widely and national issues are of more public concern than is the case in most other faculties. Since the 1944 revolution (in which the students and faculty played a role), the student organization has attempted from time to time to provide legal services to the poor and especially to those who find themselves suffering from restrictions of the labor system. The AED and the law faculty operate a *bufete popular*, providing free legal service to anyone who wants it. Where the licensed notary or lawyer is required, the students take care of getting this service. Since it is a requirement in the faculty that students practice at least six penal cases before a tribunal, this means that much of the work that is done is in the area of criminal, rather than civil, law. Such a service is also offered by the students of the faculty in Quezaltenango, and another legal service is run by the general students association, the AEU.

Young lawyers who are politically concerned and who recognize the inequities in the system often begin professional practice for workers and labor organizations. In more cases than not, however, the structure of the society forces them out of this service. The average laborer can pay almost nothing for law services, and the labor organizations are equally poor. The idealistic lawyer finds himself faced with the alternative of seeking out clients who can afford to pay him or continuing indefinitely on an income limited by the general level of funds available in the lower sector.

The consequence of this is, first, that few lawyers remain available for long to the lower sector, and some who begin with this ideal in mind gradually turn their lower-sector experience into a good thing by becoming labor lawyers for the upper sector. So it is that the structure of the society guides lawyers into activities that benefit the upper sector. Being upper-sector aspirants themselves, they seek the appurtenances of that society; whether they be liberals or radicals, their support comes from that area. It is ironic that the Faculty of Law, the locus of such radical student manifestations, produces a population of professionals that is apparently incapable of altering the system and is, instead, deeply involved in its continuity. Since the structure tolerates only a few who are both lawyers and active supporters of the lower sector, there are many *empíricos*, untrained people who collect fees from the poor for legal "services."

The only institutional support to which a lawyer may look outside the private sector is the government itself. The political position of most recent governments has not been radical and might prove more attractive to more conservative individuals. But, as often is the case in large organizations, those in the lower echelon may reflect entirely different political attitudes, as well as a distinctive general value orientation. As a result, the young lawyer in a government post may continue to reflect radical ideas, even though unable to realize them within his current position. The government offers lawyers one of the few channels for mobility within the upper sector. It was estimated by one informant that between 150 and 200 lawyers work in nonjudiciary posts in government bureaus and ministries. They attain their positions as much through personal contacts as through political devices. Every Congress has a large number of candidates who are lawyers. It is not merely the poorer and those with no connections who turn to government work. Especially under conservative governments, individuals of experience and considerable prestige may take posts, both as a public service and as a means to consolidate and continue their power. It is hard to generalize on the public careers of such individuals, since no survey or study has ever touched on the subject. Some retire after having found that the political arena offers dangers as well as opportunities; some return when another promising opportunity comes their way.

Within the bureaucracy, the most important purely legal post is the *ministerio público*. This office represents the government in legal affairs. It may intervene in all legal affairs and participate in legal action in all tribunals, including the military. All ministries, however, also have *asesores jurídicos*, who have among their other duties the careful revision of laws and decrees that pass through their ministry. Lawyers exercise greater influence in Congress than in the lower sections of bureaucracy. To become a *diputado*, one must have connections. The pay is good, and a private practice may be retained. If supported by a political party, the candidate may not have to spend much to be elected, but if he runs alone he will have to back his candidacy with his own funds. Obviously, Congress is a place where lawyers with some background and connections may expect to operate profitably, but it is not clear how much promise it holds for the beginner.

While the term *licenciado* in Guatemala refers to a person who has received the *licenciatura*, it has also become the professional title of reference and address for lawyers. The importance of lawyers in the political life is indicated by data collected by John Sloan on the elections of 1958 through 1966 (see Table 8–18). In almost all of these elections, *licenciados* were the most numerous professionally identified group both as to the number of candidates in the field and the number of winners. In the 1964 "election," which was actually a plebiscite, since all candidates automatically won, lawyers formed 40 percent of the candidate-winners. In the other four elections, *señor* was the most numerous group; *licenciado* was second, both as winner and as candidate in all but one election. In that election (1966), *licenciado* ranked first as winner, taking sixteen out of fifty-five seats, while the second most numerous, the *señor*, had only ten. Of special interest is that not only does *licenciado* rank below only *señor* in these matters, but that, in comparing their percentage of the total as candidates and as winners, it is consistently the case that as winners they get a disproportionately large part of the total. The preponderance of lawyers from among all professions is probably due both to the fact that they are selectively chosen as candidates and to the fact that they are selectively chosen by voters.

The data brought together by Sloan also permits insight into the current status of the lawyer as politician. Until 1966 *licenciado* continued as the single most important group aside from *señor* in almost all elections. The first major divergence from this came in

TABLE 8–18
Candidates and Winners in Guatemalan Elections (1958–1966) by Title as Listed on Ballot

Title on Ballot	1958 Candidates No.	%	1958 Winners No.	%	1959 Candidates No.	%	1959 Winners No.	%	1961 Candidates No.	%	1961 Winners No.	%	1964 Candidates No.	%	1966 Candidates No.	%	1966 Winners No.	%
Señor	86	58.50	19	51.5	124	62.60	19	57.50	63	46.30	11	33.30	19	23.80	37	22.40	10	18.20
Licenciado	27	18.40	9	24.2	34	17.20	9	27.10	19	14.00	10	30.30	32	40.00	27	16.40	16	29.10
Doctor	11	7.49	4	10.8	8	4.04	1	3.03	16	11.70	2	6.05	9	11.20	20	12.10	8	14.50
Bachiller	8	5.44	2	5.4	8	4.04	1	3.03	14	10.30	4	12.10	2	2.50	10	6.06	4	7.29
Contador	2	1.36	1	2.7	4	2.10	0	0.0	4	2.94	1	3.03	2	2.50	7	4.24	5	9.10
Military	1	0.68	1	2.7	2	1.01	1	3.03	1	0.73	1	3.03	7	8.75	3	1.82	2	3.64
Agricultor	3	2.20	1	2.7	0	0.0	0	0.0	4	2.94	2	6.05	1	1.25	25	15.20	4	7.29
Periodista	2	1.36	0	0.0	3	1.52	1	3.03	0	0.0	0	0.0	4	5.00	6	3.62	1	1.82
Ingeniero	1	0.66	0	0.0	6	3.01	1	3.03	4	2.94	1	3.03	3	3.75	3	1.82	0	0
Profesor	6	4.09	0	0.0	9	4.51	0	0.0	9	6.60	1	3.03	1	1.25	11	6.68	2	3.64
Obrero	0	0.0	0	0.0	0	0.0	0	0.0	1	0.73	0	0.0	0	0.0	5	3.02	1	1.82
Piloto aviador	0	0.0	0	0.0	0	0.0	0	0.0	1	0.73	0	0.0	0	0.0	1	6.07	0	0
Comerciante	0	0.0	0	0.0	0	0.0	0	0.0	0	0.0	0	0.0	0	0.0	9	5.45	2	3.64
Arquitecto	0	0.0	0	0.0	0	0.0	0	0.0	0	0.0	0	0.0	0	0.0	1	6.07	0	0
Totals	147	100.09	37	100.00	198	100.03	33	99.78	136	99.92	33	99.92	80	100.00	165	100.97	55	100.12

SOURCE: Calculated from data in John Sloan, *The Electoral Game in Guatemala*, Ph.D. dissertation, University of Texas at Austin, 1967, Table I.

NOTE: The 1964 election was not competitive; all candidates "won."

1966 when the winning PR party fielded a different proportion. Of its seventy-eight candidates, eighteen were *agricultores*, and sixteen were *comerciantes*, whereas only thirteen were lawyers. But of the thirty PR winners, ten were lawyers, and the other two categories together accounted for only five. In other words, the PR party, while trying to be representative of a much broader political spectrum, won with a more traditional lineup, depending heavily on the lawyers.

The most important governmental area for the poorer lawyer is the judiciary (Tables 8–19, 8–20). This has a number of structural features of relevance. Perhaps most important is that most judicial posts pay very poorly and, consequently, do attract some men who do not expect great success elsewhere. Lawyers who find it difficult, for whatever reason, to make a living by practice welcome the judicial posts. Some posts, after a preliminary period, provide life tenure. Since the pay is bad, however, some use the court as a device for advancement and do not take the life appointment seriously. Law students also depend heavily upon the judicial branch for support. Many of them work in tribunals where, if clever, they can exercise a certain amount of influence. They read cases thoroughly, doing the "spade work," and the magistrates often find that they must depend upon student recommendations, since they are more familiar with the material. Contacts and friendships the student makes during these years are crucial to him in later years. The judiciary in Guatemala is weak. This stems in part from the fact that under the civil law system, judges do not carry the prestige and potential power that is the case within the common law. The Supreme Court positions carry great prestige, but those on the lower courts seldom do.

An index of the degree to which lawyers choose to derive their power from sources centralized in government and the upper sector is suggested by their regional distribution. In 1965, of the 876 lawyers listed in the Colegio de Abogados de Guatemala, 84.6 percent were in the capital. An additional 6 percent were in Quezaltenango (but sixteen of these thirty-four were in the judiciary). Table 8–21 indicates that this concentration in the capital is increasing rather than decreasing and that over half of all provincial lawyers are in the judiciary. The reason for this concentration is,

TABLE 8–19
Lawyers in the Judiciary: Provincial Distribution of Judicial Posts

Department (seated in departmental capital)	Judge, Court of the First Instance	Court of the Second Instance			Judge, Labor Court
		Magis-trates	Alter-nates	Secre-tary*	
Alta Verapaz	1				†
Baja Verapaz	1				
Chimaltenango	1				
Chiquimula	2				
El Petén	1				†
El Progreso	1				
Escuintla	2				1
Huehuetenango	1				
Izabal	1				†
Jalapa	1	3	2		†
Jutiapa	2				
Quezaltenango	2	6	4	2	1
Family Court	1				
Quiché	1				†
Retalhuleu	1				
Sacatepéquez	1	3	2		
San Marcos	2				
Santa Rosa	1				
Sololá	1				
Suchitepéquez	1				1
Totonicapán	1				
Zacapa	1	3	2	1	

Total number of professional rural judicial posts: 58

SOURCE: *Gaceta de los tribunales* 83, nos. 7–12 (Jan.–June, 1964): 225–242. Table prepared by Fredda Bullard.
* According to source, counted as professional post if occupied by a *licenciado*.
† Duties of presiding over the Labor Court assigned to the Judge of the First Instance Court.

of course, that the lawyer finds his major sources of income and power in the capital.

The most powerful and successful lawyers are those who work with the wealthier enterprises. In the past, this referred principally to the major national enterprises and the United Fruit Company. For the former, the lawyers from the wealthy families tended to handle most of the business. The company, however, developed

TABLE 8–20
Provincial Distribution of the Legal Profession

partment Municipio	Number of Lawyers Not in Judiciary	Number of Judicial Posts	Total Number of Lawyers	Department Lawyers as Percent of Total: in Departments	in Nation
Verapaz			7	4.4	0,8
bán	6	1	7		
Verapaz			1	0.6	0.1
Salamá	0	1	1		
naltenango			5	3.1	0.6
nimaltenango	4	1	5		
uimula			3	1.9	0.3
niquimula	1	2	3		
etén			1	0.6	0.1
ores	0	1	1		
rogreso			1	0.6	0.1
Progreso	0	1	1		
intla			8	5.0	0.9
scuintla	3	3	6		
quisate	2	0	2		
huetenango			6	3.7	0.7
uehuetenango	5	1	6		
al			5	3.1	0.6
erto Barrios	3	1	4		
nanera	1	0	1		
pa			7	4.4	0.8
lapa	1	6	7		
lapa	1	6	7		
tiapa	5	2	7		
altenango			53	33.1	6.0
ezaltenango	34	16	50		
atepeque	3	0	3		
hé			5	3.1	0.6
iché	4	1	5		
huleu			5	3.1	0.6
talhuleu	4	1	5		
tepéquez			10	6.2	1.1
tigua Guatemala	4	6	10		
Marcos			10	6.2	1.1
n Marcos	7	2	9		
n Pedro Sac.	1	0	1		
a Rosa			2	1.2	0.2
ilapa	0	1	1		
eblo Nuevo Viñas	1	0	1		

(Table 8–20, continued)

Department and Municipio	Number of Lawyers Not in Judiciary	Number of Judicial Posts	Total Number of Lawyers	Department Lawyers as Percent of Total:	
				in Departments	in Na
Sololá			1	0.6	0.1
Sololá	0	1	1		
Suchitepéquez			11	6.9	1.3
Mazatenango	8	2	10		
Patulúl	1	0	1		
Totonicapán			3	1.9	0.3
Totonicapán	2	1	3		
Zacapa			9	5.6	1.0
Zacapa	2	7	9		
Total	102	58	160	(100.0)	18.3

Source: *Colegio de Abogados de Guatemala* (list of members), Guatemala, Colegio de Abog 1965; updated by the secretariat. *Gaceta de los tribunales* 83, nos. 7–12 (Jan.–June 1964): 242. Table prepared by Fredda Bullard.

Note: Lawyers who listed addresses outside the capital and whose names do not appear as r bers of the judiciary in *Gaceta de los tribunales*, 1964, are tabulated in the second column. number of lawyers in Guatemala, midyear 1965, was 876.

some of its own lawyers through working with young, intelligent, and clever individuals. In so doing, it has created a corps of dependable advocates. The major new source of wealth open to lawyers has been the increase in foreign investment. As with land, so it is with legal accounts. The most lucrative business is handled by a relative few of the *bufetes* of the city. The expansion of business, however, has also tended to harness lawyers purely as adjuncts to the enterprises. One lawyer informant felt that this reflected the changing role of the lawyer and his diminishing importance. The lawyer is less able to act as an independent professional and must work increasingly in the direct service of the controllers of economic power.

This change is not, however, bringing power into the hands of the lawyers in general. The basic reason for this is that both in the new industries and in certain areas of government, the decisions are more and more influenced by the technician, the specialist, and most often, the economist. In some areas, such as banking, responsibilities that were almost entirely handled by lawyers a generation

TABLE 8–21

Distribution of Lawyers in Guatemala

	1958	1965
Total number of lawyers	634	876
Lawyers listed in capital:		
Number	526	741*
Percent of total	83.0	84.6
Lawyers listed outside capital:		
Number	108	135
Percent of total	17.0	15.4
In departamentos:		
Number	104	130
Percent of total	16.4	14.8
In foreign countries:†		
Number	4	5
Percent of total	0.6	0.6
Proportion of lawyers to total population	1:5,441	1:4,891

SOURCE: Mario Monteforte Toledo, *Guatemala*: *Monografía Sociológica*, second edition, Instituto de Investigaciones Sociales, UNAM, Mexico, 1959, p. 350; data assumed current for 1958. *Colegio de Abogados de Guatemala* (list of members), Guatemala, Colegio de Abogados, 1965; updated by the secretariat. Table prepared by Fredda Bullard.
* Includes lawyers listing addresses in the capital and those for whom no addresses were available.
† Includes exiles.

ago are now controlled by economists. The new industries that are emerging within the Central American Common Market are also largely in the hands of the economists. The key financial agencies of the government, the Ministries of Hacienda and Economy, as well as the Secretariat of the Economic Planning Council, are run by economists. Under the industrial development law, applications for new industries must be endorsed by economists and usually accompanied by economic studies. So it is that much of the overseer's role, the position of being able to control the handling of papers, is leaving the domain of the lawyer. While well organized for some purposes, the Colegio de Abogados is much too large and much too split internally along political lines to organize for defense against this "invasion" of the lawyers' domain. Also, lawyers are not trained to handle some of the financial and technical issues at stake.

The lawyer's role is undergoing structural changes as a result of development, the changing technology of living, and the increase in income and new sources of wealth. The lawyers still form an integral part of the upper sector, however, and have not seen any potential for the manipulation of power by operating within the lower sector. Because of this, it is inevitably left to the government or the revolutionaries to take the lead in this area. The failure of the legal system to operate effectively in this part of the population is of importance in evaluating the paths available to the *campesino* for his own development.

Thus far, the lawyer has been described as an individual, finding his way to prestige and wealth through a profession that is overcrowded and in which one's social origins set limits on what may be reasonably expected. The capabilities for organization among the members of the legal profession are seriously hampered by the fact that differences between the very poor and the very wealthy are extreme and that within the profession there is wide political divergence. There are, nevertheless, systematically organized efforts to coordinate activities to the benefit of the profession as a whole or of some particular subsegment. There are two major kinds: those having to do with the entire profession and those of a small group of individuals. The first includes the association of students in the university and the Colegio de Abogados de Guatemala. In the second are the joint law offices operated by a set of individuals.

The student entering on a career of law learns from his earliest days at the university that organization is important. Immediately upon attempting to matriculate, he is required to join the Asociación de Estudiantes de Derecho (AED); for this he must pay Ø3.50 and an additional Ø1.50 for membership in the more inclusive Asociación de Estudiantes Universitarios (AEU). Although the AEU is theoretically concerned with matters common to the students of all faculties of the university, the seniority and size of the law faculty and the student body make it the dominant group. The members of the AEU directive board are usually law students, as was the case in 1965, the year of this study. The AEU had a three-story building under construction at that time, and the entire top floor was to be occupied by the AED.

The student organization impresses the virtues of organization on the student in a number of ways. It is a power in the government of the faculty itself, and therefore the university; through this, it can influence and at times even take a commanding position in the employment of professors, deans, and the rector. One-third of the Junta Directiva of the faculty and the Consejo Superior Universitario of the entire university are students, and these are strongly controlled by the student organizations. By virtue of this organization, the students can expect a greater consistency in their vote than can be anticipated from either of the two other elements represented, the faculty and the professional graduates. Since deans are elected by the Junta Directiva and the rector by the Consejo Superior, the students hold a powerful voice. They can even command the retirement of faculty as they did during the military government of Peralta Azurdia, when they fired about eight law professors, among the most prominent in the faculty, for cooperating with the incumbent government.

While regular political parties may not be formed legally among students, the two student parties most recently dominant in the law faculty clearly represent issues of current concern to the politicians of the country at large. The Fuerzas Revolucionarias Unidas (FRU) is strongly radical and has been extremely antimilitary, as well as only thinly masking its open sympathy with the *guerrilleros*. The Frente Estudiantil Social Cristiana (FESC) is more moderate. It is hard to judge with accuracy, but the impression of most informants is that, while many students are less than enthusiastic about excessive student political action, they are moved by the same events that spur their student leaders. One informant guessed that at least one-third of the law students were politically independent and could not be expected to vote consistently with either one or the other student political party; the remaining 1,000 belonged to various factions. The proportion of students politically interested is suggested by the fact that of the approximately 1,500 students, 575 voted in the very hotly contested elections of 1965.

The general posture of the student organization is defensive. It regards itself as a bulwark of freedom of action, a leader in the struggle to defend not only the university and students, but the country at large against the excesses of the government, the foreign imperialists, and any other evil forces that might appear on the horizon. Its power lies in the control it claims to have over the students themselves. Some informants claimed that the AED could expel a student for failure to participate in the organization; others held that this was not true. The idea has been voiced abroad that such was the case, at least strongly enough to lead most students not to challenge it. This has provided the organization with a cash basis upon which to work and without which it would be extremely weak. The students' strength also lies in the acceptance by the nation at large of the tripartite system of university government and the fact that this permits student control and influence over the faculty and what it teaches. In the Faculty of Law, the students tend to be poorer than is the case in the others, and there is a higher proportion of older students than in all except the medical school. Both these qualities contribute to the greater action evident in this faculty than elsewhere.

The student who successfully passes his public examinations for his *licenciatura* and the technical professional examination for the title of Abogado y Notario will usually then be elected to the Colegio de Abogados de Guatemala. Although first established in 1810, the Colegio, as it now operates, was reestablished in 1945. It operates both as the national association of lawyers and as the alumni association of the law faculty of San Carlos. Membership is obligatory for the practice of law, and it thereby is a guild or closed-shop union. In the past, the Colegio represented the consensus of the nation's lawyers, and its pronouncements had a considerable effect on the implementation of the nation's laws. Recently, however, it seems not to have played a very effective role in this matter, and its concerns have turned more to such guild issues as protection for the members and collecting a five-cent tax on every document sheet sent to court and a further tax of up to five dollars on various legal instruments. In its capacity as the professional alumni association of the San Carlos faculty, the Colegio has been responsible for one-third of the effective government in the faculty.

The Colegio has no power over the political stance of its members and includes those of all political interests. It can suspend a member (thereby prohibiting him from practice) for malpractice or failure to pay dues, but not for political action. As a result, the Colegio's own political position is merely that which is consonant with its own governing body and the consensus of the members. While this leads it to focus its public attention on matters pertaining to law, these concerns at times have political ramifications. In 1964 it held its Third National Juridical Congress on the same topic as had been set for the previous two, the problem of the "rule of law." In early 1965 a round-table forum was held on this subject, with open criticism of the incumbent military government, aimed especially at meddling with the constitution. The fact that an *estado de sitio* (martial law) was declared immediately following this was taken by some as the government's response to the criticism. Since the Colegio must respond to the general and common interests of its members, its more consistent activities are in those areas directly concerning the practice of the profession and less with matters bordering on the political.

Another organizational effort found among lawyers is that which involves a select set of individuals who band together to share an office. The law office, or *bufete*, in Guatemala may be either individual or joint. The joint *bufete*, involving a number of lawyers, is not too common, but it has been growing in importance. It gives a public impression of greater competence and power and does have the practical value of having consultant law specialists available within the same office. Civil, penal, administrative, and labor law are all currently specialties. Members of the *bufete* also tend to complement one another in other matters: some will be "idea men," others will be public figures and effective orators. Finally, and perhaps most important from the point of view of power manipulation by the lawyer, *bufetes* frequently have sufficient friendship to try to maintain a wide network of connections, including the major political variations, so that at least one of their members will have a series of relations that permits access to the incumbent government.

There are perhaps not more than a dozen broadly effective joint *bufetes* in Guatemala, but these handle many of the more lucrative accounts and, between them, serve as nodes of a series of relations that operate extensively through the economic and political power of the country. The effectiveness of a particular *bufete* at any point in time becomes a matter of the tactical application of power and influence, combined with the necessary knowledge and skill. Sometimes, as under the Peralta government, the members of a single *bufete* will occupy posts within the government or have specifically close relations with high government officials. Clearly such a mother lode does not last beyond the particular regime, but it serves to widen the powers of a particular *bufete* for a time.

Fundamentally, the organization for power within the legal profession is oriented along one of two major lines: it is either for the defense of the profession as such or for the increased power of some particular group. The organization of the joint *bufetes* does not destroy the bonds among lawyers in general and seems in no way to conflict with the larger organizations. The Colegio, however, does not have the weapons in hand to materially affect the general decline in power of the legal profession. As is the case with other operators in the networks of power, the lawyers who become involved in development stand to gain individually because their skills are necessary. They no longer have the extensive powers they once had, however, because foreign capital and skills are requiring new kinds of manipulators. Bankers do not need to be lawyers, and economists can exercise their skills independently of the law. In the meantime, lawyers are becoming aware of important new legal problems that need to be solved in the face of development itself and of the specific expansion in the Central American region. The international complexities of Central American integration, industries specifically, are becoming a matter of real concern. At the other end of the spectrum, lawyers continue to show little interest in the *campesino* and rural laborer.

The presence and power of the lawyer in Guatemala is an excellent weather vane of power. When and if power begins to crawl into the hands of the *campesino*, it will be signaled by the appearance of lawyers in that area. While the lawyer is a manipulator and purveyor of power, he must depend upon others to put the power in his hands.

4. *Access to Law: Labor and Justice*

There is no area in which the structure of power becomes so manifest as that involving labor, *patrones*, and government. It is here that the bare bones of self-interest inevitably show themselves. In order to see the general direction that the power structure is taking, however, it is necessary to distinguish the operation of a given regime from the structure on which it is based. The only possible way to separate operation from structure is to look at the internal strategy of change over a period of time, to analyze from this the nature of the structure, and then to compare it with the actual regime and events currently under way. We will, therefore, first review some of the changes that have taken place in the relations between *patrones*, labor, and government, and then explore the current scene in terms of the existing public and private power domains.[16]

A labor movement emerged in Guatemala prior to 1920, but it was eliminated under Ubico. Consequently, when the revolution of 1944 occurred, labor organizations had little recent experience upon which to draw (see Chapter 9). The Ubico regime had, however, instituted an important structural shift in the relation between *patrón* and worker by eliminating debt peonage (see Chapter 3). The revolution of 1944 and the regime of Arévalo that followed attempted to bring startling changes into the entire system. Other than specific laws and decrees, Guatemala had never had a labor code. The elimination of debt peonage, together with his personalistic call upon the Indian, gave Ubico prestige as an ultimate authority to whom Indians could appeal if things really became intolerable, but there was little legal basis that provided access to even the few laws that were relevant. Under the Arévalo government, a labor code was established, along with special labor courts, and labor law was introduced into the curriculum of the Faculty of Law at San Carlos.

With the introduction of a revolutionary labor code, the workers were allowed to organize and to bring complaints against their employers, whether the latter was a private concern or a government agency. In valuable but unpublished data on labor cases reaching the First and Second Labor Courts of Appeals in Guatemala City, Emilio Zebadúa[17] has shown that there was a gradual increase in *juicios ordinarios laborales* against the government (both at the national and municipal levels) until 1952; beginning the next year, they decreased in number and were of little consequence after 1957 (see Table 8–22). Zebadúa's research suggests that the

---

[16] Almost all the materials in this section were collected by Fredda Bullard.
[17] Emilio Zebadúa, typescript materials, summer, 1965.

TABLE 8–22
Juicios Ordinarios Laborales, Court of Appeals,
Guatemala City, 1947–1964

Year	Juicios Ordinarios Laborales Brought Against			Total
	The State	Municipalities	Private Enterprise	
1947	5	3	148	156
1948	82	11	264	357
1949	38	9	246	293
1950	85	30	312	427
1951	200	17	370	587
1952	239	27	463	729
1953	138	37	466	641
1954	98	24	431	553
1955	33	11	334	378
1956	16	12	270	298
1957	4	7	258	269
1958	1	1	289	291
1959	5	0	269	274
1960	0	1	289	290
1961	5	2	275	282
1962	5	2	337	344
1963	0	0	459	459
1964	0	0	427	427

SOURCE: Emilio Zebadúa, typescript materials, summer 1965.

problem with labor's rights against the government was an issue independent of any particular regime. If the government was to exercise the power formerly held by the *patrones*, then the government could not well accept rising challenges to its own authority. In contrast to other defendants, the state was able to gradually apply pressure on its employees and to resist legal attack on its position.

Clearly, a distinction must be drawn between the government as a structural element and the regime as the organizational form. The government's power over labor has definitely been increasing. Government treatment of labor at a given point, however, varies with a particular regime and the particular circumstances of the time; a regime may favor the *patrones* or favor labor. From Ubico's time through the revolutionary decade and into the postrevolutionary period, the government became increasingly powerful. The result was to improve the structural position of the laborer before the law, but the particular regime determined whether the law would be exercised in a form that really granted derivative power to labor as well as the *patrones*.

Until approximately thirty years ago, the Guatemalan *campesino* would have had an advantage in a free labor market.[18] There was, under the liberal spurt initiated by García Granados and J. R. Barrios, a demand for labor in the growing coffee fincas of the piedmont and Alta Verapaz. *Patrones* could, under laws issued at that time, force Indians to work on the farms.[19] The market was not allowed to become free until the rural population had grown equal to or beyond the national needs in export agriculture. As a result, *campesinos*, primarily Indians, today need the work available on the fincas and plantations more than the plantations need them. There are, it is true, complaints from owners and administrators of large farms that labor is not adequate in either quality or quantity. These comments are usually localized, however. There have been no serious losses of crops because of lack of hands to harvest them, although cheaper labor or better labor is often sought. A study issued by the Committee of Nine of the Alliance for Progress[20] estimates that while the absolute size of the employed rural population grew from 660,000 to 824,000 between 1950 and 1962, the increase did not change the proportion of the employed rural population to the total rural population; it remained about 31 percent. The employed urban population in the same period increased from 308,000 to 402,000, but that of the total urban population suited for work increased to 645,000, or seven times the additional number employed. This suggests that the heavy migration to urban areas is due in part to the fact that the rural labor market is sat-

[18] This is a broad guess; one finca owner is reported to have said that they needed workers twenty years ago to keep up the finca population, but that at present there is a surplus. Cf. Schmid, "Migratory Labor," p. 282.

[19] See "Circular" dated November 3, 1876, and Governmental Decree 177 of April 3, 1877, in Skinner-Klée, *Legislación Indigenista de Guatemala*, pp. 33–42.

[20] Comité de los Nueve, Alianza para el Progreso, "Evaluación del Plan de Desarrollo Económico y Social de Guatemala, 1965–1969: Informe Presentado al Gobierno de Guatemala por el Comité Ad Hoc," p. 54.

urated and that the possibilities for survival are regarded as being better in the cities.

The Guatemalan *campesinos*, then, did not have a free labor market during the historical period when it would have been to their advantage, and now that they are forced to work in a free market, it is strongly disadvantageous for them. This labor-market situation is important, since it places the *campesino* in a position where he cannot use a labor shortage as a means of pressure to better his circumstances. The *patrón*, in turn, assumes that it is totally unnecessary to bargain with employees about their interests, since there are always others available who need the work. This has, therefore, effectively prevented any development of private bargaining, and the laborer has continued at the mercy of the employer. The government has evolved as a distinct and higher authority to which both *patrón* and laborer must turn. Whether one prefers to see this as developing coincidentally with nationalism or feels that the nation-building process itself is a partial product of population expansion is not an issue at this point. It is clear that the Guatemalan *patrón*'s participation in improving the laborer's condition is almost negligible, and the government has gradually evolved into the only mechanism that can do it.

To say, however, that the government is in the position to do this is to speak of structure. Whether it will, how fast, and in what ways rests on organization and strategy and how these stand in a broader structure. Indices show that the speed with which improvements are being made varies distinctly with the regime and widely with local conditions. For instance, there are extreme examples of organizational relics from the Ubico period. In the San Pedro Carchá vagrancy system described earlier, the laborers tend to be largely under the control of local employers. This can be contrasted with the situation in the United Fruit Company holdings at Bananera, where there is a labor union and salaries and living conditions are relatively good. The variation is orderly in the sense that the *campesino* laborer is in almost every way worse off in the more rural and underdeveloped areas and somewhat better off in the urban zones and in those regions where development is taking place. According to incomplete reports (see Table 8–7), the highest agricultural wages are paid in the departments of Guatemala and Escuintla. Among the highest are Retalhuleu, Quezaltenango, and

Suchitepéquez; whereas among the lowest are Huehuetenango, Alta Verapaz, Baja Verapaz, Jalapa, and Chiquimula.

Another kind of index is the use of the labor courts. Referring again to Table 8–22, one sees that the end of the Arbenz regime in 1954 brought a sharp decline in the number of cases against private owners. The total, however, did not even drop by one-half and had started to rise again significantly when the military government took over in 1963. The total number of cases brought to the court of appeals increased greatly from 1949 to 1952, showed no real increase in 1953, and then decreased. The number of cases stemming from labor unions did not decrease in this manner, but followed a different pattern (see Table 8–23). It is clear that even

TABLE 8–23
Three Types of Labor Cases, Court of Appeals,
Guatemala City, 1947–1964

Year	Punishment of Patrones	Contract Termination Due to Death of Worker	Collective Conflict over Socioeconomic Issues (union cases)
1947	6	11	3
1948	46	7	12
1949	75	7	15
1950	92	7	22
1951	89	0	28
1952	61	21	42
1953	56	66	77
1954	116	70	50
1955	98	72	0
1956	189	82	0
1957	204	128	2
1958	199	117	9
1959	322	101	17
1960	365	82	11
1961	390	90	9
1962	191	125	8
1963	211	27	2
1964	303	30	11

SOURCE: Emilio Zebadúa, typescript materials, summer 1965.

TABLE 8-24
Number of Cases Handled by Labor Inspectors,
January, 1964, to August, 1965

Department	Municipio of the Departmental Capital	Other Municipios in the Department	Total
Escuintla	233	202	435
Quezaltenango	116	54	170
Izabal	113	17	130
Sacatepéquez	84	30	114
San Marcos	1	56	57
Zacapa	37	2	39
Alta Verapaz	12	18	30
Chimaltenango	4	18	22
Santa Rosa	1	14	15
Suchitepéquez	1	11	12
Chiquimula	8	0	8
Totonicapán	3	2	5
Sololá, Baja Verapaz	1 each	0	2
Retalhuleu, El Quiché, and Jutiapa	0	1 each	3
Total	615	427	1,042

SOURCE: Data provided by the Ministry of Labor.

with the change in regimes and with a severe cutback in cases, the individual laborer continued to initiate legal action. Unfortunately, it is not possible from these data to determine what proportion came from Guatemala City and what proportion from the provincial areas.

Other data that bear on this matter (see Table 8-24) are taken from a series of materials[21] that provide basic information on cases

[21] These data were obtained by Fredda Bullard from the Ministerio de Trabajo. The minister kindly arranged to have the Inspección General de Trabajo collect information on all the cases from all over the country (except Guatemala City) for six alternate months beginning in August, 1964. Various provincial agents sent in additional cases from January, 1964, through August, 1965. The present regional distributional comments are made from the set of cases thus submitted. As in other matters, we are indebted to the minister and his office for this extraordinary service.

handled over a limited period of time in the regional offices of the Inspección General de Trabajo. (It should be noted that these data are imperfect because they do not include comparable cases from the city and the sample is not representative.) From these provincial areas, the greatest single number of cases came from Escuintla. An examination shows that the relation between a departmental capital and its surrounding region is not necessarily consistent, however. Quezaltenango, Izabal, San Marcos, and Zacapa show great disparity between the capital figures and those for the rest of the department. This indicates that the nature of the departmental capital labor situation may be quite independent of that in the rest of the department. San Marcos is a particularly good case in point. Presumably, most of the cases from that department are from coffee farms in the piedmont, as there is little activity in the departmental capital. In Quezaltenango most of the activity in the *municipios* was in coastal Coatepeque and piedmont Colomba, ecologically quite unrelated to the highland capital.

Also important is the fact that almost all the cases come from a limited set of areas. The central south coast leads the rest, and Quezaltenango–San Marcos and Izabal are secondary centers. Of tertiary importance are the Chimaltenango-Sacatepéquez highlands, Alta Verapaz, and the *municipios* of Zacapa and Chiquimula. Aside from scattered individual cases, there were no other areas of importance in the sample, which suggests that there is great variation in the amount of knowledge, the amount of preparation to engage in labor disputes, the differences in labor agitation, and the efforts of the agents of the Ministry to handle such cases.

Finally, even excluding the material from Guatemala City, as these data do, 59 percent of the cases come from departmental capitals and are quite likely to be somewhat marginal to what might be regarded a *campesino* situation. Of the remaining rural cases, 73 percent come from the three areas of Escuintla, Quezaltenango, and neighboring San Marcos.

One final set of data suggests that there has tended to be a general increase in the number of cases resulting in punishment of *patrones* except for certain periods of time when there were changes in regimes. Table 8–23 shows that from 1947 to 1950 there was a regular increase, but during the Arbenz administration such judgments declined, a fact of which social commentators and the *pa-*

trones of the period were apparently unaware. There was then a sharp rise in 1956 and another in 1959, with a severe drop in 1962. It is hard to relate these changes precisely to the political events of the period, but it is clear that the operation of the labor courts was, to some degree, independent of those events. The increase in such judgments during the 1959–1961 period and again in 1964 under the military government indicates that the labor courts of appeal continued to act with some independence once the cases reached them.[22]

The general picture is, then, as follows: the number of laborers has increased steadily; the labor market in the rural areas is almost entirely in favor of the employer; judgments in the courts have increased against the *patrón* independently of the political regime; and whether or not a laborer brings a case to court at all varies with the regions of the country and is much more common in towns and cities. To this picture may be added information reported by a number of lawyer informants who were (as far as could be judged) unprejudiced against the laborer. The informants reported that labor-court action, once initiated, is usually fairly swift and that in one kind of case especially (that concerning the firing of an employee) the employer must prove that the firing was justified. If he fails, then he must pay the indemnification. Apparently the most common decision in such cases favors the laborer, and the labor code is written in such a way as to promote this.

Why, then, with these circumstances, did the investigators on the present project encounter repeated comments, statements, and histories of labor's inferiority and inability to function in the face of the available laws? The answer to this seems to be that a variety of obstacles prevents labor from having access to the most effective legal procedures. These obstacles are of two kinds: structural and

---

[22] There are five types of procedures in labor tribunals, all but the first of which may pass to the Court of Appeals; in the first, only those cases involving more than ₡100 could be appealed. The five kinds are (1) ordinary labor cases involving unjustified firing, nonpayment of salaries, and so forth, (2) ordinary procedures for social protection, (3) offenses against the labor laws and laws of social protection, (4) procedures on collective conflicts of a socioeconomic character, and (5) matters incidental to the termination of labor contract due to death of the worker.

political. The structural obstacles are present because of some set of relationships within the total system; the political obstacles are derived from the stance of a specific regime or state of competition at a given point in time.

Among the structural obstacles, those related to lack of income are the most common, and, of these, the major problem is the lack of available professional legal help for laborers. The system in 1965 was such that only unions could expect to employ lawyers. There were few lawyers in the country who handled cases for laborers, and most laborers obviously had no access to them. The idealistic young attorney who began defending labor often gave it up simply because he could not live off the returns. Laborers could seldom pay a small fee if they won, and they could never be expected to pay anything if they lost. This meant that not only were such lawyers hard to retain, but they usually did not continue the practice for long and therefore could not accumulate experience in favor of labor. Lawyers for the *patrones* would have had continuing and long experience and would know (often through their own earlier defense of workers) weaknesses in labor's position. Furthermore, over the years, they would come to know well the differences between various judges and would choose the judge who would be most likely to give them a favorable decision in that particular case.

Another structural problem faced by laborers is their lack of reserves. They cannot afford to stay unemployed for an indefinite period while litigation is in progress. The clever labor lawyer in the employ of the *patrón* can take various steps to extend this period so that the laborer faces an increasing financial crisis. This usually works directly to the advantage of the *patrón* by making the laborer willing to accept a far smaller settlement than he might ultimately obtain in court. The *patrón*, on the other hand, seldom faces this type of structural pressure.

At another level the labor inspectors and labor judges face a problem within their own context. Inspectors are supposed to be so familiar with the rights of labor under the labor code that they can ascertain whether abuses are occurring and bring these to the attention of the *patrón* and the laborers involved. They are, in addition, supposed to be able to act as a conciliator, to try to obtain a satisfactory solution without going to court. If they find a laborer who is not receiving just treatment at the hands of his employer, they are supposed to act as the laborer's defender if the case goes to court. In short, the inspectors of labor and their men in the field are supposed to be superhuman, and to be so on a minimum education and very small salary. Few are really sufficiently familiar with labor law to handle a case systematically in a professional manner. In fact, courts have often had to throw out cases that the laborer might have won because of errors in the inspector's presentation. Also, to act as a counselor between a *patrón* and a laborer places the inspector in a position of "authority" over the two parties involved. Since many subinspectors are lower on the social scale than the *patrones*, they are often not seriously heeded. They can win favor only by subordinating themselves and playing the proper social role of deference. Under these circumstances, the difficulty in communication varies directly with the social distance that separates the inspector and the *patrón*. Some inspectors become subservient and simply do not interfere with the labor relationships in their zones. They prefer to get along well with the local upper sector.

Labor judges, too, find themselves in structural difficulties. Judiciary posts are not highly paid, and they are not of great prestige. The individual who has one and cannot move on to better things may well find himself in this position because of lack of ability as well as lack of influence. Under such circumstances, and with the changing code of labor law, it is not surprising to find that judges themselves are sometimes incompetent in the law and are therefore unable to provide the kind of justice that a case warrants. All this leaves out of consideration the possibility that the judge might be subject to bribes or simply predisposed to favor either the *patrones* or labor.

Individual laborers generally have not confronted political obstacles unless they were seen as part of a broader collective activity. The numerous cases reported of finca workers being jailed have, in most cases, been individuals who were attempting to promote unions or who had been elected as officers to unions. The major development of unionism in Guatemala occurred during the revolutionary period when the governments of Arévalo and Arbenz encouraged their growth through legal devices and, especially under Arbenz, overlooked excesses of organizers. The period is a complex one, and its history has yet to be fully explored.[23] With the exception of those in the United Fruit Company center, the strongest unions were urban-based. There was, however, a widespread network of farm unions, and these became extremely active, especially in the latter years of the Arbenz period. The advent of Castillo brought about a sharp restriction of organizational activity. Most *campesino* organizations were put out of operation, and farm owners often did not await legal process before throwing out the major union leaders who had been plaguing them so effectively. More important, many of the union leaders, along with those of political parties and *campesino* organizations, were jailed immediately after the fall of Arbenz. On the farms, the owners and administrators, unable to get rid of all "troublesome" labor, discriminated against the remainder in various ways, such as giving them onerous tasks.

Under the law at the time of the present study (1965), the organization of a union could not be denied by the government if it fulfilled the proper requirements. Recognition could be refused only if there already existed another such organization that had three-quarters of the employees of the establishment. Further, if at least one-quarter of the laborers belong to a *sindicato* and wish to have a collective pact written with the employer, the latter is obliged by law to make such a pact with his laborers. Such a pact sets forth the basic conditions of relations that must exist between the laborer and the employer.[24] The inhibiting, legally based restrictions on unions are simple, and only one is really decisive. The real problems lie in the nature of the social environment in which organizing must take place. There are three major phases: the lack of leadership, the factors that have made rural unionizing difficult every-

[23] See Archer C. Bush, "Organized Labor in Guatemala, 1944–1949"; Edwin Bishop, "The Guatemalan Labor Movement," Ph.D. dissertation, University of Wisconsin, 1959.

[24] The *pacto colectivo* must not be confused with the *contrato*. The former establishes the basis for relations between employer and laborer but does not say that they are in effect. A contract is the statement that a given worker(s) will be obligated to do certain things and the *patrón* will be obligated in turn to give certain things.

where, and, most important, the legal restriction on political activity.[25]

Leadership in the lower sector presents problems because the values relevant to advancement and improvement of the individual's position vary, depending upon one's position in the social structure. In the upper sector, the concern with one's own achievement of increasing power is important; among rural laborers and *campesinos*, the individual is much more concerned with survival, with the achievement of only enough to get along at some given level. There is rarely motivation to achieve something beyond this. Leadership cannot elicit a steady following when the goals are distant, and it is unlikely that leaders will readily emerge from such a situation. A leader must have vision beyond this, even if it is merely to see his own long-range needs as being satisfied through the efforts of others. But to see things in this light, the leader must exhibit upper-sector values, that is, he must be interested in achieving power. So it is that the lower-sector leaders rarely exist; and when they do, they do so through having taken over the values of the upper sector but choosing to use the lower sector as the means to accomplish their ends.

Labor leadership during the Arbenz period was derived almost entirely from upper-sector individuals. The leaders at the local level were beginning to emerge in some numbers just at the time that Castillo arrived and put an effective stop to the process. In a situation in which leadership was structurally difficult, this was a political event of catastrophic proportions, and it temporarily ended the process of forming rural leaders. The suppression of unions and collective leadership discouraged the nascent efforts through "showing" the new leaders that they had been wrong in their attempt to venture into the values of the upper sector; also, many of the upper-sector leaders themselves fled the country and never returned to labor organizing.

The success of the attempted rebirth of the labor movement in Guatemala is illustrated by Zebadúa's data in Table 8–23. The accelerating rise (that began in 1947) of collective cases brought against employers naturally dropped to nothing in 1955 and 1956.

---

[25] Details concerning specific discrimination against *campesino* organizations are discussed in Chapter 9.

Following this, it did not significantly rise again. Although individual cases (Table 8–22) started to increase again in 1962 and punitive judgments against employers followed their own pattern (Table 8–23), the cases brought by unions remained low.

The second feature alluded to earlier, the fact that rural union development is difficult anywhere, lies in the character of rural labor. It (1) is unskilled, (2) involves additional seasonal labor, (3) tends to be scattered (as opposed to being in easy contact with other labor organizing as is the case in cities), and (4) tends to involve a poorly educated or totally uneducated population. In addition to these features, the Guatemalan rural laborer may also be Indian, with little or no command of Spanish. That these characteristics are not entirely restrictive was illustrated by the successful beginnings of unionism during the revolutionary period. Beginning from a situation in which most laborers had never even heard of unions, a large number of Guatemalans became familiar with them in less than ten years. This, however, was achieved only through the change in the power structure under the revolutionary governments: the government provided support. Without this feature, it is difficult to guess when rural unionism would have emerged.

The third restriction is the prohibition against political action placed on union organization by the postrevolutionary governments. Essentially, the government policy was "go ahead with union organization, providing that the unions keep hands strictly off politics; they must act only in economic matters." This restriction is political, since it obviously changes with the policy of the government in power. It is structural, however, in that it imposes an obstacle on the only kind of activity through which labor can expect to engender significant change.

In a society where power is controlled by a specific sector and the organization of that society is such as to perpetuate the control by that sector, change can only occur through action that removes some of that power and distributes it more widely in the society. Quite clearly, there is nothing in the normal course of a capitalistic economy that tends toward wider proportional distribution of the total wealth. This means that the only device available to the lower sector is political action that may help obtain a government that has as its policy the wider distribution of this power. By denying political activity to the unions, the postrevolutionary governments completely removed from the laboring population the only viable tool they might have for their own concerted action in behalf of their own interests—the political action to bring a government into power that would support their own interests.

In matters pertaining to unions in Guatemala, then, postrevolutionary structure and politics are congruent. The official stance—the politics of repression—acts in harmony with a variety of structural obstacles to inhibit politically significant unionization. This was clearly evident in the rural unions in 1965. The chapter on *campesino* organizations describes the process whereby unions were discouraged, and mention was made in the chapter on the military of the role played by the *comisionados militares* in this situation. An obvious question arises from these facts, however: Why does this oppression of union organization not extend to individual labor conflict or to the actions of labor courts or the permissiveness for "economic" activity by unions?[26]

The most likely answer has to do with the organization of politics to support a structure. For the government to remain strong, it must have some degree of support from the laboring sector. If it does not, it can fall in an election, and, even more, it would be easily subverted by the upper-sector agrarian, commercial, industrial, and military interests. But if it gets this support from labor through the formation of unions, the unions themselves may well become pressure groups equally or more threatening than those currently working elsewhere for the upper sector. The strategy, whether clearly enunciated or not, effectively tries to divide and conquer. By giving laborers access to some measure of justice, by requiring that they gain this through individual competitive action with the clearly entrenched upper sector (even more strongly organized by virtue of the increase in upper-sector interest groups), the government provides a mechanism whereby individuals may occasionally be successful. At the same time, the political power of unions is viewed as a threat. They might overthrow the government (even legally through elections) or they might so scare the

---

[26] The question as to why the unions were discriminated against while other organizations received some support is explored in Chapter 9.

upper sector that the latter would react through a further military coup. In either case, the incumbent government might fall.

So, while unions are legal and farm owners and other employers are enjoined to accept them and the government itself says it cannot reject them, there is little movement through this door opened by the law. The Escuela Sindical (still in existence in 1965), established in an attractive building, pays professors (who are presumably specialists in these matters) twenty-five quetzales a month, surely the lowest wage of any government-paid teachers in the country. Such teachers can, presumably, be trusted to follow the traditional irregular attendance practiced in the national university, thereby discouraging a student body that is ill-prepared for adult formal education anyway. The students must be elected from existent *sindicatos*, and this avoids the possibility of people learning how to form unions where none may currently exist.

Unions in Guatemala, then, find themselves in a dilemma. Their structural weakness is augmented because contemporary politics is congruent with it. To be strong, to be able to exercise their role as bargaining for the improvement of the laborer's situation, they must have derived power, and the only source of this is the government (barring the intervention of outside powers). The government, as a regime, does not wish a union to have any more political support than is good for the regime in question and will allow only that which is deemed useful. The situation, to those familiar with Mexico, will appear quite similar, although it is less formalized in its development. The focus of control, then, is the government, both as a state and as a regime. It is this domain that holds the key to the future of labor.

9 | The Stunted Growth of Campesino Organizations

by Brian Murphy

THIS CHAPTER WILL DISCUSS the growth, virtual disappearance, and regrowth of rural lower-sector organizations. It will deal only with selected organization types,[1] and, within those types, only with organizations that have achieved a formal legal status or juridic personality.[2] It will examine historical variations in interaction between the local organization and its supralocal "parents" at the regional, national, and international levels. And it will explore the relationship between (a) the government as political regime, (b) the legal framework, and (c) the environment of competing power units, as determinants of the exercise of *campesino* pressure. The general historical frame employed will be the

NOTE: This chapter, in essentially its present form, was the author's M.A. thesis at The University of Texas at Austin. Much of the research was carried out in Guatemala, June through September, 1967, and during a two-week revisit in January, 1968. Translations of Spanish sources, unless otherwise noted, are by the author.

[1] Excluded from the study are such organizations as *campesino* social and sports clubs, religious societies, *cofradías*, cooperatives, *Comités pro* (*escuela, mejoramiento, carretera*, etc.), and ephemeral community associations or committees that exist only during the resolution of a single specific issue.

[2] Juridic personality (*personalidad jurídica*) is roughly equivalent to the North American concept of corporate legal personality. In Guatemala, no organization of any type may function as a legal unit—in the sense of signing contracts or negotiating loans—until receipt of that recognition.

three-period division set forth in Chapter 3: prerevolution, revolution, and postrevolution.

Two principal organization types will be discussed here: (1) *sindicatos* of finca workers, and (2) *campesino* leagues (*ligas campesinas*). Local agrarian committees founded in the revolutionary period will be described primarily as agents reinforcing participation in these two organization types.

Sindicatos and leagues are formal interest or pressure group associations in that they represent individuals legally organized for the promotion of their own well-being. As is the case with upper-sector interest groups (see Chapter 6), they are nonprofit in nature, and participation is voluntary. *Campesino sindicatos* are labor organizations granted a mandate for existence under the constitution of 1945 and the labor code of 1947. They have a direct focus for pressure exercise in the person of the employer or *patrón*, and under the provisions of the labor code they may negotiate for a variety of labor relational benefits, such as wage and salary increases, shorter hours, smaller work tasks, and better working conditions. They are the rural counterparts of urban company (as opposed to craft) unions.

Campesino leagues, while currently granted legal recognition under the labor code, are not labor organizations. They are associations of independent agriculturalists—small owners, renters, sharecroppers—that, like the *sindicatos*, are organized for political action in the largest sense (for competitive promotion of common interests). They pursue such community development programs as the building of a road or bridge, the construction of a school or clinic, the development of a potable water supply, or whatever. Unlike *sindicatos*, the leagues do not focus on a specific economic group, such as employers; instead they contend with government officials and with representatives of a variety of national and international agencies.

1. *Organization Growth*

Precursors to both organization types may be found in the mutual aid societies of the late nineteenth century and in the labor agitation of the 1920's. The first *campesino* associations to receive legal recognition were apparently league-like, rather than labor, organizations, but little is known about their numbers or activities.

Following the revolution, *sindicatos* and leagues proliferated; but in 1954 the counterrevolution choked off that growth and systematically all but eliminated existing organizations. They only began to reappear in significant numbers in 1964.

The limited available data suggest that the Sociedades de Agricultores that existed with legal personality from the time of Barrios (1871–1885) were upper-sector associations designed to provide additional controls to the labor-generating legislation of that period. The 1920's saw the real birth of lower-sector organizations, both in the cities and, on a far more limited scale, in the countryside. Presumably as a reward for the urban workers' role in the overthrow of the dictator Estrada Cabrera, constitutional amendments dealing with workers' rights were published on March 11, 1921. Article 20 was revised to read:

Work is free and should be justly remunerated. Provisions through which individual liberty is lost or human dignity sacrificed are null. Industrial workers and operators are individually and collectively empowered to suspend their work so long as they do not employ coercion or violent or illegal means, or contravene that which is legally stipulated in contracts. . . . The State shall develop instruments of social assistance and solidarity and shall issue legislation concerning the general organization of labor and to guarantee the life and health of the worker.[3]

Thus the state not only recognized the concepts of free contract and the right to strike, but also accepted a protective responsibility for the general welfare of the worker.

At least four league-like associations received juridic personality in the early 1920's. The Sociedad de Empleados de Agricultura de Retalhuleu, recognized in 1921, was followed by the Sociedad de Empleados de Agricultura, Ahorro y Protección Mutua in 1923. This latter organization sought, among other things, to acquire land for distribution to its members at a fair price, to use influence to locate work for members in need, to provide assistance in cases of "sickness, firing, or personal disgrace," and to pursue for its mem-

---

[3] Constitution of 1921 in Kalman Silvert, *A Study in Government: Guatemala*, p. 176. According to Silvert, a new series of amendments in 1927 "virtually wiped out the work which had been done in 1921" (p. 109).

bers "a non-alcoholic development."[4] The Sociedad de Agricultores "Nuevo Progreso" in San Marcos and the Sociedad Rural y Obrera "La Concordia" were recognized in 1924.[5] A fifth organization, the Liga Obrera de Tejutla in San Marcos, was recognized on May 29, 1922, but it has not been possible to ascertain whether it included *campesino* membership.

The decade also witnessed considerable extralegal agitation in the countryside. In a presidential message dated March 1, 1922, General Orellana made reference to an incipient "caste war." Government troops were sent in to repress disturbances in eight "Indian" communities located in five departments: San Pedro Pinula in Jalapa, San Vicente Pacaya and the town of Escuintla in Escuintla, San Agustín Acasaguastlán in El Progreso, Ciudad Vieja and Antigua, Sacatepéquez, and San José del Golfo and Palencia in the department of Guatemala.[6] Chester Lloyd Jones reported that "disputes were constant" on the coffee fincas during this period. *Jefes políticos* persecuted, arrested, and imposed a variety of punishments on the leaders, yet revolts continued to break out that had to be put down with mounted troops. Disturbances were reported in the departments of Sololá, Quezaltenango, and El Quiché, while Suchitepéquez experienced four serious uprisings in 1931 alone.[7] Only with the increasingly effective repressive measures instituted by Jorge Ubico and the added pressure of the world depression did this period come to a close.

DECADE OF REVOLUTION, 1944–1954

Restrictive constitutional amendments published in 1927—which abrogated the prolabor provisions of 1921—and Ubico's persistent repression of competitive associations of whatever kind[8] combined

---

[4] Estatutos (excerpts) in Alfonso Bauer Paiz, *Catalogación de leyes y disposiciones de trabajo de Guatemala del periodo 1872–1930*, p. 49.

[5] Ibid., pp. 50–51.

[6] Presidential Message, March 1, 1922, T. 41, p. 4 in ibid., p. 37.

[7] Chester Lloyd Jones, *Guatemala: Past and Present*, p. 161. Alvarado Monzón also states that in 1930, "an important movement developed among the workers on the coffee fincas in the West and South of the country" (cited in Bauer Paiz, *Catalogación*, p. 37).

[8] Even the conservative Asociación General de Agricultores (AGA) was denied legal status by Ubico (see Chapter 6).

for more than a decade to successfully inhibit *campesino* organization. By 1944 only a few relatively innocuous mutualistic workers'
societies remained in the capital city; but these, nonetheless, provided the initial base for organizational development.

A new constitution[9] was published on March 15, 1945, concur-
rent with the presidential inauguration of Juan José Arévalo. Despite the conciliatory phraseology of several articles, the constitution
did provide a preliminary map of many of the social reforms to follow. Labor was defined as both individual right and social obligation, and vagrancy was declared a punishable offense;[10] no sanctions
were provided for the regulation of that latter evil. Article 32 stated
that "the right of association toward the various ends of human
life" is guaranteed in conformity with those laws regulating "the
right of free organization for exclusive purposes of the socioeconomic protection of employers, private employees, teachers, and
workers in general." The constitution sought to bring all organizations within operating legal structure: "Organizational associations
must secure authorization from competent authority before initiating their activities. This registration will establish the legal personality of the associations" (Article 61). Restrictions were placed on
the organizing process: "Religious societies or groups and their respective members and ministers of cults may not intervene in pol-

[9] The articles cited were extracted from the Constitution of March 15, 1945,
as translated by Kalman Silvert, *A Study in Government*, pp. 207–239.

[10] Vagrancy laws had existed in Guatemala at least since the time of Barrios
(see Bauer Paiz, *Catalogación*, p. 91). In 1934, concomitant with the abolition
of debt peonage, Ubico passed a comprehensive vagrancy law, which then became the primary standard for coercion and control of agricultural labor. That
law defined as vagrants everyone from the man who lacks "profession, position, rentals, salary, occupation or legitimate means of livelihood" to the habitual beggar, the drunkard, anyone convicted of a previous crime, and those
loitering on corners, in the streets, and in "inns, taverns, or billiard halls" after
the required hours of closing. Anyone could denounce a vagrant, and the recent
cessation of employment was not an acceptable excuse beyond a fifteen-day
"period of grace" (Decree # 1996). In 1935 a *reglamento* expanded the definition of vagrancy to require all day laborers (including those who cultivated
some land of their own) to work for wages either 100 or 150 days per year
(from Jorge Skinner-Klée, *Legislación Indigenista de Guatemala*, pp. 110–114
and 118).

itics or in matters related to the organization of labor" (Article 29). "Foreigners are prohibited from intervening in matters related to the organization of workers" (Article 61).

Since no distinction has been made between urban and rural workers, it was assumed that these provisions applied equally to both, and organization continued in the countryside. The Sindicato de Empresa de Trabajadores de la Compañía Agrícola de Guatemala (SET-CAG), the union of agricultural workers on the United Fruit Company plantation at Tiquisate, Escuintla, became, in August, 1944, Guatemala's second labor organization. It was followed shortly by its sister union (SETUFCO) at the United Fruit plantation at Bananera, on the Atlantic coast.[11] Some preliminary organization also occurred on national[12] and private fincas, but on September 27, 1945, a government order required the suspension of "all campaigns for the organization of farm workers into unions pending the issuance of the Labor Code."[13]

The much anticipated code became law on May 1, 1947. Article 206 declared that *sindicatos* might be of "laborers, employers, or persons of independent occupation or profession," and that they must be organized "exclusively for the study, betterment and protection of their respective common economic and social interests." Upon receipt of juridic personality, the *sindicato* was free to contract financial obligations, to acquire goods, to negotiate collective labor contracts, to "create, administer or subsidize institutions, establishments or social works of collective utility for its

[11] Archer C. Bush, "Organized Labor in Guatemala: 1944–49," section II, pp. 22–23.

[12] The national fincas were estates confiscated primarily from German owners according to an F.B.I. blacklist prepared in 1942; the majority were coffee fincas in the departments of Alta Verapaz and Guatemala (ibid., section II p. 43). Bush states (section II, pp. 45–46) that the finca Concepción was organized in 1946; its *sindicato* was legally recognized in the following year (*Registro, Libro* #1, p. 58, Archivo, Departamento Administrativo de Trabajo, Guatemala—hereafter cited as Archivo, DAT, Guatemala).

[13] Edwin Bishop, "The Guatemalan Labor Movement, 1944–59," p. 26. Bishop notes that Víctor Manuel Gutiérrez, later the most powerful labor leader in Guatemala, cautioned his more impatient followers to "go slow" until changes in the legal structure would provide a new framework within which to function.

members, such as cooperatives, and sports, cultural, and educational entities," and in general, to perform "all those activities that do not conflict either with its own essential ends or with the law" (Articles 210 and 214). Involvement in "matters of electoral or party politics" was expressly forbidden (Article 226a).

The provisions delineating the requisites for legal recognition did, however, clearly discriminate against *campesino* labor organizations. Whereas urban *sindicatos* could organize with a minimum of twenty workers over the age of fourteen and only elected officers needed to provide proof of literacy, these conditions were sufficient only for *campesino* organizations founded on farms employing at least five hundred workers. *Sindicatos* of workers on farms employing less than that number could only organize with an initial minimum of fifty members, 60 percent of whom had to provide proof of ability to read and write (Articles 235–238). In 1949, Guatemala could claim twenty-nine agricultural enterprises, other than those of the United Fruit Company, with five hundred or more workers;[14] and in a country where in 1950, 71.9 percent of the national population over seven years of age was illiterate,[15] the universe for organization in the countryside had been legislated almost out of existence. By January, 1948, only eleven *campesino sindicatos* had achieved legal status: those on the United Fruit Company plantations at Tiquisate and Bananera, three organizations on national fincas, and six on fincas privately owned.[16]

An important initial change occurred in June, 1948, when Decree 526 eliminated the discriminatory provisions of the labor code and made the requisite for legal organization uniform for both agricultural and urban workers. The passage of two additional laws signaled a new intervention by the national government in established local and national power relationships. Decree 712 of December 21, 1949, known as the Ley de Arrendamiento Forzoso (Law of Forced Rental), was intended to bring into production lands lying idle on large fincas and also, by fixing maximum rental rates at 5

[14] Bush, "Organized Labor," section II, p. 43, citing Alfonso Bauer Paiz, "El Gobierno de Guatemala y el Conflicto de la United Fruit Company," *El mes económico y financiero* 111 (Feb.–March 1949): 2–3.

[15] Mario Monteforte Toledo, *Guatemala: Monografía sociológica*, p. 609.

[16] Bush, "Organized Labor," section II, p. 43.

percent of the annual crop value, to protect the renter from exploitation by the landlord.[17] In practice, however, the law was not generally applied to idle lands on large estates, but rather to such areas as the Ladino region of eastern Guatemala, where land leasing by medium-sized landholders was more common. As noted by Adams: "The law struck rather at the body of customs involved in the relations between established social classes within a locality and the pattern of labor related to these classes.[18]

In contrast, the Agrarian Reform Law was employed specifically to undermine, through redistribution of the land, the principal power resource of the large landholders. The preamble to this law, approved by the national Congress on June 17, 1952, cited as a consideration in its creation "[that] the laws enacted to assure the forced rental of idle lands have not satisfied fundamentally the most urgent needs of the great majority of the Guatemalan people."[19] The stated purposes of the law included the abolition of a feudal land system and the establishment of new tenurial arrangements—viewed as prerequisites for the rationalization of agricultural production and the promotion of industrialization. The entire reform program was made the immediate responsibility of the president of the republic, and the majority of the newly landed *campesinos* became state tenants in that they received lifetime use of the land rather than actual property rights.[20] The role of the national government as landlord was greatly expanded.

Given the changing local power relationships and the new role of the national government relative to the *campesino,* lower-sector pressure organizations proliferated. Whereas in the period June, 1944, through June, 1948, only 23 *campesino sindicatos* received juridic personality—all obviously having received such recognition after publication of the labor code in May, 1947—by February, 1950, that number had increased to 96. In the final four years of the decade, 249 *sindicatos* were recognized, bringing the total as of

[17] Richard N. Adams, *Encuesta sobre la cultura de los ladinos en Guatemala,* p. 71; cf. Nathan L. Whetten, *Guatemala: The Land and the People,* p. 153.

[18] Adams, *Encuesta,* p. 71.

[19] *Ley de reforma agraria, Decreto número 900,* Guatemala, 1952, p. 4, cited in Whetten, *Guatemala,* p. 153.

[20] For the complete discussion of the agrarian reform program from which these comments were drawn, see Whetten, *Guatemala,* pp. 152–163.

May 18, 1954, to 345 organizations. This total included 26 so-called *sindicatos* (actually *campesino* leagues in the terminology of this paper) of independent agriculturalists—small-scale farmers not directly dependent on a *patrón*. The remaining 319 organizations were all *sindicatos* of finca workers.[21] Some were probably nominal or paper entities and others may well have ceased to function before the counterrevolution of 1954.[22] However, it is also probable that additional solicitations for legal recognition were still in process.

The revolutionary period also witnessed the appearance of *uniones campesinas*, predecessors of the contemporary leagues. The *uniones* multiplied more slowly than *sindicatos*, perhaps in part because (1) there had been no legislation dealing specifically with their formation, and (2) in this period of experimentation, it may not have been initially clear what ends they might serve. The 1947 labor code stated that *sindicatos* might be of "persons of independent occupation or profession," as well as of workers responsible to an employer, and of the employers themselves. Presumably, it was under the former provision that the twenty-six *"sindicatos"* of independent agriculturalists (mentioned above) had received juridic personality. Only one of these, the Sindicato de Campesinos de Antigua Guatemala, was recognized prior to 1950, and eighteen of the twenty-six received that recognition after February, 1953.[23]

A far larger number of similar organizations, specifically called *uniones* rather than *sindicatos*, were approved and recognized by the ministry of government, not by the ministry of economy and labor—an implicit acknowledgment, it would seem, of their distinctive orientation.[24] The first 5 *uniones* were founded in Chiquimula in 1948, and between 1950 and 1953, 315 additional organizations

[21] These figures represent combined tabulations from the *Libro de Sindicatos no reorganizados*, Archivo, DAT, Guatemala, and from the *expedientes* on *sindicatos* presently reorganized, Archivo, DAT, Guatemala.

[22] Cf. Bush, "Organized Labor," section II, p. 54; and Bishop, "Guatemalan Labor Movement," p. 77.

[23] Archivo, DAT, Guatemala.

[24] The rationale behind the inconsistent approval of twenty-six organizations under the Labor Code and of the rest as specifically nonlabor associations is not clear; it may only reflect the general inexperience of all government agencies in dealing with the new organization forms.

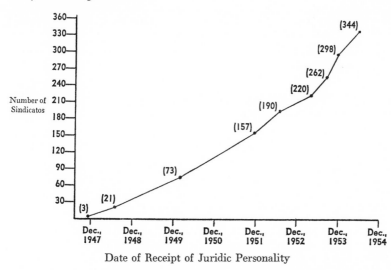

FIGURE 9–1. Campesino Sindicatos with Juridic Personality, 1947–1954

NOTE: Based on 344 *campesino sindicatos* that received juridic personality during the revolutionary period. One additional organization (for which I have no data) received legal recognition during this period, bringing the total to 345. Compiled by the author from the *Libro de sindicatos no-reorganizados* and individual *expedientes* on reorganized sindicatos. Archivo, Departamento Administrativo de Trabajo, Guatemala.

received juridic personality. The rate of recognition, as was the case with *campesino sindicatos,* increased late in Arevalo's term of office, then accelerated markedly with the election of Arbenz.

Arbenz also promoted the development of local agrarian committees. According to the law of 1952, the functions of reform were to be carried out by a nine-member National Agrarian Council appointed by the president, by departmental committees in all departments but El Petén, and by local agrarian committees on the *municipio* or *aldea* level.[25] The local committee ordinarily initiated expropriation proceedings, although anyone could denounce, before the committee, land that he considered liable for expropriation. By law the committees were to be organized so that already exist-

[25] Whetten, *Guatemala*, pp. 156–160.

TABLE 9-1

Uniones Campesinas with Juridic Personality, 1948–1954

Year of Receipt of Juridic Personality	1948	1949	1950	1951	1952	1953	1954	Total
Number of organizations	5	0	55	100	80	80	0	320

SOURCE: Figures compiled by the author from the *Libro de registro, Ministerio de Gobernación,* Guatemala.

NOTE: The lack of entries for 1949 or for the first six months of 1954 remains unexplained. The official now responsible for the processing of juridic personalities in the Ministry of Government told this writer that a number of applications for legal recognition, both ministry approved and in process, were awaiting presidential approval at the time of the Castillo victory in 1954.

Neale J. Pearson ("The Confederación Nacional Campesina de Guatemala (CNCG) and Peasant Unionism in Guatemala 1944–54," M.A. thesis, George-town University, 1964, p. 41) has estimated that 1,500 organizations pertained to the CNCG in June, 1954. The estimate was based on an undated *Nomina de Personerias Tramitadas de los Departamentos* listing 1,541 "unions" that Pearson claimed "had been given legal status."

While the present writer did not have access to this document, Pearson's citation raises two points of possible confusion: (1) the Spanish verb *tramitar,* in the sense used, means "to process" rather than "to approve," and (2) Pearson uses the English word "union" to denote an organization type distinct from *sindicato* (when, in fact, the English "union" most closely translates *sindicato*). It is not clear whether Pearson's Nomina listed all applications (i.e., those for unions—meaning *sindicatos*—as well as for *uniones*), approved and in process, or just those for *uniones.* The total number of *sindicatos* canceled or suspended in 1954 was 533 (Bishop, *Guatemalan Labor Movement,* p. 169), and only 320 juridic personalities are now recorded for *uniones;* thus the discrepancy between the Pearson figure and that now officially recorded for both organization types (granting even the widest margin for growth in numbers of *uniones* in the first six months of 1954) remains very large.

ing *campesino* organizations (primarily the *sindicatos* and *uniones campesinas*) would have a determining vote in the proceedings. Each local committee was to number five members: one chosen by the departmental governor, one by the mayor of the *municipio,* and three by the local *campesino* association or *sindicato.*[26] Thus, by establishing a legal tie between organization and the promotion of the redistribution of the land, the Agrarian Reform Law reinforced participation in *sindicatos* and *campesino* leagues.

[26] Ibid.

POSTREVOLUTION

With the counterrevolution of Castillo Armas, organization growth was choked off almost immediately. On July 16, 1954, the Junta de Gobierno (headed by Castillo) published Decree #21, which stated that: "The infiltration of persons of communist tendencies is evident in the directive organism of the urban and campesino sindicatos, whose only objective ought to be the protection of the workers." Hence the decree declared that all representatives of the workers must be "totally apolitical and noncommunist" and canceled the inscription of officers of all "confederations, federations, and *sindicatos* of urban and *campesino* workers." If new officers acceptable to the regime were not elected within three months,[27] the juridic personalities of these organizations would automatically be voided. Two weeks later, a *disposición* for the implementation of Decree #21 declared that any organization seeking official recognition must submit a list of twenty names to the Departamento Administrativo de Trabajo (DAT). The lists were then passed to the Comité de Defensa Nacional Contra el Comunismo, which checked its burgeoning blacklist to preclude the reemergence of undesirable elements. Once approved, the list was returned to the DAT, which then selected three *sindicato* members to be responsible for the calling of a general assembly and for the election of new officers.

A second decree (#48) was applied only to those organizations considered most blatantly Communistic, and under its application, juridic personalities were declared permanently dissolved. It is not known exactly how many[28] organizations fell victim to Decree #48, but that number evidently included no local *campesino* organiza-

---

[27] This time allowance was extended three months by Decree #120, on October 22, 1954; an additional two months by Article 217 (January 28, 1955); then further by Decrees 261, 380, and 521. In the end, no juridic personalities were voided under the original decree, and unless specifically canceled by the later Decree #48, all are still viable, whether the organizations themselves actually exist or not.

[28] A list currently available at the DAT cites less than a dozen organizations "permanently dissolved," but included on the list is SAMF, the railroad workers' union, which in fact reorganized almost immediately after the counterrevolution.

tions. While the de jure viability of individual organizations continued as before, the Castillo rulings effected the de facto death of almost all local organizations in the countryside.

Chapter 5 of the 1956 constitution further revised the official labor policy. Article 116 stated that "the law will regulate [the right of association] according to the nature of the means *and to the differences between the situations of the rural and urban worker or patrón"* (emphasis added). In February, 1955, Decree #217 reintroduced the 1947 restrictions on rural organization in their original form.[29] Articles 236–238 again required that *campesino* organizations have fifty initial members, 60 percent of whom were to be literate (while that literacy ratio was to remain constant with membership growth and was to be subject to annual verification), and only on agricultural enterprises with more than five hundred employees could workers organize under the more lenient provisions applicable to urban *sindicatos* (that is, a minimum of twenty initial members, literacy required only for elected officers, and no restrictions based on size of enterprise). Article 207 was subsequently amended to include the statement that "sindicatos and their directors, as such, may not engage in politics."[30]

From 1954 through 1961, only seven *sindicatos* of finca workers successfully reorganized, and one new organization received juridic personality. On August 16, 1961, Decree #1441 superseded the original labor code and, just as had occurred in 1948, declared the provisions discriminatory to *campesino* organizations *derogado* (void). The Ydígoras administration (1959–1963) was, however, only slightly more amenable to lower-sector organizations than had been that of Castillo Armas, and few were recognized. Despite reports of some initial repression, it was the Peralta military regime (1963–1966) that permitted a moderate redevelopment of the *campesino* movement—a redevelopment that accelerated with the election of Méndez Montenegro. Whereas only twenty-four *sindicatos* of finca workers received legal recognition in the decade subsequent to the Castillo counterrevolution, forty-two organizations were recognized in the two years 1966–1967.

Of the 66 operating *sindicatos* with juridic personality as of Janu-

[29] Bishop, "Guatemalan Labor Movement," p. 170.
[30] Decreto #570, February 28, 1956.

ary 31, 1968, only 18 were new organizations. The remaining 48 were reorganized under juridic personalities granted during the revolutionary period.[31] In weighing this regrowth it is important to remember that 345 *campesino sindicatos* had received legal recognition in the revolutionary period. Since apparently none of these suffered de jure cancellation, it may be assumed that 297 *sindicatos* (86.3 percent of the total) still retain valid juridic personalities but lack organization and officers.

Uniones campesinas, the nonlabor community organizations, were also thoroughly repressed by the Castillo government. At the time of the study, none had reappeared with legal personality. However, in December, 1962, some fifty *campesinos* from the *municipio* of San Pedro Ayampuc in the department of Guatemala met to form an association called a *liga campesina*, but identical in nature to the earlier *unión*. The initiative for organization came from the Christian Democratic party (then in the process of building new power bases within the lower sector). The league was named El Carrizal and on August 23, 1963, it received juridic personality. The grant of legal recognition was made under the labor code in 1961. Yet this change in legal status from nonlabor *unión* to specifically "labor league" (indicated by a shift in the locus of approval from the Ministry of Government to the Ministry of Labor) was accompanied by no change in the organizational form. Two leagues received juridic personality in 1964 and three more in 1965; grants of legal recognition accelerated to thirteen in 1966 and by January of 1968 there were twenty-seven organizations with juridic personality.[32]

In the revolutionary period, the passage of laws promoting the forced rental of idle lands and the redistribution of large holdings, in combination with the 1948 labor code revisions, precipitated the breakdown of established *patrón-mozo* relationships in the countryside. The new laws undermined the pattern of control of land and labor, the power base of the landed oligarchy, and opened legal

[31] Figures compiled by the author from individual *expedientes*, Archivo, DAT, Guatemala. As of January 31, 1968, there were fifteen *campesino sindicatos* whose juridic personalities remained in process either at the DAT or at the Ministry of Labor; all but five of these had been in process for more than one full year, and there was no indication when they would be approved.

[32] From individual *expedientes*, Archivo, DAT, Guatemala.

TABLE 9–2
Campesino Organizations With Juridic Personality, 1920–1967

	Sindicatos	Leagues	Total
Prerevolution	—	[5]	[5]
Revolution	345	320	665
Postrevolution	66	27	93

NOTE: The present study has not attempted to explore the prerevolutionary period in detail; the figures for this period are probably incorrect.

channels for direct manipulation, by the national government, of local power relationships. The victory of Castillo Armas, on the other hand, presaged a rebuilding of the power position of the large land-holder, in part (as is discussed in Chapter 6) through the promotion of upper-sector interest groups. Of the postrevolutionary governments, at least the first three apparently viewed *campesino* organizations as a power threat, rather than resource, and thus maintained legislation discriminatory to their reappearance. Government support for the 1961 labor code has only recently, and only temporarily, included support for organization regrowth; and, as will be discussed below, regrowth has occurred in an environment very different from that of the revolutionary period.

2. *Local and Parent Organizations*

Local *campesino* organizations have seldom operated without an affiliation to a larger unit, and then generally only when in transition from one to another. The larger entities have been relied on for procedural advice, for the provision of lawyers, for technical assistance (in such things as book- and record-keeping) and for a variety of other skills. Prior to the 1944 revolution, it is unlikely that *campesino* organizations (or their leadership) played any but a very subordinate role in the national federations, for rural associations were few in number and could claim no experience in the exercise of pressure. The national federations themselves were, however, already clearly aligned with representatives of competing international ideologies—thus participating early in a power structure extending beyond the national boundaries.

IDEOLOGY AND THE INTERNATIONAL CENTRALS

The first supralocal pressure organization in Guatemala, the Federación de Sociedades Obreras, was founded in 1912 and two years later became the Federación Obrera para la Protección Legal de Trabajo.[33] It subsequently affiliated with the Pan American Federation of Labor,[34] an international central founded in 1918 under the joint sponsorship of the American Federation of Labor (AFL) and the Confederación Regional Obrero Mexicana (CROM). This international central was dominated by representatives from the United States: of the seventy-six delegates to the initial convention, forty-six represented U.S. organizations, twenty-one were from Mexico, and the remaining five from Guatemala, El Salvador, Costa Rica, and Colombia.[35] Samuel Gompers of the AFL was elected federation president.

In opposition to this U.S. influence, the 1920's also witnessed the emergence of a Communist-oriented labor leadership. The Unificación Obrera Socialista, founded in 1921 as the Unificación Obrera, was abolished by the coup d'état of Generals Orellana, Larrave and Lima, but some of its leaders regrouped to found the Partido Comunista de Centro América: Sección Guatemala in 1922.[36] In 1924 the Guatemalan Communist party was recognized by the Comintern;[37] and the periodical *Vanguardia Proletaria* began promoting labor agitation in 1925.[38] Under Communist leadership, the Federación Regional de Trabajadores de Guatemala (FRTG) was founded in 1926 to pressure for the rescinding of Decree #914, which had voided the right to strike. The FRTG became an affiliate of the Third International,[39] and in 1929 sent two delegates to a Pan-Latin American conference in Montevideo, at which the Con-

---

[33] Victor Alba, *Politics and the Labor Movement in Latin America*, p. 283.

[34] Bush, "Organized Labor," section III, p. 2.

[35] Alba, *Politics and the Labor Movement*, p. 319.

[36] Antonio Obando Sánchez cited in Bauer Paiz, *Catalogación*, p. 37. The current writer was unsuccessful in locating a copy of the Obando Sánchez study, although its existence was confirmed by a member of the U.S. embassy in Guatemala.

[37] Robert Alexander, *Communism in Latin America*, p. 351.

[38] Alvarado Monzon in Bauer Paiz, *Catalogación*, p. 36.

[39] Bush, "Organized Labor," section III, p. 2.

federación Sindical de Trabajadores de América Latina was founded (see Table 9–3). In the following year, Antonio Obando Sánchez, a leader of the Guatemalan Communist party, traveled to Moscow for the Fifth Congress of the Internacional Sindical Roja, and upon his return was imprisoned by Ubico, not to be released until the revolution of 1944.[40]

Immediately following the revolution, new local and supralocal organizations began to appear, and the ideological bifurcation of the postwar world increasingly shaped their development. On December 15, 1944, the Confederación de Trabajadores de Guatemala (CTG) was founded with Gumercindo Tejada as secretary general.[41] The Confederación de Trabajadores de América Latina (CTAL), Communist-led affiliate of the World Federation of Trade Unions (WFTU), sent representatives to Guatemala in 1945, and the Cuban Angel Cofiño began to promote CTG affiliation with CTAL. He met substantial resistance in this effort from Gumercindo Tejada, but in late 1945, Tejada was removed from the top post.[42]

At the same time, Antonio Obando Sánchez used his new freedom to promote the foundation of a Communist ideological training school, the Escuela Claridad.[43] A segment of the labor leadership strongly opposed the representation of the Escuela Claridad on the CTG executive committee[44] and in January, 1945, ten *sindicatos* that had withdrawn from the CTG over this question joined five unaffiliated organizations to found the Federación Sindical de Guatemala (FSG). This left the CTG with the teachers' union, a number of considerably weaker urban unions, and an amorphous group of unstable rural organizations.[45] According to Schneider: "until the middle of 1950, the FSG was more important and influential than the CTG."[46]

---

[40] Bauer Paiz, *Catalogación*, p. 37; Bishop, "Guatemalan Labor Movement," p. 15.

[41] Ronald M. Schneider, *Communism in Guatemala: 1944–1954*, p. 215.

[42] Ibid.

[43] Bishop, "Guatemalan Labor Movement," p. 17.

[44] Schneider, *Communism in Guatemala*, p. 12.

[45] Ibid.; Bush, "Organized Labor," section III, p. 6; Bishop, "Guatemalan Labor Movement," p. 17.

[46] Schneider, *Communism in Guatemala*, p. 129; Bush, Organized Labor," section III, p. 5.

CTAL representatives, including Cofiño, argued for unification, but the question of ideology continued to provide a focus for factional dissension. In 1950, when the FSG federated with CTAL and WFTU, the FSG's strongest member organization[47] expelled its top officer (who was then head of the federation as well) and renounced its FSG affiliation. A year later, in August, 1951, the much weakened FSG merged with its progenitor, the CTG.

In the same year, CTAL and WFTU sponsored a Conference of Transportation Workers' Unions of Latin America, at which international Communist leaders (including Louis Saillant, head of the WFTU) met with Guatemalan labor leaders. A Unity Congress was planned for October 12–14, 1951, and on those dates, the Confederación General de Trabajadores de Guatemala (CGTG) was founded, with Víctor Manuel Gutiérrez, the radical urban organizer, elected to the top post.[48]

Four months after the conference, ideological conflicts caused a split within the CGTG.[49] Leaders of two member federations withdrew with all their organizations. The agricultural *sindicato* SET-CAG, allegedly angered by a lack of support from the CGTG in a dispute with the United Fruit Company, was "on the verge" of leaving; and four members of its executive committee publicly charged that the CGTG was trying to undermine SET-CAG because "they had been unable to plant seeds of Communism in its ranks."[50] The splinter group tried to build an independent anti-Communist national federation, but their principal leader was alleged to have regularly exploited his position for personal gain and hence was discredited by the ascetic Gutiérrez.[51]

From this point until the Castillo counterrevolution, the CGTG dominated all labor organizations,[52] while the nonlabor *uniones campesinas* were united from 1950 under the Confederación Na-

---

[47] SAMF, the railroad workers' union.

[48] From Schneider, *Communism in Guatemala*, pp. 138–194.

[49] Pearson, "Confederación," p. 147.

[50] Schneider, *Communism in Guatemala*, p. 144.

[51] Pearson, "Confederación," p. 147.

[52] Daniel James (*Red Design for the Americans: Guatemalan Prelude*, p. 122) has stated that one additional "vigorously anti-Communist" labor organization, called the Unión Nacional de Trabajadores Libres (UNTL), was founded in late 1953, but was soon repressed by the Arbenz government.

cional Campesina de Guatemala (CNCG).[53] Founded by Leonardo Castillo Flores and two other former members of the CTG, the CNCG operated, until late 1953, in an organizational and political orbit distinct from that of the CGTG. It did not attempt to compete directly in the organization of finca workers, but instead concentrated on independent agriculturalists.[54] In August, 1953, the CGTG voted affiliation with CTAL and WFTU, and shortly the CNCG executive committee voted to seek the same affiliation. From this point the two centrals (incorporating virtually all lower-sector organizations in the country) became indistinguishable, and they began issuing joint statements on national and international questions.[55] Within Guatemala, the supralocal organizational structure had become monolithic.

Meanwhile, CTAL continued to send representatives to Guatemala, and Vicente Lombardo Toledano, CTAL director, maintained close ties with Guatemalan labor leaders. Víctor Manuel Gutiérrez the CGTG was elected to the central committee of CTAL in 1948 and in the following year was named an alternate member of the WFTU central committee.[56] Trips to Moscow by Guatemalan leaders, including both Gutiérrez and Castillo Flores, helped solidify international Communist influence within the CGTG-CNCG.[57]

During the revolutionary period, influences from the non-Communist world were considerably less significant. In late 1948, three officers of the FSG were invited to Argentina, perhaps as the first step in an unsuccessful attempt by Perón to establish a Latin American labor federation under Argentine direction. Two other leaders traveled to Israel, in the summer of 1949, as the guests of Histadruth, the Israeli labor federation, where they remained for approximately one month; and in the fall of the same year, Israeli workers sent financial aid for use in rehabilitation of flood-stricken regions of Guatemala. U.S. organizations played almost no role at all. The AFL consistently opposed CTAL and in 1947, Serafino Ro-

---

[53] For the history and growth of this organization see Pearson, "Confederación," p. 147.

[54] Ibid., p. 40.

[55] Schneider, *Communism in Guatemala*, p. 165.

[56] Bush, "Organized Labor," section IV, p. 28.

[57] Schneider, *Communism in Guatemala*, pass.

mualdi, AFL representative for Latin America, visited Guatemala
in an unsuccessful attempt to enlist local cooperation in the formation of a competitive inter-American labor confederation.[58] The AFL
sponsored Confederación Interamericana de Trabajadores (CIT)
established no following in Guatemala and, like its predecessor, the
Pan American Federation of Labor, was criticized as an AFL pawn
"playing the game of the United States State Department."[59] The
CIO, however, did establish some measure of cooperation; the secretary general of the FSG visited the United States in 1949 and successfully enlisted CIO aid in the conflicts with the United Fruit Company.[60]

In the subsequent period, the situation has been reversed. Communist inputs have been all but eliminated, and the U.S. government and its representative agencies have successfully dominated
much of the organizational framework above the local level. That
domination has been achieved not in a context of open competition
but rather through manipulation by a superior power of the elements within its domain. Since 1954 there have appeared four
principal national federations, each of which includes *campesino*
member organizations:

   (1) Federación Autónoma Sindical Guatemalteca (FASGUA)
   (2) Confederación Sindical de Guatemala (CONSIGUA)
   (3) Confederación de Trabajadores de Guatemala
       (CONTRAGUA)
   (4) Federación Central de Trabajadores de Guatemala–
       Federación Campesina de Guatemala (FECETRAG–FCG)

The FASGUA grew out of an organization founded by Castillo
Armas in 1955, the Federación Autónoma Sindical (FAS). It pro-
claimed on its letterhead to be "apolitical and of a social Christian
ideological orientation"; yet the Guatemalan press reported that

[58] Bush, "Organized Labor," section IV, p. 34.

[59] Bishop, "Guatemalan Labor Movement," p. 29.

[60] Bush, "Organized Labor," section IV, p. 30. There seems to be little evidence that U.S. labor organizations received direction from the U.S. government. Serafino Romualdi noted (Pearson, *Confederación*, p. 21) that during the
revolutionary period, AFL organizers were neither supported by nor welcome
in the U.S. Embassy in Guatemala; and a permanent labor attaché was not
assigned to Guatemala until after the counterrevolution (ibid., p. 96).

TABLE 9–3
Summary of International Centrals and
Guatemalan Member Federations

Period	U.S.-Oriented Organizations	Socialist-Oriented Organizations	Others
Prerevolution			
a. *1920–1930* (relatively open competition)	*Pan-Amer. Fed. of Labor* Fed. Obrera— grew out of Fed. de Sociedades Obreras	*Confed. Sindical de Trabajadores de Amer. Latina* Fed. Regional de Trabaja- dores de Guate. (FRTG)—grew out of Unifi- cación Obrera)	
b. *1931–1944*		Ubico suppresses all organizations	
Revolution			
a. *1945–1950* (open competition)	Romualdi of A.F. of L. and CIT in Guate.; CIO con- tacts with the Fed. Sindical de Guate. (FSG)	*CTAL-WFTU* Confed. de Trabajadores de Guate. (CTG)	Fed. Sin- dical de Guate. (FSG)—no internat'l affiliation
b. *1951–1954* (Arbenz adopts anti-U.S. position)		*CTAL-WFTU* Confed. General de Trabajadores de Guate./Con- fed. Nacional Campesina de Guate. (CGTG/ CNCG)	
Postrevolution			
1955–1967 ("Communism" outlawed)	*ORIT-ICFTU* Confed. Sindical Guatemalteca (CONSIGUA) Confed. de Trabajadores de Guate. (CON- TRAGUA)—no internat'l affiliation but strong ties with U.S. agencies and programs	Fed. Autonóma Sindical Guatemalteca (FASGUA)	*CISC-CLASC-FCL* Fed. Cen- tral de Trabaja- dores de Guate.—Fed. Campesina de Guate. (FECETRAG-FCG)

Castillo was paying FAS leaders as much as $300 per month in salary.[61] Whether or not the report is true in detail, this federation's subordination to the national government is suggested by the organizational stagnation during the Castillo regime. The FAS leadership was, nonetheless, gradually taken over by more leftist leaders, and on March 6, 1957, FAS officers applied to the DAT for recognition of a new legal personality under the name Federación Autónoma Sindical Guatemalteca (FASGUA). A FASGUA official told this writer in the summer of 1967 that his organization was the direct heir of the CGTG and the CNCG of the revolutionary period, and noted the life-size photographs of Gutiérrez and Castillo Flores that decorate the rostrum of the FASGUA conference hall. While FASGUA leaders deny the oft-repeated charge of ties to national or international Communist movements, they continue to suffer a repression predicated on the alleged affiliations.

The CONSIGUA began some rather limited activity in 1955 under the name Consejo Sindical de Guatemala (CSG). From 1955 through 1965 it had no juridic personality, but its development was promoted by the Organización Regional Interamericano de Trabajadores (ORIT), the Western Hemisphere affiliate of the International Confederation of Free Trade Unions (ICTU). The ORIT is strongly based in the AFL-CIO labor combine, and the CSG early received the active assistance of Serafino Romualdi, and of Andrew McClellan, an American officer of ORIT assigned to the Central American region.[62] Bishop has also suggested that ORIT may provide financial aid, but the CSG has consistently denied this.[63]

An important change in the supralocal organizational structure occurred in 1962 when the Christian Democratic party undertook the active promotion of *campesino* organizations. Early leadership was provided by a worker who split with the Federación "Textil," a CONSIGUA affiliate, to found the Federación Central de Trabajadores de Guatemala (FECETRAG). This organization then sub-

---

[61] Bishop, "Guatemalan Labor Movement," p. 187.

[62] Ibid., p. 191.

[63] Ibid. In January, 1968, an official of the U.S. Embassy in Guatemala told this writer that funds very probably still reach the CSG (now CONSIGUA) via ORIT channels, although the amounts are probably small.

divided into FECETRAG (urban *sindicatos*) and the Federación
Campesina de Guatemala (FCG), the latter composed exclusively
of *campesino* member organizations. The FECETRAG-FCG is advised by IDESAC,[64] the Christian Democratic coordinating body
for Central America, and is an affiliate of the Christian Democratic
international entities, the Federación Campesina Latinoamericana
(FCL) and the Confederación Latinoamericana de Sindicalistas
Cristianos (CLASC). The FCL is the *campesino* subdivision of
CLASC; the latter was founded in 1954 to provide an independent
alternative to the U.S.-based ORIT and the pro-Communist CTAL.[65]
CLASC is, in turn, affiliated with the European-based Confederación
Internacional de Sindicatos Cristianos (CISC). Financial aid is pro-
vided, through IDESAC, to the FECETRAG-FCG by the German
bishops' fund, Miserior.[66]

The fourth central organization, CONTRAGUA, claims no international affiliation. Its officers include several men with (non-
Communist) organizational experience dating back to the revolutionary period, and the CONTRAGUA newspaper makes frequent
reference to the "democratic" orientation of its leadership. The
CONTRAGUA is currently the most favored central, both in dealings with the national government and in its relations with U.S.
agencies in Guatemala.

LEADERSHIP AND LOCAL AUTONOMY

In each of the three historical periods, the influence of extranational entities has been supported through the presence of foreign
"advisers." In the late 1920's, Juan Pablo Wainwright (an American native of Honduras) disseminated Communist literature in
Guatemala and aided in the foundation of the Salvadorean Communist movement prior to 1930.[67] In 1931 he was arrested and exe-

[64] Instituto de Desarrollo Económico y Social de Centro América headed by
Lic. René de León Schlotter, a long-time Christian Democratic Leader.

[65] Alba, *Politics and the Labor Movement*, p. 189.

[66] At the time of the study, the FCG had used Miserior funds to purchase office space and operating equipment and to pay the salaries of three *campesino*
organizers (at seventy-five dollars per man per month).

[67] Alba, *Politics and the Labor Movement*, p. 109.

cuted by Jorge Ubico.[68] In the subsequent period, Obando Sánchez received assistance in the formation of the Escuela Claridad from Virgilio Guerra, a Guatemalan long in exile in El Salvador and Costa Rica, and from Miguel Mármol, the Salvadorean reputed to be a member of the Communist party active in the 1932 uprising, and like Obando Sánchez, a long-time resident of the Ubico prisons.[69] CTAL leaders arrived in Guatemala within two months of the October revolution, and Angel Cofiño (who also sat on the administrative committee of the parent WFTU) began playing a major role as early as June, 1945.[70] CTAL figures Juan Vargas Puebla and César Godoy Urrutia, both Chilean deputies, plus Roberto Moreno of Brazil and Vicente Saenz of Costa Rica all made advisory visits.[71] And, as we have already noted, Lombardo Toledano continued to make periodic visits, while Gutiérrez and Castillo Flores were courted directly by Moscow.

With the advent of the counterrevolution, Moscow-oriented advisers were displaced, and U.S. organizers began to play a more important role. We have mentioned the frequent presence in Guatemala of Serafino Romualdi and of Andrew McClellan of ORIT, and later we will discuss the specific activities of U.S. agencies concerned with direction of the lower-sector movement.

Native leadership of the supralocal entities has, in each period, originated in the capital city, and, until recently, few *campesinos* had risen to positions of prominence. Some exceptions, such as CNCG leader Amor Velasco de León,[72] did occur during the revolutionary period, and a local *campesino* leadership had begun to emerge on the United Fruit Company plantations and on a few large south coastal fincas at the time of the counterrevolution. How-

---

[68] Alexander, *Communism in Latin America*, p.353; cf. Schneider, *Communism in Guatemala*, p. 56.

[69] Bush, "Organized Labor," section III, p.3; Bishop, "Guatemalan Labor Movement," p.17, has stated that the Escuela Claridad teaching staff also included "various Nicaraguan . . . refugees."

[70] See Bishop, "Guatemalan Labor Movement," pp. 14–16.

[71] Bush, "Organized Labor," section IV, p. 39.

[72] Pearson, "Confederación," p. 37 states that Velasco de León was "apparently of a peasant background [and] became a self-taught peasant intellectual and spokesman" for organizations in Castillo Flores' home base, Chiquimula.

ever, the post-1954 repression eliminated (by putting to flight or death) leaders at all levels and made lower-sector association almost synonymous with "communism"—and thus unallowable.

The regrowth of a native *campesino* leadership has been tortuous, and urban leadership has dominated the federations and confederations. The CONSIGUA was led for more than a decade by a one-time congressional deputy (just as both the CGTG and the CNCG had been led by Deputies Gutiérrez and Castillo Flores) who held, concurrently, the top offices in his own *sindicato*, in the federation to which the *sindicato* was affiliated, and in the multifederation CONSIGUA. The national federation CONTRAGUA grew out of a conflict between this deputy and upper-sector colleagues who sought unsuccessfully to remove him from CONSIGUA's top post in 1964; these same upper-sector figures now dominate CONTRAGUA's activities.[73]

Both CONSIGUA and the FECETRAG-FCG have mobilized votes for urban politicians. The FECETRAG-FCG forms an integral part of the Christian Democratic "social promotion" nexus (headed by IDESAC and René de León Schlotter), and at least two of the original FCG officers, including the secretary general, were former party representatives in their local communities. While the Christian Democratic party now admits no formal ties with the Catholic church, of the three men who have held top office in the FCG, all came out of leadership experience in the Juventud Obrera Católica, while leaders of FCG-affiliated organizations in El Quiché had been catechists for Acción Católica Rural. (It is also interesting to note that two of those three top leaders of the FCG came originally from the *municipio* of San Pedro Ayampuc, the home of the auxiliary bishop responsible for national coordination of Acción Católica Rural.)

This does not mean, however, that the federations have operated solely as devices for the enhancement of upper-sector power control. On the contrary, in 1967 CONSIGUA member organizations ousted

---

[73] Because the FASGUA was so pressured at the time of the study, it was not possible to gather information on the background of its national leaders. However, its activity in *campesino* organization had been negligible prior to 1966 (and even then unsuccessful) and it is unlikely that *campesinos* provide any direct leadership.

the congressional deputy from that confederation's top office and re-placed him with an agricultural laborer whose organizing experi-ence dates back to the 1940's and the strikes on the United Fruit Company plantation at Tiquisate.

Furthermore, with the FCG, former *campesinos* have reached positions of some power, due both to support from upper-sector ad-visers and to their capacity to command the personal allegiance of local organizations. Two former *campesinos* gained, in five years of activity, international positions within the Federación Campesina Latinoamericana, and one became the FCL's chief propagandist, writing news stories and pamphlets on organization. This man also participated in international conventions held by CLASC, and his colleague attended a CISC conference in Rome. When, in 1967, these men (in company with two Mexican leaders) were accused of misappropriation of some $40,000 in funds belonging to a Mex-ican federation and to the FCL, they withdrew from the Guatemalan FCG and established the Movimiento Campesino Independiente (MCI).

This action led to an intense period of accusation and counter-charge between the FCG leaders and their former colleagues in the MCI. It also pointed up the importance of two secondary leaders from indigenous regions. The latter two men had founded a series of organizations in communities near their homes and could each command a personal following. Both were fluent in the indigenous languages of their regions as well as in Spanish, and, while neither could claim organizational experience, they had the advantage of being able to communicate with potential membership from the regions in question. They thus became foci in the power struggle—positions of which both were fully aware. One of them first left the FCG to join friends in the MCI, but, on becoming suspicious of the MCI leadership, returned with all his organizations to the FCG; the second also went to the MCI and has since joined that federation in affiliating with CONTRAGUA.

While many local *campesino* organizations can claim little power beyond that provided through membership in the national fed-erations, that has not been uniformly the case. In the revolutionary period, SET-CAG on the United Fruit plantation at Tiquisate exer-cised considerable independence of action and, as we have already described, threatened to disrupt the hegemony of the CGTG's control in 1953. Two regional federations, [74] composed mainly of *campesino* member organizations, appeared on the south coast in the first phase of this period and each apparently remained independent of the larger national federations until the formation of the CGTG in 1951.[75] (Other regional federations appeared in virtually every department in Guatemala but these were administrative subdivisions of the CTG or the CGTG-CNCG and enjoyed little independent life.) As we have noted, the CNCG itself grew out of a split within the CTG, and for a short time provided *campesinos* with an independent national pressure organization.

In the postrevolutionary period, the *sindicatos* on the large plantations of the central south coast—El Salto and El Baul especially, but also including Mirandilla, Palo Gordo, and others—have exercised a considerable amount of local autonomy. El Salto and El Baul provided the leadership for the regional federation, FENSIL, and with the 1967 decision of the FENSIL directive board to affiliate to CONSIGUA, El Baul led several local *sindicatos* out of FENSIL and into CONTRAGUA (where strong interpersonal ties had existed from the mid-1950's when El Baul and El Salto had both pertained to the original CSG). SETUFCO, the 2,500-member *sindicato* at Bananera, has continued since the revolutionary period to operate with little dependence on the national unit, due perhaps in part to the experience of its leadership. SETUFCO dominates the regional federation in Morales and with the election of its man, Cándido González, to the top office in CONSIGUA, it can claim an important voice at the national level. Both El Salto[76] and SETUFCO regularly

[74] The Federación Regional Central de Trabajadores based in Santa Rosa and the Federación de Trabajadores de la Costa Sur in Suchitepéquez. See Bush, "Organized Labor," section III, pp. 18–29, and Leo Suslow, "Aspects of Social Reform in Guatemala, 1944–1949," p. 98.

[75] In this regard it is interesting to note that in 1946 a proposed FRCT affiliation with CTAL was successfully resisted by FRCT head Gumercindo Tejada, the same man who had in 1945, as head of the CTG, opposed that central's affiliation to CTAL (Bishop, *Guatemalan Labor Movement*, p. 27).

[76] El Salto is a British company owned by an American family, the Dorions, and long managed by British citizen George Bellamy. Its *sindicato* counts virtually the entire permanent labor force (about 580 workers) and it has operated almost without interruption since its founding in 1947. It was the first *campe-*

renegotiate collective labor contracts, and both have achieved more comprehensive labor benefits than exist elsewhere in the countryside.

The contemporary *campesino* leagues have existed for a shorter period of time, and their development as autonomous entities has been retarded, perhaps in part because they have no direct or immediate focus for pressure exercise. At least two important exceptions do currently exist, however, both affiliated to the FCG: one in an indigenous community in highland Chimaltenango and the second in a Ladino community in Escuintla. The Ladino organization is led by a cultivator turned tailor and barber. In 1967 he promoted the invasion by his local unit of lands previously granted to community members under the Agrarian Reform Law of the revolutionary period. He also actively proselytized for new organizations that he hoped to unite in a regional federation. In much the same way, the Chimaltenango league was, in mid-1967, actively proselytizing for regional organization. The leadership, composed of at least four central figures, frequently acted as agents for nonleague members from outside the community. They brought regional problems to the FCG and actively followed them through.[77] In 1967 this league initiated an investigation of a Guatemalan decree that made membership in a *gremial*[78] compulsory for all wheat growers, and on the advice of the FCG were traveling to wheat-growing communities in the region, attempting to enlist support for the abrogation of that law.

The question of local unit autonomy was brought into very sharp focus with the 1967 FCG-MCI split. Each side tried to win over local member organizations[79] and each called independent national

---

sino organization to legally reorganize after the 1954 counterrevolution, and, in addition to comprehensive labor contracts, can claim a workers' clinic, modern school, and large worker recreation areas.

[77] During the summer of 1967, these leaders were involved in one case of a murder charge against a community member, an unjust firing of an old man from a neighboring finca, and an illegal stamp tax imposed on wheat processed by two mills in the community.

[78] See Chapter 6.

[79] In San Pedro Ayampuc, the conflict was much aggravated, for the general secretaries of each faction came from *aldeas* within that *municipio*.

conventions. No immediate stampede of local organizations occurred. Some delegates attended both conventions and, in the midst of a confusing barrage of charges and countercharges, maintained a let's-wait-and-see attitude. In the final alignment, an important factor may well have been the strongly religious backgrounds of the FCG leadership and their support by the Christian Democratic hierarchy—a background the MCI leadership denied in leaving CLASC and affiliating with CONTRAGUA. For whatever complex of reasons the majority of local organizations have remained within the FCG.

While the national federations have changed in each historical period (both in name and personnel), the principal extranational influence has been generated out of an ideological conflict between "communist" and "democratic" organizations. Each side has consistently courted a national-level following within Guatemala, and a significant new extranational influence was introduced only with the formation of the FECETRAG-FCG and its subsequent affiliation to the Christian Democratic centrals FCL and CLASC. The extranational entities, in each period, have provided important technical services as well as access to other resources, probably including money. However, the extranational organizations have played only a limited role at the local level and local organizations have moved with some freedom from one national federation to another; a few locals have exercised considerable directive pressure within regional and even national federations. Finally, the corps of *campesino* leaders that may have begun to operate above the local level late in the revolutionary period was eliminated by the counterrevolution and new leaders have only appeared with the formation of the FCG.

3. *Interaction with the Larger Environment*

To this point, we have dealt with organizational units at the four levels almost as though they operated in a closed channel independent of competitive pressures from within their environments. That, of course, is not the case. It will be recalled that in the prerevolutionary period the Pan American Federation of Labor, dominated by the AFL, supported the Guatemalan Federación Obrera, while Moscow advised the Federación Regional de Trabajadores de

Guatemala (FRTG), and promoted the development of a native Communist leadership. Within Guatemala, the two federations did not operate in a context of fully open competition, for the national government consistently favored the development of the Federación Obrera. Bauer Paiz's collection of labor laws (1872–1930) lists eighteen instances of official monetary assistance to that organization. The sums varied from $25, to cover travel expenses for a labor organizer, to a biweekly payment of $10,000 for "unanticipated expenses of development." On September 17, 1925, the government allocated $50,000 for construction of the Federation "social center" and in the following year made available an additional $51,600 for the same purpose.[80]

While Ubico firmly suppressed all organizations, Communist organizers suffered the harshest penalties. Arrests and torture had been reported as early as 1930 (pre-Ubico),[81] and in 1932 Ubico arrested seventy-six "radical" Guatemalan and Salvadorean organizers whom he accused of being Communists; ten were executed.[82] By May 20, 1935, the Communist International reported that the Guatemalan Communist party had collapsed.[83]

As noted earlier, organization growth has—until recently—closely followed the pattern of relevant legislation. This parallel has obtained because in each period the national government has actively implemented those changes which the law has outlined. During the revolution, *campesinos* were granted access to prolabor special courts where indemnification awards were regularly made to workers who had been fired. Recognition of the worker's right to associate for the promotion of his own welfare was backed with the provision of an important legal sanction—the right to strike. *Campesino* exercise of that sanction was infrequent during this period, yet major exceptions did occur in 1948–1949 on the United Fruit Company plantations at Tiquisate and Bananera. In some places unionization was resisted with floggings and even killings,[84] but, until 1954, the upper sector lacked pressure organiza-

---

[80] Bauer Paiz, *Catalogación*, pp. 53–55.
[81] Alexander, *Communism in Latin America*, p. 353.
[82] Schneider, *Communism in Guatemala*, p. 56.
[83] Alexander, *Communism in Latin America*, p. 353.
[84] Bush, "Organized Labor," section III, p. 38.

tions[85] of sufficient cohesion to compete with the growing strength of the CGTG and the CNCG (especially in the face of strong government support for the latter organizations).

Because the revolutionary governments and the new organizations were reciprocally dependent upon one another for continued development—and, in fact, for their very existence—the lower sector could command special privileges. In addition to the cases cited in Chapter 8 of CNCG pressure for the removal of objectionable *comisionados militares*,[86] Archer Bush mentions several examples of CTG intervention previous to 1951, in cases of "injustice or disaster."[87] During the floods of 1949, that organization solicited aid for *campesino* families left destitute, and, in the same year, defended two communities in Huehuetenango against the arbitrary actions of landlords who sought to displace resident *campesinos* from rental properties before they could harvest their crops. During the summer of 1950, the CTG brought before the Department of Sanitation and Public Health the cause of the children of Yepocapa, Chimaltenango, who were then threatened with blindness by a type of filariasis. The CTG also promoted an experimental collective farm at La Blanca and successfully agitated for the founding of schools on fincas lacking educational facilities.[88] *Sindicatos* on both private and national fincas successfully pressured for wage increases,[89] and in some cases where national fincas resisted organization of the workers, CTG complaints to the government brought about replacement of the administrators.[90]

Late in Arbenz's presidential term, an attempt was made to arm *campesino* organizations as a counterweight to an increasingly restless military. However, military officials intercepted the arms shipment at Puerto Barrios and upon Castillo's entry into Guatemala, no "militia of the masses" rose to resist him. What is most significant about this sequence of events is not that a possible militia

[85] See Chapter 6.

[86] See Ross K. Baker, *A Study of Military Status and Status Deprivation in Three Latin American Armies*, p. 44.

[87] Bush, "Organized Labor," section II, p. 53.

[88] Ibid.

[89] Ibid., section III, pp. 39, 47–48, 51–52.

[90] Ibid., p. 48.

aborted, but rather that it was there that the government sought support.

Because these organizations had provided such a critical power resource for the Arbenz government (and vice versa), they became one of the most susceptible targets in the postrevolutionary period. Silvert has stated that "at least 300 persons were killed in non-military action during the June 1954 revolt."[91] In San Luis Jilotepeque "nine of the younger leaders [of the local *unión*] were taken captive to Chiquimula, the 'Liberation' headquarters, where they were reported to have been summarily executed by a firing squad. . . . Numerous other small leaders fled the community into exile or hiding elsewhere."[92] Silvert suggests that the period of such reprisal was relatively short (about two weeks), but that violence in rural areas may have continued on a personal and ad hoc basis, for the Castillo government was not, at the outset, sufficiently highly centralized to control activities in the provinces.[93] The capital city did, however, control a large influx of political prisoners. Newbold[94] estimated the population of two city jails and one police school converted to handle this overflow at about 1,600 persons shortly after the Castillo takeover. Of a sample of 267 prisoners, 36 percent admitted membership in *uniones*, 30 percent in agrarian committees, and 9 percent in *sindicatos*.[95]

The Castillo government denied *campesinos* the legal potential for organization and, instead, relied for support upon the upper sector: the Church, large landholders, the military, and, of course, the U.S. government and its representative agencies. New upper-sector interest groups appeared shortly after the counterrevolution, and they increased in numbers with the military coup in 1963.[96]

[91] Kalman H. Silvert, *The Conflict Society: Reaction and Revolution in Latin America*, pp. 119, 121.

[92] John Gillin and Kalman H. Silvert, "Ambiguities in Guatemala," *Foreign Affairs* 34 (April 1956): 477.

[93] Ibid. This last cited as information received from "a member of the Instituto Indigenista."

[94] Stokes Newbold, "Receptivity to Communist Fomented Agitation in Rural Guatemala," draft of manuscript that later appeared in revised form in *Economic Development and Cultural Change* 5, no. 4 (1954): 18.

[95] Ibid. The percentages include overlapping memberships.

[96] See Chapter 6.

Pressure from one of these organizations in 1967 apparently succeeded in denying agricultural laborers a fixed minimum wage.[97]

At the same time, labor courts and labor inspectors continued to function in defense of some of the rights defined by the labor codes.[98] As indicated in the Zebadúa material cited in Chapter 8, the number of individual workers' cases before the court of appeals in Guatemala City fell by less than 50 percent in the first years subsequent to 1954 and, during 1957–1964, increased almost to the revolutionary period level. Cases brought by *sindicatos,* however, decreased to a fraction of what they had been previous to the counterrevolution. Since the Zebadúa data concludes with 1964, it has not been possible to correlate organization regrowth, which did not begin in any significant degree until 1964, and changes the number of *sindicato* cases before the courts.

Apparently, there has been no consistent attempt in the postrevolutionary period to specifically select against organizations known to have been affiliated to either the CTG or CGTG; rather, the pressure has been exercised against lower-sector organizations in general. Of the twenty-six currently reorganized *sindicatos* on which such information was available, twenty-three had been founded originally by members of the CTG or CGTG, two were organized by its chief competitor (and subsequent affiliate), the FSG, and one was founded by the Federación Regional de la Costa Sur.[99]

While the Méndez Montenegro government permitted an initial spurt of organization in the countryside, by late 1967 that regrowth had already slowed considerably. Of the more than fifty organizations with applications in process in July, 1967, only eight[100] had received legal recognition by February, 1968 (a process which in the revolutionary period took three to four months). In addition to providing little active leadership in organizational promotion (the only changes in the labor code under this government have

---

[97] A member of the minimum-wage commission of the national government told this writer in September, 1967, that the coffee growers association, ANACAFE, had pressured the government to reject that commission's recommendations on a fixed minimum wage for cotton workers (ANACAFE assuming, of course, that if cotton were regulated, coffee would probably be next).

[98] See Chapter 8.

[99] Individual *expediente,* Archivo, DAT, Guatemala.

[100] Ibid.

dealt with worker holidays and vacations), the Méndez regime has selectively favored certain organizations and inhibited the growth of others. The government seldom deals directly with the local organization but, instead, exercises its influence on the larger national entities: CONTRAGUA is currently specially favored, while the FASGUA has suffered consistent discrimination.

FASGUA-sponsored applications have been processed far more slowly than those for any other federation, and one knowledgeable informant stated that this policy had been determined at the ministerial level and passed down to the DAT. In August, 1967, in a statement to the minister of labor and social promotion,[101] the FASGUA denounced the processing delay and further stated that "various employees and supervisors of the Ministry of Labor have gone so far as to indicate to labor organizers that in order that their matters be processed, it is necessary that they renounce affiliation to the FASGUA; in other cases [the employees] have been transformed into veritable agents of patronal enterprises, encrusted within the official bureaucracy."[102]

At the opposite pole, CONTRAGUA has gained special advantages. President Méndez served during the 1950's as legal adviser to SAMF, the railroad workers' *sindicato* and CONTRAGUA's strongest single affiliate. In June, 1967, CONTRAGUA called El Primer Congreso de la Confederación de Trabajadores Centroamericanos, purportedly to unite Central American labor organizations of all types under one umbrella organization. Of the four major labor centrals in Guatemala, only CONTRAGUA was represented. The Congress was convened by President Méndez Montenegro; the welcoming address was delivered by the first secretary-general of CONTRAGUA; and among the speakers were the archbishop of Guatemala, the minister of labor and social promotion, and a representative of the Organization of American States. A CONTRAGUA delegate was elected president of the Congress, and on the twenty-fourth of July the president of the country entertained the delegates in his home.

The Congress was clearly a propaganda vehicle for CONTRAGUA and for the national government (assisted by numerous

[101] *Impacto*, August 28, 1967.
[102] Ibid.

representatives of U.S.-funded agencies, both Guatemalan and international). Naturally enough, the other major federations objected to the implication that the "Guatemalan delegation" was in any sense representative. On July 21, 1967, three Christian Democratic federations—FCG, FECETRAG, and the Federación Nacional de Obreros del Transporte (FENOT)—joined the FASGUA in issuing to the press a joint statement denouncing the Congress. That statement claimed, in part, that organizations represented at the Congress were "affiliated to the Organización Regional Interamericana de Trabajadores (ORIT) which is financed by the North American Central (AFL-CIO) which has been denounced, in turn, as being infiltrated and controlled by the Central Intelligence Agency (CIA)."[103] Further, it stated that the signees looked upon CONTRAGUA as "the official trade union spokesman of the Guatemalan government."[104] While the denunciation was itself an attempt by the four federations to make political currency of their own, the interchange did provide some insight into the anti-U.S. political stance often adopted by both the FASGUA and the Christian Democratic federations. The CONSIGUA, as an acknowledged ORIT affiliate (though not included in the Congress), could hardly participate in any such denunciation.

One highly formalized channel of selective support operative at the national level is the *campesino* "training program." US/AID sponsors a school for lower-sector leaders called the American Institute for Free Labor Development (AIFLD) based at Front Royal, Virginia, with a regional school in San Pedro Sula, Honduras; it also sends Guatemalan leaders to a program at the University of Río Piedras in Puerto Rico and to a third school at Loyola University in New Orleans. All programs are funded by AID, and at least the first two received initial assistance from the AFL-CIO.

In 1967 AID funded AIFLD/Guatemala in the amount of $51,-200, some $22,700 of which was specifically earmarked for the training of "rural labor union leaders."[105] By September, 1967, AIFLD had conducted three residential training programs involving

---

[103] Mimeographed press release dated July 21, 1967.

[104] Ibid.

[105] Project Implementation Order/Technical Services No. 520-184-3-70037, U.S. Dept. of State, Agency for International Development, p. 1.

seventy-four *campesino* leaders, most of whom were members of *ligas campesinas*—leaders of agricultural *sindicatos* were trained separately, in company with urban union leaders. The majority of all trainees pertained to *ligas* affiliated to either CONTRAGUA or CONSIGUA and six members of the third-course group pertained to the then independent (but now CONTRAGUA-affiliated) MCI. *Campesinos* from FECETRAG–FCG- or FASGUA-affiliated organizations have been conspicuous by their absence.[106] At the time of the study, of the seven Guatemalans who had attended the trade-union school at Río Piedras in Puerto Rico, three were *campesino* leaders from the United Fruit Company *sindicato*, SETUFCO, at Puerto Barrios. Once again all seven men were members of *sindicatos* affiliated with either CONTRAGUA or CONSIGUA.[107] The Loyola program had trained a number of Guatemalan *campesinos* plus at least one former urban organizer now active in the FCG. Perhaps the purpose of this program may be best illustrated through a comment made by a U.S. official concerning a *campesino* candidate for the school. Said the official: "The lack of a U.S. presence in the Cobán area is notable and it would appear to be in our best interest to send [Fulano] to the Loyola Training Program."

The Christian Democrats run their own training program at San Rafael above Mixco, department of Guatemala. Administered by the Instituto Centro Americano de Estudios Sociales (ICAES), *campesino* courses generally run one full week and include ideological indoctrination as well as some legalistic counseling and a minimum of practical training.[108] ICAES is funded through IDESAC, the Christian Democratic coordinating agency in Guatemala. Through August, 1967, in addition to courses for urban unionists, ICAES had sponsored five Guatemalan national-level *campesino* courses and one Pan–Central American course, involving approximately 160 Guatemalan *campesinos*. These courses are designed as training foci for FECETRAG-FCG member organiza-

---

[106] From data compiled by the author from AIFLD course files. That the AIFLD has concentrated its training on leaders proposed by CONTRAGUA and CONSIGUA was confirmed, in personal conversation with the author, by the Guatemalan head of that training program.

[107] From US/AID-Guatemala course files.

[108] The writer spent a week as student and observer at an ICAES *campesino* training course at Mixco in July, 1967.

tions, and little attempt is made to use the program to proselytize for new membership (although leaders of unaffiliated organizations are often invited to participate). A closed ideological position makes the ICAES program as selective as that of AIFLD, Río Piedras, or Loyola; the former is based on a philosophy that has grown up in Latin America out of European sponsorship (both ideological and monetary), while the latter three support an ideological position "acceptable to" the U.S. government.

In addition to these forces operating at the national level (through a federation or confederation) there are others affecting organizational development primarily at the local level. It is at this level that the individual *campesino* organization comes into direct confrontation with such potentially competitive power holders as the *patrón*, the *comisionado militar*, and perhaps the *guerrillero*. Under the Méndez Montenegro government the rate of legal recognition initially accelerated, yet the ambience for organizational growth in much of rural Guatemala was changed only slightly, and the acceleration was not sustained. The three political regimes in office since 1961 have taken little positive action to reinforce the more liberal labor code of that year, and thus competitive power holders at the local level have either continued arbitrarily to repress the nascent or regenerating *campesino* organizations, or have found little manifest local interest in that direction.

With very few exceptions (as, for example, on the finca El Salto in Escuintla) the *patrón* has not supported organization growth, for the new entities are reminiscent of the troubled Arbenz period, and threaten the uniqueness of his control. Although informants in the summer of 1967 (including both *campesino* organizers and local organization members) reported cases of patronal violence or threat of same, a more common tactic appeared to be the threat of firing and/or expulsion from the finca.[109] On one south coastal

---

[109] The FCG reported in June of 1967 that the officers of a new *sindicato* in Chimaltenango had been threatened with death by the armed sons of the *finquero* several days after their organization was founded (mimeographed press release, June 29, 1967, FCG). While many cases of firing were reported during that summer, the most outstanding one involved a female *patrón* who fired sixteen of the twenty-two *sindicato* members on her south coastal finca. That case was being presented to the labor court in Escuintla by a lawyer associated with the FCG.

finca that this writer visited, *sindicato* members spoke of regular harassment by the finca administrator (whose permission had to be sought before *sindicato* officers could talk to the writer). Since the founding of this organization, the administrator had taken away workers' milpa plots, had denied boys 14–18 years of age permission to join their older family members in the fields (a tradition of long standing), and had threatened and eventually bought off the secretary-general of the *sindicato*, who subsequently left the finca. *Sindicato* officers on a Quezaltenango finca reported assignment to more difficult tasks and regular verbal harassment by the finca administrator since formation of their organization.

However, the most subtle, and apparently common, strategy has been the use of legalistic delay. In examining *expedientes* for all currently recognized organizations, the writer found seven cases in which the *patrón*, when questioned by the DAT, insisted that workers elected to *sindicato* offices either did not work on his finca, were only part-time laborers, or had once worked for him but were not employed at the date of election. Sometimes such replies generated first-hand investigation by a labor inspector, but the delay in the processing of the *expedientes* might run to several months. The claim that workers were not employed at the date of election had to be countered with a second letter asking whether workers were employed "within the period" of election (because, as was usually the case, workers seldom went to the fields on the day of formation of the *sindicato*). And, in fact, even when a labor inspector was sent to investigate, administrators apologized that they could not show the finca records, because mysteriously they had been "lost," or "stolen," or they were "in the city."

Inspectors are poorly paid and educated and hence are themselves susceptible to pressure from the *patrones* (see Chapter 8). After receiving in December, 1966, a report on missing records from an inspector investigating a reorganized *sindicato* in the department of Santa Rosa, the chief of the administrative section of the General Subinspectorate of Labor ordered the same inspector to recheck his story and not to "listen so unilaterally to the representatives of the *patrón*."[110] (The second inspection showed that all *sindicato* officers were full-time employees of that finca.)

[110] Archivo, DAT, Guatemala.

Occasionally, a *patrón* will simply "forget" to respond to queries from the DAT or will question the legality of the organization per se. In 1960 a finca owner in Escuintla petitioned the DAT that a *sindicato* not be permitted to reorganize, since it had been canceled in 1954 by Castillo Armas "for having belonged to the CGTG"; in his appeal, the owner argued that "its reorganization can only be permitted if one negates the validity of the decree by which it was canceled." Since, however, the decree applied to that organization (Decree #21) had only suspended the officers of the organization and had not voided its legal personality—as was apparently the case, as we have already noted, with respect to all local *campesino sindicatos*—the DAT approved the reorganization and reinscription of officers.

Also resistant to organization growth have been the local military officials. *Comisionados militares* may report organizational activities to higher officials, who in turn may exercise pressure through a variety of channels. In 1967, in a community in the northeast, the ranking military representative ordered the arrest of several members of a local *liga campesina*, allegedly on the basis of reported contacts with the guerrillas. One of the accused suggested to this writer that the order was a result of their legitimate organizational activities, and that the charge of guerrilla contacts was simply a ruse. Both urban and *campesino* organizers have received death threats from rightist vigilante organizations (Mano Blanca, CADEG, NOA, and others) due to alleged "Communist" activities.

Outside the specific organizational structure (local unit, federation, confederation), there has been little positive promotion from within the local community. The Catholic church has, however, recently emerged as one such source. It will be remembered that the current leadership of the FCG gained experience in the Juventud Obrera Católica (JOC), and local leaders in El Quiché had been religious *catequistas* for Acción Católica Rural. Local priests in El Quiché and Chiquimula, while primarily involved in development of indigenous cooperatives, have also advised the leadership of local *ligas campesinas*.

One final input within the local context is that provided by the guerrillas (until recently active in the northeast of the country). *Campesinos* have been drawn into the conflict by both the military and the guerrilla forces (and also by the rightist vigilante bands); yet it is difficult to determine the effect of this many-sided pressure on the local *campesino* community. The presence of the military has brought in the medical and community developmental services (for example, school building and well drilling) of the Acción Cívica branch of the army—a kind of rural "pacification" program. Paramilitary bands have conscripted peasants for guerrilla hunts, while the guerrillas too (especially the Fuerzas Armadas Revolucionarias—FAR) have sought to enlist the cooperation of the peasantry. And, of course, to the extent that *campesinos* have themselves participated in guerrilla activities, they have utilized that channel for a raw and special kind of lower-sector pressure exercise, albeit none too successfully.

In conclusion, then, the organization regrowth that began in 1963 and 1964 has not signaled a return to the pattern initiated under Arévalo and Arbenz. At the most obvious level, the magnitude of the movement is markedly different: whereas 665 *sindicatos* and leagues received legal recognition between 1947 and 1954, less than 100 organizations can now make that claim. What is more important, the operating relationship between national government and lower-sector organizations has changed significantly. In the revolutionary period, the two were mutually interdependent: *campesino* organizations gained access to new power resources derived directly from the national government, while the government, in turn, utilized those organizations to counteract the traditional power of a landed oligarchy. In the subsequent period, the government has turned for support, once again, to the upper sector; *sindicatos* and leagues have become potential competitors rather than allies, and thus their regrowth has been restricted.

While the 1920's witnessed a confusing experimentation with both legal and extralegal forms of pressure exercise, organization growth in the revolutionary period provided a striking parallel to the pattern of legislated reform. That is not to deny the occurrence of much extralegal land invasion (especially on the south coast and in the eastern department of Jutiapa), but only to suggest that these actions were concomitants of, rather than competitors to, the legal organizations of the period. From 1945 to 1954, the law seems consistently to have provided an acceptable legitimacy quotient for lower-sector pressure exercise; it was used both to open and to close channels for organization growth.

In the postrevolutionary period, the law has become a less reliable index. From 1955 through 1961, the reappearance of *campesino* organizations was legally inhibited, yet the removal of selective restrictions in the latter year brought no significant change in the organizational picture. Legal reform has, in each period, required for its realization the active support of the political regime in power. Whereas, Arévalo and Arbenz actively promoted organization growth, the postrevolutionary governments (including, we must now add, that of Méndez Montenegro) have maintained (or permitted the maintenance of) de facto barriers to reorganization.

The role of government vis-à-vis lower-sector organizations has, however, never been one of blanket promotion or inhibition. The prerevolutionary governments selectively aided the Federación Obrera, while Arbenz favored the CTG and the CGTG-CNCG. Postrevolutionary governments have sponsored the FAS and provided special assistance first to CONSIGUA and then to CONTRAGUA. And with the counterrevolution of 1954, North American advisers, training programs, and monies began to exercise a direction-defining influence over organization growth. "Communist" affiliation was outlawed, and only with the appearance of the FECE-TRAG-FCG were local organizations provided an affiliation alternative based outside the United States.

Thus, despite an early history of some promise, *campesino* organizations in Guatemala show few signs of becoming effective mechanisms for the development of competitive power. To date, they remain small in number and enjoy only limited (and controlled) access to channels for the exercise of pressure. The removal of active government support has left *sindicatos* and leagues prey to more traditional power holders in their local environments; and, lacking derivative support, the local organization remains a very unequal competitor.

10 | The Social Organization of Low-Income Urban Families

by Bryan Roberts

THIS CHAPTER EXPLORES the social activity of low-income families in Guatemala City. It aims to contribute to an understanding of what are often described in the literature as the "urban masses." These sectors of the population have often been regarded as having no part in the organizations and networks of social relations that influence the direction of social change in Latin America.[1] Low-income families have thus been characterized as "marginal populations." In presenting the data from Guatemala City, certain of the

NOTE: This chapter is based on research carried out while the author was on leave of absence from the University of Manchester and in receipt of research grants from the Wenner-Gren Foundation, the Institute of Latin American Studies at The University of Texas at Austin, and the Ford Foundation. The research reported herein is still under way (May, 1968), the first part being carried out from April to December of 1966. The statistics used here refer to the preliminary stage of the investigation and must be regarded as provisional. The conclusions reached may be modified by later research, but they do reflect my position after the first period of research and writing.

[1] This viewpoint has often appeared in the writings of Gino Germani and Torcuato di Tella: Gino Germani, *Política y Sociedad en una Epoca de Transición;* Torcuato di Tella, "Populism and Reform in Latin America," in Claudio Véliz, ed., *Obstacles to Change in Latin America.* Oscar Lewis, in his writings on the culture of poverty, has also tended to concentrate on the isolation of low-income families from other sectors of the urban population (Oscar Lewis, *The Children of Sánchez*).

implications of this concept of "marginality" are examined. The concern is with the relations that exist between low-income families and other sectors of the urban population. In particular, the reciprocal influence between low-income families and urban political and economic organizations is examined. Low-income urban dwellers are regarded as having an active influence on social change in Guatemala and not as being passive recipients of change.

There is also the more general question of the extent to which low-income urban families are "integrated" into the national society. Integration has been variously defined.[2] Three of its aspects are dealt with here: (1) the extent and nature of low-income families' participation in political and social life, (2) the extent low-income families are prepared to cooperate with others of like or different social positions to effect changes in Guatemala's social and economic structure, and (3) the extent low-income families differentiate themselves from more prosperous and more powerful groups in Guatemala and do not identify their interests with those of other groups.

The focus here is on two sets of factors that influence the relations of low-income families to other sectors of the urban population. These are (1) the physical and social organization of Guatemala City and, in particular, the structure of urban occupations, organizations, and residential areas, and (2) the career experiences of low-income families, such as rural-urban and intraurban migration, employment experiences, and the recent economic and political history of Guatemala. Both the effects of an urban milieu on social behavior and the effects on low-income families of the social and political experience of urbanization are the concern of this analysis.

Mitchell has recently warned of the necessity of explaining urban behavior primarily in terms of the pressures of an urban social system.[3] The behavior of rural migrants is thus to be understood in terms of their position within an urban social organization and not in terms of their previous rural experiences. In the following

[2] Myron Weiner, "Political Integration and Political Development," in *Political Development and Social Change.*

[3] J. C. Mitchell, "Theoretical Orientations in African Urban Studies," in *The Social Anthropology of Complex Societies.*

analysis, the intent is to show that the behavior of low-income families in Guatemala City is closely related to the constraints exercised by particular forms of urban social organization. Families are not bound by previous or traditional cultural patterns to an inflexible mode of adjustment to urban life. Their social and economic behavior changes with different urban situations and with changes in their social and economic position. The importance of the particular life experiences of individual families is stressed. These are important in influencing families to choose one of several behavior patterns appropriate to an urban situation. For example, in their political and economic behavior, low-income families must often balance long- and short-term advantages. This is a dilemma faced by all regardless of their educational level or income level.

In many studies socioeconomic variables, such as income and occupation, differentiate urban families and influence an individual's participation in urban activities.[4] It is argued that membership in voluntary associations, recreation, and social visiting depend on an individual's having the financial resources and social skills to undertake such activities. The sample here is confined to low-income families, and thus the range of income, occupation, and education is not great. It is expected, however, that social and economic position will be an important influence on the social and economic activity of this sample of Guatemalan families. The higher an individual's income and education and the more his occupation brings him into contact with others, the greater will be his participation in a range of urban activities. Other variables that we must consider are the ecological set. The location of a neighborhood and its social characteristics can have relatively independent effects on the behavior of an individual family by affecting communication between neighbors and contacts with other sectors of the urban population.

Attention is also directed to other variables that have a special relevance to the social organization of low-income families in rapidly growing cities. Also considered is the degree of discontinuity

---

[4] The literature is extensive; for Latin American cities, there are among other studies the analysis of Caplow et al. of San José, Puerto Rico: Theodore Caplow et al., *The Urban Ambience.*

produced by urbanization in the life careers of low-income families. By discontinuity is meant a relatively rapid change from one set of social experiences to another. Migration from small towns and villages to a city can be an example of discontinuity. Discontinuity due to migration may arise from cultural differences between city and provinces, or it may arise from changes in work situations and social relationships. This type of discontinuity is affected by the degree to which a migrant encapsulates himself in relations with people from his town or village.[5] Likewise, movements within a city contribute to discontinuity insofar as change in physical location entails change in social relations. Historical events, such as radical changes in government or social structure, also add to discontinuity in an individual's life career. Discontinuity can be expected to be a stimulus to an individual's participation in urban social and economic life. When an individual's horizons have not been rigidly confined by one set of social experiences, he is more likely to be aware of, and seek out, the possibilities of changing his social and economic position. Discontinuity is not productive of felt integration with other sectors of the urban population. The discontinuity of life experiences stimulates low-income families to be aware of inequalities of wealth. It also weakens traditional values and social relations that provided support for the existing structure of wealth and power.

Finally, the significance of the relative degree of formality in urban organization is considered. By formality is meant the operation of urban economic and administrative organizations according to impersonal and standard rules of procedure. Urban organizations can be characterized as informal when they operate in terms of individual considerations and do not apply standardized rules in their contacts with the population. The claim is made that informality of urban organization stimulates social and economic activity and contributes to the differentiation of low-income families.

One consequence of informality of urban organization is that the social and economic situations in which an individual is placed

---

[5] An example of such encapsulation is provided in Mayer's study of migrants to a South African city. Philip Mayer, *Townsmen or Tribesmen: Conservatism and the Process of Urbanization in a South African City.*

in urban life are not integrated with each other.[6] "Situation" refers to the people and expectations that an individual meets in carrying out a part of his urban life, such as his job, religion, recreation, or political activities. When few stable jobs and urban organizations operate informally, neighborhood-based relations cannot cater to all aspects of an individual family's life. Families are likely to seek out individual means of obtaining needed services and employment. These means are likely to involve them with different sets of people. Where an individual is placed in a variety of situations in which he must deal with different sets of people and different expectations of behavior, then his social behavior is not likely to be consistent from one situation to another. Low-income families will be flexible in their interpretation of the possibilities offered by urban life and unstable in their commitments to any one urban stiuation. Furthermore, an individual's activity will not be confined by any one set of experiences or one mode of coping with urban life. This contributes to the differentiation of low-income families. They will be less likely to recognize their common interests and positions.

Informality of urban organization also entails no formal structure of educational or organizational requirements to define when an individual has failed or succeeded. The possibilities of trying to change one's social and economic position are thus not foreclosed. In this way, a city whose organization is informal contrasts with a developed city where the life chances of individuals will often be decided for them by the time they have left school.

In the following section, it is suggested that low-income families in Guatemala have had discontinuous life careers, are faced by a highly informal urban organization, and are placed in a variety of unrelated urban situations. These factors contribute to the social and economic activity of low-income families. It is the presence of these factors that is likely to differentiate the social and economic activity of our Guatemalan sample from that of families living in other types of cities under different conditions of urbanization.

---

[6] I use the concept of the integration of different social situations in the sense that Mitchell uses it. It refers to the extent to which the people that an individual interacts with in one situation will interact with him in other situations. See J. C. Mitchell, "Introduction," in *Social Networks in Urban Situations*.

1. *Two Neighborhoods in Guatemala City*

The present population of Guatemala City is approximately 600,000.[7] This population has doubled in the last fourteen years, and much of this increase has been produced by migration from small towns and villages to the city. The migration has come mainly from the eastern parts of the country, and the migrants are predominantly Ladino.[8] Before coming to the city, many had migrated seasonally to coastal areas to work on plantations. Others had traveled within and without Guatemala in search of work. Migrants often have had considerable mobility experience before arrival. Furthermore, the small size of the country and the prevalence of small trading or construction employment among the urban poor have meant that many city born have also traveled to work in the countryside. During the land-reform programs of the last twenty years, city dwellers as well as rural families have benefited from grants of farming land.

Geographical mobility between city and countryside is matched by geographical mobility within the city. The rapid expansion of the population has radically altered the urban residential distribution. Expansion has far outrun the available supply of urban housing. This has meant increasing densities in older neighborhoods, the spread of the city into outlying rural areas, and the proliferation of shantytowns. Accommodation near the center of the city is expensive. Cheap accommodation is not conveniently located near the centers of work. Low-income families move residence frequently in the course of their life cycle, searching for the accommodation whose price, size, and location best suit their needs of the moment. The expansion of the city thus means geographical discontinuity, in which neighborhood-based social relations are frequently being disrupted. This discontinuity is high even for the city born, many of whom were reared at a time when work and friendship relations were still based on relatively stable and cohesive urban neighborhoods. Several informants described the city before 1944 as composed of a number of clearly defined barrios, each with its own

---

[7] As of 1966.

[8] Alvan Zárate, "Migraciones internas de Guatemala," *Estudios Centroamericanos* No. 1. As has been noted in earlier chapters, many of these migrants will have been ladinized.

name and distinctive character. Inhabitants of one barrio felt a common identity in opposition to inhabitants of another. Relations within and between the sexes were confined to the barrio. The traditional organization of the city was thus composed of a series of communities as "closed" as the rural communities from which migrants had come. Thus, like rural migrants, those born in the city have had to cope with new forms of social organization.

Expansion in industrial activity in the city has not kept pace with the expansion of the population. Large-scale industrial enterprises are still relatively scarce and employ a minority of the working population. The majority of low-income workers find their sustenance in a variety of small industrial and commercial establishments, in urban services, or in self-employment. Self-employment, whether in craft or trading activities, has not decreased over time. Instead, it has provided one of the major means of absorbing migrants into the urban economy. This economic structure entails a wide variety of work situations requiring distinctive sets of work relations and orientations. Urban workers move quite frequently from one job to another and have few opportunities to build up extensive and lasting social relations based on their work. Residential mobility means that workers and neighbors are usually distinct sets of people.

Few secondary associations have developed to cater to low-income urban families. Labor unions include less than 5 percent of the working population. Geographical mobility and low incomes are not conducive to the formation of mutual-benefit associations or sporting clubs. There is little opportunity for workers or neighbors to cooperate together in different social situations. An individual's leisure activities and means of coping with emergencies are not often based on work place or neighborhood.

People living in Guatemala City retain close links with towns and villages outside the capital. Distances are not great, and bus services are frequent and cheap. There is considerable visiting back and forth between country and city. City dwellers will usually return at least once a year to visit relatives or friends in the places they have lived before coming to the city. Many city dwellers retain business or land interest outside the city. This is seen most dramatically in the cases of the many urban traders who extend their activities into the provinces. People outside the capital come to the city on business and will stay with relatives or friends who live in the city. This interpenetration of city and provinces contributes to diminishing the cultural discontinuity experienced by migrants. It also enables urban low-income families to compare their conditions of life with those of people living outside the city. The outlook of these families is thus not confined to the urban milieu. This is another reason why the activity and attitudes of low-income families are not circumscribed by any one urban social and economic situation.

There are few occasions when low-income families are exposed to formal organizational requirements. Education is compulsory for children between seven and fourteen, but absenteeism is rarely punished. Few jobs open to low-income families require formal qualifications, and, at best, educational attainment is an insecure means to better one's work position. The various governmental bureaucracies have few contacts with low-income families. A tax of a dollar a year is collected of all heads of family, but many of the urban working population do not fulfill this minimal requirement. Funds are short in the city and consequently the provision of urban services does not extend throughout the city. Welfare provision is also scarce. Faced with numerous applicants, it tends to be administered by informal procedures. An abundance of legal requirements exists to regulate residence and work behavior. The relative scarcity of police and the rapid expansion of the urban population have meant that these regulations have also been administered informally. This lack of formal organizational constraints on the lives of low-income families means that their ways of coping with urban life are individual and flexible. To merely survive in Guatemala City, low-income families must learn to manipulate the urban social structure. Even though the possibilities of low-income families substantially improving their position are minimal, informality of urban organization is thus conducive to the urban poor actively participating in urban life.

In the last thirty years, many Guatemalans have directly experienced radical changes in the political and social life of the country. The revolution of 1944 and the reforms of the years immediately following produced changes in the rate of urban migration, the system of landholding, the participation of low-income families in elections, and the protection given to the worker. The city has been the location since 1944 of two successful coups d'état and a host of unsuccessful ones. Under successive regimes, whether of right- or left-wing persuasion, political demonstrations and processions have been frequent and have included substantial numbers of low-income workers. Low-income families have become increasingly exposed to events with the spread of mass communications. Approximately 70 percent of the urban male population is literate. Attendance at films and ownership of radios are widespread. Despite attempts at political censorship, low-income families are likely to be aware of political events and to have directly experienced the impact of these events.

It is in the context of such a city that the study of two low-income neighborhoods is focused. One, here called San Lorenzo, is a shanty-town located near the center of the city. It was illegally invaded in the late 1950's and is composed of wooden shacks with tin roofs. It contains only the rudiments of urban services. The second neighborhood, here called Planificada, is located at some distance from the city center. It was laid out in equally spaced lots in the early 1950's and has gradually become filled by a variety of constructions ranging from spacious concrete dwellings to shacks of the type found in San Lorenzo. The inhabitants of Planificada either own or rent their homes. Planificada has been provided with some urban services, contains a public dispensary, police station, and schools, and is connected to the center by a frequent bus service.

Ecological factors make these two neighborhoods distinct from each other and not wholly representative of the low-income urban population. San Lorenzo has a high density; interaction among neighbors is fomented by the proximity of shacks and the use of communal services. It attracts the attention of urban politicians because of its central location and ambiguous legal status. San Lorenzo thus has very high levels of political awareness. It also attracts families whose work and low pay make it essential for them to live near the center of the city, but whose size is too large for the rented rooms of the center.

The distance of Planificada from the center of the city makes active participation in sport and entertainment facilities difficult. It is not densely settled and provides few occasions for interaction among neighbors. It has a higher average income and a greater range of property types, attracting more prosperous as well as low-income families. However, occupational patterns, family status, and length of urban residence are broadly similar in both neighborhoods (see Table 10–1). The combined sample is used and the neighbor-

TABLE 10–1
Social Characteristics of San Lorenzo and Planificada

Variable	San Lorenzo	Planificada
Length of urban residence:		
Born in city	25%	18%
Resident more than 20 years	33	38
Resident 10 to 20 years	23	18
Resident less than 10 years	19	26
	100%	100%
Number of respondents	108	121
Average monthly income of head of family	55 dollars	65 dollars
Family status:		
Nuclear family (husband, wife, child)	77%	76%
Woman and children	17	17
Single men or single women	6	7
	100%	100%
Number of respondents	109	127
Average number of children per family	3.5	3.5
Occupation of male head of household:		
Self-employed	33%	40%
Employed in small-scale enterprises	24	15
Employed in large-scale enterprises	32	31
White-collar worker	4	9
Unemployed	7	5
	100%	100%
Number of respondents	88	102

NOTE: Employees in small-scale enterprises include watchmen, odd-job men, and operatives small workshops and businesses. The criterion is the number of persons employed by the ente prise, which, in these cases, does not exceed ten. Employees in large-scale enterprises inclu factory operatives, construction laborers (modal occupation), bus drivers, and inspectors. No of these jobs requires high levels of skill or obtains high levels of pay. White-collar workers this sample are low-level office workers and male nurses. Self-employment covers artisans wo ing in their own houses (e.g., shoemakers), small traders, and job laborers.

hoods are differentiated only where appropriate.[9] Unless otherwise indicated, the statistics refer to interviewed heads of households.

Social and recreational life involves low-income families in city-wide activities. Guatemala City offers numerous sporting events, cinemas, and parks. Forty-two percent of male heads of households attend a sporting event once a month or more, most going to a football match every week or fortnight. Of male heads of households, 38 percent attend a movie once a month or more, and 62 percent of this sample go either to a sporting event or to a film during the month. When asked their favorite diversions, 14 percent cited doing things in the home, such as playing with the children or listening to the radio. The majority cited recreations that took them elsewhere in the city or countryside. Many neighbors are also active in religion: 61 percent attended church or chapel at least once a fortnight. These religious activities are not neighborhood based, but they take these families to chapels and churches in various parts of the city.

Families in both neighborhoods also interact quite frequently with friends and relatives. In the majority of cases, these interactions are not based on neighborhood. Sixty-six percent reported that they visited or went out at least once a week with friends made through their work or previous residence. Only 10 percent reported that their best friends lived in the same neighborhood. Sixteen percent reported that they had no known relatives in the city, and a further 19 percent said that they saw their relatives less than once a month. Of the remainder, more than half had relatives living in the neighborhood, and all visited relatives at least once a month;

[9] The statistics presented here and in later tables are drawn from interviews with a 33 percent sample of San Lorenzo and with all family heads of a representative sector of Planificada. The San Lorenzo sample was drawn randomly, and 85 percent of those selected were interviewed. Two interviews of approximately one hour were conducted with each family. There was an interval of approximately three months between the two sets of interviews. The interviews were conducted after a period of two months when families in both neighborhoods had become used to my presence. In Planificada, the sector selected represented approximately 5 percent of the neighborhood. A first interview was conducted with all families in the sector (approximately 127), and a second interview with every second family. This procedure was adopted for lack of time. The remainder of the eight and a half months of field work was spent in participant observation—mainly in San Lorenzo. The qualitative data are drawn from this observation.

most made a practice of visiting parents, siblings, or more distant relatives on Sunday or Saturday afternoon. Respondents were more likely to have relatives living in their neighborhood than to have their best friends living there.

Low-income families make extensive use of radio and newspapers. Sixty-six percent own and listen regularly to a radio, 50 percent listened to foreign stations as well as national, and 54 percent read a newspaper at least two or three times a week (17 percent do not read a newspaper at all.)

The families generally take advantage of the scarce economic opportunities and public services available in the city. Forty-five percent have used the free public medical services four or more times in the past year (25 percent had not used them at all); of those with children of school age, 37 percent had been four or more times to visit the school and talk to the teachers about their child's progress, while 34 percent had not visited the school at all. Families in both neighborhoods show enterprise in finding additional sources of revenue or improving on existing ones. In San Lorenzo there are approximately forty small shops in a neighborhood of approximately four hundred families. Most wives supplement their husband's wages by keeping shop or petty trading activities outside their neighborhood. Self-employed workers in both neighborhoods are constantly seeking new ways to improve their businesses. Several small craftsmen have utilized contacts made through religious activities or politics to develop retailing networks for their products. In San Lorenzo, several small traders have used the money they have saved on rent to invest in expanding their businesses. One has fully equipped a barber shop, and another has purchased a truck for wholesale deliveries. Employed workers in both neighborhoods are also quick to exploit opportunities to better their position. Visits with friends and relatives are often used to learn of new and better job opportunities. Of the employed workers, 73 percent got their present jobs through contacts in the city. Only 2 of the 120 male heads of household interviewed twice remained unemployed and dependent on their families in the five months of the interview period. Even in times of temporary economic depression, unemployed neighbors rapidly found new jobs.

Both these low-income neighborhoods have demonstrated quite high degrees of community organization. Betterment committees, set up mainly through local initiative, have organized neighbors to improve their neighborhoods with their own labor and to act as pressure groups on the city administration. The general survey given above indicates that these low-income families are active participants in an urban social life that is not confined to their neighborhood. At a certain point, notably through community organization and political activity, they exercise a definite influence on urban organization. They are exposed to a variety of urban situations—in recreation, in social interaction, in their occupations, and in their neighborhoods—each of which entails different patterns of social relationship and norms of conduct. We should expect, therefore, that families be affected by the problems and opportunities of the larger society.

2. Determinants and Consequences of Social Activity

We will now consider the variables that influence the social activity of low-income families. To recapitulate, these are (a) individual social and economic variables, (b) ecological variables, (c) life experiences, and (d) informality of urban organization and the degree of integration between an individual's urban situations.

SOCIAL AND ECONOMIC VARIABLES

Income, occupation, and length of residence in the city are the three social and economic variables whose effects are examined here.[10] These variables differentiate low-income families in both neighborhoods, but there is little evidence for sharp differences in behavior between different groups of low-income families. In general, the higher its level of income, the more likely a family is to participate in an activity. Newspaper reading, listening to a radio, and visiting school are directly related to level of income. Attendance at sports and films and visiting with friends, however, are not

[10] Education is one important variable that has not been examined. Most heads of family have low levels of education. Whether a person is literate (approximately 70 percent of the male heads of household) does affect his activity—notably newspaper reading and attendance at films. The illiterate are disproportionately concentrated in the lowest income group. The effect of education is a variable that is being considered in the present stage of the research. Age, another important variable in social activity, was considered in terms of its influence on income, occupation, and length of residence. Analyzing within age categories left the direction of the results reported unchanged. The general effect of age is to diminish activity.

so directly related to income (Table 10–2). In fact, in all three of these activities, it is the lowest and highest income levels that participate least. Many of the wealthier heads of household in both neighborhoods claimed that they had little time to engage in such time-consuming activities.

On most of these activities, the very poorest families—those with an income of less than 30 dollars a month—have markedly lower levels of activity than do other families. Families at this income level were the only families in the sample who were not in the majority favorable to urban life. Other families answered a question asking them to compare urban and rural life by seeing city life as being the more pleasant and having more opportunities. Only at the lowest income level were people more favorable to rural life. In understanding why families in both neighborhoods continue

TABLE 10–2
Income and Social Activity

	Monthly income of head of family			
Activity	30 dollars or less	31 to 49 dollars	50 to 89 dollars	90 to 120 dollars
Read newspaper at least once a month	30%	49%	64%	74%
Number	(11)	(19)	(32)	(23)
Listen to radio every day	38%	66%	73%	90%
Number	(13)	(26)	(33)	(28)
Have visited children at school three or more times in past year	5%	33%	45%	52%
Number	(1)	(5)	(14)	(13)
Do not attend sporting events*	80%	40%	18%	53%
Number	(12)	(10)	(4)	(7)
Attend films once a month at least	27%	38%	44%	37%
Number	(7)	(10)	(14)	(6)
Interact with friends at least every week	51%	61%	78%	74%†
Number	(23)	(27)	(48)	(28)

NOTE: The number in parentheses is the number to which the percentage refers, not the total in the category.

* Only those under forty were included, since age affects attendance at sports.

† The percentage for the highest income category (110 to 120) is 59%.

to be active participants in urban life despite difficult political and economic conditions, it is important to remember that for most of them urban life represents a definite improvement in comparison with rural communities.

Occupation influences reading of newspapers, radio listening, attendance at sports and films, and interaction with friends (Table 10–3). The size of the sample makes it difficult to take into account the influence of income and urban experience, but in the case of occupation, as with income and urban experience, analysis of the data within the categories of the other relevant variables shows that the direction of the relationship was not affected. Self-employed workers are less likely than either employees in small- or large-scale enterprises to participate in an activity. Employees in large-scale enterprises are most likely to participate. Part of the explanation of these findings lies in the type of work associated with different types of occupation. Self-employed workers in both neighborhoods have irregular hours of work that often take them outside their homes for considerable periods, day and night. They often do not have leisure time that is conducive to participation in either organized

TABLE 10–3
Occupation and Social Activity

Activity	Self-Employed*	Employed in Small-Scale Enterprises	Employed in Large-Scale Enterprises
Do not attend sporting events†	62%	41%	25%
Number (of which percentage composed)	(16)	(9)	(7)
Attend films at least once a month	27%	37%	39%
Number	(17)	(13)	(23)
Read newspapers at least once a week	50%	51%	72%
Number	(32)	(19)	(37)
Listen to a radio every day	59%	62%	82%
Number	(37)	(23)	(40)
Interact with friends at least every week	63%	77%	74%
Number	(41)	(31)	(40)

* The occupational categories used are the same as those in Table 10–1.
† Only those under forty were included, since age affects attendance at sports.

or home-based recreation. Employed workers have more regular hours of work, usually arriving home at a fixed time and ready to relax after a tiring day's work. Occupation has also a more indirect effect. Part of the reason why workers in large-scale enterprises were more active participants in these forms of recreation is that they engage in them as groups of workmates. Newspapers are shared between workers. They often attend sports and films together. Discussions between workers about films, sports, and news topics also encourage participation.

Concerning to whom respondents turned for loans and getting jobs, differences also emerge between occupational categories (Table 10–4). Self-employed workers, as might be expected, were most likely to say that they had started their present job through their own efforts. They are also more likely than employed workers to say that they have no one to go to for a loan. Employed workers, on the other hand, are more likely to say they can obtain loans from their work friends or their bosses and are able to cite a greater range of possible sources of loans.

Yet despite the apparent isolation of the self-employed, they are as resourceful manipulators of urban organization as are other categories of workers. On certain variables, self-employed workers participate as much, if not more, than other categories of workers. This is true of political activity in the neighborhoods. Self-employed workers are also as likely as other workers to visit schools to talk about their children's progress and to use urban medical facilities. When asked what recourse they would have if they wanted to obtain something that was beyond their ordinary resources, self-employed workers cited as many possible recourses as do employees in large-scale enterprises (Table 10–5). They cited more recourses than employees in small-scale enterprises. Self-employed workers were also more likely than other groups of workers to cite contacts with social and economic superiors as possible sources of aid in times of need. While the constraints of their job may make self-employed workers less able to interact or frequently exchange services with other people, they do maintain a range of relationships, many of which remain latent until they are needed. The participation of self-employed workers does not reflect a general withdrawal from urban social activity, but rather a selection of activities appropriate to their occupational situations.

TABLE 10–4
Occupation and Obtaining Loans and Jobs

| Occupation | People to whom one would turn for help to obtain loans or jobs | | | | | | | | | | | | | | | |
| | Family | | Neighbor | | Work Friend | | Other Friend | | Employer, Patrons | | Fellow Villager | | No Source | | Total | |
	Loan	Job	Loan	Job	Loan	Job	Loan	Job	Loan	Job	Loan	Job	Loan	Job	Loan	Job
Self-employed	29%	7%	12%	—	19%	—	32%	38%	7%	19%	5%	5%	26%	43%	104%	69%
Number															65	42
Employed in small-scale enterprises	24%	14%	12%	—	38%	3%	9%	27%	35%	31%	—	4%	19%	17%	118%	79%
Number															37	29
Employed in large-scale enterprises	21%	19%	13%	—	55%	2%	4%	30%	35%	21%	2%	4%	9%	25%	130%	76%
Number															52	47

NOTE: Total percentages do not add up to one hundred, since respondents could cite more than one possible recourse for loans and jobs.

TABLE 10–5
Occupation and Obtaining Help in Emergency

| | Where one would obtain help in emergency or great necessity | | | | | | | | |
Occupation	Welfare Institution	Relative	Work Friend	Other Friend	Employer, Patrons	Fellow Villager	Neighbor	No Source	Total
Self-employed	58%	14%	1%	20%	42%	8%	3%	22%	146%
Number									65
Employed in small-scale enterprises	52%	22%	—	14%	31%	6%	3%	24%	128%
Number									37
Employed in large-scale enterprises	61%	20%	2%	23%	32%	2%	8%	10%	148%
Number									51

Length of residence in the city has always been regarded as a crucial variable in understanding the participation of low-income families in urban activties. It has been argued that with increasing length of residence, migrants participate more in urban social activities.[11] The evidence from this Guatemalan sample is inconclusive on this point. Length of residence has little effect on the behavior of migrants that cannot be accounted for by age or occupation.[12] There are, however, certain differences between those born in the city and migrants. Those born in the city interact with friends more frequently, visit their children's schools more frequently, and attend sports and films more frequently (Table 10–6). Those born in the city and migrants are similar in their participation in newspaper reading and use of medical facilities. City born are less likely than migrants to listen frequently to the radio (45

[11] Gino Germani, "Inquiry into the Social Effects of Urbanization in a Working-Class Sector of Greater Buenos Aires," in Philip Hauser, ed., *Urbanization in Latin America.*

[12] Migrants with more urban experience are older and are more likely to be self-employed; this accounts for some of the differences among migrants. When younger migrants who work in small- or large-scale enterprises are compared with nonmigrants of similar age and occupational range, the differences shown in Table 6 persist.

TABLE 10–6
Length of Residence and Social Activity

Length of Residence	Interact with Friends Every Week at Least	Visited School at Least 3 or 4 Times	Have Not Attended Sports	Read Newspapers at Least Once a Week	Attend Films Once a Month at Least	Used Medical Facility 3 or More Times in Past Year
Less than ten years	72%	25%	47%	48%	37%	43%
Number	(34)	(5)	(15)	(16)	(12)	(15)
Ten to twenty years	71%	33%	47%	65%	31%	52%
Number	(32)	(7)	(18)	(26)	(12)	(21)
More than twenty years	61%	32%	67%	43%	35%	39%
Number	(44)	(12)	(40)	(30)	(18)	(24)
Born in city	85%	61%	30%	57%	44%	45%
Number	(35)	(11)	(10)	(19)	(14)	(15)

NOTE: Percentages for attendance at films are based on the sample of forty years of age and under.

percent of city born listen rarely or not at all in comparison with 31 percent of migrants). There is thus some suggestion that those born in the city are more active in the aspects of urban life involving interaction with other people. Yet, on other indicators reflecting the manner of an individual's participation in urban life, differences between migrants and nonmigrants are the reverse of what has been found in other studies. With respect to type of marital union, the city born are more likely to be united by consensual union than are migrants (87 against 66 percent). Migrants are more likely to have been married by either church or state authorities. We shall see that in San Lorenzo the politically active are migrants and that length of urban residence is not associated with voting in city elections. It is suggested that these latter findings reflect both rural social conditions in Guatemala and the different means of coping with urban life open to low-income migrants and low-income city born.

Categorizing heads of household in the two neighborhoods by their length of residence provides us with further evidence of change in an individual's social behavior related to change in urban situation. Living near relatives and interaction with friends vary directly with length of urban residence (Table 10–7). Recent migrants to the city are the most likely to have relatives living in their neighborhood. In both neighborhoods, it is usual for recent arrivals in the city to come and stay with their relatives and to find accommodation near those relatives. With longer residence in the city, migrants are less likely to have relatives living near them. Frequent residential moves throughout the city disperse relatives. Those born in the city are least likely to have relatives living in their neighborhood. Both neighborhoods are recently developed. A similar pattern emerges with respect to interaction with friends. Recent migrants have fewest friends in other neighborhoods and are most likely to have friends in their own neighborhood. With increasing urban residence, friends become spread throughout the city until, for those born in the city, the overwhelming proportion of their friends are in other neighborhoods of the city. Recent migrants were most likely

TABLE 10–7

Length of Residence and Interaction with Friends and Family

Interaction	Less than Ten Years	Ten to Twenty Years	More than Twenty Years	Born in the City
With relatives in neighborhood (weekly)	53%	37%	27%	23%
With relatives in other parts of city (weekly)	15	26	36	46
See relatives infrequently or not at all	32	37	37	31
Percentage	100%	100%	100%	100%
Number	47	46	78	47
With friends in neighborhood (weekly)	40%	38%	21%	22%
With friends in other parts of city (weekly)	32	33	40	63
Interact infrequently with friends	28	29	39	15
Percentage	100%	100%	100%	100%
Number	47	45	73	41

to cite relatives as having got them their present job. Those with longer urban residence were more likely to cite friends or workmates.

As we have seen, the two neighborhoods present very different living conditions for their inhabitants. These living conditions are important influences on the social behavior of our sample of low-income families. The contrast between Planificada and San Lorenzo is between a relatively urbanized and planned neighborhood and one that was unplanned and arose spontaneously to meet the housing needs of low-income families. The conditions that differentiate San Lorenzo and Planificada are (a) density, (b) centrality of location, (c) degree of urbanization, and (d) legal status.

Because of greater living density, people in San Lorenzo can be mobilized more rapidly for communal projects or meetings than can those in Planificada. Gossip and information travel fast in San Lorenzo. At any time of day or night its narrow streets are filled with children, young and old men, and women. In contrast, families in Planificada keep to their houses to a much greater extent. Lack of urban services has been a further stimulus to the cooperation of San Lorenzo families. They have worked together to install the urban services they lack and to put pressure on the municipal authorities to have them installed. Furthermore, the possibility that they might be evicted has encouraged San Lorenzo families to form neighborhood committees and has exposed them to the play of urban politics. Political groups in the city have seen the insecurity of such areas as San Lorenzo as providing a useful lever for the establishment and propagation of local branches of their parties. These stimuli to community organization and interaction are lacking in Planificada. Also, because of the distance of the neighborhood from the center of the city, Planificada families have less time to spend on such activities or even on recreation. In contrast, San Lorenzo's central location means that its inhabitants spend only a short time in journeys to and from work and are in easy reach of most urban services and amusements. San Lorenzo has both higher interaction among neighbors and higher exposure to outside urban social organization than Planificada.

San Lorenzo's inhabitants do participate more in urban life. Its people can be seen leaving the neighborhood to attend a sporting event or a movie more frequently than seems to be the case in Planificada. The sample of San Lorenzo heads of family claimed that they attended sports or movies more often than was claimed by the sample in Planificada. In comparison with those in Planificada, the San Lorenzo sample also claimed to interact more frequently with friends and to see their relatives more frequently (Table 10–8). We should note that these findings occur despite the fact that incomes in Planificada are higher. As we have seen, higher income affects attendance at sports or films.

The centrality of San Lorenzo's location is not the only factor affecting its inhabitants' use of recreational facilities and ability to maintain relationships outside the neighborhood. It is common in San Lorenzo for people to persuade others in the neighborhood to accompany them in their leisure activities. A small group of men will make their way up the mud street of San Lorenzo and call on those they meet to join them to see a football match or a wrestling exhibition. The spaciousness of Planificada makes such contacts less likely. Since the journey to work is longer in Planificada, heads of families arrive home later and do not wish to leave again. However, in the case of institutions located in or near the two neighborhoods, such as the public health clinic and the schools, the sample of families in both neighborhoods showed no difference in the frequency of their use of such facilities.

Community organization has been more successful in San Lo-

TABLE 10–8
Ecology and Social Activity

Neighborhood	Interact with Friends Every Week at Least	Interact with Relatives Every Week at Least	Have Not Attended Sports in Last Year	Attend Film at Least Once a Month
San Lorenzo	78%	70%	47%	41%
	(108)	(108)	(47)	(41)
Planificada	65%	60%	57%	25%
	(98)	(116)	(36)	(15)

NOTE: The change in size of sample occurs because data were available on the full sample for friends and relatives, but were available only for the reduced sample on the other two questions.

renzo than in Planificada. In San Lorenzo, families have laid their own sewage system, built chapels and a community church, and erected a community center. Pressure exercised by betterment committees and other groups has persuaded the municipality to help San Lorenzo, though it is not a legally recognized neighborhood. Water faucets have been installed, building materials provided, and a medical dispensary constructed. In comparison, the various betterment committees organized in Planificada have had less success. Planificada still lacks an adequate sewage system, and, though a legally settled neighborhood, it has been unable to secure the paving of all its streets or the provision of an adequate water supply.

Part of the reason for San Lorenzo's relative success in community organization has been the higher levels of political awareness and organization in San Lorenzo. In San Lorenzo, a neighborhood of four hundred families, there existed at least five political committees at the time of the last elections. Each of these had at least six active officeholders and many more active helpers. Similar committees existed in Planificada, but they were proportionately less numerous. Levels of political awareness are high in both neighborhoods. Most neighbors found no difficulty in discussing present and past political events. In San Lorenzo, over 80 percent of heads of family were able to give a definite preference for a past president of Guatemala. Seventy-five percent of Planificada heads of family gave definite preferences. Seventy-five percent of San Lorenzo male heads of families and 65 percent of Planificada heads of families voted in the elections.

Each low-income family has an individual experience of spatial and job mobility. Families also differ in the exposure they have had to social and political changes in Guatemala. Age, for example, is one determinant of exposure; occupation and residence are others. The cumulative life experience of an individual provides him with an orientation, whereby he interprets contemporary events and the various urban situations he is placed in. Though each experience is unique, general distinctions can be made between these life experiences and can be related to the contemporary social activity of low-income families. This section, however, is limited to providing examples of the relevance of life careers to an analysis of urban social organization.

The influence of their life experiences appears in the political attitudes of heads of families. All those heads of families over the age of thirty-five have experienced the regimes of presidents Arévalo and Arbenz. These regimes attempted to introduce a measure of agrarian and industrial reform to benefit low-income workers. Both regimes were examples of times when political parties improved the position of low-income families—if only temporarily. These improvements would have been felt most by those working in large-scale enterprises. The overwhelming majority of heads of households who were over thirty-five and had always been employed in large-scale enterprises replied positively to a question asking them if they thought a political party could improve the situation in Guatemala. These same heads of households were also overwhelmingly in favor of Arévalo as best past president of Guatemala. These were the people who in the interviews would list the achievements of the Arévalo regime in discussing the past presidents of Guatemala. Their past experience gave them more confidence in the political process than any other group. Younger heads of families working in large-scale enterprises did not think that a political party could improve the situation. The same was true of self-employed workers and employees in small-scale enterprises, whether these were over or under thirty-five. As described elsewhere, working in large-scale enterprises predisposes heads of families to be favorable to cooperating politically with fellow workers and neighbors.[13] It is only experience with successful reformist regimes that converts these attitudes arising from the work situation into confidence in the political process.

The relevance of life experience comes out sharpest in examining political activity within San Lorenzo. All those who were politically active in one of the national political parties were with one exception migrants. The one exception had spent a major part of his working life in the rural areas of Guatemala. Apart from their experience of rural areas, these political activists were similar in the range and type of job experience they had had. They had

[13] Bryan Roberts, "The Politics of an Urban Neighborhood of Guatemala City," *Sociology* (May 1968).

worked in various areas of the countryside, often in connection with such large-scale enterprises as plantations, construction, or government enterprises. The life career of these political activists had been highly discontinuous. They had experienced different types of social situations and different sets of social relations. They had also experienced political activity before coming to the city. In the neighborhood they were vigorous proponents of national as well as neighborhood political issues. Like other neighbors, they were interested in short-term gains for the neighborhood and in their own personal self-advancement. Many of them, for example, got jobs through their political activity. They were in the main self-employed, which gave them the flexibility they needed to spend time in political activity. They contrast with another group of neighbors who were almost solely concerned with neighborhood issues. This group was composed of men who were mostly migrants but who had been in the city a considerable number of years. They had obtained fairly steady, well-paid jobs and had remained in these jobs for many years. This second group had more of their children continuing into secondary education than was usual for the neighborhood. This locally orientated group had experienced events under Arévalo and Arbenz and were politically aware of and sympathetic to reform governments. Their experiences had been less discontinuous than those of the nationally orientated group. Their life had been a slow attempt to improve their own position and that of their children. They were committed to urban life, had many friends throughout the city, and felt that improvements, even on a neighborhood basis, were worthwhile.

In the complex political events of San Lorenzo, both groups, locals and nationals, responded in very similar ways to the inducements held out by the national political parties interested in the neighborhood. Both groups were influenced by the prospect of jobs, short-term benefits, and the power of competing parties. Yet, their activity was still heavily influenced by the basic orientation that they took to politics. The neighborhood orientated group always tried to limit political activity to neighborhood improvements. They gave little support to programs designed to convey the extra-local significance of what was being done. The nationally orientated group attempted to extend the significance of local activities, fostering literacy programs, cooperative schemes, and meetings designed to explain to neighbors the general significance of neighborhood improvements.

Families in both neighborhoods differ in the extent and nature of their residential and occupational mobility. Such differences would be expected to affect not only their political behavior, but also their attitudes toward their present job and neighborhood. These differences will also affect commitments to urban life as measured by such indicators as the educational level of the children. The analysis of these variables must await the collection of more detailed information concerning the life histories of these families. The aim here has been to emphasize that individual life experiences contribute to an understanding of the behavior of families placed in different social positions. Furthermore, characterizing families by the prevalent type of life experience is a necessary complement to an analysis of organization at the group level.

INFORMALITY OF URBAN ORGANIZATION AND ARTICULATION OF SOCIAL SITUATIONS

It was concluded previously that the social activity of families in the two neighborhoods is spread throughout the city. Activity is not based either on the home or on ties formed with neighbors. In the description of the city, it was noted that this is a necessary consequence of the social and economic structure of a city in which urban organizations operate informally. Family heads in the two neighborhoods work independently or in small enterprises scattered throughout the city. Few families work in the same enterprise as their neighbors. Work contacts are thus different from neighborhood contacts. Recreation is usually taken outside the neighborhood and often in the company of friends and relatives living elsewhere in the city. Religious activity is not primarily based on neighborhood. Catholics attend several churches with little opportunity to establish enduring relations with other worshipers. Protestantism involves close-knit but small communities whose relations extend to fellow believers in other parts of the city rather than to neighbors.[14] In the recent history of Guatemala,

---

[14] Bryan Roberts, "Protestantism and Coping with Urban Life in Guatemala City," *American Journal of Sociology* (May 1968).

political parties have not received consistent support from low-income families. Both neighborhoods are fragmented politically. The enduring political relationships made by a politically interested family head will not be with fellow neighbors or workmates. They will often be with middle-class political organizers who themselves may shift from political party to political party.

Neighbors are thus involved in diverse sets of relations that differ not only between individuals, but also as individuals move from one urban situation to another. Heads of households operate within one set of relations at work, within another in their religious activity, within another when cooperating for community organization, and within yet another when active in a national political party. Few relations are common to these different situations. There is thus little social pressure for neighbors to be consistent in their behavior from one situation to another. One neighbor in San Lorenzo was active in a left-wing national political group. He was also a member of the local Catholic brotherhood, most of whose members were conservative politically. He helped in community organization and was ritually related to another community organizer of opposed political persuasion. His political group was suspicious of the value of social drinking or sporting with workmates. He came from the same rural village as several other families in the neighborhood and was distantly related to them. They all maintained contacts with their home village and would exchange gossip about events there. These ties with fellow villagers were used as one base for political recruitment. However, another relative and fellow villager was one of his chief political opponents in the neighborhood. This fragmentation should not be overemphasized. Certainly common birthplace, kinship, and religion are bases for interaction that are common to many spheres of activity. In general, however, families in both neighborhoods move between urban situations in which they deal with distinct sets of people and expectations.

The social activity of low-income families is often socially heterogeneous. Most low-income families in both neighborhoods could cite social and economic superiors on whose help they counted in time of emergency. These relations are formed on a variety of bases. Often they are with former or present employers. In the case of employed workers, employers are almost as frequent sources of small loans as are workmates. Women establish loan relations with the women at whose house they work. These relations are often latent. Low-income workers do not make a frequent practice of visiting possible patrons, but they maintain the relation by visiting when the opportunity arises or the occasions demand. One man makes a practice of visiting the house of an army colonel with whom he had served. He goes about twice a year and does a small service for the colonel without expecting anything in return. He admits, however, that the colonel would be one source of aid to him should the need arise.

Coming from the same rural village, kinship, and membership in a religious group or in a political organization are also bases on which families in these neighborhoods establish relations with people in different social and economic positions. These relations become a significant frame of reference for neighbors. They estimate their possibilities of improving their position in terms of the kind and range of contacts they have. These social contacts are factors differentiating one low-income family from another. Families in the two neighborhoods do not interact frequently with each other. Their relations are often with people of different social and economic positions. The social life of these low-income families thus does not encourage them to recognize their common social and economic interests.

The social relations of low-income families in both neighborhoods described above lead them to be flexible participants in urban life. The implications of this are discussed in terms of residence, employment and politics. In both neighborhoods, some 15 percent of families leave every year for other parts of the city. Both San Lorenzo and Planificada are stopping places in the search for good urban accommodation. This residential mobility does reflect the heterogeneity of neighbors' relations. Families do not have intensive contacts with neighbors that bind them to any one urban locale. Having contacts in various parts of the city provides a family with opportunities to obtain other urban housing that suits changes in a family's size or income. Sometimes it will be rented accommodations. Sometimes a family will buy a plot of land after a period of saving in their present neighborhood or when their financial situation improves.

San Lorenzo inhabitants, and those renting in Planificada, are eager to receive information about new housing developments. They will travel considerable distances to inspect a new development and discover the costs entailed. When the local priest of San Lorenzo launched a scheme to locate shantytown inhabitants on cheap land on the far outskirts of the city, a large proportion of San Lorenzo inhabitants went singly or in groups to inspect the property. They examined the bus routes and talked with people already living in this development. They concluded that the development was too rudimentary and too distant from their places of work. Almost everyone interviewed was able to recite these facts about the development project.

It is thus not attachment to their neighborhoods or lack of knowledge of alternative possibilities that keeps these low-income families in what is often low-standard housing. In fact, their mobility constitutes a major problem for the urban planning of Guatemala. The city has expanded to suit the pressures of its mobile low-income population. Low-income families have given little credence to government promises or threats. They have not been prepared to rent overcrowded and expensive accommodations. In considerable numbers they have moved to illegally settled shantytowns scattered throughout the city. New urban administrative problems have thus arisen, and the framework of urban administration has been changed. Municipal administration has tacitly recognized the existence of shantytowns and has sponsored betterment committees in low-income areas. These committees have become an informal but important part of the administrative structure of the city.

These low-income families are also flexible in their attitudes toward employment. In these two neighborhoods, the relations a man forms at work and those he forms in his leisure are different. Consequently, there are few social pressures to keep a worker in an employment when better opportunities become available. No family head that was interviewed said that he was unprepared to change his type of work. Some men returned to the countryside to agricultural employment and others went to development projects in distant parts of the nation. Information about new job possibilities circulates quickly in these neighborhoods. As soon as a new construction project is started, for example, laborers without employment will be there seeking employment. Apart from the best-paid and securest jobs, job turnover is quite high among low-income heads of households in the sample. This introduces a flexibility into urban employment that is economically both an advantage and a disadvantage. Labor is available and flexible, but it is not stable.

The flexible behavior of low-income families is perhaps most apparent in the field of politics. Families in both neighborhoods do not cooperate politically in support of any one group. Instead, they are available to the variety of political interests that seek the support of low-income voters.

Throughout its short history, San Lorenzo has been divided between competing political committees.[15] These committees gain the temporary allegiance of groups of neighbors. They are usually sponsored by national or municipal political parties. These political parties vary in their ideology from left to right of the political spectrum. They are all controlled by middle-class Guatemalans. Political parties establish themselves by using kinship, religion, common rural origin, or work relations to approach San Lorenzo family heads. If the relation is a strong one or if sufficient favors are offered, a neighborhood political committee will be established in support of the national or municipal political party. This neighborhood committee will make use of its neighborhood relations to recruit other members to the committee.

At any one time, there are likely to be at least three or four competing political committees existing within San Lorenzo. Families shift from one committee to another or join new committees as political circumstances change. The political histories of members of both neighborhoods usually include temporary membership in three or four distinct political committees in the last five years. Members of the neighborhood betterment committee, for example, had informally sponsored candidates in the last two municipal elections. These candidates lost the elections, and the committee members switched their political allegiance to the victorious candidate. The bases of a neighborhood political committee are loose alliances of different interest groups, each based on one of the differentiating experiences to which these low-income families are exposed. Religion, occupation, life experiences, kinship, and rural origin are

---

[15] I use the term *committee* to cover the semiformal political groups that exist in the neighborhood. During the year preceding an election and for a short period afterward, these political groups are constituted as committees with officeholders and the task of inscribing supporters for their political parties.

the most common of these. The interest groups are temporarily united into a political alliance through the personal contacts that members of one interest group have with members of another interest group. They are also united in opposition to other political committees existing in the neighborhood.

An analysis of one of the political committees formed before the latest municipal election illustrates these features of the composition of a committee. This particular committee was formed when the area organizer of a national political party used the local priest to make contact with some members of San Lorenzo's religious brotherhood. These members agreed to help, and in turn they suggested that he contact another neighbor with extensive kin contacts in the neighborhood; this neighbor was known to be discontented with the activities of the neighborhood betterment committee. Members of a national political party were also included in the committee. Their support was gained partly through kinship ties with committee members, but it was mainly obtained because other committees were thought to be supporting a rival national political party. The committee also gained the support of Protestants angered at the supposed hostility of other neighborhood committees and their candidates to Protestant interests in the city. This political committee was united by the municipal election campaign. Its members shared few life situations that gave them a common and enduring political position. After the election, the area organizer attempted to maintain the committee and to use it to promote neighborhood political organization. The committee, however, split into its component parts, and some of these formed new alliances to begin new political groups around fresh political interests.

The type of political flexibility described above influences political organization in the city. It means that most political parties can find some support among low-income groups. This encourages the proliferation of political parties and means that the style of urban politics includes the use of public agitation and demonstration. The political flexibility of low-income families also contributes to the lack of organization among existing political parties. Since a political party can easily gain grass-roots support by sponsoring neighborhood committees, political parties have established only the skeleton of an organization. There are few full-time party workers dedicated to continuously fomenting support in local neighborhoods. When not in power, political parties do not have well-organized local support that makes them a continuing and important influence in national decision making. Furthermore, since political parties depend on sponsoring local political committees, they are under considerable pressure to reward their supporters by obtaining favors or jobs for them. As we have seen, local political committees are not united by an organized and common political position, but by a variety of temporary considerations. Under these conditions, urban political organization is fluid and orientated to short-term issues. Ideologically sophisticated political parties compromise their long-term political goals to the exigencies of the urban political organization under which they work. In these ways, low-income families are an active influence in urban political life. Whereas decision making remains in the hands of middle-class Guatemalans, national and municipal political parties are highly exposed to, and sensitive to, the short-term demands of low-income families.

3. *Polarization of Low-Income Families*

The interconnection and reciprocal influence of low-income families and other sectors of Guatemalan society have thus far been emphasized. These interconnections modify, but do not invalidate, a conceptualization of Guatemalan society as composed of two discrete social sectors, differentiated by life styles and access to power.[16] Indeed, low-income families do not frequently participate in urban formal organizations, and many of their relations with social and economic superiors are of a patron-client nature. In this section the argument is directly relevant to the dual-sectors model of stratification in Latin America. Here is examined the extent that low-income families in Guatemala see themselves as a distinct sector of society, with interests and life styles opposed to those of more powerful members of their society.

In Guatemala City there are few bases on which an individual obtains prestige in the eyes of his fellows. Wealth and occupation are the most visible bases of social prestige in the city, and low-income families are low on both. Almost everyone in the city can be classed as Ladino, and ethnic status is thus not effective compara-

[16] Richard Adams, "Political Power and Social Structures," in Claudio Véliz, ed., *The Politics of Conformity in Latin America*.

tive grounds for social prestige. Many low-income families in the two neighborhoods are independent in their work. Yet, they, like the employed, are dependent on others for effectively coping with urban life. Furthermore, mobility within the city and the relative absence of organizations in which low-income families participate mean that it is difficult for an individual to build up prestige through the course of long acquaintance or service in an organization. Sectarian religious organizations are almost the only organizations through which low-income families in these neighborhoods obtain prestige through service. There is thus a sharp contrast with the situation that holds in the rural areas, as described by Méndez.[17] In the village he discusses, there are several bases on which prestige is allocated and the village stratified. Individuals can be ranked high in prestige on one dimension and low on another. Wealth is only one dimension of prestige, and others include ethnic status, ownership of land, experience, and community service. There are few individuals in the village who cannot claim some measure of prestige on one of these dimensions. Conflict does exist between the various social groups in the village. Most individuals, however, feel that they have a place within the village structure and are committed to its preservation or change.

Families in San Lorenzo and Planificada attempt to maintain some basis of social discrimination. In conversation and interaction, a notion of respectability often occurs. The respectable are regarded as those with regular jobs, who wear decent clothes and keep their houses or huts in some semblance of order. Those who are not regarded as respectable are those who drink too much, do not attempt to improve their accommodations, and pay little attention to their personal appearance or that of their children. Even in the shantytown, San Lorenzo, neighbors will talk of holding a party only for the respectable people. They classify many neighbors as not respectable enough for community office. In their personal dealings, most heads of family emphasize that it is desirable to maintain reciprocity in social relations. Most stated that they preferred to borrow money either from those to whom they also lent or under some system of interest payment where the debt relation is a commercial one. Some neighbors commented that they were no longer

---

[17] Alfredo Méndez, *Zaragoza*.

able to visit certain relatives, since these relatives were rich and they could not hope to return any favors received. In these conversations, the norm that was emphasized was that of the independence of the individual family; the "respectable" made a point of not asking for any favors.

Yet the conditions of urban life in Guatemala make it impossible for any low-income family not to enter into some relations of dependence. The norm of independence is constantly being violated in practice. Also, the differentiations in prestige that these low-income neighbors make are insignificant when compared with the prestige that accrues to wealth and power in the city. The improvements any low-income family can make on their house, their clothes, and their financial status are marginal when compared with the life styles of the wealthy in Guatemala City. Consequently, almost without exception, families in both neighborhoods made their major classification of urban social groups that of rich and poor. Even the relatively highly paid among these low-income families classified themselves as among the poor. People of widely opposing political preferences referred to the gulf between rich and poor as the central problem facing Guatemala. Thus, one elderly inhabitant of San Lorenzo chose Ubico, the old dictator, as his preferred past president of Guatemala. This same man then stated that the root of Guatemala's contemporary ills lay in the fact that the rich did not help the poor. A Protestant who claimed to be apolitical stated that he sympathized with the *guerrilleros*, since the rich merchants and landowners had done nothing but exploit the poor. Neighbors of left-wing sympathies were equally vociferous in making polar distinctions between rich and poor. Polarization of urban groups into rich and poor is encouraged by an individual's life experience. Those most ready to make this distinction in the two neighborhoods were the older heads of family and those whose lives had been devoted to trying to improve their own position or that of their fellows. One political activist, in a tape recording of his life history, described the sequence of events by which he tried to improve his economic situation. At each stage, his ambitions had been thwarted by the political and economic climate of Guatemala. He told of his increasing conviction that the rich did not wish to help the poor and of his increasing pessimism that peaceful action would improve the conditions of poorer Guatemalans.

Low-income families are thus highly conscious that the major bases on which prestige is allocated in the urban social structure are irrevocably denied to them. Yet, apart from the categorical distinction between rich and poor, there is, as we have seen, no situational basis for group solidarity among low-income families. Each family has its own set of social relations that differentiates it from other low-income families. Each family attempts to improve its position individually. The consequence of polarization and differentiation among low-income families in Guatemala City is low involvement with the formal processes of urban life. Low-income families are active manipulators of urban social organization. They, however, see themselves as apart from the formal mechanisms by which this social organization is maintained or changed. The majority of heads of family in both neighborhoods had no confidence that any political party, no matter what its political complexion, could improve the economic and political situation in Guatemala. Most family heads regarded the activities of both political reformers and political reactionaries as outside their concern. Their awareness of the significance of the distinction between rich and poor thus contributed to their sense of apartness from the formal political structure.

Few of these low-income families identified with the national concerns of Guatemala. The actions of the United States or of any other foreign power, with respect to Guatemala, are evaluated in terms of how they individually affect these low-income families. Individual experiences of employment in U.S.-owned enterprises were the most important determinants of attitudes toward the United States. Protestants in both neighborhoods identified more closely with their religious brothers in the United States than they did with their fellow citizens. It is this that gives a peculiar character to urban social organization in Guatemala City. Low-income families are active members of the city, but they feel no commitment either to maintaining or to changing the urban social structure. It is this that makes it difficult to effect planned change in Guatemala City. Low-income families are neither passive recipients nor consistent supporters of change.

In looking at the social activity of low-income families in two neighborhoods of Guatemala City, the articulation of these families with the rest of the urban social structure has been emphasized. There is sufficient differentiation among them to render difficult their common organization. Each family is linked by an individual set of relations and activities to other sectors of the urban population. These families have a varied and extensive experience of both rural and urban social organization. The social activity of an individual family is determined by the orientations derived from their life careers and by the various urban situations in which they find themselves. Their experiences have led most of them to an active attempt to improve their individual positions within the city. Their activity is an important condition to the operation of urban organizations and to the behavior of other segments of the urban population. The lack of continuity in life careers and the lack of integration between different urban situations are important factors stimulating both activity and differentiation among these low-income families. In terms of prestige, their urban experience has led them to distinguish themselves as an underprivileged group that is distinct from richer sectors of the city's population. This apartness, together with their internal differentiation, causes low-income families to direct their activity toward the informal manipulation of urban life. They do not attempt to change the formal structure of power and wealth.

WORKS CITED

Adams, Richard N. "Cultural Components of Central America." *American Anthropologist* 58, no. 5 (October 1956).

———. *Encuesta sobre los ladinos de Guatemala.* Guatemala City: Seminario de Integración Social Guatemalteca, Publication No. 2, 1956.

———. *Cultural Surveys of Panama-Nicaragua-Guatemala-El Salvador-Honduras.* Washington: Pan American Sanitary Bureau, Scientific Publication No. 33, 1957.

———. *Migraciones Internas en Guatemala: Expansión Agraria de los Indígenas Kekchíes hacia El Petén.* Guatemala City: Seminario de Integración Social Guatemalteca, *Estudios Centroamericanos* No. 1, 1965.

———. "Power and Power Domains." *América Latina* 9, no. 2 (1966).

———. "Nationalization." In *Social Anthropology*, edited by Manning Nash. *Handbook of Middle American Indians*, edited by Robert Wauchope, vol. 6. Austin: University of Texas Press, 1967.

———. "Political Power and Social Structures." In *The Politics of Conformity in Latin America*, edited by Claudio Véliz. London: Royal Institute of International Affairs, 1967.

———. *The Second Sowing.* San Francisco: Chandler Publishing Co., 1967.

———, ed. *Political Changes in Guatemalan Indian Communities.* New Orleans: Middle American Research Institute, Publication 21, 1957.

Alba, Victor. *Politics and the Labor Movement in Latin America.* Stanford: Stanford University Press, 1968.

Alexander, Robert. *Communism in Latin America.* New Brunswick, N.J.: Rutgers University Press, 1967.

516   *Works Cited*

Archivo. *Registro, Libro #1*. Guatemala City: Departamento Administrativo de Trabajo.

Arias B., Jorge. "Migración interna en Guatemala." *Estadística* 20, no. 76 (1962): 519–527.

Arriola, J. L., ed. "Ladinización en Guatemala." *Integración Social en Guatemala*. Guatemala City: Seminario de Integración Social Guatemalteca, Publication No. 3, 1956.

Baker, Ross K. *A Study of Military Status and Status Deprivation in Three Latin American Armies*. Washington: American University, Center for Research in Social Systems, 1966.

Banco de Guatemala, *Informe de Guatemala, 1961–65*. Guatemala City: Cuarta Reunión Anual del Consejo Interamericano Económico y Social, 1966.

Barber, Willard F., and Ronning, Neale. *Internal Security and Military Power: Counterinsurgency and Civic Action in Latin America*. Columbus: Ohio State University Press, 1966.

Batalle, G. Bonfil. "Conservative Thought in Applied Anthropology: A Critique." *Human Organization* 25, no. 2 (1966): 92.

Bauer Paiz, Alfonso. "El Gobierno de Guatemala y el Conflicto de la United Fruit Company." *El mes económico y financiero* 111 (Feb.–March 1949).

―――. *Catalogación de Leyes y Disposiciones de Guatemala del Período 1872 a 1930*. Guatemala City: University of San Carlos, 1965.

Bennett, John. "Microcosm-Macrocosm Relationships in North American Agrarian Society." *American Anthropologist* 69, no. 5 (1967): 441–454.

Berg, Klaus. "Agricultural Structure of Guatemala." Mimeographed. Guatemala City, 1966.

Bishop, Edwin. "The Guatemalan Labor Movement, 1944–59." Ph.D. dissertation, University of Wisconsin, 1959.

Bonilla, Frank. "Cultural Elites." In *Elites in Latin America*, edited by Seymour Martin Lipset and Aldo Solari. New York: Oxford University Press, 1967.

Boulding, Kenneth E. "Dare We Take the Social Sciences Seriously?" *American Behavioral Scientist* 10, no. 10 (June 1967): 12–16.

Bryant, Mavis Ann. "Agricultural Interest Groups in Guatemala." M.A. thesis, The University of Texas at Austin, 1967.

————. "Industrial and Commercial Associations in Guatemala." Manuscript, The University of Texas at Austin, 1967.

Bunzel, Ruth. *Chichicastenango: A Guatemalan Village.* American Ethnological Society Publication No. 22, 1952.

Bush, Archer C. "Organized Labor in Guatemala, 1944–49." Mimeographed. Hamilton, N.Y.: Colgate University Area Studies, Latin American Seminar Reports No. 2, 1950.

Buttrey, Jerrold. "The Guatemalan Military, 1944–1963: An Interpretive Essay." Manuscript, The University of Texas at Austin, 1967.

Calder, Bruce. "Growth and Change in the Guatemalan Catholic Church, 1944–1964." M.A. thesis, The University of Texas at Austin, 1968.

Comité de los Nueve, Alianza para el Progreso. "Evaluación del Plan de Desarrollo Económico y Social de Guatemala, 1965–1969: Informe Presentado al Gobierno de Guatemala por el Comité Ad Hoc." Mimeographed. Washington, D.C., 1965.

Comité Interamericano de Desarrollo Agrícola. *Tenencia de la Tierra y Desarrollo Socio-económico del Sector Agrícola, Guatemala.* Washington, D.C.: Pan American Union, 1965.

Canreiro, Robert, and Tobias, Stephen F. "The Application of Scale Analysis to the Study of Cultural Evolution." *New York Academy of Sciences, Transactions* 26, second series, no. 2, 196–207.

Caplow, Theodore, et al. *The Urban Ambience.* Totowa, N.J.: Bedminster Press, 1964.

Conferencia Nacional de Religiosos y Religiosas de Guatemala. *Boletín Informativo y Tercer Informe General* 2, no. 3 (March 1965).

Coverdale, John F. "Opus Dei." *St. Joseph's Magazine* (October 1965).

Dawson, Frank Griffith. "Labor Legislation and Social Integration in Guatemala: 1871–1944." *American Journal of Comparative Law* 14 (1965): 124–142.

Delgado, Oscar, ed. *Reforma en la América Latina.* Mexico City: Fondo de Cultura Económica, 1965.

Departamento de Censos y Encuestas. *Censos 1964: Población; Resultados de Tabulación por Muestra.* Guatemala City, June 1966.

Despres, Leo A. *Cultural Pluralism and Nationalist Politics in British Guiana.* Chicago: Rand McNally, 1967.

Deutschtum in der Alta Verapaz. Stuttgart: Deutschen Verlagsanstalt, 1939.

Devons, Ely, and Gluckman, Max. "Conclusions: Modes and Consequences of Limiting a Field of Study." In *Closed Systems and Open Minds*, edited by Max Gluckman. Chicago: Aldine, 1964.

Di Tella, Torcuato. "Populism and Reform in Latin America." In *Obstacles to Change in Latin America*, edited by Claudio Véliz. London: Royal Institute of International Affairs, 1966.

Durston, John. *Power Structure in a Rural Region of Guatemala: The Department of Jutiapa*. M.A. thesis, The University of Texas at Austin, 1966.

Eisenstadt, S. N. "Anthropological Studies of Complex Societies." *Current Anthropology* 2, no. 3 (1961): 209.

Ewald, Robert H. *Bibliografía comentada sobre antropología social, 1900–1955*. Guatemala City: Seminario de Integración Social Guatemalteca, 1956.

———. "San Antonio Sacatepéquez: Culture Change in a Guatemalan Community." *Social Forces* 36 (1957): 160–165.

Firth, Raymond. *Elements of Social Organization*. London: Watts, 1951.

Fried, M. "State: The Institution." *International Encyclopedia of the Social Sciences*, vol. 15. New York, 1968.

Germani, Gino. "Inquiry into the Social Effects of Urbanization in a Working-Class Sector of Greater Buenos Aires." In *Urbanization in Latin America*, edited by Philip Hauser, New York: UNESCO, 1961.

———. *Política y Sociedad en una Epoca de Transición*. Buenos Aires: Paidós, 1962.

Gillin, John. *The Culture of Security in San Carlos*. Middle American Research Institute Publication 16. New Orleans: Tulane University, 1951.

———, and Silvert, Kalman H. "Ambiguities in Guatemala." *Foreign Affairs* 34 (1956).

Goulden, Joseph C. "Guatemala: A Democracy Falters." Alicia Patterson Fund Report JCG-10. 1966.

Harris, Marvin. *Town and Country in Brazil*. New York: Columbia University Press, 1956.

Hernández de León, F. *Viajes presidenciales*. Guatemala City, n.d.

Holleran, Mary P. *Church and State in Guatemala*. New York: Columbia University Press, 1949.

Horowitz, Irving Lewis. "The Military Elite." In *Elites in Latin America*, edited by Seymour Martin Lipset and Aldo Solari. New York: Oxford University Press, 1967.

———. "The Norm of Illegitimacy: Toward a General Theory of Latin American Political Development." *Soundings* 2, no. (1968): 8–32.

Howard, Alan. "With the Guerrillas in Guatemala." *New York Times Magazine*, June 26, 1966.

Hupp, Bruce. "The Indians of Quezaltenango City." M.A. thesis, The University of Texas at Austin, 1969.

Hutchinson, Harry W. *Village and Plantation Life in Northeastern Brazil*. Seattle: University of Washington Press, 1958.

James, Daniel. *Red Design for the Americas: Guatemalan Prelude*. New York, 1954.

———. "Subversive Document Revealed." *Latin American Times* 1:18.

Jiménez, Julio M. "A Critique of the Policies and Attitudes Affecting Cotton Agriculture in Guatemala through a Study of Its Development." M.A. thesis, The University of Texas at Austin, 1967.

Johnson, John J. *The Military and Society in Latin America*. Stanford: Stanford University Press, 1964.

Johnson, Kenneth F. *The Guatemalan Presidential Election of March 6, 1966: An Analysis*. Election Analysis No. 5. Washington, D.C.: Institute for the Comparative Study of Political Systems, n.d.

Jones, Chester Lloyd. *Guatemala: Past and Present*. Minneapolis: University of Minnesota Press, 1940.

Klausner, Samuel Z., ed. *The Study of Total Societies*. New York: Doubleday, 1967.

LaFarge, Oliver. *Santa Eulalia*. Chicago, 1947.

———, and Byers, D. *The Year Bearer's People*. Middle American Research Institute Publication 3, n.d.

LeBeau, Frances. "Agricultura de Guatemala." *Integración Social en Guatemala*, vol. 3. Guatemala City: Seminario de Integración Social Guatemalteca, 1956.

Leeds, Anthony. "Brazilian Careers and Social Structure." In *Contemporary Cultures and Societies of Latin America*, edited by D. Heath and Richard N. Adams. New York: Random House, 1965.

Lenski, Gerhard. *Power and Privilege*. New York: McGraw-Hill, 1966.

Levi-Strauss, Claude. *The Savage Mind*. London: Weidenfeld and Nicolson, 1966.

520   *Works Cited*

Lewis, Oscar. *The Children of Sánchez.* New York: Random House, 1961.

Lipset, Seymour Martin, and Solari, Aldo, eds. *Elites in Latin America.* New York: Oxford University Press, 1967.

Mayer, Philip. *Townsmen or Tribesmen: Conservatism and the Process of Urbanization in a South African City.* New York: Oxford University Press, 1961.

Mendelson, E. Michael. *Los Escándolos de Maximón.* Guatemala City: Seminario de Integración Social Guatemalteca, 1965.

Mead, Margaret. *Continuities in Cultural Evolution.* New Haven: Yale University Press, 1964.

Méndez, Alfredo. *Zaragoza.* Guatemala City: Seminario de Integración Social Guatemalteca, 1967.

Mitchell, J. C. "Theoretical Orientations in African Urban Studies." In *The Social Anthropology of Complex Societies,* edited by Michael Banton. London: Tavistock, 1966.

———, ed. *Social Networks in Urban Situations.* Manchester: Manchester University Press, 1969.

Monteforte Toledo, Mario. *Guatemala: Monografía sociología.* 2nd edition. Mexico City: Universidad Nacional Autónoma de México, 1965.

Moore, G. A. "Social and Ritual Change in a Guatemalan Town." Ph.D. dissertation, Columbia University, 1966.

Moore, Omar Khayyam. "Divination: A New Perspective." *American Anthropologist* 59, no. 1 (1957): 69–74.

Nash, Manning. *Machine Age Maya.* American Anthropological Association Memoir 87, 1958.

———. "Political Relations in Guatemala." *Social and Economic Studies* 7 (1958): 65–75.

Newbold, Stokes. "Receptivity to Communist-Fomented Agitation in Rural Guatemala." *Economic Development and Cultural Change* 5, no. 4 (1957): 360.

Noval, Joaquín. *Materiales Etnográficos de San Miguel.* Cuadernos de Antropología 3. Guatemala City: Universidad de San Carlos, 1964.

Paredes Moreira, José Luis. *Estudios sobre Reforma Agraria en Guatemala: Aplicación del Decreto 900, Cuadro No. 1.* Instituto de Investigaciones Económicas y Sociales. Guatemala City: Universidad de San Carlos, 1964.

Pearson, Neale J. "The Confederación Nacional Campesina de Guatemala (CNCG) and Peasant Unionism in Guatemala, 1944–54." M.A. thesis, Georgetown University, 1964.

Pizer, Samuel, and Cutler, Frederick. *U. S. Business Investments, Foreign Countries: A Supplement to the Survey of Current Business.* Washington, D.C.: Department of Commerce, 1960.

Redfield, Robert. "Primitive Merchants of Guatemala." *Quarterly Journal of Inter-American Relations* 1, no. 4 (1938): 42–56.

————. *The Folk Culture of Yucatan.* Chicago: University of Chicago Press, 1941.

Reina, Ruben E. "Two Patterns of Friendship in a Guatemalan Community." *American Anthropologist* 61 (1959): 44–50.

————. *Chinautla: A Guatemalan Indian Community.* Middle American Research Institute Publication 24, New Orleans: Tulane University, 1960.

————. *The Law of the Saints: A Pokoman Corporate Community and Its Culture.* Indianapolis: Bobbs Merrill, 1966.

Relatos del Normalista y Soldado, Verdadero Causas de la Caída del Poder Público del Sr. Lic. Manuel Estrada Cabrera. Quezaltenango: Tipografía Occidental, 1928.

Rivera, Alejandro. "Llamos a la toma del poder, dicen las guerrillas." *Economía* 2 (March–April 1965): 3.

Roberts, Bryan. "The Politics of an Urban Neighborhood of Guatemala City." *Sociology* (May 1968).

————. "Protestantism and Coping with Urban Life in Guatemala City." *American Journal of Sociology* (May 1968).

Russett, Bruce M., et al. *World Handbook of Political and Social Indicators.* New Haven: Yale University Press, 1964.

Sahlins, Marshall D. "Evolution: Specific and General." In *Evolution and Culture*, edited by Marshall D. Sahlins and Elman R. Service. Ann Arbor: University of Michigan Press, 1960.

Schlesinger, J. *Revolución Comunista.* Guatemala, 1946.

Schmid, Lester. "The Role of Migratory Labor in the Economic Development of Guatemala." Ph.D. dissertation, University of Wisconsin, 1967.

Schneider, Ronald. *Communism in Guatemala, 1944–54.* New York: Praeger, 1959.

Secretaría General del Consejo Nacional de Planificación Económica. *Aspectos generales del plan de desarrollo económico y social de Guatemala, 1965–1969.* Guatemala City, 1965.

———. *Diagnóstico del Sector Industrial: Período 1950–1962.* Guatemala City, 1965.

———. *La Situación del Desarrollo Económico y Social de Guatemala.* Guatemala City, 1965.

El Servicio de Alfabetización del Ejército. "La Alfabetización en el ejército: Estudio sobre la contribución del ejército en la lucha contra el analfabetismo en Guatemala." Mimeographed. Sept. 1961.

Silvert, Kalman H. *A Study in Government: Guatemala.* Middle American Research Institute Publication 21. New Orleans: Tulane University 1954.

———. *The Conflict Society: Reaction and Revolution in Latin America.* New Orleans: Hauser Press, 1961.

Skinner-Klée, Jorge. *Legislación Indigenista de Guatemala.* Mexico City: Ediciones Especiales del Instituto Indigenista Interamericano, 1954.

Sloan, John W. "The Electoral Game in Guatemala." Ph.D. dissertation, The University of Texas at Austin, 1968.

Smith, M. G. "Political Anthropology." *International Encyclopedia of the Social Sciences,* vol. 12. New York, 1968.

Stahlke, Leonardo E. *Estadística Religiosa Cristiana de Guatemala.* Guatemala City: Iglesia Luterana, 1966.

Stavenhagen, Rodolfo. "Estratificación social y estructura de clases." *Ciencias Políticas y Sociales* 27 (1962): 73–102.

———. "Clase, colonialismo y aculturación: Ensayo sobre un sistema de relaciones interétnicas en Mesoamérica." *América Latina* 6, no. 4 (1963).

Julian Steward, et al. *The People of Puerto Rico.* Urbana: University of Illinois Press, 1955.

———. *The Theory of Culture Change.* Urbana: University of Illinois Press, 1955.

———. "Perspectives on Modernization: Introduction to the Studies." In *Contemporary Change in Traditional Societies,* edited by Julian Steward, vol. 1, pp. 24–25. Urbana: University of Illinois Press, 1967.

———. "Cultural Ecology." *International Encyclopedia of the Social Sciences,* vol. 4. New York, 1968.

Suslow, Leo A. "Aspects of Social Reforms in Guatemala, 1944–1949." Latin American Seminar Reports No. 1. Mimeographed. Hamilton, N.Y.: Colgate University, 1949.

Termini, Deanne Lanoix. "Socio-Economic and Demographic Characteristics of the Population of Guatemala City with Special Reference to Migrant–Non-Migrant Differences." M.A. thesis, The University of Texas at Austin, 1968.

Tumin, Melvin. *Caste in a Peasant Society*. Princeton: Princeton University Press, 1952.

U.S. Department of Defense. *Military Assistance Facts*. February 1965.

U.S. Senate. "Hearings before the Subcommittee on American Republics Affairs." March 1968.

U.S. State Department. *Points in Explanation of U.S. Military Assistance Programs for Latin America*. 1964.

Useem, John. "The Community of Man: A Study of the Third Culture." *The Centennial Review* 7, no. 4 (1963): 481–498.

———; Useem, Ruth; and John Donoghue. "Men in the Middle of the Third Culture." *Human Organization* 22, no. 3 (1963):169–179.

Véliz, Claudio, ed. *Obstacles to Change in Latin America*. London: Oxford University Press, 1966.

Wagley, Charles. *Amazon Town: A Study of Man in the Tropics*. New York: Macmillan Co., 1953.

———. *An Introduction to Brazil*. New York: Columbia University Press, 1963.

———, ed. *Race and Class in Rural Brazil*. Paris: UNESCO, 1952.

Walterhouse, Harry F. "A Time to Build: Military Civic Action—Medium for Economic Development and Social Reform." Studies in International Affairs No. 4. Columbia: University of South Carolina, 1964.

Weiner, Myron. "Political Integration and Political Development." In *Political Development and Social Change*, edited by Jason Finkle and Richard Gable. New York: Wiley, 1966.

Whetten, Nathan L. *Guatemala: The Land and the People*. New Haven: Yale University Press, 1961.

Winter, E. H., and Beidelman, T. O. "Tanganyika: A Study of an African Society at National and Local Levels." In *Contemporary Change in Traditional Societies*, edited by Julian Steward, vol. 1, pp. 61–204. Urbana: University of Illinois Press, 1967.

Wolf, Eric. "La formación de la nación: Un ensayo de formulación." *Ciencias Sociales* 4(1953): 50–62, 98–111, 146–171.

———. "Types of Latin American Peasantry: A Preliminary Discussion." *American Anthropologist* 57, no. 3 (1955).

———. "Aspects of Group Relations in a Complex Society." *American Anthropologist* 58 (1956): 1065–1078.

———. "Closed Corporate Communities in Mesoamerica and Central Java." *Southwestern Journal of Anthropology* 13 (1957): 1–18.

———. "Kinship, Friendship, and Patron-Client Relations in Complex Societies." In *The Social Anthropology of Complex Societies*, edited by Michael Banton. New York: Praeger, 1966.

———. "Levels of Communal Relations." In *Social Anthropology*, edited by Manning Nash. *Handbook of Middle American Indians*, edited by Robert Wauchope, vol. 6. Austin: University of Texas Press, 1967.

Zamora Castellanos, P. *El grito de independencia*. Guatemala City: Tipografía Nacional, 1935.

Zárate, Alvan. "Migraciones internas de Guatemala." *Estudios Centroamericanos* No. 1. Guatemala City: Seminario de Integración Social Guatemalteca, 1967.

INDEX

Acción Católica: purpose of, 294–295; membership of Presidencia General of, 295; organization of, 295; operation of Universitaria of, 297–298; role of Professional of, 298; significance of activities of, 309. SEE ALSO Acción Católica Rural; Movimiento Familiar Cristiana de Guatemala

Acción Católica Rural: role of, 295–297; within FCG, 476

—*catequistas* of: training of, 295; role of, 296; lead FCG-affiliated organizations, 462

Acción Cívica: 477

ACOGUA. SEE Asociación de Cafecultores del Oriente de Guatemala

adaptation: and social organization, 46–47; to habitat, 70, 71; to total environment, 70–71; to society, 70–71; levels of, described, 74; features affecting, 74–75; and power, 75–76; process of, in complex societies, 116

—methods of: physical mobility, 76, 77; fragmentation, 77; expansion, 78–80; socioeconomic mobility, 79–80

AED. SEE Asociación Estudiantes de Derecho

Aero Club: 233

AEU. SEE Asociación de Estudiantes Universitarios

AFL. SEE American Federation of Labor

AGA. SEE Asociación General de Agricultores

Agency for International Development. SEE United States Agency for International Development

agrarian committees: arming of, to neutralize military, 191; confiscation of arms for, 192, 266; organization of, 447–448. SEE ALSO Agrarian Reform Law; *campesinos*, organizations of

Agrarian Reform Law: issued by Arbenz, 185; agency to operate, employs Communists, 186; sets up local agrarian committees, 190; committees of, responsible to president, 190; rescinded by postrevolutionary government, 198; effect of, on AGA, 336; and land for *campesinos*, 395; compared to colonization program, 395–396; expropriation of land under, 395, 396, 398–401; application of, 445; reinforces participation in *sindicatos* and leagues, 448. SEE ALSO agrarian committees

agriculture: as major Guatemalan resource, 149–150, 151, 153; growth of, 152; importance of, 394. SEE ALSO *campesinos*; conservation practices; land; *finqueros*; *patrones*

AGSA. SEE Algodonera Guatemalteca, S.A.

AGUAPA. SEE Asociación Guatemalteca de Productores de Algodón

AID. SEE United States Agency for International Development

AIFLD. SEE American Institute for Free Labor Development

air force. SEE military

alcaldes: 176

sympathy during World War II, 183; bishops' fund of, supports Guatemalan Church, 291; and importance of coffee, 354. SEE ALSO Miserior

Gluckman, Max: 32

Godoy Urrutia, César: 461

Gompers, Samuel: 453

González, Cándido: 464

"Good Neighbor" era: 260

government: organization, structure, and power of, described, 85; ways of increasing concentration of power of, 86; organizational goals of, 92; nation-state, as beneficiary of nationalism, 92; determination of regions by, 218

—Guatemalan: reasons for failure of, to change Indian way of life, 102–103; increased growth of, 147, 149; expansion of power of, 265–266; rule of, by military, 275; influence of, on interest group goals, 322; control of interest groups by, 327–329; power of, over labor, 424–425, 426. SEE ALSO postrevolutionary governments; revolutionary governments; specific administrations

governor, departmental: appointment of, 220; power of, in Jutiapa, 222, 223

Gremial de Cafecultores: 347. SEE ALSO Asociación General de Agricultores

Gremial de Cañeros: 339. SEE ALSO Asociación General de Agricultores

Gremial de Cañeros de Escuintla: 350

Gremial de Distribuidores Vehículos Automotores: 345

Gremial de Fabricantes de Acumuladores: 321

Gremial de Fabricantes y Convertidores de Papel Centroamericano: 345

Gremial de Paneleros: 342, 343

Gremial de Productos Farmecéuticas y Anexos: 336

Gremial de Transportes: 344

Gremial de Transportes Marítimos: 344

Gremial de Trigueros: membership of, 325; financing for, 326; organization of, 342–343

gremiales: establishment of, 196; defined, 325; of the Cámara de Comercio; Cámara de Industria; interest groups; specific *gremiales*

group formation: 46–47

growth rate: of Guatemala, 125; conditions for, 157

Guatemala (department): migration from, 112, 115; industry in, 172, 173; support of PR in, 207; in 1966 election, 207, 208. SEE ALSO Guatemala City

Guatemala City: pollution in, 71; population growth of, 126, 130–131, 134–135; described, 165; as national center, 170; importance of location of, 170; support of PR in, 207; in 1966 election, 207, 208; as part of *guerrillero* strategy, 216; and Chimaltenango elite, 226, 227; importance of, to Escuintla, 227, 228; concentration of population in, 265; seminaries in 285, 286; radio broadcast by priest in, 303–304; migration to, 484; population of, 484; geographical mobility within, and discontinuity, 484–485; industrial activity within, 485; residents of, and other towns, 485–486; urban services in, 486; effect on, of changes in political and social life, 486–487; and low-income family political participation, 509–510; bases in, for gaining individual prestige, 510–511; mentioned, 223. SEE ALSO families, low-income urban; Guatemala (department)

—"Planificada" neighborhood of: general description of, 487–488; social characteristics of, 488; compared to "San Lorenzo" neighborhood, 499–501

—"San Lorenzo" neighborhood of: general description of, 487; social characteristics of, 488; community organization of, 490; compared to "Planificada" neighborhood, 499–501; political activity within, 502–504

Guatemalan Club: 233

Guatemalan Church. SEE Catholic church

ORIT. See Organización Regional Interamericano de Trabajadores

Palín: 227

Panama Canal: 183, 260

Pan American Federation of Labor: 453, 457

Pan American highway system: 192

Pan–Central American organizations: 345, 351–352

Partido Comunista de Centro América: 453

Partido Guatemalteco de Trabajo. See Communist party

Partido Revolucionario (PR): political orientation of, 198; as opposition party in 1958, 198–199; not allowed to participate in 1957 elections, 206; strong showing by, in cities, 207; national support of, in 1966 election, 207–212; relationship of variables with vote for, 212, 213, 214; dependence upon lawyers by, 413; mentioned, 91

party: defined, 16

patrones: role of, in debt peonage practice, 176; in control of *campesinos*, 177; prohibited from paying wages in advance, 178; and labor regulation, 178; loss of power of, 191; under García Granados and Barrios, 425; and availability of labor, 426; punishment of, 429; attitudes of, toward *campesino* organizations, 474–476. See also *finqueros*; upper sector

Patzicía: 191

Paul VI: 300

Peace Corps: 107, 201

Peralta Azurdia, Enrique: refuses title of president, 275; effect of personality of, 276; mentioned, 86, 91, 155

—administration of: and labor union organizers, 107–108; political parties under, 206–207; and *guerrillero* activity, 215, 268; and power structure, 231; and anti-U.S. feeling, 261–262; power of, and nationalization, 265; changes procedure for reporting by *comisionados*, 272; relationship of, with the Church, 303; local banks started under, 348; interest groups

established under, 349–351; power of students under, 419; *bufete* members in, 422; and *campesino* organizations, 450. See also postrevolutionary governments

Perón, Juan: 456

personalidad juridica: granted to the Church by Castillo, 195; revocation of, 278. See also *campesinos*, organizations of; *campesino sindicatos*

petroleum: 341

PGT. See Communist party

pharmaceutical industry: 336

Philippines: 273

Pieters, Franz: 323 n.

Planificada. See Guatemala, "Planificada" neighborhood of

Pochuta: 208, 209

Pocoman: 167

Poland: 192

Politécnica. See Escuela Politécnica

political organizing: 203

political parties: influence of, 189–190; removal of, 194, 195; varying orientation of, 198; determination of regions by, 218; activities of, under Peralta, 206–207; position of, under postrevolutionary governments, 231; of students, 419; mentioned, 188

Polochic River: 180

Poptún, El Petén: 236

population: distribution of, 125; growth of, 125–126, 128, 130, 134–136; native, by department, 127; of Guatemala, ranked among world's nations, 137; growth of, in Escuintla, 228

postrevolutionary governments: devices of, to centralize power, 91; features of, contrasted with revolutionary governments, 194; changes instituted by, 194–195; formation of interest groups under, 195–196, 331–333, 338–352 *passim*; polarization of attitudes under, 197–198; efforts of, to promote industrialization and colonization, 199; position of *campesinos* under, 199; role of *comisionado militar* under, 199–200; union organizing under, 200; reappearance of cooperative movement under, 200–201; political activity under, 203, 435–436; elections held under, 206;

and the Church, 289, 310–311; attempts of, to take over ANACAFE, 327–328; and the cotton-growing sector, 362–364; effects of events under, 400–401; *campesino* organizations under, 440–441, 449–451; decrees issued by, 449–450; effects of policy of, 452; principal national labor federations under, 457–460. SEE ALSO Castillo Armas, Carlos, administration of; colonization programs; Peralta Azurdia, Enrique, administration of; Ydígoras Fuentes, Miguel, administration of

power: of social unit, importance of to study, 5; as basis for study, 8; as common factor in studies, 36; individual access to, 57; and operating units, 57–58; independent and derivative, 58; of elite sets, 60; allocation and application of, 64; controls used to increase, 75–76; defined, 117; elements affecting exercise of, 117–119; features crucial for understanding and utilization of, 119; kinds of, 120; sources of independent, 143–144

—base: importance of, in adaptation of units, 75; of interest groups, 322. SEE ALSO power domains; power structure

—concentration of: in Guatemala, 74; effects of, at higher levels, 86, 87, 88–89; in complex societies, 95

—derived: sources of, 143; and cultural potential, 143; in complex societies, 143–144; dependence upon, 407

power domains: defined, 54, 56, 119–120; and levels of articulation, 56–57; vertical relationships within, 60–61, 120, 121; new units formed between, 60, 62, 64; relationships between, 60–63, 120–123; unitary, defined and illustrated, 65; influence of, upon relations between units, 66, 67, 68; and formation of third culture, 69; effects of environment upon, 70; and investigator of complex societies, 99; and individual operator, 100; control of, and possibilities for change, 105–106; effects of revolution on, 107; restricting of choice by,

107–108; restrictiveness of, 115–116; kinds of, 120; structural patterns of, 122; independence of, 123; factors affecting, 168; effects on, of Guatemalan regionalization, 170; in defining regions, 218–219; in defining elites, 219–220; *guerrillero* effect on, 231, 232; in rural farm population, 232. SEE ALSO levels of articulation; power; power structure

—multiplicity of: illustrated, 65; described, 66; of nations, 96; and possibilities for individual operators, 101

power structure: and social structure, 7; in Guatemala, 8; features of, 119–120; during Ubico period, 179; under revolutionary governments, 187–193 *passim*; under postrevolutionary governments, and effects on lower sector, 195; and position of elites, 231; and expansion of power of central government, 265–266; and the Church, 279, 309; and interest groups, 352; and distribution of increase in wealth, 380–381; and support of labor, 436–437. SEE ALSO power; power domains

PR. SEE Partido Revolucionario

preliminary map. SEE conceptual map

prerevolutionary period: 109. SEE ALSO Cabrera, Manuel Estrada; Ubico, Jorge

priests. SEE clergy

printers: 342

private ownership: 140, 141

Progreso: 221

promoción: 257, 258

provincial territory: 220 n.

public administration: 245

Puerto Barrios: control of, by United Fruit Company, 183; effects of arms shipment to, 266; interception of arms at, 468

Quezaltenango: population of, 20; population growth in, 134; coffee production in, 138, 223, 350–351; Indian control in, 160, 166–167; subordination of, 170; industry in, 172, 173; in 1966 elections, 207, 208, 209, 214; minor seminary in, 286